Data Intensive Distributed Computing:

Challenges and Solutions for Large-scale Information Management

Tevfik Kosar
University at Buffalo, USA

A volume in the Advances in Systems
Analysis, Software Engineering, and High
Performance Computing (ASASEHPC)
Book Series

Information Science
REFERENCE
An Imprint of IGI Global

Managing Director:	Lindsay Johnston
Senior Editorial Director:	Heather Probst
Book Production Manager:	Sean Woznicki
Development Manager:	Joel Gamon
Development Editor:	Hannah Abelbeck
Acquisitions Editor:	Erika Gallagher
Typesetters:	Milan Vracarich, Jr.
Cover Design:	Nick Newcomer, Greg Snader

Published in the United States of America by
Information Science Reference (an imprint of IGI Global)
701 E. Chocolate Avenue
Hershey PA 17033
Tel: 717-533-8845
Fax: 717-533-8661
E-mail: cust@igi-global.com
Web site: http://www.igi-global.com

Library of Congress Cataloging-in-Publication Data

Data intensive distributed computing: challenges and solutions for large-scale information management / Tevfik Kosar, editor.
    p. cm.
  Includes bibliographical references and index.
  Summary: "This book focuses on the challenges of distributed systems imposed by the data intensive applications, and on the different state-of-the-art solutions proposed to overcome these challenges"--Provided by publisher.
  ISBN 978-1-61520-971-2 -- ISBN 978-1-61520-972-9 (ebk.) 1. Expert systems (Computer science) 2. Computer systems. I. Kosar, Tevfik, 1974-
  QA76.76.E95D378 2012
  006.3--dc22
                        2010006730

This book is published in the IGI Global book series Advances in Systems Analysis, Software Engineering, and High Performance Computing (ASASEHPC) Book Series (ISSN: 2327-3453; eISSN: 2327-3461)

British Cataloguing in Publication Data
A Cataloguing in Publication record for this book is available from the British Library.

Advances in Systems Analysis, Software Engineering, and High Performance Computing (ASASEHPC) Book Series

Vijayan Sugumaran
Oakland University, USA

ISSN: 2327-3453
EISSN: 2327-3461

MISSION

The theory and practice of computing applications and distributed systems has emerged as one of the key areas of research driving innovations in business, engineering, and science. The fields of software engineering, systems analysis, and high performance computing offer a wide range of applications and solutions in solving computational problems for any modern organization.

The **Advances in Systems Analysis, Software Engineering, and High Performance Computing (ASASEHPC) Book Series** brings together research in the areas of distributed computing, systems and software engineering, high performance computing, and service science. This collection of publications is useful for academics, researchers, and practitioners seeking the latest practices and knowledge in this field.

COVERAGE
- Computer Graphics
- Computer Networking
- Computer System Analysis
- Distributed Cloud Computing
- Enterprise Information Systems
- Metadata and Semantic Web
- Parallel Architectures
- Performance Modeling
- Software Engineering
- Virtual Data Systems

IGI Global is currently accepting manuscripts for publication within this series. To submit a proposal for a volume in this series, please contact our Acquisition Editors at Acquisitions@igi-global.com or visit: http://www.igi-global.com/publish/.

Titles in this Series

For a list of additional titles in this series, please visit: www.igi-global.com

Service-Driven Approaches to Architecture and Enterprise Integration
Raja Ramanathan (Independent Researcher, USA) and Kirtana Raja (Independent Researcher, USA)
Information Science Reference • copyright 2013 • 367pp • H/C (ISBN: 9781466641938) • US $195.00 (our price)

Progressions and Innovations in Model-Driven Software Engineering
Vicente García Díaz (Universidad de Oviedo, Spain) Juan Manuel Cueva Lovelle (University of Oviedo, Spain) B. Cristina Pelayo García-Bustelo (University of Oviedo, Spain) and Oscar Sanjuan Martinez (University of Oviedo, Spain)
Engineering Science Reference • copyright 2013 • 352pp • H/C (ISBN: 9781466642171) • US $195.00 (our price)

Knowledge-Based Processes in Software Development
Saqib Saeed (Bahria University Islamabad, Pakistan) and Izzat Alsmadi (Yarmouk University, Jordan)
Information Science Reference • copyright 2013 • 318pp • H/C (ISBN: 9781466642294) • US $195.00 (our price)

Distributed Computing Innovations for Business, Engineering, and Science
Alfred Waising Loo (Lingnan University, Hong Kong)
Information Science Reference • copyright 2013 • 369pp • H/C (ISBN: 9781466625334) • US $195.00 (our price)

Data Intensive Distributed Computing Challenges and Solutions for Large-scale Information Management
Tevfik Kosar (University at Buffalo, USA)
Information Science Reference • copyright 2012 • 352pp • H/C (ISBN: 9781615209712) • US $180.00 (our price)

Achieving Real-Time in Distributed Computing From Grids to Clouds
Dimosthenis Kyriazis (National Technical University of Athens, Greece) Theodora Varvarigou (National Technical University of Athens, Greece) and Kleopatra G. Konstanteli (National Technical University of Athens, Greece)
Information Science Reference • copyright 2012 • 330pp • H/C (ISBN: 9781609608279) • US $195.00 (our price)

Principles and Applications of Distributed Event-Based Systems
Annika M. Hinze (University of Waikato, New Zealand) and Alejandro Buchmann (University of Waikato, New Zealand)
Information Science Reference • copyright 2010 • 538pp • H/C (ISBN: 9781605666976) • US $180.00 (our price)

IGI GLOBAL
DISSEMINATOR OF KNOWLEDGE
www.igi-global.com

701 E. Chocolate Ave., Hershey, PA 17033
Order online at www.igi-global.com or call 717-533-8845 x100
To place a standing order for titles released in this series, contact: cust@igi-global.com
Mon-Fri 8:00 am - 5:00 pm (est) or fax 24 hours a day 717-533-8661

Table of Contents

Section 1
New Paradigms in Data Intensive Computing

Esma Yildirim, State University of New York at Buffalo (SUNY), USA

Mehmet Balman, Lawrence Berkeley National Laboratory, USA

Tevfik Kosar, State University of New York at Buffalo (SUNY), USA

Ioan Raicu, Illinois Institute of Technology, USA & Argonne National Laboratory, USA

Ian Foster, University of Chicago, USA & Argonne National Laboratory, USA

Yong Zhao, University of Electronic Science and Technology of China, China

Alex Szalay, Johns Hopkins University, USA

Philip Little, University of Notre Dame, USA

Christopher M. Moretti, University of Notre Dame, USA

Amitabh Chaudhary, University of Notre Dame, USA

Douglas Thain, University of Notre Dame, USA

Arcot Rajasekar, University of North Carolina at Chapel Hill, USA

Mike Wan, University of California at San Diego, USA

Reagan Moore, University of North Carolina at Chapel Hill, USA

Wayne Schroeder, University of California at San Diego, USA

Section 2
Distributed Storage

Section 3
Data & Workflow Management

Section 4
Data Discovery & Visualization

Detailed Table of Contents

Section 1
New Paradigms in Data Intensive Computing

Chapter 1

    Esma Yildirim, State University of New York at Buffalo (SUNY), USA
    Mehmet Balman, Lawrence Berkeley National Laboratory, USA
    Tevfik Kosar, State University of New York at Buffalo (SUNY), USA

With the continuous increase in the data requirements of scientific and commercial applications, access to remote and distributed data has become a major bottleneck for end-to-end application performance. Traditional distributed computing systems closely couple data access and computation, and generally, data access is considered a side effect of computation. The limitations of traditional distributed computing systems and CPU-oriented scheduling and workflow management tools in managing complex data handling have motivated a newly emerging era: data-aware distributed computing. In this chapter, the authors elaborate on how the most crucial distributed computing components, such as scheduling, workflow management, and end-to-end throughput optimization, can become "data-aware." In this new computing paradigm, called data-aware distributed computing, data placement activities are represented as full-featured jobs in the end-to-end workflow, and they are queued, managed, scheduled, and optimized via a specialized data-aware scheduler. As part of this new paradigm, the authors present a set of tools for mitigating the data bottleneck in distributed computing systems, which consists of three main components: a data-aware scheduler, which provides capabilities such as planning, scheduling, resource reservation, job execution, and error recovery for data movement tasks; integration of these capabilities to the other layers in distributed computing, such as workflow planning; and further optimization of data movement tasks via dynamic tuning of underlying protocol transfer parameters.

Many-task computing aims to bridge the gap between two computing paradigms, high throughput computing and high performance computing. Traditional techniques to support many-task computing commonly found in scientific computing (i.e. the reliance on parallel file systems with static configurations) do not scale to today's largest systems for data intensive application, as the rate of increase in the number of processors per system is outgrowing the rate of performance increase of parallel file systems. In this chapter, the authors argue that in such circumstances, data locality is critical to the successful and efficient use of large distributed systems for data-intensive applications. They propose a "data diffusion" approach to enable data-intensive many-task computing. They define an abstract model for data diffusion, define and implement scheduling policies with heuristics that optimize real world performance, and develop a competitive online caching eviction policy. They also offer many empirical experiments to explore the benefits of data diffusion, both under static and dynamic resource provisioning, demonstrating approaches that improve both performance and scalability.

Service-oriented architectures (SOA) enable orchestration of loosely-coupled and interoperable functional software units to develop and execute complex but agile applications. Data management on a distributed data grid can be viewed as a set of operations that are performed across all stages in the life-cycle of a data object. The set of such operations depends on the type of objects, based on their physical and discipline-centric characteristics. In this chapter, the authors define server-side functions, called micro-services, which are orchestrated into conditional workflows for achieving large-scale data management specific to collections of data. Micro-services communicate with each other using parameter exchange, in memory data structures, a database-based persistent information store, and a network messaging system that uses a serialization protocol for communicating with remote micro-services. The orchestration of the workflow is done by a distributed rule engine that chains and executes the workflows and maintains transactional properties through recovery micro-services. They discuss the micro-service oriented architecture, compare the micro-service approach with traditional SOA, and describe the use of micro-services for implementing policy-based data management systems.

Section 2
Distributed Storage

Chapter 4

    Sudharshan S. Vazhkudai, Oak Ridge National Laboratory, USA
    Ali R. Butt, Virginia Polytechnic Institute and State University, USA
    Xiaosong Ma, North Carolina State University, USA

In this chapter, the authors present an overview of the utility of distributed storage systems in supporting modern applications that are increasingly becoming data intensive. Their coverage of distributed storage systems is based on the requirements imposed by data intensive computing and not a mere summary of storage systems. To this end, they delve into several aspects of supporting data-intensive analysis, such as data staging, offloading, checkpointing, and end-user access to terabytes of data, and illustrate the use of novel techniques and methodologies for realizing distributed storage systems therein. The data deluge from scientific experiments, observations, and simulations is affecting all of the aforementioned day-to-day operations in data-intensive computing. Modern distributed storage systems employ techniques that can help improve application performance, alleviate I/O bandwidth bottleneck, mask failures, and improve data availability. They present key guiding principles involved in the construction of such storage systems, associated tradeoffs, design, and architecture, all with an eye toward addressing challenges of data-intensive scientific applications. They highlight the concepts involved using several case studies of state-of-the-art storage systems that are currently available in the data-intensive computing landscape.

Chapter 5

    Ismail Akturk, Bilkent University, Turkey
    Xinqi Wang, Louisiana State University, USA
    Tevfik Kosar, State University of New York at Buffalo (SUNY), USA

The unbounded increase in the size of data generated by scientific applications necessitates collaboration and sharing among the nation's education and research institutions. Simply purchasing high-capacity, high-performance storage systems and adding them to the existing infrastructure of the collaborating institutions does not solve the underlying and highly challenging data handling problem. Scientists are compelled to spend a great deal of time and energy on solving basic data-handling issues, such as the physical location of data, how to access it, and/or how to move it to visualization and/or compute resources for further analysis. This chapter presents the design and implementation of a reliable and efficient distributed data storage system, PetaShare, which spans multiple institutions across the state of Louisiana. At the back-end, PetaShare provides a unified name space and efficient data movement across geographically distributed storage sites. At the front-end, it provides light-weight clients the enable easy, transparent, and scalable access. In PetaShare, the authors have designed and implemented an asynchronously replicated multi-master metadata system for enhanced reliability and availability. The authors also present a high level cross-domain metadata schema to provide a structured systematic view of multiple science domains supported by PetaShare.

Chapter 6

Douglas Thain, University of Notre Dame, USA
Michael Albrecht, University of Notre Dame, USA
Hoang Bui, University of Notre Dame, USA
Peter Bui, University of Notre Dame, USA
Rory Carmichael, University of Notre Dame, USA
Scott Emrich, University of Notre Dame, USA
Patrick Flynn, University of Notre Dame, USA

Over the last few decades, computing performance, memory capacity, and disk storage have all increased by many orders of magnitude. However, I/O performance has not increased at nearly the same pace: a disk arm movement is still measured in milliseconds, and disk I/O throughput is still measured in megabytes per second. If one wishes to build computer systems that can store and process petabytes of data, they must have large numbers of disks and the corresponding I/O paths and memory capacity to support the desired data rate. A cost efficient way to accomplish this is by clustering large numbers of commodity machines together. This chapter presents Chirp as a building block for clustered data intensive scientific computing. Chirp was originally designed as a lightweight file server for grid computing and was used as a "personal" file server. The authors explore building systems with very high I/O capacity using commodity storage devices by tying together multiple Chirp servers. Several real-life applications such as the GRAND Data Analysis Grid, the Biometrics Research Grid, and the Biocompute Facility use Chirp as their fundamental building block, but provide different services and interfaces appropriate to their target communities.

Section 3
Data & Workflow Management

Chapter 7

Suraj Pandey, The Commonwealth Scientific and Industrial Research Organisation (CSIRO),
Australia
Rajkumar Buyya, The University of Melbourne, Australia

This chapter presents a comprehensive survey of algorithms, techniques, and frameworks used for scheduling and management of data-intensive application workflows. Many complex scientific experiments are expressed in the form of workflows for structured, repeatable, controlled, scalable, and automated executions. This chapter focuses on the type of workflows that have tasks processing huge amount of data, usually in the range from hundreds of mega-bytes to petabytes. Scientists are already using Grid systems that schedule these workflows onto globally distributed resources for optimizing various objectives: minimize total makespan of the workflow, minimize cost and usage of network bandwidth, minimize cost of computation and storage, meet the deadline of the application, and so forth. This chapter lists and describes techniques used in each of these systems for processing huge amount of data. A survey of workflow management techniques is useful for understanding the working of the Grid systems providing insights on performance optimization of scientific applications dealing with data-intensive workloads.

Scientific applications such as those in astronomy, earthquake science, gravitational-wave physics, and others have embraced workflow technologies to do large-scale science. Workflows enable researchers to collaboratively design, manage, and obtain results that involve hundreds of thousands of steps, access terabytes of data, and generate similar amounts of intermediate and final data products. Although workflow systems are able to facilitate the automated generation of data products, many issues still remain to be addressed. These issues exist in different forms in the workflow lifecycle. This chapter describes a workflow lifecycle as consisting of a workflow generation phase where the analysis is defined, the workflow planning phase where resources needed for execution are selected, the workflow execution part, where the actual computations take place, and the result, metadata, and provenance storing phase. The authors discuss the issues related to data management at each step of the workflow cycle. They describe challenge problems and illustrate them in the context of real-life applications. They discuss the challenges, possible solutions, and open issues faced when mapping and executing large-scale workflows on current cyberinfrastructure. They particularly emphasize the issues related to the management of data throughout the workflow lifecycle.

Chapter 9

Management of the large data sets produced by data-intensive scientific applications is complicated by the fact that participating institutions are often geographically distributed and separated by distinct administrative domains. A key data management problem in these distributed collaborations has been the creation and maintenance of replicated data sets. This chapter provides an overview of replica management schemes used in large, data-intensive, distributed scientific collaborations. Early replica management strategies focused on the development of robust, highly scalable catalogs for maintaining replica locations. In recent years, more sophisticated, application-specific replica management systems have been developed to support the requirements of scientific Virtual Organizations. These systems have motivated interest in application-independent, policy-driven schemes for replica management that can be tailored to meet the performance and reliability requirements of a range of scientific collaborations. The authors discuss the data replication solutions to meet the challenges associated with increasingly large data sets and the requirement to run data analysis at geographically distributed sites.

Section 4
Data Discovery & Visualization

Data intensive computing, cloud computing, and multicore computing are converging as frontiers to address massive data problems with hybrid programming models and/or runtimes including MapReduce, MPI, and parallel threading on multicore platforms. A major challenge is to utilize these technologies and large-scale computing resources effectively to advance fundamental science discoveries such as those in Life Sciences. The recently developed next-generation sequencers have enabled large-scale genome sequencing in areas such as environmental sample sequencing leading to metagenomic studies of collections of genes. Metagenomic research is just one of the areas that present a significant computational challenge because of the amount and complexity of data to be processed. This chapter discusses the use of innovative data-mining algorithms and new programming models for several Life Sciences applications. The authors particularly focus on methods that are applicable to large data sets coming from high throughput devices of steadily increasing power. They show results for both clustering and dimension reduction algorithms, and the use of MapReduce on modest size problems. They identify two key areas where further research is essential, and propose to develop new O(NlogN) complexity algorithms suitable for the analysis of millions of sequences. They suggest Iterative MapReduce as a promising programming model combining the best features of MapReduce with those of high performance environments such as MPI.

An effective visualization is best achieved through the creation of a proper representation of data and the interactive manipulation and querying of the visualization. Large-scale data visualization is particularly challenging because the size of the data is several orders of magnitude larger than what can be managed on an average desktop computer. Large-scale data visualization therefore requires the use of distributed computing. By leveraging the widespread expansion of the Internet and other national and international high-speed network infrastructure such as the National LambdaRail, Internet-2, and the Global Lambda Integrated Facility, data and service providers began to migrate toward a model of widespread distribution of resources. This chapter introduces different instantiations of the visualization pipeline and the historic motivation for their creation. The authors examine individual components of the pipeline in detail to understand the technical challenges that must be solved in order to ensure continued scalability. They discuss distributed data management issues that are specifically relevant to large-scale visualization. They also introduce key data rendering techniques and explain through case studies approaches for scaling them by leveraging distributed computing. Lastly they describe advanced display technologies that are now considered the "lenses" for examining large-scale data.

Chapter 12

    Huadong Liu, University of Tennessee, USA
    Jinzhu Gao, University of The Pacific, USA
    Jian Huang, University of Tennessee, USA
    Micah Beck, University of Tennessee, USA
    Terry Moore, University of Tennessee, USA

The emergence of high-resolution simulation, where simulation outputs have grown to terascale levels and beyond, raises major new challenges for the visualization community, which is serving computational scientists who want adequate visualization services provided to them on-demand. Many existing algorithms for parallel visualization were not designed to operate optimally on time-shared parallel systems or on heterogeneous systems. They are usually optimized for systems that are homogeneous and have been reserved for exclusive use. This chapter explores the possibility of developing parallel visualization algorithms that can use distributed, heterogeneous processors to visualize cutting edge simulation datasets. The authors study how to effectively support multiple concurrent users operating on the same large dataset, with each focusing on a dynamically varying subset of the data. From a system design point of view, they observe that a distributed cache offers various advantages, including improved scalability. They develop basic scheduling mechanisms that were able to achieve fault-tolerance and load-balancing, optimal use of resources, and flow-control using system-level back-off, while still enforcing deadline driven (i.e. time-critical) visualization.

Preface

MOTIVATION AND ORGANIZATION OF THE BOOK

Scientific applications generate increasingly large amounts of data, often referred as the "data deluge," which necessitates collaboration and sharing between national and international research institutions. Simply purchasing high-capacity, high-performance storage systems and adding them to the existing infrastructure of the collaborating institutions does not solve the underlying and highly challenging data handling problem. Scientists are often forced to spend a great deal of time and energy on solving basic data-handling issues, such as the physical location of data, how to access it, and/or how to move it to visualization and/or compute resources for further analysis.

In this book, experts on data intensive computing discuss the challenges imposed by data-intensive applications on distributed systems, and present state-of-the-art solutions proposed to overcome these challenges. This book is intended to be a reference for research scientists and application developers working with complex, data intensive, and data-driven applications on distributed environments. It can also be used as a textbook for advanced distributed systems, data management, and related courses.

This book is organized in four sections: i) New Paradigms in Data Intensive Computing; ii) Distributed Storage; iii) Data and Workflow Management; and iv) Data Discovery and Visualization.

Section 1, New Paradigms in Data Intensive Computing, focuses on new generation of computing paradigms proposed to overcome the challenges of complex, data intensive, and data-driven applications running on distributed environments. It includes three chapters: "Data-Aware Distributed Computing," "Towards Data Intensive Many-Task Computing," and "Micro-Services: A Service-Oriented Paradigm for Scalable, Distributed Data Management."

Chapter 1, "Data-Aware Distributed Computing," elaborates on how the most crucial distributed computing components such as scheduling, workflow management, and end-to-end throughput optimization can become "data-aware." In this new computing paradigm, called data-aware distributed computing, data placement activities are represented as full-featured jobs in the end-to-end workflow, and they are queued, managed, scheduled, and optimized via a specialized data-aware scheduler. As part of this new paradigm, the authors present a set of tools for mitigating the data bottleneck in distributed computing systems, which consists of three main components: a data-aware scheduler, which provides capabilities such as planning, scheduling, resource reservation, job execution, and error recovery for data movement tasks; integration of these capabilities to the other layers in distributed computing, such as workflow planning; and further optimization of data movement tasks via dynamically tuning of underlying protocol transfer parameters.

Chapter 2, "Towards Data Intensive Many-Task Computing," presents a new computing paradigm called many-task computing, which aims to bridge the gap high throughput computing and high performance computing. Many task computing denotes high-performance computations comprising multiple distinct activities, coupled via file system operations. The aggregate number of tasks, quantity of computing, and volumes of data may be extremely large. The authors also propose a "data diffusion" approach to enable data-intensive many-task computing. Data diffusion acquires compute and storage resources dynamically, replicates data in response to demand, and schedules computations close to data, effectively harnessing data locality in application data access patterns.

Chapter 3, "Micro-Services: A Service-Oriented Paradigm for Scalable, Distributed Data Management," defines micro-services, which are orchestrated into conditional workflows for achieving large-scale data management specific to collections of data. Micro-services communicate with each other using parameter exchange, in memory data structures, a database-based persistent information store, and a network messaging system that uses a serialization protocol for communicating with remote micro-services. The orchestration of the workflow is done by a distributed rule engine that chains and executes the workflows and maintains transactional properties through recovery micro-services. The authors discuss the micro-service oriented architecture, compare the micro-service approach with traditional service-oriented architectures (SOA), and describe the use of micro-services for implementing policy-based data management systems.

Section 2, Distributed Storage, focuses on design and implementation of advanced storage systems for sharing large amounts of data between distantly collaborating researchers. It includes three chapters: "Distributed Storage Systems for Data Intensive Computing," "Metadata Management in PetaShare Distributed Storage Network," and "Data Intensive Computing with Clustered Chirp Servers."

Chapter 4, "Distributed Storage Systems for Data Intensive Computing," presents an overview of the utility of distributed storage systems in supporting modern applications that are increasingly becoming data intensive. The coverage of distributed storage systems in this chapter is based on the requirements imposed by data intensive computing and not a mere summary of storage systems. To this end, the authors delve into several aspects of supporting data-intensive analysis, such as data staging, offloading, checkpointing, and end-user access to terabytes of data, and illustrate the use of novel techniques and methodologies for realizing distributed storage systems therein. The data deluge from scientific experiments, observations, and simulations is affecting all of the aforementioned day-to-day operations in data-intensive computing. Modern distributed storage systems employ techniques that can help improve application performance, alleviate I/O bandwidth bottleneck, mask failures, and improve data availability. The authors present key guiding principles involved in the construction of such storage systems, associated tradeoffs, design, and architecture, all with an eye toward addressing challenges of data-intensive scientific applications.

Chapter 5, "Metadata Management in PetaShare Distributed Storage Network," presents the design and implementation of a reliable and efficient distributed data storage system, PetaShare, which spans multiple institutions across the state of Louisiana. At the back-end, PetaShare provides a unified name space and efficient data movement across geographically distributed storage sites. At the front-end, it provides light-weight clients the enable easy, transparent, and scalable access. In PetaShare, the authors have designed and implemented an asynchronously replicated multi-master metadata system for enhanced reliability and availability. The authors also present a high level cross-domain metadata schema to provide a structured systematic view of multiple science domains supported by PetaShare.

Chapter 6, "Data Intensive Computing with Clustered Chirp Servers," presents Chirp as a building block for clustered data intensive scientific computing. Chirp was originally designed as a lightweight file server for grid computing and was used as a "personal" file server. The authors explore building systems with very high I/O capacity using commodity storage devices by tying together multiple Chirp servers. Several real-life applications such as the GRAND Data Analysis Grid, the Biometrics Research Grid, and the Biocompute Facility use Chirp as their fundamental building block, but provide different services and interfaces appropriate to their target communities.

Section 3, Data and Workflow Management, focuses on the challenges of managing and scheduling complex workflows and large-scale data replication for data intensive applications. It includes three chapters: "A Survey of Scheduling and Management Techniques for Data-Intensive Application Workflows," "Data Management in Scientific Workflows," and "Replica Management in Data Intensive Distributed Science Applications."

Chapter 7, "A Survey of Scheduling and Management Techniques for Data-Intensive Application Workflows," presents a comprehensive survey of algorithms, techniques, and frameworks used for scheduling and management of data-intensive application workflows. Many complex scientific experiments are expressed in the form of workflows for structured, repeatable, controlled, scalable, and automated executions. This chapter focuses on the type of workflows that have tasks processing huge amount of data, usually in the range from hundreds of mega-bytes to petabytes. Scientists are already using Grid systems that schedule these workflows onto globally distributed resources for optimizing various objectives: minimize total makespan of the workflow, minimize cost and usage of network bandwidth, minimize cost of computation and storage, meet the deadline of the application, and so forth. This chapter lists and describes techniques used in each of these systems for processing huge amount of data. A survey of workflow management techniques is useful for understanding the working of the Grid systems providing insights on performance optimization of scientific applications dealing with data-intensive workloads.

Chapter 8, "Data Management in Scientific Workflows," describes a workflow lifecycle as consisting of a workflow generation phase where the analysis is defined, the workflow planning phase where resources needed for execution are selected, the workflow execution part, where the actual computations take place, and the result, metadata, and provenance storing phase. The authors discuss the issues related to data management at each step of the workflow cycle. They describe challenging problems and illustrate them in the context of real-life applications. They discuss the challenges, possible solutions, and open issues faced when mapping and executing large-scale workflows on current cyberinfrastructure. They particularly emphasize the issues related to the management of data throughout the workflow lifecycle.

Chapter 9, "Replica Management in Data Intensive Distributed Science Applications," provides an overview of replica management schemes used in large, data-intensive, distributed scientific collaborations. Early replica management strategies focused on the development of robust, highly scalable catalogs for maintaining replica locations. In recent years, more sophisticated, application-specific replica management systems have been developed to support the requirements of scientific Virtual Organizations. These systems have motivated interest in application-independent, policy-driven schemes for replica management that can be tailored to meet the performance and reliability requirements of a range of scientific collaborations. The authors discuss the data replication solutions to meet the challenges associated with increasingly large data sets and the requirement to run data analysis at geographically distributed sites.

Section 4, Data Discovery and Visualization, focuses on techniques for mining, discovering, and visualization of large data sets. It includes three chapters: "Data Intensive Computing for Bioinformatics,"

"Visualization of Large-Scale Distributed Data," and "On-Demand Visualization on Scalable Shared Infrastructure."

Chapter 10, "Data Intensive Computing for Bioinformatics," discusses the use of innovative data-mining algorithms and new programming models for several Life Sciences applications. The authors particularly focus on methods that are applicable to large data sets coming from high throughput devices of steadily increasing power. They show results for both clustering and dimension reduction algorithms, and the use of MapReduce on modest size problems. They identify two key areas where further research is essential, and propose to develop new $O(NlogN)$ complexity algorithms suitable for the analysis of millions of sequences. They suggest Iterative MapReduce as a promising programming model combining the best features of MapReduce with those of high performance environments such as MPI.

Chapter 11, "Visualization of Large-Scale Distributed Data," introduces different instantiations of the visualization pipeline and the historic motivation for their creation. The authors examine individual components of the pipeline in detail to understand the technical challenges that must be solved in order to ensure continued scalability. They discuss distributed data management issues that are specifically relevant to large-scale visualization. They also introduce key data rendering techniques and explain through case studies approaches for scaling them by leveraging distributed computing. Lastly they describe advanced display technologies that are now considered the "lenses" for examining large-scale data.

Chapter 12, "On-Demand Visualization on Scalable Shared Infrastructure," explores the possibility of developing parallel visualization algorithms that can use distributed, heterogeneous processors to visualize cutting edge simulation datasets. The authors study how to effectively support multiple concurrent users operating on the same large dataset, with each focusing on a dynamically varying subset of the data. From a system design point of view, they observe that a distributed cache offers various advantages, including improved scalability. They developed basic scheduling mechanisms that were able to achieve fault-tolerance and load-balancing, optimal use of resources, and flow-control using system-level back-off, while still enforcing deadline driven (i.e. time-critical) visualization.

Tevfik Kosar
State University of New York at Buffalo (SUNY), USA

Section 1
New Paradigms in Data Intensive Computing

Chapter 1
Data–Aware Distributed Computing

Esma Yildirim
State University of New York at Buffalo (SUNY), USA

Mehmet Balman
Lawrence Berkeley National Laboratory, USA

Tevfik Kosar
State University of New York at Buffalo (SUNY), USA

ABSTRACT

With the continuous increase in the data requirements of scientific and commercial applications, access to remote and distributed data has become a major bottleneck for end-to-end application performance. Traditional distributed computing systems closely couple data access and computation, and generally, data access is considered a side effect of computation. The limitations of traditional distributed computing systems and CPU-oriented scheduling and workflow management tools in managing complex data handling have motivated a newly emerging era: data-aware distributed computing. In this chapter, the authors elaborate on how the most crucial distributed computing components, such as scheduling, workflow management, and end-to-end throughput optimization, can become "data-aware." In this new computing paradigm, called data-aware distributed computing, data placement activities are represented as full-featured jobs in the end-to-end workflow, and they are queued, managed, scheduled, and optimized via a specialized data-aware scheduler. As part of this new paradigm, the authors present a set of tools for mitigating the data bottleneck in distributed computing systems, which consists of three main components: a data-aware scheduler, which provides capabilities such as planning, scheduling, resource reservation, job execution, and error recovery for data movement tasks; integration of these capabilities to the other layers in distributed computing, such as workflow planning; and further optimization of data movement tasks via dynamic tuning of underlying protocol transfer parameters.

Copyright © 2012, IGI Global. Copying or distributing in print or electronic forms without written permission of IGI Global is prohibited.

INTRODUCTION

Scientific applications and experiments are becoming increasingly complex and more demanding in terms of computational and data requirements. Large experiments, such as high-energy physics simulations (ATLAS, 2010; CMS, 2010), genome mapping (Altshul et al, 1990), and climate modeling (Kiehl et al, 1998) generate data volumes reaching hundreds of terabytes per year (Hey & Trefethen, 2003). Data collected from remote sensors and satellites, dynamic data-driven applications, digital libraries and preservations are also producing extremely large datasets for real-time or offline processing (Ceyhan & Kosar, 2007; Tummala & Kosar, 2007). To organize and analyze these data, scientists are turning to distributed resources owned by collaborating parties or national facilities to provide the computing power and storage capacity needed. But the use of distributed resources imposes new challenges (Kosar, 2006). Even simply sharing and disseminating subsets of the data to the scientists' home institutions is difficult and not yet routine — the systems managing these resources must provide robust scheduling and allocation of storage resources, as well as efficient and reliable management of data movement.

Although through the use of distributed resources the institutions and organizations gain access to the resources needed for their large-scale applications, complex middleware is required to orchestrate the use of these compute, storage, and network resources between collaborating parties, and to manage the end-to-end processing of data. The majority of existing research has been on the management of compute tasks and resources, as they are widely considered to be the most expensive. As scientific applications become more data intensive, however, the management of data resources and data flow between the storage and compute resources is becoming the main bottleneck. Many jobs executing in distributed environments are failed or are inhibited by over-loaded storage servers, congested network links, or incomplete data transfers. These failures prevent scientists from making progress in their research.

According to the 'Strategic Plan for the US Climate Change Science Program (CCSP)', one of the main objectives of the future research programs should be *"Enhancing the data management infrastructure"*, since *"The users should be able to focus their attention on the information content of the data, rather than how to discover, access, and use it."* (CCSP, 2003). This statement by CCSP summarizes the goal of many cyberinfrastructure efforts initiated by NSF, DOE and other federal agencies, as well the research direction of several leading academic institutions. This is also the main motivation for our work presented in this chapter.

Traditional distributed computing systems closely couple data handling and computation. They consider data resources as second class entities, and access to data as a side effect of computation. Data placement (i.e., access, retrieval, and/or movement of data) is either embedded in the computation and causes the computation to delay, or is performed by simple scripts which do not have the same privileges as compute jobs. The inadequacy of traditional distributed computing systems in dealing with complex data handling problems in our new data-rich world has motivated a new paradigm called *data-aware distributed computing* (Kosar et al, 2009).

We have previously introduced the concept that the data placement activities in a distributed computing environment need to be first class entities just like computational jobs, and presented the first batch scheduler specialized in data placement and data movement: Stork (Kosar & Livny, 2004). This scheduler implements techniques specific to queuing, scheduling, and optimization of data placement jobs, and provides a level of abstraction between the user applications and the underlying data transfer and storage resources. Stork is considered one of the very first examples of "data-aware scheduling" and has been very actively used in many e-Science application areas including coastal hazard prediction and storm surge modeling (SCOOP, 2010); oil flow and reservoir uncertainty analysis (UCoMS, 2010); numerical relativity and black hole collisions (NumRel, 2010); educational video processing and behavioral assessment (WCER, 2010); digital sky imaging (DPOSS, 2010); and multiscale computational fluid dynamics (MSCFD, 2010).

Our previous work in this area has also been acknowledged by the strategic reports of federal agencies. The DOE Office of Science report on 'Data Management Challenges' defines data movement and efficient access to data as two key foundations of scientific data management technology (DOE, 2004). The DOE report says: *"In the same way that the load register instruction is the most basic operation provided by a CPU, so is the placement of data on a storage device... It is therefore essential that at all levels data placement tasks be treated in the same way computing tasks are treated."* and refers to our previous work (Kosar & Livny, 2004). The same report also states that *"Although many mechanisms exist for data transfer, research and development is still required to create schedulers and planners for storage space allocation and the transfer of data."*

In this chapter, we elaborate on how we can bring the concept of 'data-awareness' to several most crucial distributed computing components such as scheduling, workflow management, and end-to-end throughput optimization. In this new paradigm, data placement activities are represented as full-featured jobs in the end-to-end workflow, and they are queued, managed, scheduled, and optimized via a specialized data-aware scheduler. As part of this new paradigm, we have developed a set of tools for mitigating the data bottleneck in distributed computing systems, which consists of three main components: a data-aware scheduler which provides capabilities such as planning, scheduling, resource reservation, job execution, and error recovery for data movement tasks *(see "Data Scheduling" section)*; integration

of these capabilities to the other layers in distributed computing such as workflow planning *(see "Integration with Workflow Planning" section)*; and further optimization of data movement tasks via dynamically tuning of underlying protocol transfer parameters *(see "Throughput Optimization" section)*.

BACKGROUND

Several previous studies address data management for large-scale applications (Tierney et al, 1999; Johnston et al, 2000; Allcock et al, 2001a,b,c; Ranganathan et al, 2002, 2004; Venugopal et al, 2004; ROOT, 2006). However, scheduling of data storage and networking resources and optimization of data transfer tasks has been an open problem.

In an effort to achieve reliable and efficient data placement, high level data management tools such as the Reliable File Transfer Service (RFT) (Ravi et al, 2002), the Lightweight Data Replicator (LDR) (Koranda & Moe, 2007), and the Data Replication Service (DRS) (Chervenak et al, 2005) were developed. The main motivation for these tools was to enable byte streams to be transferred in a reliable manner, by handling possible failures such as dropped connections, machine reboots, and temporary network outages automatically via retrying. Most of these tools are built on top of GridFTP (Allcock et al, 2001a,b), which is a secure, and reliable data transfer protocol especially developed for high-bandwidth wide-area networks.

Beck et al. (1999) introduced Logistical Networking which performs global scheduling and optimization of data movement, storage and computation based on a model that takes into account all the network's underlying physical resources. Systems such as the Storage Resource Broker (SRB, 2010), the Integrated Rule Oriented Data System (iRODS, 2010), and the Storage Resource Manager (SRM, 2010) were developed to provide a uniform interface for connecting to heterogeneous data resources and accessing replicated data sets.

Thain et al. (2004) introduced the Batch-Aware Distributed File System (BAD-FS), which was followed by a modified data-driven batch scheduling system (Bent, 2005). Their goal was to achieve data-driven batch scheduling by exporting explicit control of storage decisions from the distributed file system to the batch scheduler. Using some simple data-driven scheduling techniques, they have demonstrated that the new data-driven system can achieve better throughput both over current distributed file systems such as AFS as well as over traditional CPU-centric batch scheduling techniques which are using remote I/O.

According to Stockinger (2005a,b), the entire resource selection problem requires detailed cost models with respect to data transfer. A cost model for data-intensive applications is presented in (Stockinger et al, 2001) where theoretical models for data-intensive job scheduling are discussed. In that work, a cost model is created that can determine if it is more efficient to transfer the data to a job or vice versa. The metric for measuring efficiency is the effective time seen by the client application. The model includes all important factors in a distributed Data Grid and takes various storage and access latencies into account to determine optimal data access. More general performance engineering approaches are discussed in (Stockinger et al, 2005b). In that work, they analyze a typical Grid system and point out performance analysis aspects in order to improve the overall job execution time of the system. Their focus is on the performance issues regarding data and replica management.

Babu, Shivam & Chase (2006) present Non-Invasive Modeling for Optimization (NIMO) system which automatically learns cost models for predicting the execution time of computational science application on distributed environments. NIMO first generates training samples for distributed applications, and using these samples learns cost models with statistical learning techniques.

NIMO is an active system which deploys and monitors the sampled application un- der different conditions. NIMO is also noninvasive so collects training data from passive streams without effecting not only the operating system or the application, but also the application source or library. On the other hand, there are some challenges arise based on this system. According to Babu, Shivam & Chase (2006), sampling acquiring may have high overhead. Also, the number of samples needed to get given level of accuracy increase exponentially. Last but not least, the training sample set may not represent the entire operating range of the system.

The studies that try to find the optimal number of streams for data scheduling are limited and they are mostly based on approximate theoretical models (Crowcroft et al, 1998; Hacker et al, 2002; Lu et al, 2005; Altman et al, 2006). They all have specific constraints and assumptions. Also the correctness of the model is proved with simulation results mostly. Hacker et al. (2002) claim that the total number of streams behaves like one giant stream that transfers in capacity of total of each streams' achievable throughput. However, this model only works for uncongested networks. Thus it is not be able to predict when the network will be congested. An- other study (Crowcroft et al., 1998) declares the same theory but develops a protocol which at the same time provides fairness. Lu et al. (2005) models the bandwidth of multiple streams as a partial second order polynomial equation and needs two different throughput measurement of different stream numbers to predict the others. In another model, the total throughput always shows the same characteristics (Altman et al., 2006) depending on the capacity of the connection as the number of streams increases and 3 streams are sufficient to get 90% utilization. None of the existing studies are able to accurately predict optimal number of parallel streams for best data throughput in a congested network.

In dynamic TCP buffer size tuning, the techniques that need modifications to the kernel (Cohen & Cohen, 2002; Semke, Madhavi & Mathis, 1998; Torvalds, 2008; Weigle & Feng, 2001) is usually based on changes to the buffer size during the transfer based on the congestion window or flow control window parameters. The approach presented in (Cohen & Cohen, 2002) requires changes to the Kernel Stack. Based on the current congestion window, RTT and server Read Time, they calculate the next congestion window and set the buffer variables based on the current and next congestion window sizes. Another study (Semke, Madhavi & Mathis, 1998) is also similar to the previous where the sender buffer size is adjusted based on the congestion window. Other two competitive techniques are Dynamic Right-Sizing (Weigle & Feng, 2001) and Linux 2.4 Auto-Tuning (Torvalds, 2008). DRS is basically a receiver-based approach where the receiver tries to estimate the bandwidth × delay product by using TCP packet header information and time stamps. Linux auto-tuning is a memory management technique in which it increases or decreases window size continuously based on the available memory and socket buffer space.

Although a decent number of studies have been presented in buffer size tuning, there are only a few studies that try to derive a mathematical model to find the relationship between buffer size and number of parallel streams. The study in (Ito, Ohsaki & Imase, 2008) models the throughput of parallel streams as multiple continuous time models of TCP congestion control mechanism. Another study represents the relationship between number of parallel streams, buffer size and round trip time by a single regression equation (Choi, Huh & Choo, 2005). However this equation again considers a no-loss network. The existing models are scarce and derived for no-loss networks and they consider the cases where the buffer size is not properly tuned but they do not consider the case where the buffer is also properly tuned and also using the parallel streams for tuned buffers

as in (Dunigan, Mathis & Tierney, 2002). There is no result comparing a less tuned buffer size with using more streams or a properly tuned buffer and using less number of streams.

DATA SCHEDULING

Data management and I/O has been a crucial problem in every area of science as well as computer science/engineering including operating system and microprocessor design (Balman & Kosar, 2007), and it is not surprising that there are similar challenges at the distributed system level. In the old days, the stress was mostly on performing calculations successfully and efficiently, and storage was controlled by the CPU, including fetching data back and forth between main memory and hard disk. Currently, we have reached the age of multi-core machines and distributed clusters. Data storage requirements per day, have reached terabyte scale.

Accessing and transferring widely distributed data can be extremely inefficient and can degrade reliability. For instance, an application may suffer from insufficient storage space when staging-in the input data, generating the output, and staging-out the generated data to a remote storage. This can lead to thrashing of the storage server and subsequent timeout from too many concurrent read data transfers, ultimately causing server crashes due to an overload of write data transfers. Other third party data transfers may stall indefinitely due to loss of acknowledgment. And even if the transfer is performed efficiently, any faulty hardware can cause data corruption. Furthermore, remote access can suffer from unforeseeable contingencies such as performance degradation due to unplanned data transfers, and intermittent network outages.

In designing a data-aware distributed system, it is helpful to learn from developments in data access and management issues in different layers of computing systems from the microprocessor (e.g. pipelining, superscalar, latency hiding) to the operating system level (e.g. I/O scheduling) and look for their analogy for distributed systems. Although the scale of the problems is very different at each of these levels, conceptually they show a lot of similarities.

In microprocessors, efficient data access is the most important issue affecting performance (Flynn, 1999). One strategy to improve execution throughput is to hide memory latency, for example Intel's memory disambiguation architecture uses special algorithms to predict whether a load instruction depends on a previous store operation, so it can be scheduled out of program or- der to improve performance (Wechsler, 2006). To allow these optimizations, the instructions in modern microprocessors are classified into arithmetic instructions or memory-access (e.g. load/store) instructions (Hyde, 2003), where both sets are equally important (Yu, 1996). Similarly, we classify operations in a distributed computing system into either computational tasks or data access/movement tasks (referred also as data placement).

At the operating system level, many strategies are used to access data efficiently, including DMA, simultaneous resource sharing, I/O scheduling, disk management, file systems, and low-level parallelism such as disk striping. Additional challenges and solutions arise providing efficient I/O in parallel computer systems. In an operating system kernel, an I/O scheduling and control subsystem interacts with I/O devices, dealing with the queuing and scheduling of I/O operations, handling interrupts, and collecting and reporting status information. Main memory buffers are used for I/O requests, and disk requests can be scheduled taking into account e.g. seek time to improve performance. Two example approaches are Linus Elevator and Deadline I/O scheduling. In Elevator scheduling, a single queue maintains a list of requests sorted by the block number, whereas Deadline scheduling separates read and write request queues with requests having an expiration time. Read and write requests have different characteristics at the operating system level,

where write requests are usually asynchronous, read requests are in small one-by-one chunks.

In traditional distributed systems, scheduling of I/O requests is usually not considered independently of compute tasks. The 'data-aware scheduling' framework that we develop provides a clear separation of computation and data placement tasks each with a different scheduler, enabling asynchronous execution of the two different classes of tasks. The data-aware scheduler implements techniques specific to queuing, scheduling, and optimization of data placement jobs, and provides a level of abstraction between the user applications and the underlying data transfer and storage resources. In this sense, the system resembles the I/O control system from an operating system, or a "data placement subsystem" for a distributed computing environment.

We have introduced the concept that the data placement activities in a distributed computing environment need to be first class entities just like computational jobs (Kosar & Livny, 2004; Kosar, 2005; Kosar, 2006). In that work, we have presented a framework in which data placement activities are considered as full-edged jobs which can be queued, scheduled, monitored, and even check-pointed. We have introduced the first batch scheduler specialized in data placement and data movement: Stork. This scheduler implements techniques specific to queuing, scheduling, and optimization of data placement jobs; provides high reliability in data transfers; and creates a level of abstraction between the user applications and the underlying data transfer and storage resources (including FTP, HTTP, GridFTP, SRM, SRB, and iRODS) via a modular, uniform interface. Stork is considered one of the very first examples of "data-aware scheduling" and has been very actively used in many application areas including coastal hazard prediction (SCOOP), reservoir uncertainty analysis (UCoMS), digital sky imaging (DPOSS), and educational video processing (WCER) (Ceyhan et al, 2008; Kosar et al, 2005; Kola, Kosar & Livny, 2004).

Figure 1. a) Data-aware scheduler "Stork" and its interaction with other components in an end-to-end system; b) Preliminary results using different optimization techniques of Stork

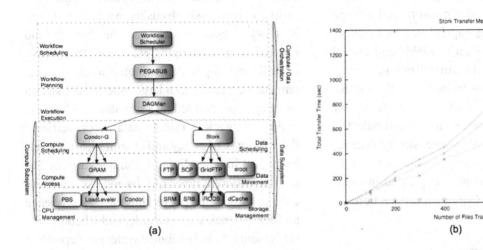

(a)   (b)

Our initial end-to-end implementation using Stork consists of two parallel universes: a data subsystem, and a compute subsystem. These two sub-systems are complimentary, the first specializing in data management and scheduling and the latter specializing in compute management and scheduling. The orchestration of these two parallel subsystems is performed by the upper layer workflow planning and execution components. In cases where multiple workflows need to be executed on the same system, users may want to prioritize among multiple workflows or make other scheduling decisions. This is handled by the workflow scheduler at the highest level. An example for such a case would be hurricanes of different urgency levels arriving at the same time. Figure 1a shows the illustration of this framework, and Figure 1b shows the effect of using different optimization schemes in Stork (such as connection caching, concurrent transfers, and data fusion) on the end-to-end data transfer performance. For this specific application (UCoMS), data fusion (merging many small files into a single large file before transfer) resulted in the best performance since UCoMS data set consists of thousands of small files. On the other hand, generalizing this

approach and selecting the right scheme for any application still remains an open issue.

The Stork data-aware scheduler takes the responsibility of managing data resources and scheduling data tasks from the user and perform these tasks transparently. In existing approaches, users must deal with the complexities of linking to different libraries and using different interfaces of data transfer protocols and storage servers. Stork data-aware scheduler provides a uniform interface for all different protocols and storage servers, and will grant a level of abstraction between them and the user.

The data-aware scheduler can also interact with higher level workflow planning and management tools for optimal end-to-end application performance and ensure that neither the storage system nor the network links become overloaded. It provides a flexible and extensible data model to represent different data management services and constraints. In this framework, the data storage resources advertise themselves, their attributes, and their access policies as well (e.g. the maximum number of concurrent connections allowed). This reduces the common problem of storage server thrashing and crashing due to too many concurrent file transfer connections. This component is explained in more detail in "Integration with Workflow Planning" section.

The scheduler includes network and storage bandwidth monitoring capabilities that collect statistics on the maximum available end-to-end band-width, actual bandwidth utilization, latency, and the number of hops to be traveled. In order to estimate the speed at which data movement can take place, it is necessary to estimate the bandwidth capability at the source storage system, at the target storage system, and the network in between. This component is explained in more detail in "Throughput Optimization" section.

INTEGRATION WITH WORKFLOW PLANNING

Workflow systems that map task execution to highly distributed, dynamic runtime environments must all deal with the low-level data handling issues that we address in this chapter. To effectively schedule, a workflow planner must either send jobs to sites where data resides, or should include stage-in and stage-out steps in the workflow to make sure that the data arrives to the execution site before the computation starts. In the latter case, several other steps may need to be included in the workflow, such as allocating the disk space needed by the jobs, and deleting the data once it is no longer required, at optimal points. These strategies must recognize caching needs and each workflow's unique data access pattern, as well as predicting the future needs for cached files.

When developing data-aware workflow systems, we can make use of similarities to instruction pipelining in microprocessors, where the lifecycle of an instruction consists of steps such as fetch, decode, execute, and write (Hennessy & Jouppi, 1991). In microprocessor level instruction pipeline, data retrieval from memory to the execution unit is generally the bottleneck due to the slow memory access speed (compared with register and internal cache access speeds) and the latency in

the bus between memory and CPU (Flynn, 1999). Pipelining helps in in- creasing the throughput of instruction processing by using smaller sub-stages. Memory access instructions are then buffered and ordered with overlapping executions to improve overall throughput. A distributed workflow system can be viewed as a large pipeline consisting of many tasks divided into sub-stages, where the main bottleneck is remote data access/retrieval due to network latency and communication overhead. Just like pipelining techniques are used to overlap different types of jobs and execute them concurrently while preserving the task sequence and dependencies, we can order and schedule data movement jobs in distributed systems independent of compute tasks to exploit parallel execution while preserving data dependencies.

For this purpose, we expand the scientific workflows to include the necessary data-placement steps such as stage-in and stage-out, as well as other important steps which support data movement, such as allocating and de- allocating storage space for the data, and reserving and releasing the net- work links. This workflow expansion is illustrated in Figure 2. Similar to load/store operations being scheduled and executed by different components in modern processor architectures (Ramanathan, 2006), we schedule and execute data placement and compute jobs using different schedulers specialized for each.

Like the data forwarding between pipeline stages is used to avoid wasting pipeline cycles when writing to a register and reading it again for the next instruction in the pipeline order (Stokes, 2003; Sun, 2005a,b), the data-aware workflow planner communicates with the data placement scheduler and computational job scheduler via the workflow execution tool to order jobs so that data stage-in and stage-out are managed to minimize system overhead. For example, one approach is to schedule and send jobs to compute nodes that are "close" to the requested data (Ranganathan, 2002; Ranganathan & Foster, 2004).

Figure 2. Expansion of a scientific workflow to include data-placement steps

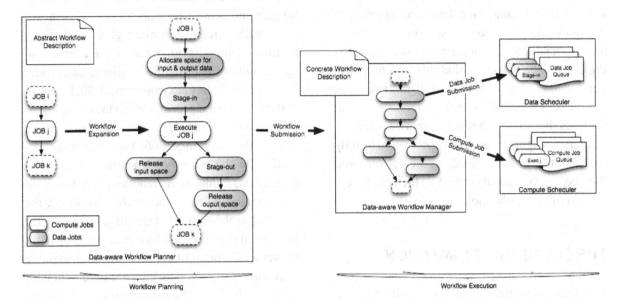

We have done a preliminary implementation of data-aware workflow management where data-awareness components were added to workflow planning tool Pegasus (Deelman et al, 2006) and workflow execution tool Condor DAGMan (Figure 1). This preliminary implementation was used in coastal hazard prediction (SCOOP) and reservoir uncertainty analysis (UCoMS) applications (Ceyhan et al, 2008). We have developed a preliminary model (Suslu & Kosar, 2007; Suslu et al, 2008) to choose between remote I/O versus staging for particular applications. As one of the results of that work, we suggest that for remote I/O to be more efficient than staging, the following equation should hold true:

$$Nr - Ns < Wl + Rl \qquad (1)$$

where Rl is the time to read from local disk to local memory, Wl is the time to write from local memory to local disk, Ns is the time to send data over network via a staging protocol, and Nr is the time to send data over network via a remote I/O protocol This equation shows that the time difference coming from using a specialized data transfer protocol versus a remote I/O protocol should be less than the overhead of extra read/write to the disk in staging. In other words, if your remote I/O library performs good in data transfer over network, or your local disk performance is slow, remote I/O might be advantageous over staging. Otherwise, staging method would perform better. One challenge would be estimating these parameters without actually running the application.

We have created a synthetic program to simulate the effects of different parameters such as input and output data size, data access pattern, and data access ratio on the performance of staging vs remote I/O. This program can simulate four different data access patterns which are i) read all blocks in the dataset sequentially (full), ii) read every other blocks in the dataset sequentially (jump) iii) read first half of the dataset sequentially (half), and iv) read half of the dataset in random blocks (random). In our testbed, we had a fast end-to-end network connection (1Gbps) but the disk on the execution site was old and slow. Confirming our conclusion from equation 1, remote I/O performed better in this setting since the overhead of extra write and read to/from the local disk in case of staging was too high compared with network data transfer gain. But when we changed the data access pattern of the application from sequential to non-sequential and especially to random, staging starts becoming better. The reason behind this is, remote I/O per- forms extremely bad in case of multiple small remote seek and read/write operations. Our initial findings showed that the decision between remote I/O versus staging for an application would heavily depend on i) relative speeds of the network and the disk on the execution host ii) the data access pattern of the application.

THROUGHPUT OPTIMIZATION

In a data-aware distributed system, effective use of available network throughput and optimization of data transfer speed is crucial for end-to-end application performance. With the recent developments in the optical network technology, that provides up to 100Gbps transport and promising a higher level capacity in the future, the utilization of network resources has brought a challenge to the current middleware solutions to provide distributed Petascale science (DOE, 2008). Using the existing techniques, achieving multiple Gbps throughput conventionally over TCP-based networks has become a burden. The throughput rate achieved by today's IP networks is limited by the performance of TCP, which is a reliable data transport protocol and the basis of default application-level transport protocols (e.g. FTP, GridFTP). Over the years many variants of TCP have been implemented to improve its performance however still it has remained the most-widely adopted protocol.

Apart from the low-level transport protocols implemented, there have been a number of high-level methods to optimize the throughput of data transfers regardless of the underlying protocol used. Tuning underlying end-system parameters and opening parallel streams is a way of doing it and widely used in many application areas from data-intensive scientific computing to live multimedia and peer-to-peer paradigms. It is shown that parallel streams achieve high throughput by mimicking the behavior of individual streams and get an unfair share of the available bandwidth (Sivakumar, Bailey & Grossman, 2000; Lee et al, 2001; Balakrishman et al, 1998; Hacker, Noble & Atley, 2005; Eggert, Heideman & Touch, 2000; Karrer, Park & Kim, 2006; Lu, Qiao & Dinda, 2005). On the other hand, using too many simultaneous connections reaches the network on a congestion point and after that threshold; the achievable throughput starts to drop down for low-speed networks. Unfortunately it is difficult to predict the point of congestion and is variable over some parameters, which are unique in both time and domain. The prediction of the optimal number of streams is hence very challenging and almost impossible without some parameters of current network conditions such as available bandwidth, RTT, packet loss rate, bottleneck link capacity and data size.

It is easier to optimize the network parameters in the case of bulk data transfers. After some point in time, enough historical information is gathered and the parameters are optimized according to the condition of the network. This type of optimization has been already used with Stork data scheduler (Kosar & Livny, 2004) before. However, for individual data transfers, the optimization becomes harder. Instead of relying on historical information, the transfer should be optimized based on instant feedback. This optimization can be done by achieving optimal number of parallel streams to get the highest throughput. However, an optimization technique not relying on historical data in this case must not cause overhead of gathering instant data that is larger than the speed up gained with multiple streams for a particular data size. Gathering instant information for prediction models can be done by using network performance measurement tools. However it is very difficult to choose a measurement tool for efficient and accurate information collection. Although difficult, the prediction of the optimal parallelism level for a data transfer regardless of the underlying network characteristics is not impossible (whether it is a HS network or a low-speed WAN or LAN). We have already developed mathematical models to find the near-optimal parallel stream number and applied their accuracy against actual data transfers. We also have developed algorithms to perform the prediction in the most cost-effective way without relying on much historical data or instant prediction information obtained from prediction tools (Pathload, 2010; Pathchirp, 2010; NWS, 2010; Iperf, 2010). We have gained promising results and will work for finer predictions.

Another important parameter to be tuned for high throughput is the TCP buffer size. It is important in the sense that it affects the maximum number of bits that could be on the fly before an acknowledgement is received. Usually the buffer size is tuned as setting it to twice the value of bandwidth × delay product (BDP) (Jain, Prasad & Davrolis, 2003). However there are also different interpretations of bandwidth and delay concepts. Most of the current buffer size tuning work either require changes to the kernel stack (Cohen & Cohen, 2002; Semke, Madhavi & Mathis, 1998; Torvalds, 2008; Weigle & Feng, 2001) or is based on estimations made on bandwidth and delay values in the application level (Jain, Prasad & Davrolis, 2003; Prasad, Jain & Davrolis, 2004; Hasegawa et al, 2001; Morajko, 2004).

Although the buffer size parameter is properly tuned, it does not show a better performance than using parallel streams, as parallel streams tend to recover from packet loss more quickly rather than a buffer tuned single stream. When a packet loss event occurs only one of the streams goes into a window reduction and the other streams go unaffected. Also the recovery time for a small stream is quicker than a large buffer-tuned stream. There are a few studies that try to derive a mathematical model to find the relationship between buffer size and number of parallel streams (Ito, Ohsaki & Imase, 2008; Choi, Huh & Choo, 2005). The

study in (Ito, Ohsaki & Imase, 2008) models the throughput of parallel streams as multiple continuous time models of TCP congestion control mechanism. Another study represents the relationship between number of parallel streams, buffer size and round trip time by a single regression equation (Choi, Huh & Choo, 2005). However this equation again considers a no-loss network. Mostly the models are derived for no-loss networks and they do not present an optimal value for both parameters.

In this section, we provide a new model that can predict the behavior of the throughput of parallel streams with accuracy and historical or prediction information and analyze the behavior of throughput with respect to buffer size and parallel streams to set a way to balance them.

PARALLEL TCP STREAM OPTIMIZATION

We have chosen TCP as our underlying transport protocol for our models since it is the most widely adapted protocol and one of the most important reasons of bottleneck in network because of its design goals. TCP is designed for optimizing the network bandwidth as well as provide fairness among the flows sharing the network. It has two phases that are named Slow start and Congestion Avoidance (Figure 3). In this figure, the CWND refers to congestion window, which is the number of packets the sender is allowed to send. The higher the congestion window, the higher is the throughput. In the slow start phase, the congestion window starts from 1 packet and is exponentially increased to utilize the throughput quickly until a packet loss event occurs. Then the congestion window is divided by half and starts to increase linearly. This is known as the additive increase - multiplicative decrease property (AIMD) (Tierney, 2005). When a timeout occurs the loop turns to the beginning congestion window size and enters the slow start phase again. This property of TCP en-

Figure 3. TCP behavior

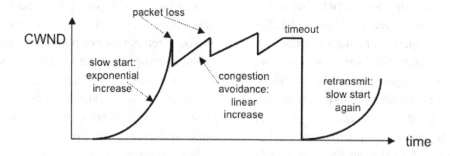

sures fairness, however it gives poor performance in terms of throughput. Therefore other methods are tried to compensate its poor performance.

There has been a number of studies that try to optimize the network and the end-systems to obtain the maximal end-to-end throughput in terms of several parameters such as the parallel stream number, window size, I/O block size, I/O scheduler, MTU (Maximum Transmission Unit) size, load sharing with IRQ (Interrupt ReQuest) bonding and interrupt coalescing. Most of the optimizations are done manually and dynamic optimization methods are scarce.

Throughput of Parallel Streams for Uncongested Networks

The Mathis throughput equation (Mathis et al, 1997) states that the achievable throughput depends on three parameters: Round-trip time (RTT), Packet loss rate (p) and Maximum segment size (MSS). Equation 2, presents an upper bound on the achievable throughput. In this equation, MSS is the IP maximum transmission unit (MTU) size - TCP header. RTT is the time it takes for the segment to reach the receiver and for a segment carrying the generated acknowledgment to return to the sender. p is the ratio of missing packets over total number of packets while c is a constant.

$$Th \leq \frac{MSS}{RTT}\frac{c}{\sqrt{p}} \quad (2)$$

Hacker, Nobel & Atley, (2005) claim that the total number of streams behaves like one giant stream that transfers in capacity of total of each streams' achievable throughput. Hence an application opening n connections actually gains n times the throughput of a single connection, assuming all connections experiencing equal packet losses and RTTs of all connections are equivalent since they most likely follow the same path. So Mathis throughput equation for n streams becomes as follows:

$$Th_n \leq \frac{MSS \times c}{RTT}\left(\frac{n}{\sqrt{p}}\right) \quad (3)$$

However this equation is valid for only uncongested networks in which packet loss rate is stable and does not change as the number of streams changes. On the contrary, at the point where the network gets congested, the packet loss rate starts to increase exponentially and the achievable throughput starts to drop down. In Figure 4, the average throughput of wide area data transfers with respect to the number of streams is presented. In these transoceanic wide area transfers, *RTT* is around 155ms while the size of the file to be

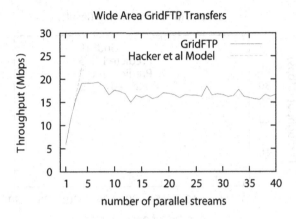

Figure 4. Hacker et al. model application over wide area transfers

transferred is 512MB. The throughput starts to increase linearly as suggested by the Hacker et al model, however, after reaching a peak point, the network becomes congested and it starts to decrease. If we apply that model, we cannot assume that the packet loss rate will not change; therefore we have to know the exact values of packet loss rate and RTT at the time of congestion, which is difficult to predict. As the Figure 4 denotes, the curve of Equation 3 continues to increase linearly and cannot predict the throughput behavior when the network gets congested. Another downside of this model is that collection of the variables p, RTT and MSS information is quite difficult.

Modeling Parallel Streams Throughput with a Partial Second Order Polynomial

The problem about the prediction of throughput with Equation 3 is that when the network gets congested, RTT and p parameters will all become dependent on n. Therefore the new equation will transform into the following:

$$Th_n \leq \frac{MSS \times c}{RTT_n} \left(\frac{n}{\sqrt{p_n}} \right) \qquad (4)$$

If a model can be presented that will relate these three parameters with only small number of measurements, then Th_n could be calculated easily. In the model proposed by Lu et al (2005), considering that p will increase exponentially starting from the point of congestion, this relationship is presented by a new variable p'_n which is equalized to a partial second order polynomial:

$$p'_n = p_n \frac{RTT_n^2}{c^2 MSS^2} = a'n^2 + b' \qquad (5)$$

When we replace p'_n in Equation 4, the total throughput of n streams could be calculated as follows:

$$Th_n = \frac{n}{\sqrt{p'_n}} = \frac{n}{\sqrt{a'n^2 + b'}} \qquad (6)$$

In this equation, a' and b' are variables to be found by measurements. To find the values of these variables, two achievable throughput measurements for two different parallelism levels are needed. The only possible way to find those throughput values is either use a tool that has the capability to do parallel transfers or to use information about past transfers. The experimental results claim that the parallelism level correctly

Figure 5. Lu et al. model application over wide area transfers

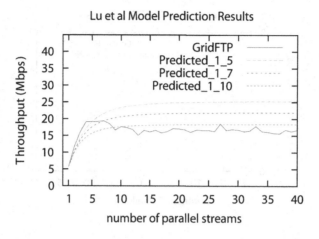

can be predicted, however in those results the aggregated throughput of connections increases and then becomes stable but never falls down. Hence it does not take into account that opening too many streams can place a burden over the network and the end-system and causes the throughput to decrease after the optimal point. In Figure 5, we apply this model over the wide area results we received from our experiments. The prediction curve calculated with throughput results of 1 and 5 parallel streams presents higher results than the ones calculated with 1 and 7, and also 1 and 10. The closest results, given for low number of streams, are 1 and 5; and also for high number of streams 1 and 10. All of the prediction curves have a logarithmic ascent behavior and then becomes stable for high number of streams but never fall down.

Dynamic Extraction of Model Equation Order

The reason to use a partial second order equation is because of the assumption that the packet loss rate starts to increase exponentially and also their experiments showed that best results were taken with a partial second order polynomial comparing to linear and full second order polynomials. However it is not a proven fact that a certain order

equation should be used to get accurate results. If we increase the number of parallelism levels to be used to three and derive the model equation order dynamically based on the throughput of those levels, we are able to get the characteristics of a throughput curve that increases first, after reaching its maximum point starts to decrease with a minimum bound. In this case, we assign the following equation to p'_n variable:

$$p'_n = a'n^{c'} + b' \tag{7}$$

In this equation, c' variable is the unknown order of the equation additional to a' and b'. When we replace this into our throughput equation for n streams, the resulting formula becomes as follows:

$$Th_n = \frac{n}{\sqrt{a'n^{c'} + b'}} \tag{8}$$

To solve this equation, we need three measurements Th_{n1}, Th_{n2} and Th_{n3} on the throughput curve for stream values $n1$, $n2$ and $n3$. Also c' being to the power n makes the solving of the equation much harder. After several substitutions we come up with the following equations for a', b' and c':

Figure 6. Dynamic model order extraction with Newton's iteration over wide area transfers

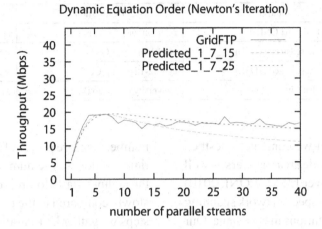

$$\frac{n_3^{c'} - n_1^{c'}}{n_2^{c'} - n_1^{c'}} = \frac{\dfrac{n_3^2}{Th_{n_3}^2} - \dfrac{n_1^2}{Th_{n_1}^2}}{\dfrac{n_2^2}{Th_{n_2}^2} - \dfrac{n_1^2}{Th_{n_1}^2}} \qquad (9)$$

$$a' = \frac{\dfrac{n_2^2}{Th_{n_2}^2} - \dfrac{n_1^2}{Th_{n_1}^2}}{n_2^{c'} - n_1^{c'}} \qquad (10)$$

$$b' = \frac{n_1^2}{Th_{n_1}^2} - a' n_1^{c'} \qquad (11)$$

The derivation of a' and b' depends on c'. However since it is in the power of the equation, it is not possible to solve it with an exact solution. Therefore we applied a mathematical approximate root finding method called Newton's Iteration. We revised the method to be suitable to our own problem:

$$c'_{x+1} = c'_x - \frac{f(c'_x)}{f'(c'_x)} \qquad (12)$$

According to this approach, after x+1 iterations we are able to find a very close approximation of c'. Starting with a small number for c'_0, we continue to calculate through c'_{x+1}. The value of the most approximate c' depends on only $f(c')$, in this case Equation 9, and its derivative. After calculating a most approximate c' which is possible with only a few iterations, the value of a' and b' can easily be derived with Equations 10 and 11.

Figure 6 shows the results of the predicted throughput by using dynamic equation order extraction over the wide area results. The best predicted results are taken with 1,7 and 25 parallelism levels although 1,7 and 15 give pretty close results. We are able to predict the actual throughput curve with a smooth transition between the increasing and decreasing part of the curve and with a good approximation overall. With this method the peek point of the curve will give us the optimal stream number to open for maximum throughput only with three data points either gathered from past transfers or immediate samplings with prediction tools.

Experiments over LAN/WAN and LONI

It is important to prove that the model we propose is accurate and adaptive to different environments

Table 1. Testbed categories and settings

Category	Source	Destination	System
LONI	neptune.loni.org(LONI)	zeke.loni.org (LONI)	IBM AIX
LAN-LONI	dsl-condor.csc.lsu.edu (DSL)	eric1.loni.org (LONI)	Redhat Linux
LAN	dsl-condor.csc.lsu.edu (DSL)	eyildi2-1.lsu.edu (CCT)	Redhat Linux
WAN	eyildi2-1.lsu.edu (CCT)	University of Trento (Italy)	Redhat and Suse Linux

and settings. Henceforth we construct a testbed that includes local and wide area transfers as well as transfers conducted over LONI (LONI, 2010) which is a statewide high-speed network spanning the universities and institutions in Louisiana. Our testbed consists of 2 IBM AIX 256-processor clusters over LONI network, two Linux workstations in DSL Laboratory and CCT at Louisiana State University and a workstation at University of Trento in Italy. The test cases are divided into four categories: transfers between LONI clusters, transfers between DSL and a LONI cluster, local area transfers between CCT and DSL and finally wide area transfers between CCT and Italy. The details of the test cases and environment are presented in Table 1. In all of the cases we use GridFTP as our transfer protocol.

The model we propose can show its best performances if the sample throughput data to calculate the predicted throughput can be chosen from appropriate parallelism levels. Since it needs three data points, there exists many kinds of combinations if we have more than three pairs (n, Th_n) of data and it is important for us to find the best combination to minimize the distance between historical or immediate sampling data and calculated throughput of n streams based on the model presented. In this case, the number of combinations is too large, therefore we provide an intelligent selection strategy, which decides on less number of data and can be used with an online model as well. Our previous experiences showed that it is better if we choose the parallelism levels not close to each other. So we applied an exponential increase strategy by selecting the stream

numbers that are power of 2: $1,2,2^2,2^3,...,2^k$. Each time we double the number of streams until the throughput starts to drop down or increase very slowly compared to the previous level. After k+1 steps we gather k+1 parallelism level throughput data.

In the first test case, we apply our model to the data transfers over 2 LONI clusters with 10Gbps NICs. In Figure 7, the averaged throughput starts to increase as we increase the number of streams. After going in the same level for a range of stream numbers, it starts to drop down as a result of further increasing the number of streams. Lu et al model cannot predict this behavior. However, Dynamic Equation Order (Newton's Iteration Method) model can predict the optimal stream number where the throughput first reaches the optimal point.

Figure 8 presents the results of the second test case where the transfers occur between a workstation in LAN and a cluster over LONI network. In this case, since the workstation in DSL has lower capabilities comparing to the other, its performance will limit overall throughput and the throughput will not fall down but become stable. Nevertheless, our model is able to predict this curve better than Lu et al model again.

For the third case, we have conducted the experiments in LAN environment and the characteristic of the curve is interesting (Figure 9). After falling down in two streams the throughput started to increase reaching a peak point and then started to decrease coming to a stable point. The Lu et al Model is far from predicting this unusual behavior. However Dynamic Equation

Figure 7. Comparison of prediction models over LONI network

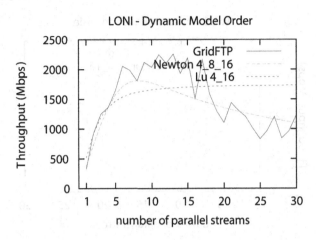

Figure 8. Comparison of prediction models between LAN and LONI network

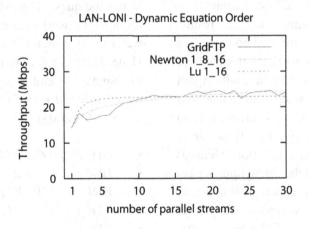

Figure 9. Comparison of prediction models over LAN

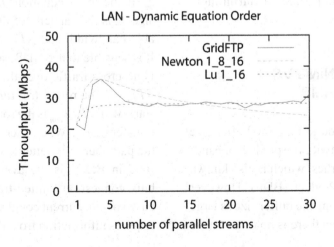

Figure 10. Comparison of prediction models over WAN

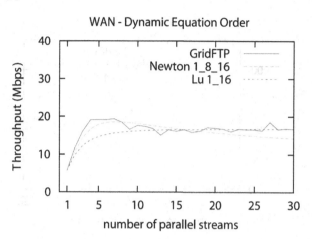

Order (Newton's Iteration Method) Model could predict this behavior with the best accuracy.

In the final case the same wide area results that were used in Figure 6 are used however this time we apply the intelligent selection strategy of parallelism levels on the prediction results. Again the throughput increased steeply up to reaching the peak point then started to decrease due to congestion in the network (Figure 10). Dynamic Equation Order (Newton's Iteration Method) Model was able to predict the throughput behavior very accurately with the exponential selection strategy and Lu et al Model was not able to predict the characteristics of the curve. With these results, we have seen that our models can adapt to different network environments and end-system characteristics and predict the parallel stream throughput behavior accurately.

BUFFER SIZE TUNING VS PARALLEL STREAMS

A very common method to tune the buffer size parameter is to set it to twice the product of bandwidth and delay properties, which is also known as Bandwidth-Delay Product (BDP). However this assumption of making the buffer size as large as BDP only holds when there is no cross traffic

along the path, which is quite impossible. So it brings the question of whether to use the capacity of the network or the available bandwidth as well as minimum RTT or maximum RTT values. Hence there is a variety in the understandings of the bandwidth and delay concepts. Below is a list of different meanings of BDP (Jain, Prasad & Davrolis, 2003):

- BDP1: $B = C \times RTT_{max}$
- BDP2: $B = C \times RTT_{min}$
- BDP3: $B = A \times RTT_{max}$
- BDP4: $B = A \times RTT_{min}$
- BDP5: $B = BTC \times RTT_{ave}$
- BDP6: $B = B_\infty$

In the above equations B represents the buffer size, C is the capacity of the link, A is the available bandwidth and RTT is the round-trip time. It is sensible to use BDP1 and BDP2 when there is no cross traffic over the network path. Here, RTT_{max} is the round-trip time before the transfer starts while RTT_{min} is the round-trip time after the transfer starts. When there is cross traffic over the path then it is better to use BDP4 and BDP5. *BTC* in BDP5 is the average throughput of a bulk congestion-limited transfer and calculated based on the current congestion window size and requires information from the protocol layer. *RT-*

Figure 11. Comparison of throughput in terms of optimized parallel streams and tuned buffers

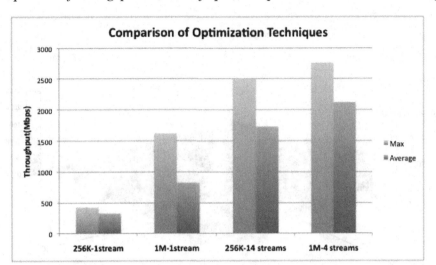

T_{ave} represents the average round-trip time. In the final case, BDP6 is a large value which is always greater that the congestion window so that the connection will always be congestion-limited.

There have been extensive studies that tune the buffer size, unfortunately there are not any practical work to balance the buffer size and parallel stream number to achieve the optimal throughput. We believe that a good combination of tuned buffer size and parallel streams could even give more effective results than the single applications of these two techniques. In Figure 11, a comparison of tuning techniques is presented in terms of optimal parallel streams and tuned buffer size. These tests are conducted in the LONI network between two IBM clusters with 10Gbps interfaces. In the first column, a non-optimized buffer size of 256K and only single stream is used and both maximum and average throughput is below 500Mbps. In the second column, the buffer size is tuned based on the average throughput results and it shows that if only buffer size of 1M is used than about 750Mbps throughput in average and over 1.5 Gbps in maximum is achieved. Instead of tuning the buffer size, if we tune the number of parallel streams, which is shown in column 3, in average more than 1.5 Gbps and in maximum

2.5 Gbps throughput is achieved. It can clearly be seen that parallel streams perform better than tuned buffer size. In column 4, a balanced combination of tuned buffers with parallel streams is presented and while the average throughout is more than 2Gbps, the maximum can reach up to 2.75 Gbps.

To understand the characteristics of throughput based on the buffer size and parallel streams parameters, we have conducted some experiments by ranging the buffer size between 64KB-4M and the parallel streams between 1- 50. The average and maximum behavior of throughput could be seen in Figure 12 and Figure 13. The average throughput starts to increase as both parallel streams and buffer size increases. It demonstrates higher values for high- buffer/low-stream number and low-buffer/high-stream number. The peak is reached with a stream number value between 5-10 and a buffer size value 256K-512K. After that point a sharp decrease is seen in throughput value and a large fluctuation for large buffer size and stream number values as well. On the other hand this sharp decrease is not seen in maximal throughput (Figure 13) although a decrease can also be seen. The highest values for throughput are presented with the light yellow area, where the highest number resides in around 1M buffer

Figure 12. Buffer size vs parallel streams (average throughput)

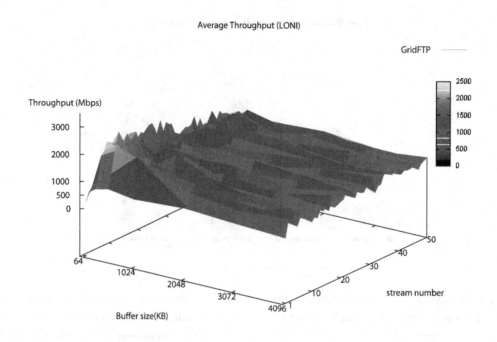

Figure 13. Buffer size vs parallel streams (maximal throughput)

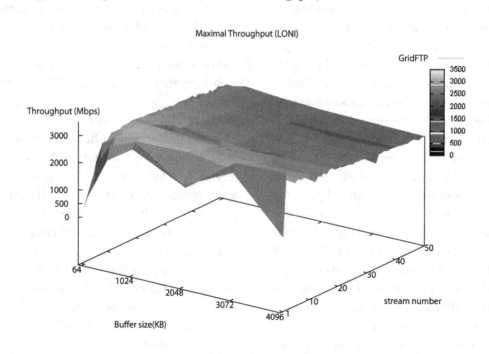

Figure 14. First technique for balancing buffer size and stream number

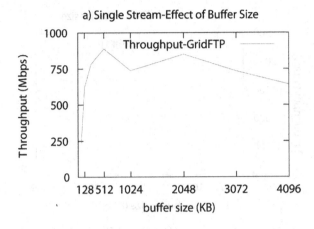

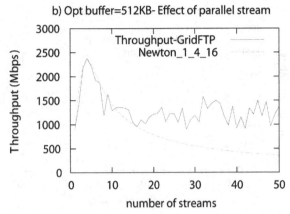

and 10 streams. Then again, the maximal achievable areas of both maximal and average throughput are close to each other.

We have considered a rather practical set of approaches to predict the optimal combinations for buffer size and stream number. In the first approach, we conducted some sampling transfers by increasing the buffer size exponentially using only single stream. In Figure 14a, the optimal buffer size that gives the highest throughput is 512KB. By setting the buffer size to this value we have ranged the number of streams between 1-30 and applied the Dynamic Equation Order (Newton's Iteration Method) model (Figure 14b). The optimal stream number that is decided by the model, in this case 4 streams, with a buffer size of 512KB gave us a throughput of almost 2.5 Gbps, which is the maximum throughput that was achieved in our previous tests.

As a second approach we reversed the order of the procedure. But for applying the optimization model on parallel streams we have to choose a random buffer size to do the transfers. If we by chance choose the optimal number for single stream and apply the model (Figure 15a) and get an optimal parallelism level, then ranging the buffer size over that value to see if it has any effect, it is shown that the throughput is not improved at all (Figure 15b). On the other hand, if we ran-

domly choose a non-optimal buffer size and apply the model (Figures 13c and 13e), we may get an improvement by ranging the buffer size over that throughput as in Figures 13d and 13f, however we may not always get as high throughput as we can get with the optimal buffer size value. Hence the first technique is a better approach to achieve the maximized throughput.

CONCLUSION

In this chapter, we have discussed the limitations of the traditional CPU-oriented batch schedulers in handling the challenging data management problem of large-scale distributed applications. We have elaborated on how we can bring the concept of 'data-awareness' to several most crucial distributed computing components such as scheduling, workflow management, and end-to-end throughput optimization. In this new paradigm, data placement activities are represented as full-featured jobs in the end-to-end workflow, and they are queued, managed, scheduled, and optimized via a specialized data- aware scheduler.

As part of this new paradigm, we have developed a set of tools for mitigating the data bottleneck in distributed computing systems, which consists of three main components: a data-aware

Figure 15. Second technique for balancing buffer size and stream number

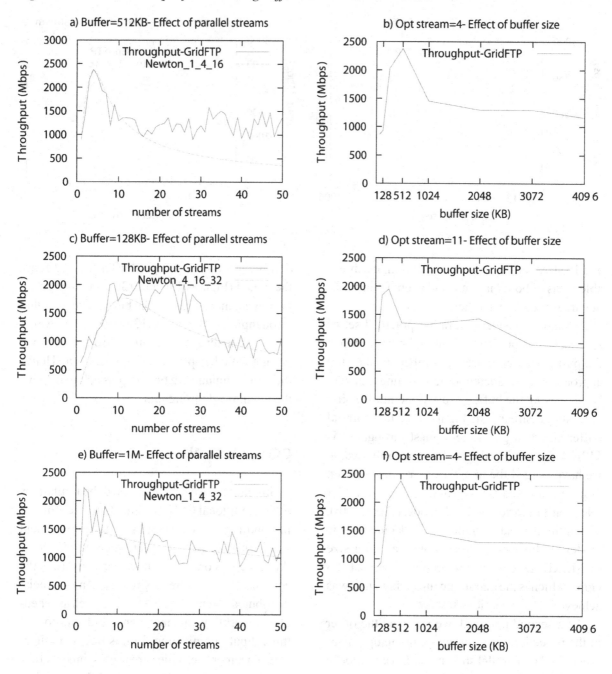

scheduler which provides capabilities such as planning, scheduling, resource reservation, job execution, and error recovery for data movement tasks; integration of these capabilities to the other layers in distributed computing such as workflow planning; and further optimization of data move-ment tasks via dynamically tuning of underlying protocol transfer parameters. Our preliminary results show that the optimizations performed by the data-aware scheduler help to achieve much higher end-to-end throughput in data transfers compared to non-optimized approaches.

We believe that this new 'data-aware distributed computing' paradigm will impact all traditionally compute and data intensive disciplines from science and engineering, as well as new emerging computational areas in the arts, humanities, business and education which need to deal with increasingly large amounts of data.

ACKNOWLEDGMENT

This work was supported in part by the National Science Foundation under award numbers CNS-1131889 (CAREER), CNS-0619843 (MRI-PetaShare), OCI-0926701 (STCI-Stork), and CCF-1115805 (CiC-Stork).

REFERENCES

Allcock, B., Bester, J., Bresnahan, J., Chervenak, A., Foster, I., & Kesselman, C. ... Tuecke, S. (2001). Secure, efficient data transport and replica management for high-performance data-intensive computing. *Proceedings of IEEE Mass Storage Conference*.

Allcock, B., Bester, J., Bresnahan, J., Chervenak, A., Foster, I., & Kesselman, C. (2001). Data management and transfer in high performance computational grid environments. *Parallel Computing, 28*(5).

Allcock, B., Foster, I., Nefedova, V., Chervenak, A., Deelman, E., & Kesselman, C. ... Williams, D. (2001). High-performance remote access to climate simulation data: a challenge problem for data grid technologies. *Proceedings of the 2001 ACM/IEEE Conference on Supercomputing*.

Altman, E., Barman, D., Tuffin, B., & Vojnovic, M. (2006). Parallel tcp sockets: Simple model, throughput and validation. *Proceedings of IEEE Conference on Computer Communications (INFOCOM06),* (pp. 1-12).

Altschul, S. F., Gish, W., Miller, W., Myers, E. W., & Lipman, D. J. (1990). Basic local alignment search tool. *Journal of Molecular Biology, 3*(215), 403–410.

ATLAS. (2010). A *Toroidal LHC ApparatuS Project* (ATLAS). Retrieved from http://atlas.web.cern.ch/

Babu, S., Shivam, P., & Chase, J. (2006). Active and accelerated learning of cost models for optimizing scientific applications. *Proceedings of International Conference on Very Large Data Bases (VLDB)*.

Balakrishman, H., Padmanabhan, V. N., Seshan, S., Katz, R. H., & Stemm, M. (1998). TCP behavior of a busy internet server: Analysis and improvements. *Proceedings of IEEE Conference on Computer Communications (INFOCOM98),* (pp. 252-262).

Balman, M., & Kosar, M. (2007). From micro- to macro-processing: A generic data management model. *Proceedings of the 8th IEEE/ACM International Conference on Grid Computing, (Grid2007)*, Austin, TX, USA.

Beck, M., Elwasif, W. R., Plank, J., & Moore, T. (1999). The Internet backplane protocol: Storage in the network. *Proceedings of the 1999 Network Storage Symposium NetStore99,* Seattle, WA, USA.

Bent, J. (2005). *Data-driven batch scheduling.* PhD thesis, University of Wisconsin- Madison.

CCSP. (2003). *Strategic plan for the US climate change science program.* CCSP Report.

Ceyhan, E., Allen, G., White, C., & Kosar, T. (2008). A grid-enabled workflow system for reservoir uncertainty analysis. *Proceedings of Challenges of Large Applications in Distributed Environments (CLADE 2008) Workshop,* Boston, MA, USA.

Ceyhan, E., & Kosar, T. (2007). Large scale data management in sensor networking applications. *Proceedings of Secure Cyberspace Workshop*, Shreveport, LA, USA.

Chervenak, A., Schuler, C., Kesselman, C., Koranda, S., & Moe, B. (2005). Wide area data replication for scientific collaborations. *Proceedings of the 6th IEEE/ACM International Workshop on Grid Computing.*

Choi, K. M., Huh, E., & Choo, H. (2005). Efficient resource management scheme of TCP buffer tuned parallel stream to optimize system performance. *Proceedings of Embedded and Ubiquitous Computing.*

CMS. (2010). *The US Compact Muon Solenoid Project.* Retrieved from http://uscms.fnal.gov/

Cohen, A., & Cohen, R. (2002). A dynamic approach for efficient TCP buffer allocation. *IEEE Transactions on Computers*, *5*(3), 303–312. doi:10.1109/12.990128

Crowcroft, J., & Oechslin, P. (1998). Differentiated End-to-end Internet services using a weighted proportional fair sharing TCP. *ACM SIGCOMM Computer Communication Review*, *28*, 53–69. doi:10.1145/293927.293930

Deelman, E., Kosar, T., Kesselman, C., & Livny, M. (2006). What Makes Workflows Work in an Opportunistic Environment? *Concurrency and Computation: Practice and Experience*, *18*(10), 1187-1199.

DOE. (2004). *The data management challenge. Report from the DOE Office of Science Data-Management Workshops.* US Department of Energy.

DOE. (2008). *Advanced networking for distributed petascale science. Technical report.* US Department of Energy.

DPOSS. (2010). *The Palomar Digital Sky Survey* (DPOSS). Retrieved from http://www.astro.caltech.edu/~george/dposs/

Dunigan, T., Mathis, M., & Tierney, B. (2002). A TCP tuning daemon. *Proceedings of IEEE Super Computing Conference (SC02).*

Eggert, L., Heideman, J., & Touch, J. (2000). Effects of ensemble TCP. *ACM Computer Communication Review*, *30*(1), 15–29. doi:10.1145/505688.505691

Flynn, M. J. (1999). Basic issues in microprocessor architecture. *Journal of System Architecture*, *45*(12-13), 939–948. doi:http://dx.doi.org/10.1016/S1383- 7621(98)00045-9.

Hacker, T. J., Noble, B. D., & Atley, B. D. (2002). The end-to-end performance effects of parallel tcp sockets on a lossy wide area network. *Proceedings of IEEE International Symposium on Parallel and Distributed Processing (IPDPS02)*, (pp. 434-443).

Hacker, T. J., Noble, B. D., & Atley, B. D. (2005). Adaptive data block scheduling for parallel streams. *Proceedings of IEEE International Symposium on High Performance Distributed Computing (HPDC05)*, (pp. 265-275).

Hasegawa, G., Terai, T., Okamoto, T., & Murata, M. (2001). Scalable socket buffer tuning for high-performance Web servers. *Proceedings of the International Conference on Network Protocols (ICNP01)*, (p. 281).

Hennessy, J. L., & Jouppi, N. P. (1991). Computer technology and architecture: An evolving interaction. *IEEE Computer*, *24*(9), 18–29. doi:10.1109/2.84896

Hey, T., & Trefethen, A. (2003). The data deluge: An e-science perspective. In Berman, F., Fox, G., & Hey, A. J. G. (Eds.), *Grid computing - Making the global infrastructure a reality* (pp. 809–824). Wiley and Sons Publishers.

Hyde, R. (2003). *The art of assembly language programming - CPU architecture.* No Starch Press. Retrieved from http://web- ster.cs.ucr.edu/AoA/Windows/PDFs/CPUArchitecture.pdf

IPERF. (2010). *Website*. Retrieved from http://iperf.sourceforge.net

IRODS. (2010). *The Integrated Rule Oriented Data System*. Retrieved from http://www.irods.org/

Ito, T., Ohsaki, H., & Imase, M. (2008). On parameter tuning of data transfer protocol GridFTP for wide-area networks. *International Journal of Computer Science and Engineering, 2*(4), 177–183.

Jain, M., Prasad, R. S., & Davrolis, C. (2003). *The Tcp bandwidth-delay product revisited: Network buffering, cross traffic, and socket buffer auto-sizing. Technical report.* Georgia Institute of Technology.

Johnston, W. E., Gannon, D., Nitzberg, B., Tanner, L. A., Thigpen, B., & Woo, A. (2000). Computing and data grids for science and engineering. *Proceedings of Supercomputing Conference (SC00)*, (p. 52).

Karrer, R. P., Park, J., & Kim, J. (2006). *Adaptive data block scheduling for parallel streams. Technical report.* Deutsche Telekom Laboratories.

Kiehl, J. T. (1998). The national center for atmospheric research community climate model: CCM3. *Journal of Climate, 11*(6), 1131–1149. doi:10.1175/1520-0442(1998)011<1131:TNCFAR>2.0.CO;2

Kola, G., Kosar, T., & Livny, M. (2004). A fully automated fault-tolerant system for distributed video processing and off-site replication. *Proceedings of the 14th ACM International Workshop on Network and Operating Systems Support for Digital Audio and Video (NOSSDAV 2004)*, Kinsale, Ireland.

Koranda, S., & Moe, M. (2007). Lightweight data replicator. Retrieved from http://www.ligo.caltech.edu/docs/G/G030623-00/G030623-00.pdf

Kosar, T. (2005). *Data placement in widely distributed systems*. Ph. D. Thesis, University of Wisconsin-Madison.

Kosar, T. (2006). A new paradigm in data intensive computing: Stork and the data-aware schedulers. *Proceedings of Challenges of Large Applications in Distributed Environments (CLADE 2006) Workshop*, Paris, France.

Kosar, T., Balman, M., Suslu, I., Yildirim, E., & Yin, D. (2009). Data-aware distributed computing with stork data scheduler. *Proceedings of the SEE-GRID- SCI'09*, Istanbul, Turkey.

Kosar, T., Kola, G., Livny, M., Brunner, R. J., & Remijan, M. (2005). Reliable, automatic transfer and processing of large scale astronomy data sets. In *Proceedings of Astronomical Data Analysis Software and Systems*. ADASS.

Kosar, T., & Livny, M. (2004). Stork: Making data placement a first class citizen in the grid. *Proceedings of IEEE International Conference on Distributed Computing Systems (ICDCS04)*, (pp. 342-349).

Lee, J., Gunter, D., Tierney, B., Allcock, B., Bester, J., Bresnahan, J., & Tuecke, S. (2001). Applied techniques for high bandwidth data transfers across wide area networks. *Proceedings International Conference on Computing in High Energy and Nuclear Physics (CHEP01)*.

LONI. (2010). *Louisiana Optical Network Initiative*. Retrieved from http://www.loni.org

Lu, D., Qiao, Y., & Dinda, P. A. (2005). Characterizing and predicting TCP throughput on the wide area network. *Proceedings of IEEE International Conference on Distributed Computing Systems (ICDCS05)*, (pp. 414-424).

Lu, D., Qiao, Y., Dinda, P. A., & Bustamante, F. E. (2005). Modeling and taming parallel TCP on the wide area network. *Proceedings of IEEE International Symposium on Parallel and Distributed Processing (IPDPS05)*, (p. 68b).

Mathis, M., Semke, J., Mahdavi, J., & Ott, T. (1997). The macroscopic behavior of the TCP congestion avoidance algorithm. *Computer Communication Review*, *27*(3), 67–82. doi:10.1145/263932.264023

Morajko, A. (2004). *Dynamic tuning of parallel/distributed applications*. PhD thesis, Universitat Autonoma de Barcelona.

MSCFD. (2010). *Multiscale Computational Fluid Dynamics at LSU*. Retrieved from http://www.cct.lsu.edu/IGERT/

NumRel. (2010). *Numerical relativity at LSU*. Retrieved from http://www.cct.lsu.edu/numerical/

NWS. (2010). *The Network Weather Service*. Retrieved from http://nws.cs.ucsb.edu/

Pathchirp. (2010). *Website*. Retrieved from http://www.spin.rice.edu/Software/pathChirp/

Pathload. (2010). *A measurement tool for the available bandwidth of network paths*. Retrieved from http://www.cc.gatech.edu/fac/Constantinos.Dovrolis/pathload.html

Prasad, R. S., Jain, M., & Davrolis, C. (2004). Socket buffer auto-sizing for high- performance data transfers. *Journal of Grid Computing*, *1*(4), 361–376. doi:10.1023/B:GRID.0000037554.67413.52

Ramanathan, R. M. (2006). *Extending the world's most popular processor architecture - New innovations that improve the performance and energy efficiency of Intel architecture*. Retrieved from http://download.intel.com/technology/architecture

Ranganathan, R., & Foster, I. (2002). Decoupling computation and data scheduling in distributed data-intensive applications. *Proceedings of the 11th IEEE International Symposium on High Performance Distributed Computing HPDC-11*, (p. 352).

Ranganathan, R. & Foster, I. (2004). Computation scheduling and data replication algorithms for data Grids. *Journal of Grid Resource Management: State of the Art and Future Trends, 359-373.*

Ravi, M. K., Cynthia, H. S., & William, E. A. (2002). Reliable file transfer in grid environments. *Proceedings of the 27th Annual IEEE Conference on Local Computer Networks*, (pp. 737-738).

ROOT. (2006). *Object oriented data analysis framework*. European Organization for Nuclear Research Journal. Retrieved from http://root.cern.ch.

SCOOP. (2010). *SURA Coastal Ocean Observing and Prediction*. Retrieved from http://scoop.sura.org

Semke, J., Madhavi, J., & Mathis, M. (1998). Automatic TCP buffer tuning. *Proceedings of ACM SIGCOMM'98, 28*(4), 315-323.

Sivakumar, H., Bailey, S., & Grossman, R. L. (2000). Psockets: The case for application-level network striping for data intensive applications using high speed wide area networks. In *Proceedings of IEEE Super Computing Conference (SC00)*, (p. 63).

SRB. (2010). *The Storage Resource Broker*. Retrieved from http://www.sdsc.edu/srb/

SRM. (2010). *The Storage Resource Managers*. Retrieved from http://sdm.lbl.gov/srm

Stockinger, H. (2005). *Data management in data Grids - Habilitation overview*. Research Lab for Computational Technologies and Applications.

Stockinger, H., Laure, E., & Stockinger, K. (2005). Performance engineering in data Grids. *Journal of Concurrency and Computation: Practice and Experience, 17*(2-4), 171–191. doi:10.1002/cpe.923

Stockinger, K., Schikuta, E., Stockinger, H., & Willers, I. (2001). Towards a cost model for distributed and replicated data stores. *Proceedings of 9th Euromicro Workshop on Parallel and Distributed Processing (PDP 2001),* IEEE Computer Society Press, Mantova, Italy.

Stokes, J. M. (2003). *Inside the machine - An illustrated introduction to microprocessors and computer architecture* (p. 320). No Starch Press.

Sun. (2005). *Sun Microsystems, Ultra Sparc III Cu Processor - Overview.* Retrieved from http://www.sun.com/processors/whitepapers/USIIIC-uoverview.pdf

Sun. (2005). *Sun Microsystems, Ultra Sparc III Cu - User manual.* Retrieved from http://www.sun.com/processors/manuals/USIIIv2.pdf

Suslu, I., & Kosar, T. (2007). Balancing the use of remote i/o versus staging in distributed environments. *Proceedings of the 9th International Conference on Enterprise Information Systems Doctoral Symposium (DCEIS 2007),* Madeira, Portugal.

Suslu, I., Turkmen, F., Balman, M., & Kosar, T. (2008). Choosing between remote i/o versus staging in large scale distributed applications. *Proceedings of International Conference on Parallel and Distributed Computing and Communication Systems,* New Orleans, LA, USA.

Thain, D., Arpaci Dusseau, A., Bent, J., & Livny, M. (2004). Explicit control in a batch aware distributed file system. *Proceedings of the First USENIX/ACM Conference on Networked Systems Design and Implementation,* San Francisco, CA, USA.

Thomas, M. (2008). *Ultralight planets tutorial.*

Tierney, B. L. (2005). *TCP tuning techniques for high-speed wide-area networks.* nfnn2 talk.

Tierney, B. L., Lee, J., Crowley, B., Holding, M., Hylton, J., & Drake, F. L. (1999). A network-aware distributed storage cache for data-intensive environments. *Proceedings of the Eighth IEEE International Symposium on High Performance Distributed Computing,* (pp. 185-189).

Torvalds, L. (2010). *The Linux kernel.* Retrieved from http://www.kernel.org

Tummala, S., & Kosar, T. (2007). Data management challenges in coastal applications. *Journal of Coastal Research, 50*(Special Issue), 1188–1193.

UCoMS. (2010). *Ubiquitous computing and monitoring system for discovery and management of energy resources.* Retrieved from http://www.ucoms.org

Venugopal, S., Buyya, R., & Winton, L. (2004). A grid service broker for scheduling distributed data-oriented applications on global grids. *Proceedings of the 2nd workshop on Middleware for grid computing,* Toronto, Canada, (pp. 75-80).

WCER. (2010). *Wisconsin Center for Education research digital video processing project.* Retrieved from http://www.wcer.wisc.edu/

Wechsler, O. (2006). *Inside Intel Core microarchitecture – Setting new standards for energy efficient performance.* Retrieved from http://download.intel.com/technology/architecture

Weigle, E., & Feng, W. (2001). Dynamic right-sizing: A simulation study. *Proceedings of IEEE International Conference on Computer Communications and Networks (ICCCN01).*

Yu, A. (1996). The future of microprocessors. *IEEE Micro, 16*(6), 46–53.

Chapter 2
Towards Data Intensive Many-Task Computing

Ioan Raicu
Illinois Institute of Technology, USA & Argonne National Laboratory, USA

Philip Little
University of Notre Dame, USA

Ian Foster
University of Chicago, USA & Argonne National Laboratory, USA

Christopher M. Moretti
University of Notre Dame, USA

Yong Zhao
University of Electronic Science and Technology of China, China

Amitabh Chaudhary
University of Notre Dame, USA

Alex Szalay
Johns Hopkins University, USA

Douglas Thain
University of Notre Dame, USA

ABSTRACT

Many-task computing aims to bridge the gap between two computing paradigms, high throughput computing and high performance computing. Traditional techniques to support many-task computing commonly found in scientific computing (i.e. the reliance on parallel file systems with static configurations) do not scale to today's largest systems for data intensive application, as the rate of increase in the number of processors per system is outgrowing the rate of performance increase of parallel file systems. In this chapter, the authors argue that in such circumstances, data locality is critical to the successful and efficient use of large distributed systems for data-intensive applications. They propose a "data diffusion" approach to enable data-intensive many-task computing. They define an abstract model for data diffusion, define and implement scheduling policies with heuristics that optimize real world performance, and develop a competitive online caching eviction policy. They also offer many empirical experiments to explore the benefits of data diffusion, both under static and dynamic resource provisioning, demonstrating approaches that improve both performance and scalability.

DOI: 10.4018/978-1-61520-971-2.ch002

Figure 1. Problem types with respect to data size and number of tasks

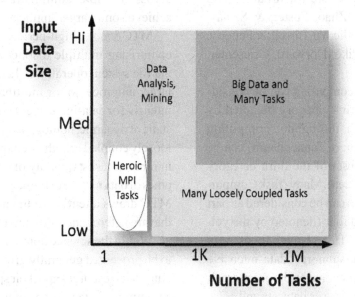

INTRODUCTION

We want to enable the use of large-scale distributed systems for task-parallel applications, which are linked into useful workflows through the looser task-coupling model of passing data via files between dependent tasks. This potentially larger class of task-parallel applications is precluded from leveraging the increasing power of modern parallel systems such as supercomputers (e.g. IBM Blue Gene/L (Gara et al, 2005) and Blue Gene/P (IBM BlueGene/P (BG/P), 2008)) because the lack of efficient support in those systems for the "scripting" programming model (Ousterhout, 1998). With advances in e-Science and the growing complexity of scientific analyses, more scientists and researchers rely on various forms of scripting to automate end-to-end application processes involving task coordination, provenance tracking, and bookkeeping. Their approaches are typically based on a model of loosely coupled computation, in which data is exchanged among tasks via files, databases or XML documents, or a combination of these. Vast increases in data volume combined with the growing complexity of data analysis procedures and algorithms have rendered traditional manual processing and exploration unfavorable as compared with modern high performance computing processes automated by scientific workflow systems (Zhao, Raicu, & Foster, 2008).

The problem space can be partitioned into four main categories (see Figure 1). 1) At the low end of the spectrum (low number of tasks and small input size), we have tightly coupled Message Passing Interface (MPI) applications (white). 2) As the data size increases, we move into the analytics category, such as data mining and analysis (blue); MapReduce (Dean & Ghemawat) is an example for this category. 3) Keeping data size modest, but increasing the number of tasks moves us into the loosely coupled applications involving many tasks (yellow); Swift/Falkon (Zhao et al., 2007; Raicu, Zhao, Dumitrescu, Foster, & Wilde 2007) and Pegasus/DAGMan (Deelman et al., 2005) are examples of this category. 4) Finally, the combination of both many tasks and large datasets moves us into the data-intensive Many-Task Computing (Raicu, Foster, & Zhao, 2008) category (green);

examples of this category are Swift/Falkon and data diffusion (Raicu, Zhao, Foster, & Szalay, 2008), Dryad (Isard, Budie, Yu, Birrell, & Fetterly, 2007), and Sawzall (Pike, Dorward, Griesemer, & Quinlan, 2005).

High performance computing can be considered to be part of the first category (denoted by the white area). High throughput computing (Livny, Basney, Raman, & Tannenbaum) can be considered to be a subset of the third category (denoted by the yellow area). Many-Task Computing (Raicu et al., 2008a) can be considered as part of categories three and four (denoted by the yellow and green areas). This chapter focuses on techniques to enable the support of data-intensive many-task computing (denoted by the green area), and the challenges that arise as datasets and computing systems are getting larger and larger.

Clusters and Grids (Foster & Kesselman, 1999; Foster, Kesselman, & Tuecke, 2001) have been the preferred platform for loosely coupled applications that have been traditionally part of the high throughput computing class of applications, which are managed and executed through workflow systems or parallel programming systems. Various properties of a new emerging applications, such as large number of tasks (i.e. millions or more), relatively short per task execution times (i.e. seconds to minutes long), and data intensive tasks (i.e. tens of MB of I/O per CPU second of compute) have lead to the definition of a new class of applications called Many-Task Computing. MTC emphasizes on using much large numbers of computing resources over short periods of time to accomplish many computational tasks, where the primary metrics are in seconds (e.g., FLOPS, tasks/sec, MB/sec I/O rates), while HTC requires large amounts of computing for long periods of time with the primary metrics being operations per month (Livny et al., 1997). MTC applications are composed of many tasks (both independent and dependent tasks) that can be individually scheduled on many different computing resources

across multiple administrative boundaries to achieve some larger application goal.

MTC denotes high-performance computations comprising multiple distinct activities, coupled via file system operations. Tasks may be small or large, uniprocessor or multiprocessor, compute-intensive or data-intensive. The set of tasks may be static or dynamic, homogeneous or heterogeneous, loosely coupled or tightly coupled. The aggregate number of tasks, quantity of computing, and volumes of data may be extremely large. The new term MTC draws attention to the many computations that are heterogeneous but not "happily" parallel.

Within the science domain, the data that needs to be processed generally grows faster than computational resources and their speed. The scientific community is facing an imminent flood of data expected from the next generation of experiments, simulations, sensors and satellites. Scientists are now attempting calculations requiring orders of magnitude more computing and communication than was possible only a few years ago. Moreover, in many currently planned and future experiments, they are also planning to generate several orders of magnitude more data than has been collected in the entire human history (Hey & Trefethen, 2003).

For instance, in the astronomy domain the Sloan Digital Sky Survey (SDSS: Sloan Digital Sky Survey, 2008) has datasets that exceed 10 terabytes in size. They can reach up to 100 terabytes or even petabytes if we consider multiple surveys and the time dimension. In physics, the CMS detector being built to run at CERN's Large Hadron Collider (CERN's Large Hadron Collider, 2008) is expected to generate over a petabyte of data per year. In the bioinformatics domain, the rate of growth of DNA databases such as GenBank (GenBank, 2008) and European Molecular Biology Laboratory (EMBL) (European Molecular Biology Laboratory, 2008) has been following an exponential trend, with a doubling time estimated to be 9-12 months. A large class of applications in Many-Task Computing will be applications that analyze large quantities of data, which in turn would require that data and computations be distributed over many hundreds and thousands of nodes in order to achieve rapid turnaround times.

Many applications in the scientific computing generally use a shared infrastructure such as TeraGrid (Catlett et al., 2006) and Open Science Grid (Open Science Grid (OSG), 2008), where data movement relies on shared or parallel file systems. The rate of increase in the number of processors per system is outgrowing the rate of performance increase of parallel file systems, which requires rethinking existing data management techniques. For example, a cluster that was placed in service in 2002 with 316 processors has a parallel file system (i.e. GPFS (Schmuck & Haskin)) rated at 1GB/s, yielding 3.2MB/s per processor of bandwidth. The second largest open science supercomputer, the IBM Blue Gene/P from Argonne National Laboratory, has 160K processors, and a parallel file system (i.e. also GPFS) rated at 8GB/s, yielding a mere 0.05MB/s per processor. That is a 65X reduction in bandwidth between a system from 2002 and one from 2008. Unfortunately, this trend is not bound to stop, as advances multi-core and many-core processors will increase the number of processor cores one to two orders of magnitude over the next decade (Zhao et al., 2008a).

We believe that data locality is critical to the successful and efficient use of large distributed systems for data-intensive applications (Szalay, Bunn, Gray, Foster, & Raicu, 2006; Gray, 2003) in the face of a growing gap between compute power and storage performance. Large scale data management needs to be a primary objective for any middleware targeting to support MTC workloads, to ensure data movement is minimized by intelligent data-aware scheduling both among distributed computing sites, and among compute nodes.

We propose an alternative *data diffusion* approach (Raicu et al., 2008c; Raicu et al., 2009), in which resources required for data analysis are acquired dynamically from a local resource man-

ager (LRM), in response to demand. Resources may be acquired either "locally" or "remotely"; their location only matters in terms of associated cost tradeoffs. Both data and applications "diffuse" to newly acquired resources for processing. Acquired resources and the data that they hold can be cached for some time, allowing more rapid responses to subsequent requests. Data diffuses over an increasing number of processors as demand increases, and then contracts as load reduces, releasing processors back to the LRM for other uses.

Data diffusion involves a combination of dynamic resource provisioning, data caching, and data-aware scheduling. The approach is reminiscent of cooperative caching (Podlipnig & Böszörmenyi, 2003), cooperative web-caching (Lancellotti, Colajanni, & Ciciani, 2002), and peer-to-peer storage systems (Hasan, Anwar, Yurnik, Brumbaugh, & Campbell, 2005). Other data-aware scheduling approaches tend to assume static resources (Xiaohui et al., 2005; Fuhrmann, 2004), in which a system configuration dedicates nodes with roles (i.e. clients, servers) at startup, and there is no support to increase or decrease the ratio between client and servers based on load. However, in our approach we need to acquire dynamically not only storage resources but also computing resources. In addition, datasets may be terabytes in size and data access is for analysis (not retrieval). Further complicating the situation is our limited knowledge of workloads, which may involve many different applications. In principle, data diffusion can provide the benefits of dedicated hardware without the associated high costs. The performance achieved with data diffusion depends crucially on the characteristics of application workloads and the underlying infrastructure.

This chapter is a culmination of a collection of papers (Raicu et al., 2007; Raicu et al., 2008a; Raicu et al., 2008c; Szalay et al., 2006; Raicu et al., 2009; Raicu, Zhang, Wilde, & Szalay, 2007; Raicu et al. 2008b; Raicu, 2007; Zhang et al., 2008) dating back to 2006, and includes a deeper analysis of previous results as well as some new results. "Data Diffusion Architecture" section covers our proposed support for data-intensive many-task computing, specifically through our work with the Falkon (Raicu et al., 2007; Raicu et al., 2008b) light-weight task execution framework and its data management capabilities in data diffusion (Raicu et al., 2008c; Raicu et al., 2009; Fuhrman, 2004; Raicu, 2007). This section also discusses the data-aware scheduler and scheduling policies. "Theoretical Evaluation" section defines a data diffusion abstract model; towards developing provable results we offer 2Mark, an *O(NM)*-competitive caching eviction policy, for a constrained problem on *N* stores each holding at most *M* pages. This is the best possible such algorithm with matching upper and lower bounds (barring a constant factor). "Micro-benchmarks" section offers a wide range of micro-benchmarks evaluating data diffusion, our parallel file system performance, and the data-aware scheduler performance. "Synthetic Workloads" section explores the benefits of both static and dynamic resource provisioning through three synthetic workloads. The first two workloads explore dynamic resource provisioning through the Monotonically-Increasing workload and the Sin-Wave workload. We also explore the All-Pairs workload (Moretti, Bulosan, Tahin, & Flynn, 2008) which allows us to compare data diffusion with a best model for active storage (Thain, Moretti, & Hemmes, 2008). "Large-scale Astronomy Application Performance Evaluation" section covers a real large-scale application from the astronomy domain, and how data diffusion improved its performance and scalability. "Related Work" section covers related work, which have addressed data management issues to support data intensive applications. We finally conclude the chapter with the "Conclusions" section.

DATA DIFFUSION ARCHITECTURE

We implement data diffusion (Raicu et al., 2008c) in the Falkon task dispatch framework (Raicu et al., 2007). We describe Falkon and data diffusion, offer justifications to why we chose a centralized scheduler approach, and finally discuss the data-aware scheduler and its various scheduling policies.

Falkon and Data Diffusion

To enable the rapid execution of many tasks on distributed resources, Falkon combines (1) multi-level scheduling (Banga, Druschel, & Mogul, 1999) to separate resource acquisition (via requests to batch schedulers) from task dispatch, and (2) a streamlined dispatcher to achieve several orders of magnitude higher throughput (487 tasks/sec) and scalability (54K executors, 2M queued tasks) than other resource managers (Raicu et al., 2007). Recent work has achieved throughputs in excess of 3750 tasks/sec and scalability up to 160K processors (Raicu et al., 2008b).

Figure 2 shows the Falkon architecture, including both the data management and data-aware scheduler components. Falkon is structured as a set of (dynamically allocated) *executors* that cache and analyze data; a *dynamic resource provisioner* (DRP) that manages the creation and deletion of executors; and a *dispatcher* that dispatches each incoming task to an executor. The provisioner uses tunable allocation and de-allocation policies to provision resources adaptively. Falkon supports the queuing of incoming tasks, whose length triggers the dynamic resource provisioning to allocate resources via GRAM4 (Feller, Foster, & Martin, 2007) from the available set of resources, which in turn allocates the resources and bootstraps the executors on the remote machines. Individual executors manage their own caches, using local eviction policies, and communicate changes in cache content to the dispatcher. The scheduler sends tasks to compute nodes, along with the

Figure 2. Architecture overview of Falkon extended with data diffusion (data management and data-aware scheduler)

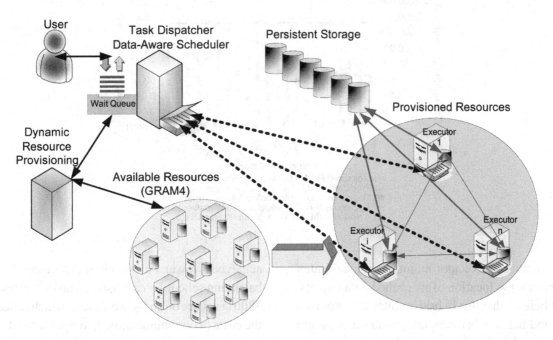

necessary information about where to find related input data. Initially, each executor fetches needed data from remote persistent storage. Subsequent accesses to the same data results in executors fetching data from other peer executors if the data is already cached elsewhere. The current implementation runs a GridFTP server (Allcock et al., 2005) at each executor, which allows other executors to read data from its cache. This scheduling information are only hints, as remote cache state can change frequently and is not guaranteed to be 100% in sync with the global index. In the event that a data item is not found at any of the known cached locations, it attempts to retrieve the item from persistent storage; if this also fails, the respective task fails. In Figure 2, the black dotted lines represent the scheduler sending the task to the compute nodes, along with the necessary information about where to find input data. The red thick solid lines represent the ability for each executor to get data from remote persistent storage. The blue thin solid lines represent the

ability for each storage resource to obtain cached data from another peer executor.

In our experiments, we assume data follows the normal pattern found in scientific computing, which is to write-once/read-many (the same assumption as HDFS makes in the Hadoop system (Bialecki, Cafarella, Cutting, & O'Malley, 2005)). Thus, we avoid complicated and expensive cache coherence schemes other parallel file systems enforce. We implement four cache eviction policies: *Random*, *FIFO*, *LRU*, and *LFU* (Podlipnig & Böszörmenyi, 2003). Our empirical experiments all use LRU, and we will study the other policies in future work.

To support data-aware scheduling, we implement a centralized index within the dispatcher that records the location of every cached data object; this is similar to the centralized NameNode in Hadoop's HDFS (Bialecki et al., 2005). This index is maintained loosely coherent with the contents of the executor's caches via periodic update messages generated by the executors. In

Figure 3. P-RLS vs. hash table performance for 1M entries

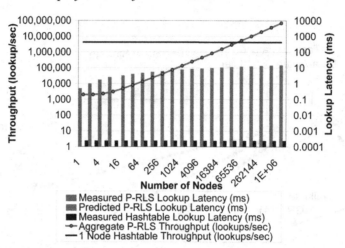

addition, each executor maintains a local index to record the location of its cached data objects. We believe that this hybrid architecture provides a good balance between latency to the data and good scalability. The next subsection covers a deeper analysis in the difference between a centralized index and a distributed one, and under what conditions a distributed index is preferred.

Centralized vs. Distributed Cache Index

Our central index and the separate per-executor indices are implemented as in-memory hash tables. The hash table implementation in Java 1.5 requires about 200 bytes per entry, allowing for index sizes of 8M entries with 1.5GB of heap, and 43M entries with 8GB of heap. Update and lookup performance on the hash table is excellent, with insert times in the 1~3 microseconds range (tested on up to 8M entries), and lookup times between 0.25 and 1 microsecond (tested on up to 8M entries) on a modern 2.3GHz Intel Xeon processor. Thus, we can achieve an upper bound throughput of 4M lookups/sec.

In practice, the scheduler may make multiple updates and lookups per scheduling decision, so the effective scheduling throughput that can be achieved is lower. Falkon's non-data-aware load-balancing scheduler can dispatch tasks at rates of 3800 tasks/sec on an 8-core system, which reflects the costs of communication. In order for the data-aware scheduler to not become the bottleneck, it needs to make decisions within 2.1 milliseconds, which translates to over 3700 updates or over 8700 lookups to the hash table. Assuming we can keep the number of queries or updates within these bounds per scheduling decision, the rate-liming step remains the communication between the client, the service, and the executors.

Nevertheless, our centralized index could become saturated in a sufficiently large enough deployment. In that case, a more distributed index might perform and scale better. Such an index could be implemented using the peer-to-peer replica location service (P-RLS) (Chervenak, Palavalli, Bharathi, Kesselman, & Schwartzkopf, 2004) or distributed hash table (DHT) (Stoica, Morris, Karger, Kaashoek, & Balakrishnan, 2001). Chervenak et al. (2004) report that P-RLS lookup latency for an index of 1M entries increases from 0.5 ms to just over 3 ms as the number of P-RLS nodes grows from 1 to 15 nodes. To compare their data with a central index, we present in Figure 3. We see that although P-RLS latencies do not increase significantly with number of nodes (from

0.5 ms with 1 node to 15 ms with 1M nodes) (Raicu et al., 2008c), a considerable number of nodes are required to match that of an in-memory hash table. P-RLS would need more than 32K nodes to achieve an aggregate throughput similar to that of an in-memory hash table, which is 4.18M lookups/sec. In presenting these results we do not intend to argue that we need 4M+ lookups per second to maintain 4K scheduling decisions per second. However, these results do lead us to conclude that a centralized index can often perform better than a distributed index at small to modest scales.

There are two disadvantages to our centralized index. The first is the requirement that the index fit in memory. Single SMP nodes can be bought with 256GB of memory, which would allow 1.3B entries in the index. Large-scale applications that are data intensive (Moretti et al., 2008, Raicu, Foster, Szalay, & Turcu, 2006; Berriman et al., 2004; ASC/ Alliances Center for Astrophysical Thermonuclear Flashes, 2008) typically have terabytes to tens of terabytes of data spread over thousands to tens of millions of files, which would comfortably fit on a single node with 8GB of memory. However, this might not suffice for applications that have datasets with many small files. The second disadvantage is the single point of failure; it is worth noting that other systems, such as Hadoop (Bialecki et al., 2005), also have a single point of failure in the NameNode which keeps track of the global state of data. Furthermore, our centralized index load would be lower than that of Hadoop as we operate at the file level, not block level, which effectively reduces the amount of metadata that must be stored at the centralized index.

We have investigated distributing the entire Falkon service in the context of the IBM Blue Gene/P supercomputer, where we run N dispatchers in parallel to scale to 160K processors; we have tested N up to 640. However, due to limitations of the operating systems on the compute nodes, we do not yet support data diffusion on this system. Furthermore, the client submitting the workload is currently not dispatcher-aware to optimize data locality across multiple dispatchers, and currently only performs load-balancing in the event that the dispatcher is distributed over multiple nodes. There is no technical reason for not adding this feature to the client, other not having the need for this feature so far. An alternative solution would be to add support for synchronization among the distributed dispatchers, to allow them to forward tasks amongst each other to optimize data locality. We will explore both of these alternatives in future work.

Data-Aware Scheduler

Data-aware scheduling is central to the success of data diffusion, as harnessing data-locality in application access patterns is critical to performance and scalability. We implement four dispatch policies.

The **first-available** (FA) policy ignores data location information when selecting an executor for a task; it simply chooses the first available executor, and provides the executor with no information concerning the location of data objects needed by the task. Thus, the executor must fetch all data needed by a task from persistent storage on every access. This policy is used for all experiments that do not use data diffusion.

The **max-cache-hit** (MCH) policy uses information about data location to dispatch each task to the executor with the largest amount of data needed by that task. If that executor is busy, task dispatch is delayed until the executor becomes available. This strategy is expected to reduce data movement operations compared to first-cache-available and max-compute-util, but may lead to load imbalances where processor utilization will be sub optimal, if nodes frequently join and leave.

The **max-compute-util** (MCU) policy leverages data location information, attempting to maximize resource utilization even at the potential higher cost of data movement. It sends a task to an available executor, preferring executors with the most needed data locally.

Figure 4. Pseudo code for part #1 of algorithm which sends out the notification for work

```
1  while Q !empty
2      foreach files in T₀
3          tempSet = Imap(fileᵢ)
4          foreach executors in tempSet
5              candidates[tempSetⱼ]++
6          end
7      end
8      sort candidates[] according to values
9      foreach candidates
10         if Eset(candidateᵢ) = freeState then
11             Mark executor candidateᵢ as pending
12             Remove T₀ from wait queue and mark as pending
13             sendNotificatoin to candidateᵢ to pick up T₀
14             break
15         end
16         if no candidate is found in the freeState then
17             send notification to the next free executor
18         end
19     end
20 end
```

Figure 5. Pseudo code for part #2 of algorithm which decides what task to assign to each executor

```
21 while tasksInspected < W
22     fileSetᵢ = all files in Tᵢ
23     cacheHitᵢ = |intersection fileSetᵢ and Emap(executor)|
24     if cacheHitᵢ > minCacheHit || CPUutil < minCPUutil then
25         remove Tᵢ from Q and add Tᵢ to list to dispatch
26     end
27     if list of tasks to dispatch is long enough then
28         assign tasks to executor
29         break
30     end
31 end
```

The **good-cache-compute** (GCC) policy is a hybrid MCH/MCU policy. The GCC policy sets a threshold on the minimum processor utilization to decide when to use MCH or MCU. We define processor utilization to be the number of processors with active tasks divided by the total number of processors allocated. MCU used a threshold of 100%, as it tried to keep all allocated processors utilized. We find that relaxing this threshold even slightly (e.g., 90%) works well in practice as it keeps processor utilization high and it gives the scheduler flexibility to improve cache hit rates significantly when compared to MCU alone.

The scheduler is a window based one, that takes the scheduling window W size (i.e. $|W|$ is the number of tasks to consider from the wait queue when making the scheduling decision), and starts to build a per task scoring cache hit function. If at any time, a best task is found (i.e. achieves a 100% hit rate to the local cache), the scheduler removes this task from the wait queue and adds it to the list of tasks to dispatch to this executor. This is repeated until the maximum number of tasks were retrieved and prepared to be sent to

the executor. If the entire scheduling window is exhausted and no best task was found, the m tasks with the highest cache hit local rates are dispatched. In the case of MCU, if no tasks were found that would yield any cache hit rates, then the top m tasks are taken from the wait queue and dispatched to the executor. For MCH, no tasks are returned, signaling that the executor is to return to the free pool of executors. For GCC, the aggregate CPU utilization at the time of scheduling decision determines which action to take. Pre-binding of tasks to nodes can negatively impact cache-hit performance if multiple tasks are assigned to the same node, and each task requires the entire cache size, effectively thrashing the cache contents at each task invocation. In practice, we find that per task working sets are small (megabytes to gigabytes) while cache sizes are bigger (tens of gigabytes to terabytes) making the worst case not a common case.

We define several variables first in order to understand the scheduling algorithm pseudo-code (see Figure 4 and Figure 5); the algorithm is separated into two sections, as the first part (Figure 4) decides which executor will be notified of available tasks, while the second part (Figure 5) decides which task to be submitted to the respective executor:

Q wait queue

T_i task at position i in the wait queue

E_{set} executor sorted set; element existence indicates the executor is free, busy, or pending

I_{map} file index hash map; the map key is the file logical name and the value is an executor sorted set of where the file is cached

E_{map} executor hash map; the map key is the executor name, and the value is a sorted set of logical file names that are cached at the respective executor

W scheduling window of tasks to consider from the wait queue when making the scheduling decision

The scheduler's complexity varies with the policy used. For FA, the cost is constant, as it simply takes the first available executor and dispatches the first task in the queue. MCH, MCU, and GCC are more complex with a complexity of $O(|T_i| + min(|Q|, W))$, where T_i is the task at position i in the wait queue and Q is the wait queue. This could equate to many operations for a single scheduling decision, depending on the maximum size of the scheduling window and queue length. Since all data structures used to keep track of executors and files use in-memory hash maps and sorted sets, operations are efficient (see the previous subsection).

THEORETICAL EVALUATION

We define an abstract model that captures the principal elements of data diffusion in a manner that allows analysis. We first define the model and then analyze the computational time per task, caching performance, workload execution times, arrival rates, and node utilization. Finally, we present an O(NM)-competitive algorithm for the scheduler as well as a proof of its competitive ratio.

Abstract Model

Our abstract model includes computational resources on which tasks execute, storage resources where data needed by the tasks is stored, etc. Simplistically, we have two regimes: the working data set fits in cache, $S \geq W$, where S is the aggregate allocated storage and W is the working data set size; and the working set does not fit in cache, $S < W$. We can express the time T required for a computation associated with a single data access as follows (see Equation 1), both depending on H_l (data found on local disk), H_c (remote disks), or H_s (centralized persistent storage):

$$S \geq W : (R_l + C) \leq T \leq (R_c + C)$$

$$S < W : (R_c + C) \leq T < (R_s + C) \tag{1}$$

Where R_l, R_c, R_s are the average cost of accessing local data (l), cached data (c), or persistent storage (s), and C is the average amount of computing per data access. The relationship between cache hit performance and T can be found in Equation 2.

$$S \geq W : T = (R_l + C)*HR_l + (R_c + C)*HR_c$$

$$S < W : T = (R_c + C)*HR_c + (R_s + C)*HR_s \tag{2}$$

Where HR_l is the cache hit local disk ratio, HR_c is the remote cache ratio, and HR_s is the cache miss ratio; $HR_{l/c/s} = H_{L/C/S}/(H_L + H_C + H_S)$. We can merge the two cases into a single one, such as the average time to complete task i is (see Equation 3):

$$TK_i = (R_l + C)*HR_l + (R_c + C)*HR_c + (R_s + C)*HR_s \tag{3}$$

Which can also be expressed as (see Equation 4):

$$TK_i = C + R_l*HR_l + R_c*HR_c + R_s*HR_s \tag{4}$$

The time needed to complete an entire workload *D* with *K* tasks on *N* processors is, where D is a function of K, W, A, C, and L (see Equation 5):

$$T_N(D) = \sum_{i=1}^{K} TK_i \qquad (5)$$

Having defined the time to complete workload D, we define speedup as Equation 6:

$$SP = T_1(D) / T_N(D) \qquad (6)$$

And efficiency can be defined as (see Equation 7):

$$EF = SP / N \qquad (7)$$

What is the maximum task arrival rate (*A*) that a particular scenario can sustain? We have (see Equation 8):

$$S \geq W : N*P/(R_1+C) \leq A_{max} \leq N*P/(R_c+C)$$

$$S < W : N*P/(R_c+C) \leq A_{max} < N*P/(R_s+C) \qquad (8)$$

Where *P* is the execution speed of a single node. These regimes can be collapsed into a single formula (see Equation 9):

$$A = (N*P/T)*K \qquad (9)$$

We can express a formula to evaluate tradeoffs between node utilization (*U*) and arrival rate; counting data movement time in node utilization, we have (see Equation 10):

$$U = A*T/(N*P) \qquad (10)$$

Although the presented model is quite simplistic, it manages to model quite accurately an astronomy application with a variety of workloads (the topic of subsection on "Abstract Model Validation").

O(NM)-Competitive Caching

Among known algorithms with provable performance for minimizing data access costs, there are none that can be applied to data diffusion, even if restricted to the caching problem it entails. For instance, LRU maximizes the local store performance, but is oblivious of the cached data in the system and persistent storage. As a step to developing a provably sound algorithm we present an online algorithm that is *O(NM)*-competitive to the offline optimum for a constrained version of the caching problem. For definitions of competitive ratio, online algorithm, and offline optimum see (Torng, 1998). In brief, an online algorithm solves a problem without knowledge of the future, an offline optimal is a hypothetical algorithm that has knowledge of the future. The competitive ratio is the worst-case ratio of their performance and is a measure of the quality of the online algorithm, independent of a specific request sequence or workload characteristics.

In the constrained version of the problem there are *N* stores each capable of holding *M* objects of uniform size. Requests are made sequentially to the system, each specifying a particular object and a particular store. If the store does not have the object at that time, it must load the object to satisfy the request. If the store is full, it must evict one object to make room for the new object. If the object is present on another store in the system, it can be loaded for a cost of R_c which we normalize to *1*. If it is not present in another store, it must be loaded from persistent storage for a cost of R_s, which we normalize to $s=R_s/R_c$. Note that if $R_s<R_c$ for some reason, we can use LRU at each node instead of 2Mark to maintain competitive performance. We assume R_l is negligible.

All stores in the system our allowed to cooperate (or be managed by a single algorithm with complete state information). This allows objects to be transferred between stores in ways not directly required to satisfy a request (e.g., to back up an object that would otherwise be evicted). Specifically, two stores may exchange a pair of objects for a cost of *1* without using an extra memory space. Further, executors may write to an object in their store. To prevent inconsistencies, the system is not allowed to contain multiple copies of one object simultaneously on different stores.

We propose an online algorithm 2Mark (which uses the well known marking algorithm (Torng, 1998) at two levels) for this case of data diffusion. Let the corresponding optimum offline algorithm be OPT. For a sequence σ, let 2Mark(σ) be the cost 2Mark incurs to handle the sequence and define OPT(σ) similarly. 2Mark may mark and unmark objects in two ways, designated *local-marking* an object and *global-marking* an object. An object may be local-marked with respect to a particular store (a bit corresponding to the object is set only at that store) or global-marked with respect to the entire system. 2Mark interprets the request sequence as being composed of two kinds of phases, *local-phases* and *global-phases*. A local-phase for a given store is a contiguous set of requests received by the store for *M* distinct objects, starting with the first request the store receives. A global-phase is a contiguous set of requests received by the entire system for *NM* distinct objects, starting with the first request the system receives. We prove Equation11 which establishes that 2Mark is *O(NM)-competitive*. From the lower bound on the competitive ratio for simple paging (Torng, 1998), this is the best possible deterministic online algorithm for this problem, barring a constant factor.

$$2Mark(\sigma) \leq (NM + 2M / s + NM / (s + v)) \cdot OPT(\sigma)$$
$$\textit{for all sequences } \sigma$$

(11)

2Mark essentially uses an *M*-competitive marking algorithm to manage the objects on individual stores and the same algorithm on a larger scale to determine which objects to keep in the system as a whole. When a store faults on a request for an object that is on another store, it exchanges the object it evicts for the object requested (see Figure 6). We will establish a bound on the competitive ratio by showing that every cost incurred by 2Mark can be correlated to one incurred by OPT. These costs may be *s-faults* (in which an object is loaded from persistent storage for a cost of *s*) or they may be *1-faults* (in which an object is loaded from another cache for a cost of *1*). The number of 1-faults and s-faults incurred by 2Mark can be bounded by the number of 1-faults and s-faults incurred by OPT in sequence σ, as described in the following.

To prevent multiple copies of the same object in different caches, we assume that the request sequence is *renamed* in the following manner: when some object *p* requested at a store *X* is requested again at a different store *Y* we rename the object once it arrives at *Y* to *p'* and rename all future requests for it at *Y* to *p'*. This is done for all requests. Thus if this object is requested at *X* in the future, the object and all requests for it at *X* are renamed to *p"*. This ensures that even if some algorithm inadvertently leaves behind a copy of *p* at *X* it is not used again when *p* is requested at *X* after being requested at *Y*. Observe that the renaming does not increase the cost of any correct algorithm.

Consider the *ith* global phase. During this global phase, let OPT load objects from persistent storage *u* times and exchange a pair of objects between stores *v* times, incurring a total cost of *su+v*.

Every object loaded from persistent storage by 2Mark is globally-marked and not evicted from the system until the end of the global phase. Since the system can hold at most *NM* objects, the number of objects loaded by 2Mark in the *ith* global phase is at most *NM*. We claim OPT loads at least one object from persistent storage during this global phase. This is trivially true if this is the first global phase as all the objects loaded by 2Mark have to be loaded by OPT as well. If this is not the first global phase, OPT must satisfy each of the requests for the distinct *NM* objects

Figure 6. Algorithm 2Mark

```
Input:   Request for object p at store X from sequence σ
1  if p is not on X then
2     if X is not full then /* No eviction required */
3        if p is on some store Y then
4           Transfer p from Y to X
5        else
6           Load p to X from persistent storage
7        end
8     else /* Eviction required to make space in X */
9        if all objects on X are local-marked then
10          local-unmark all  /*Begins new local phase */
11       end
12       if p is on some store Y then
13          Select an arbitrary local-unmarked object q on X
14          Exchange q and p on X and Y
            /* X now has p and Y has q */
15          if p was local-marked on Y then
16             local-mark q on Y
17          end
18       else /* p must be loaded from persistent storage */
19          if all objects in system are global-marked then
20             global-unmark and local-unmark all objects
               /*Begins new global phase & local phases at each store */
21          end
22          if all objects on X are global-marked then
23             Select an arbitrary local-unmarked object q on X
24             Select an arbitrary store Y with at least one global-unmarked object or empty space
25             Transfer q to Y, replacing an arbitrary global-unmarked object or empty space
26          else
27             Evict an arbitrary global-unmarked object q on X
28          end
29          Load p to X from persistent storage
30       end
```

in the previous global phase by objects from the system and thus must s-fault at least once to satisfy requests in this global phase.

Within the *ith* global phase consider the *jth* local phase at some store X. The renaming of objects ensures that any object p removed from X because of a request for p at some other store Y is never requested again at X. Thus the first time

an object is requested at X in this local phase, it is locally marked and remains in X for all future requests in this local phase. Thus X can 1-fault for an object only once during this local phase. Since X can hold at most M objects, it incurs at most M 1-faults in the *jth* local phase. We claim that when $j \neq 1$ OPT incurs at least one 1-fault in this local phase. The reasoning is similar to

Table 1. Platform descriptions

Name	# of Nodes	Processors	Memory	Network
TG_ANL_IA32	98	Dual Xeon 2.4 GHz	4GB	1Gb/s
TG_ANL_IA64	64	Dual Itanium 1.3 GHz	4GB	1Gb/s
UC_x64	1	Dual Xeon 3GHz w/ HT	2GB	100Mb/s

that for the *ith* global phase: since OPT satisfies each of the requests for M distinct objects in the previous local phase from cache, it must 1-fault at least once in this local phase. When $j=1$, however, it may be that the previous local phase did not contain requests for M distinct objects. There are, however, at most NM 1-faults by 2Mark in all the local phases in which $j=1$, for the N stores each holding M objects, in the *ith* global phase.

Since OPT has the benefit of foresight, it may be able to service a pair of 1-faults through a single exchange. In this both the stores in the exchange get objects which are useful to them, instead of just one store benefiting from the exchange. Thus since OPT has v exchanges in the *ith* global phase, it may satisfy at most $2v$ 1-faults and 2Mark correspondingly has at most $2vM + NM$ 1-faults. The second term is due 1-faults in the first local phase for each store in this global phase.

Thus the total cost in the *ith* global phase by 2Mark is at most $sNM + 2vM + NM$, while that of OPT is at least $s+v$, since $u \geq 1$ in every global phase. This completes the proof.

MICRO-BENCHMARKS

This section describes our performance evaluation of data diffusion using micro-benchmarks.

Testbed Description

Table 1 lists the platforms used in the micro-benchmark experiments. The UC_x64 node was used to run the Falkon service, while the TG_ANL_IA32 and TG_ANL_IA64 clusters

(ANL/UC TeraGrid Site Details, 2007) were used to run the executors. Both clusters are connected internally via Gigabit Ethernet, and have a shared file system (GPFS) mounted across both clusters that we use as the "persistent storage" in our experiments. The GPFS file system has 8 I/O nodes to handle the shared file system traffic. We assume a one-to-one mapping between executors and nodes in all experiments. Latency between UC_x64 and the compute clusters was between one and two milliseconds.

File System Performance

In order to understand how well the proposed data diffusion works, we decided to model the shared file system (GPFS) performance in the ANL/UC TG cluster where we conducted all our experiments. The following graphs represent 160 different experiments, covering 19.8M files transferring 3.68TB of data and consuming 162.8 CPU hours; the majority of this time was spent measuring the GPFS performance, but a small percentage was also spent measuring the local disk performance of a single node. The dataset we used was composed of 5.5M files making up 2.4TB of data. In the hopes to eliminate as much variability or bias as possible from the results (introduced by Falkon itself), we wrote a simple program that took in some parameters, such as the input list of files, output directory, length of time to run experiment (while never repeating any files for the corresponding experiment); the program then randomized the input files and ran the workload of reading or reading+writing the corresponding files in 32KB chunks (larger buffers

Figure 7. Comparing performance between the local disk and the shared file system GPFS from one node

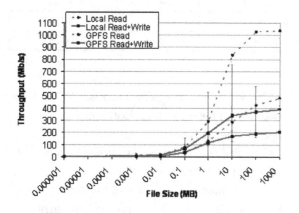

Figure 8. Read performance for GPFS expressed in Mb/s; only the x-axis is logarithmic; 1-64 nodes for GPFS; 1B – 1GB files

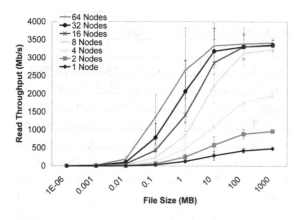

Figure 9. Read+write performance for GPFS expressed in Mb/s; only the x-axis is logarithmic; 1-64 nodes for GPFS; 1B – 1GB files

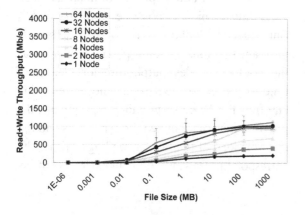

than 32KB didn't offer any improvement in read/write performance for our testbed). Experiments were ordered in such a manner that the same files would only be repeated after many other accesses, making the probability of those files being in any cache of the operating system or parallel file system I/O nodes small. Most graphs (unless otherwise noted) represent the GPFS read or read+write performance for 1 to 64 (1, 2, 4, 8, 16, 32, 64) concurrent nodes accessing files ranging from 1 byte to 1GB in size (1B, 1KB, 10KB, 100KB, 1MB, 10MB, 100MB, 1GB).

As a first comparison, we measured the read and read+write performance of one node as it performed the operations on both the local disk and the shared file system. Figure 7 shows that local disk is more than twice as fast when compared to the shared file system performance in all cases, a good motivator to favor local disk access whenever possible.

Notice that the GPFS read performance (Figure 8) tops out at 3420 Mb/s for large files, and it can achieve 75% of its peak bandwidth with files as small as 1MB if there are enough nodes concurrently accessing GPFS. It is worth noting that the performance increase beyond 8 nodes is only apparent for small files; for large files, the difference is small (<6% improvement from 8 nodes to 64 nodes). This is due to the fact that there are 8 I/O servers serving GPFS, and 8 nodes are enough to saturate the 8 I/O servers given large enough files.

The read+write performance (Figure 9) is lower than that of the read performance, as it tops out at 1123Mb/s. Just as in the read experiment, there seems to be little gain from having more than 8 nodes concurrently accessing GPFS (with the exception of small files).

These final two graphs (Figure 10 and Figure 11) show the theoretical read+write and read throughput (measured in Mb/s) for local disk access.

These results are theoretical, as they are simply a derivation of the 1 node performance (see

Figure 7), extrapolated to additional nodes (2, 4, 8, 16, 32, 64) linearly (assuming that local disk accesses are completely independent of each other across different nodes). Notice the read+write throughput approaches 25GB/s (up from 1Gb/s for GPFS) and the read throughput 76Gb/s (up from 3.5Gb/s for GPFS). This upper bound potential is a great motivator for applications to favor the use of local disk over that of shared disk, especially as applications scale beyond the size of the statically configured number of I/O servers servicing the shared file systems normally found in production clusters and grids.

Data Diffusion Performance

We measured performance for five configurations, two variants (read and read+write), seven node counts (1, 2, 4, 8, 16, 32, 64), and eight file sizes (1B, 1KB, 10KB, 100KB, 1MB, 10MB, 100MB, 1GB), for a total of 560 experiments. For all experiments (with the exception of the 100% data locality experiments where the caches were warm), data was initially located only on persistent storage, which in our case was GPFS parallel file system. The six configurations are: Model (local disk), Model (persistent storage), FA Policy, MCU Policy (0% locality), and MCU Policy (100% locality).

Figure 12 shows read throughput for 100MB files, seven of the eight configurations, and varying numbers of nodes. Configuration (8) has the best performance: 61.7Gb/s with 64 nodes (~94% of ideal). Even the first-cache-available policy which dispatches tasks to executors without concern for data location performs better (~5.7Gb/s) than the shared file system alone (~3.1Gb/s) when there are more than 16 nodes. With eight or less nodes, data-unaware scheduling with 100% data locality performs worse than GPFS (note that GPFS also has eight I/O servers); one hypothesis is that data is not dispersed evenly among the caches, and load imbalances reduce aggregate throughput, but we need to investigate further to better understand

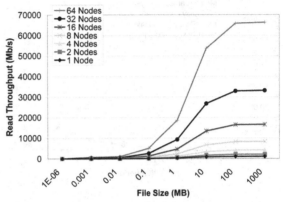

Figure 10. Theoretical read performance of local disks expressed in Mb/s; only the x-axis is logarithmic; 1-64 nodes for local disk access; 1B – 1GB files

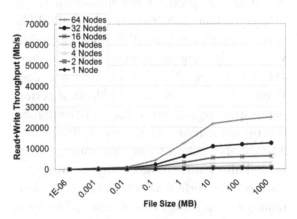

Figure 11. (local model 1-64 nodes r+w): Theoretical read+write performance of local disks expressed in Mb/s; only the x-axis is logarithmic; 1-64 nodes for local disk access; 1B – 1GB files

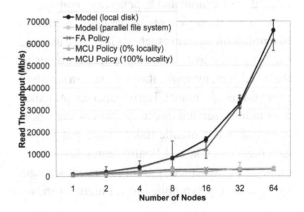

Figure 12. Read throughput (Mb/s) for large files (100MB) for seven configurations for 1 – 64 nodes

Figure 13. Read+Write throughput (Mb/s) for large files (100MB) for seven configurations and 1 – 64 nodes

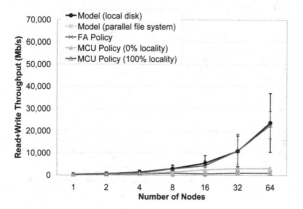

Figure 14. Read and Read+Write throughput (Mb/s) for a wide range of file sizes for three configurations on 64 nodes

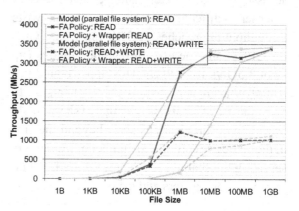

the performance of data-unaware scheduling at small scales.

Figure 13 shows read+write performance, which is also good for the max-compute-util policy, yielding 22.7Gb/s (~96% of ideal). Without data-aware scheduling, throughput is 6.3Gb/s; when simply using persistent storage, it is a mere 1Gb/s. In Figure 12 and Figure 13, we omit configuration (4) as it had almost identical performance to configuration (3). Recall that configuration (4) introduced a wrapper script that created a temporary sandbox for the application to work in, and afterwards cleaned up by removing the sandbox. The performance of these two configurations was so similar here because of the large file sizes (100MB) used, which meant that the cost to create and remove the sand box was amortized over a large and expensive operation.

In order to show some of the large overheads of parallel file systems such as GPFS, we execute the FA policy using a wrapper script similar to that used in many applications to create a sandbox execution environment. The wrapper script creates a temporary scratch directory on persistent storage, makes a symbolic link to the input file(s), executes the task, and finally removes the temporary scratch directory from persistent storage, along with any symbolic links. Figure 14 shows

read and read+write performance on 64 nodes for file sizes ranging from 1B to 1GB and comparing the model performance with the FA policy with and without a wrapper. Notice that for small file sizes (1B to 10MB), the FA policy with wrapper had one order of magnitude lower throughput than those without the wrapper. We find that the best throughput that can be achieved by 64 concurrent nodes with small files is 21 tasks/sec. The limiting factor is the need, for every task, to create a directory on persistent storage, create a symbolic link, and remove the directory. Many applications that use persistent storage to read and write files from many compute processors use this method of a wrapper to cleanly separate the data between different application invocations. This offers further example of how GPFS performance can significantly impact application performance, and why data diffusion is desirable as applications scale.

Overall, the shared file system seems to offer good performance for up to eight concurrent nodes (mostly due to there being eight I/O nodes servicing GPFS), however when more than eight nodes require access to data, the data diffusion mechanisms significantly outperform the persistent storage system. The improved performance can be attributed to the linear increase in I/O bandwidth with compute nodes, and the effective data-aware scheduling performed.

Scheduler Performance

In order to understand the performance of the data-aware scheduler, we developed several micro- benchmarks to test scheduler performance. We used the FA policy that performed no I/O as the baseline scheduler, and tested the various scheduling policies. We measured overall achieved throughput in terms of scheduling decisions per second and the breakdown of where time was spent inside the Falkon service. We conducted our experiments using 32 nodes; our workload consisted of 250K tasks, where each task accessed a random file (uniform distribution) from a dataset of 10K files of 1B in size each. We use files of 1 byte to measure the scheduling time and cache hit rates with minimal impact from the actual I/O performance of persistent storage and local disk. We compare the FA policy using no I/O (sleep 0), FA policy using GPFS, MCU policy, MCH policy, and GCC policy. The scheduling window size was set to 100X the number of nodes, or 3200. We also used 0.8 as the CPU utilization threshold in the GCC policy to determine when to switch between the MCH and MCU policies. Figure 15 shows the scheduler performance under different scheduling policies.

We see the throughput in terms of scheduling decisions per second range between 2981/sec (for FA without I/O) to as low as 1322/sec (for MCH). It is worth pointing out that for the FA policy, the cost of communication is significantly larger than the rest of the costs combined, including scheduling. The scheduling is quite inexpensive for this policy as it simply load balances across all workers. However, we see that with the 3 data-aware policies, the scheduling costs (red and light blue areas) are more significant.

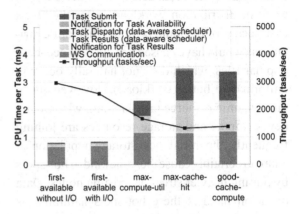

Figure 15. Data-aware scheduler performance and code profiling for various scheduling policies

SYNTHETIC WORKLOADS

We measured the performance of the data-aware scheduler on various workloads, both with static (SRP) and dynamic (DRP) resource provisioning, and ran experiments on the ANL/UC TeraGrid [48] (up to 100 nodes, 200 processors). The Falkon service ran on an 8-core Xeon@2.33GHz, 2GB RAM, Java 1.5, 100Mb/s network, and 2 ms latency to the executors. The persistent storage was GPFS [23] with <1ms latency to executors.

The three subsections that follow cover three diverse workloads: Monotonically-Increasing (MI), Sine-Wave (SI), and All-Pairs (AP). We use workloads MI and SI to explore the dynamic resource provisioning support in data diffusion, and the various scheduling policies (e.g. FA, GCC, MCH, MCU) and cache sizes (e.g. 1GB, 1.5GB, 2GB, 4GB). We use the AP workload to compare data diffusion with active storage (Moretti et al., 2008).

All our workloads were generated at random, using uniform distribution. Although this might not be representative of all applications, we believe workloads with uniform distribution will stress the data-aware scheduler far more than if the distribution followed zipf where few files were extremely popular and many files were unpopular. In general, zipf distribution workloads require a smaller aggregate cache in relation to the workload working set. From data locality perspective, uniform distribution workloads offer the worst case scenario. It should be noted that zipf distributions would have caused hot-spots to occur for popular files, which does not naturally occur in uniform distribution workloads. However, due to our dynamic resource provisioning, when many new compute and storage resources are joining frequently, the initial local storage population of data can certainly cause the same kind of hot-spots by putting heavier stress on existing nodes. Data diffusion handles these hot-spots naturally, as temporarily popular data (due to new nodes joining and having an empty cache) get replicated at the new storage locations, and subsequent accesses to this data can be served locally. Therefore, in our system, these hot-spots are only temporary, while the popular data diffuses to other storage nodes, and subsequent accesses to this data is then localized effectively eliminating the hot-spot (even in the face of continuing access patterns that favor several popular files).

Monotonically Increasing Workload

The MI workload has a high I/O to compute ratio (10MB:10ms). The dataset is 100GB large (10K x 10MB files). Each task reads one file chosen at random (uniform distribution) from the dataset, and computes for 10ms. The arrival rate is initially 1 task/sec and is increased by a factor of 1.3 every 60 seconds to a maximum of 1000 tasks/sec. The increasing function is shown in Equation12.

$$A_i = \min\left[ceiling(A_{i-1} * 1.3), 1000\right], 0 \leq i < 24 \tag{12}$$

This function varies arrival rate A from 1 to 1000 in 24 distinct intervals makes up 250K tasks and spans 1415 seconds; we chose a maximum arrival rate of 1000 tasks/sec as that was within the limits of the data-aware scheduler (see subsection

on "Centralized vs. Distributed Cache Index"), and offered large aggregate I/O requirements at modest scales. This workload aims to explore a varying arrival rate under a systematic increase in task arrival rate, to explore the data-aware scheduler's ability to optimize data locality with an increasing demand. This workload is depicted in Figure 16.

We investigated the performance of the FA, MCH, MCU, and GCC policies, while also analyzing cache size effects by varying node cache size (1GB to 4GB). Several measured or computed metrics are relevant in understanding the following set of graphs:

Demand (Gb/s): throughput needed to satisfy arrival rate

Throughput (Gb/s): measured aggregate transfer rates

Wait Queue Length: number of tasks ready to run

Cache Hit Global: file access from a peer executor cache

Cache Hit Local: file access from local cache

Cache Miss: file accesses from the parallel file system

Speedup (SP): $SP = T_N(FA) / T_N(GCC|MCH|MCU)$

CPU Time (CPU_T): the amount of processor time used

Performance Index (PI): $PI = SP/CPU_T$, normalized $[0...1]$

Average Response Time (AR_i): time to complete task i, including queue time, execution time, and communication costs

Slowdown (SL): measures the factor by which the workload execution times are slower than the ideal workload execution time

Cache Size Effects on Data Diffusion

The baseline experiment (FA policy) ran each task directly from GPFS, using dynamic resource provisioning. Aggregate throughput matches demand for arrival rates up to 59 tasks/sec, but remains flat at an average of 4.4Gb/s beyond

Figure 16. Monotonically increasing workload overview

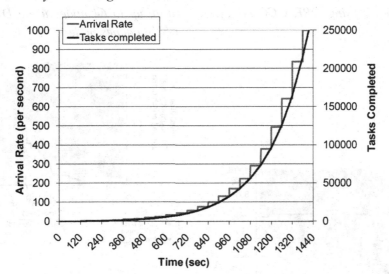

that. At the transition point when the arrival rate increased beyond 59, the wait queue length also started growing to an eventual maximum of 198K tasks. The workload execution time was 5011 seconds, yielding 28% efficiency (ideal being 1415 seconds).

We ran the same workload with data diffusion with varying cache sizes per node (1GB to 4GB) using the GCC policy, optimizing cache hits while keeping processor utilization high (90%). The dataset was diffused from GPFS to local disk caches with every cache miss (the red area in the graphs); global cache hits are in yellow and local cache hits in green. The working set was 100GB, and with a per-node cache size of 1GB, 1.5GB, 2GB, and 4GB caches, we get aggregate cache sizes of 64GB, 96GB, 128GB, and 256GB. The 1GB and 1.5GB caches cannot fit the working set in cache, while the 2GB and 4GB cache can.

Figure 18 shows the 1GB cache size experiment. Throughput keeps up with demand better than the FA policy, up to 101 tasks/sec arrival rates (up from 59), at which point the throughput stabilizes at an average of 5.2Gb/s. Within 800 seconds, working set caching reaches a steady state with a throughput of 6.9Gb/s. The overall cache hit rate was 31%, resulting in a 57% higher

Figure 17. MI workload, 250K tasks, 10MB:10ms ratio, up to 64 nodes using DRP, FA policy

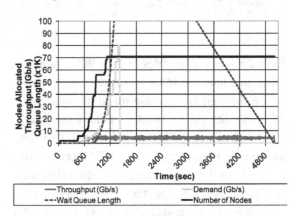

throughput than GPFS. The workload execution time is reduced to 3762 seconds, down from 5011 seconds for the FA policy, with 38% efficiency.

Figure 19 increases the per node cache size from 1Gb to 1.5GB, which increases the aggregate cache size to 96GB, almost enough to hold the entire working set of 100GB. Notice that the throughput hangs on further to the ideal throughput, up to 132 tasks/sec when the throughput increase stops and stabilizes at an average of 6.3Gb/s. Within 350 seconds of this stabilization, the cache hit performance increased significantly

Figure 18. MI workload, 250K tasks, 10MB:10ms ratio, up to 64 nodes using DRP, GCC policy, 1GB caches/node

Figure 19. MI workload, 250K tasks, 10MB:10ms ratio, up to 64 nodes using DRP, GCC policy, 1.5GB caches/node

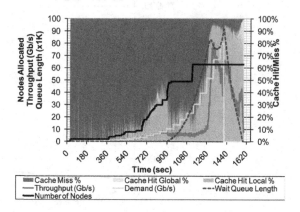

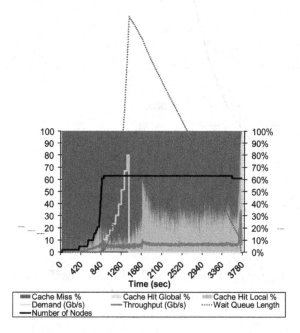

Figure 20. MI workload, 250K tasks, 10MB:10ms ratio, up to 64 nodes using DRP, GCC policy, 2GB caches/node

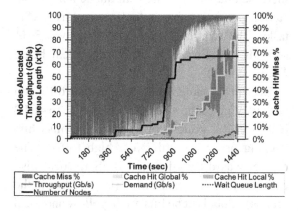

from 25% cache hit rates to over 90% cache hit rates; this increase in cache hit rates also results in the throughput increase up to an average of 45.6Gb/s for the remainder of the experiment. Overall, it achieved 78% cache hit rates, 1% cache hit rates to remote caches, and 21% cache miss rates. Overall, the workload execution time was reduced drastically from the 1GB per node cache size, down to 1596 seconds; this yields an 89% efficiency when compared to the ideal case. Both the 1GB and 1.5GB cache sizes achieve reasonable cache hit rates, despite the fact that the cache sizes are smaller than the working set; this is due to the fact that the data-aware scheduler looks deep (i.e. window size set to 2500) in the wait queue to find tasks that will improve the cache hit performance.

Figure 20 shows results with 2GB local caches (128GB aggregate). Aggregate throughput is close to demand (up to the peak of 80Gb/s) for the entire experiment. We attribute this good performance to the ability to cache the entire

working set and then schedule tasks to the nodes that have required data to achieve cache hit rates approaching 98%. Note that the queue length never grew beyond 7K tasks, significantly less than for the other experiments (91K to 198K tasks long). With an execution time of 1436 seconds, efficiency was 98.5%.

Investigating if it helps to increase the cache size further to 4GB per node, we conduct the experiment whose results are found in Figure 21. We see no significant improvement in performance from the experiment with 2GB caches. The execution time is reduced slightly to 1427 seconds

Figure 21. MI workload, 250K tasks, 10MB:10ms ratio, up to 64 nodes using DRP, GCC policy, 4GB caches/node

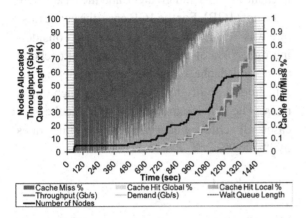

Figure 22. MI workload, 250K tasks, 10MB:10ms ratio, up to 64 nodes using DRP, MCH policy, 4GB caches/node

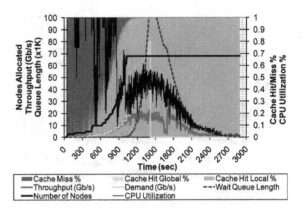

(99.2% efficient), and the overall cache hit rates are improved to 88% cache hit rates, 6% remote cache hits, and 6% cache misses.

Comparing Scheduling Policies

To study the impact of scheduling policy on performance, we reran the workload for which we just gave GCC results using MCH and MCU with 4GB caches. Using the MCH policy (see Figure 22), we obtained 95% cache hit performance % (up from 88% with GCC), but poor processor utilization (43%, down from 95% with GCC). Note that the MCH policy always schedules tasks according to where the data is cached, even if it has to wait for some node to become available, leaving some nodes processors idle. Notice a new metric measured (dotted thin black line), the CPU utilization, which shows clear poor CPU utilization that decreases with time as the scheduler has difficulty scheduling tasks to busy nodes; the average CPU utilization for the entire experiment was 43%. Overall workload execution time increased, to 2888 seconds (49% efficiency, down from 99% for GCC).

Figure 23 shows the MCU policy, which attempts to maximize the CPU utilization at the expense of data movement. We see the workload

execution time is improved (compared to MCH) down to 2037 seconds (69% efficient), but it is still far from the GCC policy that achieved 1436 seconds. The major difference here is that the there are significantly more cache hits to remote caches as tasks got scheduled to nodes that didn't have the needed cached data due to being busy with other work. We were able to sustain high efficiency with arrival rates up to 380 tasks/sec, with an average throughput for the steady part of the experiment of 14.5 Gb/s.

It is interesting to see the cache hit local performance at time 1800~2000 second range spiked from 60% to 98%, which results in a spike in throughout from 14Gb/s to 40Gb/s. Although we maintained 100% CPU utilization, due to the extra costs of moving data from remote executors, the performance was worse than the GCC policy when 4.5% of the CPUs were left idle. The next several subsections will summarize these experiments, and compare them side by side.

Cache Performance

Figure 24 shows cache performance over six experiments involving data diffusion, the ideal case, and the FA policy which does not cache any data.

Figure 23. MI workload, 250K tasks, 10MB:10ms ratio, up to 64 nodes using DRP, MCU policy, 4GB caches/node

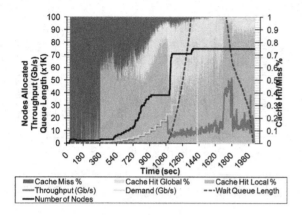

Figure 24. MI workload cache performance

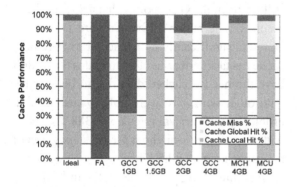

Figure 25. MI average and peak (99 percentile) throughput

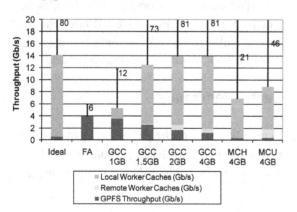

We see a clear separation in the cache miss rates (red) for the cases where the working set fit in cache (1.5GB and greater), and the case where it did not (1GB). For the 1GB case, the cache miss rate was 70%, which is to be expected considering only 70% of the working set fit in cache at most, and cache thrashing was hampering the scheduler's ability to achieve better cache miss rates. The other extreme, the 4GB cache size cases, all achieved near perfect cache miss rates of 4%~5.5%.

Throughput

Figure 25 summarizes the aggregate I/O throughput measured in each of the seven experiments. We present in each case first, as the solid bars, the average throughput achieved from start to finish, partitioned among local cache, remote cache, and GPFS, and second, as a black line, the "peak" (actually 99th percentile) throughput achieved during the execution. The second metric is interesting because of the progressive increase in job submission rate: it may be viewed as a measure of how far a particular method can go in keeping up with user demands.

We see that the FA policy had the lowest average throughput of 4Gb/s, compared to between 5.3Gb/s and 13.9Gb/s for data diffusion (GCC, MCH, and MCU with various cache sizes), and 14.1Gb/s for the ideal case. In addition to having higher average throughputs, data diffusion also achieved significantly throughputs towards the end of the experiment (the black bar) when the arrival rates are highest, as high as 81Gb/s as opposed to 6Gb/s for the FA policy.

Note also that GPFS file system load (the red portion of the bars) is significantly lower with data diffusion than for the GPFS-only experiments (FA); in the worst case, with 1GB caches where the working set did not fit in cache, the load on GPFS is still high with 3.6Gb/s due to all the cache misses, while FA tests had 4Gb/s load. However, as the cache sizes increased and the working set

Figure 26. MI workload PI and speedup comparison

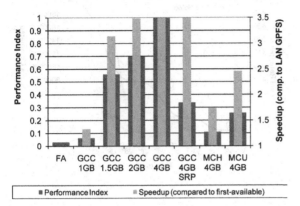

Figure 27. MI workload slowdown as we varied arrival rate

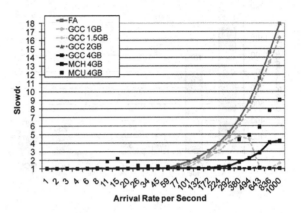

fit in cache, the load on GPFS became as low as 0.4Gb/s; similarly, the network load was considerably lower, with the highest values of 1.5Gb/s for the MCU policy, and less than 1Gb/s for the other policies.

Performance Index and Speedup

The performance index attempts to capture the speedup per CPU time achieved. Figure 26 shows PI and speedup data. Notice that while GCC with 2GB and 4GB caches each achieve the highest speedup of 3.5X, the 4GB case achieves a higher performance index of 1 as opposed to 0.7 for the 2GB case. This is due to the fact that fewer resources were used throughout the 4GB experiment, 17 CPU hours instead of 24 CPU hours for the 2GB case. This reduction in resource usage was due to the larger caches, which in turn allowed the system to perform better with fewer resources for longer durations, and hence the wait queue did not grow as fast, which resulted in less aggressive resource allocation. Notice the performance index of the FA policy which uses GPFS solely; although the speedup gains with data diffusion compared to the FA policy are modest (1.3X to 3.5X), the performance index of data diffusion is significantly more (2X to 34X).

Slowdown

Speedup compares data diffusion to the base case, but does not tell us how well data diffusion performed in relation to the ideal case. Recall that the ideal case is computed from the arrival rate of tasks, assuming zero communication costs and infinite resources to handle tasks in parallel; in our case, the ideal workload execution time is 1415 seconds. Figure 27 shows the slowdown for our experiments as a function of arrival rates. *Slowdown (SL)* measures the factor by which the workload execution times are slower than the ideal workload execution time; the ideal workload execution time assumes infinite resources and 0 cost communication, and is computed from the arrival rate function.

These results in Figure 27 show the arrival rates that could be handled by each approach, showing the FA policy (the GPFS only case) to saturate the earliest at 59 tasks/sec denoted by the rising red line. It is evident that larger cache sizes allowed the saturation rates to be higher (essentially perfect for some cases, such as the GCC with 4GB caches). It interesting to point out the GCC policy with 1.5GB caches slowdown increase relatively early (similar to the 1GB case), but then towards the end of the experiment the slowdown is reduced from almost 5X back down

Figure 28. MI workload average response time

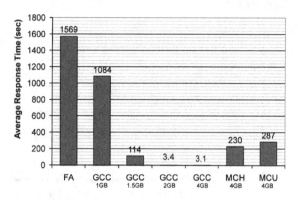

Figure 29. SW workload overview

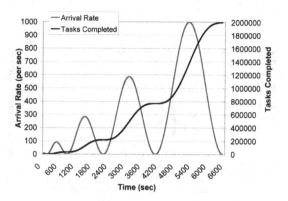

to an almost ideal 1X. This sudden improvement in performance is attributed to a critical part of the working set being cached and the cache hit rates increasing significantly. Also, note the odd slowdown (as high as 2X) of the 4GB cache DRP case at arrival rates 11, 15, and 20; this slowdown matches up to the drop in throughput between time 360 and 480 seconds in Figure 23 (the detailed summary view of this experiment), which in turn occurred when an additional resource was allocated. It is important to note that resource allocation takes on the order of 30~60 seconds due to LRM's overheads, which is why it took the slowdown 120 seconds to return back to the normal (1X), as the dynamic resource provisioning compensated for the drop in performance.

Response Time

The response time is probably one of the most important metrics interactive applications. *Average Response Time (AR)* is the end-to-end time from task submission to task completion notification for task i; $AR_i = WQ_i + TK_i + D_i$, where WQ_i is the wait queue time, TK_i is the task execution time, and D_i is the delivery time to deliver the result. Figure 28 shows response time results across all 14 experiments in log scale.

We see a significant different between the best data diffusion response time (3.1 seconds per task) to the worst data diffusion (1084 seconds) and

the worst GPFS (1870 seconds). That is over 500X difference between the data diffusion GCC policy and the FA policy (GPFS only) response time. A principal factor influencing the average response time is the time tasks spend in the Falkon wait queue. In the worst (FA) case, the queue length grew to over 200K tasks as the allocated resources could not keep up with the arrival rate. In contrast, the best (GCC with 4GB caches) case only queued up 7K tasks at its peak. The ability to keep the wait queue short allowed data diffusion to keep average response times low (3.1 seconds), making it a better for interactive workloads.

Sine-Wave Workload

The previous subsection explored a workload with monotonically increasing arrival rates. To explore how well data diffusion deals with decreasing arrival rates as well, we define a sine-wave (SW) workload (see Figure 29) that follows the function shown in Equation 13 (where time is elapsed minutes from the beginning of the experiment):

$$A = \left| \left(\sin\left(sqrt\left(time + 0.11\right) * 2.859678 \right) + 1 \right) * \left(time + 0.11 \right) * 5.705 \right|$$

(13)

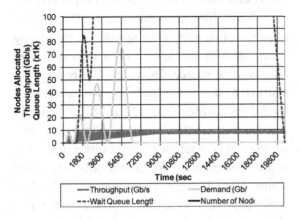

Figure 30. SW workload, 2M tasks, 10MB:10ms ratio, 100 nodes, FA policy

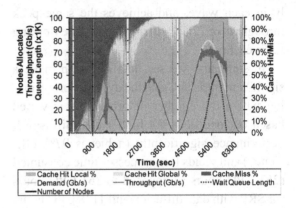

Figure 31. SW workload, 2M tasks, 10MB:10ms ratio, 100 nodes, GCC policy, 50GB caches/node

This workload aims to explore the data-aware scheduler's ability to optimize data locality in face frequent joins and leaves of resources due to variability in demand. This function is essentially a sine wave pattern (red line), in which the arrival rate increases in increasingly stronger waves, increasing up to 1000 tasks/sec arrival rates. The working set is 1TB large (100K files of 10MB each), and the I/O to compute ratio is 10MB:10ms. The workload is composed of 2M tasks (black line) where each task accesses a random file (uniform distribution), and takes 6505 seconds to complete in the ideal case.

Our first experiment consisted of running the SW workload with all computations running directly from the parallel file system and using 100 nodes with static resource provisioning. We see the measured throughput keep up with the demand up to the point when the demand exceeds the parallel file system peak performance of 8Gb/s; beyond this point, the wait queue grew to 1.4M tasks, and the workload needed 20491 seconds to complete (instead of the ideal case of 6505 seconds), yielding an efficiency of 32%. Note that although we are using the same cluster as in the MI workload (previous subsection), GPFS's peak throughput is higher (8Gb/s vs. 4Gb/s) due to a major upgrade to both hardware and software in the cluster between running these experiments.

Enabling data diffusion with the GCC policy, setting the cache size to 50GB, the scheduling window size to 2500, and the processor utilization threshold to 90%, we get a run that took 6505 seconds to complete (see Figure 31), yielding an efficiency of 100%. We see the cache misses (red) decrease from 100% to 0% over the course of the experiment, while local cache hits (green) frequently making up 90%+ of the cache hits. Note that the data diffusion mechanism was able to keep up with the arrival rates throughout with the exception of the peak of the last wave, when it was only able to achieve 72Gb/s (instead of the ideal 80Gb/s), at which point the wait queue grew to its longest length of 50K tasks. The global cache hits (yellow) is stable at about 10% throughout, which is reflected from the fact that the GCC policy is oscillating between optimizing cache hit performance and processor utilization around the configured 90% processor utilization threshold.

Enabling dynamic resource provisioning, Figure 32 shows the workload still manages to complete in 6697 seconds, yielding 97% efficiency. In order to minimize wasted processor time, we set each worker to release its resource after 30 seconds of idleness. Note that upon releasing a resource, its cache is reset; thus, after every wave, cache performance is again poor until caches are rebuilt. The measured throughput does not fit the demand line as well as the static resource provisioning did, but it increases steadily in each wave, and achieves the same peak throughput of 72Gb/s after enough of the working set is cached.

In summary, we see data diffusion make a significant impact. Using the dynamic provisioning where the number of processors is varied based on load does not hinder data diffusion's performance significantly (achieves 97% efficiency) and yields less processor time consumed (253 CPU hours as opposed to 361 CPU hours for SRP with data diffusion and 1138 CPU hours without data diffusion).

All-Pairs Workload Evaluation

In previous work, several of the co-authors addressed large scale data intensive problems with the Chirp (Thain et al., 2008) distributed filesystem. Chirp has several contributions, such as

delivering an implementation that behaves like a file system and maintains most of the semantics of a shared filesystem, and offers efficient distribution of datasets via a spanning tree making Chirp ideal in scenarios with a slow and high latency data source. However, Chirp does not address data-aware scheduling, so when used by All-Pairs (Moretti et al., 2008), it typically distributes an entire application working data set to each compute node local disk prior to the application running. We call the All-Pairs use of Chirp *active storage*. This requirement hinders active storage from scaling as well as data diffusion, making large working sets that do not fit on each compute node local disk difficult to handle, and producing potentially unnecessary transfers of data. Data diffusion only transfers the minimum data needed per job. This subsection aims to compare the performance between data diffusion and a best model of active storage.

Variations of the AP problem occur in many applications, for example when we want to understand the behavior of a new function F on sets A and B, or to learn the covariance of sets A and B on a standard inner product F (see Figure 33). (Moretti et al., 2008) The AP problem is easy to express in terms of two nested for loops over some parameter space (see Figure 34). This regular structure also makes it easy to optimize its data access operations. Thus, AP is a challenging benchmark for data diffusion, due to its on-demand, pull-mode data access strategy. Figure 35 shows a sample 100x100 problem space, where each black dot represents a computation computing some function F on data at index i and j; in this case, the entire compute space is composed of 10K separate computations.

Figure 32. SW workload, 2M tasks, 10MB:10ms ratio, up to 100 nodes with DRP, GCC policy, 50GB caches/node

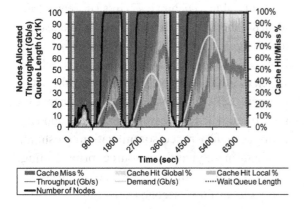

Figure 33. All-Pairs definition

All-Pairs(set A, set B, function F) returns matrix M:
Compare all elements of set A to all elements of set B via function F, yielding matrix M, such that M[i,j] = F(A[i],B[j])

In previous work (Moretti et al., 2008), we conducted experiments with biometrics and data mining workloads using Chirp. The most data-intensive workload was where each function executed for 1 second to compare two 12MB items, for an I/O to compute ratio of 24MB:1000ms. At the largest scale (50 nodes and 500x500 problem size), we measured an efficiency of 60% for the active storage implementation, and 3% for the demand paging (to be compared to the GPFS performance we cite). These experiments were conducted in a campus wide heterogeneous cluster with nodes at risk for suspension, network connectivity of 100Mb/s between nodes, and a shared file system rated at 100Mb/s from which the dataset needed to be transferred to the compute nodes.

Due to differences in our testing environments, a direct comparison is difficult, but we compute the best case for active storage as defined in (Moretti et al., 2008), and compare measured data diffusion performance against this best case. Our environment has 100 nodes (200 processors) which are dedicated for the duration of the allocation, with 1Gb/s network connectivity between nodes, and

a parallel file system (GPFS) rated at 8Gb/s. For the 500x500 workload (see Figure 36), data diffusion achieves a throughput that is 80% of the best case of all data accesses occurring to local disk (see Figure 40). We computed the best case for active storage to be 96%, however in practice, based on the efficiency of the 50 node case from previous work (Moretti et al., 2008) which achieved 60% efficiency, we believe the 100 node case would not perform significantly better than the 80% efficiency of data diffusion. Running the same workload through Falkon directly against a parallel file system achieves only 26% of the throughput of the purely local solution.

In order to push data diffusion harder, we made the workload 10X more data-intensive by reducing the compute time from 1 second to 0.1 seconds,

Figure 34. All-Pairs workload script

```
1  foreach $i in A
2      foreach $j in B
3          submit_job F $i $j
4      end
5  end
```

Figure 35. Sample 100x100 AP problem, where each dot represents a computation at index i,j

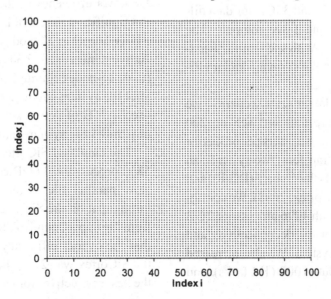

Figure 36. AP workload, 500x500=250K tasks, 24MB:1000ms, 100 nodes, GCC policy, 50GB caches/node

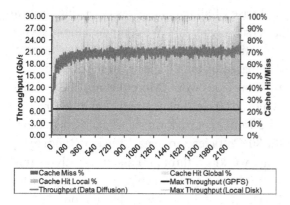

Figure 37. AP workload, 500x500=250K tasks, 24MB:100ms, 100 nodes, GCC policy, 50GB caches/node

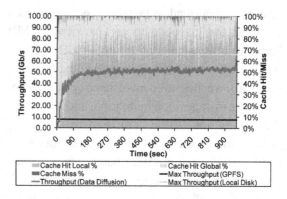

yielding a I/O to compute ratio of 24MB:100ms (see Figure 37).

For this workload, the throughput steadily increased to about 55Gb/s as more local cache hits occurred. We found extremely few cache misses, which indicates the high data locality of the AP workload. Data diffusion achieved 75% efficiency. Active storage and data diffusion transferred similar amounts of data over the network (1536GB for active storage and 1528GB for data diffusion with 0.1 sec compute time and 1698GB with the 1 sec compute time workload) and to/from the parallel file system (12GB for active storage and 62GB and 34GB for data diffusion for the 0.1 sec and 1 sec compute time workloads respectively). With such similar bandwidth usage throughout the system, similar efficiencies were to be expected.

In order to explore larger scale scenarios, we emulated (ran the entire Falkon stack on 200 processors with multiple executors per processor and emulated the data transfers) two systems, an IBM Blue Gene/P (IBM BlueGene/P (BG/P)) and a SiCortex SC5832 (SiCortex, 2008). We configured the Blue Gene/P with 4096 processors, 2GB caches per node, 1Gb/s network connectivity, and a 64Gb/s parallel file system. We also increased the problem size to 1000x1000 (1M tasks), and

set the I/O to compute ratios to 24MB:4sec (each processor on the Blue Gene/P and SiCortex is about ¼ the speed of those in our 100 node cluster). On the emulated Blue Gene/P, we achieved an efficiency of 86%. The throughputs steadily increased up to 180Gb/s (of a theoretical upper bound of 187Gb/s). It is possible that our emulation was optimistic due to a simplistic modeling of the Torus network, however it shows that the scheduler scales well to 4K processors and is able to do 870 scheduling decisions per second to complete 1M tasks in 1150 seconds. The best case active storage yielded only 35% efficiency. We justify the lower efficiency of the active storage due to the significant time that is spent to distribute the 24GB dataset to 1K nodes via the spanning tree. Active storage used 12.3TB of network bandwidth (node-to-node communication) and 24GB of parallel file system bandwidth, while data diffusion used 4.7TB of network bandwidth, and 384GB of parallel file system bandwidth (see Table 2).

The emulated SiCortex was configured with 5832 processors, 3.6GB caches, and a relatively slow parallel file system rated at 4Gb/s. The throughput on the SiCortex reached 90Gb/s, far from the upper bound of 268Gb/s. It is interesting that the overall efficiency for data diffusion on the SiCortex was 27%, the same efficiency that the best case active storage achieved. The slower

Table 2. Data movement comparing the best case active storage and Falkon data diffusion

Experiment	Approach	Local Disk/Memory (GB)	Network (node-to-node) (GB)	Shared File System (GB)
500x500x 200 CPUs 1 sec	Best Case (active storage)	6000	1536	12
	Falkon (data diffusion)	6000	1698	34
500x500 200 CPUs 0.1 sec	Best Case (active storage)	6000	1536	12
	Falkon (data diffusion)	6000	1528	62
1000x1000 4096 CPUs 4 sec	Best Case (active storage)	24000	12288	24
	Falkon (data diffusion)	24000	4676	384
1000x1000 5832 CPUs 4 sec	Best Case (active storage)	24000	12288	24
	Falkon (data diffusion)	24000	3867	906

parallel file system significantly reduced the efficiency of the data diffusion (as data diffusion performs the initial cache population completely from the parallel file system, and needed 906GB of parallel file system bandwidth), however it had no effect on the efficiency of the active storage as the spanning tree only required one read of the dataset from the parallel file system (a total of 24GB). With sufficiently large workloads, data diffusion would likely improve its efficiency as the expensive cost to populate its caches would get amortized over more potential cache hits.

There are some interesting oscillations in the cache hit/miss ratios as well as the achieved. We believe the oscillation occurred due to the slower parallel file system of the SiCortex, which was overwhelmed by thousands of processors concurrently accessing tens of MB each. Further compounding the problem is the fact that there were twice as many cache misses on the SiCortex than there were on the Blue Gene/P, which seems counter-intuitive as the per processor cache size was slightly larger (500MB for Blue Gene/P and

Figure 38. AP workload on emulated Blue Gene/P, 1000x1000=1M tasks, 24MB:4000ms, 1024 nodes (4096 processors), GCC policy, 2GB caches/node

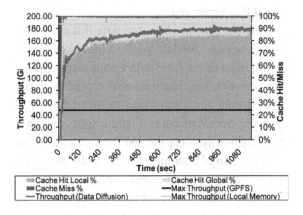

600MB for the SiCortex). We will investigate these oscillations further to find their root cause, which might very well be due to our emulation, and might not appear in real world examples.

In reality, the best case active storage would require cache sizes of at least 24GB, and the existing 2GB or 3.6GB cache sizes for the Blue

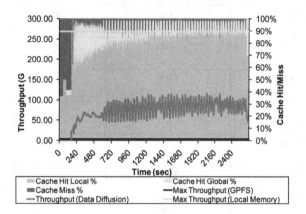

Figure 39. AP workload on emulated SiCortex, 1000x1000=1M tasks, 24MB:4000ms, 972 nodes (5832 processors), GCC policy, 3.6GB caches/ node

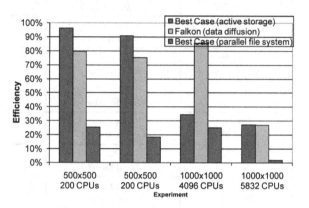

Figure 40. AP workload efficiency for 500x500 problem size on 200 processor cluster and 1000x1000 problem size on the Blue Gene/P and SiCortex emulated systems with 4096 and 5832 processors respectively

Gene/P and SiCortex respectively would only be sufficient for an 83X83 problem size, so this comparison (Figure 38 and Figure 39) is not only emulated, but also hypothetical. Nevertheless, it is interesting to see the significant difference in efficiency between data diffusion and active storage at this larger scale.

Our comparison between data diffusion and active storage fundamentally boils down to a comparison of pushing data versus pulling data. The active storage implementation pushes all the needed data for a workload to all nodes via a spanning tree. With data diffusion, nodes pull only the files immediately needed for a task, creating an incremental spanning forest (analogous to a spanning tree, but one that supports cycles) at runtime that has links to both the parent node and to any other arbitrary node or persistent storage. We measured data diffusion to perform comparably to active storage on our 200 processor cluster, but differences exist between the two approaches. Data diffusion is more dependent on having a well balanced persistent storage for the amount of computing power (as could be seen in comparing the Blue Gene/P and SiCortex results), but can scale to larger number of nodes due to the

more selective nature of data distribution. Furthermore, data diffusion only needs to fit the per task working set in local caches, rather than an entire workload working set as is the case for active storage.

LARGE-SCALE ASTRONOMY APPLICATION PERFORMANCE EVALUATION

Previous two sections covered micro-benchmarks and synthetic workloads to show how well data diffusion works, and how it compares to parallel file systems such as GPFS and active storage. This section takes a specific example of a data intensive application, from the astronomy domain, and shows the benefits of data diffusion in both performance and scalability of the application.

The creation of large digital sky surveys presents the astronomy community with tremendous scientific opportunities. However, these astronomy datasets are generally terabytes in size and contain hundreds of millions of objects separated into millions of files—factors that make many analyses impractical to perform on small computers. To address this problem, we have developed a Web Services-based system, AstroPortal, that uses grid computing to federate large computing and storage resources for dynamic analysis of large datasets. Building on the Falkon framework, we have built an AstroPortal prototype and implemented the "stacking" analysis that sums multiple regions of the sky, a function that can help both identify variable sources and detect faint objects. We have deployed AstroPortal on the TeraGrid distributed infrastructure and applied the stacking function to the Sloan Digital Sky Survey (SDSS), DR4, which comprises about 300 million objects dispersed over 1.3 million files, a total of 3 terabytes of compressed data, with promising results. AstroPortal gives the astronomy community a new tool to advance their research and to open new doors to opportunities never before possible on such a large scale.

The astronomy community is acquiring an abundance of digital imaging data, via sky surveys such as SDSS (SDSS:Sloan Digital Sky Survey, 2008), GSC-II (GSC-II:Guide Star Catalog II, 2008), 2MASS (2MASS: Two Micron All Sky Survey, 2008), and POSS-II (POSS-II: Palomar Observatory Sky Survey, 2008). However, these datasets are generally large (multiple terabytes) and contain many objects (100 million +) separated into many files (1 million +). Thus, while it is by now common for astronomers to use Web Services interfaces to retrieve individual objects, analyses that require access to significant fractions of a sky survey have proved difficult to implement efficiently. There are five reasons why such analyses are challenging: (1) *large dataset size*; (2) *large number of users* (1000s); (3) *large number of resources* needed for adequate performance (potentially 1000s of processors and 100s of TB of disk); (4) *dispersed geographic distribution of the users and resources*; and (5) *resource heterogeneity*.

Definition of "Stacking"

The first analysis that we have implemented in our AstroPortal prototype is "stacking," image cutouts from different parts of the sky. This function can help to statistically detect objects too faint otherwise. Astronomical image collections usually cover an area of sky several times (in different wavebands, different times, etc). On the other hand, there are large differences in the sensitivities of different observations: objects detected in one band are often too faint to be seen in another survey. In such cases we still would like to see whether these objects can be detected, even in a statistical fashion. There has been a growing interest to re-project each image to a common set of pixel planes, then stacking images. The stacking improves the signal to noise, and after coadding a large number of images, there will be a detectable signal to measure the average brightness/shape etc of these objects. While this has been done for years manually for a small number of pointing fields, performing this task on wide areas of sky in a systematic way has not yet been done. It is also expected that the detection of much fainter sources (e.g., unusual objects such as transients) can be obtained from stacked images than can be detected in any individual image. AstroPortal gives the astronomy community a new tool to advance their research and opens doors to new opportunities.

AstroPortal

AstroPortal provides both a Web Services and a Web portal interface. Figure 41 is a screenshot of the AstroPortal Web Portal, which allows a user to request a "stacking" operation on an arbitrary set of objects from the SDSS DR4 dataset. The AstroPortal Web Portal is implemented using Java Servlets and Java Server Pages technologies; we used Tomcat 4.1.31 as the container for our web portal.

Figure 41. Left: AstroPortal Web portal stacking service; Right: Stacking service results

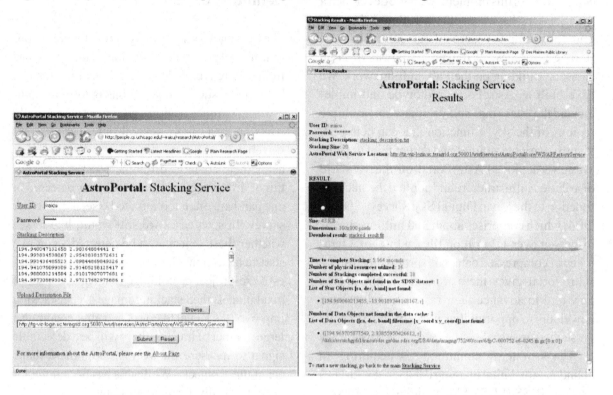

User input comprises user ID and password, a stacking description, and the AstroPortal Service location. The user ID and password are currently created out-of-band; in the future, we will investigate alternatives to making this a relatively automated process. The stacking description is a list of objects identified by the tuple {ra dec band}. The AstroPortal Web Service location is currently statically defined in the web portal interface, but in the future we envision a more dynamic discovery mechanism.

Following submission (see Figure 41, left), the user gets a status screen showing the progress of the stacking, including percentage completed and an estimated completion time. Once the stacking is complete, the results are returned along with additional information about performance and any errors encountered. Figure 41 (right) shows an example result from the stacking of 20 objects. The results include summary, results, and statistics and errors. The results displays a JPEG equivalent

of the result for quick interpretation, along with the size of the result (in KB), the physical dimensions of the result (in pixels x pixels), and a link to the result in FIT format (Hanish et al., 2001).

The final section specifies the completion time, number of computers used, number of objects found, the number (and address) of star objects not found in the SDSS dataset, and the number (and address) of data objects not found in the data cache. Some star objects might not be found in SDSS since the SDSS dataset does not cover the entire sky; other objects might not be found in the data cache due to inconsistencies (e.g., read permission denied, corrupt data, data cache inaccessible) between the original data archive and the live data cache actually used in the stacking.

Workload Characterization

Astronomical surveys produce terabytes of data, and contain millions of objects. For example,

Figure 42. SQL command to identify interesting objects for a quasar search from the SDSS DR5 dataset

```
select SpecRa, SpecDec
from QsoConcordanceAll
where bestMode=1
    and SpecSciencePrimary=1
    and SpecRa<>0
```

the SDSS DR5 dataset (which we base our experiments on) has 320M objects in 9TB of images (SDSS:Sloan Digital Sky Survey, 2008). To construct realistic workloads, we identified the interesting objects (for a quasar search) from SDSS DR5; we used the CAS SkyServer (CAS, SkyServer, 2007)to issue the SQL command from Figure 42. This query retrieved 168,529 objects, which after removal of duplicates left 154,345 objects per band (there are 5 bands, u, g, r, I, and z) stored in 111,700 files per band.

The entire working set consisted of 771,725 objects in 558,500 files, where each file was either 2MB compressed or 6MB uncompressed, resulting in a total of 1.1TB compressed and 3.35TB uncompressed. From this working set, various workloads were defined (see Table 3) that had certain data locality characteristics, varying from the lowest locality of 1 (i.e., 1-1 mapping between objects and files) to the highest locality of 30 (i.e., each file contained 30 objects on average of).

Stacking Code Profiling

We first profile the stacking code to see where time is spent. We partition time into four categories, as follows.

open: open Fits file for reading
radec2xy: convert coordinates from RA DEC to X Y
readHDU: reads header and image data
getTile: perform extraction of ROI from memory

Table 3. Workload characteristics

Locality	Number of Objects	Number of Files
1	111700	111700
1.38	154345	111699
2	97999	49000
3	88857	29620
4	76575	19145
5	60590	12120
10	46480	4650
20	40460	2025
30	23695	790

curl: convert the 1-D pixel data (as read from the image file) into a 2-dimensional pixel array
convertArray: convert the ROI from having SHORT value to having DOUBLE values
calibration: apply calibration on ROI using the SKY and CAL variables
interpolation: do the appropriate pixel shifting to ensure the center of the object is a whole pixel
doStacking: perform the stacking of ROI that are stored in memory
writeStacking: write the stacked image to a file

To simplify experiments, we perform tests with a simple standalone program on 1000 objects of 100x100 pixels, and repeat each measurement 10 times, each time on different objects residing in different files. In Figure 43, the Y-axis is time per task per code block measured in milliseconds(ms).

Having the image data in compressed format affects the time to stack an image significantly, increasing the time needed by a factor of two. Similarly, accessing the image data from local disk instead of the shared file system speeds up processing 1.5 times. In all cases, the dominant operations are file metadata and I/O operations. For example, calibration, interpolation, and doStacking take less than 1 ms in all cases. Radec2xy consumes another 10~20% of total time, but the rest is spent opening the file and reading the image data to memory. In compressed format

Figure 43. Stacking code performance profiling for 1 CPU

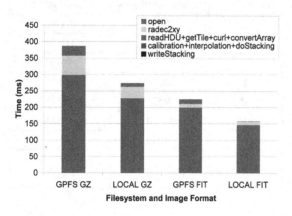

Figure 44. Performance of the stacking application for a workload data locality of 1.38 using data diffusion and GPFS while varying the CPUs from 2 to 128

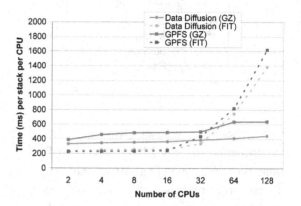

(GZ), there is only 2MB of data to read, while in uncompressed format (FIT) there are 6MB to read. However, uncompressing images is CPU intensive, and in the case of a single CPU, it is slower than if the image was uncompressed. In the case of many CPUs, the compressed format is faster mostly due to limitations imposed by the shared file system. Overall, Figure 43 shows the stacking analysis to be I/O bound and data intensive.

Performance Evaluation

All tests performed in this section were done using the testbed described in Table 1, using from 1 to 64 nodes, and the workloads (described in Table 3) that had locality ranging from 1 to 30. The experiments investigate the performance and scalability of the stacking code in four configurations: 1) Data Diffusion (GZ), 2) Data Diffusion (FIT), 3) GPFS (GZ), and 4) GPFS (FIT). At the start of each experiment, all data is present only on the persistent storage system (GPFS). In the data diffusion experiments, we use the MCU policy and cache data on local nodes. For the GPFS experiments we use the FA policy and perform no caching. GZ indicates that the image data is in compressed format while FIT indicates that the image data is uncompressed.

Figure 44 shows the performance difference between data diffusion and GPFS when data locality is small (1.38). We normalize the results here by showing the time per stacking operation (as described in previous subsection and Figure 43) per processor used; with perfect scalability, the time per stack should remain constant as we increase the number of processors.

We see in Figure 44 that data diffusion and GPFS perform quite similarly when locality is low, with data diffusion slightly faster; data diffusion has a growing advantage as the number of processors increases. This similarity in performance is not surprising because most of the data must still be read from GPFS to populate the local disk caches. Note that in with small number of processors, it is more efficient to access uncompressed data; however, as the number of processors increases, compressed data becomes preferable. A close inspection of the I/O throughput achieved reveals that GPFS becomes saturated at around 16 CPUs with 3.4Gb/s read rates. In the compressed format (which reduces the amount of data that needs to be transferred from GPFS by a factor of three), GPFS only becomes saturated at 128 CPUs. We also find that when working in the compressed format, it is faster (as

Figure 45. Performance of the stacking application for a workload data locality of 30 using data diffusion and GPFS while varying the CPUs from 2 to 128

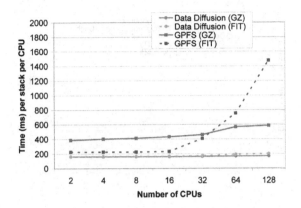

Figure 46. Cache hit performance of the data-aware scheduler for the stacking application using 128 CPUs for workloads ranging from 1 to 30 data locality using data diffusion

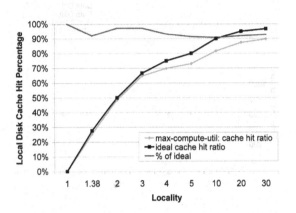

much 32% less per stack time) to first cache the compressed files, uncompress the files, and work on the files in uncompressed format, as opposed to working directly on the uncompressed files from GPFS.

While the previous results from Figure 44 shows an almost worst case scenario where the data locality is small (1.38), the next set of results (Figure 45) shows a best case scenario in which the locality is high (30). Here we see an almost ideal speedup (i.e., a flat line) with data diffusion in both compressed and uncompressed formats, while the GPFS results remain similar to those presented in Figure 44.

Data diffusion can make its largest impact on larger scale deployments, and hence we ran a series of experiments to capture the performance at a larger scale (128 processors) as we vary the data locality. We investigated the data-aware scheduler's ability to exploit the data locality found in the various workloads and its ability to direct tasks to computers on which needed data was cached. We found that the data-aware scheduler can get within 90% of the ideal cache hit ratios in all cases (see Figure 46). The ideal cache hit ratio is computed by $1 - 1/locality$; for example, with locality 3 (meaning that each file is

access 3 times, one cache miss, and 2 cache hits), the ideal cache hit ratio is $1 - 1/3 = 2/3$.

The following experiment (Figure 47) offers a detailed view of the performance (time per stack per processor) of the stacking application as we vary the locality. The last data point in each case represents ideal performance when running on a single node. Note that although the GPFS results show improvements as locality increases, the results are far from ideal. However, we see data diffusion gets close to the ideal as locality increases beyond 10.

Figure 48 shows aggregate I/O throughput and data movement for the experiments of Figure 47. The two dotted lines show I/O throughput when performing stacking directly against GPFS: we achieve 4Gb/s with a data locality of 30. The data diffusion I/O throughput is separated into three distinct parts: 1) local, 2) cache-to-cache, and 3) GPFS, as a stacking may read directly from local disk if data is cached on the executor node, from a remote cache if data is on other nodes, and from GPFS as some data may not have been cached at all.

GPFS throughput is highest with low locality and lowest with high locality; the intuition is that

Figure 47. Performance of the stacking application using 128 CPUs for workloads with data locality ranging from 1 to 30, using data diffusion and GPFS

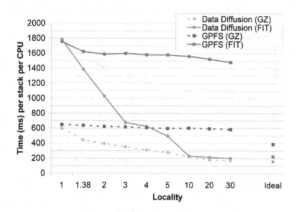

Figure 49. Data movement for the stacking application using 128 CPUs, for workloads with data locality ranging from 1 to 30, using data diffusion and GPFS

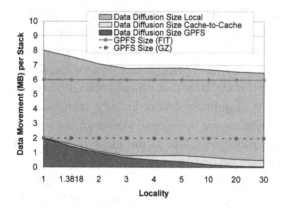

with low locality, the majority of the data must be read from GPFS, but with high locality, the data can be mostly read locally. Note that cache-to-cache throughput increases with locality, but never grows significantly; we attribute this result to the good performance of the data-aware scheduler, always gets within 90% of the ideal cache hit ratio (for the workloads presented in this subsection). Using data diffusion, we achieve an aggregated I/O throughput of 39Gb/s with high

Figure 48. I/O throughput of image stacking using 128 CPUs, for workloads with data locality ranging from 1 to 30, and using both data diffusion and GPFS

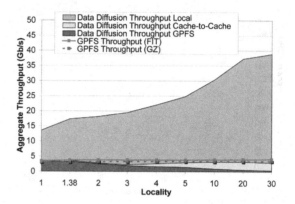

data locality, a significantly higher rate than with GPFS, which tops out at 4Gb/s. Finally, Figure 49 investigates the amount of data movement that occurs per stacking as we vary data locality.

In summary, data diffusion (using compressed data) transfers a total of 8MB (2MB from GPFS and 6MB from local disk) for a data locality of 1; if data diffusion is not used, we need 2MB if in compressed format, or 6MB in uncompressed format, but this data must come from GPFS. As data locality increases, data movement from GPFS does not change (given a large number of processors and the small probability of data being re-used without data-aware scheduling). However, with data diffusion, the amount of data movement decreases substantially from GPFS (from 2MB with a locality of 1 to 0.066MB with a locality of 30), while cache-to-cache increases from 0 to 0.421MB per stacking respectively. These results show the decreased load on shared infrastructure (i.e., GPFS), which ultimately allows data diffusion to scale better.

Abstract Model Validation

We perform a preliminary validation of our abstract model (presented in the subsection on

Figure 50. Model error for varying number of processors

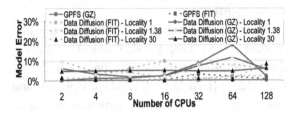

Figure 51. Model error for varying data-locality

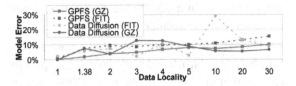

"Abstract Model") with results from a real large-scale astronomy application (Raicu et al., 2006). We compared the model expected time $T_N(D)$ to complete workload D (with varying data locality and access patterns) on the measured completion time for N equal from 2 to 128 processors incrementing in powers of 2. For 92 experiments (Raicu et al., 2008c), we found an average (and median) model error 5%, with a standard deviation of 5% and 29% worst case.

Figure 50 and Figure 51 shows the details of the model error under the various experiments, presented earlier in this section. These experiments were from the stacking service and had a working set of 558,500 files (1.1TB compressed and 3.35TB uncompressed). From this working set, various workloads were defined that had certain data locality characteristics, varying from the lowest locality of 1 (i.e., 1-1 mapping between objects and files) to the highest locality of 30 (i.e., each file contained 30 objects). Experiments marked with FIT represents ones performed on uncompressed image data, GZ represents experiments on compressed image data, GPFS represents experiments ran accessing data directly on the parallel file system, and data diffusion are experiments using the data-aware scheduler. Figure 50 shows the model error for experiments that varied the number of CPUs from 2 to 128 with locality of 1, 1.38, and 30. Note that each model error point represents a workload that spanned 111K, 154K, and 23K tasks for data locality 1, 1.38, and 30 respectively.

Figure 51 shows the model error with a fixed the number of processors (128), and varied the data locality from 1 to 30. The results show a larger model error with an average of 8% and a standard deviation of 5%. We attribute the model errors to contention in the parallel file system and network resources that are only captured simplistically in the current model, and due to not having dedicated access to the 316-CPU cluster.

Overall, the model seems to be a good fit for this particular astronomy application at modest scales of up to 128 processors. We did not investigate the model's accuracy under varying arrival rates, nor did we investigate the model under other applications. We plan to further the model analysis in future work, by implementing the model in a simple simulator to allow more dynamic scenarios, such as the ones found in subsections on "Monotonically Increasing Workload" and "Sine-Wave Workload".

RELATED WORK

There has been much work in the general space of data management in distributed systems over the last decade. This section is placed at the end, as some of the comparisons to other systems get into subtle details, which are better appreciated after being familiar with data diffusion.

The Stork (Kosar, 2006), scheduler seeks to improve performance and reliability when batch scheduling by explicitly scheduling data placement operations. While Stork can be used with other system components to co-schedule CPU and storage resources, there is no attempt to retain nodes and harness data locality in data access patterns between tasks. Please see Chapter 2 for more on Stork scheduler.

The GFarm team implemented a data-aware scheduler in Gfarm using an LSF scheduler plugin (Xiaohui et al., 2005; Tatebe et al., 2004, Wei et al., 2005, Tatebe, Morita, Matsuoka, Soda, & Sekiguchi, 2002). Their performance results are for a small system in comparison to our own results and offer relatively slow performance (6 nodes, 300 jobs, 900 MB input files, 0.1–0.2 jobs/sec, and 90MB/s to 180MB/s data rates); furthermore, the papers present no evidence that their system scales. In contrast, we have tested our proposed data diffusion with 200 processors, 2M jobs, input data ranging from 1B to 1GB per job, working sets of up to 1TB, workflows exceeding 1000 jobs/sec, and data rates exceeding 9GB/s.

The NoW (Culler et al.) project aimed to create massively parallel processors (MPPs) from a collection of networked workstations; NoW has its similarities with the Falkon task dispatching framework, but it differs in the level of implementation, Falkon being higher-level (i.e. cluster local resource manager) and NoW being lower-level (i.e. OS). The proceeding River (Arpaci-Dusseau, 2003) project aimed to address specific challenges in running data intensive applications via a data-flow system, specifically focusing on database operations (e.g. selects, sorts, joins). The Swift (Zhao et al., 2007; Zhao et al., 2008b) parallel programming system, which can use Falkon as an underlying execution system, is a general purpose parallel programming system that is data-flow based, and has all the constructs of modern programming languages (e.g. variables, functions, loops, conditional statements). One of the limitations of River is that one of its key enabling concepts, graduated declustering (GD), requires data to be fully replicated throughout the entire cluster. This indicates that their scheduling policies are simpler than those found in data diffusion, as all data can be found everywhere; this assumption also incurs extra costs for replication,

and has large wastage in large-scale systems. River is a subset of the combination of Swift, Falkon and data diffusion.

BigTable (Chang et al., 2006), Google File System (GFS) (Ghemawat, Gobioff, & Leung, 2003), MapReduce (Dean & Ghemawat, 2004), and Hadoop (Bialecki et al., 2005) couple data and computing resources to accelerate data-intensive applications. However, these systems all assume a dedicated set of resources, in which a system configuration dictates nodes with roles (i.e., clients, servers) at startup, and there is no support to increase or decrease the ratio between client and servers based on load; note that upon failures, nodes can be dynamically removed from these systems, but this is done for system maintenance, not to optimize performance or costs. This is a critical difference, as these systems are typically installed by a system administrator and operate on dedicated clusters. Our work (Falkon and data diffusion) works on batch-scheduled distributed resources (such as those found in clusters and Grids used by the scientific community) which are shared by many users. Although MapReduce/Hadoop systems can also be shared by many users, nodes are shared by all users and data can be stored or retrieved from any node in the cluster at any time. In batch scheduled systems, sharing is done through abstraction called jobs which are bound to some number of dedicated nodes at provisioning time. Users can only access nodes that are provisioned to them, and when nodes are released there are no assumptions on the preservation of node local state (i.e. local disk and ram). Data diffusion supports dynamic resource provisioning by allocating resources from batch-scheduled systems when demand is high, and releasing them when demand is low, which efficiently handles workloads which have much variance over time. The tight coupling of execution engine (MapReduce, Hadoop) and file system (GFS, HDFS) means that scientific applications must be modified, to use these underlying non-POSIX compliant filesystems to read and write files. Data diffusion coupled with the Swift parallel programming system (Zhao et al., 2007; Zhao et al, 2008b) can enable the use of data diffusion without any modifications to scientific applications, which typically rely on POSIX compliant file systems. Furthermore, through the use of Swift's check-pointing at a per task level, failed application runs (synonymous with a job for MapReduce/Hadoop) can be restarted from the point they previously failed; although tasks can be retried in MapReduce/Hadoop, a failed task can render the entire MapReduce job failed. It is also worth mentioning that data replication in data diffusion occurs implicitly due to demand (e.g. popularity of a data item), while in Hadoop it is an explicit parameter that must be tuned per application. We believe Swift and data diffusion is a more generic solution for scientific applications and is better suited for batch-scheduled clusters and grids.

Two systems that often compare themselves with MapReduce and GFS are Sphere (Grossman & Gu, 2008) and Sector (Gu, GrossmanSzalay, & Thakar, 2006). Sphere is designed to be used with the Sector Storage Cloud, and implements certain specialized, but commonly occurring, distributed computing operations. For example, the MapReduce programming model is a subset of the Sphere programming model, as the Map and Reduce functions could be any arbitrary functions in Sphere. Sector is the underlying storage cloud that provides persistent storage for the data required by Sphere and manages the data for Sphere operations. Sphere is analogous to Swift, and Sector is analogous with data diffusion, although they each differ considerably. For example, Swift is a general purpose parallel programming system, and the programming model of both MapReduce and Sphere are a subset of the Swift programming model. Data diffusion and Sector are quite similar in function, both providing the underlying data management for Falkon and Sphere, respectively. However, Falkon and data diffusion has been mostly tested within LANs, while Sector seems to be targeting

WANs. Data diffusion has been architected to run in non-dedicated environments, where the resource pool (both storage and compute) varies based on load, provisioning resources on-demand, and releasing them when they are idle. Sector seems to be running on dedicated resources, and only handles decreasing the resource pool due to failures. Another important difference between Swift running over Falkon and data diffusion, as opposed to Sphere running over Sector, is the capability to run "black box" applications on distributed resources without any need to modify legacy applications, and access to files are done over POSIX read and write operations. Sphere and Sector seem to take the approach of MapReduce, in which applications are modified to support the read and write operations of applications.

Our work is motivated by the potential to improve application performance and even enable the ease of implementation of certain applications that would otherwise be difficult to implement with adequate performance. This section covers an overview of a broad range of systems used to perform analysis on large datasets. The DIAL project that is part of the PPDG/ATLAS project focuses on the distributed interactive analysis of large datasets (Branco, 2004; Adams, Harrison, & Tan, 2006). Chervenak et al. (2003) developed the Earth System Grid-I prototype to analyze climate simulation data using data Grid technologies. The Mobius project developed a sub-project DataCutter for distributed processing of large datasets (Beynon et al., 2001). A database oriented view for data analysis is taken in the design of GridDB, a data-centric overlay for the scientific Grid (Liu & Franklin, 2004). Finally, Olson et al. discusses Grid service requirements for interactive analysis of large datasets (Olson & Perl, 2002).

With respect to provable performance results, several online competitive algorithms are known for a variety of problems in scheduling (see Pruhs, Sgall and Torng (2004) for a survey) and for some problems in caching (see Torng (1998) for a survey), but there are none, to the best of our knowledge, that combine the two. The closest problem in caching is the two weight paging problem (Irani, 2002); it allows for different page costs but assumes a single cache.

Finally, there has been some interest from the database community to do multi-query optimization. One such effort is the active semantic caching (Andrade, Kurc, Sussman, & Saltz, 2007), which performs the identification and transparent reuse of data and computation in the presence of multiple queries. They explore a similar space of applications for which Falkon and data diffusion is most suitable for, namely scientific applications; furthermore, they draw similar conclusions that we do, such as that data locality is critical to obtaining good performance. However, their work centers on databases, which inherently limits the types of operations and applicability of their proposed system. We argue that the Falkon system in conjunction with the Swift parallel programming system is a much more general, powerful, and accepted set of tools for the broader scientific community.

In summary, we have seen very little work that tries to combine data management and compute management to harness data locality down to the node level, and to do this in a dynamic environment that has the capability to expand and contract its resource pool. Data aware scheduling has typically been done at the site level (within Grids), or perhaps rack level (for MapReduce and Hadoop), but no work has addressed data-aware scheduling down to the node or processor core level. Exploiting data locality in access patterns is the key to enabling scalable storage systems to efficiently scale to petascale systems and beyond. Furthermore, most of other work lack the assumption that Grid systems are managed by batch schedulers, which can complicate the deployment of permanent data management infrastructure such as Google's GFS (or Hadoop's HDFS) and the GFarm file system, making them impractical to be operated in a non-dedicated environment at the user level. Another assumption of batch scheduled

systems is the ability to run "black box" applications, an assumption that is not true for systems such as MapReduce, Hadoop, or Sphere.

Much of our work is pushing the limits of the traditional scientific computing environments which heavily rely on parallel file systems for application runtimes, which are generally separated from the computer resources via a high speed network. Our work strives to make better use of the local resources found on most compute nodes (i.e. local memory and disk) and to minimize the reliance on shared infrastructure (i.e. parallel file systems) that can hamper performance and scalability of data-intensive applications at scale.

CONCLUSION

We have defined a new paradigm – MTC – which aims to bridge the gap between two computing paradigms, HTC and HPC. MTC applications are typically loosely coupled that are communication-intensive but not naturally expressed using standard message passing interface commonly found in high performance computing, drawing attention to the many computations that are heterogeneous but not "happily" parallel. We believe that today's existing HPC systems are a viable platform to host MTC applications. We also believe MTC is a broader definition than HTC, allowing for finer grained tasks, independent tasks as well as ones with dependencies, and allowing tightly coupled applications and loosely coupled applications to co-exist on the same system.

Furthermore, having native support for data intensive applications is central to MTC, as there is a growing gap between storage performance of parallel file systems and the amount of processing power. As the size of scientific data sets and the resources required for analysis increase, data locality becomes crucial to the efficient use of large scale distributed systems for scientific and data-intensive applications (Szalay et al., 2006). We believe it is feasible to allocate large-scale computational resources and caching storage resources that are relatively remote from the original data location, co-scheduled together to optimize the performance of entire data analysis workloads which are composed of many loosely coupled tasks.

When building systems to perform such analyses, we face difficult tradeoffs. Do we dedicate computing and storage resources to analysis tasks, enabling rapid data access but wasting resources when analysis is not being performed? Or do we move data to compute resources, incurring potentially expensive data transfer costs? We envision "data diffusion" as a process in which data is stochastically moving around in the system, and that different applications can reach a dynamic equilibrium this way. One can think of a thermodynamic analogy of an optimizing strategy, in terms of energy required to move data around ("potential wells") and a "temperature" representing random external perturbations ("job submissions") and system failures. This chapter proposes exactly such a stochastic optimizer. Our work is significant due to the support data intensive applications require with the growing gap between parallel file system performance and the increase in the number of processors per system. We have shown good support for MTC on a variety of resources from clusters, grids, and supercomputers through our work on Swift (Zhao et al., 2007; Zhao et al., 2008b; Swift Workflow System, 2008) and Falkon (Raicu et al., 2007; Raicu et al., 2008b). Furthermore, we have addressed data-intensive MTC by offloading much of the I/O away from parallel file systems and into the network, making full utilization of caches (both on disk and in memory) and the full network bandwidth of commodity networks (e.g. gigabit Ethernet) as well as proprietary and more exotic networks (Torus, Tree, and Infiniband) (Raicu et al., 2008c; Zhang et al., 2008).

We believe that there is more to HPC than tightly coupled MPI, and more to HTC than embarrassingly parallel long running jobs. Like HPC applications, and science itself, applications are becoming increasingly complex opening new doors for many opportunities to apply HPC in new ways if we broaden our perspective. We hope the definition of Many-Task Computing leads to a stronger appreciation of the fact that applications that are not tightly coupled via MPI are not necessarily embarrassingly parallel: some have just so many simple tasks that managing them is hard, some operate on or produce large amounts of data that need sophisticated data management in order to scale. There also exist applications that involve MPI ensembles, essentially many jobs where each job is composed of tightly coupled MPI tasks, and there are loosely coupled applications that have dependencies among tasks, but typically use files for inter-process communication. Efficient support for these sorts of applications on existing large scale systems, including future ones will involve substantial technical challenges and will have big impact on science.

ACKNOWLEDGMENT

This work was supported in part by the NASA Ames Research Center GSRP Grant Number NNA06CB89H and by the Mathematical, Information, and Computational Sciences Division subprogram of the Office of Advanced Scientific Computing Research, Office of Science, U.S. Dept. of Energy, under Contract DE-AC02-06CH11357. This research was also supported in part by the National Science Foundation through TeraGrid resources provided by UC/ANL. We thank the Computation Institute at University of Chicago for hosting part of the experiments. We also thank the numerous people that have contributed to ideas, papers, implementations that have made this chapter possible; in no particular order, Jim Gray, Julian Bunn, Catalin Dumitrescu, Mike Wilde, Zhao Zhang, Ben Clifford, and Mihael Hategan.

REFERENCES

Adams, D. L., Harrison, K., & Tan, C. L. (2006). *DIAL: Distributed interactive analysis of large datasets*. Conference for Computing in High Energy and Nuclear Physics (CHEP 06).

Allcock, W., Bresnahan, J., Kettimuthu, R., Link, M., Dumitrescu, C., Raicu, I., & Foster, I. (2005). *The Globus striped GridFTP framework and server*. ACM/IEEE SC05.

Andrade, H., Kurc, T., Sussman, A., Saltz, J. (2007). Active semantic caching to optimize multidimensional data analysis in parallel and distributed environments. *Parallel Computing Journal, 33*(7-8).

ANL/UC. (2007). *TeraGrid site details*. Retrieved from http://www.uc.teragrid.org/tg-docs/tg-tech-sum.html

Arpaci-Dusseau, R. (2003). Run-time adaptation in river. *ACM Transactions on Computer Systems, 21*(1), 36–86. doi:10.1145/592637.592639

ASC. (2008). *Alliances Center for Astrophysical Thermonuclear Flashes*. Retrieved from http://www.flash.uchicago.edu/website/home/

Banga, G., Druschel, P., & Mogul, J. C. (1999). *Resource containers: A new facility for resource management in server systems*. Symposium on Operating Systems Design and Implementation.

Berriman, G. B., et al. (2004). *Montage: A Grid enabled engine for delivering custom science-grade image mosaics on demand*. SPIE Conference on Astronomical Telescopes and Instrumentation.

Beynon, M., Kurc, T. M., Catalyurek, U. V., Chang, C., Sussman, A., & Saltz, J. H. (2001). Distributed processing of very large datasets with DataCutter. *Parallel Computing, 27*(11), 1457–1478. doi:10.1016/S0167-8191(01)00099-0

Bialecki, A., Cafarella, M., Cutting, D., & O'Malley, O. (2005). *Hadoop: A framework for running applications on large clusters built of commodity hardware*. Retrieved from http://lucene.apache.org/hadoop/

Branco, M. (2004). *DonQuijote - Data management for the ATLAS automatic production system*. Computing in High Energy and Nuclear Physics (CHEP04).

CAS. (2007). *SkyServer*. Retrieved from http://cas.sdss.org/dr6/en/tools/search/sql.asp

Catlett, C. (2006). TeraGrid: Analysis of organization, system architecture, and middleware enabling new types of applications. In Grandinetti, L. (Ed.), *High performance computing and Grids in action*. IOS Press.

CERN. (2008). *Large hadron collider*. Retrieved from http://lhc.web.cern.ch/lhc

Chang, F., Dean, J., Ghemawat, S., Hsieh, W. C., Wallach, D. A., & Burrows, M. … Gruber, R. E. (2006). *Bigtable: A distributed storage system for structured data*. Symposium on Operating System Design and Implementation (OSDI'06).

Chervenak, A., Deelman, E., Kesselman, C., Allcock, B., Foster, I., & Nefedova, V. (2003). High-performance remote access to climate simulation data: A challenge problem for data Grid technologies. *Parallel Computing. Special Issue: High Performance Computing with Geographical Data, 29*(10), 1335–1356.

Chervenak, A. L., Palavalli, N., Bharathi, S., Kesselman, C., & Schwartzkopf, R. (2004). *The replica location service*. International Symposium on High Performance Distributed Computing Conference (HPDC-13).

Culler, D., et al. (1997). *Parallel computing on the Berkeley now*. Symposium on Parallel Processing.

Dean, J., & Ghemawat, S. (2004). *MapReduce: Simplified data processing on large clusters.* USENIX OSDI'04.

Deelman, E., Singh, G., Su, M., Blythe, J., Gil, A., & Kesselman, C. (2005). Pegasus: A framework for mapping complex scientific workflows onto distributed systems. *Scientific Programming Journal, 13*(3), 219–237.

European Molecular Biology Laboratory. (2008). Retrieved from http://www.embl.org

Feller, M., Foster, I., & Martin, S. (2007). *GT4 GRAM: A functionality and performance study.* TeraGrid Conference.

Foster, I., & Kesselman, C. (Eds.). (1999). Chapter 2: Computational Grids. In I. Foster (Ed.), *The Grid: Blueprint for a future computing infrastructure.* Morgan Kaufmann Publishers.

Foster, I., Kesselman, C., & Tuecke, S. (2001). The anatomy of the Grid. *The International Journal of Supercomputer Applications, 15*(3), 200–222. doi:10.1177/109434200101500302

Fuhrmann, P. (2004). *dCache, the commodity cache.* Twelfth NASA Goddard and Twenty First IEEE Conference on Mass Storage Systems and Technologies.

Gara, A., Blumrich, M. A., Chen, D., Chiu, G. L.-T., Coteus, P., & Giampapa, M. E. (2005). Overview of the Blue Gene/L system architecture. *IBM Journal of Research and Development, 49*(2/3).

GenBank. (2008). Retrieved from http://www.psc.edu/general/software/packages/genbank

Ghemawat, S., Gobioff, H., & Leung, S.T. (2003). *The Google file system.* 19th ACM SOSP.

Gray, J. (2003). *Distributed computing economics.* Technical Report MSR-TR-2003-24, Microsoft Research, Microsoft Corporation.

Grossman, R. L., & Gu, Y. (2008). Data mining using high performance clouds: Experimental studies using Sector and Sphere. *Proceedings of the 14th ACM SIGKDD International Conference on Knowledge Discovery and Data Mining (KDD 2008).*

GSC-II. (2008). *Guide star catalog II.* Retrieved from http://www-gsss.stsci.edu/gsc/GSChome.htm

Gu, Y., Grossman, R. L., Szalay, A., & Thakar, A. (2006). Distributing the Sloan digital sky survey using udt and sector. In *Proceedings of e-Science 2006.*

Hanisch, R. J. (2001). Definition of the flexible image transport system (FITS). *Astronomy & Astrophysics, 376,* 359–380. doi:10.1051/0004-6361:20010923

Hasan, R., Anwar, Z., Yurcik, W., Brumbaugh, L., & Campbell, R. (2005). A survey of peer-to-peer storage techniques for distributed file systems. *International Conference on Information Technology: Coding and Computing* (ITCC'05), (p. 2).

Hey, T., & Trefethen, A. (2003). The data deluge: An e-sicence perspective. In Berman, F., Fox, G., & Hey, A. J. G. (Eds.), *Grid computing: Making the global infrastructure a reality.* Wiley.

IBM. (2008). *BlueGene/P* (BG/P). Retrieved in 2008 from http://www.rcscarch.ibm.com/bluegene/

Irani, S. (2002). Randomized weighted caching with two page weights. *Algorithmica, 32*(4), 624–640. doi:10.1007/s00453-001-0095-6

Isard, M., Budiu, M., Yu, Y., Birrell, A., & Fetterly, D. (2007). *Dryad: Distributed data-parallel programs from sequential building blocks.* European Conference on Computer Systems (EuroSys).

Kosar, T. (2006). *A new paradigm in data intensive computing: Stork and the data-aware scheduler.* IEEE CLADE.

Lancellotti, R., Colajanni, M., & Ciciani, B. (2002). *A scalable architecture for cooperative Web caching*. Workshop in Web Engineering, Networking 2002.

Liu, D. T., & Franklin, M. J. (2004). The design of GridDB: A data-centric overlay for the scientific grid. *VLDB04*, (pp. 600-611).

Livny, M., Basney, J., Raman, R., & Tannenbaum, T. (1997). Mechanisms for high throughput computing. *SPEEDUP Journal, 1*(1).

2MASS. (2008). *Two Micron all sky survey*. Retrieved from http://irsa.ipac.caltech.edu/Missions/2mass.html

Moretti, C., Bulosan, J., Thain, D., & Flynn, P. (2008). *All-Pairs: An abstraction for data-intensive cloud computing*. IPDPS'08.

Olson, D., & Perl, J. (2002). *Grid service requirements for interactive analysis*. PPDG CS11 Report.

Open Science Grid (OSG). (2008). Retrieved from http://www.opensciencegrid.org/

Ousterhout, J. (1998). Scripting: Higher level programming for the 21st century. *IEEE Computer Magazine*, March 1998.

Pike, R., Dorward, S., Griesemer, R., & Quinlan, S. (2005). Interpreting the data: Parallel analysis with Sawzall. *Scientific Programming Journal. Special Issue on Grids and Worldwide Computing Programming Models and Infrastructure, 13*(4), 227–298.

Podlipnig, S., & Böszörmenyi, L. (2003). A survey of Web cache replacement strategies. *ACM Computing Surveys, 35*(4), 374–398. doi:10.1145/954339.954341

POSS-II. (2008). *Palomar observatory sky survey*. Retrieved from http://taltos.pha.jhu.edu/~rrg/science/dposs/dposs.html

Pruhs, K., Sgall, J., & Torng, E. (2004). Online scheduling. In Leung, J. Y.-T., & Anderson, J. H. (Eds.), *Handbook of scheduling: Algorithms, models, and performance analysis*.

Raicu, I. (2007). *Harnessing Grid resources with data-centric task farms. Technical Report*. University of Chicago.

Raicu, I., Foster, I., Szalay, A., & Turcu, G. (2006). *AstroPortal: A science gateway for large-scale astronomy data analysis*. TeraGrid Conference.

Raicu, I., Foster, I., & Zhao, Y. (2008a). *Many task computing: Bridging the gap between high throughput computing and high performance computing*. IEEE Workshop on Many-Task Computing on Grids and Supercomputers (MTAGS08).

Raicu, I., Foster, I., Zhao, Y., Little, P., Moretti, C., Chaudhary, A., & Thain, D. (2009). *The quest for scalable support of data intensive applications in distributed systems*. To appear at ACM HPDC09.

Raicu, I., Zhang, Z., Wilde, M., Foster, I., Beckman, P., Iskra, K., & Clifford, B. (2008b). *Towards loosely-coupled programming on Petascale systems*. IEEE/ACM International Conference for High Performance Computing, Networking, Storage and Analysis (SuperComputing/SC08).

Raicu, I., Zhao, Y., Dumitrescu, C., Foster, I., & Wilde, M. (2007). *Falkon: A Fast and Lightweight tasK executiON framework*. IEEE/ACM International Conference for High Performance Computing, Networking, Storage, and Analysis (SC07).

Raicu, I., Zhao, Y., Foster, I., & Szalay, A. (2007). *A data diffusion approach to large-scale scientific exploration*. Microsoft eScience Workshop at RENCI.

Raicu, I., Zhao, Y., Foster, I., & Szalay, A. (2008c). *Accelerating large-scale data exploration through data diffusion*. ACM International Workshop on Data-Aware Distributed Computing.

Schmuck, F., & Haskin, R. (2002). *GPFS: A shared-disk file system for large computing clusters.* FAST'02.

SDSS. (2008). *Sloan digital sky survey.* Retrieved from http://www.sdss.org/

SiCortex. (2008). Retrieved from http://www.sicortex.com/.

Stoica, I., Morris, R., Karger, D., Kaashoek, M. F., & Balakrishnan, H. (2001). *Chord: A scalable peer-to-peer lookup service for internet application.* ACM SIGCOMM.

Swift. (2008). *Swift workflow system.* Retrieved from http://www.ci.uchicago.edu/swift

Szalay, A., Bunn, A., Gray, J., Foster, I., & Raicu, I. (2006). *The importance of data locality in distributed computing applications.* NSF Workflow Workshop.

Tatebe, O., Morita, Y., Matsuoka, S., Soda, N., & Sekiguchi, S. (2002). Grid datafarm architecture for petascale data intensive computing. *IEEE/ACM International Symposium on Cluster Computing and the Grid* (CCGrid 2002), (pp. 102-110).

Tatebe, O., Soda, N., Morita, Y., Matsuoka, S., & Sekiguchi, S. (2004). *Gfarm v2: A Grid file system that supports high-performance distributed and parallel data computing.* Computing in High Energy and Nuclear Physics (CHEP04).

Thain, D., Moretti, C., & Hemmes, J. (2008). Chirp: A practical global file system for cluster and grid computing. *Journal of Grid Computing, 7*(1).

Torng, E. (1998). A unified analysis of paging and caching. *Algorithmica, 20,* 175–200. doi:10.1007/PL00009192

Wei, X., Li, W. W., Tatebe, O., Xu, G., Hu, L., & Ju, J. (2005). *Integrating local job scheduler – LSF with Gfarm. Parallel and Distributed Processing and Applications, LNCS 3758/2005* (pp. 196–204). Berlin, Germany: Springer.

Xiaohui, W., Li, W. W., Tatebe, O., Gaochao, X., Liang, H., & Jiubin, J. (2005). Implementing data aware scheduling in Gfarm using LSF scheduler plugin mechanism. *International Conference on Grid Computing and Applications* (GCA'05), (pp. 3-10).

Zhang, Z., Espinosa, A., Iskra, K., Raicu, I., Foster, I., & Wilde, M. (2008). *Design and evaluation of a collective I/O model for loosely-coupled Petascale programming.* IEEE Workshop on Many-Task Computing on Grids and Supercomputers (MTAGS08).

Zhao, Y., Hategan, M., Clifford, B., Foster, I., von Laszewski, G., & Raicu, I. … Wilde, M. (2007). *Swift: Fast, reliable, loosely coupled parallel computation.* IEEE Workshop on Scientific Workflows.

Zhao, Y., Raicu, I., & Foster, I. (2008a). *Scientific workflow systems for 21st century e-science. New bottle or new wine?* IEEE Workshop on Scientific Workflows.

Zhao, Y., Raicu, I., Foster, I., Hategan, M., Nefedova, V., & Wilde, M. (2008b). Realizing fast, scalable and reliable scientific computations in grid environments. In Wong, J. (Ed.), *Grid computing research progress.* Nova Publisher.

Chapter 3
Micro–Services:
A Service–Oriented Paradigm for Scalable, Distributed Data Management

Arcot Rajasekar
University of North Carolina at Chapel Hill, USA

Mike Wan
University of California at San Diego, USA

Reagan Moore
University of North Carolina at Chapel Hill, USA

Wayne Schroeder
University of California at San Diego, USA

ABSTRACT

Service-oriented architectures (SOA) enable orchestration of loosely-coupled and interoperable functional software units to develop and execute complex but agile applications. Data management on a distributed data grid can be viewed as a set of operations that are performed across all stages in the life-cycle of a data object. The set of such operations depends on the type of objects, based on their physical and discipline-centric characteristics. In this chapter, the authors define server-side functions, called micro-services, which are orchestrated into conditional workflows for achieving large-scale data management specific to collections of data. Micro-services communicate with each other using parameter exchange, in memory data structures, a database-based persistent information store, and a network messaging system that uses a serialization protocol for communicating with remote micro-services. The orchestration of the workflow is done by a distributed rule engine that chains and executes the workflows and maintains transactional properties through recovery micro-services. They discuss the micro-service oriented architecture, compare the micro-service approach with traditional SOA, and describe the use of micro-services for implementing policy-based data management systems.

DOI: 10.4018/978-1-61520-971-2.ch003

INTRODUCTION

Traditional data management requires the application of administrative functions to enforce management policies such as backup, retention, and disposition, and to validate assessment criteria such as authenticity, integrity, and chain of custody. The administrative functions require the management of state information about each file including the location, owner, and access controls. Service Oriented Architectures provide mechanisms to tune environments to implement specific data management policies by chaining procedures together. We explore whether a policy-based data management environment can be created that provides the extensibility of SOA while managing state information normally associated with digital libraries. We demonstrate that data analysis environments can be tightly integrated with data management environments. Indeed, for petabyte-scale collections, it is not feasible to move the entire collection to a compute server. Data analysis procedures will need to be applied at the storage location to extract the data sets of interest. In practice, it is more effective to execute low-complexity operations (that have a small number of operations compared to the size of the data in bytes) at the remote storage location. A simple example is the extraction of a subset of a file. It is faster to extract the data subset at the storage location through partial I/O commands than it is to move the entire file to a remote compute engine. Data analysis can be significantly accelerated through the execution of services at remote storage locations.

These are the driving motivations behind the integration of data processing functions into the data management infrastructure, and the execution of the functions under the control of a service oriented orchestration. We have integrated the SOA paradigm with collection management functions within the integrated Rule Oriented Data System (iRODS), and applied the technology in support of data sharing environments, data processing pipelines, data publication systems, data preservation systems, and data federation environments for long-term sustainability.

Massive Data Collections

We address the data management challenges of large-scale data systems that manage Petabytes of data and store hundreds of millions of files in a distributed environment composed from heterogeneous storage resources ranging from file systems to archives to relational databases. We automate execution of administrative functions, enforce management policies, and validate assessment criteria in order to minimize the amount of labor needed to manage massive collections. A generic solution is needed that is capable of handling discipline-centric data and catalog services for data types from high-definition video to real-time sensor data streams to simulation output. The diversity of support requirements - from small to large file sizes, from blobs to highly structured files, from static files to dynamic and active data streams, from single user systems to large-scale, distributed community-sharing networks, from free, public sites to systems with high levels of authentication and authorizations – poses a challenge that needs an intelligent and integrated operating system, executing coordinated workflows on collections of millions of digital objects stored across wide-area networks. Service-oriented architectures provide a solution for tackling this problem and catering to the distributed processing needs of such large-scale data management systems. Examples of large-scale data sharing systems at the large enterprise level can be found in business organizations as well as in the scientific/ academic communities. The following provides a small list of such scientific data systems that are currently being assembled and that will exceed several Petabytes in size in production operation.

- Astronomical data: The National Virtual Observatory (US National Virtual

Observatory (n.d)) is assembling standard mechanisms for sharing catalog information and sky survey images. They have established interoperability mechanisms for querying catalogs and for accessing data within a storage system.

- Oceanographic data: The Ocean Observations Initiative (OOI) (Ocean Observatories Initiative (n.d)) is exploring the integration of cloud computing systems and cloud storage caches with institutional repositories. One goal is to manage extraction of previous observations from an archive, caching of the data on a cloud resource, and on –demand analysis of the data.
- Science of Learning Centers: The NSF Science of Learning Centers (Temporal Dynamics of Learning Center (n.d)) support six research areas in cognitive science. They have the challenge of both sharing data within a research area, and sharing data between research areas.
- Earth Systems Data: DataOne (DataOne: (n.d)) is an NSF datanet initiative that will provide universal access to data about life on earth and the environment.
- ARCS: The Australian Research Collaboration Service provides long-term eResearch support through federation of shared collections across research institutions in Australia.
- LSST: The Large Synoptic Survey Telescope is developing a data grid to manage transport of images from a telescope in Chile to the US, analysis of the images, and archiving of more than 150 petabytes of data.
- NCDC: The National Climatic Data Center is building a data grid to manage 150 petabytes of satellite images of the earth. The data grid will link computing resources with data archives.

- CERN LHC: The Large Hadron Collider experiment will generate 15 petabytes of data per year, and distribute the data around the world to data analysis platforms.

Data Management as a Distributed Processing System

Data grids organize distributed data into shareable collections. Both the sources of the data, the storage locations, and the users may be distributed across a wide-area-network. Production examples of data grids include regional data grids that span sites across a state, national data grids that build shared collections that span institutions on both the East and West Coasts, and international data grids. The data grid should enable execution of low complexity operations at each storage location when the transfer of the data files is too expensive, while ensuring that the remote processing can be conducted efficiently. Consider the following example. An astronomer wants to check all images of a particular region of the sky to gather details of a newly discovered super novae event. She wants to check images taken by multiple observatories, taken in multiple wavelengths (from infra-red to radio waves), taken in multiple resolutions, and over a long period of time (say over the past two years). Her aim is to find information from older images before the super novae event and recent images after the event. The images are scattered over several resources, under multiple administrative domains. Since data sub-setting and object-detection are common tools in an astronomers repertoire, we can assume that such services exists in every observatory and can be applied to the specific types of images stored there in. The astronomer can launch a workflow that is highly distributed and gather the set of images that are promising candidates for her search. The processing of this workflow over thousands of images can take several hours (depending upon the complexity of the processing being done) and should be done in parallel.

If the data and process management are performed *in situ,* at the data storage location, one can view this scenario using the model of a micro-service based SOA architecture. Data management and workflow management are intertwined because of the distributed nature as well as the need for authentication, authorization and tracking authoritative sources. For example, some of the image files might be in a tape archive and need to be staged before performing the computation. Whenever a promising image is analyzed, the authenticity and integrity of the image may need to be checked to make sure the results are based on uncorrupted data.

In this scenario, the astronomer launches a service-oriented workflow across the entire data grid. The results are gathered in a collection with notifications being sent to her periodically about the progress and/or whenever a significant discovery is made. The choreography of this distributed (and parallel) processing is dynamically interpreted and tailored to the properties of the underlying data resource capabilities Once the workflow is completed, the astronomer can change the workflow so that it becomes a monitoring tool that only operates on new image files that are being ingested into the system. She may launch another workflow, with more service components that may perform refined searches on the images selected by the first workflow. She may also re-launch the first workflow but change some of the image processing/search criteria to analyze the super novae event in a different context.

As can be realized, these types of data processing interact with data management at multiple layers. It would be helpful if a common data management and analysis framework based on a service-oriented architecture can be used. Our design and development of a micro-service based SOA is a step in that direction.

Service-Oriented Architectures

Service-Oriented Architectures (SOA) (Lawler & Howell-Barber, 2008; Papazoglu, 2007; Arsanjani, 2004) provide a set of unassociated, loosely-coupled services (or applications/functionalities) that can communicate with each other and/or client applications using well-defined interfaces and protocols. The services can be integrated or stitched together (orchestrated) to provide a larger functionality. The loose-coupling of services provides a flow of computation that can be dynamically defined at run-time rather than hard-coded during design or compile time.

The image analysis example can be viewed as an orchestration of a set of distributed services. A query is made on a collection to find images for the desired area in the sky. The storage locations are identified and processing is initiated at each storage location to extract a cut-out around the star of interest. The cut-out is re-projected to a common reference coordinate system. Multiple images are co-added to improve the signal-to-noise level, and finally images are composited across multiple wavelengths of light. As one can see, there are multiple services involved, at different geographic locations, under different administrative organizations. The loose-coupling allows a run-time choice of services and stitching of a workflow to meet the higher-level task. Many of these services might be legacy applications that are wrapped to expose a well-defined interface. Also SOAs allow new services to be added or older services withdrawn to track changes in data sources. Moreover, when a different mesh of services is needed a new workflow can be formed by rearranging the services.

An SOA can be seen as a collection of services, each with well-defined interface definitions, and a communication mechanism that allows the services to interact with each other through message passing. An SOA defines a service interface in terms of protocols and functionality instead of defining a set of APIs which is normally done in a modular, distributed client-server architecture. A client from any platform, running applications on any operating system written in any programming language, can access an SOA service to create a new application by sending appropriate messages using a standardized protocol.

Defining service orchestration requires state information, in sufficient detail, to describe not only the characteristics of the SOA services, but also the input data that are needed for execution as well as the format of the output results. The concept is similar to data type and values in traditional client-server programming but with a complication that the definitions are used at run-time rather than being hard coded at compile time. The lingua franca for this service description is currently XML. Since most of the SOA services communicate over the web (using http over SOAP as the favored communication protocol), the Web Service Description Language (WSDL) (WSDL Web Service Definition Language (n.d)) is typically used for the service definition and description. This XML based description is chosen as it enables machine interpretation and can be extended to describe any required communication structure. This enables services to be dynamically incorporated in a workflow, and invoked on demand. The description of the service per se provides a means for discovering services that are appropriate for a particular task. Ontologies for describing services are still in their infancy, and currently are better formulated for business applications. Service orchestration is done by special brokering middleware. Enterprise Service Bus (ESB) (Chappell, 2004; Keen et al.(n.d)), and BPEL4WS (Oasis Web Services Business Process Execution Language (WSBPEL) (n.d)) are accepted industry standard for incorporating legacy applications into the web services framework through a uniform messaging bus that provides a standardized orchestration language.

In "Micro-service Oriented Architecture" section, we will see how we have used the SOA model to perform orchestrated functions for data management. The main challenge is that web services are too heavy-weight for our fine-grained approach. Also, the persistent state management requirements for many of the data management services are hard to encode in the normal web services paradigm.

Data Grids

The "Grid" is the software infrastructure that links multiple computational resources such as people, computers, sensors and data (Rajasekar, Wan, & Moore, 2002). The "Data Grid" links distributed storage resources, from archival systems, to caches, to databases. The data within the Data Grid are mapped to a uniform logical name space to create global, persistent collections. Examples of data grids can be found in the physics community (PPDG (n.d); Hoscheck et al., 2000; GryPhyN, 2000; NEES, 2000), for climate prediction (Hammond, 1999), for ecological sciences (KNB, 1999) for astronomy (NVO, 2001), geography, and earthquake and plate tectonic systems (EarthScope, 2001), etc. Most of these data grids represent different proto-typical systems for building distributed data management infrastructure with unique policies for data management, sharing and distribution.

The utility of data grids can be described in terms of their ability to manage persistent data (Moore, 2002). It is possible to create and manage geographically distributed replicas of the digital entities that are registered into the collection. The naming convention for the digital entities can be global in scale, making it possible to organize into a shareable collection data objects that reside at multiple storage locations. In addition to use as data sharing environments, data grids can also be used to support publication of data and preservation of data. The Data Intensive Cyber Environments group at the University of North Carolina at Chapel Hill and the University of California, San Diego, has developed data grids that organize distributed data into shared collections.

The first generation of the data grid technology was called the Storage Resource Broker (SRB), which has been used very successfully to support multiple international collaborations. More than three petabytes of shared data are managed by SRB data grids that span North America, South America, Europe, the Far East, and Australia. The SRB data grid implemented the minimal set of remote operations needed to manipulate data, and the logical name spaces that were needed for consistent and persistent data management. An important lesson learned from the deployments is that while the SRB provides an essential set of data sharing functionality through its data virtualization paradigm, many customizations and extensions were needed to make it applicable to the policies of the underlying domains. The projects achieved the required capabilities through client-side applications built on top of the SRB deployments. For data intensive analyses, these client side applications should be executable at the remote storage location to take advantage of data locality. This minimizes data movement and is more efficient for operations that have low complexity (a small number of operations compared to the number of bytes in the file). In addition, each domain-specific data grid needs the ability to impose different data management policies. An outcome of this insight is the development of the second-generation data grid called the integrated Rule Oriented Data System (iRODS). The iRODS system, in addition to supporting virtual shared data collections, also provides a server-side rule engine that allows data providers and administrators to define, develop and enforce management policies, automate administrative tasks, and validate assessment criteria.

The evolution of data grid technology architecture has been driven by requirements for scalability, separation of policy from interactions with storage resources, and for minimizing the administrative complexity needed to maintain massive collections. During 2002 to 2008, the amount of data stored at the University of California, San Diego under SRB collection management grew from 28 terabytes to over a petabyte, and from 6 million files to more than 200 million files. These collections represent 25 projects that either support shared collections for access by project members, or publication of data for use by the broader science discipline, or preservation of data for use as reference collections. This exponential growth is expected to continue into the future. For instance, the Large Synoptic Survey Telescope will manage over 150 petabytes of data starting in 2014.

The Storage Resource Broker (SRB) (SRB:Storage Resource Broker (n.d); Moore & Rajasekar, 2001) is an exemplar data grid implemented as client-server middleware that uses collections to build a logical name space for identifying distributed data (Rajasekar et al., 2002; NVO, 2001). The SRB, in conjunction with the Metadata Catalog (MCAT, 2000), supports location transparency by accessing data sets and resources based on their attributes rather than their names or physical locations (Baru, Moore, Rajasekar, & Wan, 1998). The SRB provides access to data stored on archival resources such as HPSS, UniTree and ADSM, file systems such as the Unix File System, NT File System and Mac OSX File System and databases such as Oracle, DB2, and Sybase. The SRB provides a logical representation for describing storage systems, digital file objects, and collections and provides specific features for use in digital libraries, persistent archive systems and collection management systems. SRB also provides capabilities to store replicas of data, for authenticating users, controlling access to documents and collections, and auditing accesses. SRB also provides a facility for co-locating data together using containers. One can view containers as tar files but with more flexibility in accessing and updating files. The SRB can also store user-defined metadata at the collection and object level and provides search capabilities based on these metadata. SRB is a *federated server* system, with each SRB server managing/brokering a set of storage resources.

The federated SRB implementation provides unique advantages:

1. **Location transparency:** Users can connect to any SRB server to access data from any other SRB server, and discover data sets by either a logical path name or by collection attributes.

2. **Improved reliability and availability:** data may be replicated in different storage systems on separate hosts under control of different SRB servers to provide load balancing.

3. **Logistical and administrative support:** different storage systems may be used from different hosts under different security protocols, through implementation of a single sign-on environment and with Access Control Lists maintained for each digital entity;

4. **Fault tolerance:** data can be accessed using a global persistent identifier, with the system automatically redirecting access to a replica on a separate storage system when the first storage system is unavailable.

5. **Integrated data access:** SRB provides the same mechanisms for accessing data in distributed caches and archives, making it possible to integrate access to back-up copies into the data management environment

6. **Persistence:** data can be replicated onto new storage systems by a recursive directory movement command, without changing the name by which the data is discovered and accessed. This makes it possible to migrate collections onto new resources without affecting access.

The SRB has been implemented on multiple platforms including IBM AIX, Sun, SGI, Linux, Cray T3E and C90, Windows NT, 2000, Me, Mac OSX, etc. The SRB has been used in several efforts to develop infrastructure for GRID technologies, including the Biomedical Information Research Network (NIH), NSF/DOE Particle Physics Data Grid (Hoscheck et al.,2000), NSF NVO (NVO, 2001) and NEES (NEES, 2000). The SRB also has been used for handling large-scale data collections, including the 2-Micron All Sky Survey data (10 TB comprising 5 million files in a digital library), NPACI data collections, the Digital Embryo collection (a digital library of images) and LTER hyper-spectral datasets (a distributed data collection). More details on the SRB can be found at (SRB: Storage Resource Broker (n.d)).

The SRB has been in operation for more than a decade. The valuable experience gained from its use in production and subsequent requests for extensions to meet new user requirements compelled us to think of a more extensible programming model.

MICRO-SERVICE ORIENTED ARCHITECTURE

The need for customizability of data management operations as well as the need to perform special domain-specific server-side operations on the data implied that a service-oriented architecture paradigm is better suited for the next generation data management. We have taken this thesis to the next level in designing and implementing a data grid system called the integrated rule-oriented data system (iRODS). In this approach, we have applied concepts in service-oriented architecture (SOA) for performing data management services. Since the operations are mostly services of short duration, we have adapted and modified SOA to orchestrate "micro-services". We use a rule-execution paradigm to perform the orchestration. We discuss these two parts of our system first before describing in brief the iRODS system that is under production use by multiple communities for their data sharing and data management.

Micro-Services

A service in an SOA is a function that is well-defined, self-contained, and does not depend on the context or state of other services. In contrast to traditional programming architectures that provide a hierarchical organization of the software system through compiled sub-systems, the SOA defines a logical way of implementing end-user applications through interconnection of loosely couple services. This works well in normal SOAs such as web services where the orchestration and service-level communication and message transformation take a significant amount of time (measured in hundreds of milliseconds). But when the operations (as in data management) are of very short duration (10s of milliseconds) and their interaction requires sharing of a lot of metadata, the web-service architecture becomes a bottle-neck. What is needed is a light-weight version of the SOA that can easily deal with dynamic orchestration of short duration functions. In addition to message passing, we also needed inter-service interactions that take advantage of in-core data structures to meet performance goals.

Micro-services are small, well-defined procedures/functions that perform a specific task. These functions can be written as C functions or as Perl or Python scripts, or as system-executable binaries or java snippets (support for java-based micro-services is under development). Each micro-service has a well-defined description based on doxygen-type tagging. This allows for ease of publication and discovery by users. A micro-service has four different ways of interacting with other micro-services and client applications:

1. *Parameters:* Each micro-service can have a set of parameters. This is similar to parameter passing in normal programming, but with a difference. Each parameter has a name, a type and a value associated with it. For input parameters, the value is filled (and checked by the micro-service for type-compliance).

For output parameters, the value and type are filled in by the micro-service. Hence, there is no requirement for hard-coded typed parameters as in normal programming. A micro-service can take one parameter of a particular type as input, transform it into another type and pass it on for the next micro-service. Also, one can write micro-services that can take a variety of types as inputs for the same parameter.

2. *Whiteboard:* Apart from the parameters, a common memory area is utilized for passing information between micro-services. One can view this as a "session memory" that is available for micro-services throughout an orchestrated workflow. The whiteboard can be used by the micro-services as a means of transferring large amounts of structured or unstructured data among themselves. In the case of data management, we have identified a standard structure that holds information that is relevant to data processing. This includes meta information about a file or collection of files that are being operated on by the micro-services, as well as associated storage resources and other information useful during the session such as user identity, authentication, etc.

3. *Messaging System:* The orchestration system that we have implemented has a message bus as one of its components. The message bus enables micro-services to send and receive messages, provides support for asynchronous communication, parallel synchronization points, data flow streams, and exception handling between distributed micro-service that are executed on different servers.

4. *Persistent database:* The orchestration system also has access to a metadata catalog that is implemented on a relational database. The catalog holds information about data, collections, resources, and users as well as information about rules, micro-services and

reserved keywords (an internal ontology). This database is available for access by the micro-services using a simple query and modify mechanism. The persistent database can be used to share system state information (such as a file checksum that can be used by an appropriate micro-service for detecting bit corruption) as well as descriptive meta-data that can be used to support discovery. The persistent database can also be used to communicate among micro-services over long periods of time in a transactional manner such as information needed for a long-running workflow. The persistent database is an essential component when performing distributed and parallel processing for management of state information.

Facilities are provided to checkpoint the parameters and in-memory data structures so that a micro-service can be deferred for later invocation (we call this concept delayed execution). Another facility serializes (packs and unpacks) the parameters and the whiteboard for transmission over a network for use in remote processing. Hence, the orchestration might include migrating the whole session memory in the whiteboard to a remote host (possibly running a different operating system) and rebuilding it there and continuing processing of the micro-service at that host.

The above features provide a very rich communication interface for micro-services and actually go beyond what is normally associated with SOA systems. The main reason behind adopting this model is to take advantage of "local memory" interactions when micro-services communicate on the same host. When this happens the orchestrator does not perform any structure migration or translation, but just invokes the next micro-service providing the parameters and white board locations for use by that micro-service. This provides very efficient execution that takes advantage of the locality of the computation. When the micro-service being invoked is at a remote site, the local orchestrator

automatically performs the data migration and hands over the orchestration to the remote site for continuation of execution. The user (developer of the workflow of micro-services) need not be aware of this migration and execution and designs the workflow in a host-agnostic manner – hence a workflow (or parts thereof) can be invoked from and run at any site.

In the micro-service oriented architecture, we also have a concept of recovery micro-services. A micro-service can change the data collection (such as creating a new file or deleting an old file), the persistent state information, and the whiteboard session memory. When a micro-service fails, it may leave the system in an inconsistent state. In an SOA architecture, since the services operate in isolation, if a service fails, it will not effect the other components of the operation; indeed the orchestrator can run the service on possibly a different service provider and continue the workflow. In data management systems, however, it is essential to maintain consistent state across all operations. Because of the side effects that can be caused by a micro-service, it is important to provide a recovery mechanism. The recovery micro-services are similar to the workflow micro-services. They are coded to handle any type of errors that can cause a micro-service to fail. In the case that a subsequent micro-service fails within a workflow, recovery is also needed across successful completion of each prior micro-service to roll back an entire workflow chain. In this system, it is considered good practice to define a recovery micro-service for every micro-service that changes system state.

Rules-Based Orchestration

Orchestration is an important aspect of the SOA paradigm. Since services are invokable in a dynamic manner, and an end-user goal can be achieved by integrating a chain of services (such as a directed graph) orchestration of the workflow is a necessary part of the design and implementation. As noted earlier the BPEL-WS (Business

Process Execution Language-Web Services) provides a standard orchestration language for SOA and implementations such as Open ESB (OpenESB(n.d)), WebSphere (Websphere (n.d)) (among others) provide alternate means of interpreting the language and providing orchestration.

Since, we are dealing with a light-weight SOA, we decided that the orchestration provided by BPEL-WS is too expensive in terms of time and processing power. Most of our micro-services are of short execution span and the power of the system comes from dynamically chaining such services. So, we opted for a different type of orchestration provided by a distributed rule engine paradigm.

The language that we provide for orchestration is a simple rule language that is adapted from ECA (Event-Condition-Action) rules of active databases (Dayal, 1994). One can view each rule as defining a workflow. Each rule composes the action part from micro-services and can invoke other rules. We based our language on the following assumption:

1. A data management operation is a triggering event that can result in different sets of actions based on the context in which the event occurs. Hence there can be more than one rule defined for an event with its guard clause given by "C" of the ECA rule. The guard clause will use the invocation context (defined by the parameters of the rule, the white board and information from the persistent database) to either accept a rule definition for invocation or reject it and try another rule definition.

2. Departing from normal ECA semantics, by default only one orchestration rule per event can succeed. The rules are prioritized and applied in a specified order and the rule invocation completes when an ECA rule succeeds. (If needed, there is syntax sugar in the language which allows application of all rules)

3. Extending ECA semantics, an orchestration rule is transactional in nature: it returns the distributed system to the original state if the action sequence fails at any part. This is necessary to make sure that the data grid is not left in an unstable state. As noted earlier, to enable this transactional nature, every micro-service used in a rule is associated with *a recovery micro-service*. Most of the side-effects can be rolled back except for a few external effects that will be discussed later. With this, we have an extended ECAR type of rule (R standing for recovery). In relational databases, transactional properties are handled with commits and rollbacks, even extending them into triggers. But in the case of a data grid, because of the complexity of the operations involved and the diversity of the side effects, explicit recovery is needed.

4. Operationally the sub-events and actions can happen serially, in parallel, in a distributed execution environment and/or in a time-delayed mode.

5. The set of iRODS rules that are applied is normally fixed for each session within a user connection to the iRODS system. But flexibility is built into the system to allow different sets of rules to be used for different users and groups. Hence a data grid can apply one set of rules for the seismic community and another set for the astronomy community.

With the above principles in mind, we defined a rule system with rules of the form:

$$E\text{:-} C \mid A_1, ..., A_n \mid R_1, ..., R_n$$

where E is the name triggering event,

C is the guard condition for the rule to fire
A_i is a micro-service or a rule, and

Box 1.

```
a.   OnIngest:- userGroup == astro
        | findResource, storeFile, registerInIcat, replicateFile
        | nop, removeFile, rollback, unReplicate.
b.   OnIngest:- userGroup == seismic  &&  size > 1GB
        | findTapeResource, storeFile,  registerInIcat, seisEv1
        | nop, removeFile, rollback.
c.   OnIngest:- userGroup == seismic  &&  size <= 1GB
        | findTinyResource, storeFile,  registerInIcat, seisEv2
        | nop, removeFile, rollback.
```

R_i is a recovery micro-service corresponding to every micro-service A_i.

As an example, consider an ingestion event, where a new dataset is being uploaded into the data grid. There is a sequence of actions that need to be performed for the data to be stored in the grid. First, the user's permission for performing the action in the data collection needs to be checked, then the users permission to store the file in a particular physical location is checked, then depending upon the type and size of the file, a data movement protocol is selected (to do the move in parallel, in multiple hops by staging, etc.) and finally the dataset is stored into the system. Information about this new addition is entered into the metadata catalog (iCAT) such as the physical location, the logical name, ownership, size, type, etc. Moreover, if other events are triggered by this ingestion (such as extraction of metadata, replication of the data into other distributed resources, or performance of some transform or integrity check) these events can lead to more rules being fired and actions taken therewith. We show in Box 1 a simpler example rule that can be used for such an ingestion event where contextual information plays a role. In this case, the context is based on either the group to which the ingesting user belongs or the type of data being ingested. [Many of the details of the parameters are not shown for clarity purposes. In each of the rules, the first line defines the event and the guard condition, the second line shows the action sequence and the third line shows the recovery action sequence.]

Rule (a) is applied for users within user group "astro". When a file is put into the data grid, a storage resource is selected, the file is stored, the state information is registered into the iCAT catalog, and the file is replicated. Note that this can be a sequence of images from a telescope that is being ingested.

Rule (b) is applied for users within user group "seismic" for file sizes greater than 1 Gigabyte. When a file is put into the data grid, a tape storage system is selected, the file is stored, the state information is registered into the iCAT catalog, and an additional micro-service called "seisEv1" is executed. This might trigger a delayed or asynchronous action on the newly ingested file such as extraction of metadata, searching for some seismic markers, etc. The input may consist of a stream of packets from a sensor network.

Rule (c) is also applied for users within user group "seismic", but for files smaller than 1 Gigabyte. When a file is put into the data grid, a "small" storage system is selected, the file is stored, the state information is registered into the iCAT catalog, and an additional micro-service called "seisEv2" is executed.

The language of the ECAR rules is simple. But in order to accommodate the definition of

Figure 1. iRODS distributed data management architecture

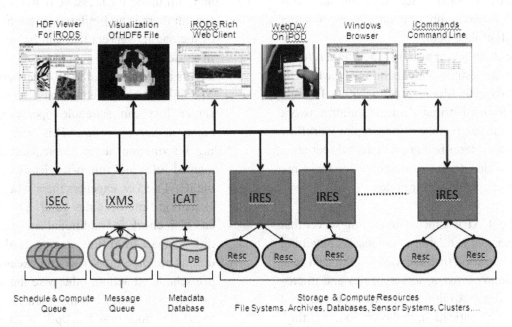

powerful workflows, aggregation constructs such as conditional branches, looping on conditions, looping over a set, etc are implemented as micro-services. Rules can also be recursive, providing a way to encode complex workflows. Also concepts such as remote execution, delayed execution and parallel execution are supported to provide rich distributed processing power. With the four kinds of interactions (including messaging) that are possible between micro-services, the ECAR rule system provides a language that can accommodate all SOA functionality.

iRODS: INTEGRATED RULE-ORIENTED DATA SYSTEMS

The integrated Rule-oriented Data Systems (iRODS) (Rajasekar, Wan, Moore, & Schroeder, 2006; iRODS: integrated Rule Oriented Data System (n.d); Moore & Rajasekar, 2007) is a data management system that is being developed by the Data Intensive Cyber Environments (DICE) group with collaborations from various groups and

projects all around the world. The iRODS system is a data grid that spans geographically remote sites and supports policy-oriented life cycle management for digital artifacts. It is based on experience in managing large collections of data using the Storage Resource Broker discussed earlier.

The iRODS system (see Figure 1) is a network of loosely connected nodes of resource servers, called iRES servers that provide access to data and computational resources. Each resource server can be viewed as a node providing data management capabilities through sets of micro-services. These servers manage the protocol interchange that is needed for interfacing with exotic devices and mapping storage-specific protocols onto a uniform API that is used by the micro-services.

The iRES servers are the workhorse of the grid and perform data movement between the servers and between the client and the servers. Also they are responsible for managing multiple types of data transfer modes (parallel, sequential, bundled, etc), multiple transfer protocols (XML, binary, TCP/IP, UDP, etc.), and operations related to manipulation of complex collections. iRES servers are also responsible for providing data management functionality and interfacing to other servers described below.

Each iRES server also incorporates a rule engine that orchestrates the execution of the ECAR-rules (Rajasekar, Moore, & Wan, 2009). The rule engines form a distributed rule execution network and provide functionalities for complex workflow execution as described in previous subsection.

In addition to the resource nodes there are three other special server nodes.

- The iCAT is a metadata catalog server that manages a relational database containing information (metadata) about the data sets, resources, users, servers, rules and micro-services. Additional information required for authentication, authorization, auditing, accounting, etc. are also stored in the metadata catalog server. There is conceptually only one catalog server per data grid. The system allows one to have multiple catalog servers provided one is in the master mode and the rest are in the slave mode. The slave mode catalog servers are used for 'read only' operations. All catalog modifications are automatically directed to the master catalog server. The use of master-slave servers is mainly intended for load balancing and reducing access time when going across wide-area networks. All servers are aware of the location of the iCAT catalog server. The iCAT server exposes a set of metadata micro-services that can be used to perform data management and processing functions.
- The iXMS is a messaging server that provides a "mailbox" service with store and forward capability for messages between the server nodes and the micro-services that execute in these resources. This server node is used by the messaging micro-services to send, broadcast and receive messages. The server operates in both push

and pull mode for message delivery. Even though there is no limitation to the number of messaging servers that can be operated in a grid, at least one should be operational and its address known to all other servers.

- The iSEC is a scheduler and execution server that can schedule operations on resource server nodes. This server, using information about pre-scheduled and queued rules and micro-services stored in the iCAT server, executes them when their execution time becomes valid. The server can also check for additional success conditions apart from time stamps. If all conditions are met, the server can execute the pre-scheduled action; otherwise the server puts the action back in the queue with retries being done based on options set by the user and/or the administrator.

Three kinds of micro-services are available in the iRODS system:

1. System micro-services are the core services that are used for providing operational functions in the resource servers, iRES. These functions include low-level data management, data movement (e.g. data replication, copy, move), integrity and type checking (e.g. checksums such as MD5), collection-level operations, and micro-services for providing metadata management, messaging services and delayed execution and scheduling services. They also include services for authentication, authorization, auditing and for emailing users. Micro-services for user management, resource management and other administrative functions are also provided by system micro-services. The iRES high level operations (as invoked by the client) translate into a set of rule invocations that in turn invokes these micro-services. The system micro-services also include micro-services for interacting with the iXMS

messaging system, iCAT metadata catlog and the iSEC scheduler and execution server for delayed processing.

2. Rule-Language Micro-services provide workflow control functions. The iRODS rule language does not provide powerful language constructs which one normally expects when building workflows, e.g. loops and conditional forks. Semantically (and in theory) these types of constructs can be coded using the simple rule-definition syntax by a rule developer. But it is more helpful and useful if syntactic constructs are pre-programmed to make it easier for rule programmers to code these complex workflows. The design decision in providing these functionalities was not to complicate the rule engine with complex rule interpretations, but to provide these functionalities as micro-services that are executed by the rule engine. The complexity of managing the workflow constructs such as loop variables and if-then-else conditionals is left to the design of the individual "rule-language' micro-services. We support constructs including while, for, forEachInList, ifThenElse, output strings and assignment. In addition, constructs for remote execution, parallel execution and delayed execution are also coded as micro-services that can be invoked. Each construct can execute a chain of micro services defined by input parameters.

3. Domain micro-services are domain-specific functions that are organized in modules of micro-services. A community can include as many modules as they need for their data system configuration to achieve a required functionality.

The iRODS data grid is distributed as open source software under a BSD license from the wiki: http://irods.diceresearch.org. Each user community can implement their preferred procedures (as micro-services), their preferred policies (as rules)

for their shared data collection. The micro-services and the rule engine implemented in every iRES server provide the service-oriented functionality. Application managers, data providers and system administrators can customize their data grid implementation with their own set of rules by modifying existing rules and/or adding new rules and micro-services. An image cut-out micro-service might be needed in an astronomy grid, but a neuroscience grid might have an anonymization micro-service. Both may use a common set of data management micro-services for replicating, checking and migrating their files in the data grid. A suite of more than 180 micro-services are provided for download with the iRODS software. More information on iRODS can be found in the wiki at (iRODS: integrated Rule Oriented Data System(n.d)).

POLICY ENFORCEMENT

The enforcement of data management policies is traditionally done when data are ingested into a collection. Policies may specify the required data format, the required descriptive metadata, and the required retention period. In order to automate the enforcement of administrative policies, additional locations need to be checked within the data management environment to ensure that all operations comply with the desired collection properties. Examples include checking disposition policies (to control deletion), checking distribution policies (for whether files can be moved to an alternate storage location), checking approval flags on access (for whether files can be shared), checking redaction policies (for the removal of confidential information), etc. In the iRODS data grid, approximately 62 locations were identified within the data management framework where data policies should be checked (Rajasekar, Moore, Wan, & Schroeder, 2009).

The policy management enforcement locations are listed in Table 1. They support the checking

Table 1. Policy enforcement locations within iRODS

Policy Enforcement Point	Description
acChkHostAccessControl	Set policy for host access control
acCreateCollByAdmin	Create a new collection with name "childColl" under the parent collection "parColl"
acCreateDefaultCollections	Create default collections (home,trash)
acCreateUser	Create a new user
acCreateUserZoneCollections	Create collections in Data Grid Zone
acDataDeletePolicy	Pre-process for file delete
acDeleteCollByAdmin	Delete the child collection "childColl" under the parent collection "parColl"
acDeleteDefaultCollections	Delete home collection
acDeleteUser	Delete user
acDeleteUserZoneCollections	Delete collections in a Data Grid Zone
acGetIcatResults	Apply the "action" to the list of files that meet the specified condition
acNoChkFilePathPerm	Set policy for checking permissions on registering a file
acPostProcForCollCreate	Post-process for collection create
acPostProcForCopy	Apply processing to file on copy
acPostProcForCreate	Post-process on file create
acPostProcForCreateResource	Post-process on resource creation
acPostProcForCreateToken	Post-process on token creation
acPostProcForCreateUser	Post-process for user create
acPostProcForDelete	Post-process for file delete
acPostProcForDeleteResource	Post-process on resource deletion
acPostProcForDeleteToken	Post-process on token deletion
acPostProcForDeleteUser	Post-process for user delete
acPostProcForFilePathReg	Post-process for registering a file path
acPostProcForModifyAccessControl	Post-process for modification of ACLs on data or collection
acPostProcForModifyAVUMetadata	Post-process for modification of AVU metadata for data/collection/resouce/user
acPostProcForModifyCollMeta	Post-process on modification of collection metadata
acPostProcForModifyDataObjMeta	Post-process on modification of data metadata
acPostProcForModifyResource	Post-process on resource modification
acPostProcForModifyResourceGroup	Post-process on resource group modification
acPostProcForModifyUser	Post-process for user modify
acPostProcForModifyUserGroup	Post-process for user group modify
acPostProcForObjRename	Post-process for object move
acPostProcForOpen	Post-process for file read or file read. $writeFlag $=$ 0 for open for read, $=$ 1 for open for write
acPostProcForPut	Apply processing to file on put
acPostProcForRmColl	Post-process for collection delete
acPreProcForCollCreate	Pre-process for collection create
acPreProcForCreateResource	Pre-process for resource creation
acPreProcForCreateToken	Pre-process on token creation

Continued on following page

Table 1. Continued

Policy Enforcement Point	Description
acPreProcForCreateUser	Pre-process for user create
acPreProcForDataObjOpen	Pre-process for file open or read, select which copy of a file to open. $writeFlag == 0 for open for read, == 1 for open for write
acPreProcForDeleteResource	Pre-process on resource deletion
acPreProcForDeleteToken	Pre-process on token deletion
acPreProcForDeleteUser	Pre-process for user delete
acPreProcForModifyAccessControl	Pre-process for modification of ACLs on data or collection
acPreProcForModifyAVUMetadata	Pre-process for modification of AVU metadata for data/collection/resource/user
acPreProcForModifyCollMeta	Pre-process on modification of collection metadata
acPreProcForModifyDataObjMeta	Pre-process on modification of data metadata
acPreProcForModifyResource	Pre-process on resource modification
acPreProcForModifyResourceGroup	Pre-process on resource group modification
acPreProcForModifyUser	Pre-process for user modify
acPreProcForModifyUserGroup	Pre-process for user Group modify
acPreProcForObjRename	Pre-process for moving a file
acPreProcForRmColl	Pre-process for collection delete
acPurgeFiles	Purge files satisfying condition on expiration time
acRenameLocalZone	Rename the Data Grid Zone from the name "oldZone" to the name "newZone"
acSetMultiReplPerResc	Specify number of copies per resource
acSetNumThreads	Set the default number of threads for data transfers
acSetPublicUserPolicy	Set policy for allowed operations by public
acSetRescSchemeForCreate	Pre-process on file create, define selection scheme for default resource
acSetVaultPathPolicy	Set policy for assigning physical path name
acTrashPolicy	Set policy for using trash can
acVacuum	Optimize the Postgresql database after waiting "arg1" specified time. See delayExec Micro-service

of policies before an operation is performed (typically to verify access permissions), and the checking of policies after an operation is performed (to generate derived data products or execute a deferred operation). By combining checks across multiple policy enforcement points, a community can tightly control all interactions with their collection, down to the individual operation level. From the perspective of a user of the system, it is possible to build interactive rules that will automate processing of files at any stage of the data life cycle, including the automated creation of derived data products on ingestion, the automated migration of files into different storage systems as retention periods expire, the automated redaction of data files to the portions that may be viewed by well-defined user groups, and the automated distribution of data between caches and archives.

DATA MANAGEMENT APPLICATIONS

Based on observations of the use of the SRB data grid, the iRODS data grid was designed to simplify the enforcement of management policies. The iRODS data grid expresses management policies as computer actionable rules. Procedures are expressed as sets of computer executable operations that have been aggregated into micro-services. The rules execute a chained set of micro-services and rules, under the control of a distributed rule engine. State information that is generated by application of the micro-services is stored in a metadata catalog. The state information can be queried to validate assessment criteria. Thus the iRODS environment makes it possible to define the purpose for building a shared collection, express the purpose as assessment criteria that will conserve properties about the collection, define management policies that conserve the desired collection properties, define procedures that enforce the management policies, and query resulting state information to verify the desired properties have been maintained.

The requirements for the iRODS architecture have also been driven by the rapid pace of technology evolution. The iRODS data grid is highly extensible, and capable of managing both external and internal technology evolution. This is accomplished by defining six logical name spaces to identify 1) users, 2) files, 3) storage resources, 4) management policies, 5) micro-services, and 6) persistent state information. Within iRODS, one sub-collection can be managed by an original set of rules and procedures, while a second sub-collection can be managed by a new set of rules and procedures that generate new state information. This means that the data grid itself can evolve over time, dynamically adding new policies and procedures as needed. The iRODS data grid manages external technology evolution through the use of highly modular drivers that issue the protocol required by storage devices

and databases. IRODS maps standard operations to the protocol required by each storage system.

Finally, data grids provide generic infrastructure that can be tuned to meet the needs of specific data management applications. We note that the set of operations for manipulation of data share a small but important core across application areas, but the management policies may be quite different and invoke discipline-specific procedures. By defining management policies as computer actionable rules, the wide difference in policies for access, retention, disposition, distribution, integrity, authenticity, chain of custody, and trustworthiness can be addressed. Starter kits that implement representative policies and procedures for data management applications are now being defined. The hope is that the integration of technologies such as DuraSpace Fedora digital library middleware with iRODS data grid administration will result in generic infrastructure applied at scale to support distributed scientific data collections.

An example of the application of the iRODS data management system is the integration of cloud storage with institutional repositories (Wan, Moore, & Rajasekar, 2009). Current cloud storage systems support a simple get and put interface. In order to support execution of management procedures, a disk cache is logically linked to the cloud storage resource. The file is cached on the disk system (which may be located at the user's site), the management procedures are applied, and the resulting data is then sent to the user. This makes it possible to created derived data products, sub-set data, and extract metadata efficiently from files stored in the cloud.

A second application is the development of preservation environments (Moore, Conrad, Marciano, Rajasekar, & Wan, 2009). The NARA Transcontinental Persistent Archive Prototype federates seven independent data grids to manage long-term sustainability across selected NARA digital holdings. Each data grid manages a separate independent collection. Federation policies are established that control interactions between the data grids. Users can be cross-registered between the data grids, and identified as "native" members of the data grid, or "external" users that have been a remote home data grid. Policies can be created that test the type of user, and then restrict operations accordingly. Thus an "external" user may be allowed to read selected collections, but would not be allowed to write into the collections.

Policies can also be established that periodically synchronize collections (data and metadata) between data grids, or that implement a deep archive. It is possible to implement rules that force all data ingestion to be initiated by a "native" member of the data grid, that turn off data deletion, and that turn on versioning. Thus any time a file is updated, it is stored as a version in a write once environment.

CURRENT STATUS AND CONCLUSION

In this chapter, we have shown how we have adopted techniques in Service Oriented Architectures for implementing scalable, distributed data management systems. We integrated the execution of data administration functions and the execution of data analysis functions through a loosely coupled execution paradigm, based on workflows composed from micro-services. By enabling micro-services to be chained for execution within each remote storage server, and by passing information through in-memory structures, we can implement high-performance policy-based data management systems.

The iRODS system has been in operation for nearly two years and has seen widespread usage in many user groups and projects around the world. Many of the projects listed in the "Introduction" section are using or planning to use iRODS for their data sharing and distributed data management including NARA TPAP, ARCS, TDLC, OOI and iPlant. In each of these cases, the policies for data management differ from other implementa-

tions because of internal requirements. The rule-oriented nature of iRODS, with its micro-service orchestration provides an easy way of implementing the diverse needs of the various projects. For example, the iRODS system used by the NARA TPAP project has more than 15 million files and will have more than 100 million files in the near future (the project is aggregating EOS files from NASA Distributed Active Archive Centers) as an archived collection in the testbed. Experiments performed with iRODS have shown that it is capable of handling large file ingestions (50 files/second from a single stream), and degrades gracefully as the collection size increases. This result is reported in (iRODS, n.d.). Several optimization techniques are also being tested and advocated for better performance of the iRODS system. These results give us confidence that a micro-service oriented architecture implementation of iRODS can scale to 100s of millions of files and give good performance for ingestion and access.

ACKNOWLEDGMENT

The research results in this chapter were funded by the NARA supplement to NSF SCI 0438741, "Cyberinfrastructure; From Vision to Reality" - Transcontinental Persistent Archive Prototype (TPAP) (2005-2008) and by the NSF Office of Cyberinfrastructure OCI-0848296 grant, "NARA Transcontinental Persistent Archive Prototype", (2008-2012). The iRODS technology development has been funded by NSF ITR 0427196, "Constraint-based Knowledge Systems for Grids, Digital Libraries, and Persistent Archives" (2004-2007) and NSF SDCI 0721400, "SDCI Data Improvement: Data Grids for Community Driven Applications" (2007-2010).

REFERENCES

Arsanjani, A. (2004). *Service-oriented modeling and architecture*. IBM developerWorks.

Baru, C., Moore, R., Rajasekar, A., & Wan, M. (1998). The SDSC storage resource broker. *Proceedings of CASCON'98 Conference*, Toronto, Canada.

Chappell, D. (2004). *Enterprise service bus*. O'Reilly Media, Inc. DataONE. (n.d). *Enabling data-intensive biological and environmental research through cyberinfrastructure*. Retrieved from http://mediabeast.ites.utk.edu/mediasite4/Viewer/?peid=38558e47202247bd847456b047cedfbd

Dayal, U. (1994). *Active database systems: Triggers and rules for advanced database processing*. Morgan Kaufmann Publishers Inc.

EarthScope. (2001). Retrieved from http://www.earthscope.org/

GriPhyN. (2000). *The Grid physics network*. Retrieved from http://www.griphyn.org/projdesc1.0.html.

Hammond, S. (1999). *Prototyping an Earth system Grid*. Workshop on Advanced Networking Infrastructure Needs in Atmospheric and Related Sciences, National Center for Atmospheric Research, Boulder CO.

Hoschek, W., Jaen-Martinez, J., Samar, A., Stockinger, H., & Stockinger, K. (2000). *Data management in an international data Grid project*. IEEE/ACM International Workshop on Grid Computing. *iRODS: Integrated Rule Oriented Data System*. (n.d). Retrieved from https://www.irods.org/index.php

Keen, M., Moore, B., Carvalho, A., Hamann, M., Imandi, P., Lotter, R., … Telerman, G. (n.d). *Getting started with Websphere enterprise service bus V6*. IBM Press

KNB. (1999). *The knowledge network for biocomplexity*. Retrieved from http://knb.ecoinformatics.org/

Lawler, J. P., & Howell-Barber, H. (2008). *Service-oriented architecture: SOA strategy, methodology, and technology*. Auerbach Publications.

MCAT. (2000). *Metadata catalog*. Retrieved from http://www.npaci.edu/dice/srb/mcat.html

Moore, R. (2002). Preservation of data, information, and knowledge. *Proceedings of the World Library Summit*, Singapore.

Moore, R., Conrad, M., Marciano, R., Rajasekar, A., & Wan, M. (2009). *Transcontinental preservation archive prototype*. Indo-US Workshop on International Trends in Digital Preservation. Pune, India.

Moore, R., & Rajasekar, A. (2001). *Data and metadata collections for scientific applications*. High Performance Computing and Networking (HPCN 2001). Amsterdam, NL.

Moore, R. W., & Rajasekar, A. (2007). *Rule-based distributed data management*. Grid 2007: IEEE/ACM International Conference on Grid Computing.

NEES. (2000). *Network for earthquake engineering simulation*. Retrieved from http://www.eng.nsf.gov/nees/

NVO. (2001). *National virtual observatory*. Retrieved from http://www.srl.caltech.edu/nvo/

OASIS. (n.d). *Web services business process execution language* (WSBPEL). Retrieved from http://www.oasis-open.org/committees/tc_home.php?wg_abbrev=wsbpel

Ocean Observatories Initiative. (n.d). Retrieved from http://www.oceanobservatories.org/spaces

OpenESB. (n.d). Retrieved from https://open-esb.dev.java.net/

Papazoglou, M. P. (2007). *Web services: Principles and technology*. Prentice Hall.

PPDG. (1999). *The particle physics data Grid*. Retrieved from http://www.cacr.caltech.edu/ppdg/

Rajasekar, A., Moore, R. W., & Wan, M. (2009). *Event processing in policy oriented data Grids*. AAAI Spring Symposium, Stanford, CA, USA.

Rajasekar, A., Moore, R. W., Wan, M., & Schroeder, W. (2009). *Universal view and open policy: Paradigms for collaboration in data grids*. International Symposium on Collaborative Technologies and Systems. Baltimore, MD, USA

Rajasekar, A., Wan, M., & Moore, R. (2002). *MySRB & SRB - Components of a data Grid*. The 11th International Symposium on High Performance Distributed Computing (HPDC-11). Edinburgh, Scotland.

Rajasekar, A., Wan, M., Moore, R. W., & Schroeder, W. (2006). *A prototype rule-based distributed data management system*. HPDC Workshop on Next Generation Distributed Data Management. Paris, France. SRB. (n.d). *Storage resource broker*. Retrieved from http://www.sdsc.edu/srb/index.php/Main_Page

Temporal Dynamics of Learning Center. (n.d). Retrieved from http://tdlc.ucsd.edu/portal/

US National Virtual Observatory. (n.d). Retrieved from http://www.us-vo.org/.

Wan, M., Moore, R. W., & Rajasekar, A. (2009). *Integration of cloud storage with data.* The Third International Conference on the Virtual Computing Initiative. Research Triangle Park, North Carolina, USA. *WebSphere.* (n.d). Retrieved from http://wwww.ibm.com/software/websphere/

WSDL. (n.d). *Web service definition language*. Retrieved from http://www.w3.org/TR/wsdl

Section 2
Distributed Storage

Chapter 4
Distributed Storage Systems for Data Intensive Computing

Sudharshan S. Vazhkudai
Oak Ridge National Laboratory, USA

Ali R. Butt
Virginia Polytechnic Institute and State University, USA

Xiaosong Ma
North Carolina State University, USA

ABSTRACT

In this chapter, the authors present an overview of the utility of distributed storage systems in supporting modern applications that are increasingly becoming data intensive. Their coverage of distributed storage systems is based on the requirements imposed by data intensive computing and not a mere summary of storage systems. To this end, they delve into several aspects of supporting data-intensive analysis, such as data staging, offloading, checkpointing, and end-user access to terabytes of data, and illustrate the use of novel techniques and methodologies for realizing distributed storage systems therein. The data deluge from scientific experiments, observations, and simulations is affecting all of the aforementioned day-to-day operations in data-intensive computing. Modern distributed storage systems employ techniques that can help improve application performance, alleviate I/O bandwidth bottleneck, mask failures, and improve data availability. They present key guiding principles involved in the construction of such storage systems, associated tradeoffs, design, and architecture, all with an eye toward addressing challenges of data-intensive scientific applications. They highlight the concepts involved using several case studies of state-of-the-art storage systems that are currently available in the data-intensive computing landscape.

DOI: 10.4018/978-1-61520-971-2.ch004

DATA INTENSIVE COMPUTING CHALLENGES

The advent of extreme-scale computing systems, e.g., Petaflop supercomputers, cyber-infrastructure, e.g., TeraGrid, and experimental facilities such as large-scale particle colliders, are pushing the envelope on dataset sizes. Supercomputing centers routinely generate huge amounts of data, resulting from high-throughput computing jobs. These are often result-datasets or checkpoint snapshots from long-running simulations. For example, the Jaguar petaflop machine (National Center for Computational Sciences [NCCS], 2009) at Oak Ridge National Laboratory, which is No.2 in the Top 500 supercomputers as of this writing, is generating terabytes of user data while supporting a wide-spectrum of science applications in Fusion, Astrophysics, Climate and Combustion. Another example is the TeraGrid, which hosts some of NSF's most powerful supercomputers such as Kraken (National Institute of Computational Sciences [NICS], 2008) at the University of Tennessee, Ranger (Sun constellation linux cluster, 2008) at Texas Advanced Supercomputing Center and Blue Waters at National Center for Supercomputing Applications, and are well on their way to produce large amounts of data. Accessing these national user facilities is a geographically distributed user-base with varied end-user connectivity, resource availability, and application requirements. At the same time, experimentation facilities such as the Large Hadron Collider (LHC) (Conseil Europ'een pour la Recherche Nucl'eaire [CERN], 2007) or the Spallation Neutron Source (SNS) (Spallation Neutron Source [SNS], 2008; Cobb et al., 2007] will generate petabytes of data. These large datasets are processed by a geographically dispersed user-base, often times, on high-end computing systems. Therefore, result output data from High-Performance Computing (HPC) simulations are not the only source that is driving dataset sizes. Input data sizes are growing many folds as well (SNS, 2008; CERN, 2007;

Sloan digital sky survey [SDSS], 2005; Laser Interferometer Gravitational-Wave Observatory [LIGO], 2008).

In addition to these high-end systems, commodity clusters are prevalent and the data they can process is growing manifold. Most universities and organizations host mid-sized clusters, comprising of hundreds of nodes. A distributed user base comes to these machines for a variety of data intensive analyses. In some cases, compute intensive operations are performed at supercomputing sites, while post-processing is conducted at local clusters or high-end workstations at end-user locations. Such a distributed user analysis workflow entails intensive I/O. Consequently, these systems will need to support: (i) the staging in of large input data from end-user locations, archives, experimental facilities and other compute centers; (ii) the staging out terabytes of output, intermediate and checkpoint snapshot data to end-user locations or other compute destinations (iii) the ability to checkpoint terabytes of data at periodic intervals for a long-running computation; (iv) the ability to support high-speed reads to support a running application.

In the discussion below, we will high light these key data intensive operations, the state-of-the-art and the challenges and gaps there in to set the stage for how distributed storage systems can help in optimizing them.

Data Staging and Offloading

Large input, output and checkpoint data is required to be staged in and out of these systems. With the exponential growth in application input and output data sizes, it is impractical to store all user data indefinitely at HPC centers. Traditionally, centers have operated under the premise that users come to them with all of their storage and computing needs. The legacy of this approach still weighs heavily when it comes to provisioning a center as significant portions of the operational budget is spent on large data stores and archives. End-user data services such as staging and offloading are key I/O operations that can help streamline center scratch space consumption and improve its serviceability.

Timely data offloading is necessary to both protect the job output data from center purge policies (MCCS.GOV File Systems, 2007; UC/ANL Teragrid Guide, 2004) as well as to deliver data on a deadline. This is largely left to the user and is a manual process, wherein users stage out result-data using point-to-point transfer tools such as GridFTP (Bester, Foster, Kesselman, Tedesco, & Tuecke, 1999), sftp, hsi(Gleicher(n.d)), and scp. The inherent problem with several point-to-point transfer tools, used to offload data from supercomputers, is that they are only optimized for transfers between two well-endowed sites. For example, the TeraGrid (Nsf teragrid, 2009) offers several optimizations (TCP buffer tuning, parallel flows, etc.) for GridFTP transfers between the various site pairs that makeup the TeraGrid, which are already well connected (10-40Gbps links). In contrast, data staging and offloading involve providing access to the data to the end-user. How does one move data efficiently from well-provisioned HPC centers to the outside world? More often, users come from smaller universities and organizations with varied connectivity to the HPC center. Thus, efficient and timely staging and offloading of data cannot be ignored as a "last-mile" issue.

The need for such a service is also fueled by the, often, distributed nature of computing services and users' job workflow, which implies that data needs to be shipped to where it is needed. For example, several HPC applications analyze intermediate results of a running job, through visualizations, to study the validity of initial parameters and change them if need be. This process requires the expeditious delivery of the result-data to the end-user visualization application for online feedback. A slightly offline version of this scenario is a pipelined execution, where the output from one computation at supercomputer site A is the input to the next stage in the pipeline, at site B.

Large-scale user facilities such as the Spallation Neutron Source (SNS) (SNS, 2008) and Earth System Grid (ESG) (Earth system grid [ESG], 2006) that employ distributed workflows are already facing these problems and require efficient data staging and offloading techniques.

The inverse of delivering data to the end-user is to stage the data from a source location to an HPC center. Modern applications usually encompass complex analyses, which can involve staging gigabytes to terabytes of input data, using point-to-point transfer tools (e.g., scp, hsi (Coyne & Watson, 1995)), from observations or experiments. Many times, the applications also involve comparing the above analyses data against large-scale simulation results to see how theoretical models fit real experimental results. Thus, input data can originate from multiple data sources ranging from end-user sites, remote archives (e.g., HPSS (Coyne & Watson, 1995)), Internet repositories (e.g., NCBI (National center for biotechnology information [NCBI] (n.d)), SDSS (SDSS, 2005)), collaborating sites and other clusters that run pieces of the job workflow.

Once submitted, the job waits in a *batch queue* at the HPC center until it is selected for running, while the input data "waits" on the scratch space. HPC centers are heavily crowded and it is not uncommon for a job to spend hours—or even days on end—in the queue. The time a job takes to complete, i.c., (*wall time + wait time*), is also the time the input data spends in the scratch space, in the best case when the data is staged at job submission. In the worst case, which is more common, the data waits longer as users conservatively (manually) stage it in much earlier than job submission, let alone job startup. Thus, there is the need for a timely staging in of job input data so it is able to minimize resource consumption and exposure of data to failure.

From the above usecases, we can state the problem as: *Offload by a specified deadline to avoid being purged*; Or, *Deliver by a specified deadline to ensure continuity in the job workflow.*

How can distributed storage systems help address this problem? Solutions in this regard can have a profound impact on data intensive computing.

Checkpointing

Checkpointing is an indispensable fault tolerance technique adopted by long-running data intensive applications. These applications periodically write large volumes of snapshot data to persistent storage in an attempt to capture their current state. In the event of a failure, applications recover by rolling-back their execution state to a previously saved checkpoint.

The checkpoint operation and the associated data have unique characteristics. First, applications have distinct phases where they compute and checkpoint; often, these phases occur at regular intervals. Second, checkpointing is a write I/O intensive operation. For instance, consider a 10,000 core job that runs for 12 hours and checkpoints every half hour on a system which has 2GB of memory. For this job, in the worst case, when all of the memory per core is saved as state information, 500TB of checkpoint data is produced during a run. Such data volumes can overwhelm any storage system. As we scale to petaflop systems, this problem is likely to get acute with the increase in the number of computing cores and the amount of data to be saved at each timestamp. Under these conditions, high-resolution checkpointing can easily overwhelm the I/O system. Third, checkpoint data is often written once and read only in case of failure. This suggests that checkpoint images are seldom accessed beyond the lifetime of an application run or even during the run. Finally, checkpointing, however critical it maybe for reliability, is pure overhead from an application standpoint, as time is spent away from useful computation.

Data intensive applications usually deal with checkpointing operations in the following ways. First is node-local storage. It is common practice for jobs running on the individual nodes in a dis-

tributed computing environment (e.g., cluster or a desktop grid) to checkpoint to their respective node-local storage. Local storage is dedicated and is not subject to the vagaries of network file system I/O traffic. Moreover, local I/O on even moderately endowed desktops offers around 50-100MB/s. However, local storage is bound to the volatility of the compute node itself. Thus, the locally stored data is lost when the node crashes. Moreover, there is no node-local storage on extreme-scale machines as the disk is one more component that can fail.

Second is shared file systems. Compute nodes can also checkpoint to a shared, central file server. However, shared file servers are crowded with I/O requests and often have limited space. Shared file servers, accessible to desktop grid-like distributed environments, offer merely tens of MB/s as I/O bandwidth. Clusters usually employ sophisticated SAN storage that are able to offer higher throughput. However, the hundreds of nodes in a cluster, on which processes of a parallel application run, can flood the central server with simultaneous check-pointing I/O operations. In extreme-scale systems–with thousands of processors–the I/O bandwidth bottleneck for check-pointing in writing to central file system (albeit a parallel file system), can be profound. Even though parallel file systems (e.g., Lustre, PVFS, GPFS) offer high I/O throughput (order of tens of GB/s in extreme-scale systems), historically, I/O bandwidth has not scaled with process or frequencies. Further, when the I/O channel is shared across multiple applications, the effective throughput achieved by any given application significantly deteriorates, even in such high-end storage systems. Can novel distributed storage solutions help improve the I/O bandwidth bottleneck seen in checkpointing I/O?

End-User Analysis

For most end-users of scientific data, certain stages of their data intensive tasks often require computing, data processing, or visualization at local computers and high-end personal desktop workstations. Local workstation is and will remain an indispensable part of end-to-end scientific workflow environments, for several reasons. First, it provides users with interfaces to view and navigate through data, such as images, timing and profiling data, databases, and documents. Second, users have more control over hardware and software on their personal computers compared to on shared high-end systems (such as parallel computer), which allows much greater flexibility and interactivity in their tasks. Third, personal computers provide convenience in connecting users' computing/visualization tasks with other tools used daily in their work and collaboration, such as editors, spreadsheet tools, web browsers, multimedia players, and visual conference tools. Finally, compared to high-end computing systems that are often built to last for years, desktop workstations at research institutions get updated more often and typically have higher compute power than individual nodes of a large, parallel system. This is especially advantageous for running sequential programs, and there exist many essential scientific computing tools that are not parallel. Applications that were once beyond the capability of a single workstation are now routinely executed on personal desktop computers. The combination of fast CPU and large memory provides scientists with a familiar–yet powerful–computing platform right in their office.

While personal computers are up to their important roles in scientific workflows with advantages in human-computer interface and processing power, storage nowadays usually becomes their limiting factor. Commodity desktop computers are often equipped with limited secondary storage capability and I/O rates. Shared storage in university departments and research labs are mostly provided for hosting ordinary documents such as email and web-pages, and usually comes with small quota, low bandwidth, and heavy workloads. This imbalance between compute power and storage resources leaves

scientists with the unattractive choice of remote data access when processing datasets larger than their workstations' available disk space. However, the wide-area network latencies kill performance. How can distributed storage systems help sustain end-user analysis on high-end local workstations?

DEMANDS AND REQUIREMENTS FOR DISTRIBUTED STORAGE SYSTEMS IN DATA INTENSIVE SCIENCE

Distributed storage is an increasingly important component of end-to-end scientific computing workflows, due to the fact that most of such workflows are inherently distributed themselves. In the majority of cases, data acquisition sites (observatory or experimental instruments), supercomputers or large clusters, and scientific data centers are located outside of scientists' local organization and must be accessed remotely. Data generated by the data collection, experiment, or simulation processes, on the other hand, will not be stored on the data generation site, whose storage facilities are often precious shared resources and only used for transient data storage to help the active tasks running on the facility. Scientific computing users usually have to move their data to their home institute for post-processing, or on archival system for affordable long-term storage, or, as in many cases, both. Bringing data back to their local clusters allows for more efficient data processing, analysis, and visualization, and eventually in most situations scientists view and interact with their data on their office workstations with display devices. Meanwhile, valuable datasets are often archived on tape systems to prepare for potential, while relatively infrequent, reuse.

While scientific data users have managed to get their job done with basic data movement and management tools, such as FTP, SCP, GridFTP, several factors and trends intensify the need for more powerful distributed storage support and possible paradigm shifts in data storage and movement models. First, there is a growing gap in system sizes between data generation sites (experimentation facilities and supercomputers) and consumption sites (local clusters and office workstations). Without efficient distributed storage infrastructures to aggregate capacities and bandwidths, the use of Peta-scale and Exa-scale computing enabled by cutting-edge supercomputers will be severely limited by scientists' data post-processing storage facilities. Second, the increasing complexity of scientific computing workflows makes it harder and harder to stay with labor-intensive and error-prone manual operations. In addition, such manual operations or scripts are often point-to-point processes that do not easily adapt to changes in computing/storage platforms, nor do they naturally support data sharing or collaboration. Finally, point-to-point data movement and single-site storage will not be able to effectively utilize recent technology advances, such as P2P storage and data distribution, volunteer computing, and cloud computing.

One may wonder whether existing distributed storage and data sharing solutions, mostly developed for commercial or entertainment applications, can be applied to scientific computing. Unfortunately, although the storage, processing, and sharing of scientific data can significantly benefit from many components of existing distributed storage solutions, these processes also possess many unique challenges and requirements that have not been addressed by systems in existence:

- **Level of System integration:** Distributed storage systems for data-intensive science need to locate a balance point between tightly coupled systems that resemble parallel file systems, and loosely coupled systems used in P2P data sharing. On one hand, the separation between storage resources and high-level storage structures is highly desirable to accommodate diverse and ever-changing hardware and software

components. On the other hand, data-intensive scientific applications, unlike entertainment data sharing and many other commercial applications, adopt a more tightly coupled computation model, and often demand highly optimized performance.

- **Namespace:** Distributed storage systems need to be able to identify datasets stored using well-defined names. These range from self-identifying uniform resource indices (URI) to simple filenames. These are then needed to be organized in some form of a flat or a hierarchical namespace. A flat namespace is easy to implement, but may not scale to large sizes, where as a hierarchical namespace is flexible but more involved.

- **Granularity:** Typically, media sharing is done at the granularity of entire files. However, the size of datasets involved in modern scientific computing, and the streaming approach adopted in typical workflows entail that the scientific data is handled in small fixed size portions or chunks. The size of chunks can vary from a few KBs to several hundreds of MBs. Consequently, a data transfer architecture designed for scientific computing must efficiently handle varying size chunks, as well as issues of maintaining, finding, and identifying chunks belonging to specific datasets.

- **Resource model:** While dedicated, high-end resources are universally equipped at supercomputing centers, the distributed end-to-end scientific computing workflow provides many practical use cases for contributed (or volunteer) storage, where storage resource owners donate spaces to be aggregated into large, shared storage capacities. This is partly due to that scientific data are often considered less sensitive compared to commercial data, making storage on individually owned and managed devices more acceptable. Also, often resource-constrained, scientists tend to be more open with distributed storage solutions that have low cost, in terms of both hard ware purchase and system management.

- **Performance vs. Space Utilization:** A key design consideration for distributed storage systems is to strike a balance between performance and space tradeoffs. What is the goal of the system? Is it to use a set of distributed resources to provide more storage than what is feasible? Or, is it to bring a set of distributed storage resources to provide faster data access performance? Or, can we achieve a balance between these goals?

- **Reliability:** A distributed storage system needs to be able to store data in a reliable fashion. Since such a storage system can be constructed out of dedicated or commodity components, the reliability semantics has to be robust enough to accommodate any underlying fabric. In any case, recent studies show that the rate of storage system failures is high (Schroeder & Gibson, 2007; Pinheiro, Weber, & Barroso; Shah & Elerath, 2005) and that ensuring reliability in large-scale installations is complex. Any distributed storage system will need to support a combination of standard replication and erasure coding schemes depending on space and performance tradeoffs.

- **Transparency:** Transparency is a highly desired feature for data-intensive science. In many situations, transparency translates into ease of use, portability, and reusability that can be of more value than performance. In particular, scientific application developers and users are typically domain scientists, who hesitate to invest time and effort in configuring distributed storage services, or to modify existing applications. In addition, transparent storage solutions allow existing applications and work-

flows to evolve with new hardware and software upgrades, which is worthwhile compared to the lost optimization opportunities when more lower-level design and implementation details are exposed to applications and users.

- **Deployability:** Any practical data storage scheme should provide abstractions that can be easily integrated with the application base, and should be minimally intrusive on existing software to ensure adoption by system administrators. Ease of deploying, maintaining, and using a particular service is key to its success as a practical system. For instance, a distributed storage service that uses the standard NFS (Callaghan, 200) protocol is more likely to see actual deployment compared to a service which requires users to link with customized libraries, or worse make changes to their codebase.

- **Quality of Service:** Quality of service metrics for a distributed storage system range from ensuring that the datasets are safely stored, to ensuring integrity and correctness on retrievals, to securing the datasets against malicious users and hosts and to guaranteeing performance. A loosely coupled, contributory storage poses fundamental challenges to ensuring quality of service.

- **Bulk Data Optimizations:** Distributed storage for data-intensive science has to be designed with handling massive data in mind, in terms of dataset size, access granularity, or both. In particular, with Peta-scale computing centers becoming the main stream, there is a growing disparity between a simulation site and other parts of a scientific computing workflow in storage capacity and bandwidth.

- **Leverage Commodity Components:** Finally, an ideal service will utilize commodity off-the-shelf components for realizing its goals. This is critical, as cost is a major obstacle in large-scale HPC installations, and relying on specialized hardware may make an approach economically non-viable. More and more, there is a wealth of commodity components at end-user sites, in the data path and at the HPC center. Distributed storage systems need to be able to utilize these in a concerted fashion.

The end-to-end data path in scientific computing throws open numerous opportunities to construct distributed storage systems that can be brought to bear on I/O intensive tasks. In the following case studies, we will highlight several state-of-the-art distributed storage solutions that are built from novel combinations of storage elements available in the end-to-end I/O stack and their design choices. We will highlight how the storage systems implement some of the aforementioned functionality. We will further analyze how these systems address the data intensive computing challenges.

CASE STUDIES IN DISTRIBUTED STORAGE SYSTEMS

Google File System

The Google File System (GFS) (Ghemawat, Gobioff, & Leung, 2003) is a distributed file system developed by and deployed at Google, specifically designed to its web data processing and search engine workloads. GFS' design principles are based on Google's data access workload as well as computing platform characteristics.

As Google periodically crawls the web space, downloads web contents, and indexes documents to provide continuous and scalable service to many concurrent search engine users, it creates many large files and most of its files are seldom overwritten. Instead, its write workload is heavily made up by appends, where it is common for multiple clients to concurrently append to a shared file. Meanwhile, overall Google has a read-intensive workload, with a large number of current queries processed simultaneously. Several major GFS design decisions reflect these workload requirements. First, files are partitioned into chunks, which are distributed to multiple server nodes, for better access throughput. Second, the chunk size is set at 64MB, much larger than block sizes used in traditional file systems, to reduce the metadata size and communication/management overhead. Third, GFS adopts a relaxed consistency model that targets Google's appending-oriented file mutations. In addition, the general optimization goal of GFS is made to prioritize high throughput over low latency.

Similarly, GFS is highly customized toward Google's computing environment, which consists of large collections of commodity nodes and heavily relies on hardware and software redundancy to protect against failures. GFS' architecture also reflects the same philosophy, where chunk replication plays a key role in both fault tolerance and scalable distributed data accesses. A GFS cluster is made of one master node, multiple chunk server nodes, and many client nodes. File chunks are aggressively replicated (with a configurable replication degree, which is set at 3 by default). The chunk replicas are intelligently placed to improve data availability and to enhance the network bandwidth utilization. The master node manages metadata such as the namespaces, the file-to-chunk mappings, and the chunk locations. Google has demonstrated that with its large chunk size, a single master node is capable of managing and serving large GFS clusters made of thousands of nodes. This has inspired the single-master design in other distributed storage systems such as FreeLoader.

GFS' data storage model and architecture works hand-in-hand with its application interfaces, such as the well-known MapReduce model (Dean & Ghemawat, 2004). With MapReduce, more complex operations can be partitioned into many Map operations that take input data and generate intermediate results, both in the form of key-value pairs, which are then sorted by the key and passed to nodes that perform the result merging with Reduce tasks. Many of Google's data processing tasks can be expressed as a pipeline that consists of one or more MapReduce stages. With GFS providing the underlying distributed chunk access services, MapReduce applications can easily perform distributed Map tasks and shuffle data to redistribute intermediate results to reduce tasks. Also the chunk replication mechanism naturally supports the task replication performed by MapReduce for better reliability. Hadoop (Hadoop (n.d)), a popular open-source MapReduce framework implemented by Apache, comes with an open-source counterpart of GFS, called HDFS (Hadoop Distributed File System).

Given Google's read-and append-intensive I/O workload and its loosely coupled distributed execution environments (as opposed to supercomputers or clusters running parallel batch jobs), GFS is suitable for certain classes of scientific data workloads, such as data centers that provides query, mining, and visualization services. On the other hand, though GFS is designed for massive data processing, it is not optimized for highly synchronized, write-intensive applications such as parallel simulations.

FreeLoader

FreeLoader (Vazhkudai et al., 2005; Vazhkudai et al., 2006) is a distributed volunteer storage frame work developed at North Carolina State University and Oak Ridge National Laboratory, which aggregates unused desktop storage space and I/O bandwidth into a shared cache/scratch space. It was motivated by the observation that even with the proliferation of high-end systems (high-performance parallel file systems, storage area clusters, data centers, and archival systems), there is a lack of end-to-end storage support for scientists to accommodate, prepare, or consume data in their local computing environments. In

particular, the "last mile" in many scientific computing workflows requires data processing and visualization at personal computers, where there are interactive devices as well as more user control on software/tools for viewing and navigating data. While personal computers today are equipped with unprecedented processing power, I/O and storage are more than ever the weakest link in these systems. Therefore, although recent technologies such as the multi-core architecture has brought personal computers the parallel processing capability to enable powerful desktop data processing, the lack of storage space and I/O rates easily prohibits their effective use for data intensive sciences. FreeLoader was proposed to enable these personal computers to pool not only their idle storage spaces, but also under-utilized I/O bandwidths, to create a shared space for scientists to work on their data.

With FreeLoader, workstation owners within a local area network contribute unused disk space, similar to how volunteer computing participants contribute idle CPU cycles using frameworks such as Condor (Litzkow, Livny, & Mutka, 1988) and Entropia (Calder, Chien, Wang, & Yang, 2005). To utilize today's high-speed local area networks for better data access rates, FreeLoader stripes datasets onto multiple participating nodes (called *benefactors*). The aggregate storage space managed by FreeLoader is intended as a cache or scratch space, rather than a general purpose file system or archival system that offers persistent, long-term storage of data. Instead, it targets creating a space much larger than a typical workstation's node-attached secondary storage, to enable scientists to process, analyze, and visualize their "hot" datasets generated by data-intensive experiments or applications. As interest fades on these datasets, they will be replaced by new datasets that are currently of interest to the local FreeLoader users. In addition, such a distributed storage framework would also facilitate data sharing, as colleagues in the same physical organization tend to collaborate and access common datasets (Iamnitchi, Ripeanu, &

Foster, 2004; Otoo, Rotem, & Romosan, 2004). Further, when scientists consume their data, they often work on certain datasets for a next ended period of time (typically days or weeks). Considering that data migration from archival systems is limited by transfer rates that are significantly lower than local I/O or LAN throughput (Lee, Ma, Winslett, & Yu, 2002; Lee, Ma, Ross, Thakur & Winslett, 2004, Vazhkudai, Schopf, & Foster, 2002), as a storage cache FreeLoader exploits data locality to reduce redundant and expensive remote I/O or data migration operations. In a subsequent project (Ma et al., 2006), the FreeLoader authors also exploited further in this direction by using a local FreeLoader space to only cache *prefixes* of remotely stored datasets to hide the latency in remote data access with a reduced space cost. Such prefix caching is coupled with *collective downloading* to achieve fast data transfer that makes remote data accesses feel like speedy local FreeLoader space operations.

The FreeLoader storage system contends that such a storage model is practical and cost-effective, based on several observations. First, collectively a large amount of disk space remains under-utilized on personal computers within academic or industry organizations. Studies have shown that on average, at least half of the disk space on desktop workstations is idle, and the fraction of idle space increases as the disks become larger (Adya et al., 2002; Douceur & Bolosky, 1999). In addition, most workstations are online for the vast majority of the time (Chien, Calder, Elbert, & Bhatia, 2003). Second, disks are cheap today and personal computers are more frequently updated and upgraded compared to higher-end systems. At the same time, off-the-shelf shared storage solutions such as disk arrays and SAN (Storage Area Network) systems are much more expensive and often out of reach for scientists. Therefore, frameworks like FreeLoader allows people to pool distributed storage devices in a reasonably sized organization into a considerably large, yet affordable, shared space. Third, scientific data use

patterns have unique characteristics that allow for simplified design, enabling FreeLoader as a user-level, light-weight system. For example, scientific datasets processed at scientists' local environments are often immutable and are safely archived (typically at the mass storage centers co-located with supercomputers or web data repositories (NCBI (n.d); SDSS, 2005; Szalay & Gray, 2001). Also, datasets are large and often accessed sequentially. These features provide FreeLoader with opportunities to focus more on providing a transparent shared storage space and efficiently reading and writing bulk data, rather than traditional distributed storage issues such as data consistency, concurrency control, and reliability.

The FreeLoader architecture comprises contributing benefactor nodes and a management layer that provides services such as data integrity, high performance, load balancing, and impact control. The FreeLoader prototype demonstrated that in addition to the space aggregation benefit, it was able to deliver higher data access rates than traditional storage facilities available in scientists' local computing environments. This is mainly attributed to novel data striping techniques that aggregate a workstation's network communication band width and local I/O bandwidth. The authors also show that security features such as data encryptions and integrity checks can be easily added as filters for interested clients.

Compared to more general-purpose distributed storage systems built on top of contributed devices, such as Farsite (Adya et al., 2002) and two projects to be discussed later in this chapter (Kosha (Butt, Johnson, Zheng, & Hu, 2004) and TSS(Thain et al., 2005), FreeLoader is a more specialized system specifically targeting local scientific data processing. Therefore, it does not support full file system functionality, and only implements a very small set of file I/O interfaces to enable Unix-style read/write operations in addition to whole-file operations. On the other hand, it is a very light-weight software cache/scratch space tailored for handling transient uses of bulk scientific data. In addition, the performance impact on the native workload of donor machines is small and can be effectively controlled. Finally, we demonstrate how legacy application scan use the FreeLoader API to store and retrieve datasets. Also, FreeLoader is designed with the capability to dynamically control its resource use to yield to native workloads on storage contributors. This is particularly important as FreeLoader is intended for data-intensive computing in desktop environments, where owners of contributed benefactors also conduct their day-to-day activities. The original FreeLoader development involved performance impact study (Vazhkudai et al., 2005) and a systematic performance impact control mechanism was proposed in a related study (Strickland, Freeh, Ma, & Vazhkudai, 2005).

stdchk

stdchk (developed at Oak Ridge National Laboratory and the University of British Columbia), a checkpoint storage system, extends the concept of FreeLoader aggregate storage checkpointing operations in HPC applications. Much like how stdin and stdout input/output systems are ubiquitously available to applications, stdchk argues that checkpointing is an I/O intensive operation, requiring a special 'datapath'. It ensures that this data path is being made available to HPC applications as a low-cost checkpoint-optimized storage system. stdchk is optimized for the workload: high-speed writes of incremental versions of the same file. stdchk can be used within a desktop grid, where the loosely connected workstation storage is aggregated; it can be used within a cluster where node-local storage can be aggregated; and finally, it can also be used to aggregate memory from processor cores in supercomputers. To this end, stdchk introduces several optimizations to render itself 'checkpoint-friendly' to HPC applications:

- *High write throughput.* stdchk exploits the I/O parallelism that exists inherently in

the aggregated storage to provide a suite of write-optimized protocols that enable checkpointing at throughputs higher than what is feasible in current settings.

- *Support for incremental versioning.* stdchk minimizes the size of the data stored using a novel solution to incremental checkpointing that exploits the commonality between successive checkpoint images. Since checkpoint images are chunked and striped in stdchk, it can afford to perform the following optimizations. First is a fixed-size compare-by-hash (FsCH) technique, which divides a file into equal-sized chunks, hashes them and uses the hashes to detect similar chunks. The main weakness of this approach is that it is not resilient to file insertions and deletions. An insertion of only one byte at the beginning of a file prevents this technique from detecting any similarity. Second is content-based compare-by-hash (CbCH).Instead of dividing the file into equal-sized blocks, CbCH detects block boundaries based on content. Compared to FsCH, this approach is more computationally intensive. stdchk experiments have shown that system-level checkpointing can benefit significantly from incremental checkpointing compared to application or library-level checkpointing. A desired side-effect of incremental checkpointing is that it enables applications to checkpoint at a finer granularity.

- *Tunable data availability and durability.* Since stdchk aggregates storage contributions from transient nodes, standard replication techniques are used to ensure data availability and durability. Further, applications can decide the level of data availability/durability they require. The level of redundancy needs to be balanced against overall space availability as that is a finite amount and dictates the serviceability of the storage system. stdchk choose replication against erasure coding for improving the availability of datasets as erasure coding is a compute intensive operations and applications are eager to return to perform useful computation rather than spending more time checkpointing. Consequently, stdchk conducts the replication in the background.

- *Tunable write semantics.* Additionally, stdchk gives applications the ability to choose between a write semantic that is pessimistic (the system call returns only after the desired level of replication is achieved and, consequently, slower) or optimistic (return immediately after data has been written safely once, while replication occurs in the background). This further gives applications control over the write throughput vs. data durability tradeoff.

- *Automatic pruning of checkpoint images.* stdchk offers efficient space management and automatic pruning of checkpoint images. These data management strategies lay the foundation for efficient handling of transient data.

- *Easy integration with applications.* stdchk provides a traditional file system API, using the FUSE (File system in user space) Linux kernel module, for easy integration with applications. Since the entire checkpoint storage is mounted as a file system, applications can save snapshot data seamlessly. This transparency comes with a small performance cost in the write operations. However, the flexibility offered outweighs this cost.

In extreme-scale systems, where there are no node-local disks, stdchk can be employed by aggregating memory contributions from the user's allocated processor cores. It is common in HPC job submission systems for jobs to oversubscribe for processors to prepare for failure. For example, depending on the failure rate of the machine, a particular job might ask for 12,000 cores instead of the10, 000 cores that it actually needs. The remaining cores are used for failing over processes. stdchk can create an aggregated memory device built out of such pools. This approach has the advantage that it uses the application's own oversubscribed processor allocation. However, in such an instantiation, the data striped on to stdchk is drained to a central, stable parallel file system to make room for additional checkpoint data. Thus, stdchk can be used to improve the I/O bandwidth in data intensive applications.

BAD-FS

BAD-FS (Bent, Thain, Arpaci-Dusseau, Arpaci-Dusseau, & Livny, 2004) (developed at the University of Wisconsin) is a distributed file system for handling large, I/O intensive batch workloads on remote computing clusters distributed across the wide area. BAD-FS facilitates staging of data on distributed storage resources, by allowing the users to explicitly specify the data needs of their applications and then factoring the user specifications in data scheduling decisions. BAD-FS differs from traditional distributed file systems in its approach to control data placement and movement. It exposes decisions regarding consistency, caching and replication, commonly hidden inside a file system, to the external scheduler. Using I/O scoping, BAD-FS reduces traffic over the wide area network. Through capacity-aware scheduling, BAD-FS avoids mismatch between jobs and resources, consequently preventing overflowing storage and thrashing caches. The interface exposed by BAD-FS can be leveraged to allow applications to dictate placement of data.

BAD-FS can serve as a enabler for supporting large-scale data staging and offloading. For instance, a user can specify the set of input dataset, locations where the dataset is stored or can be replicated, and locations for storing the output dataset. The scheduler can then stage the data from the specified locations before a job is started, and move the output data to the output locations after completion of the job. Additionally, although not done in BAD-FS, such interfaces can be extended with an automatic monitoring system to allow for dynamic placement of data even in the absence of explicit information from the application.

dCache

dCache (dCache.ORG, 2009) (developed at Deutsches Elektronen-Synchrotron, DESY and the Fermi National Accelerator Laboratory) is a distributed storage system to store large datasets that are disseminated from experiments such as the CERN's LHC. It uses a set of commodity nodes to store large datasets and provides access to clients using standard access protocols. Datasets are stored in their entirety on a node and may even be replicated to protect against failure of the commodity node. dCache can be tied to a tertiary storage system and can move data back and forth using LRU schemes. It offers a uniform namespace within a single file system tree for data stored across these storage elements.

Data is usually placed onto pools using pool attraction models that stores data on nodes based on properties such as reliability. Certain pools can be dedicated for interactions with tertiary storage systems. Pools can also communicate between each other to shuffle datasets in order to avoid hot spots in data accesses. Such an approach is used to load balance the dCache storage system.

dCache serves as an excellent use case for storing large data on commodity systems and can help immensely on end-user analysis. Many site have numerous commodity system that can be pooled together to offer a collective storage. However, the I/O throughput offered is limited to the bandwidth capabilities of the individual storage nodes and dCache does not exploit parallelism among the nodes to perform striping.

dCache offers support of grid transfers using the gsiftp(Bester et al., 1999) mechanism. It also supports the Storage Resource Manager (SRM)

(Shoshani, Sim, & Gu, 2003) protocol. These features make dCache a good candidate for data intensive science and extreme-scale data movement.

There are several similarities with FreeLoader and GFS in how these systems aggregate storage. Contrary to dCache, these systems chunk the datasets and stripe them for better throughput. Replication is performed at the chunk-level and not at the dataset-level as in dCache. While chunk-level operations offer more flexibility, they also entail more management overhead. dCache is fundamentally optimized for providing a large storage space for bulk datasets and accomplishes its goals elegantly.

IBP

The Internet Backplane Protocol (IBP) (Plank et al., 1999) (developed at the University of Tennessee) is a middleware for managing distributed storage depots. The basic premise behind IBP is to make use of storage in the network fabric. Just like how packets are buffered at intermediate routers on their way from source to destination in the internet, IBP byte arrays are forwarded from one storage depot to another. Therefore, IBP offers a staged approach to data movement, providing application managed communication buffers in the network with a temporal validity. This setup provides a logistical networking infrastructure supporting the scheduling and optimization of data movement for end-to-end applications.

IBP supports the following key functionality:

* Ability to allocate byte arrays for storing data. These allocations can be temporal or permanent; the client can specify whether the allocation is volatile or stable to mean whether the server can revoke the allocation or not.
* Moving data from senders to byte arrays
* Moving data from byte arrays to receivers

These features are supported using several procedure calls, based on TCP/IP, that help expose a storage to the IBP infrastructure. Distributed storage on a wide-area scale is usually managed and operated using standard file systems with a uniform namespace and strict semantics. Instead, IBP byte arrays can be viewed as files that reside in the network IBP offers applications ways to read and write byte arrays on other depots, thereby creating a shared network resource for storage. IBP byte arrays are appended only. IBP offers exNodes to aggregate storage resource across depots to present an aggregate file service over the network. This allows users to interact with IBP infrastructure at a higher-level and not using lower-level services such as storing data in the network. This is similar to users not worrying about disk blocks in file systems

The IBP approach can be used to stage data closer where it is needed or to allow applications to perform their own routing, steering the placement of data in a wide-area setting. Consider the staging in and out of job data between end-users and HPC centers. IBP storage depots can be used as a means to deliver data through the intermediate depots, while also using them as fail-over points in case of resource failure. Storage depots can be used to move data close to either the end-user or an HPC center. Thus IBP's ability to exploit locality to offer a staged delivery can be used as an alternative to point-to-point transfers in data intensive computing.

IBP's ability to stage data closer to end-user is also similar to FreeLoader's client-side caching. However, IBP is not designed as a locality-aware cache in that users need to explicitly assign temporal validity to files and retention is not based on frequent accesses.

IBP's infrastructure can also be used for distributed checkpointing. As mentioned earlier, checkpoint images are stored on disk within a LAN. However, IBP can be used to store checkpoints in a distributed environment, providing more fault tolerance for snapshot data. This allows end-user applications to control the locations and level of redundancy for checkpoint data. Unlike stdchk, IBP is not specifically geared for checkpointing, but it serves as a nice storage place for checkpoint images.

Tactical Storage Systems

One key challenge in aggregating distributed (and often heterogeneous) storage hardware for data-intensive scientific applications is to choose a balanced level for I/O interfaces. While systems with a tightly coupled storage hierarchy provides opportunities to deliver highly optimized performance and low overhead, such systems usually lack the portability or flexibility to work with diverse applications/hardware, or to adapt to changes.

TSS (Tactical Storage System) (Thain et al., 2005) was proposed with the goal of enabling flexible upper-level storage system establishment, by separating storage abstractions from physical storage resources. The TSS authors observed that shared file systems in cluster environments often become major limiting factors in the overall system productivity, in terms of policy constraints, capacity limits, and bandwidth bottlenecks. A TSS allows users to build a variety of storage structures (file systems, databases, or caches), with desired features (distributed and/or shared), on top of storage resources contributed by workstation or cluster owners. TSS was deployed at the University of Notre Dame to support two scientific applications with different storage needs and data use patterns.

Like FreeLoader, TSS operates at user level. Its authors argue that this allows great flexibility in creating different high-level storage abstractions, while the performance disadvantage caused by higher latency and overhead is reasonably small. Its basic storage unit is a file server that exports a Unix-like I/O interface, running on the machine participating in storage aggregation.

However, there are several major distinctions between TSS and FreeLoader. First, TSS is a more loosely coupled and general system compared with FreeLoader. It is intended for building diverse storage abstractions on top of a shared resource layer with well-known and consistent interfaces. FreeLoader, on the other hand, employs an architecture closer to the Google File System, with a single node acting as central manager and metadata server and participating machines serving chunks of data. Second, TSS aims at flexibility and versatility, therefore its design focus was placed on resource virtualization and abstraction construction (with mechanisms such as *adaptors*, which connect various abstractions to the resource layer). In contrast, FreeLoader is intended to be a shared cache facilitating fast data processing and consumption on desktop workstations, whose design is focused on performance and scalability issues and adopts throughput optimization techniques such as striping. Finally, the TSS prototype has the capability of building a shared file system with Unix-like interfaces, while FreeLoader supports a rather small set of Unix file I/O operations.

P2P Techniques in Distributed Storage

Peer-to-peer (p2p) overlay networks were initially popularized by file sharing systems such as Napster (Napster (n.d)), Gnutella (Frankel & Pepper, 2003), and Kazaa (Sharman Networks, 2004). The main attraction of these systems at the time was their ability to manage a large number of users without any centralized control, and user anonymity that guaranteed freedom from fears of censorship (Clarke, Sandberg, Wiley, & Hong, 1999). However, these first-generation systems used centralized servers, proprietary protocols, or controlled flooding for communication among peers in the overlay and for searching data. This led to drawbacks such as bandwidth wastage, lack of resiliency, and dependence on external entities such as *boot* servers. However, studies of p2p traffic on these networks showed their promise as storage substrates: the primary application of

these systems was file sharing (Leibowitz, Berman, Ben-Shauk, & Shavit, 2002).

The second generation p2p networks imposed some form of structure on the topology of the overlay and formalized the overlay building and maintenance protocols. Examples of such structured p2p overlays include CAN (Ratnasamy, Francis, Handley, Karp, & Schenker, 2001), Chord (Stoica, Morris, Karger, Kaashoek, & Balakrishnan, 2001), Pastry (Rowstron & Druschel, 2001a), and Tapestry (Zhao, Kubiatowicz, & Joseph, 2001), and have demonstrated the ability to serve as a robust, fault-tolerant, and scalable substrate for a variety of applications (Rowstron & Druschel, 2001b; Coyne & Watson. 1995; Castro, Druschel, Kermarrec, & Rowstron, 2002; Zhuang, Zhao, Joseph, Katz, & Kubiatowitz, 2001; Zhang & Hu, 2003; Hu, Das, & Pucha, 2003; Pucha, Das, & Hu, 2006; Butt, Johnson, Zheng, & Hu, 2006).

Structured p2p overlay networks essentially implement a *distributed hash table* (DHT) abstraction. Each node in a structured p2p network has a unique node identifier (nodeId) and each data item stored in the network has a unique key. The nodeIds and keys live in the same name space, and each key is mapped to a unique node in the network. Thus DHTs allow data to be inserted without a-priori knowledge of where it will be stored, and requests for data to be routed without requiring any knowledge of where the corresponding data items are stored, laying the foundation for developing p2p storage systems.

Scalable distributed (Howard et al., 1988) or server less (nderson et al., 1996; Thekkath, Mann, & Lee, 1997) file systems provide some p2p aspects. There are also several wide-area file system projects such as Ivy (Muthitacharoen, Morris, Gil, & Chen, 2002), Farsite (Adya et al., 2002), and Pangaea (Saito, Karamanolis, Karlsson, & Mahalingam, 2002), which also provide reliability.

The basic data sharing is extended by providing strong persistence and reliability in p2p distributed storage projects, such as Pond (Rhea et al., 2003) which is a prototype of Oceanstore (Kubiatowicz et al., 2000), CFS (Dabek, Kaashoek, Karger, Morris, & Stoica, 2001), and PAST (Rowstron & Drischel, 2001b).

PAST (Rowstron & Drischel, 2001b) is a large-scale, Internet-based, storage utility, which uses the p2p network provided by Pastry (Rowstron & Drischel, 2001a) as a communication substrate. PAST provides scalability, high availability, persistence and security. Any online machine can act as a PAST node by installing the PAST software, and joining the PAST overlay network. A collection of PAST nodes forms a distributed storage facility, and store a file as follows. First, a unique identifier for the file is created by performing a universal hashing function such as SHA-1 (F.180-1, 1995) on the filename. Next, this unique identifier is used as a key to route a message to a destination node in the underlying Pastry network. The destination node serves as the storage point for the file. Similarly, to locate a file, the unique identifier is created from the file name, and the node on which the file is stored is determined through Pastry routing. PAST utilizes the excellent distribution and network locality properties inherent in Pastry. It also automatically negotiates node failures and node additions. PAST employs replication for fault tolerance, and achieves load-balancing among the participating nodes. Our work builds on the functions provided by PAST to store and retrieve portions of file, and adapts the core PAST functions to handle large files.

CFS (Deabek et al., 2001) provides a scalable, wide-area storage infrastructure for content distribution. CFS exports a file system (hierarchical organization of files) interface to clients. It distributes a file over many servers by chopping every file into small (8KB) blocks there by solving the problem of load balancing for the storage and the retrieval of popular big files. This also results in higher download throughput for big files, which can be retrieved in parallel from many nodes. The component that stores data is referred to as a publisher. A publisher identifies a data block by a hash of its contents, and also makes this hash

value known for others. Similarly, a client uses the identifier hash of a block and Chord (Stoica et al., 2001) routing to locate and retrieve the block. To ensure authenticity of retrieved data, each block is signed using the publisher's well known public-key. Also, to maintain data integrity, blocks can only be updated by their publishers. Finally, CFS deals with fault tolerance by replicating each data block on k successors, where one successor is made in charge of regenerating new replicas when existing ones fail.

These systems share the goal of using peer nodes to establish a participant-based contributory storage facility that can be used to support decentralized data delivery and efficient staging in the context of data intensive computing.

Finally, systems such as Kosha (Butt et al., 2006) and TFS (Cipar, Corner, & Berger, 2007) provide transparent access to p2p-storage. In the following, we discuss Kosha in more detail.

Kosha

Kosha (Butt et al., 2006) (developed at Purdue University) provides a Network File system interface (Sandberg, Goldberg, Kleiman, Walsh, & Lyon, 1985; Callaghan, 2000) to a p2p storage system, and allows users and applications to transparently access their distributed files using a virtual directory hierarchy.

The design of Kosha is aimed at providing storage for individual participating sites consisting of multiple nodes, e.g., clusters connected to the grid. It provides an economical and fault-tolerant alternative to the dedicated storage within a single administrative domain. Kosha instances can provide sustainable intermediate storage locations where data can be stored in a wider end-user data-delivery scheme.

Kosha aims to utilize the cheap storage that is available in targeted environments to create a distributed file system, and to provide features of location transparency, mobility transparency, load balancing, and high availability through file replication and transparent fault handling. These features allow Kosha to run on components that can fail often. For deployability and transparency, Kosha retains the widely used NFS semantics, so that users and applications can access the distributed file system without any changes to their applications.

Kosha organizes the participating nodes into a structured p2p overlay, and uses NFS facilities to make the files available across peers. It ensures that the location of the files remains transparent to the user. Unique to the design of Kosha is that instead of distributing individual files over the distributed storage provided by the nodes in the p2p overlay, it distributes at the level of directories, i.e., files in the same directory are by default stored in the same node as that directory. Kosha also aim to leveraging unused storage space on resources available in academic or corporate settings, where a lot of disk space is wasted on desktop machines.

In Kosha, the participating nodes are assumed to run NFS servers, so that their contributed disk space can be accessed via NFS. It is assumed that only the system administrator has full access to these nodes, and the users cannot modify the system arbitrarily. Various file operations performed are handled as follows. First, Kosha determines the node on which a file is stored by performing a DHT mapping on the filename. Second, the NFS Remote Procedure Calls (RPC) are redirected to appropriate remote nodes. Third, the receiving node performs the operation and returns the results to Kosha, which then records the information needed for future accesses. Finally, Kosha returns control to the client. Hence, the client remains unaware of the underlying RPC forwarding, and the whole operation is transparent, except for a delay caused by the lookup for the appropriate storage node.

By blending the strengths of NFS with those of p2p overlays, Kosha aggregates unused disk space on many computers within an organization into a single, shared file system, while maintaining nor-

mal NFS semantics. In addition, Kosha provides location transparency, mobility transparency, load balancing, and high availability through replication and transparent fault handling. Thus, Kosha effectively implements a "Condor" (Litzkow, Livny, & Mutka, 1988) for unused disk storage.

Intermediate Storage Overlays

P2P systems discussed so far utilize loosely connected resources in local or wide area settings to create distributed storage systems. Next, we discuss how a number of such distributed storage sites can facilitate decentralized data delivery, staging and offloading of large data from the perspective of data intensive analysis within HPC centers.

An issue in using distributed resources is to ensure that data integrity and privacy is preserved during the decentralized transfer. Thus, users often only rely on trusted sites, which are determined using out-of-band agreements. An example of such collaboration can be TeraGrid (Nsfteragrid, 2009) sites. However, research on decentralized staging (Monti, Butt, & Vazhkudai, 2008a) and offloading (Monti, Butt, & Vazhkudai, 2008b) has shown that even when possible participating sites are known a-priori, their dynamic availability and policies entail a discovery process for determining the set of sites that can be used for a particular transfer. Given the scale, dynamic, and distributed nature of intermediate sites, p2p overlays can play a vital role in intermediate site discovery.

P2P Site Discovery

The process of selecting intermediate sites (N_i's) from among the participating sites, which are interested in the data transfer, proceeds as follows.

A p2p overlay, e.g., Pastry (Rowstron & Druschel, 2001a), is used to arrange the N_i's. The overlay provides reliable communication with other participants in the network, even when sites leave or join the system. The participating sites use the overlay to advertise their availability to other nodes in the overlay using random broadcast (Monti et al., 2008b). Nodes that receive these messages build local information about available nodes for offload. A given node can use its own policies and information about a remote node's capacity to make a decision regarding whether to use the remote node for the offload. For instance, to discover intermediate sites, a user site (N_s) sends out a number of discovery messages on the p2p network with random destination addresses. By virtue of the DHT abstraction provided by p2p routing, the messages are received at some N_i's. On receiving such a discovery message, an N_i replies with its IP address. Thus, N_s discovers the N_i. In case the sharing policies of the user site prohibit it from interacting with N_s, the site can simply ignore the discovery messages from N_s. Finally, to accommodate dynamic preferences of N_i's, N_s discards information about discovered N_i's after a specified period of time and starts afresh discovery process.

Data-Transfer Paths

A decentralized data transfer scheme for HPC centers that ensures timely data delivery and offloading is achieved using a combination of strategies both at the center as well as the end-user to orchestrate the transfers. To this end, the discovered intermediate sites (D_i's) provide multiple data flow paths between the center and the end-user, which lead to better orthogonal bandwidth utilization, faster retrieval speeds, as well as fault-tolerance in the face of failure.

The staging/offloading process works as follows. Let us consider data offloading. Once the job execution completes, the data-offloading process is initiated. First, the center chooses a number of nodes from the set of D_i's ordered by available bandwidth. The exact number of nodes used for this purpose, i.e., the fan-out, is chosen to achieve maximum (pre-specified) out-bound center bandwidth utilization, or to meet previously agreed-upon offload deadlines. These chosen D_i's serve

as the Level-1 intermediate nodes. Note that the selected fan-out is not static, and can vary depending on the transfer speeds achieved. Second, the result-data is split into chunks and parallel transfer of the chunks to Level-1 nodes is initiated. Since the Level-1 nodes support better transfer speeds than the user site, the offload time is expected to be much smaller than a direct transfer to the user site. Third, Level-1 intermediate nodes may also further transfer data to the Level-2 intermediate nodes (once again chosen from D_i's), and soon. Consequently, data flows towards the user site, though it is not pushed to the user site. Finally, the user site can asynchronously retrieve the data from the Level-N nodes. Decoupling the user site from the data push path allows the center to offload the data at peak (pre-specified) out-bound bandwidth without worrying about the availability (and connection speed) of the user site, while enabling the user site to pull (retrieve) data from D_i's as necessary.

Similarly, the process of data staging involves the following steps. Once the data staging is initiated, the user site chooses a number of nodes from the set of D_i's (fan-out) ordered by available bandwidth. The cardinality of the fan-out is chosen to stage-in all the necessary data before the predicted job start time. These chosen D_i's serve as the Level-S_1 intermediate nodes. Once again, the selected fan-out is not static, and can vary depending on the actual transfer speeds and the impending deadline. The staging service monitors the changing bandwidths periodically (using NWS(Wolski, Spring, & Hayes, 1999)) to determine if a chosen fan-out needs to be increased. Next, the input data is split into chunks and parallel transfer of the chunks to Level-S_1 nodes is initiated. The transfer may also involve further levels of intermediate nodes (up to Level-S_N). Alternatively, depending on the availability of intermediate nodes, the user site can also stage the data to Level-S_N nodes much earlier than the deadline.

As the job startup deadline approaches, the close proximity of the Level-S_N nodes to the center allows them to quickly move the input data to the center's scratch space. Also, this design allows the Level-S_N nodes to stage the data at peak (pre-specified) bandwidth that the most appropriate time without worrying about the availability (and connection speed) of the submission site.

The use of intermediate nodes in the decentralized data transfer systems provide multiple data-flow paths between the center and the user site, leading to several alternative options for data delivery. For instance, data may be replicated across different D_i's during the transfer from one level to the other. This will allow for pulling data from a number of locations when needed, thus providing fault tolerance against node failure, as well as better utilization of the available orthogonal bandwidth. Finally, the schedule can also be used to simultaneously deliver data to multiple interested sites in the network.

The use of intermediate nodes is similar to that of IBP. IBP offers a data distribution infrastructure with a set of strategically placed resources (storage depots) to move data, and implement what is referred to as logistical networking. The intermediate storage overlay also exploits the presence of pre-installed storage nodes for data delivery as and when they are available. However, it differs significantly in its attempt to combine both a staged as well as a decentralized data delivery. The induction of user-specified nodes also allows the system to optimize the data delivery on a per user basis, which is not possible with IBP. Further, it strives to meet a deadline in delivering as well as in timely offloading from the HPC center.

SUMMARY

In this chapter, we presented some key challenges faced in data intensive analysis, the gaps in extant solutions and how novel distributed storage systems can help address them. We discussed several I/O operations in large-scale data analysis such as staging, offloading, checkpointing and end-user analysis and the problems therein, in terms of data availability, storage failure and I/O bandwidth bottleneck. We highlighted several desired features in distributed storage systems and how large-scale scientific data analysis poses unique requirements. We then presented a set of case studies, analyzing state-of-the-art distributed storage systems such as GFS, FreeLoader, stdchk, BADFS, dCache, IBP, TSS, Kosha and several other peer-to-peer systems, illustrate their design goals and analyze how they can be used in data intensive computing.

REFERENCES

Adya, A., Bolosky, W. J., Castro, M., Cermak, G., Chaiken, R., & Douceur, J. R. ... Wattenhofer, R.P. (2002). FARSITE: Federated, available, and reliable storage for an incompletely trusted environment. In *Proceedings 5th USENIX OSDI*, (pp. 1–14).

Anderson, T. E., Dahlin, M. D., Neefe, J. M., Patterson, D. A., Roselli, D. S., & Wang, R. Y. (1996). Serverless network file systems. *ACM Transactions on Computer Systems*, *14*(1), 41–79. doi:10.1145/225535.225537

Bent, J., Thain, D., Arpaci-Dusseau, A. C., Arpaci-Dusseau, R. H., & Livny, M. (2004). Explicit control in a batch-aware distributed file system. In *Proceedings of the 1st USENIX NSDI*, (pp. 365–378).

Bester, J., Foster, I., Kesselman, C., Tedesco, J., & Tuecke, S. (1999). GASS: A data movement and access service for wide area computing systems. In *Proceedings of the Sixth Workshop on I/O in Parallel and Distributed Systems*.

Butt, A., Johnson, T., Zheng, Y., & Hu, Y. (2004). Kosha: A peer-to-peer enhancement for the network file system. In *Proceedings of Supercomputing Conference*.

Butt, A. R., Johnson, T. A., Zheng, Y., & Hu, Y. C. (2006). Kosha: A peer-to-peer enhancement for the network file system. *Journal of Grid Computing: Special issue on Global and Peer-to-Peer Computing, 4*(3), 323–341.

Calder, B., Chien, A., Wang, J., & Yang, D. (2005). The Entropia virtual machine for desktop grids. In *Proceedings of the 1st ACM/USENIX International Conference on Virtual Execution Environments*.

Callaghan, B. (2000). *NFS illustrated*. Essex, UK: Addison-Wesley Longman, Inc.

Castro, M., Druschel, P., Kermarrec, A.-M., & Rowstron, A. (2002). Scribe: A large-scale and decentralised application-level multicast infrastructure. *IEEE Journal on Selected Areas in Communications, 20*(8), 100–110. doi:10.1109/JSAC.2002.803069

Chien, A., Calder, B., Elbert, S., & Bhatia, K. (2003). Entropia: Architecture and performance of an enterprise desktop grid system. *Journal of Parallel and Distributed Computing, 63*(5). doi:10.1016/S0743-7315(03)00006-6

Cipar, J., Corner, M. D., & Berger, E. D. (2007). TFS: A transparent file system for contributory storage. In *Proceedings of the 5th USENIX FAST*, (pp. 215–229).

Clarke, I., Sandberg, O., Wiley, B., & Hong, T. W. (1999). *Freenet: A distributed anonymous information storage and retrieval system*. Retrieved from http://freenetproject.org/freenet.pdf

Cobb, J. W., Geist, A., Kohl, J. A., Miller, S. D., Peterson, P. F., & Pike, G. G. (2007). The neutron science teragrid gateway: A teragrid science gateway to support the spallation neutron source: Research articles. *Concurrency and Computation, 19*(6), 809–826. doi:10.1002/cpe.1102

Conseil Europ'een pour la Recherche Nucl'eaire (CERN). (2007). *LHC– The large hadron collider*. Retrieved from http://lhc.web.cern.ch/lhc/

Coyne, R., & Watson, R. (1995). The parallel i/o architecture of the high-performance storage system (hpss). In *Proceedings of the IEEE MSS Symposium*.

Dabek, F., Kaashoek, M. F., Karger, D., Morris, R., & Stoica, I. (2001). Wide-area cooperative storage with CFS. In *Proceedings of SOSP*, (pp. 202–215).

dCache.org. (2009). Retrieved from http://www.dcache.org/.

Dean, J., & Ghemawat, S. (2004). Mapreduce: Simplified data processing on large clusters. In *Proceedings of the Sixth Symposium on Operating System Design and Implementation (OSDI'04)*.

Douceur, J., & Bolosky, W. (1999). A large-scale study of file-system contents. In *Proceedings of SIGMETRICS*.

Earth System Grid (ESG). (2006). Retrieved from http://www.earthsystemgrid.org

F. 180-1. (1995). *Secure hash standard*. Technical Report Publication 180-1, Federal Information Processing Standard (FIPS), NIST. Washington D.C.: US Department of Commerce.

Frankel, J., & Pepper, T. (2003). *The Gnutella protocol specification* v0.4. Retrieved from http://www9.limewire.com/developer/gnutella protocol 0.4.pdf

Ghemawat, S., Gobioff, H., & Leung, S. (2003). The Google file system. In *Proceedings of the 19th Symposium on Operating Systems Principles*.

Gleicher, M. (n.d). *HSI: Hierarchical storage interface for HPSS*. Retrieved from http://www.hpss-collaboration.org/hpss/HSI/

Hadoop. (n.d). Retrieved from http://hadoop.apache.org/core/

Howard, J. H., Kazar, M. L., Menees, S. G., Nichols, D. A., Satyanarayanan, M., Sidebotham, R. N., & West, M. J. (1988). Scale and performance in a distributed file system. *ACM Transactions on Computer Systems, 6*(1), 51–81. doi:10.1145/35037.35059

Hu, Y. C., Das, S. M., & Pucha, H. (2003). Exploiting the synergy between peer-to-peer and mobile ad hoc networks. In *Proceedings of HotOS IX*.

Iamnitchi, A., Ripeanu, M., & Foster, I. (2004). Small-world file-sharing communities. In *Proceedings of Infocom*.

Kubiatowicz, J., et al. (2000). Oceanstore: An architecture for global-scale persistent store. In *Proceedings of ASPLOS*, (pp. 190–201).

Laser Interferometer Gravitational-Wave Observatory (LIGO). (2008). Retrieved from http://www.ligo.caltech.edu/

Lee, J., Ma, X., Ross, R., Thakur, R., & Winslett, M. (2004). RFS: Efficient and flexible remote file access for MPI-IO. In *Proceedings of the IEEE International Conference on Cluster Computing*.

Lee, J., Ma, X., Winslett, M., & Yu, S. Active buffering plus compressed migration: An integrated solution to parallel simulations' data transport needs. In *Proceedings of the 16th ACM International Conference on Supercomputing*.

Leibowitz, N., Bergman, A., Ben-Shaul, R., & Shavit, A. (2002). Are file swapping networks cacheable? Characterizing p2p traffic. In *Proc. 7th International Workshop on Web Content Caching and Distribution (WCW7)*.

Litzkow, M., Livny, M., & Mutka, M. (1988). Condor - A hunter of idle workstations. In *Proceedings of the 8th International Conference on Distributed Computing Systems*.

Ma, X., Vazhkudai, S., Freeh, V., Simon, T., Yang, T., & Scott, S. L. (2006). Coupling prefix caching and collective downloads for remote data access. In *Proceedings of the ACM International Conference on Supercomputing*.

Monti, H., Butt, A. R., & Vazhkudai, S. S. (2008a). Just-in-time staging of large input data for supercomputing jobs. In *Proceedings ACM Petascale Data Storage Workshop*.

Monti, H., Butt, A. R., & Vazhkudai, S. S. (2008b). Timely offloading of result-data in HPC centers. In *Proceedings of 22nd ACM International Conference on Supercomputing (ICS'08)*.

Muthitacharoen, A., Morris, R., Gil, T. M., & Chen, B. (2003). *Ivy: A read/write peer-to-peer file system*. In *Proc. 5th USENIX OSDI*, (pp. 31–34).

Napster. (n.d). Retrieved from http://www.napster.com/

National Center for Biotechnology Information (NCBI) (n.d). Retrieved from http://www.ncbi.nlm.nih.gov/

National Center for Computational Sciences (NCCS). (2009). Retrieved from http://www.nccs.gov/

National Institute of Computational Sciences (NICS). (2008). Retrieved from http://www.nics.tennessee.edu/computing-resources/kraken

NCCS.GOV File Systems. (2007). Retrieved from http://info.nccs.gov/computing-resources/jaguar/file-systems

NSF Teragrid. (2009). Retrieved from http://www.teragrid.org.

Otoo, E. J., Rotem, D., & Romosan, A. (2004). Optimal file-bundle caching algorithms for data-grids. In *Proceedings of Supercomputing.*

Pinheiro, E., Weber, W.-D., & Barroso, L. A. (2007). Failure trends in a large disk drive population. In *Proceedings of USENIX FAST.* USENIX Association.

Plank, J., Beck, M., Elwasif, W., Moore, T., Swany, M., & Wolski, R. (1999). The Internet backplane protocol: Storage in the network. In *Proceedings of the Network Storage Symposium.*

Pucha, H., Das, S. M., & Hu, Y. C. (2006). Imposing route reuse in mobile ad hoc network routing protocols using structured peer-to-peer overlay routing. *IEEE Transactions on Parallel and Distributed Systems*, *17*(12), 1452–1467. doi:10.1109/TPDS.2006.174

Ratnasamy, S., Francis, P., Handley, M., Karp, R., & Schenker, S. (2001). A scalable content-addressable network. In *Proceedings of SIGCOMM.*

Rhea, S., Eaton, P., Geels, D., Weatherspoon, H., Zhao, B., & Kubiatowicz, J. (2003). Pond: The Oceanstore prototype. In *Proceedings of 2nd USENIX FAST*, (pp. 1–14).

Rowstron, A., & Druschel, P. (2001a). Pastry: Scalable, distributed object location and routing for large-scale peer-to-peer systems. In *Proceedings of IFIP/ACM Middleware*, (pp. 329–350).

Rowstron, A., & Druschel, P. (2001b). Storage management and caching in PAST, a large-scale, persistent peer-to-peer storage utility. In *Proceedings of SOSP*, (pp. 188–201).

Saito, Y., Karamanolis, C., Karlsson, M., & Mahalingam, M. (2002). Taming aggressive replication in the Pangaea wide-area file system. In *Proceedings of 5th USENIX OSDI*, (pp. 15–30).

Sandberg, R., Goldberg, D., Kleiman, S., Walsh, D., & Lyon, B. (1985). Design and implementation of the Sun network file system. In *Proceedings of Summer USENIX*, (pp. 119–130).

Schroeder, B., & Gibson, G. A. (2007). Disk failures in the real world: What does an MTTF of 1,000,000 hours mean to you? In *Proceedings of USENIX FAST.*

Shah, S., & Elerath, J. (2005). Reliability analysis of disk drive failure mechanisms. In *Proceedings of RAMS.*

Sharman Networks. (2004). *Kazaa media desktop.* Retrieved from http://www.kazaa.com/index.htm

Shoshani, A., Sim, A., & Gu, J. (2003). Storage resource managers: Essential components for the grid. In Nabrzyski, J., Schopf, J., & Weglarz, J. (Eds.), *Grid resource management: State of the art and future trends.*

Sloan Digital Sky Survey (SDSS). (2005). Retrieved from http://www.sdss.org

Spallation Neutron Source (SNS). (2008). Retrieved from http://www.sns.gov/

Stoica, I., Morris, R., Karger, D., Kaashoek, M. F., & Balakrishnan, H. (2001). Chord: A scalable peer-to-peer lookup service for Internet applications. In *Proceedings of SIGCOMM.*

Strickland, J., Freeh, V., Ma, X., & Vazhkudai, S. (2005). Governor: Autonomic throttling for aggressive idle resource scavenging. In *Proceedings of the 2nd IEEE International Conference on Autonomic Computing.*

Sun Constellation Linux Cluster. (2008). Retrieved from http://www.tacc.utexas.edu/resources/hpcsystems/#constellation

Szalay, A., & Gray, J. (2001). The world-wide telescope. *Science*, *293*(14), 2037–2040. doi:10.1126/science.293.5537.2037

Thain, D., Klous, S., Wozniak, J., Brenner, P., Striegel, A., & Izaguirre, J. (2005). Separating abstractions from resources in a tactical storage system. In *Proceedings of Supercomputing*.

Thekkath, C. A., Mann, T., & Lee, E. K. (1997). Frangipani: A scalable distributed file system. In *Proceedings of SOSP*, (pp. 224–237).

UC/ANL Teragrid Guide. (2004). Retrieved from http://www.uc.teragrid.org/tg-docs/user-guide.html#disk

Vazhkudai, S., Ma, X., Freeh, V., Strickland, J., Tammineedi, N., & Scott, S. (2005). Scavenging desktop storage resources for bulk, transient data. In *Proceedings of Supercomputing, 2005*. Freeloader.

Vazhkudai, S., Ma, X., Freeh, V., Strickland, J., Tammineedi, N., Simon, T., & Scott, S. (2006). Constructing collaborative desktop storage caches for large scientific datasets. *ACM Transactions on Storage*, *2*(3), 221–254. doi:10.1145/1168910.1168911

Vazhkudai, S., Schopf, J., & Foster, I. (2002). Predicting the performance of wide-area data transfers. In *Proceedings of the 16th Int'l Parallel and Distributed Processing Symposium (IPDPS 2002)*.

Wolski, R., Spring, N., & Hayes, J. (1999). The network weather service: A distributed resource performance forecasting service for metacomputing. *Future Generation Computer Systems*, *15*(5), 757–768. doi:10.1016/S0167-739X(99)00025-4

Zhang, R., & Hu, Y. C. (2003). Borg: A hybrid protocol for scalable application-level multicast in peer-to-peer networks. In *Proceedings of the 13th NOSSDAV Workshop*.

Zhao, B. Y., Kubiatowicz, J. D., & Joseph, A. D. (2001). *Tapestry: An infrastructure for fault-resilient wide-area location and routing*. Technical Report UCB//CSD-01-1141, U. C. Berkeley.

Zhuang, S. Q., Zhao, B. Y., Joseph, A. D., Katz, R. H., & Kubiatowicz, J. (2001). Bayeux: An architecture for scalable and fault-tolerant wide-area data dissemination. In *Proceedings of 11th NOSSDAV Workshop*.

Chapter 5
Metadata Management in PetaShare Distributed Storage Network

Ismail Akturk
Bilkent University, Turkey

Xinqi Wang
Louisiana State University, USA

Tevfik Kosar
State University of New York at Buffalo (SUNY), USA

ABSTRACT

The unbounded increase in the size of data generated by scientific applications necessitates collaboration and sharing among the nation's education and research institutions. Simply purchasing high-capacity, high-performance storage systems and adding them to the existing infrastructure of the collaborating institutions does not solve the underlying and highly challenging data handling problem. Scientists are compelled to spend a great deal of time and energy on solving basic data-handling issues, such as the physical location of data, how to access it, and/or how to move it to visualization and/or compute resources for further analysis. This chapter presents the design and implementation of a reliable and efficient distributed data storage system, PetaShare, which spans multiple institutions across the state of Louisiana. At the back-end, PetaShare provides a unified name space and efficient data movement across geographically distributed storage sites. At the front-end, it provides light-weight clients the enable easy, transparent, and scalable access. In PetaShare, the authors have designed and implemented an asynchronously replicated multi-master metadata system for enhanced reliability and availability. The authors also present a high level cross-domain metadata schema to provide a structured systematic view of multiple science domains supported by PetaShare.

DOI: 10.4018/978-1-61520-971-2.ch005

INTRODUCTION

The unbounded increase in the size of data generated by scientific applications, such as high energy physics (Carena et al., 2008) (Newman, 2003), computational biology (Ponomarev, Bishop, & Putkaradze, 2009) (Yang & Yang, 2008), coastal modeling (Chen, Zhao, Hu, & Douglass, 2005) (Stamey, Wang, & Koterba, 2007), computational fluid-dynamics (Gaither, 2007) numerical relativity (Allen, Goodale, Masso, & Seidel, 1999), and astrophysics (Tyson, 2002) necessitates collaboration and sharing data among the nation's education and research institutions. Having stringent performance requirements, large volume of data sets, and geographically distributed human, computational and storage resources makes existing data management infrastructures insufficient (Chervenak, Foster, Kesselman, Salisbury, & Tuecke, 1999). Simply purchasing high-capacity, high-performance storage systems and adding them to the existing computing infrastructure of the collaborating institutions do not solve the underlying and highly challenging data handling problems. Scientists are compelled to spend a great amount of time and energy on solving basic data-handling issues, such as how to find physical location of data, how to access it, and/or how to move it to visualization and/or compute resources for further analysis.

There is a wide variety of distributed file systems developed to alleviate data management challenges in cluster environment, such as AFS (Howard et al., 1988), NFS (Shepler et al., 2003), Lustre (Lustre, 2010), PVFS (Ligon, & Ross, 1996), GPFS (Schmuck, & Haskin, 2002) and Panasas (Nagle, Serenyi, & Matthews, 2004). These file systems are sufficient and widely used in LANs as a cluster file system. However, when the volume of generated data sets increases and data sets are distributed over the clusters through WANs, it becomes very expensive to maintain a unified shared file system running across distributed clusters. This is due to the constraints of

WAN, heterogeneity of distributed resources and environments, and authorization/authentication policies of different administration domains. To address the challenges of data handling issues in geographically distributed and heterogeneous environments, distributed data storage systems have been proposed and implemented.

Distributed data storage systems provide flexible mechanisms for controlling, organizing, sharing, accessing and manipulating data sets over widely distributed resources that are under the control of different administration domains. One of the important features of distributed storage systems is providing global unified name space across distributed resources, which enables easy data sharing and accessing without the knowledge of actual physical location of data. This is known as 'location transparency'. The location transparency of distributed data sets is provided efficiently by distributed data storage systems. Distributed storage systems enable scalable, efficient and transparent access to the distributed resources including replicated data sets in different resources to enable fast access while ensuring data coherency. They can issue fine-grained authentication and authorization policies over shared and distributed resources as well as data sets. In general, the data sets stored in distributed resources are accessed through data servers, while metadata is managed separately by metadata servers in distributed data storage systems for efficiency.

The NSF funded PetaShare project aims to enable transparent handling of underlying data sharing, archival, and retrieval mechanisms, and make data available to scientists for analysis and visualization on demand. The goal is to enable scientists to focus on their primary research problems, assured that the underlying infrastructure will manage the low-level data handling issues. In the design and implementation of PetaShare, a novel approach has been employed to solve the distributed data sharing and management problems. Unlike existing approaches, PetaShare treats data storage resources and the tasks related to data access as first class entities just like computational resources and compute tasks, and not simply the side effect of computation.

PetaShare provides scientists with simple uniform interfaces to store, access and process heterogeneous distributed data sources. The archived data is well cataloged to enable easy access to desired files or segments of files, which can then be returned to the requester in a chosen format or resolution. Multiple copies of high priority information can be stored at different physical locations to increase reliability and also enable easier retrieval by scientists in different geographical locations. The data is also indexed to enable easy and efficient access to the desired data. The requested data is moved from the source or archival sites to the computation sites for processing as required and then, results are sent back to the interested parties for further analysis or back to the long term storage sites for archival.

SYSTEM OVERVIEW

The back-end of PetaShare is based on enhanced version of iRODS to provide a global name space and efficient data access among geographically distributed storage resources. iRODS is the descendant of SRB (Moore, Wan, & Rajasekar, 2005) technology that aims to provide convenient interface for managing storage resources in data grids, digital libraries, persistent archives, and real-time data systems (Weise, Wan, Schroeder, & Hasan, 2008). iRODS consists of two main components: data server called irodsServer to manage physical accesses to the storage resources, and metadata server called iCAT to provide global name space and to keep all system related metadata information (Rajasekar, Wan, Moore, & Schroeder, 2006). Fore more information on iRODS, please see Chapter 4.

Current implementation and deployment of PetaShare involves five state universities and two health sciences centers in Louisiana. These

Figure 1. Louisiana optical network and PetaShare sites

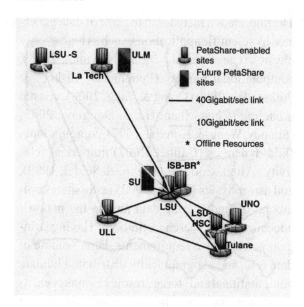

institutions are Louisiana State University, Tulane University, University of New Orleans, Louisiana Tech, University of Louisiana at Lafayette, Louisiana State University-Shreveport and Louisiana State University-Health Sciences Center in New Orleans. PetaShare manages 250 Terabytes of disk storage distributed across these sites as well as 400 Terabytes of tape storage centrally located nearby LSU campus. For connecting all of the participating institutions together, PetaShare leverages 40 Gbps high bandwidth and low-latency optical network: LONI, the Louisiana Optical Network Initiative(Allen, MacMahon, Seidel, & Tierney, 2003). The internal network connection of LONI resources and the distribution of the PetaShare resources among the LONI sites are shown in Figure 1.

In each PetaShare site, a data server is deployed. A data server is responsible for coordinating physical accesses to the resources, such as retrieving and storing data. To access relevant resource and data set, data server cooperates with metadata server. The specified global path resolved by metadata server and it identifies the resource in

Figure 2. Transparent access to the PetaShare resources

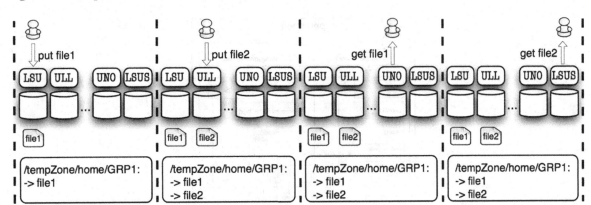

which the data set of interest is stored and its physical location. If the data set is stored in a resource that is managed by the data server to which the client is connected, then the request is handled by this data server. On the other hand, if the data set is stored in a resource that is remote and managed by some other data server, then connected data server forwards the request to the data server that is responsible for the resource in which data set is stored. The resolution of the global path, as well as forwarding the request to the desired data server is transparent to the users.

The PetaShare accounts are assigned to research groups instead of individuals which means that all members of the particular research group can access to the common group account even if group members are affiliated with different institutions. This approach makes it easy to share data between users and helps to exploit resources available in the participating institutions. Users do not need to stage in/out data to their local machines, in fact, they can utilize high-speed optical network by attaching remote data to their local applications through provided infrastructure.

The transparent access to the distributed storage resources provided by PetaShare is illustrated in Figure 2. For this example, assume that the research group called *'GRP1'* has members at LSU, ULL, UNO and LSUS. Research group *'GRP1'* has global home directory as *'\tempZone*

home\GRP1' in the global name space. Group member at LSU uploads a data set called *file1* into PetaShare. The global home directory of *'GRP1'* is updated in metadata server in a way that *file1* is represented under the global home directory of *'\tempZone\home\GRP1'*. Similarly, group member at ULL uploads a data set called *file2* into PetaShare. The same procedure is followed and *file2* is represented under the global home directory of *'GRP1'*. *At this point*, global home directory *'\tempZone\home\GRP1'* contains two files: *file1* and *file2*.

On the other hand, group member at UNO wants to retrieve the data set *file1*. The data server at UNO asks the physical location of *file1* to metadata server and figures out that *file1* in *'\ tempZone\home\GRP1'* is physically located at LSU. Then, it forwards this request to the data server at LSU. The data server at LSU retrieves the *file1* from the storage and turns it to the user. User could receive the desired data set through UNO; although, it is not physically located in there. Similarly, group member at LSUS can obtain data set *file2* through LSUS by specifying the global path of the file.

At the front-end, PetaShare provides light weight clients based on FUSE, Parrot and icommand technologies which enable easy, transparent, and scalable access to the data sets at the user level. Petashell is an interactive shell interface

Figure 3. Mapping system I/O calls to remote I/O calls via Petashell

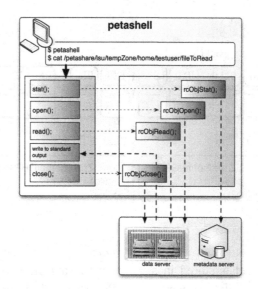

that virtualizes global namespace provided by PetaShare within a shell and attaches data set stored in PetaShare to running applications. Petafs is a user space virtual file system that enables users to mount PetaShare resources to the local machines. Pcommands are a set of unix-like commands that are specialized for accessing to and managing resources in PetaShare. In addition to these three clients, a web portal is provided that enables access to resources in Petashare through a web browser.

CLIENT TOOLS

PetaShare provides three main client tools for the users: petashell, petafs and pcommands.

Petashell is an interactive shell interface that attaches data sets stored in PetaShare to the locally running applications. Basically, petashell catches system I/O calls made by an application and maps them to the relevant remote I/O calls. Petafs is a user space virtual file system that enables users to mount PetaShare resources to the local machines. Pcommands are a set of unix-like commands that are specialized for interacting with PetaShare.

Petashell

Petashell is an interactive shell interface that allows users to run their applications on their machines while data resides on remote PetaShare resources. That means, there is no need to move data sets to the machine in where applications run, or port the applications on machines where data sets are stored. Petashell attaches application and data together while both are physically separated.

Petashell is based on *Parrot* that is a tool for attaching running programs to remote I/O systems through the file system interface (Thain, & Livny, 2005). The main idea behind Parrot is to catch system I/O calls of the application and translate these calls into the corresponding I/O operations of the remote system. Basically, the system calls of an application are trapped through the *ptrace* and corresponding I/O calls are sent to the remote system. For example, if a user runs *cat* program to read a file stored in PetaShare resource, then Parrot captures the relevant I/O calls (i.e. fstat, open, read, write, close) made by *cat*, and maps these I/O calls to corresponding remote calls (i.e. rcObjStat, rcDataObjOpen, rcDataObjRead, rcDataObjClose). This is illustrated in Figure 3.

Figure 4. Interaction between Petafs and FUSE kernel module

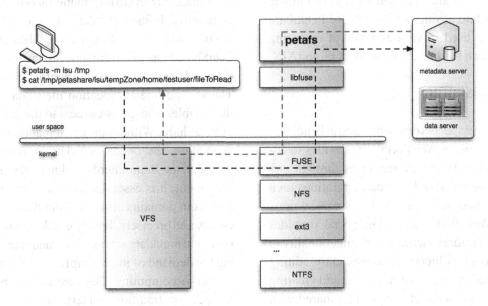

Petashell installation requires no kernel modification, so unprivileged users can run it without worrying about low-level system and permission issues. Petashell can be used in linux-based systems.

Petafs

Petafs is a virtual file system that allows users to access PetaShare resources as a local file system after being mounted to their machines. By using petafs, PetaShare resources can be seen in the directory hierarchy of an existing file system of local machine and can be accessed as local directory.

Petafs is based on FUSE (File system in User space) that is a simple interface to export a virtual file system to the Linux kernel in user space ("FUSE," n.d.). FUSE interacts with the existing file system at the kernel level and maps virtual file system calls to the corresponding file system calls. Whenever system I/O calls are made towards mounted PetaShare resource, FUSE captures these I/O calls in the kernel and forwards them to the user space library called libFuse. This library maps system I/O calls into remote I/O calls. The

interaction between FUSE and petafs is shown in Figure 4.

Installation of petafs requires kernel support for FUSE, so it is appropriate for privileged users. Petafs can be used in linux-based systems and MacOS if FUSE module is provided in the kernel.

PCommands

Pcommands are a set of commands that enable to access and manipulate data sets stored in PetaShare resources. They are evoking the basic unix commands, such as *pls*, *pcp*, *pmkdir* where unix counterparts are *ls*, *cp*, *mkdir* respectively. Also, pcommands provide advance utilities to manage data set and storage resources, such as replication of particular data set in more than one storage resource, physical movement of data sets between storage resources and inserting user-defined metadata for data sets. There are two basic commands which are used heavily: *pput* and *pget*. Users can store their data sets in PetaShare resources by using *pput* command, and retrieve data sets from PetaShare resources by using *pget* command.

Pcommands are a revised version of built-in command line utilities of iRODS for PetaShare and can be used in various types of operating systems; such as Linux, Solaris, MacOS, and AIX.

Web Portal

Another way to access data sets stored in PetaShare resources is using Web Portal[1]. It provides seamless access to PetaShare resources through any modern web browser. Basic data operations such as storing and retrieving data sets can be done through Web Portal, also. The portal provides additional features such as search functionality to explore directory hierarchy conveniently, editing user-defined metadata of data sets, and creating HTML links to data sets that can be shared with other users.

CROSS-DOMAIN METADATA MANAGEMENT IN PETASHARE

One of the key problems in scientific computing is the interoperability between different data sources and management of metadata for cross-domain projects. Metadata enables physical data to be effectively discovered, interpreted, evaluated, and processed. Today, the scientific research community faces new challenges in metadata management as computing environments become increasingly large and complex and science requires more interdisciplinary collaboration. These large collaborations involve not only domain scientists, but also computer scientists, engineers, and visualization experts who need to access the data to advance research in their own fields. Traditional catalogue based metadata services have limitations in such application scenarios. It is difficult to handle data integration across different domains; management of domain schema evolution often leads to confusion; and performance under petascale computing environment is often not satisfactory.

Metadata refers to information about data itself, commonly defined as "data about data". There are two main types of metadata of data stored in PetaShare. One is "semantic metadata" that is essential for cross-domain scientific computing. The second one is "location metadata" of data that enables transparent access to the data stored in PetaShare. Without proper semantic metadata annotation, the underlying data is meaningless to scientists. In an interdisciplinary research environment, it is essential for scientists to access data from domains different from their own efficiently and precisely. Traditional domain-specific semantic metadata schema is inadequate in meeting the demand of interdisciplinary collaborative scientific computing. Because of difference in perspective, tradition and terms used, same item might be described completely differently in different domains. Therefore, it is important to establish conceptual and semantic mapping among concepts from different domains to facilitate cross-domain data access. On the other hand, it is unrealistic to expect to establish a completely unified view of everything and reconcile all the differences among all the domains without sacrificing relevance. Semantic metadata schema also needs to take into consideration possible future extension to address possible addition of scientific domains. As discussed above, in cross-domain semantic metadata management, proper balance of integration, relevance and extensibility is essential for enabling efficient and precise access to cross-domain data archive.

Another factor must be take into consideration is the issue of scalability and performance, in petascale computing, metadata schema must also be able to scale to petascale while still provide reasonably satisfactory performance. A balanced approach is needed in both high-level architecture as well as low-level implementation in order to reach the desired scalability and performance targets.

To accommodate modern science's demands for cross-domain data access without compromising on scalability and performance in the face of petascale computing, in collaboration with four different science projects, a high level cross-domain metadata schema has been developed to provide a structured systematic view of domains involved as well as to establish conceptual and semantic mapping among related concepts and terms of different domains; on the other hand, PetaShare adopts a layered approach in implementing metadata management infrastructure based on the concept of separating high-level cross-domain access from individual data object access to reduce overhead associated with metadata management in petascale data sets.

Cross-Domain Metadata Schema

Currently, cross-domain metadata schema in PetaShare incorporates domain-independent, domain-dependent and provenance metadata of four science drivers: coastal hazard protection (The SURA coastal ocean observing and prediction, n.d), reservoir uncertainty analysis (Ubiquitous computing and monitoring system, n.d), numerical relativity (The numerical relativity group, n.d) as well as scientific visualization at Center for Computation and Technology, LSU. The following are brief introductions of the four current guiding application scenarios:

Coastal Modeling - SCOOP Archive

The SURA Coastal Ocean Observing and Prediction (SCOOP) program builds a modeling and observation cyber-infrastructure to provide new enabling tools for a virtual community of coastal researchers. Two goals of the project are to enable effective and rapid fusion of observed oceanographic data with numerical models and to facilitate the rapid dissemination of information to operational, scientific, and public or private users. As part of the SCOOP program, the team at LSU has built an archive to store simulation and observational data sets. Currently the archive

contains around 300,000 data files with a total size of around 7 Terabytes. Three main types of data files are held in the archive: wind file; surge (water height) file; and data model file. The basic metadata information for these files are: the file type, the model used to generate the file, the institution where the file was generated, the starting and ending date for the data, and other model related information.

Astrophysics - NumRel Archive

The Numerical Relativity group at LSU is building an archive of simulation data generated by black hole models. One of the motivations is to analyze experimental data from gravitational wave detectors such as LIGO. These simulations are typical of many other science and engineering applications using finite element or finite difference methods to solve systems of partial differential equations. The simulations often take many CPU hours on large supercomputers and generate huge volumes of data. Software packages such as Cactus enable scientists to develop their code in a modular fashion. Each numerical library in the package defines a set of attribute names that can be used as controlled vocabulary. The attribute names could describe input parameters or computation flags. Such information is crucial for user's later retrieval.

Petroleum Engineering - UCoMS Archive

Reservoir simulations in petroleum engineering are used to predict oil reservoir performance. This often requires parameter sweeping, where large numbers (thousands) or runs are performed. In this scenario, users need to provide the initial range of parameter settings. In such a setting, the important metadata can be expressed as follows: parameter name; the range of the parameter in the simulation; the particular parameter value that is set for the run.

Visualization - DMA Archive

Scientific data, after being generated by simulations, needs to be further analyzed. One important tool to help scientists is visualization. The Digital Media Archive (DMA) at Center for Computation and Technology at LSU is built to store the resulting images from scientific visualization, along with other media such as movies, sound tracks, and associated information. Visualization metadata can be fairly simple: Image Name, Image Size, Image Width, Image Height, and File Format.

As evidenced by the projects involved, cross-domain metadata schema in PetaShare currently covers multiple scientific domains. Metadata described in the metadata schema spans simple domain-independent metadata such as file type (txt, jpg, png, etc.), location (physical location or logical location) and file size, domain-dependent metadata such as different observation in SCOOP (SURGE, WIND or Trans), drilling and reservoir metadata in UCoMS, as well as provenance metadata that describes the steps involved in the generation of data file. The schema also maps files from different domains via content-describing metadata such as the mapping of hurricane observation data from SCOOP to data visualization produced by DMA. The schema is modeled as taxonomy of classes, instances and properties connected through relations such as subClassOf, equivalent-to and disjoint-with. Figure 5 illustrates the classes, properties and relations available in current schema for the description of aforementioned science domains.

Metadata Management Implementation

Currently, two layer of metadata management in PetaShare based on Protégé (Protégé ontology editor, n.d) and iRODS respectively to accommodate need for interdisciplinary access and petascale data set.

Protégé-Based Layer

The reason one layer of metadata system in PetaShare is implemented based on Protege-API and Protege-based database back-end is to take advantage of the semantic expressive power of ontology. As the de facto standard for ontology design, Protege supports almost all the W3C standards and provides support for the whole range of of ontology related functionalities, from graphic ontology design interface to built-in reasoner all the way to ontology serialization into relational database, which make Protege and Protege-related technologies good candidate for implementing an semantic enabled metadata system.

As shown in Figure 6, two different interfaces are available in the system. They are browser-based and command line based respectively. The purposes of browser-based metadata interface to PetaShare is to provide an easy-to-use, easy-to-understand method of access so that scientists can query and obtain small amount of experimental files, while command line based interface can be combined with scripts and other programming tools so that more flexible, more powerful access to bulk files is also available in the system.

The cores of systems are Protege Query Parser and Semantic Metadata Store. Protege Query Parser is implemented to parse queries entered by users into Sparql (Sparql query language for rdf, n.d) queries understandable to Protege query engine; In Semantic Metadata Store, metadata definitions in the forms of ontological classes and ontological individuals are stored. Protege itself provides two ways of storing ontology: file-based and relational database-based. The first approach essentially stores ontological class and individual definition into text files, although it is easier to implement and access text file based ontology, experiments (Wang & Kosar, 2009) showed that text-based ontology cannot scale to satisfy the data intensive requirement of PetaShare.

The causes of the failure to scale include:

Figure 5. Cross-domain metadata schema

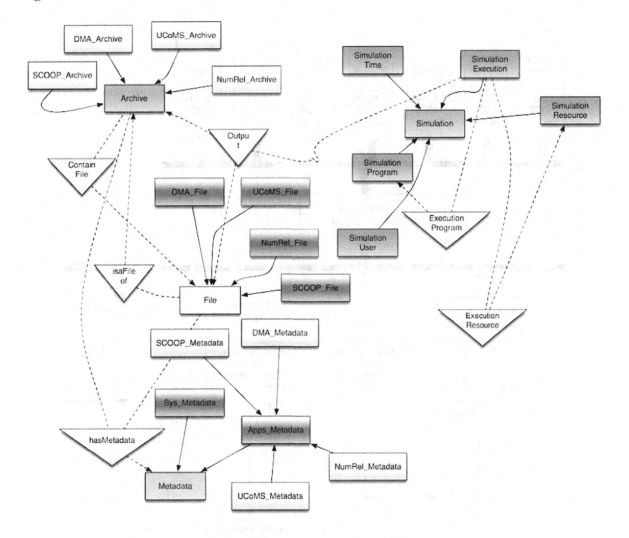

1. The amount of memory required exceeds the maximum size of memory Java Virtual Machine is capable of handling.
2. System is saddled with too high a performance overhead as a result of large numbers of file accesses.

To overcome the above mentioned problems, decision is made to take advantage of the second approach and store the ontology in regular relational databases, in the system, MySQL is chosen as the back end database in which all metadata are stored in ontological forms. Experiments showed that MySQL-based system is capable of handling 300000+ individuals; further experiments also indicated that as many as 700000 to 1 million individuals can be stored and accessed. More experiments are needed to assess the upward limit of relational database-based ontology store.

Another part of the system is called metadata-insertion interface, it is a Java-based command line program that can be utilized, with the help of script languages such as Perl, to automatically insert metadata about newly created experiment files. For example, in large science experiments, when an experiment file is created, Metadata-

Figure 6. Protégé-based architecture

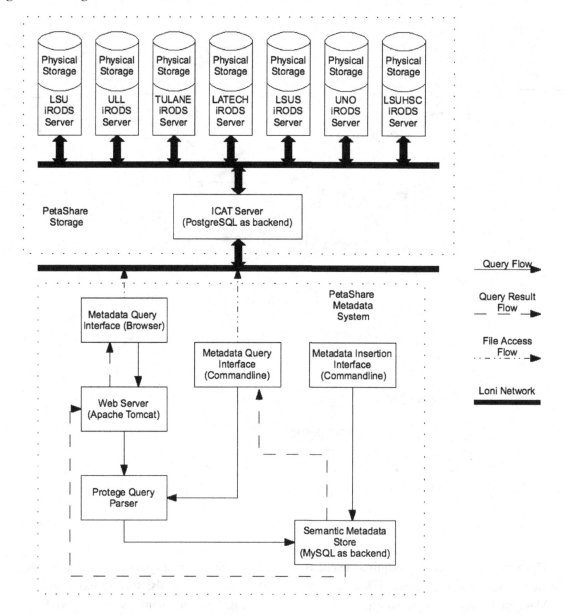

insertion interface can be triggered to automatically add appropriate metadata information, such as name, keyword, time of creation, file type, etc, into Semantic Metadata Store. The system administrator can also choose to do bulk-insertion of up to 1 million files.

So far, Protege-based metadata system implementation offers support for ontology-based metadata query, ontology-based automatic metadata insertion, as well as ontology-based file access through both browser and command-line interfaces.

iRODS-based Layer

Unlike ontology-based system, iRODS-based metadata system does not support a richly representative scheme, namely ontology, like Protege

Figure 7. iRODS-based architecture

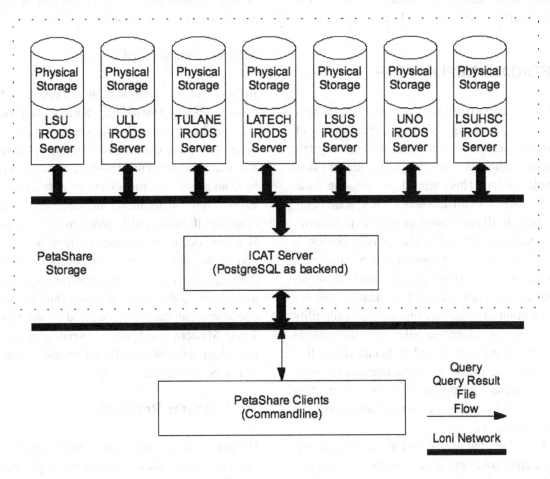

does. However, iRODS and its corresponding iCAT metadata system serve as the backbone of PetaShare, as a result, metadata system based on iRODS and iCAT is naturally integrated into PetaShare seamlessly. ICAT is used as a metadata server to provide global name space which ensures transparent access to heterogeneous and distributed data storage resources. Also, unlike ontology technology, which is Java-based and was originally designed for Semantic Web with little prior consideration for performance, iCAT was designed with the requirement by data-intensive computing in mind. Better performances can be achieved as a result.

As Figure 7 shows, the framework of iCAT metadata system is far simpler. Only one extra layer

of system is added to the existing iCAT PetaShare storage. PetaShare clients have been developed to parse and remote-execute various iRODS commands. One such command is "imeta", which is used for inserting and accessing metadata stored in iCAT. Command "imeta" can be used to insert metadata about iRODS files, collections, resource and users in the form of attribute-value-unit triples (AVUs). Because iCAT also employs relational database as back end storage and the fact that iCAT deals with metadata far less expressive than ontology, it is expected to be able to be at least as scalable as Protege-based system, experiment indicates that iCAT can easily handle file metadata in the order of hundreds of thousands of files. In current implementation, command "imeta" can only insert metadata one AVU at a time.

METADATA REPLICATION

One of the important features of distributed storage systems is providing global name space across all participating institutions, which enables easy data sharing without the knowledge of actual physical location of data. This feature depends on the 'location metadata' of all data sets in the system being available to all participating institutions. Centralized metadata server is widely used approach to provide global name space in distributed data storage systems. Although it is simple to implement and maintain, a central metadata server is a single point of failure leading to low availability of the system. Moreover, all read/write requests need to go through central metadata server that decreases the overall performance and the scalability suffers as the number of participating institutions increases due to increased load on the metadata server.

Ensuring high availability as well as increasing performance and sustain scalability requires replication of metadata across multiple locations. To do so, a metadata server should be deployed along with a data server on each storage site and metadata should be replicated among metadata servers. This enables a data server to have the advantage of cooperating with a local metadata server which minimizes the cost of metadata retrieval. If a metadata server fails in one of the storage sites, there are available metadata servers located in the other storage sites that ensure high availability.

The existence of multiple metadata servers requires to define the role of each of the metadata servers. A metadata server can be either a master which has the capability of updating metadata, or a slave which can only read metadata. There are two main metadata server layouts: either all metadata servers are masters called multi-master, or only one metadata server is master while others are slaves called master-slave.

Master-Slave Replication

In the master-slave replication, any operation that requires updating metadata, such as writing a data set, must be processed by the master server which is similar to the central metadata server layout. The main benefit of master-slave replication is to have an alternative metadata server to use in the case of failure in the master metadata server which alleviates the availability problem of the system. If failure occurs in the master metadata server, one of the slaves temporarily becomes master. Although, master-slave replication provides better availability, it does not scale well since the write operations can only be processed by the master server. Master server becomes overwhelmed when the volume of write operations increases and drifts to low performance.

Multi-Master Replication

Having a master metadata server in each storage site relieves the burden on the single master metadata server that is the case in central and master-slave metadata server layouts. However, it is challenging to find the balance between performance, scalability and consistency while updating multi-master metadata servers. Metadata servers can be updated either synchronously or asynchronously. In synchronous replication, an incoming request that requires metadata update is propagated to all metadata servers before it is committed. Metadata information is updated if and only if all metadata servers agree to commit the incoming request. Propagating incoming requests to all metadata servers and receiving corresponding acknowledgments take time which degrades the performance. However, asynchronous replication can be employed to eliminate the overhead of synchronous replication while updating metadata servers. Asynchronous replication allows a metadata server to process incoming request on its own without propagating the request to others immediately. Metadata servers are updated asynchronously in the background by delaying update messages. This increases performance, especially for write operations since immediate synchronization is not enforced. A challenge of asynchronous multi-master metadata server replication is that it yields to have inconsistent metadata unless all metadata servers are synchronized. The implications of asynchronous replication in multi-master layout on metadata consistency and conflict resolution are discussed in the following section.

Asynchronous Metadata Replication across Multi-Master Servers

In asynchronous replication, an incoming request is processed and get committed on the metadata server without propagating it to other replicating servers simultaneously. Instead, committed requests are deferred and sent to all other replicating servers asynchronously. Once replicating servers receive these deferred requests, they process them and make themselves synchronized. Asynchronous replication utilizes network resources intelligently, creates less traffic, and provides higher performance. Deferring multiple requests and propagating them all as a big chunk of requests are much more efficient rather than to propagate each of them separately (Keating, 2001). Operation latency is reduced as opposed to synchronous replication because a server can process a request without need to negotiate with other servers to commit. It also provides better scalability since response time of a server is independent from the number of replicating servers, and generated network traffic is proportional to the number of replicating servers. Moreover, network latency introduced due to the geographical distance between replicating servers can be tolerated since requests are deferred and propagated asynchronously.

Allowing each metadata server to update metadata information on its own and deferring the propagation of update messages to other metadata servers brings the issue of inconsistency between replicating metadata servers. As opposed to the synchronous replication, asynchronous replication does not enforce updating metadata servers immediately. Instead, each metadata server processes and commits an update request by its own, and propagates the committed updates to other metadata servers asynchronously. If a metadata server updates metadata information of an object, such as file, that has been already updated by another metadata server, but respective update request has not been received yet, then conflict occurs on replicating metadata servers. In such case, metadata servers receive two update requests for the same object with different values, so they need to know which one is correct and must be committed.

Conflict Avoidance and Resolution

In general there are three types of conflicts that may cause inconsistency of metadata:

- Uniqueness conflicts: occur if two or more metadata server try to insert new objects with the same ID.
- Update conflicts: occur if two or more metadata server try to update the same object simultaneously.
- Delete conflicts: occur if one metadata server deletes an object from the system while another metadata server tries to update this object simultaneously.

Each object in the system, such as files, directories, physical storage resources and users, is associated with a unique ID which is a value obtained from monotonically increasing sequence of numbers. If an object is assigned an ID that has a value x, then the next object will be assigned with an ID has a value x+1. If two metadata servers create new objects in their sites before receiving metadata create request of each other's, then both metadata servers will assign the same ID for created objects. In this case, uniqueness conflict occurs when they propagate create requests to all metadata servers, because there are two requests which assign same ID for different objects.

Uniqueness conflicts can be avoided by partitioning the ID space among the metadata servers. The ID space can be partitioned into the mutually exclusive sub-spaces and each sub-space can be associated with one of the metadata servers. Each metadata server is restricted to assign an ID to a new object from its ID sub-space. This ensures that metadata servers assign different IDs when they create new objects; although, they have not received metadata create request one from the other. It is worth to mention that although metadata servers are associated with mutually exclusive ID sub-spaces (i.e. they can only assign an ID from their ID sub-spaces), they still have capability of updating metadata information of objects created in other metadata servers.

Other than ID conflict, there is a possibility of having uniqueness conflict if more than one metadata server creates a new file in the same global directory with the same file name in different storage resources; although the files have different IDs (i.e. ID conflict is avoided by ID space partitioning). These conflicts are resolved by renaming the conflicted files. For example, metadata server X creates a file called F1 in storage resource S1 under logical directory called DIR. Similarly, metadata server Y creates a file called F1 in storage site S2 under logical directory DIR before it receives metadata create request from metadata server X. When both metadata servers X and Y propagate metadata create requests, all metadata servers receive conflicting requests. Two different files have been mapped by the same file name under the same logical directory. It is undesirable to discard any one of the requests. If any one of the requests is discarded, then there would be no way to access the file which has been already stored in storage resources since metadata information is missing for the file. Thus, to make

both files accessible and to resolve the conflict, renaming is used. In the given example, file created in S1 is renamed as F1.X.S1 (i.e. metadata server name and storage name are appended), and the file created in S2 is renamed as F1.Y.S2. This renaming are also done in originating metadata servers.

Update conflicts occur only when more than one metadata server update the same metadata information before any one of the update requests has been received by all metadata servers. For example, a metadata server X updates the file size of file F1 and commits this update. It defers to propagate the update request to the other metadata servers. Assume that metadata server Y updates the file size of the same file F1 before metadata server X propagates the update request. When both metadata server X and Y propagate their update requests, other metadata servers will have two update requests for the same file. It is not known which update request is correct, thus causing a conflict. This conflict cannot be avoided; however, it is straightforward to resolve such conflicts by using timestamps. Metadata servers need to check the timestamps of both update requests when a conflict is detected. Then, they must process the update request that has the most recent time stamp and discard the other one.

There are update conflicts that timestamps are not sufficient to resolve them. Data servers in storage sites do not allow simultaneous updates for the same file, so timestamps of update requests will be different. For this reason, using timestamps is sufficient for metadata update requests which are generated due to physical access to the data, such as editing a file. However, there are operations that do not involve physical access to the data, but update metadata information of an object, such as changing permission of the file. For such operations, it is possible to update metadata information of the same object from different metadata servers simultaneously, which results in having exactly the same time stamp for both of the metadata update requests for the same object which are propagated from different metadata servers. Update conflict occurs when metadata servers receive these update requests with the same time stamp. A solution is to use site-priority to resolve this kind of conflicts which is a unique numeric value assigned to all metadata servers. The metadata update request is accepted of whose site-priority is highest and the others are discarded.

Delete conflict occurs when a file is deleted in one metadata server while it is updated in another metadata server. A temporary location is maintained for deleted files before moving them out from the system permanently. Deleted files are kept in temporary location unless all the metadata servers are synchronized and any one of the metadata servers ask for it. If there is a request made for a deleted file, then it is possible to roll-back the delete request, and file can be restored.

Implementation of Asynchronous Metadata Replication across Multi-Master Server

Implementing replication logic in metadata server itself is complicated and creates extra work for metadata server. For this reason, an external tool called MASREP (Multi-master ASynchronous REPlication) was implemented in PetaShare. MASREP runs on the background and lets metadata server to run on its own. This makes metadata servers not to deal with replication, and makes all replication related issues transparent to the metadata servers and users. Moreover, it provides flexibility of changing replication settings without interrupt or stop metadata servers.

The replication is based on transaction logs generated by metadata servers. The metadata servers are configured to log only metadata modification statements (i.e. insert, update, delete) in their transaction logs. All statements in the transaction log correspond to one of the metadata update made in that metadata server. For this reason, these statements have to be replicated among all other metadata servers to make them all consistent and synchronized. Other operations, such as read

operations do not change metadata information of any object, so they are not needed to be replicated.

MASREP is responsible for processing transaction logs and sending/receiving them to/from its counterparts in all other replicating metadata servers. MASREP acts as a client when it processes requests received from other metadata servers. It consists of five main components which are coordinating replication and synchronization related operations in the system. These components are extractor, dispatcher, collector, injector and conflict resolver. Along with these components, MASREP maintains two types of statement queues: outgoing-queues and incoming-queue. Outgoing-queues are used to store the statements that must be propagated to metadata servers to make them synchronized. There are separate outgoing-queues for each replicating metadata server. On the other hand, incoming queue is used to store the statements that have been received from other metadata servers.

A replication cycle is defined as duration of time in which all replication related functions have been completed. It also identifies the sequence of actions have to be made to replicate and synchronize metadata servers. Replication cycle starts with executing statements stored in incoming-queue (i.e. by injector), and goes on with extracting statements from transaction log of metadata server, and filling them into the respective outgoing-queues (i.c. by extractor). Then, statements in outgoing-queues are sent to the respective metadata servers (i.e. by dispatcher). After this step, there is a sleeping period. A replication cycle finishes when the sleeping period is over, and a new replication cycle starts. It is expected that all metadata servers become synchronized at the end of the replication cycle.

Feasibility of Asynchronous Metadata Replication across Multi-Master Servers

In general, distributed data storage systems are dealing with processing huge volume of data sets that enforces to have stringent performance requirements. In such systems, the basic access pattern to the storage resources is *'write once, read many'*. This pattern basically implies that a data set is not likely to change so often; however, it is likely to be accessed many times after it has been written into the storage resource. This means that the probability of having update and delete conflicts in asynchronously replicated multi-master metadata servers is extremely low, because of editing a data set during its life time is rare. Addition to the low probability of editing data set, it has even less probability of editing a data set from more than one metadata server within the same replication cycle which may cause an update conflict.

Although the probability of editing a data set from more than one metadata server within the same replication cycle is low, adding a new file from more than one metadata server is more likely. This does not imply any conflict, but implies the existence of inconsistencies between metadata servers unless all metadata servers are synchronized. If replication cycle is too long that keeps metadata servers inconsistent for a long time, then inconveniences may occur for the users. For example, a metadata server creates metadata information for a data set that is written into the storage resource, but does not propagate it until replication cycle is over. If a user asks to another metadata server for this data set before related metadata information has been propagated, then metadata server cannot locate it. User has to wait until the end of replication cycle to be able to access this data set through different metadata server. Fortunately, short replication cycles can easily avoid such inconvenience. Also, immediate access through other metadata servers is unlikely. It is observed that replication cycle is much smaller than the time passed until data set is asked through other metadata servers. This is also true for editing data sets. Immediate access of edited data set through other metadata servers is not expected.

Addition to the possibility of resolving the conflicts as mentioned, having low probability of occurring conflicts makes asynchronous replication of metadata across multi-master servers feasible in distributed data storage systems. Overall, it can be said that having replication cycle small enough, the users of distributed data storage systems do not feel the inconvenience of inconsistencies and conflicts occurred in the system while synchronizing metadata servers.

Evaluation of Asynchronous Multi-Master Replication

In the very first deployment of PetaShare, along with data servers in each storage site to manage storage resources there was a single central metadata server that provided global name space to assure location transparency of data sets. This deployment suffered from the drawbacks of central metadata server mentioned before (i.e being single point of failure, limited scalability, low performance) that made replication of metadata necessary. Master-slave replication was not considered because it also suffers from the existence of single master metadata server. For this reason, multi-master replication solutions were chosen to achieve high availability and performance. First, synchronous metadata replication across multi-master servers was employed in PetaShare. Although it fulfills the requirements of high availability, since it degrades the performance due to the synchronization overhead. Eventually, asynchronous metadata replication across multi-master servers was employed in PetaShare to achieve increased availability, scalability and performance.

In the current deployment of PetaShare, there are metadata server and data server in each storage site. The motivation behind doing this is to maximize availability of metadata servers, and minimize the cost of retrieving metadata information from the metadata server. A data server in storage site can cooperate with local metadata

Table 1. Average duration of writing to remote petashare resources

	Central Metadata Server	Synchronous Replication	Asynchronous Replication
10K * 1000 files	75.94	240.32	38.81
10M(single file)	1.38	1.48	1.34
100K * 1000 files	83.53	247.43	47.76
100M(single file)	2.51	2.96	2.83
1M * 1000 files	156.61	320.96	144.53
1G(single file)	9.91	11.68	10.31

server which is faster than cooperating with remote metadata server. It is more likely that users store their data sets in PetaShare resources that are deployed in their site. Thus, if they find a metadata server nearby data server in their sites, this would reduce the overhead of connecting to remote metadata server and give better performance for both read and write operations. Also, having metadata server in each PetaShare site naturally distributes the load, since all incoming requests from respective site can be processed within that site.

Test Cases and Results

The test results of read/write operations in PetaShare are shown in here for three replication scenarios: no replication (i.e. there is only one metadata server), synchronous replication and asynchronous replication of the multi-master metadata servers. During the experiments it was assumed assumed that a client is in one of the PetaShare site and trying to do the one of the following operations:

- client is writing to remote PetaShare resource
- client is writing to local PetaShare resource
- client is reading from remote PetaShare resource
- client is reading from local PetaShare resource

Two data sets were used in the experiments: a data set contains 1000 files, and a data set contains a single file. Three different data sizes were used for each data set: 10KB, 100KB and 1000KB files for the first data set, and 10MB, 100MB and 1000MB files for the second data set.

The comparison of these two data sets enables to understand the effect of the number of files on overall operation performance under all replication scenarios. It is observed that the performance is hurt by the number of files, even though the file size is small. This is because the necessary metadata operations become performance bottleneck in the system. Overall, asynchronously replicated metadata servers give better performance in all cases.

Table 1 shows the average time of writing data sets into the remote resource in three replication scenarios. As it can be seen from the Table 1, the time spent on metadata operation has big impact on the performance. Although the same size of data sets are written into the remote resource, the data set which contains 1000 files takes longer time to write. This is because writing 1000 files need creating 1000 data objects and related metadata information on metadata server, as opposed to one data object and corresponding metadata information in the case of single file.

Synchronous replication takes longer time for the first data set. This is because it needs to initiate a synchronization process and propagate a write request to all metadata servers and wait for their replies for each file. The overhead of syn-

Table 2. Average duration of writing to local PetaShare resource

	Central Metadata Server	Synchronous Replication	Asynchronous Replication
10K * 1000 files	63.51	221.33	19.92
10M(single file)	0.25	0.46	0.15
100K * 1000 files	64.42	223.06	21.38
100M(single file)	0.58	1.02	0.47
1M * 1000 files	75.02	232.48	36.75
1G(single file)	8.37	9.18	5.16

chronous replication is more than the cost of accessing to central metadata server. On the other hand, asynchronously replicated metadata server takes less time to finish compared to synchronously replicated metadata server. This is because asynchronous replication does introduce an overhead for updating metadata servers. It performs better than central metadata server because the client is not required to connect remote metadata server; instead it connects to local metadata server which reduces accessing time. For the data set that contains single file, all replication scenarios have similar performance. This is because the overall time is dominated by sending file to remote resource rather than updating metadata server. There is a single write request that have to be processed by metadata server which takes less time compared to sending a file itself.

Similar to the previous one, Table 2 makes it clear that write requests result low performance in synchronously replicated metadata servers. It

is slightly better than the performance of writing into the remote storage resources, because data set is written into the local storage resource. This reduces the time spent to write the data set. In central metadata server case, network is used only for metadata operations. Conversely, both data operation (i.e. writing files into the resource) and metadata operations are performed locally in asynchronously replicated metadata servers that minimizes the overall time of the operation.

In general, reading is less expensive request compared to writing from the metadata operation point of view. It does not require any metadata update, but just retrieving metadata information of the data object. For this reason, the overhead of updating metadata servers simultaneously seen for write operations does not appear for read operations in synchronous replication in this case. Table 3 shows that central metadata server takes more time than the others while reading the first data set. This is because metadata information of

Table 3. Average duration of reading from remote PetaShare resource

	Central Metadata Server	Synchronous Replication	Asynchronous Replication
10K * 1000 files	46	40.75	26.51
10M(single file)	1.58	1.74	1.47
100K * 1000 files	55	48.92	34.13
100M(single file)	3.44	3.54	3.29
1M * 1000 files	166.98	157.43	144.98
1G(single file)	14.47	11.55	9.57

Table 4. Average duration of reading from local PetaShare resource

	Central Metadata Server	Synchronous Replication	Asynchronous Replication
10K * 1000 files	24.33	23.63	17.08
10M(single file)	0.2	0.36	0.14
100K * 1000 files	25.57	25.23	19.43
100M(single file)	0.42	1.4	0.43
1M * 1000 files	31.94	38.08	25.43
1G(single file)	7.34	14.06	3.25

each file is retrieved from central metadata server which is located in remote site. Conversely, metadata information is retrieved from local metadata server in both synchronously and asynchronously replicated metadata servers. This reduces the time of retrieving metadata information and gives better performance. An interesting point is that although metadata information is stored in local metadata server in both synchronously replicated metadata servers and asynchronously replicated metadata servers, it takes more time in synchronously replicated metadata servers than asynchronously replicated metadata servers. This is because the overhead introduced by the synchronous replication middleware to balance the load across metadata servers. However, the tool used in asynchronous replication does not introduce such overhead, thus results better performance.

Table 4 shows that the overhead of synchronous replication is comparable to the overhead of retrieving metadata information from central metadata server while reading data set from local storage resource. On the other hand, asynchronously replicated metadata server outperforms central metadata server since it retrieves metadata information locally; thus, it eliminates the overhead of retrieving metadata information from remote metadata server. Similarly, it outperforms synchronously replicated metadata server since it directly process the read requests. Synchronously replicated metadata servers spend more

time to retrieve metadata information compared to central metadata server and asynchronously replicated metadata servers.

The results shown above enable to conclude that asynchronous replication of metadata servers outperforms central metadata server and synchronous replication of metadata servers for both write and read operations. The synchronously replicated metadata servers suffer from high synchronization overhead for write operations, and metadata information retrieval delay for read operations due to having middleware to employ synchronization in front of the metadata servers.

On the other hand, central metadata server is a single point of failure in the system and increases metadata update and retrieval time because of being a remote server.

CONCLUSION

In this chapter, we have presented the design and implementation of a reliable and efficient distributed data storage system, PetaShare, which spans multiple institutions across the state of Louisiana. PetaShare provides an asynchronously replicated multi-master metadata system for enhanced reliability and availability. Our results show that our asynchronous multi-master replication method can achieve both high performance, reliability, and availability at the same time. We gave a brief overview of the benchmarking tests we did for key metadata operations. For future work, we plan to improve conflict resolver in asynchronous replication to ensure stability of our production PetaShare system.

ACKNOWLEDGMENT

This work was supported in part by the National Science Foundation under award numbers CNS-1131889 (CAREER), CNS-0619843 (MRI-PetaShare), and OCI-0926701 (STCI-Stork). This work benefits from the use of resources of the Louisiana Optical Network Initiative (LONI). We also would like to thank iRODS and Parrot teams for their contributions.

REFERENCES

Allen, G., Goodale, T., Masso, J., & Seidel, E. (1999). The Cactus computational toolkit and using distributed computing to collide neutron stars. *Proceedings of Eighth IEEE International Symposium on High Performance Distributed Computing*, HPDC-8. IEEE Computer Society.

Allen, G., MacMahon, C., Seidel, E., & Tierney, T. (2003). *LONI: Louisiana optical network initiative*. Received from http://www.cct.lsu.edu/~gallen/Reports/LONI ConceptPaper.pdf

Carena, F., Carena, W., Chapeland, S., Divia, R., Fuchs, U., & Makhlyueva, I. … Vyvre, P. V. (2008). The ALICE DAQ online transient data storage system. *Journal of Physics: Conference Series, 119*(2), 022016 (7pp).

Chen, Q., Zhao, H., Hu, K., & Douglass, S. L. (2005). Prediction of wind waves in a shallow estuary. *Journal of Waterway, Port, Coastal, and Ocean Engineering, 131*(4), 137–148. doi:10.1061/(ASCE)0733-950X(2005)131:4(137)

Chervenak, A., Foster, I., Kesselman, C., Salisbury, C., & Tuecke, S. (1999). The data grid: Towards an architecture for the distributed management and analysis of large scientific datasets. *Journal of Network and Computer Applications, 23*, 187–200. doi:10.1006/jnca.2000.0110

FUSE. (n.d.). *Filesystem in userspace*. Retrieved from http://fuse.sourceforge.net

Gaither, K. (2007). Visualization's role in analyzing computational fluid dynamics data. *IEEE Computer Graphics and Applications, 24*(3), 13–15. doi:10.1109/MCG.2004.1297005

Howard, J. H., Kazar, M. L., Menees, S. G., Nichols, D. A., Satyanarayanan, M., Sidebotham, R. N., & West, M. J. (1988). Scale and performance in a distributed file system. *ACM Transactions on Computer Systems, 6*(1), 51–81. doi:10.1145/35037.35059

Keating, B. (2001). *Challenges involved in multimaster replication*. Retrieved from http://www.dbspecialists.com/files/presentations/mm_replication.html

Ligon, W. B., & Ross, R. B. (1996). Implementation and performance of a parallel file system for high performance distributed applications. *HPDC '96: Proceedings of the 5th IEEE International Symposium on High Performance Distributed Computing*, IEEE Computer Society, (p. 471).

Lustre. (2010). *A scalable, high performance file system*. Retrieved from http://wiki.lustre.org/index.php/Main_Page

Moore, R. W., Wan, M., & Rajasekar, A. (2005). Storage resource broker; generic software infrastructure for managing globally distributed data. *International Symposium on Mass Storage Systems and Technology*, IEEE Computer Society, (pp. 65 – 69).

Nagle, D., Serenyi, D., & Matthews, A. (2004). The Panasas ActiveScale storage cluster: Delivering scalable high bandwidth storage. *SC '04: Proceedings of the 2004 ACM/IEEE conference on Supercomputing*, IEEE Computer Society, (p. 53).

Newman, H. (2003). Data intensive grids and networks for high energy and nuclear physics. *Nuclear Physics B - Proceedings Supplements, 120*, 109–112. doi:10.1016/S0920-5632(03)01889-9

Ponomarev, S. Y., Bishop, T. C., & Putkaradze, V. (2009). DNA relaxation dynamics in 1ID3 yeast nucleosome MD simulation. (n.d). Retrieved from http://protege.stanford.edu/. *Biophysical Journal, 96*, doi:10.1016/j.bpj.2008.12.3019

Rajasekar, A., Wan, M., Moore, R., & Schroeder, W. (2006). *A prototype rule-based distributed data management system.* HPDC Workshop on Next Generation Distributed Data Management.

Schmuck, F., & Haskin, R. (2002). GPFS: A shared-disk file system for large computing clusters. *FAST '02: Proceedings of the 1st USENIX Conference on File and Storage Technologies.* USENIX Association, 19.

Shepler, S., Callaghan, B., Robinson, D., Thurlow, R., Beame, C., Eisler, M., & Novec, D. (2003). *Network file system version 4 protocol.* Retrieved from http://tools.ietf.org/html/rfc3530

Sparql Query Language for RDF. (n.d). Retrieved from http://www.w3.org/TR/rdf-sparql-query/

Stamey, B. H., Wang, V., & Koterba, M. (2007). Predicting the next storm surge flood. *Sea Technology*, 10–15.

Thain, D., & Livny, M. (2005). Parrot: An application environment for data intensive computing. *Scalable Computing: Practice and Experience, 6*(3), 9–18.

The Numerical Relativity Group. (n.d). Retrieved from http://www.cct.lsu.edu/numerical/index.php

The SURA Coastal Ocean Observing and Prediction. (n.d). Retrieved from http://scoop.sura.org/

Tyson, J. A. (2002). Large synoptic survey telescope: Overview, survey and other telescope technologies and discoveries. *Proceedings of the Society for Photo-Instrumentation Engineers, 4836*, 10–20.

Ubiquitous Computing and Monitoring System. (n.d). Retrieved from http://www.ucoms.org/

Wang, X., & Kosar, T. (2009) Design and implementation of metadata system in petashare. *SSDBM09: Proceeding of the 21st Scientific and Statistical Database Management Conference*, (pp. 191-199).

Weise, A., Wan, M., Schroeder, W., & Hasan, A. (2008). Managing groups of files in a rule oriented data management system (iRODS), *ICCS '08: Proceedings of the 8th international conference on Computational Science*, Part III, (pp. 321–330). Springer-Verlag.

Yang, M. Q., & Yang, J. Y. (2008). High-performance computing for drug design. *IEEE International Conference on Bioinformatics and Biomedicine Workshops*, (p. 120).

ENDNOTE

[1]   http://dsl-yoda.csc.lsu.edu/petashare

Chapter 6
Data Intensive Computing with Clustered Chirp Servers

Douglas Thain
University of Notre Dame, USA

Peter Bui
University of Notre Dame, USA

Michael Albrecht
University of Notre Dame, USA

Rory Carmichael
University of Notre Dame, USA

Hoang Bui
University of Notre Dame, USA

Scott Emrich
University of Notre Dame, USA

Patrick Flynn
University of Notre Dame, USA

ABSTRACT

Over the last few decades, computing performance, memory capacity, and disk storage have all increased by many orders of magnitude. However, I/O performance has not increased at nearly the same pace: a disk arm movement is still measured in milliseconds, and disk I/O throughput is still measured in megabytes per second. If one wishes to build computer systems that can store and process petabytes of data, they must have large numbers of disks and the corresponding I/O paths and memory capacity to support the desired data rate. A cost efficient way to accomplish this is by clustering large numbers of commodity machines together. This chapter presents Chirp as a building block for clustered data intensive scientific computing. Chirp was originally designed as a lightweight file server for grid computing and was used as a "personal" file server. The authors explore building systems with very high I/O capacity using commodity storage devices by tying together multiple Chirp servers. Several real-life applications such as the GRAND Data Analysis Grid, the Biometrics Research Grid, and the Biocompute Facility use Chirp as their fundamental building block, but provide different services and interfaces appropriate to their target communities.

DOI: 10.4018/978-1-61520-971-2.ch006

INTRODUCTION

It is not enough to have raw hardware for data intensive computing. System software is also needed to manage the system and make it accessible to users. If data is scattered all over the disks of a cluster, then it must be tracked, replicated, and periodically validated to ensure survival in the face of failures. Programs that execute on the system must be able to locate the relevant data and preferably execute on the same node where it is located. Users must have a reasonably simple interface for direct data access as well as for computation on the data itself.

Over the last five years, we have gained experience in designing, building, and operating data intensive clusters at the University of Notre Dame. Working closely with domain experts in physics, biometrics, and bioinformatics, we have created several novel systems that collect data captured by digital instruments, make it easy to search and access, and provide high level facilities for processing the data in ways that were not previously possible. This chapter outlines our experience with each of these repositories.

Chirp (Thain, Moretti, & Hemmes, 2009) is our building block for clustered data intensive scientific computing. Chirp was originally designed as a lightweight file server for grid computing. It was first used as a "personal" file server that could be easily deployed on a user's home machine or temporarily on a computing grid to allow a remotely executing application to access its data. However, we quickly discovered that the properties that made Chirp suitable for personal use – rapid deployment, flexible security, and resource management – also made it very effective for building storage clusters. By tying together multiple Chirp servers, we could easily build a system with very high I/O capacity using commodity storage devices.

Chirp is currently deployed on a testbed of over 300 commodity storage devices at the University of Notre Dame, in is in active use at other research institutions around the world. Using this testbed, we have constructed a number of scalable data storage and analysis systems. Each uses Chirp as its fundamental building block, but provides different services and interfaces appropriate to the target community:

- The **GRAND Data Analysis Grid** provides a scalable archive for data produced by the GRAND cosmic ray experiment at Notre Dame. It provides a conventional filesystem interface for direct access, a shell-like capability for parallel processing, and a web portal for high level data exploration.
- The **Biometrics Research Grid** archives all of the photographic and video data collected in the lab by the Computer Vision Research Lab at Notre Dame. It provides a combination database-filesystem interface for batch processing, several abstractions for high level experimental work, and a web portal for data exploration.
- The **Biocompute** facility provides a web interface to large scale parallel bioinformatics applications. Large input databases are obtained from national repositories and local experimental facilities, and replicated across opportunistic storage devices. Users may run large queries using standard tools which are decomposed and executed across the storage cluster.

In this chapter, we will explain the architecture of each of these systems, along with our experience in constructing, deploying, and using each one. We begin by describing the fundamental building block, the Chirp file server.

THE CHIRP FILE SERVER

Chirp is a practical global filesystem designed for cluster and grid computing. An overview of the main components of the filesystem is shown in the Figure 1. The core component of the system is the **chirp server**, which is a user-level process that runs as an unprivileged user and exports an existing local Unix filesystem. That is, the actual files exported by a Chirp server are stored on the underlying filesystem as regular files and directories. Although this limits the capacity and performance of the Chirp server to that of the underlying kernel-level filesystem, this approach has the advantage of allowing existing data to be exported by the Chirp server without requiring importing or moving the data into the Chirp storage namespace.

In a cluster or grid configuration, there is normally one Chirp server per storage machine or resource, although it is possible for multiple servers to run on the same node. Each Chirp server periodically sends status updates consisting of server address, owner, available space, and similar details to a well-known **catalog server** using UDP. This catalog server acts as directory and may be queried via HTTP to obtain a global list of available Chirp servers.

There are three main ways for applications to interact with Chirp servers, shown in Figure 1. The first is through a library **libchirp** that implements the Chirp networking protocol and enables direct access to the network filesystem. Using this library directly would require modifications to applications, however, which is rarely desirable or even possible. The second is through a command line tool called **chirp** that allows users to get and put files, change access controls, and so forth. It is typically invoked by scripts or web portal code where it is convenient to invoke an external tool. The third is through a tool called **parrot** (Thain & Livny, 2005), which captures the system calls of unmodified applications, and connects them remote chirp servers. Parrot effectively allows an application to mount Chirp servers under the path /chirp, but does not require any special privileges or kernel modifications to deploy.

Figure 1. Overview of the Chirp Filesystem

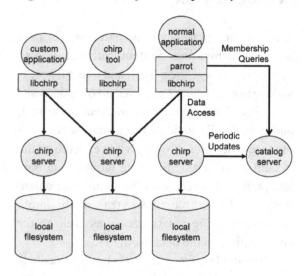

Chirp uses a custom network protocol carried over TCP to connect clients to servers. During the initial client request to a Chirp server, libchirp makes a TCP connection to that server, performs authentication, and then proceeds to issue various RPC requests. Clients can obtain connections to multiple servers, and servers can maintain connections to many clients. Any disruption in the network that would lead to the client TCP connection to hang or fail is handled by libchirp transparently. On the server side, connections that idle beyond a set timeout are automatically dropped. The use of a single persistent connection for both control and data enables optimized access to small files (Thain & Moretti, 2007), while also allowing for large TCP windows to be maintained for high bandwidth transfers.

The Chirp protocol and API contain operations that correspond roughly to each of the Unix I/O system calls. Figure 2 shows a commonly used subset of the API to open and access files. Each operation is reliable from the client side, in the sense that network outages and server crashes will be transparently retried, up to the time limit specific by the user. This aspect is important for constructing higher level reliable services, which often combine short timeout operations to test

Figure 2. Chirp file access API (partial)

```
chirp_reli_open( host, path, mode, flags, timeout );
chirp_reli_pread( file, data, length, offset, timeout );
chirp_reli_pwrite( file, data, length, offset, timeout );
chirp_reli_close( file );
chirp_reli_stat( host, path, metadata, timeout );
chirp_reli_unlink( host, path, timeout );
```

for availability with long timeout operations to complete a task reliably.

Active Storage Interface

In a conventional computing cluster, the storage and computational services are implemented on separate hardware, and the compute nodes pull data from the storage nodes on demand. For problems that are compute-intensive and have low data requirements, this arrangement is satisfactory. However, as the amount of data scales up, the network bandwidth between the storage nodes and the compute nodes increasingly becomes a bottleneck. Eventually, the data requirements become so large as in the case of data intensive problems that the compute nodes spend most of their time waiting for data rather than performing any work.

To address the problem of data intensive workloads, Chirp provides **active storage** (Riedel, Gibson, & Faloutsos, 1998) capabilities. The active storage approach seeks to minimize network data transfers by moving computations to the location where needed data are stored. To accomplish this, all nodes in the system are used for both data storage and job execution. Higher level services must identify the data needed by a given job, and then direct the job to the appropriate storage device. If a single node contains all of the needed data, then no further network transfers are needed to execute the job. If the job requires data from multiple nodes, then it can still access data from other nodes over the network. Since most executables are quite small (megabytes) compared to input data sets (hundreds of megabytes to gigabytes), it is usually more efficient to transfer the application than it is to move the data for each task.

The Chirp server provides both storage and computational services and thus serves as a flexible active storage solution. Figure 3 shows the active storage API used by Chirp. The API relies on the concept of a **transaction** to manage jobs. The client must first put the desired executable on the storage node, using normal file operations from Figure 2. Once the executable is in place, the client uses **chirp_job_begin** to create a new job transaction on the server. This creates a job and returns a job identifier (**jobid**), but does not actually start it running. To actually make the job runnable, the client must issue **chirp_job_com-**

Figure 3. Chirp job execution API

```
chirp_job_begin  (host, workingdir, command, timeout)
chirp_job_commit (host, jobid, timeout)
chirp_job_wait   (host, jobid, wait_time, timeout)
chirp_job_kill   (host, jobid, timeout)
chirp_job_remove (host, jobid, timeout)
chirp_job_list   (host, callback, arg, timeout)
```

Figure 4. Active storage model

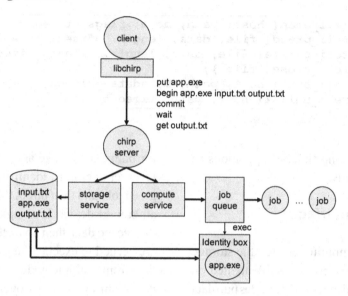

mit. The server maintains a list of jobs to run and as one finishes it checks to see if there are any available tasks. If so, it moves the job off the list and executes the task using the specifications provided by the client in command. For security reasons, the application is placed in an **identity box** (Thain, 2005), which restricts the application to the identity of the submitting client.

Once a job has been created on a remote Chirp server, the Chirp client can query the status of the task using the **chirp_job_list**, which returns the set of all jobs on a server, and **chirp_job_wait**, which waits for a job to complete (or until a timeout expires), and then returns the job status. The user may also stop a job with **chirp_job_kill**. Because jobs continue to run when the client is disconnected, terminated jobs and jobs that have completed are not automatically removed from the server's job queue. Rather, their exit status and states are stored for retrieval using **chirp_job_wait**. To remove the job record from the Chirp server queue, the user must explicitly issue **chirp_job_remove**. All together, these commands provide users the ability to execute and manage data intensive jobs on Chirp servers.

Active Storage Queue

To simplify the management and deployment of active storage tasks across multiple Chirp servers, we also provide a workflow abstraction called *ChirpQueue*, which is modeled after our Work Queue framework (Figure 4). This execution engine provides the user with a master/worker programming interface to the active storage services in a cluster of Chirp servers. As described previously, the client application must take care to call *wait* or *list* to check on the status of the remote active storage job and must remove the job when it is completed using the *remove* command. Such monitoring can be quite cumbersome for most users, so we provide *ChirpQueue*, an execution engine that provides automatic job submission and monitoring.

To use this master/worker framework, the user programs an application that utilizes the *Chirp-Queue* API as demonstrated in the pseudo-code shown in Box 1.

In this example pseudo-code, the user first creates a *ChirpQueue* which setups of various data structures used to monitor the active storage servers and tasks. Next, the programmer creates

Box 1.

```
cq = chirp_queue_create();
ct = chirp_task_create("app.exe input.txt output.txt");
chirp_task_specify_input_file(ct, "app.exe");
chirp_task_specify_target_file(ct, "/chirp/host/p/input.txt");
chirp_task_specify_output_file(ct, "output.txt");
chirp_queue_submit(cq, ct);
do {
    rt = chirp_queue_wait(cq, timeout);
    if (rt) {
            // handle completed returned task.
    }
} while (!rt);
```

a task by specifying command line the Chirp server should execute and the input, target, and output files in this task. The input file is any file that needs to be transferred to the remote Chirp server. Normally, this is the application executable, but may include other necessary files. The target file is the input data that is already on the Chirp server. Based on the location of these target files, the *ChirpQueue* will automatically submit a job to the Chirp server where the data is located. In the case where the target data is replicated across multiple servers, the user may specify which heuristic to use to select the appropriate Chirp server (i.e. random server, server with the least amount of jobs, etc.).

After the task has been fully specified, the user then submits the task to the *ChirpQueue*, which simply makes the task ready for submission to the selected Chirp server. To actually begin execution, the client must perform a wait on the queue. This action forces the *ChirpQueue* to submit any ready tasks to the remote Chirp servers for execution and monitor the active storage nodes for any completed or terminated jobs. If a job completes within the timeout specified by the user in the wait command, then a task object is returned to the user with the information about the completed task. The user can then perform any post-execution operations

such as fetching the results. Otherwise, if a timeout is reached, then an empty object is found, and the user can continue waiting until the submitted tasks complete. Of course, the client application can create and submit multiple tasks at any time and the *ChirpQueue*, will handle submission and tracking of all of these jobs for the user.

Using this active storage execution engine removes the need for the user to manage all of the intricacies of active storage job management and monitoring. The *ChirpQueue* provides a simple and easy to use master/worker framework that enables access to the active storage capabilities of a cluster of Chirp servers.

CASE STUDY: THE GRAND DATA LAB

The GRAND project (Gamma Ray Astrophysics at Notre Dame) is a long running physics experiment at the University of Notre Dame that consists of an array of 64 detectors than can detect the passage of charged subatomic particles. Most events record the passage of muons, which are generated by both solar and cosmic gamma rays interacting with the upper atmosphere. Thus, the collected data is of interest to both astronomy and meteorology.

Figure 5. Accessing data in a chirp cluster filesystem

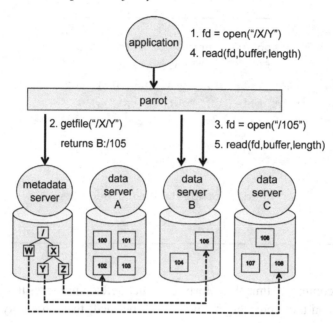

GRAND produces approximately 2GB of data each day, divided into four types of files: dayfiles, which are day-long summaries of the muon activity for each detector binned in 10 minute increments, totaling about 80KB each, muon shower data totaling an average of 20MB per file, muon data averaging 70MB per file, and pressure data totaling about 200KB per month. From 2005 to 2009, a total of 2.8 TB of data has been collected and stored for the GRAND project. In absolute terms, this is not an enormous amount of data simply to store: in the near future, it will be able to fit on one disk. However, most scientific queries against the data involve a summary computation across the entire dataset, which can only be performed efficiently if the data is partitioned across multiple disks.

To support interactive exploration of this data, we have constructed the GRAND Data Lab (GDL). The GDL keeps one complete copy of the data on a cluster of eight Chirp servers, joined together into a single clustered filesystem. For backup, a second copy of the data is kept on a conventional high capacity file server and made accessible by a

Chirp server. A custom middleware layer is used to perform efficient queries on the data, and is made user-accessible via an interactive web portal.

Figure 5 shows how multiple Chirp servers can be combined into a clustered file system: one Chirp server is set aside as a metadata server, and the others are used as data servers. The metadata server stores the entire directory tree for the filesystem. The metadata server does not contain the actual file data, but contain sub files that indicate the host and path on data servers where the data are actually stored. The permissions for any file in the cluster are a logical intersection of the permissions of the metadata file and the actual data file. The metadata server can be an independent server or it can also be used to store data (Moretti, 2007).

Opening a file stored on a Chirp cluster works as follows: first, Parrot contacts the metadata server and retrieves the metadata file. The metadata is parsed, and the location of the file's data is identified. Parrot then opens the appropriate file on a data server, and directs further calls to the appropriate data file.

Figure 6. The Grand Data Lab Web interface

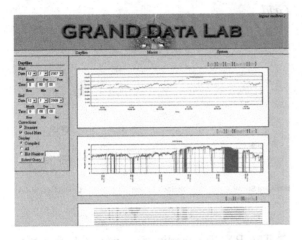

Simply storing the data is not useful without analysis tools. The interesting science comes from analyzing two things: trends over long timescales and short-term abnormalities. However, there are two obstacles that the physicists face. The first is due to file formats. The dayfiles are human-readable but difficult to scan, and the muon and shower files are binary data. Second, the experimental apparatus used to collect the data is rather finicky, and detectors will frequently, but irregularly, break. In addition, each detector has varying sensitivity, so merely averaging the results isn't sufficient. The solution is to provide an interface that allows the physicists to glance quickly through the data and identify interesting events or time periods, then download the relevant data in an easy-to-manipulate format.

The GDL provides this interface as a web portal, shown in Figure 6, with a backend of purpose-built data parsing applications and the gnuplot package. The portal provides a high-level view of the data, either as a graph of muon activity over time when looking at the dayfiles or as a histogram of incident angles when viewing the muon files, with controls for the time interval to be viewed and the level of analysis to be done. In addition, the portal provides links to the raw data in csv format, as well as the displayed graph in various formats. The separation of display from

analysis allows long-running jobs to be transparently parallelized, avoiding unnecessary overhead on short tasks while achieving good performance for queries on longer time intervals.

For queries on the dayfile data, the data to be parsed rarely exceeds more than a few megabytes, and the bulk of the analysis is highly serial, with value of each data point highly dependent upon all of the previous data points. Therefore, when performing a dayfile query, the analysis is done on the web server itself. Running in Parrot, the dayfile parsing application opens each of the dayfiles relevant to the requested time interval and reads the content into memory. Parrot traps each filesystem related system call, and when the request is related to a non-local filesystem, it translates the system call into the system-specific function call. Once the files are retrieved, the web server uses a function provided by the physicists to clean up the muon counts, removing any bad or suspect data and calibrating each reading to the previous one in order to provide a coherent view of the muon activity. This data is plotted and presented to the user graphically, using a cache to speed up common requests.

Queries on the muon files involve much larger data sets. With potentially up to terabytes of data, and no interdependence between data points, parallelizing the computation becomes a highly attractive option. When a muon-file query is performed, first the necessary data files are identified on the clustered file system. Using Parrot to locate each file system call, the files are grouped by which data server is holding them and a job is dispatched to each such node. The files are then analyzed where the data is located, avoiding the cost of transferring the files over the network. The results of each job are then combined, stored, and plotted for the user.

By using clusters of Chirp servers, the GRAND Data Lab is able to exploit parallel active storing using cost-effective commodity storage devices. Complex workloads consisting of conventional Unix programs can be split into components according to data locality, and run in parallel close to the data that they consume. From the designer's perspective, parallel processing can be achieved without custom programming languages. From the user's perspective, a single click of the mouse easily triggers a large scale data analysis.

CASE STUDY: THE BIOMETRICS RESEARCH GRID

The Computer Vision Research Lab at the University of Notre Dame collects enormous amounts of digital data to support basic research in biometrics. Hundreds of campus volunteers sit for brief weekly recording sessions in order to provide data in many different modes, such as digital finger prints, iris images, 3D recordings, and full motion videos. Researchers developing new identification algorithms can use this large body of data to explore the effectiveness of new algorithms across different populations, and can use data collected over time to perform longitudinal studies.

However, as the scale of data has grown over the years from gigabytes of image data to terabytes of video data, it has become increasingly difficult to manage the data collection, and to select and process appropriate subsets of data. Further, as acquisitions continue over time, the number of instruments and settings increases to the point where it is difficult to evaluate how new collections differ from the old.

To address this data management problem, we have created BXGrid, the Biometrics Research Grid. BXGrid assists with the entire lifecycle of data, from acquisition in the lab, through data inspection and validation, exploration and comparison, composition of workloads, generation of results, and dissemination to outside parties. By providing a structured path for the entire data lifecycle, BXGrid has dramatically increased the performance and accuracy of the entire scientific process.

Figure 7. Architecture of the Biometrics Research Grid

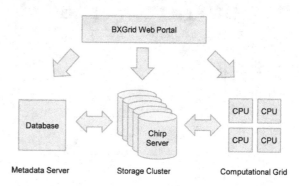

The BXGrid facility consists of four major components shown in Figure 7: a web portal, a relational database, a storage cluster, and a computational grid. Most users interact with the system via a front end web portal, which allows for the interactive browsing of datasets. A typical user might begin by exploring a very large set of data (e.g. all irises), and then successively refine the search based on metadata (e.g. subject demographics or camera type). The results may be browsed visually, saved within the system, or extracted for outside processing. Each recording has a significant amount of metadata stored in the relational database. Some collections have upwards of 50 items per recording, including camera type, subject data, and so forth. Each recording is replicated multiple times in the storage cluster, to ensure both performance and disaster recovery. Small computations are performed directly on the storage cluster, while extensive computations are carried out on the computational grid.

Figure 8 shows more detail of the relationship between the database and the storage cluster. Each scientific data object is known is a **recording**, and is represented as an entry in a table for the corresponding data type. Each recording consists of the metadata in that row of the table, with an associated **file** that contains the actual image or movie data. The file table holds information common to all files, such as the size and checksum. Each file has multiple **replicas**, so a replica table

Figure 8. Relationship between database and storage cluster

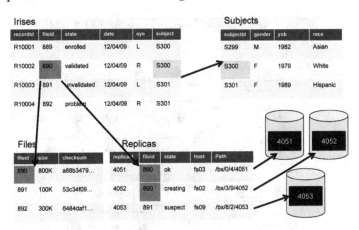

keeps track of the location and status of each one. Replicated data across number of Chirp servers provide multiple access points of the same raw data which allows scalable parallel data paging and fault tolerance. A distributed application can take full advantage of this parallelism to eliminate the data bottleneck. By default, each data object is replicated three times. When application issues a read request, one of the three replicas is chosen to satisfy the request. In case the chosen replica is not reachable for any reason, another replica will be attempted. Likewise, when importing data, if a particular file server is not ready for writing, another one will be employed.

Users access BXGrid through a web portal. The web portal let users navigate the system, validate metadata, and perform other operations. Figure 9 shows an example of a validate page. Validating data is necessary to make sure the metadata is correct and consistent. There are many ways that errors can creep into the manual process of marshalling people into the data collection lab, and capturing a picture or a movie. The validation process confirms metadata by answering metadata questions such as: does image belong to the right subject? or is subject wearing glasses? To ensure high data quality, each recording imported into the system must be validated by a student worker, and then enrolled by a supervisor.

Finally, the system allows users to compose computational workflows that use the archival data as a starting point. A biometrics workflow typically consists of the following steps:

1. **Select** a set S of images and metadata from the repository using the portal.
2. **Transform** the data by applying function F to all members of set S, yielding a set T with the same metadata, but new data.
3. **Compare** all elements in set T using function G, producing a matrix M where each element M[x][y] = G(T[x],T[y]).
4. **Analyze** matrix M to yield a statistic such as an ROC curve.

Each step in the workflow is carried out in a different component of the system: Select occurs in the web portal, Transform occurs in the storage cluster, Compare on the computational grid, and Analyze on the storage cluster again. Using this system, we have carried out the largest known experiment on public iris data, comparing 58,939 iris codes all to each other. The overall workload took 10 days to complete on the computational

Figure 9. Validating irises with the BXGrid Web portal

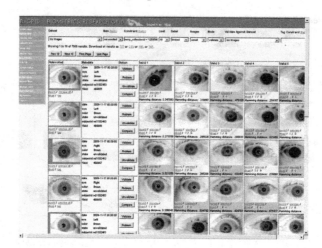

grid, and would have taken years to complete on a single CPU.

CASE STUDY: THE BIOCOMPUTE WEB PORTAL

Bioinformatics research is highly data intensive. Researchers studying problems as varied as evolution, phylogeny, and pathology rely on large databases of genetic information. These databases contain millions of entries, each a DNA string annotated with metadata describing its name, source, location, and function (if known.) Such datasets may be acquired in the lab using sequencing machines, obtained from national data repositories, or derived from other data sets using computational means. Most algorithms that operate on these datasets are I/O bound, and executing them in the ordinary way on a single machine may result in weeks or months of computer time.

To address this problem, we have created Biocompute, a web-based facility for running large scale data intensive bioinformatics tasks (Figure 10). The system allows end users to upload, manage, and share large datasets, alleviating many of the difficulties of data handling. Each dataset is replicated multiple times across a cluster of Chirp

servers, thus maximizing the I/O path to each dataset. Conventional bioinformatics applications are then parallelized, and run close to each copy of the data, dramatically reducing run times. Using Biocompute, applications that would normally take months to run can be completed in hours.

Biocompute includes a modular design that can incorporate a number of conventional bioinformatics tools. It currently supports the widely used tools BLAST and SSAHA, and we are adding support for SHRIMP as well as the SAND genome assembler developed at Notre Dame. In this section, we will describe how Biocompute handles the BLAST application, which is the most widely known and the most heavily used on our system.

Basic Local Alignment Search Tool (BLAST) (Altschul et al., 1990) is a commonly used bioinformatics tool that implements a linear time heuristic to align a set of one or more **query sequences** against a set of **reference sequences** contained in a pre-formatted database. The sequences can be either DNA or amino acid strings, and BLAST has options that permit comparison of any query type to any database type. Since biologists often wish to compare hundreds of thousands of sequences against databases containing up to seven gigabytes of sequence data, these jobs can take

Figure 10. The Biocompute Web portal

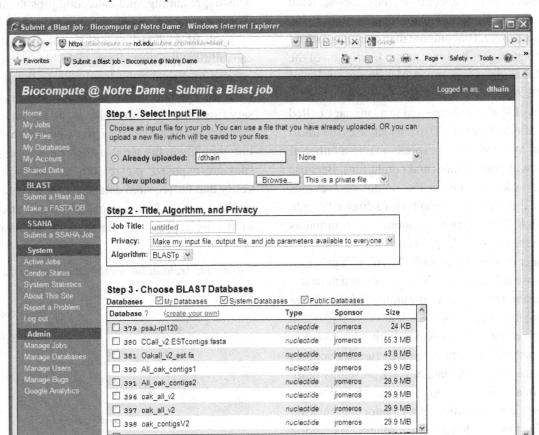

prohibitively long if executed linearly. However, BLAST jobs are naturally parallel in that the output of a BLAST of a set of sequences against a given database is identical to the concatenation of the output of the BLASTs of all disjoint subsets of the query sequences against the same reference database. Since most BLAST jobs are run against the same small subset of databases, it is possible for Biocompute to avoid considerable data transfer overhead by pre-staging BLAST databases to the machines where the subcomputations are expected to take place.

In order to support this type of workload, Biocompute is arranged into three primary components. A single server hosts the website itself, runs the scripts responsible for batch job submission, and stores data from those jobs, including input,

output, logfiles, and executables. A relational database stores metadata for the system including user data, job status, runtime and disk usage statistics, and the name, size, type, permissions, and location of any datasets available through Biocompute. The datasets themselves are stored on a Chirp cluster of 32 machines, which have also been integrated into the Condor distributed computing environment.

A typical Biocompute job is started when a user uploads a set of DNA sequences and selects a reference database against which to compare them. Upon submission, Biocompute copies a template folder containing the set of executables necessary to complete a distributed BLAST into a well known path on the web server. It populates this template folder with the user defined input file and a small file codifying any user-selected job parameters, including the identity of the reference database. Biocompute then executes a script which generates and executes a description of the workflow necessary to complete the execution of the BLAST.

Workloads are expressed in a language called Makeflow (Yu et al., 2010), which uses the traditional Make syntax to express a large number of tasks with related input and output files. Because some tasks depend on the output of previous tasks, the entire workload forms a directed graph. A BLAST Makeflow contains the commands necessary to split the reference sequences into a number of subsets, execute the BLAST program on those subsets using the appropriate databases, concatenate the resulting output, and notify the user of the completion of their job via email. Each subjob in the Makeflow is submitted to Condor, with instructions to preferentially run on machines with the necessary data already present (Figure 11). In addition, the long-running Makeflow coordinator is submitted as a Condor job, making it robust to a wide variety of failures. By having both the Makeflow, which generates and submits jobs, and the jobs themselves in Condor, we are able to maintain a single consistent interface for modifying the job during runtime. This facilitates

pausing, resuming, and canceling jobs in an efficient and intuitive manner.

Each BLAST task makes use of two special capabilities in Chirp. First, the Chirp server is queried to discover the local path to the stored datasets. This permits the job to access the necessary files directly, without having to use an intermediary such as Parrot or the Chirp command line tool. Once the local paths of the necessary files are exposed, the remote task attempts to verify that the required databases are still present on the machine. If not, it makes a single attempt to acquire any missing databases from another

Figure 11. Architecture of the Biocompute facility

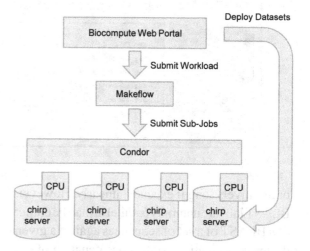

Figure 12. Timeline of a large biocompute workload

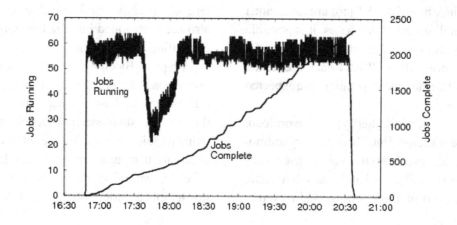

server using third party transfer. If, following this attempt, the machine still lacks necessary files, the process exits and is rescheduled elsewhere via Condor. Otherwise, it runs BLAST on the given query and reference, and returns output or error as appropriate. In some cases, jobs may be interrupted or pre-empted by higher priority users or jobs. Under these circumstances the job reenters the queue and waits to be scheduled to another available machine. Such events affect the performance of the system, shown below. Upon the completion of all job subcomponents, the Makeflow concatenates the results and notifies the user.

Figure 12 shows a graphical depiction of a large biocompute BLAST job that compared 22,767 sequences (total size of 77.3 MB) against a 169.8 MB reference database. Biocompute split this input into 2338 distinct jobs and would have taken 8 days, 17 hours, and 22 minutes if run sequentially. Using biocompute, this job completed in 3 hours and 50 minutes, for a speedup of 53x. Interestingly, a total of 5 hours and 41 minutes of CPU time were lost because a large number of jobs were preempted by a higher priority user at approximately 17:30. However, the system clearly compensated for this problem and robustly completed with workload.

CONCLUSION

As individual CPUs continue to increase in performance and parallelism, we expect that more and more applications that were once CPU-bound will become I/O-bound. To satisfy such applications, cluster design will change from parallel computing devices to parallel I/O devices. We have demonstrated several initial designs for data intensive scientific computing services. Each makes use of the Chirp file server to provide low level storage management, but each uses a different high level interface: GRAND provides a file system, BXGrid provides a database, and Biocompute

provides a batch interface. The appropriate high level interface for such clusters remains an open research question, and we hope to see new and creative solutions emerge from research.

ACKNOWLEDGMENT

We gratefully acknowledge the following people who contributed to the work described in this chapter. Christopher Moretti initially constructed the GRAND repository, contributed to the development of the cluster filesystem, and created the All-Pairs facility used in BXGrid. Robert McKeon and Karen Hollingsworth were early users of the All-Pairs framework. Carl Beyer, Clarence Helm, Christopher Lyon, Michael Kelly, Kameron Srimounghach, Rachel Witty, and Diane Wright contributed to the implementation of BXGrid. Patrick Braga-Henebry created the first version of Biocompute, and Joey Rich, Ryan Jansen, and Andrew Thrasher contributed to its development. This work was supported in part by National Science Foundation grants 0621434 and 0643229

REFERENCES

Altschul, S. F. (1990). Basic local alignment search tool. *Journal of Molecular Biology, 3*(215), 403–410.

Moretti, C. (2007). *Flexible object based filesystems for scientific computing*. M.S. Thesis, University of Notre Dame.

Riedel, E., Gibson, G., & Faloutsos, C. (1998). Active storage for large scale data mining and multimedia. In *Proceedings of Very Large Databases*. VLDB.

Thain, D. (2005). Identity boxing: A new technical for consistent global identity. *IEEE/ACM Supercomputing,* 51-61.

Thain, D., & Livny, M. (2005). Parrot: An application environment for data-intensive computing. *Scalable Computing: Practice and Experience, 6*(3), 9–18.

Thain, D., & Moretti, C. (2007). Efficient access to many small files in a filesystem for Grid computing. In *Proceedings of IEEE Grid Computing,* (pp. 243-250).

Thain, D., Moretti, C., & Hemmes, J. (2009). Chirp: A practical global filesystem for cluster and Grid computing. *Journal of Grid Computing, 7*(1), 51–72. doi:10.1007/s10723-008-9100-5

Yu, L., Moretti, C., Thrasher, A., Emrich, S., Judd, K., & Thain, D. (2010). Harnessing parallelism in multicore clusters with the all-pairs, wavefront, and makeflow abstractions. *Journal of Cluster Computing, 13*(3). doi:10.1007/s10586-010-0134-7

Section 3
Data & Workflow Management

Chapter 7
A Survey of Scheduling and Management Techniques for Data-Intensive Application Workflows

Suraj Pandey
The Commonwealth Scientific and Industrial Research Organisation (CSIRO), Australia

Rajkumar Buyya
The University of Melbourne, Australia

ABSTRACT

This chapter presents a comprehensive survey of algorithms, techniques, and frameworks used for scheduling and management of data-intensive application workflows. Many complex scientific experiments are expressed in the form of workflows for structured, repeatable, controlled, scalable, and automated executions. This chapter focuses on the type of workflows that have tasks processing huge amount of data, usually in the range from hundreds of mega-bytes to petabytes. Scientists are already using Grid systems that schedule these workflows onto globally distributed resources for optimizing various objectives: minimize total makespan of the workflow, minimize cost and usage of network bandwidth, minimize cost of computation and storage, meet the deadline of the application, and so forth. This chapter lists and describes techniques used in each of these systems for processing huge amount of data. A survey of workflow management techniques is useful for understanding the working of the Grid systems providing insights on performance optimization of scientific applications dealing with data-intensive workloads.

DOI: 10.4018/978-1-61520-971-2.ch007

INTRODUCTION

Scientists and researchers around the world have been conducting simulations and experiments as a part of medium to ultra large-scale studies in high-energy physics, biomedicine, climate modeling, astronomy and so forth. They are always seeking cutting-edge technologies to transfer, store and process the data in a more systematic and controlled manner as the data requirements of these applications range from megabytes to petabytes. Thus, to help them manage the complexity of execution, transfer and storage of results of these large-scale applications, the use of a Workflow Management Systems (WfMS) is in wide practice (Yu & Buyya, 2005).

Scheduling and managing computational tasks of a workflow were the main focus of WfMS in the past. With the emergence of globally distributed computing resources and increasing output data from scientific experiments, scientists began to realize the necessity of handling data in conjunction with computational tasks. Scientific workflows were then modeled taking into account the flow of data. However, even with a plethora of techniques and systems, many challenges remain in the area of data management related to workflow creation, execution, and result management (Deelman & Chervenak, 2008; Gil et al., 2007).

Some challenges for managing data-intensive application workflows are:

- High throughput data transfer mechanisms
- Massive, cheap, green and low latency storage solutions and their interfaces
- Composition of scientific applications as workflows
- Multi-core technology and workflow management systems
- Standards for Interoperability between workflow systems
- Globally distributed data and computation resources

In this chapter, we classify and survey techniques that have been used for managing and scheduling data-intensive application workflows to meet the challenges listed above. The classification is based on techniques that take into account data, storage, platform and application characteristics. We sub-divide each general heading into more specific techniques. We then list and describe several work under each sub-heading. Most systems use a combination of existing techniques to achieve the objectives of an application workflow.

The rest of the chapter is organized as follows. In next section, we present previous studies that focused more on systems side of Grid workflows and Data Grids along with their taxonomy. We then describe the terms and definitions used in this chapter followed by an abstract model of a WfMS and its component responsible for data and computation management. In the rest of the chapter, we present the survey. We finally conclude identifying some future trends in management of data-intensive application workflows.

RELATED WORK

Over the last few years, we can find much work being done on data-intensive environments and workflow management systems. We list taxonomies for Data Grid Systems and Workflow management Systems that present the grounds for our survey.

Venugopal, Buyya, & Ramamohanarao (2006) proposed a comprehensive taxonomy of data Grids for distributed data sharing, management and processing. They characterize, classify and describe various aspects of architecture, data transportation, data replication and resource allocation, and scheduling for Data Grids systems. They list the similarities and differences between Data Grids and other distributed data-intensive paradigms such as content delivery networks, peer-to-peer networks, and distributed databases.

Yu & Buyya (2005) proposed taxonomy of workflow management systems for Grid computing. They characterize and classify different approaches for building and executing workflows on Grids. They present a survey of representative Grid workflow systems highlighting their features and pointing out the differences. Their taxonomy focuses on workflow design, workflow scheduling, fault management and data movement.

Bahsi, Ceyhan & Kosar (2007) presented a survey and analysis on conditional workflow management. They studied workflow management systems and their support for conditional structures such as *if, switch and while*. With case studies on existing WfMS, they listed the differences in implementation of common conditional structures. They show that the same structure is implemented in completely different ways by different WfMS. A system or a user can define explicit conditions in the structure of a workflow to manage the data flow across resources and between tasks for data-intensive application workflows.

Yu, Buyya, & Ramamohanarao (2008) listed and described several existing workflow scheduling algorithms developed and deployed in various Grid environments. They categorized the scheduling algorithms as either best effort based or Quality of Service (QoS) constraint based scheduling. Under best-effort scheduling, they presented several heuristics and meta-heuristics based algorithms, which intend to optimize workflow execution times on community Grids. Under QoS constraint based scheduling algorithms, they examined algorithms, which intend to solve performance optimization problems based on two QoS constraints, deadline and budged. They also list some of the techniques we have explicitly described for data-intensive workflows in this chapter.

Kwok & Ahmad (1999) surveyed different static scheduling techniques for scheduling application Directed Acyclic Graphs (DAGs) onto homogeneous platforms. In their model, tasks are scheduled onto multiprocessor systems. The model also assumes that communication is achieved solely by message passing between processing elements. They proposed taxonomy that classified the scheduling algorithms based on their functionality. Their survey also provides examples for each algorithm along with the overview of the software tools for scheduling and mapping.

TERMS AND DEFINITIONS

In this section, we define the terms *data-intensive*, *scientific workflow* and *workflow scheduling* as applicable for scientists working on distributed, heterogeneous, large-scale platforms such as Grids and Clouds.

Data-Intensive

A data-intensive computing environment consists of applications that produce, manipulate, or analyze data in the range of hundreds of megabytes (MB) to petabytes (PB) and beyond (Moore, Prince, & Ellisman, 1998). A data-intensive application workflow has higher data workloads to manage than its computational parts. In other words, the requirements of resource interconnection bandwidth for transferring data outweigh the computational requirements for processing tasks. This, as a consequence, demands more time to transfer and store data as compared to task execution of a workflow. It is common to characterize the distinction between data-intensive and compute-intensive by defining a threshold for the Computation to Communication Ratio (CCR). Applications with lower values of this ratio are distinctly data-intensive in nature.

Scientific Workflow

Standard application components of scientific, data-intensive applications can be combined to process the data in a structured way in contrast to executing monolithic codes (Deelman et al., 2003).

The application is represented as a workflow structure, which consists of tasks, data elements, control sequences and their dependencies. According to Zhao et al. (2008), scientific workflow management systems are engaged and applied to the following aspects of scientific computations: 1) describing complex scientific procedures, 2) automating data derivation processes, 3) high performance computing (HPC) to improve throughput and performance, and 4) provenance management and query.

Workflow Scheduling

In simple terms, a process of mapping of tasks in a workflow (or an entire workflow) to compute resources for execution (preserving dependencies between tasks) is termed as scheduling of workflows. Once the workflow is instantiated in the form of a DAG, middleware technologies, such as Pegasus (Deelman et al., 2005), Gridbus Workflow Management System (Yu & Buyya, 2004) and so forth, are used to schedule the jobs described in the nodes of the DAG onto the specified resources in their specified order. The objectives of scheduling a workflow can vary from application to application. Most often, a data-intensive application workflow is scheduled to optimize the data-transfer time/cost, storage space, total execution time or a combination of these.

Resource Broker

A resource broker is an intermediate entity that acts as a mediator between Grid resources and end users. It performs resource allocation and/or scheduling, and manages execution of applications on behalf of one or multiple users. For instance, the Grid Service Broker (Venugopal, Buyya, & Winton, 2006) developed as part of the Gridbus Project, mediates access to distributed resources by discovering resources, scheduling tasks, monitoring and collating results.

ABSTRACT MODEL OF A WORKFLOW MANAGEMENT SYSTEM

Figure 1 shows the architecture of a Grid workflow system based on the workflow reference model (Hollingsworth, 1994) proposed by Workflow Management Coalition (WfMC) (www.wfmc. org) in 1994. We have extended it to include components that manage data in addition to tasks.

Yu et al. (2005) have described the abstract model in detail, but without the data-centric components. The *build time* and *run time* borders separate the functionality of the design to defining and executing tasks, respectively. At the core of the *run time*, we propose components to actively process both data and tasks equally, different from the model presented by Yu et al. (2005), where data was not given as high priority as tasks.

The scheduler, that forms the core of the engine, handles data flow schedules on top of task schedules. For example, if a workflow is modeled such that the data transfer tasks are separate from computation tasks, the scheduler may apply a different scheduling policy to the data transfer tasks. Similarly, when there is no distinction between these tasks, the scheduler may prioritize data transfers between certain tasks over computation depending on the structure of the workflow, scheduling objectives, and so forth.

We propose to add a *data provenance* (also referred to as lineage and pedigree) manager component to the architecture. It keeps the record of data entities associated with the tasks in a workflow. The scheduler may interact with this component for determining specific data flow paths between tasks and distributed resources. For example, when a workflow is executed a number of times, previously produced data may exist that could be reused. In such cases, intermediate data transfer may not be scheduled for some tasks. Similarly, the scheduler may take reference of provenance data to create/dissolve data transfer and data cleanup tasks for storage aware sched-

Figure 1. An abstract model of a workflow management system

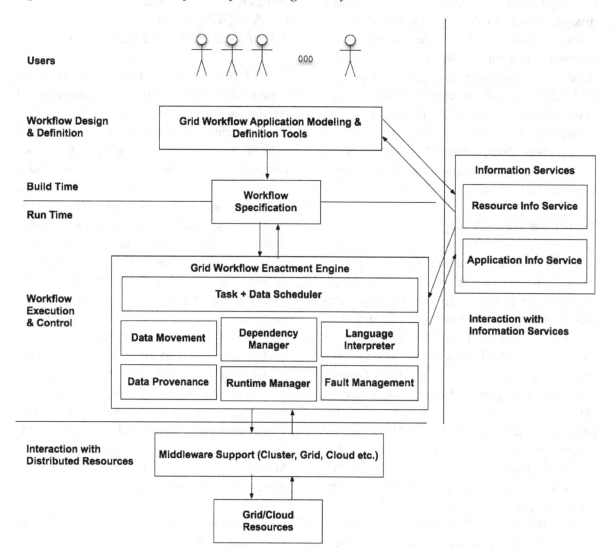

uling. Simmhan, Plale, & Gannon (2005) have surveyed and described systems using provenance for data-intensive environments in greater detail.

We envision each component in the core architecture to handle data as a first class citizen as also proposed by Kosar & Livny (2004). Data movement component, in particular, should be smart enough to overlap data transfer tasks with computation so that wait-times for data-availability is minimized. Data-transfer tasks could be prioritized for different tasks. Similarly, fault tolerance policies should be capable of handling

frequent failures of data transfer tasks. Scheduling steps heavily depend on the capability of data movement and fault tolerance components for data-intensive applications as the repercussions of failure of data transfer tasks can affect the performance of the entire workflow. Different from generic WfMS models, a higher and more sophisticated coordination mechanism is required between these components for handling data-intensive application workflows.

New models for IT service delivery (e.g. Clouds Computing) are emerging. Workflow systems should be capable of interacting with these types of service oriented architectures so that it can better utilize the storage and compute facilities provided by them for optimized data delivery, storage and distributed access. Access and security policies may different than existing Grid infrastructures when resources are from centralized data centers.

SURVEY

In this section, we characterize and classify key concepts and techniques used for scheduling and managing data-intensive application workflows. As shown in Figure 2, we have classified the techniques into seven major categories: (a) data locality, (b) data transfer, (b) data-footprint, (c) granularity, (d) model, (e) platform, (f) miscellaneous technologies. In this section, we describe each of these categories and their branches in detail.

Data Locality

In data-intensive computing environments, the amount of data involved is huge. Transferring data between computing nodes takes significant amount of time depending on the size of data and network capacity between participating nodes. Hence, most scheduling techniques target on optimizing data transfers by exploiting the locality of data. These techniques can be classified into: (a) spatial clustering, (b) task clustering, and (c) worker centric.

Spatial Clustering

Spatial clustering creates a task workflow based on the spatial relationship of files in the input data set. In spatial clustering, clusters of jobs are created based on spatial proximity, each job then assigned to a cluster, each cluster to a grid site and during the execution of the workflow, all jobs scheduled belonging to the cluster to the same site

(Meyer, Annis, Wilde, Mattoso, & Foster, 2006). It improves data reuse and reduces total number of file transfers by clustering together tasks with high input-set overlap. These clustered tasks are scheduled to the resource with the maximum overlap of input data. This reduction benefits the Grid as a whole by reducing traffic between the sites. It also benefits the application by improving its performance.

Meyer et al. (2006) presented a generalized approach to planning spatial workflow schedules for Grid execution based on the spatial proximity of files and the spatial range of jobs. They proposed *SPCL* (for "spatial clustering") algorithm that takes advantage of data locality through the use of dynamic replication and schedule jobs in a manner that reduces the number of replicas created and the number of file transfers performed when executing a workflow. They evaluated their solution to the problem using the file access pattern of an astronomy application that performs *coaddition* of images from the Sloan Digital Sky Survey (SDSS) (*SDSS Project*, 2000).

Brandic, Pllana & Benkner (2006) developed QoS-aware Grid Workflow Language (QoWL), by extending the Business Process Execution Language (BPEL) that allows users to define preferences regarding the execution *location affinity* for activities with specific security and legal constraints. Using QoS parameters that directs the WfMS to restrict the movement of sensitive and proprietary data to only agreed domains is very important for certain kinds of applications. A set of QoS-aware service-oriented components is provided for workflow planning to support automatic constraint-based service negotiation and workflow optimization.

Task Clustering

With task clustering, small tasks are grouped together as one executable unit such that the overhead of data movement can be eliminated. Task clustering groups tasks so that the intermediate

Figure 2. Classification of management techniques for data-intensive application workflows

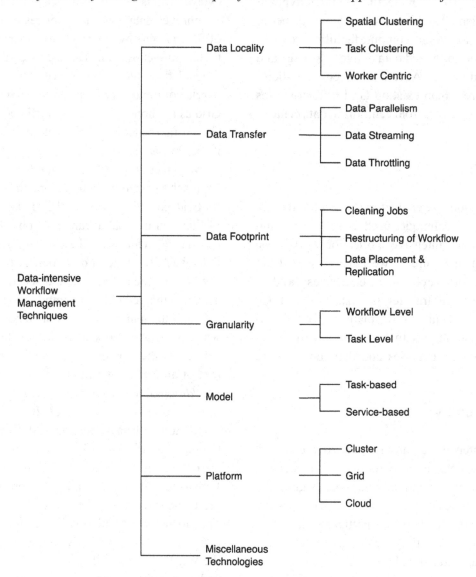

files produced by each task in the group remains in the same computing node the grouped task was submitted to. Other tasks in the same group can now access the file locally. This scheme reduces the need to transfer the intermediate output files in case the tasks in the group were scheduled to different computing nodes. Clustering also eliminates the overhead of running small tasks.

Singh, Kesselman, & Deelman (2005) explored approaches for restructuring of workflows so that the dependencies in the workflow graph can

be reduced. They group independent jobs at the same level into clusters. Their task clustering does not imply that the tasks in a group is scheduled to one processor or executed sequentially. They show workflow performance using clustering with centralized (single submit host) and distributed (multiple submit hosts) job submission. In the centralized submission, the whole workflow is submitted and executed using a single submit host. In order to increase the dispatch rate of jobs for execution, their distributed job submission strategy has a central manager, multiple submit hosts and worker nodes. The workflow is restructured with multiple clusters at each level. The number of clusters at each level is equal to the number of submit hosts in the pool. The schedulers on the submit hosts then try to find suitable nodes for the submitted jobs.

Pandey et al. (2009) used task clustering to schedule data-intensive tasks for a medical application workflow. They clustered tasks based on their execution time, data transfer and level. If tasks were having high deviation and value of average execution time, they were executed without clustering. Tasks with lower deviation and value of execution time were clustered together. They showed that clustering tasks for data-intensive application workflows has better makespan than scheduling the workflow without clustering, mainly attributed to the decrease in file transfers between tasks in the same cluster.

Worker Centric

Worker centric approaches exploit locality of interest present in data-intensive environments. Ko, Morales, & Gupta (2007) presented an algorithm where one global scheduler, upon receiving a request from a worker (computation node), calculates the weight of each unscheduled task and chooses the best task to assign to the requesting worker. The weight calculation procedure takes into account the set of files already present at the worker's site and additional files required by the worker for the task. This scheme exploits locality of file access, and thus minimizes both the number of files that need to be transferred as well as prefers workers that accessed the same files in the past. They proposed both deterministic and randomized metrics that can be used with worker-centric scheduling and found that metrics considering the number of file transfers generally gave better performance over metrics considering the overlap between a task and a storage. They experiment with traces of *Coadd* (*SDSS Project*, 2000).

Data Transfer

Researchers have proposed several mechanisms for transferring data so that data transfer time is minimized. These techniques are: (a) data parallelism, (b) data streaming, and (c) data throttling.

Data Parallelism

Data Parallelism denotes that a service is able to process several data fragments simultaneously with a minimal performance loss. This capability involves the processing of independent data on different computing resources. Glatard, Montagnat, Lingrand, & Pennec (2008) designed and implemented a workflow engine named *MOTEUR*. They propose algorithms that combine well-defined data composition strategies and fully parallel execution. They adopted the Simple Concept Unified Flow Language (SCUFL) as the workflow description language for conveniently describing data flows. In their system, tasks and data are scheduled such that most data sets are processed by independent computing resources, but by preserving the precedence constraints. They evaluated the system using a medical imaging application run on the EGEE (Enabling Grids for E-Science EU IST project, http://www.eu-egee.org) grid.

Data Streaming

In data streaming, real-time data generated through simulation or experiment is delivered in an asynchronous, high-throughput, low-latency and robust way to data analysis and storage machines. Bhat et al. (2007) investigated data streaming for executing scientific workflows on the Grid. They proposed the design, implementation and experimental evaluation of an application level self-managing data streaming service that enables efficient data transport to support Grid-based scientific workflows. The system provides adaptive buffer management mechanisms and proactive QoS management strategies based on model-based online control and user-defined policies. They showed that online data streaming could have significant impact on the performance and robustness of the data-intensive application workflow applications in Grids. They used a fusion simulation workflow consisting of long-running coupled simulations to evaluate the data streaming service and its self-managing behaviors.

Bhat, Parashar, & Klasky (2007) investigated reactive management strategies for in-transit data manipulation for data-intensive scientific and engineering workflows. Their framework for in-transit manipulation consists of processing nodes in the data path between the source and the destination. Each node is capable of processing, buffering and forwarding the data. Each node processes the data depending on its capabilities and the amount of processing still remaining. The data is dynamically buffered as it flows through the node. Eventually the processed data is forwarded until it reaches the sink. The choice between forwarding and further processing is dependent upon the network congestion. They used application level online controllers for high throughput data streaming.

Korkhov et al. (2007) & Afsarmanes et al. (2002) proposed Grid-based Virtual Laboratory AMsterdam (VLAM-G), a data-driven WfMS. Their system uses Globus services (*Globus Project*, 1996) to allow data streams to be established efficiently and transparently between remote processes composing a scientific workflow. The execution engine initiates 'point-to-point' data streams between workflow components allowing intermediate data to flow along the workflow pipeline, without requiring local storage. They use unidirectional, typed streams to ensure that proper connection can be established. Control and monitoring communication is not transmitted on such typed streams. They model the system such that all the resources needed for data stream driven distributed processing have to be made available (e.g. by advance reservation) simultaneously in

contrast to the scenario where Grid resources join and leave anytime.

Data Throttling

Data throttling is a process of describing and controlling when and at what rate data is to be transferred in contrast to moving data from one location to another as early as possible. In scientific workflows with data-intensive workload, individual tasks may have to wait for large amounts of data to be delivered or produced by other tasks. Instead of transferring the data immediately to a task, it can be delayed or transferred using lower capacity links so that the resources can be dedicated to serve other critical tasks.

Park & Humphrey (2008) identified the limitation of current systems in that there is no control available regarding the arrival time and rate of data transfer between nodes. They designed and implemented new capabilities for higher efficiency and balance in Grid workflows by creating a data-throttling framework that regulates the rate of data transfers between the workflow tasks via a specially created QoS-enabled GridFTP server. Their workflow planner constructs a schedule that both specify when/where individual tasks are to be executed, as well as when and at what rate data is to be transferred. The planner allows a workflow programmer/engine to specify the requirements on the data movement delay. This delay helps keep a balance between execution time of workflow branches by eliminating unnecessary bandwidth usage, resulting in more efficient execution.

DAGMan (Directed Acyclic Graph MANager) (*DagMan*, 2002) is a workflow engine under the Pegasus (Deelman et al., 2005) WfMS. It supports job and data throttling using parameters. Pegasus uses DAGMan to run the executable workflow. In DAGMan a "prescript" and a "postscript" step, associated with each workflow job, are responsible for transferring input files and deleting output files, respectively. It controls the number of prescripts that can be concurrently (across all jobs) started using the MAXPRE parameter. This serves as a convenient workflow-wide throttle on the data transfer load that the workflow manager can impose on the Grid from the submit host.

Data Footprint

Workflow systems adopt several mechanisms to track and utilize the data footprint of the application. These mechanisms can be classified into: (a) cleaning jobs, (b) restructuring of workflow, (c) data placement & replication.

Cleaning Jobs

Cleaning jobs are introduced in the workflow to remove the data from the resources once its no longer needed. When applications require large amount of data storage, tasks in the workflow can only be scheduled to those compute resources that can provide temporary storage large enough to hold the input and output files the tasks need. Scheduling decisions should take into consideration the storage capability of the compute resource for all tasks with data-intensive workloads.

Singh et al. (2007) presented two algorithms for reducing the data footprint of workflow type applications. The first algorithm adds a cleanup job for a data file when that file is no longer required by other tasks in the workflow or when it has already been transferred to permanent storage. Given the possibility of data being replicated on multiple resources, the cleanup jobs are made on a per resource basis. The algorithm is applied after the executable workflow has been created, but before it is executed. The second algorithm is an improvement in terms of the number of cleanup jobs and dependencies it adds to the workflow. As the workflow engine has to spend considerable amount of time in managing job execution for every added job or dependency, the authors design the algorithm to reduce the number of cleanup tasks at the possible cost of workflow footprint. This is achieved by adding at most one cleanup node per

computational workflow task in contrast to one cleanup job for every file required or produced by tasks mapped to the resource as done in the first algorithm. They reduce data footprint but as a consequence the workflow execution time increases as a result of the increased number of workflow levels.

Ramakrishnan et al. (2007) proposed an algorithm for scheduling data-intensive application workflows onto storage-constrained resources. Their algorithm first takes into account disk space availability in resources and then prioritizes resources depending on performance. The algorithm starts by identifying all resources that can accommodate the data files needed for a task to be scheduled. If no resource is available that satisfies the space requirement of any ready task, the algorithm halts. It then tries to allocate the task to the resource, which can achieve the earliest finish time (data transfer time and execution time) for the task. Finally it cleans up any unnecessary data file remaining in the resource.

Restructuring of Workflows

The structure of the workflow defines the data footprint. Restructuring of workflows is a transformation of the workflow structure such that it influences the way input/output data is placed, deleted, transferred or replicated during the execution of the workflow. Task clustering, workflow partitioning are common ways to restructure workflows. Tasks can be clustered and dependencies re-defined in such a way that data transfer is minimized, data re-use is maximized, storage resources and compute resources have well-balanced load and so forth.

Singh et al. (2007) defined workflow restructuring as the ordering or sequencing of the execution of the tasks within the workflow. They restructure the workflow primarily to reduce the data footprint of the workflow. They introduce dependencies between stage-in tasks and the previous-level computational tasks. This prevented multiple data transfers from occurring at the same time as soon as tasks become ready.

Pegasus (Deelman et al., 2005) has the capability to map and schedule only portions of the entire workflow at a given time, using partitioning techniques. Deelman et al. (2005) demonstrate the technique using level-based partitioning of the workflow. The levels refer to the depth of the tasks in the workflow. In their Just-in-time planning algorithm (Deelman et al., 2004), Pegasus waits (using DAGMan) to map the dependent workflow until the preceding workflow finishes its execution. Original dependencies are maintained even after partitioning. They also investigate partition-level failure recovery. When resources fail during execution, the entire task is retried and new partitions are not submitted to that resource.

Duan, Prodan, & Fahringer (2006) proposed an algorithm for partitioning a scheduled workflow for distributed coordination among several slave enactment engine services. They incorporated the algorithm in the ASKALON distributed workflow Enactment Engine (Duan et al., 2005). Their purpose of workflow partitioning was to minimize the communication between the master and the slave engines that coordinates the individual partitions of the entire workflow. The partitioning algorithm is based on a graph transformation theory. Partitioning reduced the number of workflow activities and, therefore, the job submission and management latencies and eliminated the data dependencies within partitions. However, the algorithm was used for compute intensive scientific workflows with large numbers of small sized data dependencies. In contrast to Pegasus (Deelman et al., 2005), which partitions the workflow before the scheduling phase, they partition the workflow after scheduling. This results in reduced overheads for job submissions and aggregated file transfers.

Data Placement and Replication

Data placement techniques try to strategically manage placement of data before or during the execution of a workflow. Data placement schedulers can either be coupled or decoupled from task schedulers. Replication of data onto distributed resources is a common way to increase the availability of data. Replication also occurs when scientists download and share the data for experimental purposes, in contrast to explicit replications done by workflow systems. In data-intensive applications, replication may or may not be feasible. Schedulers make the decision of data placement and replication based on the objectives to be optimized. If data analysis workloads have locality of reference, then it is feasible to cache and replicate data at each individual compute node, as high initial data movement costs can be offset by many subsequent data operations performed on cached data (Raicu, Zhao, Foster, & Szalay, 2008).

Kosar et al. (2004) presented Stork, a scheduler for data placement activities in the Grid. They propose to make data placement activities a first class citizen in the Grid. In Stork, data placement is a full-fledged job and decoupled from computational jobs. Users describe the data placement job explicitly in the *classads*. DAGMan (*DagMan*, 2002), a workflow scheduler for Condor, uses Stork for managing these data placement jobs. It manages the dependencies between Condor and Stork jobs as defined by the dependencies in a DAG (Couvares, Kosar, Roy, Weber, & Wenger, 2007). Under Stork, data placement jobs are categorized into three types. *Transfer* jobs are for transferring a complete or partial file from one physical location to another. *Allocate* jobs are used for allocating storage space at the destination site, allocating network bandwidth, or establishing a light-path on the route from source to destination. *Release* jobs are used for releasing the corresponding resource, which was allocated before.

Chervenak et al. (2007) studied the relationship between data placement services and workflow management systems for data-intensive applications. They propose an *asynchronous* mode of data placement in which data placement operations are performed as data sets become available and according to the policies of the virtual organization and not according to the directives of the WfMS. The WfMS can however assist the placement services on placement of data based on information collected during task executions and data collection. Their approach is proactive as it examines current workflow needs to make data placement decisions rather than depending on the popularity of data in the past. They evaluated the benefits of pre-staging data using the data replication service versus using the native data stage-in mechanisms of the Pegasus WfMS (Deelman et al., 2005). Using the Montage astronomy example, they conclude that as the size of data sets increases, pre-staging data increases the performance of the overall analysis.

Shankar & DeWitt (2007) presented architecture for Condor in which the input, output and executable files of jobs are cached on the local disks of machines in a cluster. Caching can reduce the amount of pipeline and batch I/O that is transferred across the network. This in turn significantly reduces the response time for workflows with data-intensive workloads. With caching enabled, data-intensive applications can reuse the files and also be able to compare between old and new versions of the file. They presented a planning algorithm that takes into account the location of cached data together with data dependencies between jobs in a workflow. Their planning algorithm produces a schedule by comparing the time saved by running jobs in parallel with the time taken for transferring data when dependent jobs are scheduled on different machines. By executing the BLAST (http://blast.ncbi.nlm.nih.gov.gov/) application workflow they showed that storing files on the disks of compute nodes significantly improves the performance of data-intensive application workflows.

Ranganathan & Foster (2001, 2002, 2003) conducted extensive studies for identifying dynamic replication strategies, asynchronous data placement and job and data scheduling algorithms for Data Grids. Their replication process at each site periodically generates new replicas for popular datasets. For dataset placement scheduler they define three algorithms: *Data-DoNothing*- no active replication takes place, *DataRandom*- popular datasets are replicated to a random site on the Grid, *DataLeastLoaded*- popular datasets are replicated to a least loaded neighboring site. They proposed to decouple data movement from computation scheduling, also known as asynchronous data placement. This provides opportunity for optimizing both data placement and scheduling decisions, also simplifying the design and implementation of the Data Grid system. They concluded through simulations on independent jobs that scheduling jobs to locations that contain the data they need and asynchronously replicating popular data sets to remote sites achieves better performance than coupled systems.

Granularity

Workflow schedulers can make scheduling decisions based on either: (a) task level, or (b workflow level.

Task level schedulers map individual tasks to compute resources. The decision of resource selection and data movement is based on the characteristics of individual task and its dependencies with other tasks.

Workflow level schedulers map the entire workflow rather than a set of available tasks to compute resources. A workflow's compute and storage requirements guide the scheduler to make a decision on resource selection and data movement.

Blythe et al. (2005) compared several task-based and workflow-based approaches to resource allocation for workflow applications. In their workflow-based approach, the entire workflow is mapped a priori to the resources to minimize the makespan of the whole workflow. The mapping is changed according to the changing environment, if necessary. The mapping of the jobs does not imply scheduling all the jobs ahead of time.

They use a local search algorithm for workflow allocation based on generalized GRASP procedure (Greedy randomized adaptive search) (Feo & Resende, 1995). The final schedule is chosen after an iterative and greedy comparison between alternative schedules. On each iteration, task to resource is mapped based on the minimum margin of increase to the current makespan of the workflow if the task was to be allocated to that resource. This approach is based on the *min-min* (Braun et al., 2001) heuristic. They noticed that during large file transfers, resources spent significant time waiting for all the files to arrive before they could start executing the scheduled jobs. They proposed a *weighted min-min* heuristic that takes into account the idle times of all the resources if a job were to be scheduled to a resource. Based on the weighted sum of the idle times and estimated completion time, a job is mapped to the resource that gives the minimum weighted sum. The step is repeated until all the jobs have been mapped. Due to the pre-mapping, the workflow-based approach could pre-position the data to the known destination by transferring a large file immediately after it is created. In the task-based approach, transfers could not begin until the job is scheduled which happened only after its parent was scheduled. They also simulated the impact of inaccurate estimates of transfer times for data-intensive application workflows. They show that the performance of task-based approach degrades rapidly with increasing uncertainty in comparison to workflow-based approach. Based on these facts, they conclude that workflow-based approaches perform better for data-intensive applications than task-based approaches.

Model

Workflow scheduling model depends on the way the tasks and data are composed and handled. They can be classified into two categories: (a) task-based, and (b) service-based.

Task Based

Task based approaches mention data dependencies explicitly. The workflows are generally complex in structure. Optimizations used by most systems are simple in nature. The WfMS has greater control over the data flow as it can define data placement, cleanup and transfer tasks separately from the workflow tasks. DAGMan (*DagMan*, 2002), Pegasus (Deelman et al., 2005), GridAnt (Laszewski, Amin, Hategan, Hampton, & Rossi, 2004), GrADS (Berman et al., 2005), and Grid-Flow (Cao, Jarvis, Saini, & Nudd, 2003) are some of the workflow systems that support task based approaches. These have been described individually in preceding sections.

Service Based

Service based approaches, also referred to as *meta computing*, wrap application codes into standard interfaces. Such services are hidden from the users and only invocation interface is known. Various interfaces such as Web Services (Alonso, Casati, Kuno, & Machiraju, 2003) or gridRPC (Nakada et al., 2007) have been standardized (Glatard et al., 2008). In this model, the application is described separately from the data. Data is declared as parameters to the service. In this approach, workflows are generally simple in structure. In contrast to task based approaches, workflow systems use complex optimizations. This model is useful when an application workflow is to be repeatedly executed over a large number of varying data sets. Instead of replicating the task for each data set, service based model has the ability to define different data composition strategies over the input data of a service. Kepler system (Ludäscher et al., 2006), the Taverna workbench (Oinn et al., 2004) and the Triana workflow manager (Taylor, Wang, Shields, & Majithia, 2005), are some of the service based workflow systems.

The myGrid project (http://www.mygrid.org.uk/) has developed a comprehensive loosely coupled suite of middleware components specifically to support data-intensive in-silico experiments represented as workflows, using distributed resources. The main tool is the Taverna workbench (Oinn et al., 2004). Taverna allows for the automation of experimental methods through the integration of varying services, including WSDL-based single operation web services, into workflows. It uses FreeFluo (FreeFluo, 2003) as a workflow enactment engine that facilitates intermediate data transfers and service invocations. Workflows are represented using the Simple Conceptual Unified Flow Language (SCUFL). A workflow graph consists of processors, each of which transforms a set of data inputs into a set of data outputs. Using SCUFL, implicit iteration over incoming data sets can be carried out based on user specified strategy. Users can use the Thread property to specify the number of concurrent instances that can send parallel requests to the iteration processor for handling simultaneous processing. This can help reduce the service wait time as workflow engine can send data at the time when the service is still working on previously sent data.

Kepler (Ludäscher et al., 2006) provides support for web service-based workflows. Using an extension of PTOLEMY II (Buck, Ha, Lee, & Messerschmitt, 2002), it uses an actor-oriented design approach for composing and executing scientific application workflows. Computational components are termed as actors, which are linked together to form a workflow. A director represents the interaction between these components. It specifies and mediates all inter-actor communication, separating workflow orchestration and scheduling from individual actor execution. Two of the directors (namely, Synchronous Data Flow (SDF) and Process Networks (PN)) work primarily by controlling the sequencing of actors according to the data availability, to preserve the order of execution of the workflow. The *WebService* actor provides a simple plug-in mechanism to execute any WSDL defined web service. An instantiation of the actor acts as a proxy for the web service

being executed and links to other actors through its ports. Using this component, any application that can be deployed as a remote service, can be used as a Kepler component (Jaeger et al., 2005).

Kalyanam, Zhao, Park, & Goasguen (2007) proposed a web service-enabled distributed data-driven workflow system on top of the TeraGrid (http://www.teragrid.org) infrastructure. The workflow system is based on an existing data management architecture that provides easy access to scientific data collections via the TeraGrid network. It leverages JOpera (Pautasso, 2005), an open-source workflow engine that integrates web services into a processing pipeline. Users can construct data-driven workflows using local or TeraGrid data and computation resources. Their system helps automate the operations such as data discovery, movement, filtering, computationally intensive data processing and so forth, by organizing them as a pipeline so that researchers can execute applications with minimal user interaction.

Brandic, Pllana & Benkner (2008) presented a service-oriented environment, named as Amadeus, for QoS-aware Grid workflows. For data-intensive application workflows QoS parameters may be defined for data-transfer time, reliability, storage requirements, cost and so forth. It allows users to specify QoS constraints at workflow composition, planning and execution stages. Various QoS-aware service components are provided for workflow planning to support automatic constraint-based service negotiation and workflow optimization.

Platform

Data-intensive application workflows could be executed in different resource configuration and environments (e.g. Cluster, Data Grids, Clouds etc.) depending on the requirements of the application.

Clusters are generally composed of homogeneous processors and are under a single domain. For data-intensive applications, clusters provide a viable platform for low cost and enhanced performance. When the data produced and stored are local and not globally shared, cluster based platforms is more feasible than Grids or Clouds.

Data Grids are globally distributed resources for volunteering computing designed for data intensive computing. Data is generated and/or used in research labs distributed globally, giving rise to sharing and re-use. Data grids are feasible for large-scale experiments that are a result of worldwide collaboration of resources and scientists.

Clouds are emerging model for centralized but highly available and powerful infrastructure. Large-scale storage and computation is provided by data-centers. Computing power is achieved by using virtualization technology. Data-intensive applications can highly benefit from using services provided by Clouds as compared to Data Grids and Clusters when factors such as scalability, cost, performance and reliability are important.

In the past, scientific workflows were generally executed on a shared infrastructure such as TeraGrid (http://www.teragrid.org), Open Science Grid (http://www.opensciencegrid.org), and dedicated clusters. In such systems, file system is usually shared for easy data movement. However, this can be a bottleneck for data-intensive operations (Zhao, Raicu, & Foster, 2008).

Deelman, Singh, Livny, Berriman, & Good (2008) presented a simulation-based study of costs involved when executing scientific application workflows using Cloud services. They studied the cost performance tradeoff of different execution and resource provisioning plans, and storage and communication fees of Amazon S3 in the context of an astronomy application Montage. They showed that for a data-intensive application with a small computational granularity, the storage costs were insignificant as compared to the CPU costs. They concluded that cloud computing is cost-effective solution for data-intensive applications.

Broberg, Buyya, & Tari (2008) introduced MetaCDN, which uses 'Storage Cloud' resources to deliver content to content creators at low cost but with high performance (in terms of throughput and response time). Data could be delivered to tasks in a workflow using tools provided by CDN.

In our work with data-intensive application workflows, we studied the performance characteristics of a brain Image Registration workflow (IR) (Pandey et al., 2009). We executed the application on an experimental Grid platform, Grid'5000 (Cappello & Bal, 2007), and profiled each task's execution and data flow. We were able to decrease the makespan of the workflow significantly by using Grid resources. We also used partial data retrieval technique to retrieve data from distributed storage resources while scheduling data-intensive application workflows (Pandey & Buyya, 2011). We proposed static and dynamic heuristics that incorporated the retrieval techniques. We experimented with two synthetic and one real data-intensive application workflow (IR workflow). Executions were done using Virtual Machines (VM) connected through a simulated network environment. Experimental results showed that retrieving data from multiple sources significantly improves the time taken to download data to the execution sites. Cumulative effect thus decreased the total makespan of all the workflows.

Ramakrishnan & Reed (2008) studied the impact of varying resource availability on application performance. They applied *performability* analysis (i.e., a measure of the system's performance in the event of failures) at two levels - computational resources and the network, to obtain the application workflow's overall execution time, given the failure level of resources. They used these values to estimate task completion times during each iteration of the workflow-scheduling algorithm. Their *HYBRID* approach, which takes resource failure and repair into account, performs better than the approach that does not take failures into account, when the failure-to-repair rates increase. Through simulation results, they concluded that the joint analysis of performance and reliability should improve dynamic workflow scheduling and fault tolerance strategies required for Grid and cloud environments.

Miscellaneous

In this Section, we list some technologies that have been used for enhancing the performance of data-intensive application workflows.

Semantic Technology

The myGrid project (http://www.mygrid.org.uk/) exploits semantic web technology to support data-intensive bioinformatics experiments in a grid environment. The semantic description of services in RDF and OWL is used for service discovery and matchmaking. Kepler (Ludäscher et al., 2006) is a data-driven workflow system (as described under the sub heading "Service Based" workflows), which allows semantic annotations of data and actors, and can support semantic transformation of data.

Database Technology

GridDB (Liu & Franklin, 2004) is a grid middleware based on a data centric model for representing workflows and their data. It uses database to store *memo* and *process* tables that store the inputs and outputs of a program that has completed, and process state of executing programs, respectively. It provides functional data modeling language (FDM) for expressing the relationship between programs and their inputs and outputs.

Shankar, Kini, DeWitt, & Naughton (2005) have pointed out the advantages of tightly coupling workflow management systems with data-manipulation for data-intensive scientific programs. They also presented a language for modeling workflows that is tightly integrated with SQL. Data products from workflows are defined in relational format. They use SQL for invocation and querying of programs.

FUTURE DIRECTIONS

Most workflow systems in the past focused on performance of tasks rather than data management. The reason might have been due to cluster management systems and shared storage space. But with globally distributed resources, it is a must these systems take into account the data flow management along with computational tasks. Composition of workflows that is scalable thus remains a challenge. Distributed coordinated execution of globally distributed scientific workflows can then be possible without much hurdle.

Requirements of data-intensive applications can be specified using QoS parameters at all levels of a WfMS. To meet QoS requirements of e-Research application workflows, we need technologies that support (a) QoS-based scheduling of e-Research application workflows on distributed resources, (b) mechanisms for formulating, negotiating and establishing service level agreements (SLA) with resource providers and (c) SLA-based allocation and management of resources. Specifically, we need to:

- Define an architectural framework and principles for the development of QoS-based workflow management and SLA-based resource allocation systems,
- Develop QoS-based algorithms for scheduling e-Research workflow applications,
- Develop SLA-based negotiation protocols and resource allocation algorithms.

With the advent of virtualization technologies, Cloud storage systems, content delivery networks (CDN) and so forth, it is likely that big scientific projects will start using services provided by third parties for storing and processing application data. As companies such as Amazon, IBM, and Google are innovating the use of their huge data centers for commercial use as Cloud services, data-intensive applications may leverage their utilities and not depend on conventional, error-prone, costly and unreliable solutions (Buyya, Yeo and Venugopal, 2008). However, due to higher usage and access costs of these commercial services, small-scale scientific projects may still need to rethink of deploying their application on Clouds.

CONCLUSION

In this chapter, we classified and surveyed techniques for managing and scheduling data-intensive application workflows. Under each classification, there were several specific techniques that workflow systems used for executing data-intensive application workflows on globally distributed resources. We listed and described each such work in detail. We found that most systems focused on minimizing data transfers and optimally structuring model of execution to subdue the effect of large data requirements of most scientific data-intensive applications. We also found that many systems used a combination of techniques we listed to achieve higher scalability, fault tolerance, lower costs and increase performance. A single technique alone would not suffice to minimize the effect of increasing data processing requirements of scientific applications. Due to the lack of standardization and interoperability, many of the systems were developed in isolation. As a result, techniques for managing data for data-intensive workflows were mixed and duplicated. Nevertheless, scientific community has been able to successfully achieve the goals of all scientific projects with promising results, where PetaByes of data play a major role. This was only possible due to the seamless effort put on for the development of workflow management systems that manages data and tasks for most scientific applications.

ACKNOWLEDGMENT

This work is partially supported through Australian Research Council (ARC) Discovery Project grant. We also thank Ivona Brandic from University of Vienna, Austria; Marcos Assunção, Srikumar Venugopal, Rajiv Ranjan and Marco A.S. Netto from The University of Melbourne, Australia for their valuable comments.

REFERENCES

Afsarmanesh, H., Belleman, R. G., Belloum, A. S. Z., Benabdelkader, A., Brand, J. F. J., & van den Eijkel, G. B. (2002). Vlam-g: A grid-based virtual laboratory. *Science Progress*, *10*(2), 173–181.

Alonso, G., Casati, F., Kuno, H., & Machiraju, V. (2003). *Web services - Concepts, architectures and applications*. Springer.

Bahsi, E. M., Ceyhan, E., & Kosar, T. (2007). Conditional workflow management: A survey and analysis. *Science Progress*, *15*(4), 283–297.

Berman, F., Casanova, H., Chien, A., Cooper, K., Dail, H., & Dasgupta, A. (2005). New grid scheduling and rescheduling methods in the grads project. *International Journal of Parallel Programming*, *33*(2), 209–229. doi:10.1007/s10766-005-3584-4

Bhat, V., Parashar, M., & Klasky, S. (2007). Experiments with in-transit processing for data intensive grid workflows. In *GRID* (pp. 193-200). IEEE.

Bhat, V., Parashar, M., Liu, H., Kandasamy, N., Khandekar, M., & Klasky, S. (2007). A self-managing wide-area data streaming service. *Cluster Computing*, *10*(4), 365–383. doi:10.1007/s10586-007-0023-x

Blythe, J., Jain, S., Deelman, E., Gil, Y., Vahi, K., Mandal, A., et al. (2005). Task scheduling strategies for workflow-based applications in grids. In *CCGRID '05: Proceedings of the Fifth IEEE International Symposium on Cluster Computing and the Grid (CCGrid'05) - Volume 2* (pp. 759–767). Washington, DC: IEEE.

Brandic, I., Pllana, S., & Benkner, S. (2006). An approach for the high-level specification of qos-aware grid workflows considering location affinity. *Science Progress, 14*(3/4), 231–250.

Brandic, I., Pllana, S., & Benkner, S. (2008). Specification, planning, and execution of qos-aware grid workflows within the Amadeus environment. *Concurrent Computing: Practice and Experience, 20*(4), 331–345. doi:10.1002/cpe.1215

Braun, T. D., Siegel, H. J., Beck, N., Boloni, L. L., Maheswaran, M., & Reuther, A. I. (2001). A comparison of eleven static heuristics for mapping a class of independent tasks onto heterogeneous distributed computing systems. *Journal of Parallel and Distributed Computing, 61*(6), 810–837. doi:10.1006/jpdc.2000.1714

Broberg, J., Buyya, R., & Tari, Z. (2008, August). *MetaCDN: Harnessing 'storage clouds' for high performance content delivery* (Tech. Rep. No. GRIDS-TR-2008-11). GRIDS Lab: The University of Melbourne.

Buck, J., Ha, S., Lee, E. A., & Messerschmitt, D. G. (2002). *Ptolemy: A framework for simulating and prototyping heterogeneous systems* (pp. 527–543). Norwell, MA: Kluwer Academic Publishers.

Buyya, R., Yeo, C. S., & Venugopal, S. (2008). Market-oriented cloud computing: Vision, hype, and reality for delivering it services as computing utilities. In *HPCC '08: Proceedings of the 2008 10th IEEE International Conference on High Performance Computing and Communications,* (pp. 5-13). Washington, DC: IEEE.

Cao, J., Jarvis, S. A., Saini, S., & Nudd, G. R. (2003). Gridflow: Workflow management for grid computing. In *CCGRID '03: Proceedings of the 3st International Symposium on Cluster Computing and the Grid* (pp. 198–205). Washington, DC, USA.

Cappello, F., & Bal, H. (2007). Toward an international "computer science grid". In *CCGRID '07: Proceedings of the Seventh IEEE International Symposium on Cluster Computing and the Grid* (pp. 3–12). Washington, DC: IEEE.

Chervenak, A., Deelman, E., Livny, M., Su, M.-H., Schuler, R., Bharathi, S., et al. (2007, September). Data placement for scientific applications in distributed environments. In *Proceedings of the 8th IEEE/ACM International Conference on Grid Computing (Grid 2007)*. Austin, TX: IEEE.

Couvares, P., Kosar, T., Roy, A., Weber, J., & Wenger, K. (2007, January). Workflow management in condor. In Workflows for e-Science (pp. 357–375). London, UK: Springer. doi:10.1007/978-1-84628-757-2_22

DagMan. (2002). *Online*. Retrieved from http://www.cs.wisc.edu/condor/dagman/

Deelman, E., Blythe, J., Gil, Y., Kesselman, C., Mehta, G., Patil, S., et al. (2004). Pegasus: Mapping scientific workflows onto the grid. In *European Across Grids Conference* (vol. 3165, pp. 11–20). Springer.

Deelman, E., Blythe, J., Gil, Y., Kesselman, C., Mehta, G., & Vahi, K. (2003). Mapping abstract complex workflows onto grid environments. *Journal of Grid Computing, 1*(1), 25–39. doi:10.1023/A:1024000426962

Deelman, E., & Chervenak, A. (2008). Data management challenges of data-intensive scientific workflows. In *CCGRID '08: Proceedings of the 2008 Eighth IEEE International Symposium on Cluster Computing and the Grid (CCGRID)* (pp. 687–692). Washington, DC: IEEE Computer Society.

Deelman, E., Singh, G., Livny, M., Berriman, B., & Good, J. (2008). The cost of doing science on the cloud: The montage example. In *SC '08: Proceedings of the 2008 ACM/IEEE Conference on Supercomputing* (pp. 1–12). Piscataway, NJ: IEEE.

Deelman, E., Singh, G., Su, M.-H., Blythe, J., Gil, Y., & Kesselman, C. (2005). Pegasus: A framework for mapping complex scientific workflows onto distributed systems. *Science Progress, 13*(3), 219–237.

Duan, R., Fahringer, T., Prodan, R., Qin, J., Villazon, A., & Wieczorek, M. (2005, February). *Real world workflow applications in the Askalon grid environment.* In European Grid Conference (EGC 2005). Springer Verlag.

Duan, R., Prodan, R., & Fahringer, T. (2006). Runtime optimisation of grid workflow applications. In *GRID* (pp. 33-40). IEEE.

Feo, T. A., & Resende, M. G. (1995, March). Greedy randomized adaptive search procedures. *Journal of Global Optimization, 6*(2), 109–133. doi:10.1007/BF01096763

FreeFluo. (2003). *Online.* Retrieved from http://freefluo.sourceforge.net/

Gil, Y., Deelman, E., Ellisman, M., Fahringer, T., Fox, G., & Gannon, D. (2007). Examining the challenges of scientific workflows. *Computer, 40*(12), 24–32. doi:10.1109/MC.2007.421

Glatard, T., Montagnat, J., Lingrand, D., & Pennec, X. (2008). Flexible and efficient workflow deployment of data-intensive applications on grids with moteur. *International Journal of High Performance Computing Applications, 22*(3), 347–360. doi:10.1177/1094342008096067

Globus Project. (1996). *Online.* Retrieved from http://www.globus.org/

Hollingsworth, D. (1994). *The workflow reference model. (Tech. Rep. No. TCOO- 1003).* Workflow Management Coalition.

Jaeger, E., Altintas, I., Zhang, J., Ludäscher, B., Pennington, D., & Michener, W. (2005). A scientific workflow approach to distributed geospatial data processing using web services. In *SSDBM'2005: Proceedings of the 17th International Conference on Scientific and Statistical Database Management* (pp. 87–90). Berkeley, CA: Lawrence Berkeley Laboratory.

Kalyanam, R., Zhao, L., Park, T., & Goasguen, S. (2007). A web service-enabled distributed workflow system for scientific data processing. In *FTDCS '07: Proceedings of the 11th IEEE International Workshop on Future Trends of Distributed Computing Systems* (pp. 7–14). Washington, DC: IEEE.

Ko, S. Y., Morales, R., & Gupta, I. (2007). New worker-centric scheduling strategies for data-intensive grid applications. In Cerqueira, R., & Campbell, R. H. (Eds.), *Middleware* (*Vol. 4834*, pp. 121–142). Springer. doi:10.1007/978-3-540-76778-7_7

Korkhov, V., Vasyunin, D., Wibisono, A., Belloum, A. S. Z., Inda, M. A., & Roos, M. (2007). Vlam-g: Interactive data driven workflow engine for grid-enabled resources. *Science Progress, 15*(3), 173–188.

Kosar, T., & Livny, M. (2004). Stork: Making data placement a first class citizen in the grid. In *ICDCS '04: Proceedings of the 24th International Conference on Distributed Computing* Systems *(ICDCS'04)* (pp. 342–349). Washington, DC: IEEE.

Kwok, Y. K., & Ahmad, I. (1999). Static scheduling algorithms for allocating directed task graphs to multiprocessors. *ACM Computing Surveys, 31*(4), 406–471. doi:10.1145/344588.344618

Laszewski, G. V., Amin, K., Hategan, M., Hampton, N. J. Z. S., & Rossi, A. (2004, January). Gridant: A client-controllable grid workflow system. In *37th Hawaii International Conference on System Science (HICSS'04)* (pp. 5–8). IEEE.

Liu, D. T., & Franklin, M. J. (2004). Griddb: A data-centric overlay for scientific grids. In *VLDB '04: Proceedings of the Thirtieth International Conference on Very Large Data Bases* (pp. 600–611). VLDB Endowment.

Ludäscher, B., Altintas, I., Berkley, C., Higgins, D., Jaeger, E., & Jones, M. (2006). Scientific workflow management and the kepler system: Research articles. *Concurrency and Computation, 18*(10), 1039–1065.

Meyer, L., Annis, J., Wilde, M., Mattoso, M., & Foster, I. (2006). Planning spatial workflows to optimize grid performance. In *SAC '06: Proceedings of the 2006 ACM Symposium on Applied Computing* (pp. 786–790). New York, NY: ACM.

Moore, R., Prince, T. A., & Ellisman, M. (1998). Data-intensive computing and digital libraries. *Communications of the ACM, 41*(11), 56–62. doi:10.1145/287831.287840

Nakada, H., Matsuoka, S., Seymour, K., Dongarra, J., Lee, C., & Casanova. (2007, June). *A GridRPC model and API for end-user applications.* GridRPC Working Group of Global Grid Forum.

Oinn, T., Addis, M., Ferris, J., Marvin, D., Senger, M., & Greenwood, M. (2004, November). Taverna: A tool for the composition and enactment of bioinformatics workflows. *Bioinformatics (Oxford, England), 20*(17), 3045–3054. doi:10.1093/bioinformatics/bth361

Pandey, S, & Buyya. R. (2011, in press). Scheduling Workflow Applications based on Multi-Source Parallel Data Retrieval in Distributed Computing Networks, *The Computer Journal.*

Pandey. S, Voorsluys, W., Rahman, M., Buyya, R., Dobson, J., Chiu, K. (2009, November) A Grid Workflow Environment for Brain Imaging Analysis on Distributed Systems. *Concurrency and Computation: Practice and Experience, 21*(16), 2118-2139.

Pautasso, C. (2005). Jopera: An agile environment for Web service composition with visual unit testing and refactoring. In *VLHCC '05: Proceedings of the 2005 IEEE Symposium on Visual Languages and Human-Centric Computing* (pp. 311–313). Washington, DC: IEEE Computer Society.

Raicu, I., Zhao, Y., Foster, I. T., & Szalay, A. (2008). Accelerating large-scale data exploration through data diffusion. In *DADC '08: Proceedings of the 2008 International Workshop on Data-Aware Distributed Computing* (pp. 9–18). New York, NY: ACM.

Ramakrishnan, A., Singh, G., Zhao, H., Deelman, E., Sakellariou, R., Vahi, K., et al. (2007). Scheduling data-intensive workflows onto storage-constrained distributed resources. In *CCGrid '09: Proceedings of the 7th IEEE Symposium on Cluster Computing and The Grid* (pp. 14–17). Brazil: IEEE.

Ramakrishnan, L., & Reed, D. A. (2008). Performability modeling for scheduling and fault tolerance strategies for scientific workflows. In *HPDC '08: Proceedings of the 17th International Symposium on High Performance Distributed Computing* (pp. 23–34). New York, NY: ACM.

Ranganathan, K., & Foster, I. (2002). Decoupling computation and data scheduling in distributed data-intensive applications. In *Proceedings of the 11th IEEE International Symposium on High Performance Distributed Computing*. USA: IEEE.

Ranganathan, K., & Foster, I. (2003, March). Simulation studies of computation and data scheduling algorithms for data grids. *Journal of Grid Computing, 1*(1), 53–62. doi:10.1023/A:1024035627870

Ranganathan, K., & Foster, I. T. (2001). Identifying dynamic replication strategies for a high- performance data grid. In *Proceedings of the Second International Workshop on Grid Computing*. UK: Springer-Verlag.

SDSS Project. (2000). *Online*. Retrieved from https://www.darkenergysurvey.org

Shankar, S., & DeWitt, D. J. (2007). Data driven workflow planning in cluster management systems. In *HPDC '07: Proceedings of the 16th International Symposium on High Performance Distributed Computing* (pp. 127–136). New York, NY: ACM.

Shankar, S., Kini, A., DeWitt, D. J., & Naughton, J. (2005). Integrating databases and workflow systems. *SIGMOD Record, 34*(3), 5–11. doi:10.1145/1084805.1084808

Simmhan, Y. L., Plale, B., & Gannon, D. (2005, September). A survey of data provenance in e-science. *SIGMOD Record, 34*(3), 31–36. doi:10.1145/1084805.1084812

Singh, G., Kesselman, C., & Deelman, E. (2005, September). Optimizing grid-based workflow execution. *Journal of Grid Computing, 3*(3-4), 201–219. doi:10.1007/s10723-005-9011-7

Singh, G., Vahi, K., Ramakrishnan, A., Mehta, G., Deelman, E., & Zhao, H. (2007). Optimizing workflow data footprint. *Science Progress, 15*(4), 249–268.

Taylor, I., Wang, I., Shields, M., & Majithia, S. (2005). Distributed computing with triana on the grid: Research articles. *Concurrency and Computation, 17*(9), 1197–1214. doi:10.1002/cpe.901

Venugopal, S., Buyya, R., & Ramamohanarao, K. (2006). A taxonomy of data grids for distributed data sharing, management, and processing. *ACM Computing Surveys, 38*(1). doi:10.1145/1132952.1132955

Venugopal, S., Buyya, R., & Winton, L. (2006). A grid service broker for scheduling e-science applications on global data grids: Research articles. *Concurrency and Computation, 18*(6), 685–699. doi:10.1002/cpe.974

Yu, J., & Buyya, R. (2004). A novel architecture for realizing grid workflow using tuple spaces. *Proceedings of the Fifth IEEE/ACM International Workshop on Grid Computing*.

Yu, J., & Buyya, R. (2005). A taxonomy of scientific workflow systems for grid computing. *SIGMOD Record, 34*(3), 44–49. doi:10.1145/1084805.1084814

Yu, J., Buyya, R., & Ramamohanarao, K. (2008). Workflow scheduling algorithms for grid computing. In *Metaheuristics for Scheduling in Distributed Computing Environments* (*Vol. 146*, pp. 173–214). Berlin, Germany: Springer. doi:10.1007/978-3-540-69277-5_7

Zhao, Y., Raicu, I., & Foster, I. (2008). Scientific workflow systems for 21st century, new bottle or new wine? In *SERVICES '08: Proceedings of the 2008 IEEE Congress on Services - Part I* (pp. 467–471). Washington, DC: IEEE.

Chapter 8
Data Management in Scientific Workflows

Ewa Deelman
University of Southern California, USA

Ann Chervenak
University of Southern California, USA

ABSTRACT

Scientific applications such as those in astronomy, earthquake science, gravitational-wave physics, and others have embraced workflow technologies to do large-scale science. Workflows enable researchers to collaboratively design, manage, and obtain results that involve hundreds of thousands of steps, access terabytes of data, and generate similar amounts of intermediate and final data products. Although workflow systems are able to facilitate the automated generation of data products, many issues still remain to be addressed. These issues exist in different forms in the workflow lifecycle. This chapter describes a workflow lifecycle as consisting of a workflow generation phase where the analysis is defined, the workflow planning phase where resources needed for execution are selected, the workflow execution part, where the actual computations take place, and the result, metadata, and provenance storing phase. The authors discuss the issues related to data management at each step of the workflow cycle. They describe challenge problems and illustrate them in the context of real-life applications. They discuss the challenges, possible solutions, and open issues faced when mapping and executing large-scale workflows on current cyberinfrastructure. They particularly emphasize the issues related to the management of data throughout the workflow lifecycle.

DOI: 10.4018/978-1-61520-971-2.ch008

INTRODUCTION

Scientific applications such as those in astronomy, earthquake science, gravitational-wave physics, and others have embraced workflow technologies to do large-scale science (Taylor, et al. editors, 2006). Workflows enable researchers to collaboratively design, manage, and obtain results that involve hundreds of thousands of steps, access terabytes of data, and generate similar amounts of intermediate and final data products. Although workflow systems are able to facilitate the automated generation of data products, many issues still remain to be addressed (Gil, Deelman et al. 2007). These issues exist in different forms in the *workflow lifecycle* (Deelman and Gil 2006). We describe the workflow lifecycle as consisting of a workflow generation phase where the analysis is defined, the workflow planning phase where resources needed for execution are selected, the workflow execution part, where the actual computations take place, and the result, metadata, and provenance storing phase.

During workflow creation, appropriate input data and workflow components need to be discovered. During workflow mapping and execution, data need to be staged-in and staged-out of the computational resources. As data are produced, they need to be archived with enough metadata and provenance information so that they can be interpreted and shared among collaborators. This chapter describes the workflow lifecycle and discusses the issues related to data management at each step. We describe challenge problems and, where possible, illustrate them in the context of the following applications: the Southern California Earthquake Center (SCEC) CyberShake (Maechling, Chalupsky et al. 2005), an earthquake science computational platform; Montage (Berriman, Deelman et al. 2004), an astronomy application; and the Laser Interferometer Gravitational Wave Observatory's (LIGO) binary inspiral search (Brown, Brady et al. 2006), a gravitational-wave physics application. These computations, rep-

resented as workflows, are running on today's national cyberinfrastructure and use workflow technologies such as Pegasus (Deelman, Mehta et al. 2006) and DAGMan (Couvares, Kosar et al. 2006) to map high-level workflow descriptions onto the available resources and execute the resulting computations. This chapter describes the challenges, possible solutions, and open issues faced when mapping and executing large-scale workflows on current cyberinfrastructure. We particularly emphasize the issues related to the management of data throughout the workflow lifecycle. In addition to presenting these issues, we describe particular solutions and existing approaches to the problem.

WORKFLOW CREATION

From the point of view of data, the workflow lifecycle includes the following transformations (see Figure 1): data discovery, setting up the data processing pipeline, generation of derived data, and archiving of derived data and its provenance. Data analysis is often a collaborative process or is conducted within the context of a scientific collaboration. An example of such a large-scale collaboration is the LIGO scientific Collaboration (LSC), which brings together physicists from around the world in a joint effort to detect gravitational waves emitted by celestial objects (Barish and Weiss 1999). In astronomy, projects such as Montage develop community-wide image services. In earthquake science, scientists bring together community models to understand complex wave propagation phenomena.

Data and Software Discovery

Scientists in a collaboration frequently submit workflows to process data sets and derive scientific knowledge. These collaborators may submit related workflows and build upon earlier work by other scientists. Thus, scientists need to be able to

Figure 1. Data lifecycle in a workflow

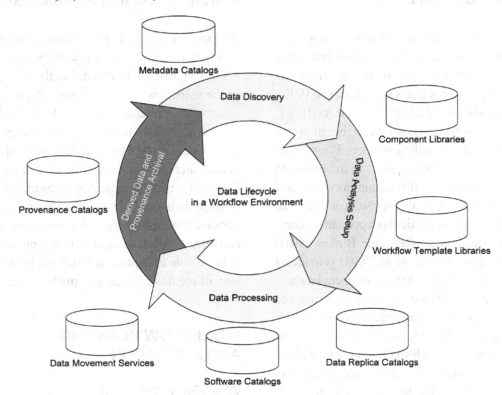

discover information about workflows that have been run in the past, identify data sets of interest, and locate analysis code and workflow templates. In the workflow creation stage, they identify data sets and analysis code of interest by unique logical identifiers or metadata, independent of where these data sets or analysis codes may be physically located in the distributed environment. Discovery of data sets, application codes, workflow templates, etc., is often done by querying various catalogs. *Metadata catalogs* store attributes that describe the contents of data sets. *Provenance catalogs* (Miles, Groth et al. 2006) store information about computations and workflows to provide a detailed record of how analyses are run, including information about inputs to computations, application parameters used, calibration values for equipment, versions of workflow and analysis software used, etc.

Community Standards

A challenging aspect of setting up these discovery catalogs is the need for communities to agree on standards for specifying metadata and provenance. Often, scientists in an application domain spend great effort to agree on a metadata ontology that is rich enough to describe the meaning of data sets used and generated in the domain. Some of the most successful efforts have been made in bioinformatics, where scientists are not only defining metadata standards but also sharing descriptions of services used in workflows as well as workflows themselves, for example, as part of myExperiment (Goble and De Roure 2007). Similar standards need to be defined in other scientific domains, including standards to describe software characteristics, inputs, outputs, and versions.

Metadata Catalogs

Many application communities have deployed their own metadata catalogs to store and query metadata attributes using relational databases or RDF triple stores (Lassila and Swick 1999), including LIGO and the Earth System Grid (ESG) (Middleton 2006), a scientific collaboration that supports climate modeling science. The schema for these databases corresponds to the metadata ontology defined by the community. Several systems provide general metadata catalogs that are independent of particular application communities. The Storage Resource Broker (SRB) system (Rajasekar, Wan et al. 2003) provides a catalog called MCAT that stores metadata and is also used to coordinate data accesses, enforce access permissions and maintain consistency for replicated data. The Metadata Catalog Service (Deelman 2004) provides a set of generic and extensible metadata attributes. Even though metadata technologies exist, the biggest challenge is for the scientific communities to decide on common definitions of terms.

Data Provenance

Data provenance technologies are still being developed (Moreau and Ludaescher 2007). A challenge in the provenance area is the ability of users and workflow systems to interpret provenance information produced by a different or unfamiliar workflow system. To facilitate data discovery where data have been produced by different systems, an effort to standardize on data provenance representation is underway (Moreau, Freire et al. 2007; Moreau, Lud et al. 2007). Recently, the W3C Provenance Interchange Working Group took up the standardization effort. Once standards are in place, the challenge for the workflow systems will be to implement them.

Workflow Creation Provenance

An interesting aspect of workflow creation is the ability to re-trace how a particular workflow has been designed, or to determine the provenance of the workflow creation process. A particularly interesting approach is taken in Vistrails (Freire, Silva et al. 2006) where the user is presented with a graphical interface for workflow creation and the system incrementally saves the state of the workflow as it is being designed. As a result, users may re-trace their steps in the design process, choose various "flavors" of the same workflow and try and retry different designs. An ongoing challenge is to be able to capture not only the how but the why of the design decisions made by the users.

WORKFLOW PLANNING AND EXECUTION

Workflow Data and Component Selection

During workflow creation, scientists specify the applications or workflows they want to run and the input data sets for these computations using unique logical identifiers. In the workflow planning stage, these logical identifiers for applications and data must be mapped to resources in the distributed environment (see Figure 2). For data sets that are inputs to workflows or analysis, this requires discovering the location of one or more copies of the desired data sets, selecting among them, and often copying or staging the data sets onto resources where computations will run. For analysis codes, this requires finding where the code exists and possibly transferring the code to the location where the computation will run. A scheduler is responsible for selecting among available data sets, selecting appropriate computational resources to run each task of a workflow, and orchestrating the movement of data sets and the execution of workflow tasks. Schedulers or

Figure 2. View of the distributed data environment

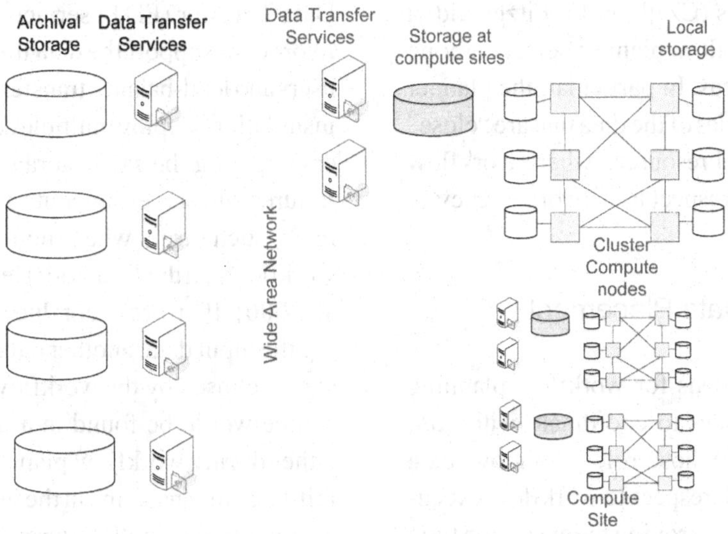

workflow mappers attempt to optimize workflows based on user-specified criteria (Sakellariou, Zhao et al.; Wieczorek, Prodan et al. 2005).

Data Dependencies

In the workflow execution stage, an execution manager such as DAGMan keeps track of tasks that must run and the dependencies among them. Earlier tasks in the workflow may produce intermediate data products that are consumed by tasks that run later. These intermediate data products may need to be staged from the resource where the earlier task ran to the resource on which the later task will run. The workflow execution system delays execution of a particular task until all its input data products are available on the computational resources where the task will run.

Challenges of workflow planning and execution include finding available resources whose capabilities match the requirements of the workflow. This in turn requires up-to-date information about the current state of each resource, so that computational tasks or data transfer jobs are not assigned to resources that are already heavily loaded or are temporarily unavailable.

Distributed Data Environment

A major challenge in today's applications is the physical management of data in the distributed environment. Although the processing power may be available, getting the data to that computational resource may be time consuming and error-prone. Most often, data are stored in archives and staged to the computational sites on demand. In case of LIGO, data are archived at each computational site within the collaboration. If the workflows execute on the Open Science Grid, data need to be staged-in from one of the LIGO sites. Within the computational site, often a cluster, we also distinguish between shared storage and storage local to a computational node.

Identifying the location of desired data sets is a challenge in this type of distributed environment. Typically, replica location (Chervenak 2002; Chervenak 2004; Chervenak 2009) or metadata catalogs (Rajasekar, Wan et al. 2003; Deelman 2004) record mappings from logical identifiers for data to one or more physical locations where copies of the data sets are stored. Based on knowledge of the state of resources (the latency, bandwidth and load of storage systems, network bandwidth among nodes, etc.) that may be provided by information services (Czajkowski, Fitzgerald et al. 2001), the workflow planner selects among available data replicas. In particular, the planner may try to select copies of the data that are "close" to the computational resources where workflow tasks will run, with respect to network latency or other metrics.

Asynchronous Data Placement

It may be advantageous for workflow planning and execution services to coordinate with *data placement services*, whose role is to move data asynchronously with respect to workflow execution with the goal of improving the execution time of workflows. For example, a workflow engine might provide hints to a data placement service about required data sets as well as the expected ordering of data set access, based on knowledge or dependencies in the workflow. Based on these hints, the placement engine can asynchronously stage some of the data required by the workflow engine onto shared storage resources near where the workflow tasks will execute. In earlier work, we demonstrated the potential advantage of pre-staging data sets that are needed for workflow execution (Chervenak 2007). We showed that such pre-staging of input data reduced the execution time of data-intensive workflows considerably.

In current work, we are exploring a range of data placement algorithms for staging data off of storage resources after execution is complete as well as for pre-staging data onto resources before execution begins. We are interested in various approaches to the design of placement services, ranging from workflow and placement services that are tightly integrated to those that have relatively little communication or interaction.

Data Transfer Challenges

Workflows rely on a variety of data transfer mechanism over the wide area. These include such tools as GridFTP (Allcock, Bester et al. 2001), the Fast Data Transfer (FDT) service (2007), and others. In order to support the data transfer needs of their users and load-balance transfer requests, many grid installations deploy multiple data movement servers targeting the same storage system. However, failures and server timeouts still occur. We found many such errors when running the CyberShake workflows on the TeraGrid (Deelman, Callaghan et al. 2006). If errors occur due to problems accessing the input data, another data source (if it exists) can be chosen by the workflow system. This data source would be found in a data replica catalog either during workflow planning or as part of the fall-back mechanisms in the workflow execution. In order to deal with failures at the destination, a simple retry can be performed by the workflow system, or a different data transfer server can be chosen for the data movement. Retries are able to deal with temporary server overloads, transient network failures, and other intermittent problems. However, other types of failures are harder to deal with.

Data Storage Challenges

When applications access terabyte-size data sets, storage available at the execution sites can be a limiting factor for successful data staging and thus for successful workflow execution. This problem is particularly challenging because there are few systems deployed today that support disk space reservation, so applications compete with each other for space on a first-come-first-serve basis. Even if there are disk quotas present on the execution sites, these quotas are usually maintained at the Virtual Organization (VO)-level (Foster, Kesselman et al. 2001), and therefore, users within the VO compete for space. In LIGO, for example, binary inspiral workflows require a minimum of 221 gigabytes of gravitational-wave data and approximately 70,000 computational workflow tasks (Singh, Vahi et al. 2007). In 2007, the resources of the Open Science Grid provided on average

258 gigabytes of shared scratch disk space that was used by approximately 20 VOs. Thus, LIGO workflows must be carefully mapped onto the available OSG resources, and new algorithms are needed to manage the size of the workflow data footprint during execution.

It is possible for workflow systems to take into account the storage space available at a particular site when making task scheduling decisions (Ramakrishnan, Singh et al. 2007). The workflow system can find out how much space is available at a remote site, estimate the amount of space needed by the workflow tasks and consider only the sites that provide a suitable amount of space for resource selection. One of the challenges in this case is the ability to receive accurate information from the resources. Another challenge is the ability to estimate the amount of storage needed for the output data of workflow tasks. Also, because the available space can change before or during data transfer operations, workflow systems need to be able to recover from disk space failures and re-plan the workflow for execution elsewhere. The ability of the workflow system to clean up data sets when they are no longer needed can reduce the workflow footprint (Singh, Vahi et al. 2007) and thus is an important factor in successful workflow execution.

Data Management inside the Resource

In distributed environments, clusters are often managed by schedulers such as Condor (Epema, Livny et al. 1996) or PBS (Henderson and Tweten 1996). As the clusters grow larger, the issue of data management within the cluster becomes important. If workflow tasks access data via the shared file system, then the overall application may suffer if the file server becomes overloaded. A solution to this problem is for the workflow tasks to compute on data that reside on a local disk. The issue is then to provide mechanisms within the workflow to perform the staging of data from a shared location to the local file system.

Most resource management systems support a way of specifying this type of data staging in the submission scripts. In a distributed environment, these scripts are usually generated automatically by remote submission software. The challenge for the workflow system is to be able to identify the properties of the remote execution site and to pass the appropriate information to the submission software.

Dealing with Data too Large to Move

In some cases, the data sets that workflows operate on are too large to move efficiently and process at a remote location. It is necessary for the workflow scheduling algorithms to take this into account when deciding which resources to use for the computation. A challenge for the algorithms is trying to figure out the costs involved in moving the data over the network, which can vary greatly based on network load and the latency and bandwidth of source and destination storage systems. Workflow systems depend on monitoring and information systems for current information on network and storage performance.

Virtual Data

When dealing with large numbers of workflows and large VOs, it is often the case that multiple workflows may use the same input data sets or intermediate data products. For example, raw data managed by a VO is often in a form that needs to be calibrated first to be scientifically viable. Thus, many workflows incorporate the calibration step in their computations. As a result, the intermediate, calibrated data can be shared by other workflows and users within the collaboration, provided the data are correctly tagged with metadata and provenance information. The challenge for the workflow system is then to recognize when intermediate data already exist; to determine whether it is more efficient to access the existing data rather than re-compute it; and to make use of this information to possibly reduce the workflow execution time.

DERIVED DATA AND PROVENANCE

Both final and intermediate workflow results are typically staged out to a permanent storage location. In order for this data to be interpretable both by the user and his/her colleagues, metadata and provenance information about the data need to be stored as well.

Metadata Management

In some scientific disciplines, such as astronomy, there are standard data formats that include metadata about an image as part of the image file header. Community codes then have the obligation to generate and save the metadata inside the files they generate. In Montage, for example, the application reads input files in the FITS format that contain image data and later writes new images in the same format with new metadata included in the headers. However, it may be difficult to search for specific data by opening and reading the file headers. Thus, additional workflow components can be provided to extract and save metadata in a metadata catalog. In general, it is very difficult for workflow systems to appropriately catalog metadata associated with derived data, as there is no standard way for software components to generate the metadata, and most of the time, the software components do not provide any metadata for the results. New capabilities need to be developed for communities to define standards and formats. One challenge is to determine how to retrofit existing legacy codes to provide metadata information, or more likely to wrap them with metadata capabilities. Another challenge is to have incentives for community members to develop new metadata-compliant codes.

Provenance Management

Having metadata information is often not sufficient to fully validate scientific results or to reproduce them. Additional provenance information is needed to support both scientific and engineering reproducibility (Gil, Deelman et al. 2007). Provenance captures information about which data were used during the workflow execution, which software was run, and which computing, storage, and other resources were used to obtain the results. Detailed information will include the various parameter settings, environmental variables, etc., used during the execution. All this information can and should be captured by the workflow management system while the workflow is executing. In terms of scientific reproducibility, where a scientist wants to share and verify research findings with colleagues inside or outside the VO, the user may need to know which data sets were used, what type of analysis was run, and with what parameters. However, in cases where the results need to be reproduced "bit-by-bit", more detailed information about the hardware architecture of the resources, environment variables used, library versions, etc. are needed. Finally, provenance can also be used to analyze workflow performance, as was done, for example, in the context of CyberShake (Deelman, Callaghan et al. 2006), where the provenance records were mined to determine the number of tasks executed, their runtime distribution, where the execution took place, etc.

In some cases, the workflow management system may modify the executable workflow to the point that it is not easy to map between what has been executed and what the user originally specified (Deelman, Singh et al. 2005). As a result, information about the workflow restructuring process needs to be recorded as well (Miles, Deelman et al. 2007). This information allows us not only to relate the user-created and the executable workflow but is also the foundation for workflow debugging, where the user can trace how the specification they provided evolved into an executable sub-workflow.

One of the challenges in managing provenance, and especially workflow provenance where the information can be significant in size (petabyte scale), is the necessity to determine what to store. Workflow management system designers need to work with application developers to define the important provenance components. Also, some other methods of periodically reducing, compressing, and otherwise managing provenance information may need to be employed. As a result, there is a risk of not having the needed information and thus being unable to verify and thoroughly analyze or reproduce the results. Another challenge related to the size of provenance is the efficient navigation of the information. Tools such as PASOA (Miles, Groth et al. 2006) and others are addressing these issues.

CONCLUSION

In this chapter, we examined the data lifecycle as it relates to the scientific workflow lifecycle. We discussed challenges in data and software discovery, data and component selection, physical data movement, and the management of derived data, metadata and provenance. We believe that data management issues are critical to scientific workflows, and although many technologies and point solutions exist today, much work remains to be done in that area. With the advent of multi-core processors, data management is increasing in importance. The need to bring data reliably and quickly to where the computation takes place is critical. In cases where the cost of data transfer is too expensive, we need to bring software and the necessary computation environment to the data. In either case, issues related to metadata, provenance, and workflow mapping techniques remain.

ACKNOWLEDGMENT

This work was supported in part by the NSF OCI-0438712 grant and by the Department of Energy's SciDAC II program under grant DE-FC02-06ER25757. The authors would like to thank the ESG, LIGO, Montage, and SCEC collaborators for helpful discussions and fruitful collaborations.

REFERENCES

Allcock, W., Bester, J., et al. (2001). Secure, *efficient data transport and replica management for high-performance data-intensive computing*. Mass Storage Conference.

Barish, B. C., & Weiss, R. (1999). LIGO and the detection of gravitational waves. *Physics Today, 52*(10), 44. doi:10.1063/1.882861

Berriman, G. B., Deelman, E., et al. (2004). Montage: A Grid enabled engine for delivering custom science-grade mosaics on demand. *SPIE Conference, 5487, Astronomical Telescopes.*

Brown, D. A., & Brady, P. R. (2006). A case study on the use of workflow technologies for scientific analysis: Gravitational wave data analysis. In Taylor, I., Deelman, E., Gannon, D., & Shields, M. (Eds.), *Workflows for e-Science*. Springer. doi:10.1007/978-1-84628-757-2_4

Chervenak, A., Deelman, E., Foster, I., Guy, L., Hoschek, W., & Iamnitchi, A..... Tierney, B. (2002). *Giggle: A framework for constructing sclable replica location services*. SC2002 Conference, Baltimore, MD.

Chervenak, A., Deelman, E., Livny, M., Su, M., Schuler, R., & Bharathi, S. ... Vahi, K. (2007). *Data placement for scientific applications in distributed environments*. 8th IEEE/ACM Int'l Conference on Grid Computing (Grid 2007), Austin, Texas.

Chervenak, A. L., Palavalli, N., Bharathi, S., Kesselman, C., & Schwartzkopf, R. (2004). *Performance and scalability of a replica location service*. Thirteenth IEEE Int'l Symposium High Performance Distributed Computing (HPDC-13), Honolulu, HI.

Chervenak, A. L., & Schuler, R. (2009). The Globus replica location service: Design and experience. *IEEE Transactions on Parallel and Distributed Systems, 20*(9), 1260–1272. doi:10.1109/TPDS.2008.151

Couvares, P., & Kosar, T. (2006). Workflow management in Condor. In Taylor, I., Deelman, E., Gannon, D., & Shields, M. (Eds.), *Workflows in e-Science* (pp. 357–375). Springer.

Czajkowski, K., Fitzgerald, S., et al. (2001). *Grid information services for distributed resource sharing*. 10th IEEE International Symposium on High Performance Distributed Computing, IEEE Press.

Deelman, E., Callaghan, S., et al. (2006). Managing large-scale workflow execution from resource provisioning to provenance tracking: The CyberShake example. *E-SCIENCE '06: Proceedings of the Second IEEE International Conference on e-Science and Grid Computing,* (p. 14).

Deelman, E., & Gil, Y. (2006). *Managing large-scale scientific workflows in distributed environments: Experiences and challenges*. Amsterdam, The Netherlands: Workflows in e-Science.

Deelman, E., Mehta, G., et al. (2006). Pegasus: Mapping large-scale workflows to distributed resources. I. Taylor, E. Deelman, D. Gannon & M. Shields (Eds.),*Workflows in e-Science.* Springer.

Deelman, E., & Singh, G. (2005). Pegasus: A framework for mapping complex scientific workflows onto distributed systems. *Scientific Programming Journal, 13*(3), 219–237.

Deelman, E., Singh, G., Atkinson, M. P., Chervenak, A., Chue Hong, N. P., & Kesselman, C. … Su, M.-H. (2004). *Grid-based metadata services*. 16th International Conference on Scientific and Statistical Database Management.

Epema, D. H. J., & Livny, M. (1996). A worldwide flock of condors: Load sharing among workstation clusters. *Future Generation Computer Systems, 12.*

Foster, I., & Kesselman, C. (2001). The anatomy of the Grid: Enabling scalable virtual organizations. *International Journal of High Performance Computing Applications, 15*(3), 200–222. doi:10.1177/109434200101500302

Freire, J., & Silva, C. T. (2006). Managing rapidly-evolving scientific workflows. *IPAW, 4145,* 10–18.

Gil, Y., & Deelman, E. (2007). *Examining the challenges of scientific workflows*. IEEE Computer.

Goble, C. A., & De Roure, D. C. (2007). myExperiment: Social networking for workflow-using e-scientists. *Proceedings of the 2nd workshop on Workflows in support of large-scale science,* (pp. 1-2).

Henderson, R., & Tweten, D. (1996). *Portable batch system: External reference specification.*

Lassila, O., & Swick, R. R. (1999). *Resource description framework (RDF) model and syntax specification.*

Maechling, P., & Chalupsky, H. (2005). Simplifying construction of complex workflows for non-expert users of the Southern California Earthquake Center Community Modeling Environment. *SIGMOD Record, 34*(3), 24–30. doi:10.1145/1084805.1084811

Middleton, D. E., Bernholdt, D. E., Brown, D., Chen, M., Chervenak, A. L., & Cinquini, L.…. Williams, D. (2006). Enabling worldwide access to climate simulation data: the earth system grid (ESG). *Scientific Discovery Through Advanced Computing (SciDAC 2006), Journal of Physics: Conference Series, 46,* (pp. 510-514).

Miles, S., Deelman, E., et al. (2007). *Connecting scientific data to scientific experiments with provenance*. e-Science.

Miles, S., & Groth, P. (2006). The requirements of using provenance in e-science experiments. *Journal of Grid Computing, 5*(1).

Moreau, L. (2007). The first provenance challenge. *Concurrency and Computation, 20*(5).

Moreau, L., & Freire, J. (2007). *The open provenance model*. University of Southampton.

Moreau, L., & Ludaescher, B. (2007). *Concurrency and Computation: Practice and Experience*. Special Issue on the First Provenance Challenge.

Rajasekar, A., & Wan, M. (2003). Storage resource broker-managing distributed data in a Grid. *Computer Society of India Journal. Special Issue on SAN, 33*(4), 42–54.

Ramakrishnan, A., Singh, G., et al. (2007). *Scheduling data -intensive workflows onto storage-constrained distributed resources*. Seventh IEEE International Symposium on Cluster Computing and the Grid — CCGrid 2007.

Sakellariou, R., & Zhao, H. (2007). Scheduling workflows with budget constraints. In Gorlatch, S., & Danelutto, M. (Eds.), *Integrated research in Grid computing. CoreGrid series*. Springer-Verlag. doi:10.1007/978-0-387-47658-2_14

Singh, G., Vahi, K., et al. (2007). Optimizing workflow data footprint. *Scientific Programming Journal, Special issue on Dynamic Computational Workflows: Discovery, Optimization, and Scheduling, 15*(4).

Wieczorek, M., & Prodan, R. (2005). Scheduling of scientific workflows in the ASKALON Grid environment. *SIGMOD Record, 34*(3), 56–62. doi:10.1145/1084805.1084816

Chapter 9
Replica Management in Data Intensive Distributed Science Applications

Ann L. Chervenak
University of Southern California, USA

Robert Schuler
University of Southern California, USA

ABSTRACT

Management of the large data sets produced by data-intensive scientific applications is complicated by the fact that participating institutions are often geographically distributed and separated by distinct administrative domains. A key data management problem in these distributed collaborations has been the creation and maintenance of replicated data sets. This chapter provides an overview of replica management schemes used in large, data-intensive, distributed scientific collaborations. Early replica management strategies focused on the development of robust, highly scalable catalogs for maintaining replica locations. In recent years, more sophisticated, application-specific replica management systems have been developed to support the requirements of scientific Virtual Organizations. These systems have motivated interest in application-independent, policy-driven schemes for replica management that can be tailored to meet the performance and reliability requirements of a range of scientific collaborations. The authors discuss the data replication solutions to meet the challenges associated with increasingly large data sets and the requirement to run data analysis at geographically distributed sites.

DOI: 10.4018/978-1-61520-971-2.ch009

Figure 1. Distributed collaboration or virtual organization

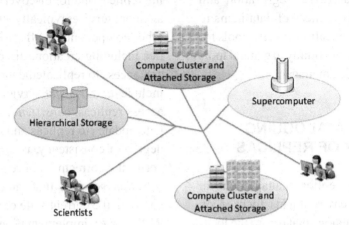

INTRODUCTION

In the last decade, a large number of distributed scientific collaborations have generated an ever-increasing amount of application data. These scientific collaborations include projects in high energy physics, gravitational wave physics, neuroscience, earthquake science, astronomy, and many others. Collaborations that span multiple institutions (see Figure 1) are typically called Virtual Organizations (Foster, Kesselman et al. 2001). Management of the large data sets produced by these data-intensive scientific applications is complicated by the fact that participating institutions are often geographically distributed and separated by distinct administrative domains. A key data management problem in these distributed collaborations has been the creation and maintenance of replicated data sets.

Data sets are replicated among the institutions of a scientific collaboration for a variety of reasons. One goal of replication is to provide high availability for data sets, so that if there are hardware failures at one site or if one region is affected by a network outage or a natural disaster, additional copies of the data sets may still be accessed at other locations. Another goal of replication is to improve performance by allowing a data set to be accessed at multiple locations. A client fetch-ing the desired data can choose a particular site based on resource characteristics, such as the available bandwidth on storage systems or networks. Alternatively, clients can access portions of the file at multiple replica sites in parallel to increase the aggregate bandwidth available for downloading the data. Other reasons for replicating data may be the desire of scientists to have a copy of essential data sets at their home institutions. In addition, data sets may be replicated to improve the performance of scientific computations or workflows running on particular computational resources, such as a supercomputer or computation cluster. In this case, the data sets needed for the computation are frequently replicated or staged in to storage resources on or near the computational site.

Scientific data sets are frequently read-only, but in some cases, they may be updated to reflect corrections or recalibrations of data sets. When an original data set is updated, its replicas must also be updated using a consistency scheme agreed upon by the Virtual Organization. This may include a versioning scheme that keeps all versions of a data item and gives them increasing version numbers as data items are updated.

In this chapter, we trace the evolution of replica management techniques for distributed scientific collaborations, from an early focus on

189

creating scalable catalogs for registration and discovery of read-only replicas of data items to more sophisticated, application-specific tools for distributed replication and finally to general tools for policy-driven replica management.

SYSTEMS FOR CATALOGUING AND DISCOVERY OF REPLICAS

Early approaches to replica management in distributed scientific environments focused on developing scalable catalogs that record the locations of replicas and allow them to be discovered. These efforts include the Replica Location Service (RLS) framework that was jointly developed by the Globus project and the European DataGrid (EDG) project (Chervenak 2002). This framework was the basis for two RLS implementations by the Globus and EDG (Kunszt 2003) teams. We describe the implementation and usage of the Globus Replica Location Service below.

Other early approaches to replica management in distributed environments include the Storage Resource Broker (Rajasekar 2003) and GridFarm (Tatebe 2003) systems that manage replicas using a centralized metadata catalog. Unlike RLS, these catalogs maintain logical metadata to describe the content of data in addition to attributes related to physical replicas; these catalogs are also used to maintain replica consistency. The LHC Computing Grid project (LCG) and the Enabling Grids for E-SciencE (EGEE) projects at CERN have implemented *file catalogs* that combine replica location functionality and hierarchical file system metadata management (Baud, Casey et al. 2005; Kunszt, Badino et al. 2005; Munro and Koblitz 2006).

The Globus Replica Location Service

The Replica Location Service (RLS) (Chervenak 2002; Chervenak 2004; Chervenak, Schuler et al. 2009) provides a scalable mechanism for register-

ing replicas and for discovering them. Data management services typically integrate the RLS with other components to offer higher-level capabilities including creation, discovery, maintenance, and access to replicated data. These components include *data transfer* services used to create and access replicas, *consistency* services that propagate updates to replicas and maintain a specified degree of consistency, *verification* services that verify the correctness of registered replicas, and *selection* services that choose among replicas based on the current state of Grid resources. The RLS server implementation performs well in distributed environments, scaling to register millions of entries and supporting up to one hundred simultaneous clients.

The RLS design consists of two types of servers: the Local Replica Catalog and the Replica Location Index.

The *Local Replica Catalog* (LRC) stores mappings between logical names for data items and the physical locations of replicas of the data items. (Alternatively, the catalog may contain mappings from logical names to another layer of logical names, providing an additional layer of indirection.) Clients query the LRC to discover replicas associated with a logical name. The simplest RLS deployment consists of a single LRC that acts as a registry of mappings for one or more storage systems. Typically, when an RLS is deployed on a site, an administrator populates it to reflect the contents of a local file or storage system. If a data publishing service or a workflow manager produces new data files, these services will register the newly created files with the RLS as part of their publication process.

For distributed RLS deployments, we also provide a higher-level *Replica Location Index* (RLI) server. By distributing the RLS, we are able to increase the overall scale of the system to store more mappings and support more queries and updates than would be possible in a single, centralized catalog. We also avoid creating a single point of failure in the Grid data management

Figure 2. Configuration options for RLS

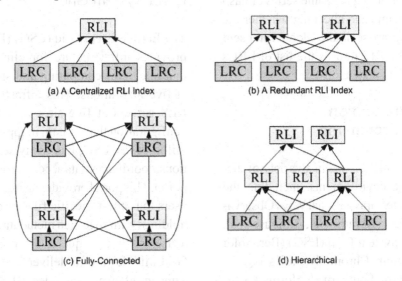

(a) A Centralized RLI Index

(b) A Redundant RLI Index

(c) Fully-Connected

(d) Hierarchical

system. In addition to satisfying the availability and performance demands of a distributed system, the loosely coupled nature of the distributed RLS design allows for local administrative control over the Local Replica Catalog servers.

Each Replica Location Index server collects information about the logical name mappings stored in one or more Local Replica Catalogs. An RLI also answers queries about those mappings. When a client wants to discover replicas that may exist at multiple locations, the client will pose that query to an RLI server rather than to an individual Local Replica Catalog. In response to a query, the RLI will return a list of all the LRCs it is aware of that contain mappings for the logical name contained in the query. The client then queries these LRCs to find the physical locations of replicas.

Figure 2 shows several possible configurations for a distributed RLS deployment, including a centralized RLI that receives updates from several LRCs; two redundant RLIs that avoid a single point of failure; a fully-connected distributed RLS, where each LRC updates an RLI at every site; and a hierarchical RLS deployment, in which RLIs aggregate information from several underlying LRC or RLI servers.

Information is sent from the LRCs to the RLIs using soft-state update protocols. Each LRC periodically sends information about its logical name mappings to a set of RLIs. The RLIs collect this mapping information and respond to queries regarding the mappings. Information in RLIs times out and gets periodically refreshed by subsequent updates. An advantage of using such soft-state update protocols is that if an RLI fails and later resumes operation, its contents can be reconstructed using these updates.

Because each LRC may hold millions of logical file name mappings, updates from LRCs to RLIs can become large. Sending them around the network may be slow, especially in the wide area; when updates arrive at an RLI, they may consume considerable storage space there. One option for making these updates more efficient is to compress their contents. The RLS implementation supports compression of LRC updates. Each LRC periodically creates a bit map called a Bloom filter that summarizes its contents by applying a series of hash functions to each logical name registered in the LRC and setting the corresponding bits in the bit map. An RLI stores Bloom filter summaries from one or more LRCs in memory and optionally on disk. The RLI answers a query about a logical name by applying the same series of hash functions to the name and checking whether the corresponding bits are set in the Bloom filter sent by each LRC. The RLI returns the list of LRCs for which these bits match.

The RLS in Production Scientific Environments

The RLS is in production use in a variety of distributed scientific environments, including the Laser Interferometer Gravitational Wave Observatory (LIGO) project (Abramovici, Althouse et al. 1992), the Earth System Grid (ESG) (Bernholdt 2005), the Quantum Chromodynamics (QCD) Grid (2005), and the Southern California Earthquake Center (2005).

LIGO

The Laser Interferometer Gravitational Wave Observatory (LIGO) collaboration (Abramovici, Althouse et al. 1992; LIGO Project 2004) conducts research to detect gravitational waves. LIGO uses data replication extensively to make terabytes of data available at ten LIGO sites. To meet LIGO data publication, replication and access requirements, researchers developed the Lightweight Data Replicator (LDR) system, which integrates RLS with the GridFTP data transfer service (Globus Project 2002) and a distributed metadata service. LDR provides rich functionality, including pull-based file replication; efficient data transfer among sites; and a validation component that verifies that files on storage systems are correctly registered in each Local Replica Catalog.

The LIGO deployment registers RLS mappings from more than 25 million logical file names to 120 million physical files. The LIGO deployment is a fully-connected RLS: each RLI collects state updates from LRCs at all ten sites. Thus, a query to any RLI identifies all LRCs that contain mappings for a logical file name.

Earth System Grid

The Earth System Grid (ESG) (Bernholdt 2005) provides infrastructure for climate researchers that integrates computing and storage resources at five institutions. This infrastructure includes RLS servers at five sites in a fully-connected configuration that contain mappings for over one million files. ESG, like many scientific applications, coordinates data access through a web-based portal. This portal provides an interface that allows users to request specific files or query ESG data holdings with specified metadata attributes. After a user submits a query, the portal coordinates Grid middleware to deliver the requested data. This middleware includes RLS, a centralized metadata catalog, and services for data transfer (Globus Project 2002) and subsetting (Bernholdt 2005). In addition to using RLS to locate replicas, the ESG web portal uses size attributes stored in RLS to estimate transfer times.

RLS and Workflow Management Systems

The Pegasus (Planning for Execution in Grids) workflow mapping system (Deelman 2004) is used by scientific applications to manage complex executions. Components of workflows are often scientific applications and data movement operations; dependencies among these components are reflected in the workflow. Pegasus maps from a high-level, abstract definition of a workflow to a concrete or executable workflow in the form of a Directed Acyclic Graph (DAG), which is then passed to the Condor DAGMan execution system (Frey 2002). During workflow mapping, Pegasus queries the RLS to identify and select physical replicas specified as logical files in the abstract workflow. When Pegasus produces new data files during execution, it registers them in the RLS.

Pegasus is used for production analysis by a number of scientific applications, including the LIGO (Abramovici, Althouse et al. 1992) project, the Montage mosaic (Berriman 2003) and the Galaxy morphology (Deelman 2003) astronomical applications, and the Southern California Earthquake Center (2005) project.

Peer-to-Peer Replica Location Services

In recent years, there has been extensive research in peer-to-peer (P2P) systems, in which the nodes of a system act as peers that create an overlay network to exchange information. Peer-to-peer systems have several desirable properties, including high scalability and reliability and the capability of self-healing the P2P overlay when nodes fail or join the network (Ratnasamy 2001; Stoica, Morris et al. 2001; Zhao 2001). There are significant challenges in applying peer-to-peer techniques to Grid resource discovery services, including performance and security issues (Chervenak and Bharathi 2008). Two groups have studied peer-to-peer organizations of RLS servers.

Cai et al. designed and implemented a Peer-to-Peer Replica Location Service (P-RLS) (Cai 2004) that uses a *structured overlay* network, Chord (Stoica 2001), to organize participating P-RLS servers. A structured peer-to-peer overlay typically uses a mechanism such as a distributed hash table to deterministically identify the node on which a particular <key, value> pair will be stored and retrieved. Thus, structured P2P approaches are usually concerned with locating resources that can be named or identified by keys (Iamnitchi 2002). Therefore, a structured P2P approach may be particularly well-suited to replica location services, where clients query for information associated with a globally unique logical or physical data identifier. A P-RLS server consists of an unchanged Local Replica Catalog (LRC) and a peer-to-peer Replica Location Index node called a P-RLI. The network of P-RLIs uses the Chord routing algorithm to store mappings from logical names to LRC sites. A P-RLI server responds to queries for the mappings it contains and routes

other queries to the P-RLI nodes that contain the corresponding mappings. The prototype system extended the RLS server with Chord protocols.

Ripeanu et al. implemented and evaluated a decentralized, adaptive replica location mechanism (Ripeanu 2002) based on an *unstructured overlay,* Bloom filter compression and soft state updates. An unstructured P2P overlay network usually does not impose any constraints on links between nodes in the system; the choice of neighbors to peer with is less restrictive and is often probabilistic or randomized. Queries are propagated in the system using flooding based algorithms, and responses are routed back on the same path as the queries. Ripeanu's work uses the unstructured overlay to distribute Bloom filter digests to all nodes in the overlay. Thus, each node maintains a compressed image of the global system. When a client queries a node for an LFN mapping, the node first checks its locally stored mappings and its stored digests that summarize the contents of remote nodes. If the node finds a match for the LFN in a digest for a remote node, it contacts that node to obtain the mappings. Network traffic generated using this approach is comparable to the traffic generated in query forwarding schemes. Query performance improves significantly because all queries are resolved in at most two network hops.

CUSTOM REPLICA MANAGEMENT SYSTEMS FOR LARGE SCIENTIFIC COLLABORATIONS

Over time, applications and middleware groups have recognized the need for more sophisticated replica management in addition to providing tools for cataloguing and discovery. Large scientific collaborations have developed complex systems for management of data distribution and replication. The Virtual Organization for a scientific collaboration may have well-defined policies for dissemination and management of replicated data. At present, most replica management system

Figure 3. Tiered distribution of high energy physics data

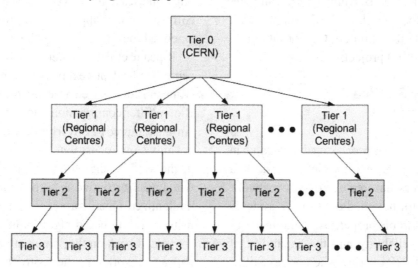

for scientific collaborations have been custom developed to meet the specific needs of a single application.

Existing replica management systems include the Physics Experiment Data Export (PheDEx) (Barrass 2004; Rehn, Barrass et al. 2006) system for high-energy physics and the Lightweight Data Replicator (LDR) (LIGO Project 2004) for gravitational-wave physics. In both collaborations, the Virtual Organization has developed policies to distribute and replicate data sets widely so that they will be available to scientists at their individual institutions or near where computations are likely to run and so that the system will provide a high degree of availability.

Replica Management in High Energy Physics

The high energy physics scientific community includes several experiments that will make use of terabytes of data collected from the Large Hadron Collider (LHC) (CMS Project 2005) at CERN. The data sets generated by these experiments will be distributed to many sites where scientists need access to the raw and processed data products. The high energy physics community has a

hierarchical or tiered model for data distribution (Barrass 2004), as illustrated in Figure 3. At the Tier 0 level at CERN, the data will be collected, pre-processed and archived. From there, data products will be replicated and disseminated to multiple sites. Tier 1 sites are typically large national computing centers that will have significant storage resources and will store and archive large subsets of the data produced at the Tier 0 site. At the next level, Tier 2 sites will have less storage available and will store a smaller subset of the data. At lower levels of the Tier system, smaller subsets of data are stored and made accessible to scientists at their individual institutions.

The PheDEx system manages data distribution for the Compact Muon Solenoid (CMS) high energy physics experiment (CMS Project 2005). The goal of the system is to automate data distribution processes as much as possible. Data operations that must be performed include staging data from tape storage (for example, at the Tier 0 site) into disk buffers; wide area data transfers (to Tier 1 or Tier 2 sites); validation of these transfers; and migration from the destination disk buffer into archival storage at those sites. The PheDEx system design includes a collection of agents or daemons running at each site, where

Figure 4. Distribution of gravitational wave data

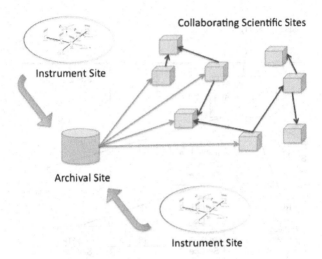

each agent performs a unique task. For example, there are agents that stage data from tape to disk and agents that perform data transfers. The agents communicate through a central database running on a multi-server Oracle database platform. The PheDEx data distribution system supports three use cases for CMS. First, it supports the initial "push-based" hierarchical distribution from the Tier 0 site at CERN to the Tier 1 sites. It also supports subscription-based transfer of data, where sites or scientists subscribe to data sets of interest, and those data sets are sent to the requesting sites as they are produced. Finally, PheDEx supports on-demand access to data by individual sites or scientists.

Replica Management in Gravitational Wave Physics

The Lightweight Data Replicator (LDR) system (LIGO Project 2004) distributes data for the Laser Interferometer Gravitational Wave Observatory (LIGO) project (Abramovici, Althouse et al. 1992; LIGO Project 2004). LIGO produces large amounts of data and distributes data sets to LIGO sites based on metadata queries by scientists at those sites. Currently, the collaboration stores

more than 120 million files across ten locations. Experimental data sets are initially produced at two LIGO instrument sites, archived at CalTech, and published in the replica catalog; they are then replicated at other LIGO sites that subscribe to specific data sets based on metadata queries in order to provide scientists with local access to data, as illustrated in Figure 4. LIGO researchers developed the LDR system to manage the data distribution process. LDR is built on top of standard Grid data services, including the Globus Replica Location Service (Chervenak 2002; Chervenak 2004) and the GridFTP data transport protocol (Allcock 2005). LDR provides a rich set of data management functionality, including replicating necessary files to a LIGO site. Each LDR site initiates local data transfers using a pull model. A scheduling daemon queries the site's local metadata catalog to request sets of files with specified metadata attributes. These sets of files are called *collections,* and each collection has a priority level that determines the order in which files from different collections will be transferred to the local site. For each file in a collection, the scheduling daemon checks whether the desired file already exists on the local storage system. If not, the daemon adds that file's logical name

Figure 5. Operation of the data replication service

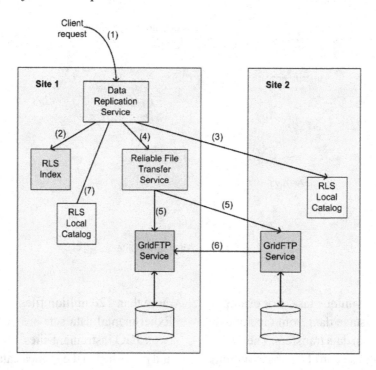

to a priority-based scheduling queue. Each LDR site also runs a transfer daemon that initiates data transfers of files on the scheduling queue in priority order. The transfer daemon queries replica catalogs to find locations in the Grid where the desired file exists and randomly chooses among the available locations. Then the transfer daemon initiates data transfer operations from the remote site to the local site using the GridFTP data transport protocol.

Generalizing Replica Management: The Data Replication Service

Based on work with the LIGO group, the Data Replication Service (DRS) (Chervenak 2005) was designed to provide an application-independent version of some of the functionality provided by the Lightweight Data Replicator System. The function of DRS is to replicate a specified set of files onto a storage system and register the new files in appropriate replica catalogs. DRS builds

on lower-level Grid data services, including the Globus Reliable File Transfer (RFT) service, which provides reliable multi-file transfer requests using the GridFTP data transfer service and the Replica Location Service (RLS). The operations of the DRS include *discovery*, identifying where desired data files exist on the Grid by querying the RLS; *transfer*, copying the desired data files to the local storage system efficiently using the RFT service; and *registration*, adding location mappings to the RLS so that other sites may discover newly created replicas. Throughout DRS replication operations, the service maintains state about each file, including which operations on the file have succeeded or failed.

Figure 5 illustrates the operation of the Data Replication Service. When a client requests a data replication operation (1), the DRS first queries the RLI to find the LRCs that may contain the desired replica locations. The RLI returns the locations of one or more LRCs, and the DRS next queries those LRCs (3) in order to get the file transfer

URLs of the desired files. Next, the DRS issues a file transfer request to the RFT Service (4), which initiates third-party transfer operations (5) between GridFTP servers at the source and destination sites. After the file transfers complete (6), the DRS registers the new replicas in its LRC (7).

POLICY-DRIVEN DATA REPLICATION

The PheDEx and LDR examples suggest that replica management systems for large scientific collaborations must support dissemination of experimental data according to well-defined strategies or policies determined by the Virtual Organization. Typically, the institutions that make up a scientific Virtual Organization build a shared understanding over time regarding how data sets should be distributed and replicated. This understanding is based on knowledge of how scientists access data sets, which storage and computational resources are available at each site, and how these resources will be used to carry out the data analysis tasks of the collaboration. This shared understanding can be expressed as policies for the VO. These policies are enforced to carry out the desired strategy for data distribution and replication. Policy expression and enforcement at the VO level requires cooperation by the collaborating sites. For example, if a VO policy specifies that copies of certain data sets must be made at particular sites in the collaboration, enforcement of this policy depends on the cooperation of the individual sites, since those sites maintain control over their local resources. Thus, policy enforcement is more complicated than simply dictating requirements at the VO level. A *Policy-Driven Data Replication Service* is responsible for replicating and distributing data items in conformance with policies or preferences of a VO.

As already discussed, data distribution and replication strategies can have significant availability and performance consequences for a scientific collaboration. Replication policies might focus on making data sets highly available, and thus require that a certain number of replicas of each data item must be maintained on distributed storage systems to avoid data loss if any storage system or disk fails. These policies might further require that replicas be maintained in distinct geographical regions to avoid data loss due to a major network outage or a significant natural disaster. A VO might also specify replication policies that are based on performance goals. For example, a VO may receive an allocation to run an application on a supercomputer or on shared cyberinfrastructure resources such as the Open Science Grid or the Teragrid. To maximize application performance and minimize delays required for data staging operations, the VO may enforce data staging policies that require that data sets needed for application execution must be replicated to storage systems associated with the allocated computational resources before execution begins. These newly created replicas may be permanent or temporary copies. Once execution is complete, additional policies enforced by the replication system may remove the staged data files to make room for other data sets needed for subsequent computations. To enforce such policies, enforcement schemes may need to interact closely with workflow management systems or computational schedulers to understand their data staging requirements.

Another performance-related policy for a VO might require that key data sets be mirrored in each major geographical region for institutions participating in the collaboration to provide faster or less costly access to users in those regions, by avoiding long data access delays and sometimes high network usage costs. Global-scale replication requires particular attention to the high cost and relatively poor reliability of long-distance, international network links. Under such circumstances, replication strategies cannot afford to replicate data without regard to the priority of select subsets of application data.

Most current replication strategies address only performance and other issues related to systems resources. However, as the Biomedical community increases reliance on data Grid technology, replication techniques will need to consider numerous issues beyond resource management and utilization. Many governments strictly regulate management of Biomedical data, such as patient records and research involving human subjects. Replication policies will be needed to help researchers and analytical tools effectively access data while obeying legal constraints on the dissemination of protected information. For instance, some projects include a mixture of protected and public, de-identified information. Public information may be replicated freely, and policies could be specified that allow the data to be replicated to maximize resource utilization as the sole consideration. However, for protected information, replication policies would need to replicate data based on a combination of factors including which collaborating organizations have authorization to access and to store replicas of specific data sets involving patients or human subjects participating in a research experiment or clinical trial.

Rule Engines and Policy-Driven Data Placement

One option for implementing a policy-driven data placement service is to use a rule engine, which encodes policies and knowledge as rules. A rule is typically expressed in the form, "if Condition, then Action," and a policy contains a collection of rules that must be satisfied. Given a set of inputs, the rule engine produces a decision based on the rules that have been encoded. For a policy-driven data replication service, the inputs to the rule engine would characterize the current state of the system (where replicas currently exist, the amount of available space on storage systems, etc.). Based on the data distribution policies that had been encoded, the rule engine would make

decisions that would determine where additional replicas would be created.

In recent work (Alspaugh, Chervenak et al. 2008), we integrated an open source rule engine called Drools (Drools project 2008) with existing services for grid data management (including the GridFTP data transfer service (Allcock 2005) and the Globus Replica Location Service (Chervenak 2004)). Information about existing replicas in the distributed system is queried from RLS and provided as an input to the rule engine, which then enforces policies for additional data replication. The rule engine creates new replicas using the GridFTP data transfer service and registers these new replicas in the RLS. We demonstrated that the open source Drools engine was able to enforce two realistic policies for data replication. The first policy distributed data according to a tiered model of data dissemination analogous to that used in the high energy physics domain. Subsets of the data produced at the top node (tier 0) were distributed first to nodes at the tier 1 level and then to nodes at the tier 2 level. The second policy enforced by our open source rule engine maintained a specified number of replicas for each data item in the system. We successfully demonstrated that simple data replication policies can be enforced using existing tools for distributed data management and an open source rule engine.

Other groups have investigated policy-based data distribution systems. In particular, the integrated Rule-based Data System (iRODS) system supports the specification of complex policies for data replication, consistency and metadata management using a rule engine (Rajasekar, Wan et al. 2006; Hedges, Hasan et al. 2007). Researchers at the University of Virginia have also examined policy-directed data movement in grids (Feng, Cui et al. 2006; Feng, Wasson et al. 2007).

RELATED WORK

Replica Location and Discovery

In addition to the work already cited, several research areas are relevant to replica location and discovery, including solutions for locating resources in peer-to-peer networks; distributed name systems; distributed file systems and database catalogs; and web proxy caches.

Peer-to-Peer Resource Discovery

Resource discovery is an important problem for peer-to-peer (P2P) networks. Approaches include centralized indexing, flooding-based *unstructured* schemes, and Distributed Hash Tables (DHTs) and other *structured* approaches.

Systems like Napster maintain a centralized index server, and each resource discovery operation queries this server. This approach has limited scalability and a single point of failure.

Gnutella (Ripeanu 2001; Chawathe, Ratnasamy et al. 2003) constructs an *unstructured* overlay network among nodes and uses flooding to distribute queries. Although query flooding improves fault tolerance by eliminating the single point of failure, it may introduce large message traffic and processing overheads in the network (Ripeanu 2002; Saroiu 2002; Sen 2002) and does not scale well. These overheads are reduced by bounding the number of times each message is forwarded by the time-to-live field of query messages or by employing one of several random walk and replication schemes (e.g., Gia (Lv, Cao et al. 2002; Chawathe, Ratnasamy et al. 2003)).

Distributed hash table (DHT) approaches construct a structured overlay and utilize message routing instead of flooding to discover a resource (Ratnasamy 2002). DHT systems (e.g., Chord (Stoica 2001), CAN (Ratnasamy 2001), Tapestry (Zhao 2004)) perform file location by hashing logical identifiers into keys. Each node maintains location information for a subset of the hashed keys and supports searches by passing queries according to the overlay structure. Some systems (e.g. OceanStore (Kubiatowicz 2000)) also employ probabilistic search to reduce search latencies.

Distributed Name Services

The functionality provided by RLS has some similarities to that provided by distributed name services such as the Domain Name System and the Handle System.

The Domain Name System (DNS) (Mockapetris and Dunlap 1988; Jung, Sit et al. 2002) is a highly scalable, hierarchical, globally distributed database that maps human-readable hostnames to IP addresses. Root servers at the top of the namespace hierarchy are centrally managed and replicated at multiple locations for high availability. Subdomains of the hierarchical namespace are administered locally. RLS has similarities with DNS in its hierarchical organization and local administration of name mappings in LRCs. However, RLS does not does not provide global name mappings, enforce namespaces or restrict the targets of name mappings (i.e., they need not be IP addresses).

The Handle System (HS) (Sun, Lannom et al.; Kahn and Wilensky 2006) is another scalable, efficient, distributed global name service. Its organization is hierarchical, with a top-level Global Handle Registry and an unlimited number of lower-level Local Handle Services that manage local namespaces. A handle is a globally-unique identifier that may "refer to multiple instances of a resource" (Sun, Lannom et al.), providing one-to-many mapping functionality similar to that in RLS. The HS differs from DNS in its support for general-purpose handle to attribute mappings rather than mappings from domain names to IP addresses for network routing, its administrative model, and its security features. The HS supports many features similar to RLS functionality, with an additional focus on global namespace management. We may provide an RLS implementation based on Handle in the future.

Distributed Databases

Heterogeneous distributed databases use catalogs to keep track of information that is needed to locate and manage distributed objects (Lindsay 1987; Choy, Selinger et al. 1991; Cho 1997) such as relations, views and indexes as well as information about users, query plans and access privileges (Cho 1997). Like RLS, these systems typically include local catalogs that contain information needed to manage a local Database Management System and a distributed, inter-site catalog for managing distributed resources. The R* system (Lindsay 1987) has a partitioned, distributed catalog architecture, where each site maintains a catalog with information about a set of objects for which it is responsible. Each object's name includes a "birth site" for the object that never changes. The current storage location of an object is obtained from its birth site.

Choy and Selinger extend the R* catalog (Choy, Selinger et al. 1991). Their architecture includes a Registration Site that can be inferred from an object's name and never changes. This site maps an object's name to a Catalog Site that in turn contains a mapping to the Storage Site where the object is currently stored. This additional indirection provides "flexibility in the placement of catalog information and allows a transparent relocation of catalog information" (Choy, Selinger et al. 1991). This scheme supports a variety of catalog configurations, including centralized, fully replicated and partitioned catalogs.

The Group Oriented Catalog Allocation Scheme (Cho 1997) is a hybrid catalog architecture between a strictly partitioned catalog scheme like R* and a fully replicated distributed catalog. It partitions information among groups of catalogs and fully replicates information within a group. This scheme reduces update costs compared to a fully replicated catalog and reduces query times compared to a partitioned catalog.

Internet Proxy Caches

Directory services for cooperative Internet proxy caches (Fan 2000; Beynon 2001; Harvey 2003; Squid-cache Project 2008) offer functionality similar to the RLS. In a cooperative proxy cache, the directory service receives requests for a URL and locates one proxy that caches a replica of that URL. The RLS provides additional functionality, including requests for multiple replicas of the same file and batch requests.

Hierarchical Internet proxy-caches have been extensively analyzed (Harvey 2003). Three additional solutions do not use hierarchies. In the Summary Cache (Fan 2000), each pair of participating proxies periodically exchanges Bloom filter summaries of the data stored locally. The RLS Bloom filter scheme, by contrast, uses an adaptive soft-state protocol to distribute digests. The Cache Array Routing Protocol (CARP) (Liang, Kumar et al. 2005) uses consistent hashing (Karger, Lehman et al. 1997; Karger, Sherman et al. 1999) to partition the name space and route requests in a manner similar to a DHT scheme. The CARP solution, however, does not efficiently support queries for co-located sets of files. In the Vicinity Cache (Rabinovich, Chase et al. 1998), a directory service at each node considers data exchange costs (e.g. latency or bandwidth) when disseminating information to other nodes.

Data Replication for Durability

Data replication policies may enforce policies that maintain a certain level of redundancy in the system to provide highly available or durable access to data. For example, a system where data sets are valuable and expensive to regenerate may want to maintain several copies of each data item on different storage systems in the distributed environment. Medical applications that preserve patient records could also benefit from replication services that maintain multiple copies of data items. Such replication services monitor the current state of the distributed system, and if the number of replicas of a data item falls below the threshold specified by V.O. policy, the placement service initiates creation of additional replicas on available storage nodes.

In the Oceanstore global distributed storage system (Kubiatowicz 2000), several algorithms have been studied for replication of data to maintain high levels of durability. These include a reactive replication algorithm called *Carbonite* (Chun, Dabek et al. 2006) that models replica repair and failure rates in a system as the birth and death rates in a continuous time Markov model. To provide durability, the replication rate must match or exceed the average rate of failures. Carbonite creates a new replica when a failure is detected that decreases the number of replicas below a specified minimum.

The Oceanstore group has also proposed a proactive replication algorithm called Tempo (Sit, Haeberlen et al. 2006) that creates replicas periodically at a fixed low rate. Tempo creates redundant copies of data items as quickly as possible using available maintenance bandwidth and disk capacity. Tempo provides durability for data sets comparable to that from the reactive Carbonite algorithm using a less variable amount of bandwidth, thus helping to keep maintenance costs predictable.

CONCLUSION

In this chapter, we have provided an overview of replica management schemes used in large, data-intensive, distributed scientific collaborations. Early replica management strategies focused on the development of robust, highly scalable catalogs for maintaining replica locations. In recent years, more sophisticated, application-specific replica management systems have been developed to sup-port the requirements of scientific Virtual Organizations. These systems have motivated interest in application-independent, policy-driven schemes for replica management that can be tailored to meet the performance and reliability requirements of a range of scientific collaborations.

More sophisticated data replication systems are needed to meet the challenges associated with increasingly large data sets and the requirement to run data analysis at geographically distributed sites. With the increasing popularity of new computational models such as cloud computing, the ability to stage large data sets into temporary storage associated with computational resources will become increasingly important. For a large number of biology, astronomy, physics, earthquake engineering and other scientific domains, the ability to effectively manage and replicate massive amounts of data being generated by experiments and simulations will be crucial to enabling scientific progress.

REFERENCES

Abramovici, A., & Althouse, W. (1992). LIGO: The laser interferometer gravitational-wave observatory. *Science, 256*, 325–333. doi:10.1126/science.256.5055.325

Allcock, W., Bresnahan, J., Kettimuthu, R., Link, M., Dumitrescu, C., Raicu, I., & Foster, I. (2005). *The Globus striped GridFTP framework and server. IEEE Supercomputing (SC05)*. Seattle, WA: Conference.

Alspaugh, S., Chervenak, A., et al. (2008). *Policy-driven data management for distributed scientific collaborations using a rule engine* (poster). International Conference for High Performance Computing, Networking, Storage and Analysis (SC08), Austin, TX, USA.

Barrass, T. A. (2004). *Software agents in data and workflow management. Computing in High Energy and Nuclear Physics (CHEP) 2004*. Switzerland: Interlaken.

Baud, J. P., Casey, J., et al. (2005). *Performance analysis of a file catalog for the LHC computing grid*. 14th IEEE International Symposium on High Performance Distributed Computing (HPDC-14).

Bernholdt, D., Bharathi, S., Brown, D., Chancio, K., & Chen, A. Chervenak, L..... Williams, D. (2005). The Earth system Grid: Supporting the next generation of climate modeling research. *Proceedings of the IEEE, 93*(3), 485- 495.

Berriman, G. B., et al. (2003). Montage: A Grid-enabled image mosaic service for the NVO. *Astronomical Data Analysis Software & Systems (ADASS), 13*.

Beynon, M., Kurc, T., Catalyurek, U., Chang, C., Sussman, A., & Saltz, J. (2001). Distributed processing of very large datasets with DataCutter. *Parallel Computing, 27*(11), 1457–1478. doi:10.1016/S0167-8191(01)00099-0

Cai, M., Chervenak, A., & Frank, M. (2004). *A peer-to-peer replica location service based on a distributed hash table*. SC2004 Conference, Pittsburgh, PA.

Chawathe, Y., Ratnasamy, S., et al. (2003). *Making Gnutella-like P2P systems scalable*. ACM SIGCOMM 2003, Karlsruhe, Germany.

Chervenak, A., & Bharathi, S. (2008). Peer-to-Peer approaches to grid resource discovery. In Danelutto, M., Fragopoulou, P., & Getov, V. (Eds.), *Making Grids work* (pp. 59–76). New York, NY: Springer. doi:10.1007/978-0-387-78448-9_5

Chervenak, A., Deelman, E., Foster, I., Guy, L., Hoschek, W., Iamnitchi, A., et al. (2002). *Giggle: A framework for constructing scalable replica location services*. SC2002 Conference, Baltimore, MD.

Chervenak, A., Schuler, R., et al. (2009). The Globus replica location service: Design and experience. *IEEE Transactions on Parallel and Distributed Systems*.

Chervenak, A., Schuler, R., Kesselman, C., Koranda, S., & Moe, B. (2005). *Wide area data replication for scientific collaborations*. 6th IEEE/ACM Int'l Workshop on Grid Computing (Grid2005), Seattle, WA, USA.

Chervenak, A. L., Palavalli, N., Bharathi, S., Kesselman, C., & Schwartzkopf, R. (2004). *Performance and scalability of a replica location service*. Thirteenth IEEE Int'l Symposium High Performance Distributed Computing (HPDC-13), Honolulu, HI.

Cho, H. (1997). Catalog management in heterogeneous distributed database systems. *Proceedings of IEEE Pacific Rim Conference on Communications, Computers and Signal Processing*.

Choy, D. M., Selinger, P. G., et al. (1991). A distributed catalog for heterogeneous distributed database resources. *Proceedings of the First International Conference on Parallel and Distributed Information Systems*.

Chun, B. G., Dabek, F., et al. (2006). Efficient replica maintenance for distributed storage systems. *Proceedings of the 3rd Symposium on Networked Systems Design and Implementation*.

Deelman, E., et al. (2003). *Grid-based galaxy morphology analysis for the National Virtual Observatory*. SC2003.

Deelman, E., Blythe, J., Gil, Y., Kesselman, C., Mehta, G., & Patil, G..... Livny, M. (2004). *Pegasus: Mapping scientific workflows onto the Grid*. Across Grids Conference, Nicosia, Cyprus.

Drools Project. (2008). *Drools*. Retrieved from http://www.jboss.org/drools/

Fan, L., Cao, P., Almeida, J., & Broder, A. Z. (2000). Summary cache: A Scalable wide-area Web cache sharing protocol. *IEEE/ACM Transactions on Networking*, *8*(3), 281–293. doi:10.1109/90.851975

Feng, J., Cui, L., et al. (2006). *Policy-directed data movement in Grids.* 12th International Conference on Parallel and Distributed Systems (ICPADS 2006).

Feng, J., Wasson, G., et al. (2007). *Resource usage policy expression and enforcement in Grid computing.* 8th IEEE/ACM International Conference on Grid Computing (Grid 2007).

Foster, I., & Kesselman, C. (2001). The anatomy of the Grid: Enabling scalable virtual organizations. *International Journal of High Performance Computing Applications*, *15*(3), 200–222. doi:10.1177/109434200101500302

Frey, J., Tannenbaum, T., Foster, I., Livny, M., & Tuecke, S. (2002). Condor-G: A computation management agent for multiinstitutional grids. *Cluster Computing*, *5*, 237–246. doi:10.1023/A:1015617019423

Globus Project. (2002). *The GridFTP protocol and software.*

Harvey, N., Jones, M., Saroiu, S., Theimer, M., & Wolman, A. (2003). *SkipNet: A scalable overlay network with practical locality properties.* Fourth USENIX Symposium on Internet Technologies and Systems (USITS '03), Seattle, WA.

Hedges, M., Hasan, A., et al. (2007). Management and preservation of research data with iRODS. *Proceedings of the ACM First Workshop on CyberInfrastructure: Information Management in eScience,* (pp. 17-22).

Iamnitchi, A., Foster, I., & Nurmi, D. (2002). *A peer-to-peer approach to resource discovery in Grid environments.* Eleventh IEEE Int'l Symposium High Performance Distributed Computing (HPDC-11), Edinburgh, Scotland.

Jung, J., & Sit, E. (2002). DNS performance and the effectiveness of caching. *IEEE/ACM Transactions on Networking*, *10*(5), 589–603. doi:10.1109/TNET.2002.803905

Kahn, R., & Wilensky, R. (2006). A framework for distributed digital object services. *International Journal on Digital Libraries*, *6*(2), 115–123. doi:10.1007/s00799-005-0128-x

Karger, D., Sherman, A., et al. (1999). *Web caching with consistent hashing.* The Eighth International World Wide Web Conference (WWW8), Toronto, Canada.

Karger, D. R., Lehman, E., et al. (1997). *Consistent hashing and random trees: Distributed caching protocols for relieving hot spots on the World Wide Web.* Symposium on Theory of Computing, ACM.

Kubiatowicz, J., et al. (2000). OceanStore: An architecture for global-scale persistent storage. 9th Int'l. *Conf. on Architectural Support for Programming Languages and Operating Systems (ASPLOS 2000).*

Kunszt, P., Laure, E., Stockinger, H., & Stockinger, K. (2003). Advanced replica management with Reptor. 5th International Conference on Parallel Processing and Applied Mathematics, Czestochowa, Poland, Springer Verlag.

Kunszt, P. F., & Badino, P. (2005). *Data storage, access and catalogs in gLite.* Local to Global Data Interoperability-Challenges and Technologies.

Liang, J., R. Kumar, et al. (2005). The KaZaA overlay: A measurement study. *Computer Networks Journal*, *49*(6).

LIGO Project. (2004). *Lightweight data replicator*. Retrieved from http://www.lsc-group.phys.uwm.edu/LDR/. from http://www.lsc-group.phys.uwm.edu/LDR/

LIGO Project. (2004). *LIGO - Laser interferometer gravitational wave observatory,* Retrieved from http://www.ligo.caltech.edu/. from http://www.ligo.caltech.edu/

Lindsay, B. G. (1987). A retrospective of R: A distributed database management system. *Proceedings of the IEEE, 75*(5), 668–673. doi:10.1109/PROC.1987.13780

Lv, Q., Cao, P., et al. (2002). *Search and replication in unstructured peer-to-peer networks*. 16th ACM International Conference on Supercomputing(ICS'02), New York, USA.

Mockapetris, P., & Dunlap, K. J. (1988). *Development of the domain name system*. ACM Symposium on Communications Architectures and Protocols (SIGCOMM '88), Stanford, CA, USA.

Munro, C., & Koblitz, B. (2006). Performance comparison of the LCG2 and gLite file catalogues. *Nuclear Instruments and Methods in Physics Research Section A, 559*(1), 48–52. doi:10.1016/j.nima.2005.11.103

Project, C. M. S. (2005). *The compact Muon Solenoid, an experiment for the large hadron collider at CERN*. Retrieved from http://cms.cern.ch/. from http://cmsinfo.cern.ch/Welcome.html/

Project, E. S. G. (2005). *The Earth system Grid*. Retrieved from www.earthsystemgrid.org

QCDGrid Project. (2005). *QCDGrid: Probing the building blocks of matter with the power of the Grid*. Retrieved from http://www.gridpp.ac.uk/qcdgrid/

Rabinovich, M., Chase, J., et al. (1998). *Not all hits are created equal: Cooperative proxy caching over a wide-area network*. Third International WWW Caching Workshop.

Rajasekar, A. (2003). Storage resource broker - Managing distributed data in a Grid. *Computer Society of India Journal. Special Issue on SAN, 33*(4), 42–54.

Rajasekar, A., Wan, M., et al. (2006). *A prototype rule-based distributed data management system*. Workshop on Next Generation Distributed Data Management, held in conjunction with the High Performance Distributed Computing Conference (HPDC2006), Paris, France.

Ratnasamy, S., Francis, P., Handley, M., Karp, R., & Shenker, S. (2001). *A scalable content-addressable network*. ACM SIGCOMM.

Ratnasamy, S., Shenker, S., & Stoica, I. (2002). *Routing algorithms for DHTs: Some open questions*. IPTPS02, Cambridge, USA.

Rehn, J., Barrass, T., et al. (2006). *PhEDEx high-throughput data transfer management system*. Computing in High Energy and Nuclear Physics (CHEP) 2006, Mumbai, India.

Ripeanu, M. (2001). *Peer-to-peer architecture case study: Gnutella network*. IEEE 1st International Conference on Peer-to-peer Computing (P2P2001), Linkoping, Sweden, IEEE.

Ripeanu, M., & Foster, I. (2002). *A decentralized, adaptive, replica location mechanism*. 11th IEEE International Symposium on High Performance Distributed Computing (HPDC-11), Edinburgh, Scotland.

Ripeanu, M., Foster, I., & Iamnitchi, A. (2002). Mapping the Gnutella network: Properties of large-scale peer-to-peer systems and implications for system design. *IEEE Internet Computing Journal, 6*(1), 50–57.

Saroiu, S., P. Gummadi, K., & Gribble, S. D. (2002). *A measurement study of peer-to-peer file sharing systems*. Multimedia Computing and Networking.

SCEC Project. (2005). *Southern California earth-quake center.* Retrieved from http://www.scec.org/

Sen, S., & Wong, J. (2002). Analyzing peer-to-peer traffic across large networks. *Proceedings of the Second ACM SIGCOMM Workshop on Internet Measurement.*

Sit, E., Haeberlen, A., et al. (2006). *Proactive replication for data durability.* 5th International Workshop on Peer-to-Peer Systems (IPTPS 2006).

Squid-Cache Project. (2008). *Squid: Optimizing Web delivery.* Retrieved from http://www.squid-cache.org/

Stoica, I., & Morris, R. (2001). *Chord: A scalable peer-to-peer lookup service for Internet applications.* ACM SIGCOMM.

Stoica, I., Morris, R., Karger, D., Kaashoek, M. F., & Balakrishnan, H. (2001). *Chord: A scalable peer-to-peer lookup service for internet applications.* ACM SIGCOMM.

Sun, S., Lannom, L., et al. (2003). *Handle system overview.* Internet Engineering Task Force (IETF) Request for Comments (RFC), RFC 3650, November 2003. Retrieved from http://hdl.handle.net/4263537/4069

Tatebe, O., et al. (2003). *Worldwide fast file replication on Grid Datafarm.* 2003 Computing in High Energy and Nuclear Physics (CHEP03).

Zhao, B. Y. (2004). Tapestry: A resilient global-scale overlay for service deployment. *IEEE Journal on Selected Areas in Communications, 22*(1). doi:10.1109/JSAC.2003.818784

Zhao, B. Y., Kubiatowicz, J. D., & Joseph, A. D. (2001). *Tapestry: An infrastructure for fault-resilient wide-area location and routing.* Berkeley: U.C. Berkeley.

Section 4
Data Discovery & Visualization

Chapter 10
Data Intensive Computing for Bioinformatics

Judy Qiu
Indiana University - Bloomington, USA

Saliya Ekanayake
Indiana University - Bloomington, USA

Jaliya Ekanayake
Indiana University - Bloomington, USA

Stephen Wu
Indiana University - Bloomington, USA

Thilina Gunarathne
Indiana University - Bloomington, USA

Scott Beason
Computer Sciences Corporation, USA

Jong Youl Choi
Indiana University - Bloomington, USA

Geoffrey Fox
Indiana University - Bloomington, USA

Seung-Hee Bae
Indiana University - Bloomington, USA

Mina Rho
Indiana University - Bloomington, USA

Yang Ruan
Indiana University - Bloomington, USA

Haixu Tang
Indiana University - Bloomington, USA

ABSTRACT

Data intensive computing, cloud computing, and multicore computing are converging as frontiers to address massive data problems with hybrid programming models and/or runtimes including MapReduce, MPI, and parallel threading on multicore platforms. A major challenge is to utilize these technologies and large-scale computing resources effectively to advance fundamental science discoveries such as those in Life Sciences. The recently developed next-generation sequencers have enabled large-scale genome sequencing in areas such as environmental sample sequencing leading to metagenomic studies of collections of genes. Metagenomic research is just one of the areas that present a significant computational challenge because of the amount and complexity of data to be processed. This chapter discusses the use of innovative data-mining algorithms and new programming models for several Life Sciences applications. The authors particularly focus on methods that are applicable to large data sets coming from high throughput devices of steadily increasing power. They show results for both clustering and dimension reduction algorithms, and the use of MapReduce on modest size problems. They identify two key areas where further research is essential, and propose to develop new O(NlogN) complexity

DOI: 10.4018/978-1-61520-971-2.ch010

algorithms suitable for the analysis of millions of sequences. They suggest Iterative MapReduce as a promising programming model combining the best features of MapReduce with those of high performance environments such as MPI.

INTRODUCTION

Overview

Data intensive computing, cloud computing, and multicore computing are converging as frontiers to address massive data problems with hybrid programming models and/or runtimes including MapReduce, MPI, and parallel threading on multicore platforms. A major challenge is to utilize these technologies and large scale computing resources effectively to advance fundamental science discoveries such as those in Life Sciences. The recently developed next-generation sequencers have enabled large-scale genome sequencing in areas such as environmental sample sequencing leading to metagenomic studies of collections of genes. Metagenomic research is just one of the areas that present a significant computational challenge because of the amount and complexity of data to be processed.

This chapter builds on research we have performed (Ekanayake, Gunarathne, & Qiu, Cloud Technologies for Bioinformatics Applications, 2010) (Ekanayake J., et al., 2009) (Ekanayake, Pallickara, & Fox, MapReduce for Data Intensive Scientific Analyses, 2008) (Fox, et al., 2009) (Fox, Bae, Ekanayake, Qiu, & Yuan, 2008) (Qiu, et al., 2009) (Qiu & Fox, Data Mining on Multicore Clusters, 2008) (Qiu X., Fox, Yuan, Bae, Chrysanthakopoulos, & Nielsen, 2008) (Twister, 2011) on the use of Dryad (Microsoft's MapReduce) (Isard, Budiu, Yu, Birrell, & Fetterly, 2007) and Hadoop (open source) (Apache Hadoop, 2009) to address problems in several areas, such as particle physics and biology. The latter often have the striking all pairs (or doubly data parallel) structure highlighted by Thain (Moretti, Bui, Hollingsworth,

Rich, Flynn, & Thain, 2009). We discuss here, work on new algorithms in "Innovations in Algorithms for Data Intensive Computing" section, and new programming models in "Innovations in Programming Models Using Cloud Technologies" and "Iterative MapReduce with Twister" sections.

We have a robust parallel Dimension Reduction and Deterministic Annealing clustering, and a matching visualization package. We also have parallel implementations of two major dimension reduction algorithms – the SMACOF approach to MDS and Generative Topographic Mapping (GTM) described in "Innovations in Algorithms for Data Intensive Computing" section. MDS is $O(N^2)$ and GTM $O(N)$ but, since GTM requires the points to have (high dimensional) vectors associated with them, only MDS can be applied to most sequences. Also, since simultaneous multiple sequence alignment MSA is impractical for interesting biological datasets, MDS is a better approach to dimension reduction for sequence samples, because it only requires sequences to be independently aligned in pairs to calculate their dissimilarities. On the other hand, GTM is attractive for analyzing high dimension data base records, where well defined vectors are associated with each point – in our case each database record. Distance calculations (Smith-Waterman-Gotoh) MDS and clustering are all $O(N^2)$, and will not properly scale to multi-million sequence problems and hierarchical operations to address this are currently not supported for MDS and clustering except in a clumsy manual fashion. In the final part of "Innovations in Algorithms for Data Intensive Computing" section, we propose a new multiscale (hierarchical) approach to MDS that could reduce complexity from $O(N^2)$ to $O(NlogN)$ using ideas related to approaches already well understood in $O(N^2)$ particle dynamics problems.

In "Innovations in Programming Models Using Cloud Technologies" and "Iterative MapReduce with Twister" sections, we chose to focus on the MapReduce frameworks, as these stem from the commercial information retrieval field, which is perhaps currently the world's most demanding data analysis problem. Exploiting commercial approaches offers a good chance that one can achieve high-quality, robust environments, and MapReduce has a mixture of commercial and open source implementations. In particular, we have looked at MapReduce and MPI, and shown how to analyze biological samples with modest numbers of sequence on a modern 768 core 32 node cluster. We have learnt that currently MapReduce cannot efficiently perform clustering and MDS (Multidimensional Scaling) steps, even though the corresponding MPI implementation only needs reduction and broadcast operations and so fit architecturally functions supported in MapReduce. In addition, since we need to support iterative operations, we propose the use of a modified MapReduce framework called Twister. An early prototype described in "Iterative MapReduce with Twister" section has been run on kernels but, as of this time, not on complete bioinformatics applications. Research issues include fault tolerance, performance, and support for existing MPI programs with the Twister run time supporting the subset of MPI calls. We also demonstrate in "Innovations in Programming Models Using Cloud Technologies" section how we take "all-pairs" or "doubly data parallel" computations in two important bioinformatics sequencing applications, and use the results to compare two implementations of MapReduce (Dryad and Hadoop) with MPI. We describe an interesting technology developed to support rapid changes of operating environment of our clusters. We focus on the effects of inhomogeneous data and set the scene for discussion of Twister in "Iterative MapReduce with Twister" section. One of the biological applications – se-

quence assembly by Cap3 – is purely "Map" and has no reduction operation. The other – calculation of Smith-Waterman dissimilarities for sequences – has a significant reduction phase to concentrate data for later MDS and Clustering.

Architecture for Data Intensive Biology Sequence Studies

The data deluge continues throughout science, and practically all scientific areas need analysis pipelines or workflows to propel the data from the instrument through various stages to scientific discovery, often aided by visualization. It is well known that these pipelines typically offer natural data parallelism that can be implemented within many different frameworks.

Figure 1 shows the data analysis pipeline shared by many gene sequence studies and, in particular, by our early work on metagenomics. Apart from simple data manipulation, there are three major steps – calculation of the pairwise distances between sequences, followed by MDS, and Clustering. We focus on the former here as it can use current MapReduce technologies, and exhibits a doubly data parallel structure, since the dissimilarities δ_{ij} can be calculated independently for the N distinct labels of sequences i and j. Note that, currently, one cannot reliably use multiple sequence analysis (MSA) on large samples, which means techniques that only use pairwise distances between sequences (that can be reliably calculated) must be used, instead of methods relying on vector representations of the sequences. The lack of vector representation for sequences implies that many approaches to dimension reduction (such as GTM (Bishop & Svensén, GTM: A principled alternative to the self-organizing map, 1997)) and clustering (such as original vector-based Deterministic annealing clustering (Rose K., Deterministic Annealing for Clustering, Compression, Classification, Regression, and Related Optimization Problems, 1998)) cannot be used. We have published several papers

Figure 1. Pipeline for analysis of metagenomics data

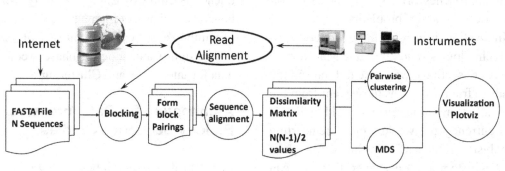

(Fox, et al., 2009) (Fox, Bae, Ekanayake, Qiu, & Yuan, 2008) (Qiu, et al., 2009) describing our earlier work on this pipeline and its related problems. The pairwise distances for metagenomics and other gene family problems are calculated using the algorithm developed by Smith-Waterman (Smith & Waterman, 1981) and Gotoh (Gotoh, 1982) (SW-G), but the process is complicated by the need to exploit the symmetry $\delta_{ij} = \delta_{ji}$, and to arrange the results in a form suitable for the next steps in the pipeline. We have obtained detailed performance measurements on MPI, Hadoop and Dryad with results summarized in "Innovations in Programming Models Using Cloud Technologies" section. This section also describes work on CAP3, which only involves the initial doubly data parallel read alignment stage.

In "Innovations in Algorithms for Data Intensive Computing" section, we use data from the NIH database PubChem (Wheeler, et al., 2006) (PubChem project, 2009) that records properties of chemical compounds. Currently there are 26 million compounds, but in our initial studies we use random subsets of up to 100,000 compounds. We then use 166 binary properties to define the 166 dimensional vectors associated with each compound. In a follow up work we are using interpolation and other methods to extend analysis to the entire NIH dataset.

INNOVATIONS IN ALGORITHMS FOR DATA INTENSIVE COMPUTING

Visualization Analysis by Using Parallel MDS and GTM

Dimension reduction and follow-up visualization of large and high-dimensional data in low dimensions is a task of growing importance in many fields of data mining and information retrieval to understand data structures, verify the results of data mining approaches, or browse them in a way that distance between points in visualization space (typically 2D or 3D) tracks the one in original high dimensional space. There are several well understood approaches to dimension reduction, but they can be very time and memory intensive for large problems. In this section we discuss parallel algorithms for Scaling by MAjorizing a COmplicated Function (SMACOF) to solve Multidimensional Scaling (MDS) problems, and Generative Topographic Mapping (GTM). The former is particularly time consuming, with complexity that grows as square of data set size. However, it does have the advantage of not requiring explicit vectors for dataset points, but only the measurement of inter-point dissimilarities. We also present a comparison between MDS and GTM by using Canonical Correlation Analysis (CCA).

Multidimensional Scaling (MDS)

MDS (Kruskal & Wish, 1978), (de Leeuw, Applications of convex analysis to multidimensional scaling, 1977), (de Leeuw, Convergence of the majorization method for multidimensional scaling, 1988), (Borg & Groenen, 2005) is a technique for mapping generally high-dimensional data into a target dimension (typically a low dimension L), such that each distance between a pair of points in the mapped configuration is an approximation to the corresponding given pairwise proximity value as measured by a weighted least squares sum. The given proximity information is represented as an $N \times N$ dissimilarity matrix $(\Delta = [\delta_{ij}], 1 \leq i, j \leq N)$, where N is the number of points (objects), and δ_{ij} is the dissimilarity between point i and j. The output of MDS algorithms can be represented as an $N \times L$ configuration matrix X, whose rows represent each data points $x_i (i=1,...,N)$ in L-dimensional space. We are able to evaluate how well the given points are configured in the L-dimensional space by using a least squares style objective functions for MDS, called STRESS (Kruskal J., 1964) or SSTRESS (Takane, Young, & de Leeuw, 1977). Definitions of STRESS (.1) and SSTRESS (2) are given in the following equations:

$$\sigma(X) = \sum_{i<j\leq N} w_{ij} \left(d_{ij}(X) - \delta_{ij} \right)^2 \qquad (1)$$

$$\sigma^2(X) = \sum_{i<j\leq N} w_{ij} \left(d_{ij}^2(X) - \delta_{ij}^2 \right)^2 \qquad (2)$$

where $d_{ij}(X) = \| x_i - x_j \|, 1 \leq i < j \leq N$ in the L-dimensional target space, and w_{ij} is a weight value, with $w_{ij} \geq 0$.

Generative Topographic Mapping (GTM)

GTM is an unsupervised learning algorithm for modeling the probability density of data, and finding a non-linear mapping of high-dimensional data in a low-dimension space. GTM is also known as a principled alternative to Self-Organizing Map (SOM) (Kohonen, 1998), which does not have any density model. GTM defines an explicit probability density model based on Gaussian distribution (Bishop & Svensén, GTM: A principled alternative to the self-organizing map, 1997) and seeks the best set of parameters associated with Gaussian mixtures by using an optimization method, notably the Expectation-Maximization (EM) algorithm (Dempster, Laird, & Rubin, 1977).

Canonical Correlation Analysis (CCA)

CCA is a classical statistical method to measure correlations between two sets of variables in their linear relationships (Hotelling, 1936). Contrary to ordinary correlation measurement methods, CCA has the ability to measure correlations of multidimensional datasets by finding an optimal projection to maximize the correlation in the subspace spanned by features. The projected values, also known as *canonical correlation variables*, can show how two input sets are correlated. In our experiments, we have measured the similarity of MDS and GTM results by measuring correlation in CCA. More details of CCA can be found in (Hardoon, Szedmak, & Shawe-Taylor, 2004) (Campbell & Atchley, 1981) (Thompson, 1984).

Parallel MDS and GTM

Running MDS or GTM with large datasets (such as PubChem) requires memory-bounded computation, and are not necessarily CPU-bounded. For example, GTM may need a matrix for 8,000 latent points, corresponding to a 20x20x20 3D grid, with 100,000 data points, which requires at least

6.4 GB memory space for holding 8-byte double precision numbers. This single requirement easily prevents us from using a single process to run GTM. Also, memory requirement of SMACOF algorithm increases quadratically as N increases. For example, if N=100,000, then one $N \times N$ matrix needs 80 GB of memory to hold 8-byte double precision numbers. To make matters worse, the SMACOF algorithm generally needs six $N \times N$ matrices, which means at least 480 GB of memory is required to run SMACOF with 100,000 data points (excluding other memory requirements). To overcome this problem, we have developed parallel MDS (SMACOF) and GTM algorithms by using MPI Message Passing Interface (MPI, 2009), which we now discuss in more detail.

Parallel SMACOF

Scaling by MAjorizing a COmplicated Function (SMACOF) (de Leeuw, Applications of convex analysis to multidimensional scaling, 1977), is an algorithm to solve MDS problem with STRESS criterion based on an iterative majorization approach, where one iteration consists of two matrix multiplications. For the mathematical details of SMACOF algorithm, please refer to (Borg & Groenen, 2005). To parallelize SMACOF, we decompose each $N \times N$ matrix with a $m \times n$ block decomposition, where m is the number of block rows and n is the number of block columns, to make use of a total of $p(=m \times n)$ processes. Thus, each process requires only approximately a $1/p$ of the sequential memory requirement of SMACOF algorithm. Figure 2 illustrates how a matrix multiplication between an $N \times N$ matrix (M) and an $N \times L$ matrix (X) is done in parallel using MPI primitives when each $N \times N$ matrix (M) is decomposed with p=6, m=2,n=3, and each arrow represents a message passing. For simplicity, we assume $N \bmod m = N \bmod n = 0$.

Figure 2. Parallel matrix multiplication of $N \times N$ matrix and $N \times L$ matrix based on the 2×3 block decomposition with 6 processes

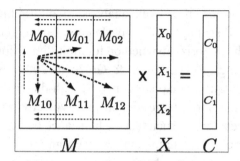

Parallel GTM

To develop the parallel GTM algorithm, we started by analyzing the original GTM algorithm. The GTM algorithm seeks a non-linear manifold embedding of user-defined K latent discrete variables y_k, mapped from a low L-dimension space called *latent space*, which can optimally represent the given N data points $x_n \in \mathbb{R}^D (n = 1, \dots, N)$ into the high D-dimension space, called *data space* (usually $L \ll D$). To define optimality, GTM uses the following log-likelihood function $\mathcal{L}$ using Gaussian noise model:

$$\mathcal{L} = \underset{\{y_k\}, \beta}{\mathrm{argmax}} \sum_{n=1}^{N} \ln \left\{ \frac{1}{K} \sum_{k=1}^{K} \left(\frac{\beta}{2\pi} \right)^{D/2} \exp \left(-\frac{\beta}{2} \left\| x_n - y_k \right\|^2 \right) \right\}$$

(3)

where β^{-1} represents the variance in Gaussian distribution. Since the detailed derivations of GTM algorithm is out of this section's scope, we recommend readers to refer to the original GTM papers (Bishop & Svensén, GTM: A principled alternative to the self-organizing map, 1997) (Bishop, Svensén, & Williams, GTM: The generative topographic mapping, 1998).

In GTM, the most memory consuming step for optimization is the process to compute the posterior probabilities, known as *responsibili-*

Figure 3. Data decomposition of parallel GTM for computing responsibility matrix R by using 2×3 mesh of 6 processes

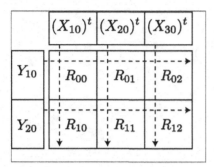

ties, between K latent points and N data points (which is represented by a $K \times N$ matrix). The core of parallel GTM algorithm is to decompose the responsibility matrix into $m \times n$ sub-blocks (Figure 3). Each sub-block holds responsibilities for only approximately K/m mapped point y_k's and N/n data point x_n's. Once the matrix is decomposed, each node of $m \times n$ mesh compute grids can process one sub-block, requiring only $1/mn$ of the memory spaces of the original full responsibility matrix.

Experimental Results

We have done a performance analysis of parallel MDS (SMACOF) and parallel GTM by using a 20K PubChem dataset having 166 dimensions, and measured the correlation of MDS and GTM results for a 100K PubChem dataset. For this performance measurement, we have used our modern cluster systems (Cluster-C, Cluster-E, and Cluster-F) as shown in Table 2.

Parallel MDS

Figure 4 shows the performance comparisons for 20K PubChem data with respect to decomposition methods for the $N \times N$ matrices with 32, 64, and 128 cores in Cluster-E and Cluster-C. A significant characteristic of those plots in Figure 4 is that skewed data decompositions (such as

$p \times 1$ or $1 \times p$, which decompose by row-base or column-base), are always worse in performance than balanced data decompositions (such as $m \times n$ block decomposition which m and n are as similar as possible). There're several reasons for these results. One reason might be the cache line effect that affects cache reusability. In general, balanced block decompositions show better cache reusability (less cache misses) than the skewed ones (Bae, 2008) (Qiu & Fox, Data Mining on Multicore Clusters, 2008). Also, the difference of overhead in message passing mechanism for different data decompositions, specially for calculating $B(X)$, is another possibility for the results in the Figure 4.

Parallel GTM

We have measured performance of parallel GTM with respect to each possible $m \times n$ decomposition of the responsibility matrix to use at most $p=mn$ cores for $p=16$ (Cluster-F), plus 32 and 64 cores in Cluster-E and using the 20k PubChem dataset.

As shown in Figure 5, the performance of parallel GTM is very sensitive on the choice of decomposition of responsible matrix R and, especially, the size of n affects greatly the performance. This is because the large n value increases the number of row-communications for exchanging sub-matrix of Y, while the submatrices of X doesn't need to re-distribute after starting processing since they are not changed throughout the whole process. Also, the results show that the worst case performance is not changed as much as we increase the number of cores. This implies that the worst performance is mainly due to the overheads caused by the use of MPI and its communications, not the process computing time in each core. The outperformance on Linux (Figure 5(a)) is because our parallel GTM implementation is using the statistics package R which is better optimized in Linux than Windows. In Windows (Figure 5(b) and (c)), we have obtained overall performance gains of about 16.89 (%) ~ 24.41 (%) by doubling the number of cores. Further current algorithm

Figure 4. Performance of Parallel SMACOF for 20K PubChem data with 32,64, and 128 cores in Cluster-E and Cluster-C w.r.t. data decomposition of N×N matrices

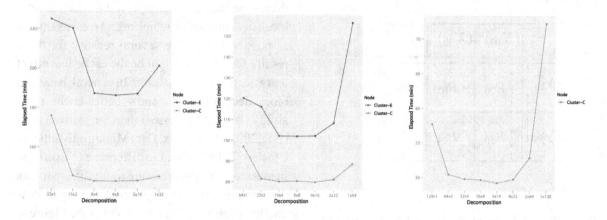

has an inherently sequential component. So we have succeeded in distributing the memory but we need further study of computational performance.

Correlation Measurement by CCA

We have processed 100,000 PubChem data points by using our parallel MDS and GTM and measured similarity between MDS and GTM outputs by using CCA. As shown in Figure 6, the correlation shows a strong linear relationship between MDS and GTM outputs.

Summary

In this subsection, we have tried to deal with large data sets using parallelism in two different data mining algorithms (MDS(SMACOF) and GTM). We found that, for MDS, skewed data decompositions are always worse in performance than balanced data decompositions. In the GTM case, the choice of the responsible matrix R matters, and the worst performance is due to the overhead caused by MPI communication. However, there are important problems for which the data set size

Figure 5. Performance of Parallel GTM for 20K PubChem data with 16, 32 and 64 cores running on Cluster-E (32 and 64 cores) and Cluster-F (16 cores) plotted with absicca defining the the data decomposition running on m×n compute grids

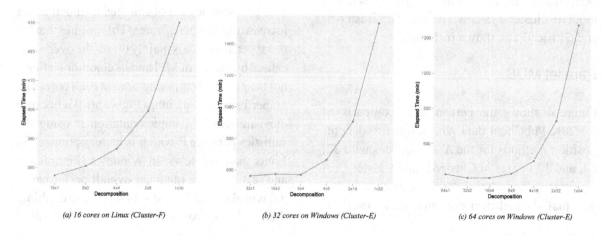

(a) 16 cores on Linux (Cluster-F)   (b) 32 cores on Windows (Cluster-E)   (c) 64 cores on Windows (Cluster-E)

Figure 6. SMACOF and GTM outputs of 100K PubChem dataset are shown in (a) and (b). SMACOF and GTM correlation computed by CCA is shown in (c) as a plot with canonical correlation variables. In this result, the optimal correlation, so-called canonical correlation coefficient, is 0.90 (maximum is 1.00) which shows strong correlation between SMACOF and GTM.

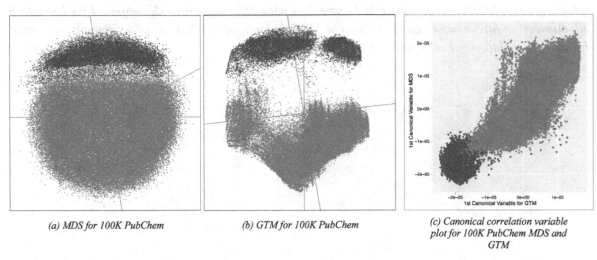

(a) MDS for 100K PubChem   *(b) GTM for 100K PubChem*   *(c) Canonical correlation variable plot for 100K PubChem MDS and GTM*

is too large for even our parallel algorithms to be practical. Because of this, we are now developing interpolation approaches for both algorithms. We are planning to run MDS or GTMs with a (random) subset of the dataset and the dimension reduction of the remaining points are interpolated, so that we can visualize many more data points without using huge amounts of memory.

Metagenomics Studies with Clustering

Our initial work on Metagenomics builds on previous clustering work on clustering (Rose K., Deterministic Annealing for Clustering, Compression, Classification, Regression, and Related Optimization Problems, 1998) (Rose, Gurewitz, & Fox, A deterministic annealing approach to clustering, 1990) (Rose, Gurewitz, & Fox, 1990) (Hofmann & Buhmann, 1997) for determining families and dimension reduction using MDS for visualization (Klock & Buhmann, 2000) (Kearsley, Tapia, & Trosset, 1995) (Kruskal J., 1964) (Takane, Young, & de Leeuw, 1977) (Kruskal & Wish, 1978) (Borg & Groenen, 2005) (de Leeuw, Applications of

convex analysis to multidimensional scaling, 1977). We will propose in "Metagenomics Studies with Hierarchical MDS" subsection to research the use of MDS to reliably divide the sequence space into regions and support fast hierarchical algorithms. Typical results are shown in Figure 7 from an initial sample of 30,000 sequences.

Figure 7 illustrates clustering of a Metagenomics sample using the robust deterministic annealing approach described in (Rose, Gurewitz, & Fox, A deterministic annealing approach to clustering, 1990) (Rose K., Deterministic Annealing for Clustering, Compression, Classification, Regression, and Related Optimization Problems, 1998) (Hofmann & Buhmann, 1997) (Klock & Buhmann, 2000) (Qiu X., Fox, Yuan, Bae, Chrysanthakopoulos, & Nielsen, 2008). This is implemented in MPI and runs in 30 minutes for 10 clusters and over 2 hours for 17 clusters on the 768 core cluster for the full 30,000 sequences. This processing time is proportional to the square of both the number of sequences and number of clusters. We need hierarchical methods to process large data samples and/or large number of clusters. This is illustrated for clusters in Figures 7 b, c, d.

Figure 7. Results of Smith-Waterman distance Computation, Deterministic Annealing Clustering and MDS visualization pipeline for 30,000 Metagenomics sequences. (a) shows 17 clusters for full sample using Sammon's version of MDS for visualization. (b) shows 10 sub-clusters with a total of 9793 sequences found from purple and green clusters in (a) using Sammon's version of MDS for visualization. Sub clustering of light brown cluster in Figure 7(a) with 2163 sequences decomposed further into 6 sub-clusters. In (c) Sammon's ansatz is used in MDS and in (d) SMACOF with less emphasis on small distances: weight(i,j) = 1 in equation 4.

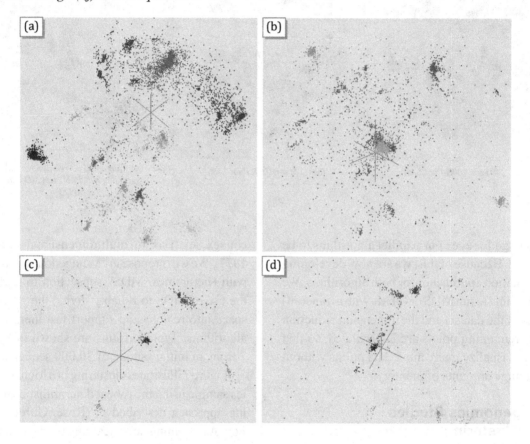

We will discuss more automatic approaches to this in "Metagenomics Studies with Hierarchical MDS" subsection.

We can generalize equations 1 and 2 to state that MDS finds the best set of vectors $\mathbf{x}_i$ in any chosen dimension d ($d=3$ in our case) by minimizing:

$$\sum_{i,j} w_{ij} \left(d_{ij}^{\,n}\left(X\right) - \delta_{ij}^{\,m} \right)^2 \qquad (4)$$

The form of the weights w_{ij} is chosen to reflect the importance of a point or perhaps a desire (Sammon's method with $w_{ij}=1/\delta_{ij}$ as opposed to SMACOF with weight $w_{ij}=1$ to fit smaller distance more precisely than larger ones. The index n is typically 1 (Euclidean distance) but 2 is also useful. The index m is 1 in Figure 7 but $m=0.5$ is also interesting. Figure 7(c and d) show the sensitivity to MDS heuristic with SMACOF producing better results than Sammon for the sub-clustering of the smallish 2163 sequence sample. Generally we use Sammon since it gives the best results overall.

We have MDS implementations with three different methods – the classic expectation maximization approach (Kruskal & Wish, 1978) (Borg & Groenen, 2005) described in "Visualization Analysis by Using Parallel MDS and GTM" subsection, a deterministic annealing version (Klock & Buhmann, 2000) (Klock & Buhmann, 2000), and a distinct version that uses nonlinear χ^2 solution methods (Kearsley, Tapia, & Trosset, 1995) which was used in Figure 7. All have efficient parallel implementations (Fox, Bae, Ekanayake, Qiu, & Yuan, 2008), and we will describe the second and third approaches in detail elsewhere.

Deterministic annealing (Rose K., Deterministic Annealing for Clustering, Compression, Classification, Regression, and Related Optimization Problems, 1998) is a powerful idea to avoid local minima in optimization methods (and both clustering and MDS can be considered this way). By calculating averages explicitly using mean field theory, we can simplify the notoriously slow simulated annealing. For clustering, Hofmann and Buhmann (Hofmann & Buhmann, 1997) first showed how to do this in a formulation that only uses pairwise distances. To see that, define an energy function

$$H_{\text{PWDA}} = 0.5 \sum_{i=1}^{N} \sum_{j=1}^{N} \delta_{ij} \sum_{k=1}^{K} M_i(k) M_j(k) / C(k)$$

(5)

where $C(k) = \sum_{i=1}^{N} M_i(k)$ is the expected number of points in the k-th cluster, and $\delta_{ij} D(i,j)$ is the pairwise distance (or dissimilarity) between points i and j. Equation 5 is minimized for the cluster probabilities $M_i(k)$ so that point i belongs to cluster k. The deterministic annealing can be derived from an informatics theoretic (Rose K., Deterministic Annealing for Clustering, Compression, Classification, Regression, and Related Optimization Problems, 1998) or a physics formalism (Hofmann & Buhmann, 1997). In latter case one smoothes out the cost function (2) by integrating it with

the Gibbs distribution exp(-H/T) over all degrees of freedom. This implies that one is minimizing not H but the free energy F at temperature T and entropy S.

$$F = H - TS$$

(6)

As explained in detail in (Rose K., Deterministic Annealing for Clustering, Compression, Classification, Regression, and Related Optimization Problems, 1998), the temperature T can be interpreted as a distance scale so that gradually reducing the temperature T in equations 5 and 6 corresponds to increasing resolution when one considers distance structure.

Our parallel implementations of equations 5 and 6 are quite mature, and have been used extensively (Fox, Bae, Ekanayake, Qiu, & Yuan, 2008) (Fox, et al., 2009), although there is ongoing activity to improve the overall infrastructure to support the many linked runs needed. There are also some sophisticated options in these methods that are still being implemented. Figure 7 indicates that we perform manual hierarchical analyses already but, as explained in the next subsection, we propose to build on current technology to dramatically improve the scaling to large numbers of sequences, which is currently limited by $O(N^2)$ complexity for all stages of the processing pipeline (Figure 1).

Metagenomics Studies with Hierarchical MDS

Even though the annealing algorithm is looking at genes with a decreasing distance scale, the current clustering algorithm is of $O(N^2)$ complexity, and its behavior (as distance scale is lowered) tracks the "worst region" because the criteria for success are not localized but rather summed over all regions. We can develop new algorithms and dissociate convergence criteria in different regions by a fully hierarchical algorithm using ideas from particle dynamics simulations O(NlogN). The essential idea is to run MDS on a subset of data (say 20,000 to 100,000 sequences) to map sequences to a 3D Euclidean space. This would take hours to days on our 768 core cluster. Then use orthogonal recursive bisection to divide 3D mapped space into geometrically compact regions. This allows both MDS mapping of the full dataset and a proper decomposition to allow efficient hierarchical clustering to find detailed sequence families. The best way to define regions is a research issue with both visual interface and automatic methods such as those described in the next paragraph possible.

We want to find a way of converting $O(N^2)$ algorithms like MDS to O(NlogN) in the same way that "Barnes-Hut trees" and "Fast Multipole" methods convert $O(N^2)$ to O(NlogN) in particle dynamics. The latter is described in many places (Barnes-Hut Simulation, 2009) including the PhD thesis of John Salmon (Salmon, 1991). The idea is illustrated in Figure 8, which shows a 2D projection of the data of Figure 7(a) with a hierarchical quad tree superimposed. This was generated by an open source Barnes Hut Tree code (Berg, 2009).

This approach can be stated as follows: consider a collection of points, which are MDS mapped points in our case, but could be galaxies or stars in astrophysics. Divide them up by "orthogonal recursive bisection" to produce quadtrees in 2D or oct-trees in 3D (as in Figure 7). This is impractical in high dimensional space (as it generates 2^d children at each node in dimension d) but quite feasible in two or three dimensions. In our case, we need to use MDS to map the original sequences, which are both high dimensional and without defined universal vector representations (until we solve Multiple Sequence Alignment MSA problem). Note that the orthogonal recursive bisection divides space into regions where all points in a region are near each other. Given the nature of MDS, "near each other" in 3D implies "near each other" in original space. Observe that this approach builds a tree,

and each internal or terminal node is a cubic region. User-defined criteria (such as number of points in region) establish if this region should be further split into 8 (in 3D) other regions. These criteria need to be designed for MDS, but are naturally the number of points as this determines the performance of part d) of algorithm below.

Our proposed algorithm proceeds as follows:

a. Perform a full $O(N_{subset}^2)$ MDS for a subset N_{subset} of points.

b. Find centers or representative (consensus) points for each region in oct-tree. The centers could be found in at least two ways. First one can use heuristic algorithms to find the center in the original space. A simple heuristic that has been successful for us is to find the point in the region with the minimum value for maximum distance from all other points in that region. A second approach is to find the geometric center in the mapped 3D MDS space (or a set of representative points around a 3D region), then find the nearest sequences to the center – these become representative points for the region. One does this for all nodes of the tree – not just the final nodes. Note that representative points are defined both in original space and in MDS mapped 3D space.

c. We now have a tree with regions and consensus points (centers) associated with all nodes. The next step is performed for remaining $N - N_{subset}$ points – call a typical point p. Take each of the points p and start at the top of the tree. Calculate distance of p to each tree node at a given level. Assign p to the node with the minimum distance from its center to p and continue down the tree looking at 8 sub-nodes below this node. Continue until you have reached bottom of tree.

d. Now we have assigned each $N - N_{subset}$ points p to a region of 3D space – let the assigned region have N_{region} points. Now one performs MDS within this region using

Figure 8. Barnes-Hut Oct tree generated from MDS dimension reduced Metagenomics data

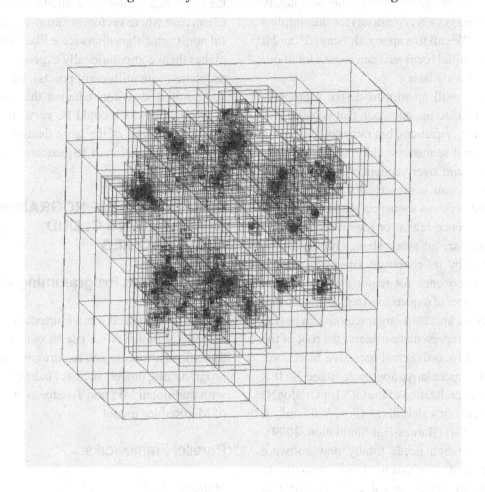

$1+ N_{region}$ points (p plus points in region) to define the MDS mapping of point p with the mapping of original N_{region} points fixed. Note our criterion for dividing nodes probably includes N_{region} < a cutoff value so we can control computational complexity of this step d). The criterion appropriate for dividing nodes is as mentioned above, an important research issue.

There are many refinements that can be evaluated. Maybe our point p is at boundary of a region. This could be addressed by either looking at quality of fit in step d) or the discrimination of distance test in step c). One would choose if necessary not a terminal node at step c) but the larger region corresponding to an internal node. There are tradeoffs between performance (which scales like the number of points in chosen region) and accuracy of method, which need to be researched. Finally all steps of the pipeline in Figure 1 have choices of heuristic parameters that can be significant and need study. In particular there is the optimal choice for weight functions and distance measures to use in equations 4 and 5.

Step a) of the above algorithm has time complexity of $O(N_{subset}^{2})$. MDS interpolation to get the full dataset mapped to 3D (steps c) and d)) has a complexity that depends on implementation — simplest is $O((N - N_{subset}) (\log N_{subset} + N_{region}))$. Clustering and MDS can use the same tree decomposition but clustering will likely use different size (larger) regions. The complexity for clustering is $O(N^2/\# \text{ regions})$ for the simplest algorithm. We call this approach "stage 1" and it will be our initial focus as it can reuse a lot of our existing software base.

Later we will attempt to derive a properly $O(N\log N)$ clustering approach that is based, not on clustering sequences, but rather on clustering "regions" and sequences. Here we will modify the double sum over sequences in equation 5. The form of sum is preserved if sequences are nearby, but replaces sequence-sequence interaction by sequence-region or region-region terms if sequences are far away. Here, a region can be represented by its consensus (mean in particle dynamics) sequence for regions with a weight equal to number of sequences in region. The further sequences are apart, the larger regions can be (i.e. one chooses representation nearer the root of the tree formed by orthogonal recursive bisection). We call this speculative approach "stage 2". It is a natural generalization of the $O(N)$ or $O(N\log N)$ particle dynamics algorithms (Fox, Williams, & Messina, 1994) (Barnes-Hut Simulation, 2009).

This approach needs totally new software and significant algorithm work — in particular to develop an error estimate to decide which level in tree (region size) to use — this is done by multipole expansion in particle case. It can possibly provide not just scalable $O(N\log N + N_{subset}^2)$ clustering but also a viable approach to Multiple Sequence Alignment for large numbers of sequences.

Summary

This section has discussed our parallel datamining algorithms for dimension reduction and clustering and their application to Metagenomics and PubChem chemical properties. We stressed the importance of methods that can be applied to cases where there is an underlying high dimension vector space and to cases where there are no defined vectors and only pairwise dissimilarities are known. We compared GTM and MDS showing

they obtained similar representations for the Pub-Chem case where vectors are known. The powerful non-vector algorithms scale like $O(N^2)$ which makes them computationally expensive for large problems (with millions of points). We discussed some initial ideas for reducing this complexity to $O(N\log N)$ which could be very important in enabling analysis of the large datasets expected from next generation of sequencers.

INNOVATIONS IN PROGRAMMING MODELS USING CLOUD TECHNOLOGIES

Runtimes and Programming Models

This section presents a brief introduction to a set of parallel runtimes we use in our evaluations. Specifically, we compare features of MapReduce programming models such as Hadoop and Dryad with traditional MPI and Twister as an extension of MapReduce model.

Parallel Frameworks

Hadoop

Apache Hadoop (Apache Hadoop, 2009) has a similar architecture to Google's MapReduce runtime (Dean & Ghemawat, 2008), where it accesses data via HDFS, which maps all the local disks of the compute nodes to a single file system hierarchy, allowing the data to be dispersed across all the data/computing nodes. HDFS also replicates the data on multiple nodes so that failures of any nodes containing a portion of the data will not affect the computations which use that data. Hadoop schedules the MapReduce computation tasks depending on the data locality, improving the overall I/O bandwidth. The outputs of the *map* tasks are first stored in local disks until later, when the *reduce* tasks access them (pull) via HTTP connections. Although this approach simplifies the fault handling mechanism in Hadoop, it adds a significant communication overhead to the intermediate data transfers, especially for applications that produce small intermediate results frequently.

Dryad

Dryad (Isard, Budiu, Yu, Birrell, & Fetterly, 2007) is a distributed execution engine for coarse grain data parallel applications. Dryad considers computation tasks as directed acyclic graphs (DAG) where the vertices represent computation tasks and the edges act as communication channels over which the data flow from one vertex to another. In the HPC version of DryadLINQ the data is stored in (or partitioned to) Windows shared directories in local compute nodes and a meta-data file is use to produce a description of the data distribution and replication. Dryad schedules the execution of vertices depending on the data locality. (Note: The academic release of Dryad only exposes the DryadLINQ (Yu, et al., 2008) API for programmers. Therefore, all our implementations are written using DryadLINQ although it uses Dryad as the underlying runtime). Dryad also stores the output of vertices in local disks, and the other vertices which depend on these results, access them via the shared directories. This enables Dryad to re-execute failed vertices, a step which improves the fault tolerance in the programming model.

Twister

Twister (Ekanayake, Pallickara, & Fox, MapReduce for Data Intensive Scientific Analyses, 2008) (Fox, Bae, Ekanayake, Qiu, & Yuan, 2008) is a light-weight MapReduce runtime (an early version was called CGL-MapReduce) that incorporates several improvements to the MapReduce programming model such as (i) faster intermediate data transfer via a pub/sub broker network; (ii) support for long running *map/reduce* tasks; and (iii) efficient support for iterative MapReduce computations. The use of streaming enables Twister to send the intermediate results directly from its producers to its consumers, and eliminates the overhead of the file based communication mechanisms adopted by both Hadoop and Dryad-LINQ. The support for long running *map/reduce* tasks enables configuring and re-using of *map/reduce* tasks in the case of iterative MapReduce computations, and eliminates the need for the re-configuring or the re-loading of static data in each iteration.

MPI Message Passing Interface

MPI (MPI, 2009), the de-facto standard for parallel programming, is a language-independent communications protocol that uses a message-passing paradigm to share the data and state among a set of cooperative processes running on a distributed memory system. The MPI specification defines a set of routines to support various parallel programming models such as point-to-point communication, collective communication, derived data types, and parallel I/O operations. Most MPI runtimes are deployed in computational clusters where a set of compute nodes are connected via a high-speed network connection yielding very low communication latencies (typically in microseconds). MPI processes typically have a direct mapping to the available processors in a compute cluster or to the processor cores in the case of multi-core systems. We use MPI as the baseline performance measure for the various algorithms that are used to evaluate the different parallel programming runtimes. Table 1 summarizes the different characteristics of Hadoop, Dryad, Twister, and MPI.

Science in Clouds: Dynamic Virtual Clusters

Deploying virtual or bare-system clusters on demand is an emerging requirement in many HPC centers. The tools such as xCAT (xCAT, 2009) and MOAB (Moab Cluster Tools Suite, 2009) can be used to provide these capabilities on top of physical hardware infrastructures. In this section

Table 1. Comparison of features supported by different parallel programming runtimes

Feature	Hadoop	DryadLINQ	Twister	MPI
Programming Model	MapReduce	DAG based execution flows	MapReduce with a *Combine* phase	Variety of topologies constructed using the rich set of parallel constructs
Data Handling	HDFS	Shared directories/ Local disks	Shared file system / Local disks	Shared file systems
Intermediate Data Communication	HDFS/ Point-to-point via HTTP	Files/TCP pipes/ Shared memory FIFO	Content Distribution Network (NaradaBrokering (Pallickara and Fox 2003))	Low latency communication channels
Scheduling	Data locality/ Rack aware	Data locality/ Network topology based run time graph optimizations	Data locality	Available processing capabilities
Failure Handling	Persistence via HDFS Re-execution of map and reduce tasks	Re-execution of vertices	Currently not implemented (Re-executing map tasks, redundant reduce tasks)	Program level Check pointing OpenMPI, FT MPI
Monitoring	Monitoring support of HDFS, Monitoring MapReduce computations	Monitoring support for execution graphs	Programming interface to monitor the progress of jobs	Minimal support for task level monitoring
Language Support	Implemented using Java. Other languages are supported via Hadoop Streaming	Programmable via C# DryadLINQ provides LINQ programming API for Dryad	Implemented using Java Other languages are supported via Java wrappers	C, C++, Fortran, Java, C#

we discuss our experience in demonstrating the possibility of provisioning clusters with parallel runtimes and use them for scientific analyses.

We selected Hadoop and DryadLINQ to demonstrate the applicability of our idea. The SW-G application described in "Pairwise Sequence Alignment Using Smith-Waterman-Gotoh" subsection is implemented using both Hadoop and DryadLINQ. With bare-system and XEN (Barham, et al., 2003) virtualization, Hadoop running on Linux, and DryadLINQ running on Windows Server 2008 operating systems, we produced four operating system configurations; namely (i) Linux Bare System, (ii) Linux on XEN, (iii) Windows Bare System, and (iv) Windows on XEN. Out of these four configurations, the fourth one did not work well due to the unavailability of the appropriate para-virtualization drivers. Therefore we selected the first three operating system configurations for this demonstration.

We selected xCAT infrastructure as our dynamic provisioning framework and set it up on top of bare hardware of a compute cluster. Figure 9 shows the various software/hardware components in our architecture. To implement the dynamic provisioning of clusters, we developed a software service that accept user inputs via a pub-sub messaging infrastructure and issue xCAT commands to switch a compute cluster to a given configuration. We installed Hadoop and DryadLINQ in the appropriate operation system configurations and developed initialization scripts to initialize the runtime with the start of the compute clusters. These developments enable us to provide a fully configured computation infrastructure deployed dynamically at the requests of the users.

We setup the initialization scripts to run SW-G pairwise distance calculation application after the initialization steps. This allows us to run a parallel application on the freshly deployed cluster automatically.

Figure 9. Software and hardware configuration of dynamic virtual cluster demonstration. Features include virtual cluster provisioning via xCAT and support of both stateful and stateless OS images.

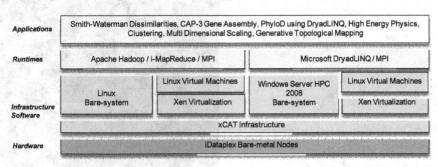

We developed a performance monitoring infrastructure to monitor the utilization (CPU, memory etc.) of the compute clusters using a pub-sub messaging infrastructure. The architecture of the monitoring infrastructure and the monitoring GUI are shown in Figure 10.

In the monitoring architecture, a daemon is placed in each computer node of the cluster, and is started with the initial boot sequence. All the monitor daemons send the monitored performances to a summarizer service via the pub-sub infrastructure. The summarizer service produces a global view of the performance of a given cluster and sends this information to a GUI that visualizes the results in real-time. The GUI is specifically developed to show the CPU and the memory utilization of the bare-system/virtual clusters when they are deployed dynamically.

With all the components in place, we implemented SW-G application running on dynamically deployed bare-system/virtual clusters with Hadoop and DryadLINQ parallel frameworks as shown in the performance chart of Figure 10. We divide cluster nodes into three groups, each has 4 nodes of 16 core to run Hadoop on Redhat bare system, Hadoop on Xen VMs, and DryadLINQ on Windows HPC respectively. The average switching time between these three settings is about 5 minutes. (Ekanayake, Gunarathne, & Qiu, Cloud Technologies for Bioinformatics Applications, 2010) observes a performance degradation be-

tween 15% and 25% for Hadoop SW-G application on Xen VMs. This dynamic virtual clusters environment will be extended in the FutureGrid project (FutureGrid Homepage, 2009).

Pairwise Sequence Alignment Using Smith-Waterman-Gotoh

Introduction to Smith-Waterman-Gotoh (SWG)

Smith-Waterman (Smith & Waterman, 1981) is a widely used local sequence alignment algorithm for determining similar regions between two DNA or protein sequences. In our studies we use Smith-Waterman algorithm with Gotoh's (Gotoh, 1982) improvement for Alu sequencing. The Alu clustering problem (Price, Eskin, & Pevzner, 2004) is one of the most challenging problems for sequencing clustering because Alus represent the largest repeat families in human genome. As in metagenomics, this problem scales like $O(N^2)$ as given a set of sequences we need to compute the similarity between all possible pairs of sequences.

Implementations

Dryad Implementation

We developed a DryadLINQ application to perform the calculation of pairwise SW-G distances for a given set of genes by adopting a coarse grain

Figure 10. Architecture of the performance monitoring infrastructure and the monitoring GUI.

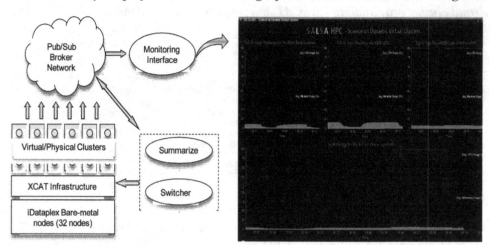

task decomposition approach which requires minimum inter-process communication to ameliorate the higher communication and synchronization costs of the parallel runtime. To clarify our algorithm, let's consider an example where N gene sequences produce a pairwise distance matrix of size NxN. We decompose the computation task by considering the resultant matrix and group the overall computation into a block matrix of size DxD, where D is a multiple (>2) of the available computation nodes. Due to the symmetry of the distances δ_{ij} and= δ_{ji} we only calculate the distances in the blocks of the upper triangle of the block matrix as shown in Figure 11(a). The blocks in the upper triangle are partitioned (assigned) to the available compute nodes, and an "Dryad Apply" operation is used to execute a function to calculate (N/D)x(N/D) distances in each block. After computing the distances, the function calculates the transpose matrix of the result matrix which corresponds to a block in the lower triangle, and writes both these matrices into two output files in the local file system. The names of these files and their block numbers are communicated back to the main program. The main program sorts the files based on their block numbers and then performs another "Apply" operation

to combine the files corresponding to a row of blocks into a single large row block as shown in the Figure 11(b).

MPI Implementation

The MPI version of SW-G calculates pairwise distances using a set of either single or multithreaded processes. We use the "Space Filling" MPI algorithm for data decomposition as shown in Figure 12(a), which runs a "space filling curve through lower triangular matrix" to produce equal numbers of pairs for each parallel unit (such as process or thread). For N gene sequences, we need to compute half of the values (in the lower triangular matrix), for a total of $M = N \times (N\text{-}1)/2$ distances. At a high level, computation tasks are evenly divided among P processes and executed in parallel. The computation workload per process is M/P. At a low level, each computation task can be further divided into subgroups and run in T concurrent threads. Our implementation in Figure 12(b) is designed for flexible use of shared memory multicore system and distributed memory clusters (tight to medium tight coupled communication technologies such threading and MPI).

Figure 11. (a) Task decomposition (b) DryadLINQ implementation and vertex hierarchy

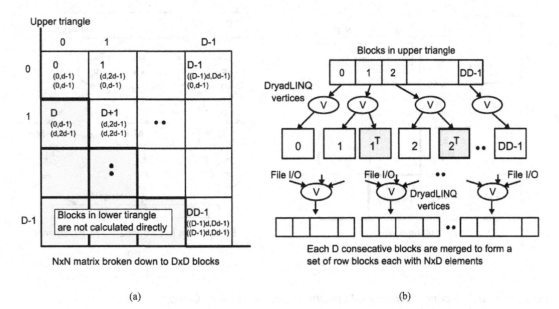

(a)

(b)

Apache Hadoop Implementation

We developed an Apache Hadoop version of the pairwise distance calculation program based on the JAligner (JAligner, 2009) program, the java implementation of the NAligner code used in Dryad version. Similar to the other implementations, the computation is partitioned in to blocks based on the resultant matrix. Each of the blocks would get computed as a map task. The block size (D) can be specified via an argument to the program. The block size needs to specified in such a way that there will be much more map tasks than the capacity of the system, so that the Apache Hadoop scheduling will happen as a pipeline of map tasks resulting in global load balancing of the application. The input data is distributed to the worker nodes through the Hadoop distributed cache, which makes them available in the local disk of each compute node.

A load balanced task partitioning strategy (as described below) is used to identify the blocks that need to be computed (dark grey) through map tasks as shown in the Figure 13(a). In addition all the blocks in the diagonal (light grey) are also computed. Even though the task partitioning mechanisms are different, both Dryad-SWG and Hadoop-SWG ends up with essentially identical computation blocks, if the same block size is given to both the programs.

When $\beta >= \alpha$, we calculate $D(\alpha,\beta)$ only if $\alpha+\beta$ is even,

When $\beta < \alpha$, we calculate $D(\alpha,\beta)$ only if $\alpha+\beta$ is odd.

Figure 13(b) depicts the run time behavior of the Hadoop-swg program. In the given example the map task capacity of the system is "k" and the number of blocks is "N". The solid black lines represent the starting state, where "k" map tasks (blocks) will get scheduled in the compute nodes. The dark dashed lines represent the state at t_1, when two map tasks, m_2 & m_6, get completed and two map tasks from the pipeline gets scheduled for the placeholders emptied by the completed map tasks. The grey dotted lines represent the future.

Figure 12. (a) Space filling data decomposition; (b) MPI runtime processes architecture

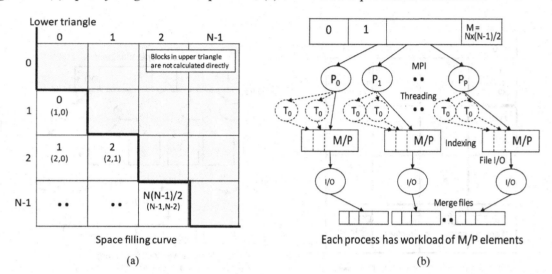

(a)   (b)

Figure 13. (a)Task decomposition; (b)Map and reduce tasks for Hadoop

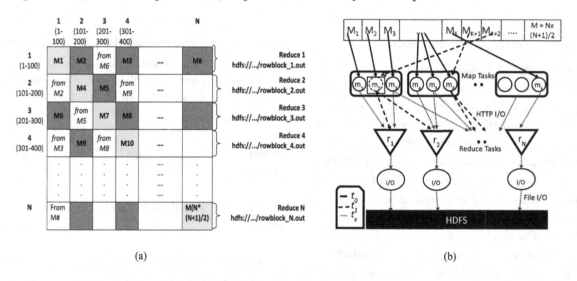

(a)   (b)

Map tasks use custom Hadoop writable objects as the output values to store the calculated pairwise distance matrices for the respective blocks. In addition, non-diagonal map tasks output the inverse distances matrix as a separate output value. Hadoop uses local files and http transfers to send the map task output key value pairs to the reduce tasks.

The outputs of the map tasks are then collected by the reduce tasks. Since the reduce tasks start

collecting the outputs as soon as the first map task finishes, and continue to do so while other map tasks are executing, the data transfers from the map tasks to reduce tasks do not present a significant performance overhead to the program. The program currently creates a single reduce task per each row block resulting in total of (no. of sequences/block size) Reduce tasks. Each reduce task to accumulate the output distances for a row block and writes the collected output to

Table 2. Different computation clusters used for this analysis

Feature	Linux Cluster (Ref A)	Windows Cluster (Ref B)	Windows Cluster (Ref C)	Windows Cluster (Ref D)	Windows Cluster (Ref E)	Linux Cluster (Ref F)
CPU	Intel(R) Xeon(R) L5420 2.50GHz	Intel(R) Xeon(R) L5420 2.50GHz	Intel(R) Xeon(R) E7450 2.40GHz	Intel(R) Xeon(R) L5420 2.50GHz	AMD Opteron 8356 2.3 GHz	Intel(R) Xeon(R) E5345 2.33 GHz
# CPU # Cores	2 8	2 8	4 6	2 8	4 16	2 4
Memory	32 GB	16 GB	48 GB	32 GB	16 GB	20 GB
# Disk	1	2	1	1	1	1
Network	Giga bit Ethernet	Giga bit Ethernet	20 Gbps Infiniband or 1 Gbps	Giga bit Ethernet	Giga bit Ethernet	Giga bit Ethernet
Operating System	Red Hat Enterprise Linux Server release 5.3 -64 bit	Microsoft Window HPC Server 2008 (Service Pack 1) - 64 bit	Microsoft Window HPC Server 2008 (Service Pack 1) - 64 bit	Microsoft Window HPC Server 2008 (Service Pack 1) - 64 bit	Microsoft Window HPC Server 2008 (Service Pack 1) - 64 bit	GNU/Linux x86_64
# Cores	256	256	768	256	128	64

a single file in Hadoop Distributed File System (HDFS). This results in N number of output files corresponding to each row block, similar to the output we produce in the Dryad version.

Performance Comparison

We compared the Dryad, Hadoop and MPI implementations of ALU SW-G distance calculations using a replicated data set and obtained the following results. The data sets were generated by taking a 10000 sequence random sample from a real data set, and replicating it 2-5 times. Dryad and MPI tests were performed in cluster *ref D* (Table 2), and the Hadoop tests were performed in cluster *ref A* (Table 2) Cluster ref A is identical to cluster *ref D*, which are two identical Windows HPC and Linux clusters. The Dryad & MPI results were scaled to account for the performance difference of the kernel programs, NAligner and the JAligner in their respective environments, for fair comparison with the Hadoop implementation.

Figure 14 indicates that all three implementations perform and scale well for this application with Hadoop implementation showing the best scaling. As expected, the times scaled proportion-

ally to the square of the number of distances. On 256 cores the average time of 0.017 milliseconds per pair for 10k data set corresponds to roughly 4.5 milliseconds per pair calculated per core used. The coarse grained Hadoop & Dryad applications perform and scale competitively with the tightly synchronized MPI application.

We notice that the Hadoop implementation shows improved performance with the increase of the data set size, while Dryad performance degrades a bit. Hadoop improvements can be attributed to the diminishing of the framework overheads, while the Dryad degradation can be attributed to the memory management in the Windows and Dryad environment.

Inhomogeneous Data Study

Most of the data sets we encounter in the real world are inhomogeneous in nature, making it hard for the data analyzing programs to efficiently break down the problems. The same goes true for the gene sequence sets, where individual sequence lengths and the contents vary among each other. In this section we study the effect of inhomoge-

Figure 14. Comparison of Dryad, MPI and Hadoop technologies on ALU sequencing application with SW-G algorithm

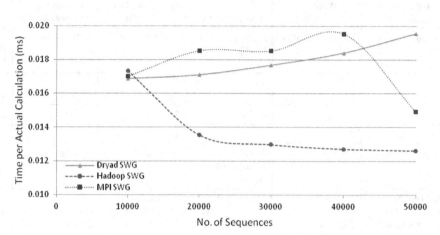

neous gene sequence lengths for the performance of our pairwise distance calculation applications.

$$SWG(A, B) = O(mn)$$

The time complexity to align and obtain distances for two genome sequences A, B with lengths m and n respectively using Smith-Waterman-Gotoh algorithm is approximately proportional to the product of the lengths of two sequences (O(mn)). All the above described distributed implementations of Smith-Waterman similarity calculation mechanisms rely on block decomposition to divide the larger problem space in to sub-problems that can be solved using the distributed components. Each block is assigned two sub-sets of sequences, where Smith-Waterman pairwise distance similarity calculation needs to be performed for all the possible sequence pairs among the two sub sets. According to the previously mentioned time complexity of the Smith-Waterman kernel used by these distributed components, the execution time for a particular execution block depends on the lengths of the sequences assigned to the particular block.

Parallel execution frameworks like Dryad and Hadoop work optimally when the load is equally partitioned among the tasks. Depending on the scheduling strategy of the framework, blocks with different execution times can have an adverse effect on the performance of the applications, unless proper load balancing measures have been taken in the task partitioning steps. For an example, in Dryad, vertices are scheduled at the node level, making it possible for a node to have blocks with varying execution times. In this case if a single block inside a vertex takes a larger amount of time than other blocks to execute, then the whole node have to wait till the large task completes, which utilizes only a fraction of the node resources.

Since the time taken for the Smith-Waterman pairwise distance calculation depends mainly on the lengths of the sequences and not on the actual contents of the sequences, we decided to use randomly generated gene sequence sets for this experiment. The gene sequence sets were obtained from a given mean sequence length (400) with varying standard deviations following a normal distribution of the sequence lengths. Each sequence set contained 10000 sequences leading to 100 million pairwise distance calculations to perform. We performed two studies using such inhomogeneous data sets. In the first study the sequences were randomly distributed in the

Figure 15. Performance of SW-G pairwise distance calculation application for randomly and skewed distibuted inhomogeneous data with '400' mean sequence length

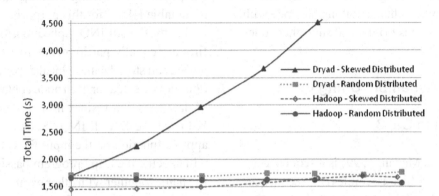

data sets. In the second one the sequences were distributed using a skewed distribution, where the sequences in a set were arranged in the ascending order of their length.

Figure 15 presents the execution time taken for the randomly distributed and skewed distributed inhomogeneous data sets with the same mean length, by the two different implementations. The Dryad results depict the Dryad performance adjusted for the performance difference of the NAligner and JAligner kernel programs. As we notice from the Figure 15, both Dryad and Hadoop performed satisfactorily for the randomly distributed inhomogeneous data, without showing significant performance degradations with the increase of the standard deviation. This behavior can be attributed to the fact that the sequences with varying lengths are randomly distributed across a data set, effectively providing a natural load balancing to the execution times of the sequence blocks. In fact Hadoop implementation showed minor improvements in the execution times, which can be attributed to the fact that the actual workload gets reduced (effect of O(mn)) with the increase of the standard deviation even

though the mean and the number of sequences stay the same.

For the skewed distributed inhomogeneous data, we notice a clear performance degradation in the Dryad implementation. Once again Hadoop performs consistently without showing significant performance degradation, even though it does not perform as well as its randomly distributed counterpart. This can be attributed to the global pipeline scheduling of the map tasks. In the Hadoop Smith-Waterman implementation, each block decomposition gets assigned to a single map task. The framework allows the administrator to specify the number of map tasks that can be run on a particular compute node. The global scheduler assigns the map tasks directly on to those placeholders in a much finer granularity than in Dryad, as and when the individual map tasks finish. This allows the Hadoop implementation to perform natural global level load balancing. In this case it might even be advantageous to have varying task execution times to iron out the effect of any trailing map tasks towards the end of the computation. Dryad implementation pre-allocates all the tasks to the compute nodes and does not perform any dynamic scheduling across the nodes.

This makes a node which gets a larger work chunk to take considerable longer time than a node which gets a smaller work chunk, making the node with a smaller work chuck to idle while the other nodes finish.

Sequence Assembly Using Cap3

Introduction to Cap3

Cap3 (Huang & Madan, 1999) is a sequence assembly program which assembles DNA sequences by aligning and merging sequence fragments. The Cap3 algorithm works in several steps after reading a collection of gene sequences from an input file in the FASTA format. In the first two steps the poor regions of the fragments are removed, and the overlaps between the fragments are calculated. The third step identifies and removes the false overlaps. In the next step, the fragments are then joined to form what are called contigs or one or more overlapping DNA segments derived from a single genetic source. Finally, the last step constructs multiple sequence alignments and generates consensus sequences. This program outputs several files as well as standard output.

Implementations

Cap3 is often used with lots of input files making it an embarrassingly parallel application requiring no inter-process communications. We implemented parallel applications for Cap3 using Microsoft DryadLINQ (Yu, et al., 2008) (Isard, Budiu, Yu, Birrell, & Fetterly, 2007) and Apache Hadoop (Apache Hadoop, 2009). This fits as a "map only" application for the MapReduce model. The Hadoop application is implemented by creating map tasks which execute the Cap3 program as a separate process on the given input FASTA file. Since the Cap3 application is implemented in C, we do not have the luxury of using the Hadoop file system (HDFS) directly. Hence the data needs to be stored in a shared file system across the nodes. Therefore, we are actively investigating the possibility of using Hadoop streaming and mountable HDFS for this purpose.

For the DryadLINQ application, the set of input files are equally partitioned across the compute nodes, and stored in their local disks. A data partition file is created for each node containing the list of data files that resides in that particular node. We used the DryadLINQ "Select" operation to apply a function on the input files. The function will execute the Cap3 program passing the input file name together with other parameters and will save the standard output from the program. All the outputs will get moved to a predefined location (an approach supported by both implementations).

Performance

First we performed a scalability test on our Cap3 implementations using a homogeneous data set. This data set is created by replicating a single file for a given number of times. The file we chose contained 458 sequences. When interpreting the results for Hadoop Cap3 implementation on Linux and DryadLINQ Cap3 implementation on windows, it should be noted that the Cap3 standalone program performed on average approximately 12.5% faster on windows than on Linux in the testing environment.

As we can see from Figure 16, both Hadoop and DryadLINQ show good scaling for the Cap3 application, with even slightly increased performance with the increase of data size. The increase must be happening due to the overheads of the framework getting diminished over the larger workload. On 256 cores the average time 0.4 seconds on Hadoop to execute Cap3 program on a single data set corresponds to approximately 102 seconds per file executed per core, while the average time 0.36 seconds for DryadLINQ Cap3 application corresponds to approximately 92 seconds per file executed per core.

Figure 16. Cap3 scalability test with homogeneous data

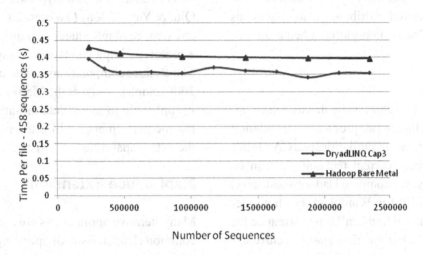

Figure 17. Cap3 inhomogeneous data performance

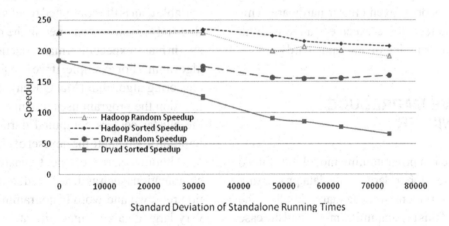

Inhomogeneous Data Study

Unlike the Smith-Waterman Gotoh case, Cap3 program execution time does not directly depend on the file size or the size of the sequences. It depends mainly on the content of the sequences. This makes it hard for us to artificially generate inhomogeneous data sets for the Cap3 program, therefore forcing us to use real data. When generating the data sets, first we calculated the standalone Cap3 execution time for each of the files in our data set. Then, based on those timings, we created data sets that have approximately similar mean times, while the standard deviation of the standalone running

times is different in each data set. We performed the performance testing for randomly distributed as well as skewed distributed (sorted according to individual file running time) data sets similar to the SWG inhomogeneous study. The speedup is taken by dividing the sum of sequential running times of the files in the data set by the parallel implementation running time.

Figure 17 depicts the Cap3 inhomogeneous performance results for Hadoop & Dryad. Hadoop shows satisfactory scaling for both random as well as sorted data sets, while the Dryad shows satisfactory scaling in the randomly distributed data set.

Once again we notice that Dryad does not perform well for the skewed distributed inhomogeneous data due to its' static non-global scheduling.

Summary

The heart of this section is the discussion of applying MapReduce to two problems – calculation of Smith-Waterman dissimilarities and CAP3 EST assembly – where current technologies can be used efficiently. We compare Hadoop (on Linux) to Dryad and MPI (on Windows). For homogeneous problems we find similar performance for all technologies but we find Hadoop currently has advantages over Dryad for inhomogeneous data. We also describe some useful technologies to allow rapid deployment of different operating environments on a given cluster hardware. This allows these tests to be executed fairly with all environments running on the same hardware.

ITERATIVE MAPREDUCE WITH TWISTER

MapReduce is a programming model introduced by Google to support large scale data processing applications (Ghemawat, January, 2008). The simplicity of this programming model and the ease of supporting quality of services make it more suitable for large scale data processing applications. Our experience in applying MapReduce for scientific analyses reveals that it is suitable for many scientific analyses as well. However, we noticed that the current MapReduce programming model and its implementations such as Apache Hadoop do not support iterative MapReduce computations efficiently. Iterative computations are common in many fields such as data clustering, machine learning, and computer vision, and many of these applications can be implemented as MapReduce computations. In Twister (an early version was known as CGL-MapReduce) (Ekanayake, Pallickara, & Fox, MapReduce for Data Intensive

Scientific Analyses, 2008) (Fox, Bae, Ekanayake, Qiu, & Yuan, 2008) (Twister, 2011), we present an extended MapReduce programming model and a prototype implementation to support iterative MapReduce computations efficiently. Note (Chu, 2006) emphasized that the MapReduce approach is applicable to many data mining applications, but the performance will often be poor without the extra capabilities of Twister.

MapReduce Extensions

Many iterative applications we analyzed show a common characteristic of operating on two types of data products called static and variable data. Static data is used in each iteration and remain fixed throughout the computation, whereas the variable data is the computed results in each iteration and typically consumed in the next iteration step in many expectation maximization (EM) type algorithms. For example, if we consider K-means clustering algorithm (MacQueen), during the nth iteration the program uses the input data set and the cluster centers computed during the $(n-1)^{th}$ iteration to calculate the next set of cluster centers.

Although some of the typical MapReduce computations such as distributed sorting, information retrieval and word histogramming consume very large data sets, many iterative applications we encounter operate on moderately sized data sets which can fit into the distributed memory of the computation clusters. This observation leads us to explore the idea of using long running map/reduce tasks similar to the long running parallel processes in many MPI applications which last throughout the life of the computation. The long running (cacheable) map/reduce tasks allow map/reduce tasks to be configured with static data and use them without loading them again and again in each iteration. Current MapReduce implementations such as Hadoop (Apache Hadoop, 2009) and DryadLINQ (Yu, et al., 2008) do not support this behavior. Hence they initiate new map/reduce tasks and load static data in each

Figure 18. Long running and short running processes in various parallel programming runtimes

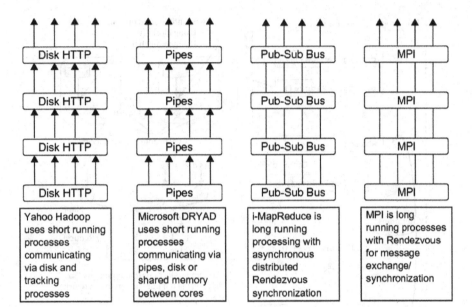

iteration step, therefore incurring considerable performance overheads. This distinction is shown in Figure 18. By supporting long running map/reduce tasks, we do not encourage users to store state information in the map/reduce tasks, which violates the "side-effect-free" nature of the map/reduce computations rather achieving considerable performance gains by caching the static data across map/reduce tasks. The framework does not guarantee the use of same set of map/reduce tasks throughout the life of the iterative computation.

In addition, we also add an optional reduction phase named "combine" to the MapReduce computation to allow programs to access the outputs of the reduce phase as a single value. Combine phase is another reduction phase which can be used to aggregate the results of the reduce phase into a single value. The user program and the combine operation run on a single process space allowing its output to be directly accessible to the user program. This enables the user to check conditions based on the output of the MapReduce computations.

Twister uses streaming for all the communication/data transfer requirements, which eliminates

the overhead in transferring data via file systems as in Hadoop or DryadLINQ. The output <Key, Value> pairs produced during the map stage get transferred directly to the reduce stage, and the output of the reduce stage get transferred directly to the combined stage via the pub-sub broker network. Currently Twister use the publish-subscribe messaging capabilities of NaradaBrokering (Pallickara & Fox, 2003) messaging infrastructure, but the framework is extensible to support any other publish-subscribe messaging infrastructure such as Active MQ (ActiveMQ, 2009).

We provide two mechanisms to access data in Twister; (i) from the local disk of the computer nodes, and (ii) directly from the pub-sub infrastructure. For the simplicity of the implementation, we provide a file based data access mechanism for the map/reduce tasks. The data distribution is left for the users to manage, and we plan to provide tools to perform such operations in the near future. Once distributed, Twister generates a meta-data file that can be used by the framework to run MapReduce computations. Apart from the above, the use of streaming enables Twister to support features such as directly sending input

Figure 19. Iterative MapReduce programming model using Twister

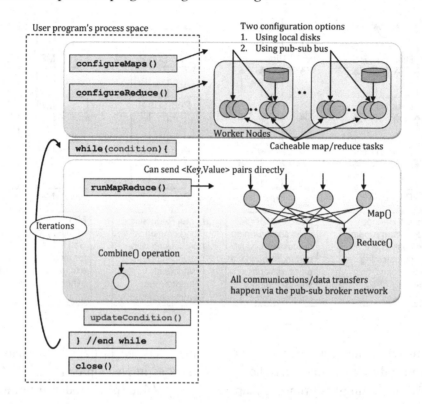

<Key,Value> pairs for the map stage, and configuring map/reduce stages using the data sent from the user program. Figure 19 shows the programming model of Twister, and how iterative MapReduce computations are executed.

Performance of Twister for Iterative Computations

We have used the Twister framework to implement a series of scientific data analyses applications ranging from simple Map-only type operations to multiple iterative computations. Here we are presenting the results of four such applications, namely (i) CAP3 (Huang & Madan, 1999) gene sequence assembly, (ii) High Energy Physics data analysis, (iii) K-means clustering, and (iv) Matrix multiplication. We have also implemented the above applications using Apache Hadoop and DryadLINQ and MPI as well. The details of these applications and the parallel implementations are

explained in more details in our previous publications (Fox, Bae, Ekanayake, Qiu, & Yuan, 2008). Figures 20 through 23 present the results of our evaluations. Notice that, to obtain these results, we have used two compute clusters as shown in Table 2. All the DryadLINQ applications were run on cluster ref. B while Hadoop, Twister and MPI applications were run on cluster ref. A. The overhead calculation is based on the formula (7) presented below.

$$\text{Overhead } f(p) = [p * T(p) - T(1)] / T(1) \qquad (7)$$

where p denotes the number of parallel processes used and T(p) denotes the time when p processes were used. T(1) gives the sequential time for the program.

The CAP3 application case is a map-only (or typically named as pleasingly parallel) application in which the parallel processes require no inter

Figure 20. Performance of CAP3 gene assembly programs under varying input sizes

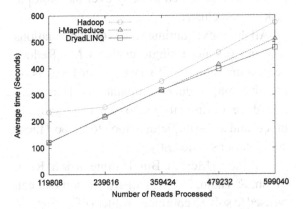

Figure 21. Performance of high energy physics programs under varying input sizes

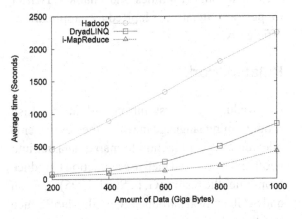

Figure 22. Overhead of K-means clustering implementations under varying input sizes

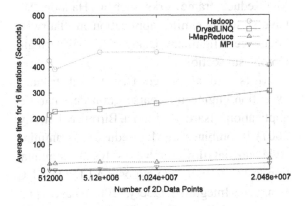

Figure 23. Overhead of matrix multiplication implementations under varying input sizes

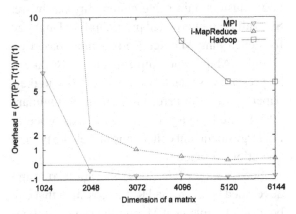

process communications. The High Energy Physics (HEP) application is a typical MapReduce application aiming to produce a histogram of identified features from a large volume of data obtained during fusion experiments. The previous results indicate that all the runtimes, Hadoop, DryadLINQ and Twister perform equally well for these two types of applications. Notice that the higher running time observed in Hadoop in the case of HEP data analysis was due to the placement of data in a different parallel file system Hadoop's built in distributed file system HDFS (Apache Hadoop, 2009). This is because the ROOT (ROOT, Data Analysis Framework, 2009) data analysis framework used for HEP analysis could

only read input files from local disks. Apart from above, these two analysis show that the Twister has not introduced any additional overheads for the typical MapReduce applications.

K-means clustering and matrix multiplication applications present typical iterative application characteristics. The graphs in Figure 22 and Figure 23 highlight the applicability of Twister to these iterative applications. The performance of Twister in the case of K-means clustering and the parallel overhead in the case of matrix multiplication are close to the values of MPI where both Hadoop and DryadLINQ shows relatively higher parallel overheads. Our approach of using long running map/reduce tasks and the use of streaming for the data transfers have eliminated many overheads present in other runtimes and enabled Twister to perform iterative MapReduce applications efficiently.

Related Work

MapReduce was first introduced in the Lisp programming language in which the developer is allowed to use a function to map a data set into another data set, and then use a function to reduce (combine) the results (G. L. Steel, 1995). J. Dean and S. Ghemawat introduced Google MapReduce and the associated programming model for large scale data intensive applications. Their framework supports fault tolerance, and is able to run on a large clusters built using commodity hardware. Swazall is an interpreted programming language for developing MapReduce programs based on Google's MapReduce implementation. R. Pike et al. present its semantics and its usability in their paper (Pike, Dorward, Griesemer, & Quinlan, 2005). The language is geared towards processing large document collections, which are typical operations for Google.

Sector/Sphere (Gu, 2009) is a parallel runtime developed by Y. Gu, and R. L. Grossman that can be used to implement MapReduce style applications. Sphere adopts a streaming based computation model used in GPUs which can be used to develop applications with parallel topologies as a collection of MapReduce style applications. Sphere stores intermediate data on files, and hence is susceptible to higher overheads for iterative applications.

Disco (Disco project, 2009) is an open source MapReduce runtime developed using a functional programming language named Erlang (Erlang programming language, 2009). Disco architecture shares clear similarities to the Google and Hadoop MapReduce architectures where it stores the intermediate results in local files and access them later using HTTP from the appropriate reduce tasks. However, Disco does not support a distributed file system as HDFS but expects the files to be distributed initially over the multiple disks of the cluster.

All the above runtimes focus on computations that can fit into a single cycle of MapReduce programming model. In Twister our focus is on iterative map reduce computations. Hence we introduce optimizations to the programming model and to the implementation to support these computations efficiently.

All-Pairs (Moretti, Bui, Hollingsworth, Rich, Flynn, & Thain, 2009) is an abstraction that can be used to solve a common problem of comparing all the elements in a data set with all the elements in another data set by applying a given function. This problem can be implemented using typical MapReduce frameworks such as Hadoop. We have shown a similar application in "Pairwise Sequence Alignment Using Smith-Waterman-Gotoh" subsection.

M. Isard et al. present Dryad - a distributed execution engine for coarse grain data parallel applications (Isard, Budiu, Yu, Birrell, & Fetterly, 2007). It combines the MapReduce programming style with dataflow graphs to solve the computation tasks. DryadLINQ exposes a LINQ (LINQ Language-Integrated Query, 2009) based programming API for Dryad. The Directed Acyclic Graph (DAG) based programming model of Dryad can support more classes of applications than pure MapReduce programming model. DryadLINQ also provides a "loop unrolling" feature that can be used to create aggregated execution graphs combing a few iterations of iterative computations. However, as we have shown in Figure 22 it could not reduce the overhead of the programming model for large (in number of iterations) iterative applications.

Future Work on Twister

In our current research we are focusing on adding fault tolerance support for the Twister runtime since this is a key feature of Hadoop and Dryad.

Saving system state at every iteration will add considerable overheads for iterative applications. Therefore we are working to add features to Twister so that it can save system state after a given number of iterations (Gropp & Lusk, 2004) (Fagg & Dongarra, 2000) (Hursey, Mattox, & Lumsdaine, 2009). Apart from the above we are researching further MapReduce extensions which will expand its use into more classes of parallel applications. We intend to support all applications that can be implemented using MPI Reduce, Broadcast and Synchronization primitives. We will present our findings under the umbrella project Twister (Twister, 2011).

Summary

In this section we have discussed our experience in developing an extended MapReduce programming model and a prototype implementation named Twister. We have shown that with *Twister* one can apply MapReduce to iterative applications and obtain considerable performance gains comparable to MPI implementations of the same applications.

CONCLUSION

We have discussed the use of innovative data-mining algorithms and new programming models for several Life Sciences applications. We are particularly interested in methods that are applicable to large data sets coming from high throughput devices of steadily increasing power. We have shown impressive results for both clustering and dimension reduction algorithms, and the use of MapReduce on modest size problems. However, we have identified two key areas where further research is essential. Therefore, we propose to develop new O(NlogN) complexity algorithms suitable for the analysis of millions of sequences. Furthermore, we suggest Iterative MapReduce as a promising programming model combining the best features of MapReduce with those of high performance environments such as MPI.

ACKNOWLEDGMENT

We would like to thank Microsoft for their collaboration and support. Tony Hey, Roger Barga, Dennis Gannon and Christophe Poulain played key roles in providing technical support. We appreciate our collaborators from IU School of Informatics and Computing. David Wild and Qian Zhu gave us important feedback on visualization for PubChem data. We are grateful for UITS system administrators Joe Rinkovsky and Jenett Tillotson who set up the infrastructure for the SALSA virtual cluster environment.

REFERENCES

ActiveMQ. (2009). Retrieved December 2009, from http://activemq.apache.org/

Apache Hadoop. (2009). Retrieved December 2009, from http://hadoop.apache.org/

Bae, S.-H. (2008). Parallel multidimensional scaling performance on multicore systems. *Proceedings of the Advances in High-Performance E-Science Middleware and Applications Workshop (AHEMA) of Fourth IEEE International Conference on eScience* (pp. 695-702). Indianapolis, IN: IEEE Computer Society.

Barham, P., Dragovic, B., Fraser, K., Hand, S., Harris, T., Ho, A., et al. (2003). Xen and the art of virtualization. *Proceedings of the Nineteenth ACM Symposium on Operating Systems Principles, Bolton Landing* (pp. 164-177). New York, NY: ACM Press.

Barnes-Hut Simulation. (2009). Retrieved December 2009, from http://en.wikipedia.org/wiki/Barnes-Hut_simulation

Berg, I. (2009). *Simulation of N-body problems with the Barnes-Hut algorithm.* Retrieved December 2009, from http://www.beltoforion.de/barnes_hut/barnes_hut_de.html

Bishop, C. M., & Svensén, M. (1997). GTM: A principled alternative to the self-organizing map. *Advances in Neural Information Processing Systems*, 354–360.

Bishop, C. M., Svensén, M., & Williams, C. K. (1998). GTM: The generative topographic mapping. *Neural Computation*, *10*, 215–234. doi:10.1162/089976698300017953

Borg, I., & Groenen, P. J. (2005). *Modern multidimensional scaling: Theory and applications.* Springer.

Campbell, N., & Atchley, W. R. (1981). The geometry of canonical variate analysis. *Systematic Zoology*, ▪▪▪, 268–280. doi:10.2307/2413249

Chu, C. T. (2006). *Map-reduce for machine learning on multicore. NIPS* (pp. 281–288). MIT Press.

de Leeuw, J. (1977). Applications of convex analysis to multidimensional scaling. *Recent Developments in Statistics*, 133-145.

de Leeuw, J. (1988). Convergence of the majorization method for multidimensional scaling. *Journal of Classification*, *5*, 163–180. doi:10.1007/BF01897162

Dean, J., & Ghemawat, S. (2008). MapReduce: Simplified data processing on large clusters. *Communications of the ACM*, *51*(1), 107–113. doi:10.1145/1327452.1327492

Dempster, A., Laird, N., & Rubin, D. (1977). Maximum likelihood from incomplete data via the EM algorithm. *Journal of the Royal Statistical Societym Series B*, 1--38.

Disco Project. (2009). Retrieved December 2009, from http://discoproject.org/

Ekanayake, J., Balkir, A., Gunarathne, T., Fox, G., Poulain, C., Araujo, N., et al. (2009). *DryadLINQ for scientific analyses.* Fifth IEEE International Conference on eScience: 2009. Oxford, UK: IEEE.

Ekanayake, J., Gunarathne, T., & Qiu, J. (2010). Cloud technologies for bioinformatics applications. *Invited paper submitted to the Journal of IEEE Transactions on Parallel and Distributed Systems*.

Ekanayake, J., Gunarathne, T., Qiu, J., Fox, G., Beason, S., & Choi, J. Y. (2009). *Applicability of DryadLINQ to scientific applications.* Community Grids Laboratory, Indiana University.

Ekanayake, J., Pallickara, S., & Fox, G. (2008). MapReduce for data intensive scientific analyses. *Fourth IEEE International Conference on eScience* (pp. 277-284). IEEE Press.

Ekanayake, J., Qiu, X., Gunarathne, T., Beason, S., & Fox, G. (2010). High performance parallel computing with clouds and cloud technologies. In Ahson, S. A., & Ilyas, M. (Eds.), *Cloud computing and software services: Theory and techniques. CRC Press*. Taylor and Francis. doi:10.1201/EBK1439803158-c12

Erlang Programming Language. (2009). Retrieved December 2009, from http://www.erlang.org/

Fagg, G. E., & Dongarra, J. J. (2000). Lecture Notes in Computer Science: *Vol. 1908. FT-MPI: Fault tolerant MPI, supporting dynamic applications in a dynamic world* (pp. 346–353). Springer Verlag.

Fox, G., Bae, S.-H., Ekanayake, J., Qiu, X., & Yuan, H. (2008). *Parallel data mining from multicore to cloudy grids*. High Performance Computing and Grids Workshop.

Fox, G., Qiu, X., Beason, S., Choi, J. Y., Rho, M., Tang, H., et al. (2009). *Biomedical case studies in data intensive computing*. The 1st International Conference on Cloud Computing (CloudCom 2009). Springer Verlag.

Fox, G. C., Williams, R. D., & Messina, P. C. (1994). *Parallel computing works!*Morgan Kaufmann Publishers, Inc.

FutureGrid Homepage. (2009). Retrieved December 2009, from http://www.futuregrid.org

Ghemawat, J. D. (2008, January). Mapreduce: Simplified data processing on large clusters.*ACM Communications, 51*, 107–113.

Gotoh, O. (1982). An improved algorithm for matching biological sequences. *Journal of Molecular Biology, 162*, 705–708. doi:10.1016/0022-2836(82)90398-9

Gropp, W., & Lusk, E. (2004). Fault tolerance in message passing interface programs. *International Journal of High Performance Computing Applications, 18*, 363–372. doi:10.1177/1094342004046045

Gu, Y. G. (2009). Sector and Sphere: The design and implementation of a high performance data cloud. *Crossing boundaries: computational science, e-Science and global e-Infrastructure I. Selected papers from the UK e-Science All Hands Meeting 2008 Philosophical Transactions of the Royal Society of America, 367*, 2429-2445.

Hadoop Distributed File System HDFS. (2009). Retrieved December 2009, from http://hadoop.apache.org/hdfs/

Hardoon, D. R., Szedmak, S., & Shawe-Taylor, J. (2004). Canonical correlation analysis: An overview with application to learning methods. *Neural Computation, 16*, 2639–2664. doi:10.1162/0899766042321814

Hofmann, T., & Buhmann, J. M. (1997). Pairwise data clustering by deterministic annealing. *IEEE Transactions on Pattern Analysis and Machine Intelligence, 19*, 1–14. doi:10.1109/34.566806

Hotelling, H. (1936). Relations between two sets of variates. *Biometrika, 28*, 321–377.

Huang, X., & Madan, A. (1999). CAP3: A DNA sequence assembly program. *Genome Research, 9(9)*, 868–877. doi:10.1101/gr.9.9.868

Hursey, J., Mattox, T. I., & Lumsdaine, A. (2009). Interconnect agnostic checkpoint/restart in Open MPI. *Proceedings of the 18th ACM International Symposium on High Performance Distributed Computing HPDC*, (pp. 49-58).

Isard, M., Budiu, M., Yu, Y., Birrell, A., & Fetterly, D. (2007). Dryad: Distributed data-parallel programs from sequential building blocks. *ACM SIGOPS Operating Systems Review, 41*, 59–72. doi:10.1145/1272998.1273005

Jaligner. (2009). Retrieved December 2009, from Smith Waterman Software: http://jaligner.sourceforge.net

Kearsley, A. J., Tapia, R. A., & Trosset, M. W. (1995). *The solution of the metric STRESS and SSTRESS problems in multidimensional scaling using Newton's method.* Houston, TX: Rice University.

Klock, H., & Buhmann, J. M. (2000). Data visualization by multidimensional scaling: A deterministic annealing approach.*Pattern Recognition, 33*, 651–669. doi:10.1016/S0031-3203(99)00078-3

Kohonen, T. (1998). The self-organizing map. *Neurocomputing, 21*, 1–6. doi:10.1016/S0925-2312(98)00030-7

Kruskal, J. (1964). Multidimensional scaling by optimizing goodness of fit to a nonmetric hypothesis. *Psychometrika, 29*, 1–27. doi:10.1007/BF02289565

Kruskal, J. B., & Wish, M. (1978). *Multidimensional scaling*. Sage Publications Inc.

LINQ Language-Integrated Query. (2009). Retrieved December 2009, from http://msdn.microsoft.com/en-us/netframework/aa904594.aspx

MacQueen, J. B. (1967). Some methods for classification and analysis of multivariate observations. *5-th Berkeley Symposium on Mathematical Statistics and Probability* (pp. 281-297). University of California Press.

Moab Cluster Tools Suite. (2009). Retrieved December 2009, from http://www.clusterresources.com/products/moab-cluster-suite.php

Moretti, C., Bui, H., Hollingsworth, K., Rich, B., Flynn, P., & Thain, D. (2009). All-Pairs: An abstraction for data intensive computing on campus grids. *IEEE Transactions on Parallel and Distributed Systems, 21*, 21–36.

MPI. (2009). Retrieved December 2009, from Message Passing Interface: http://www-unix.mcs.anl.gov/mpi/

Pallickara, S., & Fox, G. (2003). *NaradaBrokering: A distributed middleware framework and architecture for enabling durable peer-to-peer grids*. ACM/IFIP/USENIX 2003 International Conference on Middleware. Rio de Janeiro, Brazil: Springer-Verlag New York, Inc.

Pike, R., Dorward, S., Griesemer, R., & Quinlan, S. (2005). Interpreting the data: Parallel analysis with sawzall. *Scientific Programming Journal Special Issue on Grids and Worldwide Computing Programming Models and Infrastructure, 13*(4), 227–298.

Price, A. L., Eskin, E., & Pevzner, P. A. (2004). Whole-genome analysis of Alu repeat elements reveals complex evolutionary history. *Genome Research, 14*, 2245–2252. doi:10.1101/gr.2693004

PubChem Project. (2009, December). Retrieved from http://pubchem.ncbi.nlm.nih.gov/

Qiu, X., Ekanayake, J., Beason, S., Gunarathne, T., Fox, G., Barga, R., et al. (2009). *Cloud technologies for bioinformatics applications*. 2nd ACM Workshop on Many-Task Computing on Grids and Supercomputers (SuperComputing09). ACM Press.

Qiu, X., & Fox, G. C. (2008). Data mining on multicore clusters. In *Proceedings of 7th International Conference on Grid and Cooperative Computing GCC2008* (pp. 41-49). Shenzhen, China: IEEE Computer Society.

Qiu, X., Fox, G. C., Yuan, H., Bae, S.-H., Chrysanthakopoulos, G., & Nielsen, H. F. (2008). Performance of multicore systems on parallel data clustering with deterministic annealing. *Computational Science – ICCS 2008* (pp. 407-416). Kraków, Poland: Springer Berlin / Heidelberg.

ROOT, Data Analysis Framework. (2009). Retrieved December 2009, from http://root.cern.ch/

Rose, K. (1998). Deterministic annealing for clustering, compression, classification, regression, and related optimization problems. *Proceedings of the IEEE, 86*, 2210–2239. doi:10.1109/5.726788

Rose, K., Gurewitz, E., & Fox, G. (1990). A deterministic annealing approach to clustering. *Pattern Recognition Letters, 11*, 589–594. doi:10.1016/0167-8655(90)90010-Y

Rose, K., Gurewitz, E., & Fox, G. C. (1990). Statistical mechanics and phase transitions in clustering. *Physical Review Letters, 65*, 945–948. doi:10.1103/PhysRevLett.65.945

Salmon, J. K. (1991). *Parallel hierarchical N-body methods*. PhD. California Institute of Technology.

Smith, T. F., & Waterman, M. S. (1981). Identification of common molecular subsequences. *Journal of Molecular Biology, 147*(1), 195–197. doi:10.1016/0022-2836(81)90087-5

Steel, G. L. Jr. (1995). Parallelism in Lisp. *SIGPLAN Lisp Pointers*, *8*(2), 1–14. doi:10.1145/224133.224134

Takane, Y., Young, F. W., & de Leeuw, J. (1977). Nonmetric individual differences multidimensional scaling: an alternating least squares method with optimal scaling features. *Psychometrika*, *42*, 7–67. doi:10.1007/BF02293745

Thompson, B. (1984). *Canonical correlation analysis uses and interpretation*. Sage.

Twister. (2011). Retrieved July 2011, from www.iterativemapreduce.org

Wheeler, D. L., Barrett, T., Benson, D. A., Bryant, S. H., Canese, K., Chetvernin, V., et al. (2006). Database resources of the national center for biotechnology information. *Nucleic Acids Research*, *33*(1). xCAT. (2009). *Extreme cluster administration toolkit*. Retrieved December 2009, from http://xcat.sourceforge.net/

Yu, Y., Isard, M., Fetterly, D., Budiu, M., Erlingsson, U., Gunda, P., et al. (2008). *DryadLINQ: A system for general-purpose distributed data-parallel computing using a high-level language*. Symposium on Operating System Design and Implementation (OSDI).

Chapter 11
Visualization of Large–Scale Distributed Data

Jason Leigh
University of Illinois at Chicago, USA

Venkatram Vishwanath
University of Illinois at Chicago, USA & Argonne National Laboratory, USA

Andrew Johnson
University of Illinois at Chicago, USA

Tom Peterka
Argonne National Laboratory, USA

Luc Renambot
University of Illinois at Chicago, USA

Nicholas Schwarz
Northwestern University, USA

ABSTRACT

An effective visualization is best achieved through the creation of a proper representation of data and the interactive manipulation and querying of the visualization. Large-scale data visualization is particularly challenging because the size of the data is several orders of magnitude larger than what can be managed on an average desktop computer. Large-scale data visualization therefore requires the use of distributed computing. By leveraging the widespread expansion of the Internet and other national and international high-speed network infrastructure such as the National LambdaRail, Internet-2, and the Global Lambda Integrated Facility, data and service providers began to migrate toward a model of widespread distribution of resources. This chapter introduces different instantiations of the visualization pipeline and the historic motivation for their creation. The authors examine individual components of the pipeline in detail to understand the technical challenges that must be solved in order to ensure continued scalability. They discuss distributed data management issues that are specifically relevant to large-scale visualization. They also introduce key data rendering techniques and explain through case studies approaches for scaling them by leveraging distributed computing. Lastly they describe advanced display technologies that are now considered the "lenses" for examining large-scale data.

DOI: 10.4018/978-1-61520-971-2.ch011

INTRODUCTION

The primary goal of visualization is insight. An effective visualization is best achieved through the creation of a proper representation of data and the interactive manipulation and querying of the visualization. Large-scale data visualization is particularly challenging because the size of the data is several orders of magnitude larger than what can be managed on an average desktop computer. Data sizes range from terabytes to petabytes (and soon exabytes) rather than a few megabytes to gigabytes. Large-scale data can also be of much greater dimensionality, and there is often a need to correlate it with other types of similarly large and complex data. Furthermore the need to query data at the level of individual data samples is superseded by the need to search for larger trends in the data. Lastly, while interactive manipulation of a derived visualization is important, it is much more difficult to achieve because each new visualization requires either re-traversing the entire dataset, or compromising by only viewing a small subset of the whole. Large-scale data visualization therefore requires the use of distributed computing.

The individual components of a data visualization pipeline can be abstracted as:

Data Retrieval → Filter / Mine → Render → Display

The degree to which these individual components are distributed or collocated has historically been driven by the cost to deploy and maintain infrastructure and services. Early in the history of scientific computing, networking bandwidth was expensive and therefore scarce. Consequently early visualization pipelines tended to minimize the movement of data over networks in favor of collocating data storage with data processing. However, as the amount and variety of data continued to grow at an exponential pace, it became too costly to maintain full replicas of the data for each individual that needed to use it. Instead, by leveraging the widespread expansion of the Internet and other national and international high-speed network infrastructure such as the National LambdaRail[1], Internet-2[2], and the Global Lambda Integrated Facility[3], data and service providers began to migrate toward a model of widespread distribution of resources.

In this chapter we will first introduce the various instantiations of the visualization pipeline and the historic motivation for their creation. We will then examine individual components of the pipeline in detail to understand the technical challenges that must be solved in order to ensure continued scalability. We will discuss distributed data management issues that are specifically relevant to large-scale visualization. We will also introduce key data rendering techniques and explain through case studies approaches for scaling them by leveraging distributed computing. Lastly we will describe advanced display technologies that are now considered the "lenses" for examining large-scale data.

THE LARGE-SCALE DATA VISUALIZATION PIPELINE

Collocated Data, Filtering, Rendering and Display Resources

Most visualization software packages have a pipeline architecture where raw data comes in at one end of the pipeline from disk or the network, moves through a sequence of filters that process the data on the CPU and generate computer graphics primitives (e.g. lines, triangles, splats, pixels) which are rendered on the GPU, and displayed on a monitor at the other end of the pipeline. Some filters deal with accessing data or generating data. Other filters convert data from one form to another. Finally there are filters that deal with the creation of computer graphics. Each filter has an explicit input and output format allowing

Figure 1. Three views of West Lake Bonney in the McMurdo Dry Valleys of Antarctica. (ENDURANCE data collection was supported by NASA Space Sciences grant NNX07AM88G).

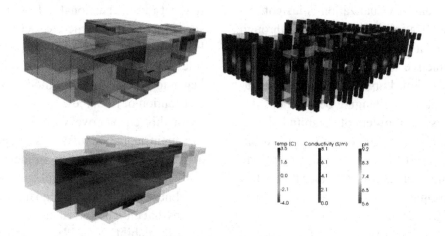

compatible filters to be linked together to move data through the pipeline, and new filters can be added to the library of filters to support new data formats, graphics formats or rendering techniques.

For example, in 2008 the NASA funded ENDURANCE project sent an autonomous underwater vehicle (AUV) into ice covered West Lake Bonney in Antarctica. The AUV took measurements of temperature, conductivity, pH, and five other values at over 18,000 points within the lake. If a scientist wants to see overall temperature trends in the lake then the pipeline could read in the data, and plot each temperature value as a box at the appropriate X, Y, Z location where each box is colored based on a transfer function that maps a given temperature value to a particular color (Figure 1). To look inside the lake, the scientist may want to see the temperature values only on a plane slicing through the lake. Here the pipeline could add a filter to interpolate raw temperature values across the surface of the plane. The scientist might also want to compare multiple values (e.g. temperature, conductivity, and pH) by plotting all three simultaneously.

The advantages of this kind of pipeline/layered approach were described in the 1987 report from the first workshop on Visualization in Scientific Computing (McCormick, 1988) that in many ways marked the official beginning of the field of Scientific Visualization. These advantages include:

- Easy adaptation to a variety of data sources and display devices;
- Software that is tailorable to the needs of diverse applications;
- The ability to add more techniques and algorithms;
- Layers that can be distributed to different computers to better leverage their capabilities and minimize cost;
- Affording economically viable development of a shared and interoperable set of tools;
- Software that can accommodate different budgets and equipment preferences of a broad community of users;
- Being able to address the demands of a broad scientific community in coherent unison rather than on a case-by-case basis.

Rendering can produce geometric primitives such as points, lines, or surfaces made of triangles that can be cached on the graphics card. When the user changes their viewpoint on the visualiza-

Figure 2. Hydrology of the Chesapeake Bay visualized in the CAVE© virtual reality environment

tion, these primitives can be quickly re-rendered without re-running the data access, data conversion, and rendering filters in the pipeline. While adequate for point, vector, or surface data, these polygonal representations are less appropriate for volumetric data. An alternative is direct rendering where there is no geometric representation and individual data points are drawn as 'splats', or volumes are rendered through raytracing each pixel on the screen. Direct rendering can give much better views of volumetric data, however as there are no graphics primitives to be cached, the entire scene must be re-rendered when the viewpoint changes.

In addition to rendering the dataset itself, supplementary graphics are often needed to put the data into context (e.g. in our example of the lake above, it might be helpful to see an outline of the lake, or a North pointing arrow, or latitude and longitude lines) and to supply information about the visualization (depth scale, legend, color bars, etc.) Filters in the pipeline generate these

supplemental graphics or read them from disk. These also must be re-drawn when the visualization is re-rendered but supplementary graphics are usually very lightweight compared to the data being visualized.

Rendering is usually done locally on the display machine. These visualizations can be viewed in 2D on a typical monitor screen or projector, or in 3D using a stereoscopic monitor, CAVE© (Figure 2) (Cruz-Neira, 1992), or other stereo projection setup. Rendering in 3D may make it easier to disambiguate complex multi-dimensional datasets but the creation of the 3D version requires rendering the dataset from two viewpoints – one for each eye. For users lacking a 3D display, the ability to quickly rotate a visualization, and the ability to view the dataset from multiple angles simultaneously can help disambiguate complex scenes. While this text focuses on rendering data visually there is also a body of work focusing on 'visualizing' data using sonification or haptics to augment visualization through the use of other senses. In these cases most of the pipeline remains the same except that there is additional rendering and display needed for these other senses.

The user interacts with the visualization by directly or indirectly modifying the filters in the pipeline – either by adding or removing filters, or changing the parameters of the existing filters. One of the major advantages of a pipeline architecture is that the entire pipeline does not need to be re-run when a change is requested. If intermediate results are stored at each of the filters then only the filters downstream from the affected filter need to be recomputed. This saves time at the cost of needing more memory to hold both the original dataset and its intermediate forms. Once the pipeline is set up correctly, similar datasets (e.g. multiple timesteps) can be fed through the pipeline without changing the filter settings.

The user can interact with the visualization in several ways. In the simplest case the user can change their point of view, or rotate and scale the visualization to see the visualization as an object from the outside looking in, or from within the visualization looking around. The user will also typically want to turn individual visualizations or supplementary graphics on and off, change the time-step in an animated sequence, change the color transfer function, or change the representation of the visualization (points, surface, glyphs.) More sophisticated users will want to dynamically change the pipeline itself. Interaction with the pipeline is typically through a graphical user interface that is linked into the pipeline, allowing the user to interact with familiar interface elements - buttons, sliders, check boxes that affect the filter parameters behind the scenes. On desktop systems interaction is typically performed with a keyboard and mouse. Immersive environments with head-tracking allow a user to more naturally change their point of view by simply moving their head, but these environments typically use a hand-held pointer instead of a mouse and keyboard making it harder to accurately change parameters quickly.

Given the large amounts of data in multi-dimensional datasets, the amount of data must be reduced at several points prior to display; there will often be more raw data points than there are pixels on the screen to display them, or space in main memory to hold them. For interactive visualization, datasets often need to be reduced so they will fit on disk at the local site, further reduced to fit in main memory at the local site, and further reduced to fit into memory on the local graphics card(s). Visualization systems often store data at multiple resolutions to allow the user to have fast interactive access to a lower resolution version of the visualization that can remain on the graphics card. This allows a user to quickly manipulate the low-resolution version, for example rotating a wireframe box showing the space the data takes up, or a visualization of only every 100th data item, while still seeing enough landmarks to do the manipulation accurately. Once the user stops manipulating the low-resolution version of the visualization, the pipeline can take the time to generate the full-resolution version, replacing the low-resolution version.

For real-time interaction with this kind of visualization there are limited filtering opportunities. Interaction is very fast if the data being visualized fits in the graphics card, for example changing the viewpoint on a polygonal surface representation or on volume data that fits in the card's 3D texture memory. If the user changes the visualization parameters on an existing visualization (e.g. generating a new polygonal iso-surface or changing the viewable subset of volume data) then various filters are going to need to be re-run. The CPU will need to use data from main memory to compute the new visualization and send it to the graphics card. If the necessary data are not currently stored in main memory then the CPU needs to move it in from disk or from the network, and the user must wait for that data to be fetched before the pipeline can execute and display the results. Prefetching data to local disk or main memory can be used to reduce this wait time, but there is only so much storage space on the graphics card, in main memory, and on local disk, so that space usage must be optimized for a given visualization. This often means that an initial preprocessing step is needed to turn large datafiles into a hierarchy of fixed sized blocks for faster transfer between the various caches.

With CPUs moving towards an increasing number of cores rather than each core becoming increasingly faster, being able to parallelize the work of the visualization pipeline on a single machine, as well as using clusters to parallelize the work across multiple machines is becoming more important in decreasing computation time for very large datasets. Shading languages such as GLSL and CG are being used to speed up the rendering on the GPUs. Languages like CUDA are being used on GPUs to speed up computation by moving some of the computation off of the CPU and onto the GPU. As with multiple CPUs, in these cases bus bandwidth can become another limiting factor- if one cannot move the data fast enough into the CPU then one cannot fully take advantage of the CPU's processing power.

Non-Interactive, Offline Rendered Visualization

When computational simulations produce extremely large datasets, and/or when raw data collected by scientific instruments, such as remote sensors, fill up storage systems, interactive exploration of the results becomes extremely difficult. A common and effective approach has been to produce animations and video files from the data that the scientist can explore at his or her home institution and can share with colleagues.

Long running simulations such as weather or earthquake simulations, protein folding, high-energy physics or astronomical computations fall in this category. They require large amounts of data as initial conditions (the starting point of the simulation) and produce greater amounts of data, often through a time series of results (a complete

solution for each time step during the length of the simulation).

When faced with such a scenario, scientists are often in a situation where the data are too large to be gathered and shipped back to his or her office computer for analysis and visualization. The data has to remain within the supercomputing facility hosting the computational simulation or the data storage in the first place.

One solution then is to schedule batch (non-interactive) jobs that produce images based on the simulation results. An image can be generated for each time step of the simulation, or an animated camera can follow a predetermined path for a given dataset. More complex visualizations can combine animations of numerous parameters (camera path, time series, change in representation, selection of variables to be visualized, etc.). While the time to render one frame can be rather large, the common approach is to apply an image-based parallelization where each processor renders a distinct complete frame. This is relatively simple to implement and fits well in the supercomputing infrastructure: a number of processor nodes can access a large commonly shared file system hosting the complete simulation results. If rendering jobs access different time step results, each processor will access unique files and maximizes I/O throughput. If rendering jobs access the same data, the read-only nature of the process also maximizes file system usage.

The end result of the rendering job is a series of frames, usually kept in a non-destructive file format, such as TIFF, to maintain data integrity. Since it's a non-interactive process, high-resolution, including stereoscopic 3D, as well as high quality images can be produced using photo-realistic rendering techniques such as raytracing. Frames can be combined in various movie formats of different resolution and quality for multiple purposes (result dissemination, education and outreach, movie production, etc.).

The software used for such approaches varies greatly from very specific home-brewed visualization software for a very narrow purpose (such as seismic wave propagation for earthquake visualization), to scientific rendering toolkits (such as the 'Visualization Toolkit', vtk.org, for medical or engineering applications), finally up to general-purpose rendering packages (such as Autodesk Maya or Pixar's Renderman). If available, graphics hardware can be used to speed up such intensive rendering jobs.

Given the non-interactive characteristics of this process, the problem resides in specifying the visualization and rendering parameters (variable selection, camera path, shading, lighting, etc.). Scientists have devised different approaches: for a well-defined visualization technique such as volume rendering, the main parameter to be selected is the transfer function that defines the mapping from data values into color and transparency. This function can be selected off-line, on a small dataset and then applied during full-scale rendering. A desktop user-interface or a web portal can be used to define rendering job characteristics (data input, image size, quality, etc.) and visualization parameters (viewpoint, transfer functions, etc.). More advanced systems let the user preview the visualization in low resolution and quality but give full access to all the parameters of the visualization (for instance Autodesk Maya). Even more advanced systems allow the user to be immersed in the visualization by using a VR device such as the CAVE©, where the scientists can interact with a proxy (reduced dataset) of the visualization and 'choreograph' the rendering to be done. Donna Cox, leading the Advanced Visualization Laboratory at the National Center for Supercomputing Applications (NCSA) at the University of Illinois at Urbana-Champaign, has pioneered such an approach with the 'Virtual Director' system (Thiebaux, 2000).

With the advent of petascale computing, where the data produced is so large that it overflows even the largest storage infrastructure, the approach of generating movies and animations directly inside the supercomputing facility is gaining renewed interest taking the model in different directions:

- Compared to petascale sized datasets, even the highest resolution uncompressed rendering is becoming attractive for its predictable and manageable size. A format gaining traction is the so-called 4K format (4096x2160 pixel resolution) adopted by the digital cinema initiative as the next generation movie distribution format. At four times the resolution of high-definition television, it becomes possible to portray a simulation dataset with exquisite detail.

- While simulations can run for an extremely long time, it is often beneficial to couple the simulation process with the visualization process, and generate early rendering results as soon as possible while the simulation is still running. This technique, referred to as computational steering if the user can interactively control simulation parameters, enables early detections of problems such as programming bugs or incorrect initial conditions in the simulation. The simulation-visualization coupling can be done through a data checkpoint on storage, or through network communication between a simulation cluster and a visualization rendering resource.

- If a tight coupling between simulation and visualization is achieved by running both programs on the same computational resource, *in situ* visualization can be performed, removing the need for any storage or data transmission, hence speeding up the generation of visual results.

- Using high-speed networking, the rendering need not to be stored for later examination, but can be streamed in full quality to the scientist at his or her desk.

The benefits of running the complete visualization pipeline all at once and generating animations or video streams are:

- Asynchronous work ("submit and forget") for the scientists;
- Non-interactive jobs where known batch optimizations can be applied, and predictable usage of resources make the visualization process efficient and acceptable by the scientist and the supercomputing community;
- Early rendering as the simulation is running can be extremely beneficial;
- The end product is much smaller than the simulation data (even for high-resolution uncompressed rendering), and can still be cut and edited into a movie production pipeline for education, dissemination and outreach.

The drawbacks of the approach are:

- Non-interactive visualization- so the scientist needs to know what to look for, hence limiting the visual exploration of simulation results.
- May require work on proxy data beforehand to determine the visualization and rendering parameters
- Data has to be reloaded and re-rendered if modifications are needed.

Examples of Offline Rendered Visualizations

- The San Diego Supercomputing Center and the Southern California Earthquake Center's TeraShake is the largest and most detailed simulation of what happens during a major earthquake on the southern San Andreas fault, computed at 3000x1500x400 resolution. Various volume renderings are used to produce movies. The parameters of visualization are submitted by scientist through a web portal, which in turn schedules and launches numerous jobs on large compute clusters such as the TeraGrid. The end results are time-series animations for various earthquake scenarios.

- The National Center for Supercomputing Applications' classic tornado simulations calculated the birth of a tornado, starting with data from weather conditions that produced a powerful tornado in South Dakota. The results are choreographed and cinematic renderings of this complex simulation data combining artistic and scientific expertise translated the data into a dynamic, high-definition animated visualization. Data representations (proxies) are loaded into software such as Maya, visualization parameters are selected interactively in pre-visualization, and then jobs are launched for rendering on a powerful cluster computer.

- Accurately modeling the dynamics and structure of the Earth's interior requires massively distributed computational techniques - the use of high-performance PC clusters generating terabytes of data which are then visualized through distributed volumetric rendering methods to produce high-quality monoscopic and stereoscopic visualizations. Global seismic wave propagation data are generated with software from the Theoretical & Computational Seismology group at the California Institute of Technology. This software produces highly accurate simulations of wave propagation. Global models for each time-step are combined to create a global model of seismic wave propagation over time. A one-hour seismic wave field divergence simulation of the 1994 earthquake in Bolivia highlighting positive amplitude compression (P) waves at progressive stages during propagation

Figure 3. Seismic wave field divergence visualization of the 1994 earthquake in Bolivia highlights positive amplitude compressional waves at progressive stages during propagation (vanKeken, 2001)

takes 21 hours to compute (Figure 3). The simulation data are redistributed across the cluster according to the requirements of the specific visualization algorithm. The 169 time steps of the simulation are sampled uniformly throughout model time, making the total time for gathering and interpolating the data 33.8 hours, producing a 512 x 512 x 512 regular grid at 16-bit resolution (40GB-worth of data). An interactive tool is used for staging and rendering monoscopic and stereoscopic 3D volumetric animations. The approach allows the user to interactively select datasets, setup camera positions, pick color, opacity and gradient transfer functions, and specify movie properties. The rendering was performed on a TeraGrid cluster at the San Diego Supercomputing Center on up to 64 nodes. Table 1 shows rendering times and speedups for a low-resolution stereoscopic rendering and high-resolution monoscopic

Table 1. Rendering time and speedups for seismic rendering on a 64-node cluster

	Stereo pairs (1024x768) Time and speedup		High-resolution (8000x3600) Time and speedup	
1 processor	2h30min	1.0	20h	1.0
32 processors	5min	30.0	52min	23.1
64 processors	2min-30sec	60.0	28min	42.0

rendering of the 169 time steps of the simulation: it shows significant acceleration, where the stereoscopic animation takes only 2 minutes and 30 seconds to generate on 64 processors, and the high-resolution animation showing all the simulation details took only 28 minutes. The end products, as shown in the following pictures, are time-series animations showing three different views of the wave propagation through the earth.

Fully Distributed Visualization

As the amount and variety of available data on the Internet grows, so will the means by which the data can be filtered or mined, visualized and displayed. There is no single data mining or visualization technique that will satisfy the needs of every application; the choice of technique is highly dependent on the fundamental question being asked about the data. The power of the Internet is maximally leveraged when storage, filtering / mining, visualization and display capabilities are presented as independent services that can be combined in a myriad different ways, distributing the visualization pipeline around the planet. Google maps is an example of how the coupling of a map service with a data service can provide wholly new forms of information and insight.

A key technological enabler for a distributed service-oriented paradigm (sometimes referred to as Grid Computing or Cloud Computing) is an abundance of high-speed networking. Traditionally, networking was considered expensive and it was therefore impractical to move large quantities of data over them. As a result, data filtering and mining algorithms were collocated with the source of the data. This made it difficult for new filtering and mining algorithms to emerge as it was not possible for the original data providers to anticipate all the different ways in which their users might want to use the data. However with the continual decrease in networking costs, a fully distributed model is quickly becoming practical.

In 2002, the National Science Foundation's OptIPuter project sought to envision how unlimited networking bandwidth could change fundamental notions of computing and the way scientists conduct basic research (Smarr, 2003). In the OptIPuter model, all computing resources were fully distributed, and the networks that tied the resources together were thought of as wide-area system busses rather than networks. Therefore a cluster of computers with massive amounts of storage was collectively considered a single virtual disk drive, and a cluster of computers with high performance graphics cards was thought of as a single graphics card. The project resulted in the creation of numerous innovations which include: ultra-high-speed network transport protocols that could routinely move data over 1-10 Gigabit/s networks between individual compute nodes at close to the full line rate of the network (Vishwanath, 2007; He, 2002; Xiong, 2005); ultra-high-speed national and international networks that could be provisioned directly by the applications through the allocation of dynamic light paths (DeFanti, 2003); wide-area RAMDisk caches that could improve I/O-bound scientific applications by five-fold (Vishwanath, 2008a); and new middleware and hardware approaches to drive network-enabled displays with hundreds of megapixels of resolution (Jeong, 2006). The OptIPuter project members were able to successfully demonstrate that these individual systems could be daisy-chained to produce a planetary-scale distributed computer (Zhang, 2003).

DATA MANAGEMENT FOR SUPPORTING DISTRIBUTED VISUALIZATION

Visual exploration of multi-terabyte and petabyte-sized datasets is critical to gain insight in scientific domains, such as astrophysics, earth sciences and biosciences. When a hurricane is about to make landfall, scientists involved in disaster management need to visualize, in real-time, climate models running on geographically distributed clusters, overlay these models with high-resolution map data, sensor data and traffic information, to make informed decisions regarding the evacuation of people. The requirements of these visualizations include access to multiple 2D, 3D, 4D and higher dimensional datasets that are geographically distributed. However, the critical challenges in achieving high performance are the access latencies of storage systems and wide-area networking, rapid access to large multi-dimensional datasets, and transparent access to both local and remote data repositories.

Scientists have traditionally copied remote datasets to local repositories in order to visualize them. However, data replication is no longer a viable solution due to the enormous data-set sizes, cost of the additional local storage, data consistency issues and real-time requirements. Prior work enabling visualization for distributed data were limited to accessing a single multi-dimensional dataset (Gao, 2005 and Ding, 2003), data present in a specific format (Prohaska, 2004) or data present on a specific storage system (Bethel, 2000 and Ding 2003). Additionally, these solutions were demonstrated on 1Gbps wide-area networks using TCP as the transport protocol to transfer data (Bethel, 2000, Ding, 2003 and Benyon, 2002). However, TCP fails to scale to the 10x Gbps wide-area networks, and novel transport protocols are needed to fully exploit the large available bandwidth. As visualization applications require access to data in multiple scientific formats present in various filesystems on distributed data repositories, a cohesive data management scheme that provides rapid and transparent access to datasets independent of their formats, storage systems, and at the same time fully exploiting the available bandwidth to provide low latency access is of paramount importance.

Case Study: LambdaRAM, a Distributed Data Cache

LambdaRAM (Vishwanath, 2009) is an approach to address the data management needs of large distributed data visualization. LambdaRAM is a high-performance, multi-dimensional, distributed cache that harnesses the memory of cluster nodes in one or more clusters that are interconnected by ultra-high-speed networks, providing data-intensive scientific visualization applications with rapid and transparent access to both local and remote data. LambdaRAM employs novel latency mitigation heuristics based on the access patterns of an application, including presending, a push-based mechanism, prefetching, a pull-based mechanism, and hybrid combinations of them, proactively fetching data before an application needs it. It uses high-performance data transfer protocols, including Celeritas (Vishwanath, 2008b), designed to fully exploit the large available bandwidth of wide-area optical networks. LambdaRAM employs multi-dimensional distributed data structures, including multi-grids and octrees, to manage multi-dimensional datasets. This enables support for 2-D, volume, time-varying volume, and parallel coordinate based visualization. LambdaRAM efficiently distributes and manages the data across the nodes of the clusters. The data distribution in LambdaRAM is configurable and can easily be tuned to the needs of an application. Scientific visualization requires access to datasets present in formats including TIFF, HDF4, NetCDF, raw and binary data. Additionally, datasets could be located on local storage, parallel filesystems or distributed filesystems. LambdaRAM has an extensible design that aids in the design of plug-ins to interface visualization applications with multiple scientific data formats and filesystems. Additionally, as a scientific dataset is typically composed of multiple files, LambdaRAM presents an intuitive API to applications to access and manipulate this dataset as without having to worry about data management. The API allows visualization applications to easily subsample, subset and interact with the data. LambdaRAM can manage multiple-datasets simultaneously. This is critical for visualization applications using multi-resolution techniques wherein each resolution is managed as a dataset in LambdaRAM. LambdaRAM provides memory quality of service guarantees necessary in interactive data visualization to ensure that the low-resolution data are always cached in memory. Additionally, As we scale towards petascale and future exascale systems, software testing is no longer sufficient to guarantee reliable performance in mission criti-

Figure 4. LambdaRAM encompassing the memory of nodes of a single cluster

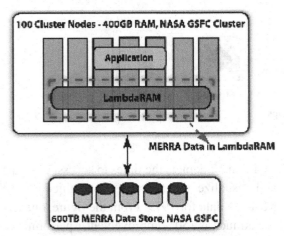

400 GB LambdaRAM encompassing a Single Cluster

Figure 5. LambdaRAM harnessing the memory of multiple clusters to provide low latency and transparent access to remote data

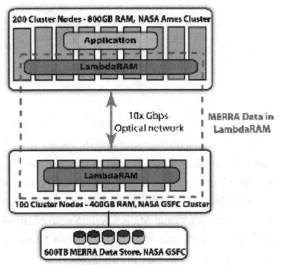

1.2 TB LambdaRAM encompassing Two Clusters

cal environments. Formal verification techniques have been applied to prove the safety and progress properties of LambdaRAM (Vishwanath, 2008a). This helped identify a deadlock condition in the memory management of LambdaRAM.

Figure 4 depicts a parallel visualization application using LambdaRAM to access the 600TB multi-dimensional national aeronautics and space administration's (NASA) modern era retrospective analysis for research and application (MERRA) data distributed on a local parallel filesystem. In this case, LambdaRAM harnesses the memory of the nodes of the cluster. LambdaRAM can harness the memory of the nodes of multiple clusters interconnected by ultra-high-speed networks to provide low-latency access to remote data. Figure 5 depicts a parallel data visualization application running at NASA Ames using LambdaRAM to rapidly and transparently access the MERRA data repository at NASA Goddard over 10 Gbps high-speed networks. LambdaRAM helps data visualization scientists spend their efforts on the visualization algorithms and facilitate scientific discovery instead of spending their efforts on data management issues including subsampling and subsetting the dataset, memory management

and copying data between sites. LambdaRAM enables time-critical, high-performance data collaboration over both the local and wide-area for data-intensive applications. Its extensible design enables high-performance highly productive scientific visualization of large distributed data.

Distributed Data Access and Visualization of NASA'S MERRA Data for Climate Analysis using LambdaRAM over Wide-Area Networks

The MERRA time period covers the modern era of remotely sensed data for the entire earth, from 1979 through the present and is key in understanding climate variability The data are published in the HDF4 format and consist of multiple 2D, 3D and 4D variables. The dataset size is approximately 600TB and is stored at NASA Goddard. Given the size of the dataset, replicating it at other sites incurs a heavy cost. Additionally, given the researchers' need to modify the dataset, replication could lead to data consistency issues. NASA would like to

Figure 6. Wide-area 10Gbps testbed to evaluate the performance of accessing data using LambdaRAM to visualize MERRA data. StarLight[4] is a 1 and 10 Gbps network connection point for both national and international research traffic.

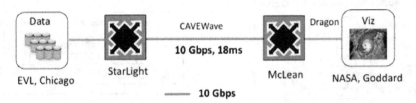

enable their researchers and collaborators at various sites to seamlessly access the data located at Goddard and use it in their weather analysis and visualizations. The ability to rapidly stride over the multidimensional MERRA data using LambdaRAM would enable earth scientists to make more informed weather predictions.

The performance of a climate analysis and visualization application accessing NASA's MERRA data using LambdaRAM over wide-are networks was evaluated. For this experiment, MERRA data for 1979 was stored on an ultra-fast storage system at Chicago. The dataset is approximately 1 Terabyte (TB) in size, and consists of 1440 data files in HDF4 format. The storage system consists of a dual-processor dual-core AMD Opteron system with 4GB of RAM, 2TB of storage and a 10GE PCI-e based network interface card (NIC). The 2TB storage was configured using eight 300 GB SATA – II disks on a PCI-e based 8-port 3ware RAID controller using RAID 0. The data analysis and visualization was performed on a node at NASA Goddard. This node consists of a dual-core dual-processor AMD Opteron with 4GB RAM and a 10GE PCI-X based Intel NIC. A dedicated 10 Gbps network was provisioned for the experiment to interconnect the two nodes. The network testbed is depicted in Figure 6 and consisted of the CAVEWave network between Chicago and McLean, Virginia, and the DRAGON network between McLean, VA and NASA Goddard. The total round trip latency for this network was around 18ms.

Figure 7 depicts the times to access, compute and visualize the average ozone thickness of MERRA data for 1979. From the figure, one can see as much as a 50% improvement in performance with a single LambdaRAM server and a 100% improvement using two LambdaRAM servers as compared to a typical ultra-fast storage system. On local storage, accessing multidimensional data involves accessing multiple noncontiguous regions on disk which incurs significant access overhead and leads to performance degradation. Improved performance was observed using presending over prefetching as it does not incur the one-way request latency in prefetching. Presending yielded 8.3% performance improvement over prefetching using a single LambdaRAM server and 21.6% using two LambdaRAM servers. Also observed is a 27% performance improvement by using Celeritas, an application-layer UDP-based reliable transport protocol, in comparison to TCP over the wide-area network. Celeritas sustained an average throughput of 3.5Gbps in the case of two LambdaRAM servers and 2.1Gbps using a single LambdaRAM server and played a key role in achieving high-performance over the Wide-area networks.

Particularly noteworthy was that it was faster to stride, compute and visualize the average ozone thickness of the *remote* MERRA data using LambdaRAM than using a *local* ultra-fast storage node. Additionally, parallel data analysis applications have demonstrated up-to a five-fold performance improvement by using LambdaRAM to access

Figure 7. Striding and computing the average ozone thickness for the entire world for 1979. The application runs at NASA Goddard and uses LambdaRAM to access data located in Chicago. Lower time indicates better performance.

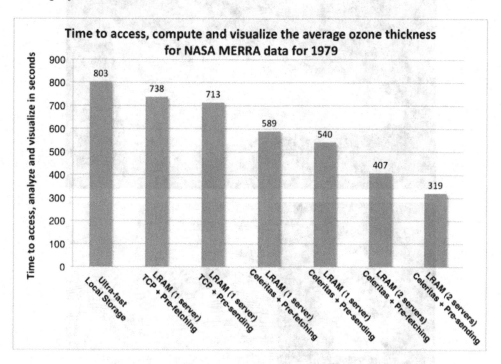

multidimensional data on a PVFS2 parallel file-system in comparison to using MPI-IO to directly access the data. This is due to the multidimensional data management and latency mitigation heuristics in LambdaRAM. At Super-computing 2004 and 2005, an interactive visualization of large 2-D imagery using LambdaRAM to access data over transatlantic networks, was demonstrated.

LambdaRAM's model of aggressively using network bandwidth to overcome latency will be crucial to ensuring the scalability of distributed computing and visualization applications whose greatest bottleneck will be in getting the data to the processing units.

DATA RENDERING FOR SUPPORTING DISTRIBUTED VISUALIZATION

So far, we have seen a number of complete examples demonstrating different instantiations of the visualization pipeline, both collocated and distributed, interactive and batch. The prior section emphasized the early stages of the pipeline, managing and staging data. We now move further down the visualization pipeline to the rendering step, again with a variety of architectures and with an emphasis on large, distributed, multivariate data. Before presenting more examples, though, we begin with a brief summary of basic methods and algorithms performed serially on a single machine. Next, we examine how these methods must be modified when datasets grow in size and complexity and architectures grow in parallelism and heterogeneity. We conclude with

Figure 8. Examples of volume rendering (top), isosurfacing (bottom left), and streamline flow visualization (bottom right). Images courtesy of H.-W. Shen, the Ohio State University.

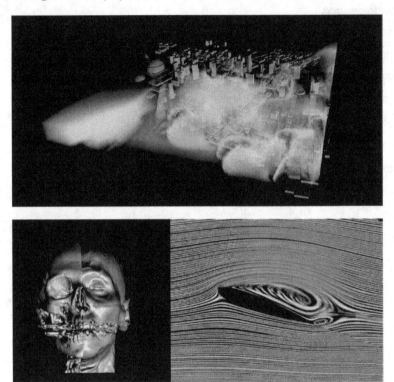

two case studies in parallel volume rendering – one in hardware on a rendering cluster another in software on a parallel supercomputer.

Rendering Techniques

Rendering methods for scientific visualization are organized according to the type of data values and grid containing those values. Data values constitute a field over the grid, $F(G)$, where $G \subset R^n$. Most often, G is two-dimensional ($n = 2$) and $F = F(x, y)$, or three-dimensional ($n = 3$) and $F = F(x, y, z)$. In the case of time-varying data, time can be treated as a fourth dimension, where $F = F(x, y, z, t)$. Alternately, a time varying dataset can be represented as a sequence of steady state 3D datasets such that $F = \{ F_0(x, y, z), F_1(x, y, z) \dots F_t(x, y, z) \}$, where time is in discrete steps from 0 to t. Each F_t is a separate time step that may be stored in a separate file on disk. G can be structured or unstructured, and F can consist of multiple scalar, vector, or tensor values at each grid point. Different rendering techniques are used depending on various combinations of F and G.

Field Types

Scalar Fields: A scalar field contains single-valued data at each grid cell, for example, temperature. Multiple scalar values can exist at each location, for example, temperature, pressure, and density. Scalar fields can be rendered by selecting a particular value (isovalue) and displaying all of the locations where the field has that isovalue. The union of these locations forms a surface (isosurface), and surface rendering techniques such as triangle meshes are used to render isosurfaces (Lorensen, 1987; Gao, 2001). See Figure 8.

Rather than extracting an isosurface, the entire volume (assuming $n = 3$ or $n = 4$) can be visualized directly using volume rendering techniques (Levoy, 1998; Ma, 2000). Volume rendering creates an image of the entire 3D space using varying color and transparency. This allows partial or complete visibility of the inside regions of the volume. Colors and opacities are mapped the data values via a user-defined transfer function. See Figure 8.

Vector Fields: A vector field contains vector-valued data at each grid cell, for example, velocity (v_x, v_y, v_z). The collection of velocity vectors represent the flow of particles in space and in time. When the flow is steady-state, a set of seed points can be numerically integrated over the velocity field to construct a set of *streamlines*. When the flow is time-varying, we call the resulting locus *pathlines*. An alternative construction for time-varying flows is *streaklines*, constructed by re-generating a constant set of seed points over time.

For rendering, each point in a streamline, pathline, or streakline can be connected to its neighbor with a line or a higher order curve. To reduce aliasing and increase visibility, these lines can be rendered as tubes or cylinders, or even semi-transparent surfaces. To further improve clarity, lighting and texturing can be applied (Johnson, 2004; vonFunck, 2008). See Figure 8.

There are direct methods of rendering a vector field without tracing particles through it, including *line integral convolution (LIC), glyphs, and topological methods*. LIC renders the result of applying an anisotropic convolution filter directly over the field (Cabral, 1993). Glyphs are representations such as arrows, cones, etc., that are placed within the field and oriented tangent to it (de Leeuw, 1993). Topological methods do not visualize the field itself, but rather the topology of the flow by evaluating ridges, saddles, and critical points in the field (Gyulassy, 2008).

Tensor Fields: Tensors are matrices; for example 3x3 tensors are common in materials science and medical imaging. Tensors that arise in science can be characterized by their eigenvalues and eigenvectors. To render such a tensor field, a set of ellipsoidal glyphs is commonly used, where the principle directions of the ellipsoid correspond to the eigenvectors, and the major and minor ellipsoid radii reflect the maximum and minimum eigenvalues. Topological methods can also be applied to tensor fields (Tricoche, 2008).

Grid Types

Structured Grids: A structured grid follows a regular pattern such that the coordinates of individual grid cells are not stored; positional and topological information is derived from a few parameters such as minimum, maximum, and spacing. Perhaps the most familiar example is a Cartesian grid, but others such as polar, cylindrical, spherical are common. Rectilinear and curvilinear grids are generalizations of these, where spacing varies across the extent of the grid (Schroeder, 2006).

A special case of variable-spacing grid is the *adaptive mesh refinement* (AMR) grid (Ma, 1999; Weber, 2001a; Weber, 2001b). In an AMR grid, block shaped regions corresponding to various data frequencies have different spatial resolution. These resolutions differ by a constant factor, for example, half-spacing in each dimension. Many combinations and varieties of structured grids exist, depending on the data requirements of the underlying simulation. Structured grids are attractive because the regularity of grid locations saves storage space and speeds access to data values. Figure 9 shows examples of structured grids.

Unstructured Grids: Some computational problems exist over a data domain that cannot be effectively modeled by a structured grid without wasting a great deal of resources. Consider simulating the airflow over an airplane. Most of the grid cells in a structured grid enveloping such an irregular shape would represent air. This is appropriate if the objective is to understand the airflow patterns surrounding the airplane. However, if the objective is to model the stress on the

Figure 9. From left to right, 2D examples of Cartesian, rectilinear, curvilinear, and AMR grids are shown. Analogies exist in 3D for each. Bottom: In 2D unstructured grids, cells are usually triangular or rectangular. In 3D unstructured grids, their counterparts are tetrahedral and hexahedral cells.

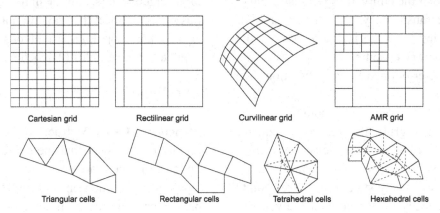

fuselage, then most of the grid cells would be wasted.

In such cases, each grid cell of interest is listed in an indexed structure. The grid coordinates of each point must be stored because they cannot be determined algorithmically. Also, topological information must be stored. In particular, links from each cell to the neighboring cells are necessary in order to traverse from one cell to an adjacent one. In 2D unstructured grids, cells are usually triangular or rectangular in shape. The 3D analogy to these cell shapes are tetrahedral and hexahedral grid cells (Nielson, 1997). See Figure 9.

Data Intensive Rendering

In computational science, simulations run for hours, days, weeks, and sometimes months at a time across thousands or tens of thousands of compute nodes. These runs produce hundreds of terabytes, even petabytes of results. Often these datasets are time varying and multivariate. The scope of modern datasets poses new challenges for rendering; we will use the term *data intensive rendering* when discussing approaches to meet these challenges, but we emphasize that this is not a special case anymore. Eventually most if not all

rendering of scientific computations will be data intensive (Mount, 2004; Ross, 2008).

Data intensive rendering can affect the visualization pipeline; in particular, overall performance depends on the successful use of parallelism and heterogeneity in the visualization workflow. The computational performance of individual CPUs and GPUs is limited by electrical consumption and heat dissipation, so parallelism is one alternative in order to continue to improve performance. This is true regardless whether parallelism is inter-core with shared memory or inter-node with distributed memory. Heterogeneity occurs when different architectures must cooperate in parallel. Combining today's multicore chips in parallel induces different types of parallelism in the same rendering algorithm. The presence of multiple GPUs within the same system is another example. Ultimately, we must use all of the architectural components in parallel, not just the homogeneous ones, in order to raise the performance level of data intensive rendering.

Most strategies used to parallelize the rendering process follow a similar form: data are first decomposed and distributed to processing units for rendering after which the output of each task is combined to form the final output image. Parallelization strategies are commonly categorized based on how data are decomposed across processing units. Parallel direct volume rendering techniques are usually categorized as either object-order or image-order techniques.

Parallel object-order techniques assign a processing unit to a section of data regardless of where the data appears in the final output image. After each section of data are rendered, a compositing step based on the theory described by Porter and Duff (Porter, 1984) constructs the final image. Much effort has been devoted to developing efficient compositing methods including Hsu's direct send method (Hsu, 1993), Camahort and Chakravarty's projection method (Camahort, 1993), the binary-swap method (Ma, 1994) and the divided-screenwise hierarchical compositing method (Ino, 2003). Object-order implementations have been developed for distributed-memory clusters (Elvins, 1992; Gribble, 2004; Müller, 2006), and specialized hardware has been developed that implements the binary-swap compositing method (Lombeyda, 2001, Muraki, 2003, Frank, 2005).

Parallel image-order rendering techniques take advantage of the fact that a contribution to a pixel in the output image is independent of other pixels in the image. These techniques break the output image into disjoint regions and assign a processing unit to render everything in that region. Image-order implementations have been developed for shared-memory systems (Palmer, 1998) as well as distributed-memory systems (Bajaj, 2000).

Object-order methods distribute input data across processing units before rendering begins. Data remains stationary even when the view transformation changes. However, object-order methods require an additional compositing phase to assemble the final output image. The cost of this phase grows with the number of processing units. Image-order methods avoid the additional compositing phase but require redistribution of some portion of the input data when the viewpoint changes. The optimal choice of parallelization strategy is heavily dependent on the implementa-

tion architecture. We will see examples of both strategies later in the section.

A common theme in data intensive rendering is heterogeneity. Heterogeneity may exist within a compute node, as in the Roadrunner architecture (Barker, 2008), or it can take the form of a rendering hierarchy, similar to a memory or storage hierarchy. We can consider three levels in this hierarchy: supercomputer, graphics cluster, and workstation. Because computing power decreases and interactivity increases as we move to different levels in the hierarchy, one may expose different system characteristics at each level by mapping different visualization algorithms and stages of the algorithm to each machine architecture and thereby optimize the end-to-end performance.

For example, in a vector flow field visualization, the supercomputer can compute particle traces and transfer finished particles to a visualization cluster for rendering. There, graphical effects such as semitransparency and lighting can be added more effectively at the GPU hardware level than in software at the supercomputer. A subset of the rendered surfaces can be transferred to the scientist's workstation for local interaction. This type of hierarchy has yet to be realized at large scales in practice, but heterogeneity of this type will likely play a role in future data intensive rendering.

Some rough guidelines for mapping algorithms to architectures are:

- **Supercomputer:** Algorithms such as ray casting that either have a software equivalent or were originated in software; large scale data-bound problems where the cost of moving data is prohibitive; high quality or large image size rendering where rendering time is long; complex mesh problems where raw rendering time is not the bottleneck; preprocessing, filtering, transforming, or numerical analysis operations performed prior to rendering

- **Graphics cluster**: Algorithms such as marching cubes that originated as triangle rendering methods; algorithms that rely heavily on triangles or textures for which the GPU rendering pipeline is optimized; algorithms that benefit from multithread parallelism that GPUs can offer, data domains that fit in GPU memory, and interactive applications.
- **Graphics workstation**: Versions of graphics cluster algorithms operating on smaller data subdomains; applications with even higher levels of interactivity; and algorithms that make local approximations to the higher levels of the hierarchy, for example, image-based rendering (Chen, 1995).

Finally, a common theme in data intensive rendering is that many algorithm design decisions are governed by the high cost of reading, writing, and transporting data. Overall performance is usually bound by the cost of data movement, rather than computation. This data movement can take the form of transporting files across a grid or the internet, reading and writing to and from storage systems, and communicating between the nodes of a cluster or supercomputer. We will see the cost of data movement reappear several times in the following examples.

Case Study: Parallel Volume Rendering on a Graphics Cluster

As the spatial size of volume data increases due to advances in scientific instrumentation, so too does the need to visualize such large data. High-resolution displays allow scientists to see their spatially large data at or nearer its native resolution. Most often, scalable high-resolution displays are composed of an array of liquid-crystal displays (LCDs) or projectors and a commodity distributed-memory cluster of computers with accelerated graphics hardware.

Schwarz and others have shown a distributed image-order volume rendering approach for high-resolution displays that scales as the output resolution of the display and the number of cluster nodes increases. This approach preprocesses data into a hierarchical structure which is distributed across the local storage of a distributed-memory cluster. The cluster is equipped with graphics cards capable of hardware accelerated 3D texture-mapping. Rendering is aborted and restarted at the lowest level in the hierarchical data structure if user interaction occurs before the highest-resolution level is completed.

The successful image-order parallelization of the rendering task relies on a data management scheme that uses a multi-level cache and distributed shared-memory system. The primary responsibility of the multi-level cache is to keep the most recently used data bricks as close to the graphics hardware as possible. The distributed shared-memory system keeps track of all data bricks loaded in memory across cluster nodes. Data bricks are transferred between cluster nodes when required via the cluster's high-speed backplane. If a data brick is not in memory on one of the nodes it is loaded from disk. Performance results show that the system scales as output resolution and cluster size increases.

The Purkinje dataset in Figure 10 is shown on a six panel, twenty-four megapixel tabletop display. The display is run by a three node cluster where each node is attached to two 2,560 x 1,600 LCDs. Each cluster node has one AMD Athlon 64 FX-60 Dual Core processor, 2 GB of RAM, and a PCI-E nVidia GeForce 7900 GT graphics card with 256 MB of texture-memory. The cluster is connected via a 10 Gbps Ethernet backplane with the MTU size set to 9,000 bytes.

The original raw data creates a 2,048 x 4,096 x 128 volume of 16-bit voxels. The real spatial extent of the data is about 80 μm x 80 μm x 15 μm. Purkinje neurons exist in the cerebellar cortex and are responsible for fine motor control. The study of Purkinje neurons may lead to treat-

Figure 10. Researcher exploring the Purkinje neuron dataset on a twenty-four megapixel tabletop display. Data courtesy of the National Center for Microscopy and Imaging Research (NCMIR) at the University of California, San Diego (UCSD).

ments for genetic mutations, such as autism, and neurodegenerative diseases, such as sporadic ataxias.

The rat kidney dataset in Figure 11 is shown on a fifty-five panel, 100 megapixel display. The display is run by a twenty-eight node cluster where all but one node is attached to two 1,600 x 1,200 LCDs. Each cluster node has two AMD Opteron 246 processors, 4 GB of RAM, 500 GB of local storage space, and an 8x AGP nVidia Quadro FX 3000 graphics card with 256 MB of texture-memory. The cluster is connected via a 1 Gbps Ethernet backplane with the MTU size set to 9,000 bytes.

The original raw data comprises a 32,768 x 32,768 x 128 volume of 24-bit samples. The real spatial extent of the data is about 8mm x 5mm x 1.5mm. Scientists are particularly interested in cell neucli which are between 5 μm and 10 μm in length.

Figure 12 shows the average time to render a single frame of the Purkinje neuron dataset. Average rendering results for the rat kidney dataset are given in Figure 13. These results reflect the average time taken to render and display all data in all levels of the tree for a given view. The results show that as the output resolution increases along with the corresponding number of rendering nodes, the time taken to render each dataset decreases.

Case Study: Parallel Volume Rendering on the IBM Blue Gene

In contrast to the previous case study, Peterka et al. (Peterka, 2008) wondered whether and how parallel supercomputers such as the IBM Blue Gene and Cray XT can operate as parallel visualization engines. Even though they do not have graphics capability, under certain conditions of data size, algorithm, number of cores, and output display resolution, we have found that a software rendering

Figure 11. Scientist examining the rat kidney dataset on a 100 megapixel display. Data courtesy of the National Center for Microscopy and Imaging Research (NCMIR) at the University of California, San Diego.

Figure 12. Average rendering results for the Purkinje neuron dataset

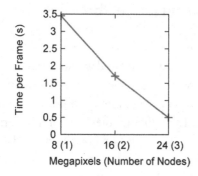

solution running in parallel on a supercomputing platform can actually be an effective alternative to hardware-accelerated graphics cluster approaches that are the *de facto* rendering method today.

Running visualization algorithms on a supercomputer also opens the door to *in situ* visualization, where visualizations are rendered simultaneously with a running simulation (Ma, 2007; Tu, 2006; Yu, 2004). This permits scientists to "see into" their computations as they proceed, even to steer them dynamically. There are many problems yet to be solved before *in situ* visualization becomes a commonly used technique, but the ability to execute parallel visualizations on the same architecture as simulations is one step in that direction.

Peterka and others are researching parallel visualization algorithms on leadership-class systems, using the IBM Blue Gene/P system as a test environment. To date, a parallel volume rendering algorithm has been successfully applied to over 32,000 BG/P compute cores. Datasets of up to 335 billion elements were successfully volume rendered on BG/P to produce images up to 16 million pixels.

Figure 14 shows an output image from volume rendering the entropy within a core-collapse supernova using this approach. Through computational simulation, Blondin and Mezzacappa (Blondin, 2003) are studying the physics of the shock wave that forms during the death of some of the largest stars.

Figure 15 shows the end-to-end performance and scalability for a range of data, image, and system sizes. Because the data are time-varying, each time step must be read from storage prior to rendering. The size of a single time step can be gigabytes or even hundreds of gigabytes, and Figure 15 shows that most of the total frame time (time to render one time step from start to finish) is spent on I/O, reading the data from storage. Various optimizations, as already discussed earlier, can help to hide the high cost of I/O (Peterka, 2008).

Excluding I/O, Figure 16 also shows that compositing is the next most expensive operation. Compositing is a many-to-many communication step among all of the compute cores to exchange partial results and merge these into a final image. Like I/O, this is a data movement operation. This example demonstrates that large scale visualization performance is dominated by the cost of data transfers, both from storage and across the interconnect between compute cores.

Returning to the original question, whether parallel volume rendering can be done within such a supercomputing architecture, the answer is yes. The strengths of Argonne's IBM Blue Gene are a large capacity parallel storage system, low-latency high-bandwidth interconnection network, and a large number of relatively low power compute nodes. Since the visualization algorithm (in this case volume rendering) is bound by data movement and not rendering speed, the algorithm properties and machine characteristics align. Data movement between supercomputer and separate visualization cluster is eliminated and future *in situ* visualization is enabled by performing visualization directly on the supercomputer.

ADVANCED DISPLAYS FOR SUPPORTING DISTRIBUTED VISUALIZATION

Traditionally data rendering and display occur together- i.e. the same computer that does the

Figure 13. Average rendering results for the rat kidney dataset

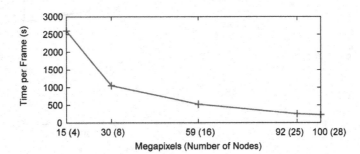

Figure 14. Volume rendering of entropy in a core-collapse supernova. Image courtesy of H. Yu, and K.-L. Ma, University of California at Davis.

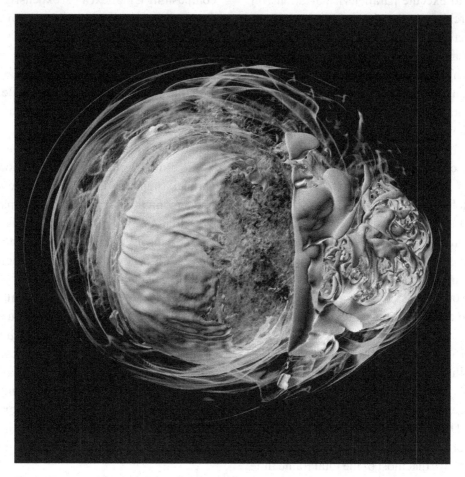

Figure 15. Total frame time is plotted for three data and image sizes, in log-log scale

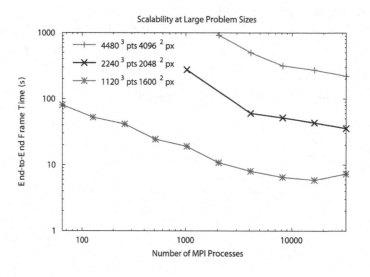

Figure 16. Percentage of time spent in I/O, rendering, and compositing. I/O dominates the overall algorithm's performance. Data size: 1120 x 1120 x 1120 Image size: 1600 x 1600.

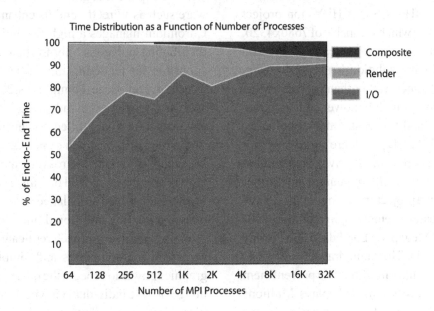

rendering, displays the result. In distributed visualization, especially as necessitated by the sheer massiveness of the data that needs to be rendered, it is ultimately more economical to separate rendering from display. This Thin Client model is actually widely used in practice today – for example every time we query Google, the "heavy lifting" of generating the result or visualization is performed by massive compute clusters at Google, and the viewer simply sees the result on their desktop computer, laptop or smartphone. This model is attractive because the large-scale (and therefore expensive) computing infrastructure that supports such services can be shared amongst large populations of users, and can be located near reliable and renewable power sources.

As the types of problems we tackle grow in scale and complexity our notion of what constitutes a Thin Client must change. The new Thin Client is a large ultra-high-resolution display interfaced with an ultra-high-speed network. Increased screen real-estate and resolution enables users to display and juxtapose more data simultaneously

and thereby enhances the users' ability to derive insight from data.

Until the mid-90s image creation for large displays (often called Power Walls) primarily used Cathode Ray Tube-based projectors. The main advantage of CRT projectors is that they maintain good brightness to 10,000 hours, are capable of generating very high resolution images (up to 1920x1200), and are able to refresh at high rates. In the mid to late 90s, LCD and DLP projectors were rapidly declining in cost as well as physical size. This was driven largely by the business graphics market which required low cost projectors for projecting presentation slides in board rooms. Tilings of LCD or DLP projectors were used to create larger walls (Funkhouser, 2000). While these projectors were relatively inexpensive it was difficult to align the geometry and color of the screens. Techniques have been developed for automatic alignment through the use of computer-vision. As a result commercial turnkey solutions are now available- but at a relatively high cost. Today DLP projectors such as Sony's SXRD are capable of 8-megapixel resolution (4096x2160) and are largely used in movie theaters. In prototype form is NHK's Super Hi-Vision project (Kanazawa, 2003) which is capable of 7680x4320.

Currently the most economical way to build scalable ultra-high-resolution displays is by using tilings of LCD panels rather than projectors due to the LCD's long life, low power consumption, high resolution and low cost. Other benefits include the fact that LCD panels are quite well color calibrated and apart from the physical alignment of the panels during tiling, require no further alignment, unlike projectors. Tilings of these have been used to create extremely high resolution walls such as the 100 Megapixel LambdaVision display (Renambot, 2005). The main drawback of LCD panels is that they have mullions that prevent them from producing truly seamless displays. Mullions do not adversely impact the viewing of an image if they are taken into account in the rendering of the image. However mullions do make the reading of text difficult when it either occludes an entire sentence or words. Driving these tilings of displays requires a cluster of computers, often each computer drives anywhere between 1 and 4 displays, and a master computer coordinates the entire cluster. By building these tiled displays using small low cost computers equipped with gigabit networking- such as Mac Minis we can leverage the Thin Client paradigm and utilize remote shared computing infrastructure to generate and stream the visualizations to the tiled display.

The major challenges in supporting tiled display environments then is how to scale graphics rendering algorithms to be able to handle the exponentially growing data volumes that are accumulated in scientific research, and how to best enable users to interact with information and visualizations in these environments.

Middleware for Scalable Displays

The traditional model for scalable rendering has assumed that faster graphics cards will be more than capable of supporting rendering to keep pace with the exponential growth of data size. Middleware such as WireGL, and its enhanced version, Chromium manages a high resolution scene by distributing polygons only to the computers responsible for rendering the particular viewport into the overall scene (Humphreys, 2001). Termed "sort-first rendering" the advantage of this scheme was that if an image filled a significant portion of the tiled display much of the geometry would be evenly distributed across all the computers. However if the image fell on only a small portion of the wall a load imbalance would result and overall rendering rate would plummet.

An alternative approach replicates all the data across all the computers and simply uses raw graphics power to process the data to generate the images for the individual viewports of the display tiles. Used in middleware such as Conduit (by VRCO) and the Cross-Platform Cluster Graphic Library (CGLX), the advantage of this approach is that many existing OpenGL applications can be easily ported without modification of the code. The primary disadvantage is that the amount of data that can be rendered is limited by the capabilities of the individual graphics card.

Evolving out of the Thin Client paradigm, a third and most scalable approach delegates the rendering to a remote cluster of computers and instead treats the tiled display simply as a large frame buffer connected via a high speed network. This approach was first pioneered in SAGE (the Scalable Adaptive Graphics Environment) (Jeong, 2006). The scheme has greater scalability than previous approaches because it allows multiple cluster computers that are potentially rendering different and very large data sets, to work concurrently and stream visualizations to be displayed on the wall as individual windows as if on an enormous desktop. This allows users to arbitrarily position and resize these windows on the wall and therefore enabling them to work with multiple visualizations simultaneously- in effect creating a *Cyber-Mashup* (Leigh, 2007). When the pixels

Figure 17. In SAGE, tiled displays are driven by multiple remote rendering pipelines that independently stream visualizations onto individual windows. Pictured is a 100-Megapixel tiled LCD display wall at the Electronic Visualization Laboratory (University of Illinois at Chicago).

of a visualization are streamed in parallel from a cluster of rendering nodes to SAGE, they are intelligently routed to the correct display cluster nodes that are managing the respective portions of the tiled display (Figure 17). As a window moves from one portion of the tiled display to another, SAGE correctly re-routes the pixels in much the same way a network router routes network packets. This approach therefore enables users to run multiple visualizations on distributed rendering clusters and display them in a tiled display environment each in its own separate window that can be independently controlled.

By contrast, the techniques used in WireGL/ Chromium and CGLX require that the entire wall be used to display only one visualization application at a time. This is acceptable for small tiled displays but becomes impractical for very large display walls, especially those that can in the future, potentially cover all the walls of a room. The SAGE model also has the advantage that far less powerful graphics cards and computers can be used to drive the display walls thereby making it more affordable and cost effective to maintain.

These display walls can then connect into global high performance networks to take advantage of large-scale computing resources that are deployed at supercomputing centers around the world.

Supporting Distance Collaboration in Scalable Display Environments

Today, remote application sharing and video conferencing using tools such as WebEx, Skype, and iChat, are making it routine for distributed users to work with each other and to work with data from their desktop computers. These solutions however do not scale to ultra-high-resolution display environments, which need to be able to share high-resolution visualizations and high-definition video and audio in real-time to facilitate group-to-group collaboration.

Visualcasting is a novel image broadcasting scheme that extends SAGE to support distance collaboration with multiple end-points without the need for traditional router-based support for multicasting which have always been difficult to deploy over wide-area networks (Renambot,

2009). Visualcasting is a scalable real-time image replication service for multiple high-resolution tiled displays. A visualization application streamed to multiple Visualcasting end-points (tiled displays) can have different window layouts on each tiled display. The window operations (moving or resizing) on each tiled display can occur independently. As windows on the tiled display are resized or repositioned, SAGE performs the non-trivial task of reconfiguring the multiple streams from the rendering source to the PC nodes that drive potentially differing tiled displays.

Visualcasting is realized via the SAGE Bridge- a high-speed intelligent bridging system that duplicates and splits pixel streams received from rendering clusters for each end-point. This allows each rendering node to stream whole images without having to be cognizant of the window layouts and tiled display configurations of multiple end-points. A single SAGE Bridge node is built from a high-performance PC equipped with 10-gigabit network interfaces. Multiples of these can be ganged together to facilitate the sharing of even higher resolution content or more varieties of content. For example one bridge could be dedicated to high-definition audio/video conferencing while another could be dedicated to sharing visualizations.

SAGE also supports audio streaming to facilitate distance collaboration. The design goal has always been to treat sound data in SAGE in a similar fashion to pixel data potentially allowing for sounds to be spatially collocated with the displays that show the visualizations. Sound buffers are captured at various sources (microphones, high-definition video capture card, audio files, or application-provided buffers), then streamed in an uncompressed form to minimize latency, and finally sent to a sound card for playback.

Figure 18 and Figure 19 show a Visualcasting trial conducted over an international network testbed called the Global Lambda Integrated Facility. In the trial ultra-high-resolution tiled displays at the SC08 conference in Austin, Texas (Figure 18),

Electronic Visualization Laboratory at the University of Illinois at Chicago (Illinois), the School of Information at the University of Michigan, and Masaryk University (Czech Republic) (Figure 19) were linked to Visualcasting servers in Chicago so that they are all able to share a 4K (4096x2048) pixel visualization stream as well as communicate over high-definition video conferencing.

CONCLUSION

The World Wide Web has been a transformative technology that has afforded its users the ability to publish and retrieve an unprecedented amount of data. Making data massively available and providing facilities for combining them stimulates the production of new insight. A crucial component to the derivation of insight is visualization- the production of a meaningful visual representation of data.

As data size continues to grow exponentially, the long-established technique of first downloading data to a desktop computer and then creating a plot on a spreadsheet has given way to distributed models of data retrieval, visualization and analysis. The majority of techniques used on the Web today

Figure 19. The views of the Visualcasting collaboration from the University of Michigan (top left), University of Illinois at Chicago (bottom left), and Masaryk University (bottom right)

have their roots in the field of High-Performance Computing (HPC). For almost two decades, the HPC community has developed innovative approaches for deriving insight from large-scale distributed data.

Large-scale data visualization is conducted via a pipeline consisting of data retrieval, filtering, rendering, and finally display. The motivation to collocate or distribute the steps of the pipeline is driven largely by the economics of meeting user demand and managing scalability. Traditionally when data was small, all the steps of the pipeline could reside on the same computer. Visualization was interactive and users could adjust the visualizations in real-time. As data sizes grew, visualization on single computers had to expand to utilize parallel processing on multiple computers in order to keep pace. However, parallel computing was still largely collocated computing because high speed wide-area networks were scarce. Furthermore, parallel computers often worked in batch mode, and therefore the results of parallel visualization algorithms consisted mainly of animated movies rather than interactive graphics. Viewing the visualization from a different point

of view was therefore not possible without time consuming re-computation.

As data volumes continued to grow, the economics of providing data management and data processing services necessitated greater wide-area distribution of resources. Serendipitously, this led to an explosion of new applications beyond scientific computing that includes e-commerce and even video gaming.

The key challenge in data visualization today is how to provide users with the interactive experience that they have grown accustomed to on their desktop computers, while offering the scalability to handle the exponential explosion of data. Experiments show that large-scale visualization is an Input/Output-bound problem. That is, the rate at which visualizations can be generated is bound by the rate at which data can be sent through the visualization pipeline. If one cannot move the data through the pipeline fast enough then one cannot process the data fast enough. When interactivity is required, data access latency becomes another major problem- especially when the data is distributed over wide-area networks. However as high-speed networks such as the National LambdaRail and Internet-2 grow in capacity, the limitation of bandwidth between distributed resources diminishes. Furthermore, through the aggressive use of bandwidth to presend and prefetch data, it becomes possible to significantly reduce data access times to the point where, surprisingly, it can be faster to access data from a remote computer than from one's local disk drive. Some researchers would argue that there will never be enough wide-area bandwidth available to keep pace with both the growth of data and the multi-core and many-core systems that are needed to process the data. In this case, researchers are examining the notion of *in situ* rendering, where the parallelized visualization and computational algorithms are collocated so that rendering the data can be done during the generation of the data. In *in situ* visualization, the computation and visualization could be either collocated on the same supercomputer or run on separate specialized resources that are collocated at the same site. In the first case, the data transfer between computers is reduced though at a cost of sharing compute resources of the supercomputer for visualization. In the latter approach, a visualization cluster, typically a GPU-based cluster, needs to be interconnected to the supercomputer via high-speed local network interconnects.

The notion of *in situ* visualization however is not a silver bullet. The rate at which a frame of visualization is generated is bound by the rate of a simulation timestep- which can be on the order of seconds to even hours. Therefore, *in situ* visualization does not lend itself to interactive visualization. *In situ* visualization's greatest value is in allowing the user to catch a glimpse of how the computation is evolving in order to determine whether it is worth allowing it to continue for days to weeks. This approach can enable computational steering where the user would directly modify the parameters of the computation. Then once the computation is complete, techniques for low-latency real-time distributed visualization can be brought to bear to provide users with a means to interactively explore the results.

REFERENCES

Bajaj, C., Ihm, I., Park, S., & Song, D. (2000). Compression-based ray casting of very large volume data in distributed environments. *Proceedings of the Fourth International Conference on High-Performance Computing in the Asia-Pacific Region* (HPC00), 2, (pp. 720–725).

Barker, K. J., Davis, K., Hoisie, A., Kerbyson, D. J., Lang, M., Pakin, S., & Sancho, J. C. (2008). Entering the petaflop era: The architecture and performance of roadrunner. *Proceedings of the 2008 ACM/IEEE conference on Supercomputing (SC'08)*, (pp. 1–11). IEEE Press.

Bethel, W., Tierney, B., Lee, J., Gunter, D., & Lau, S. (2000). Using high-speed WANs and network data caches to enable remote and distributed visualization. *Proceeding of the IEEE Supercomputing 2000 Conference*.

Beynon, M., Chang, C., Catalyurek, U., Kurc, T., Sussman, A., Andrade, H., Ferreira, R., & Saltz, J., (2002). Processing large-scale multidimensional data in parallel and distributed environments. *Parallel Computing, Special issue on Data Intensive Computing, 28*(5),827-859.

Blondin, J. M., Mezzacappa, A., & DeMarino, C. (2003). Stability of standing accretion shocks, with an eye toward core collapse supernovae. *The Astrophysical Journal, 584*(2), 971. doi:10.1086/345812

Cabral, B., & Leedom, L. C. (1993). Imaging vector fields using line integral convolution. *Proceedings of the 20th Annual Conference on Computer Graphics and Interactive Techniques (SIGGRAPH'93)* (pp. 263–270).

Camahort, E., & Chakravarty, I. (1993). Integrating volume data analysis and rendering on distributed memory architectures. *Proceedings of 1993 Symposium on Parallel Rendering* (PRS '93), (pp. 89–96).

Chen, S. E. (1995). *Quicktime VR: An image-based approach to virtual environment navigation. Proceedings of the 22nd Annual Conference on Computer Graphics and Interactive Techniques (SIGGRAPH '95)*, (pp. 29–38).

Cruz-Neira, C., Sandin, D. J., DeFanti, T. A., Kenyon, R. V., & Hart, J. C. (1992). The cave - Audio visual experience automatic virtual environment. *Communications of the ACM, 35*(6), 64–72. doi:10.1145/129888.129892

de Leeuw, W. C., & van Wijk, J. J. (1993). A probe for local flow field visualization. *Proceedings of the 4th Conference on Visualization (VIS '93)*, (pp. 39–45).

DeFanti, T. A., Brown, M. D., Leigh, J., Yu, O., He, E., & Mambretti, J. (2003, August). Optical switching middleware for the OptIPuter. *Institute of Electronics, Information and Communication Engineers (IEICE) Transactions on Communications (Special Issue on Photonic IP Network Technologies for Next Generation Broadband Access). E (Norwalk, Conn.), 86-B*(8), 2263–2272.

Ding, J., Huang, J., Beck, M., Liu, S., Moore, T., & Soltesz, S. (2003). Remote visualization by browsing image based databases with logistical networking. *In the Proceedings of SC2003*, Phoenix, AZ, USA.

Elvins, T. T. (1992). Volume rendering on a distributed memory parallel computer. *Proceedings of the 3rd Conference on Visualization '92*, (pp. 93–98).

Frank, S., & Kaufman, A. (2005). Distributed volume rendering on a visualization cluster. *Proceedings of the Ninth International Conference on Computer Aided Design and Computer Graphics*, CAD-CG '05, (pp. 371–376).

Funkhouser, T., & Li, K. (2000, July). Large format displays. *IEEE Computer Graphics and Applications, 25*(4), 20–21. doi:10.1109/MCG.2000.851745

Gao, J., & Huang, J. (2005). Distributed data management for large volume visualization. *Visualization, 2005*, 183–189.

Gao, J., & Shen, H. W. (2001). Parallel view-dependent isosurface extraction using multi-pass occlusion culling, *Proceedings of the IEEE 2001 symposium on parallel and large-data visualization and graphics (PVG '01)* (pp. 67–74).

Gribble, C., Parker, S., & Hansen, C. (2004). *Interactive volume rendering of large datasets using the silicon graphics Onyx4 visualization system. Tech. Rep.* University of Utah.

Gyulassy, G., Bremer, P.-T., Hamann, B., & Pascucci, V. (2008). A practical approach to Morse-Smale complex computation: Scalability and generality. *IEEE Transactions on Visualization and Computer Graphics, 14*(6), 1619–1626. doi:10.1109/TVCG.2008.110

He, E., Leigh, J., Yu, O., & DeFanti, T. A. (2002). Reliable blast UDP: Predictable high performance bulk data transfer. *Proceedings of IEEE Cluster Computing 2002*.

Hsu, W. M. (1993). Segmented ray casting for data parallel volume rendering. *Proceedings of the 1993 Symposium on Parallel Rendering (PRS93)*, (pp. 7–14).

Humphreys, G., Eldridge, M., Buck, I., Stoll, G., Everett, M., & Hanrahan, P. (2001). WireGL: A scalable graphics system for clusters. *Proceedings of the 28th International Conference on Computer Graphics and Interactive Techniques*, (pp. 129–140).

Ino, F., Sasaki, T., Takeuchi, A., & Hagihara, K. (2003). A divided-screenwise hierarchical compositing for sort-last parallel volume rendering. *Proceedings of the 17th International Symposium on Parallel and Distributed Processing* (IPDPS '03), (p. 141).

Jeong, B., Renambot, L., Jagodic, R., Singh, R., Aguilera, J., Johnson, A., & Leigh, J. (2006, November). High-performance dynamic graphics streaming for scalable adaptive graphics environment. *Proceedings of Supercomputing, 2006*(SC06).

Johnson, C., & Hansen, C. (2004). *Visualization handbook*. Academic Press, Inc.

Kanazawa, M., et al. (2003). *Ultrahigh-definition video system with 4000 scanning lines*. NHK Technical Report.

Leigh, J., & Brown, M. D. (2007, December). Cyber-commons: Merging real and virtual worlds. *Communications of the ACM, 51*(1), 82–85. doi:10.1145/1327452.1327488

Levoy, M. (1988). Display of surfaces from volume data. *IEEE Computer Graphics and Applications, 8*(3), 29–37. doi:10.1109/38.511

Lombeyda, S., Moll, L., Shand, M., Breen, D., & Heirich, A. (2001). Scalable interactive volume rendering using off-the-shelf components. *Proceedings of the IEEE 2001 Symposium on Parallel and Large-Data Visualization and Graphics* (PVG '01), (pp. 115–121).

Lorensen, W. E., & Cline, H. E. (1987). Marching cubes: A high resolution 3D surface construction algorithm. *ACM Computer Graphics, 21*(4), 163–169. doi:10.1145/37402.37422

Ma, K.-L. (1999). Parallel rendering of 3D AMR data on the SGI/Cray T3E, *Proceedings of 7th Annual Symposium on the Frontiers of Massively Parallel Computation 1999*, (pp. 138–145).

Ma, K. L., & Camp, D. M. (2000). High performance visualization of time-varying volume data over a wide-area network. *Proceedings of Supercomputing 2000*, (p. 29).

Ma, K.-L., Painter, J. S., Hansen, C. D., & Krogh, M. F. (1994). Parallel volume rendering using binary-swap compositing. *IEEE Computer Graphics and Applications, 14*(4), 59–68. doi:10.1109/38.291532

Ma, K.-L., Wang, C., Yu, H., & Tikhonova, A. (2007). In situ processing and visualization for ultrascale simulations. *Journal of Physics, 78*, 2007. doi:10.1088/1742-6596/78/1/012043

McCormick, B. H., DeFanti, T. A., & Brown, M. D. (1988). Visualization in scientific computing. *ACM Computer Graphics, 21*(6).

Mount, R. (2004). *The office of science data-management challenge*. Report from the DOE office of science data-management workshops, Tech. Rep.

Müller, C., Strengert, M., & Ertl, T. (2006). Optimized volume raycasting for graphics-hardware-based cluster systems. *Eurographics Symposium on Parallel Graphics and Visualization* (EGPGV06), (pp. 59–66).

Muraki, S., Lum, E. B., Ma, K.-L., Ogata, M., & Liu, X. (2003). A Pc cluster system for simultaneous interactive volumetric modeling and visualization. *Proceedings of the 2003 IEEE Symposium on Parallel and Large-Data Visualization and Graphics* (PVG '03), (pp. 95–102).

Nielson, G. M., Hagen, H., & Muller, H. (1997). *Scientific visualization, overviews, methodologies, and techniques*. IEEE Computer Society.

Palmer, M. E., Totty, B., & Taylor, S. (1998). Ray casting on shared-memory architectures: Memory-hierarchy considerations in volume rendering. *IEEE Concurrency, 6*(1), 20–35. doi:10.1109/4434.656777

Peterka, T., Ross, R., Yu, H., Ma, K.-L., Kenall, W., & Huang, J. (2008). Assessing improvements in the parallel volume rendering pipeline at large scale. *Proceedings of SC 08 Ultrascale Visualization Workshop*.

Peterka, T., Yu, H., Ross, R., & Ma, K.-L. (2008). Parallel volume rendering on the IBM blue gene/p, *Proceedings of Eurographics Parallel Graphics and Visualization Symposium 2008*.

Porter, T., & Duff, T. (1984). Compositing digital images. *Proceedings of the 11th Annual Conference on Computer Graphics and Interactive Techniques* (SIGGRAPH'84), (pp. 253–259).

Prohaska, S., Hutanu, A., Kahler, R., & Hege, H. (2004). Interactive exploration of large remote micro-CT scans. In *VIS '04: Proceedings of the conference on Visualization '04*. Washington, DC: IEEE Computer Society.

Renambot, L., Jeong, B., Hur, H., Johnson, A., & Leigh, J. (2009). Enabling high resolution collaborative visualization in display rich virtual organizations. *Future Generation Computer Systems, 25*.

Renambot, L., Johnson, A., & Leigh, J. (2005). *Techniques for Building Cost-Effective Ultra-high-resolution Visualization Instruments*. NSF CISE/CNS Infrastructure Experience Workshop 2005. Retrieved from www.cs.uiuc.edu/events/expwork-2005/Luc_Renambot_Abstract.pdf

Ross, R., Peterka, T., Shen, H.-W., Hong, Y., Ma, K.-L., Yu, H., & Moreland, K. (2008). Visualization and parallel I/O at extreme scale. *Journal of Physics, 125*(1).

Schroeder, W., Martin, K., & Lorensen, W. E. (2006). *The Visualization Toolkit* (4th ed.). Kitware, Inc.

Smarr, L. L., Chien, A. A., DeFanti, T. A., Leigh, J., & Papadopoulos, P. M. (2003, November). The OptIPuter. *Communications of the ACM, 46*(11), 58–67. doi:10.1145/948383.948410

Thiebaux, M., Cox, D., & Patterson, R. (2000). *Virtual reality 3D interface system for data creation, viewing, and editing.* (Patent No. 6,154,723).

Tricoche, X., Kindlmann, G., & Westin, C.-F. (2008). Invariant crease lines for topological and structural analysis of tensor fields. *IEEE Transactions on Visualization and Computer Graphics, 14*(6), 1627–1634. doi:10.1109/TVCG.2008.148

Tu, T., Yu, H., Ramirez-Guzman, L., Bielak, J., Ghattas, O., Ma, K.-L., & O'Hallaron, D. R. (2006). From mesh generation to scientific visualization: An end-to-end approach to parallel supercomputing. *Proceedings of Supercomputing 2006*.

Van Keken, P., & Schwarz, N. (2001). Visualizing seismic wave propagation. *EOS Transactions AGU Fall Meeting Supplement, Abstract ED31E-01, 84*(46).

Vishwanath, V., Burns, R., Leigh, J., & Seablom, M. (2008). Accelerating tropical cyclone analysis using LambdaRAM, a distributed data cache over wide-area ultra-fast networks. *Future Generation of Computer Science, The International Journal of Grid Computing: Theory, Methods and Applications, 25*(2).

Vishwanath, V., Leigh, J., Shimizu, T., Nam, S., Renambot, L., & Takahashi, H. … Kamatani, O. (2008b). *The rails toolkit (RTK) - Enabling End-system topology-aware high end computing.* 4th IEEE International Conference on e-Science.

Vishwanath, V., Shimizu, T., Takizawa, M., Obana, K., & Leigh, J. (2007, November). Towards terabit/s systems: Performance evaluation of multi-rail systems. *Proceedings of Supercomputing, 2007*(SC07).

Vishwanath, V., Zuck, L., & Leigh, J. (2008a). Specification and verification of LambdaRAM: A wide-area distributed cache for high performance computing. *In Proceedings of the 6th ACM/IEEE International Conference on Formal Methods and Models for Co-Design, 2008 (MEMOCODE 2008),* 5-7 June 2008, 187 – 198.

von Funck, W., Weinkauf, T., Theisel, H., & Seidel, H.-P. (2008). Smoke surfaces: An interactive flow visualization technique inspired by real-world flow experiments. *IEEE Transactions on Visualization and Computer Graphics, 14*(6), 1396–140. doi:10.1109/TVCG.2008.163

Weber, G. H., Hagen, H., Hamann, B., Joy, K. I., Ligocki, T. J., Ma, K.-L., & Shalf, J. M. (2001). Visualization of adaptive mesh refinement data. *Proceedings of IS&T/SPIE Visual Data Exploration and Analysis, VIII,* (pp. 121–132).

Weber, G. H., Kreylos, O., Ligocki, T. J., Shalf, J. M., Hagen, H., Hamann, B., … Ma, K.-L. (2001). *High-quality volume rendering of adaptive mesh refinement data.*

Xiong, C., Leigh, J., He, E., Vishwanath, V., Murata, T., Renambot, L., & DeFanti, T. (2005). LambdaStream – A data transport protocol for streaming network-intensive applications over photonic networks. *Proceedings of The Third International Workshop on Protocols for Fast Long-Distance Networks.*

Yu, H., Ma, K.-L., & Welling, J. (2004). A parallel visualization pipeline for terascale earthquake simulations, *Proceedings of Supercomputing 2004,* (p. 49).

Zhang, C., Leigh, J., DeFanti, T. A., Mazzucco, M., & Grossman, R. (2003). TeraScope: Distributed visual data mining of terascale data sets over photonic networks. *Journal of Future Generation Computer Systems, 19*(6). doi:10.1016/S0167-739X(03)00072-4

ENDNOTES

[1] www.nlr.net
[2] www.internet2.edu
[3] www.glif.is
[4] www.startap.net/starlight

Chapter 12
On–Demand Visualization on Scalable Shared Infrastructure

Huadong Liu
University of Tennessee, USA

Jinzhu Gao
University of The Pacific, USA

Jian Huang
University of Tennessee, USA

Micah Beck
University of Tennessee, USA

Terry Moore
University of Tennessee, USA

ABSTRACT

The emergence of high-resolution simulation, where simulation outputs have grown to terascale levels and beyond, raises major new challenges for the visualization community, which is serving computational scientists who want adequate visualization services provided to them on-demand. Many existing algorithms for parallel visualization were not designed to operate optimally on time-shared parallel systems or on heterogeneous systems. They are usually optimized for systems that are homogeneous and have been reserved for exclusive use. This chapter explores the possibility of developing parallel visualization algorithms that can use distributed, heterogeneous processors to visualize cutting edge simulation datasets. The authors study how to effectively support multiple concurrent users operating on the same large dataset, with each focusing on a dynamically varying subset of the data. From a system design point of view, they observe that a distributed cache offers various advantages, including improved scalability. They develop basic scheduling mechanisms that were able to achieve fault-tolerance and load-balancing, optimal use of resources, and flow-control using system-level back-off, while still enforcing deadline driven (i.e. time-critical) visualization.

DOI: 10.4018/978-1-61520-971-2.ch012

INTRODUCTION

The emergence of high-resolution simulation, where simulation outputs have grown to terascale levels and beyond, raises major new challenges for the visualization community, which is serving computational scientists who want adequate visualization services provided to them on-demand. For one thing, visualizing such massive datasets inevitably requires large-scale parallelism, but parallel systems of adequate size are still too scarce a resource for widespread routine use. This practical bottleneck is exacerbated by the fact that many existing algorithms for parallel visualization were not designed to operate optimally on time-shared parallel systems or on heterogeneous systems. They are usually optimized for systems that are homogeneous and have been reserved for exclusive use. Few parallel visualization algorithms now available can effectively utilize aggregated, network accessible computing resources to serve the data-intensive and on-demand visualization needs of a group of concurrent users.

To ameliorate this situation and start supporting the changing demands of simultaneous users, we need to develop parallel visualization algorithms that do not assume that the underlying processors are homogeneous or always available. Such algorithms should work well even when a parallel visualization task obtains different performances from different processors or when overloaded processors appear temporarily unavailable.

Weakening other assumptions could enable some even greater advantages. In particular, instead of assuming that all available processors are connected by a system-area network, we could develop algorithms that assume the wide-area Internet as the interconnect. Algorithms so designed could recruit all processing resources available in the distributed environment and obtain a system that scales beyond the conventional boundaries of administrative domains. Moreover, with the standard Internet providing universal access, geographically separated users could use such an inherently distributed parallel system as a shared infrastructure for collaborative data sharing and data-intensive visualization. It would be unnecessary to provision dedicated clusters and create local replicas of large data objects at each separate site.

In this chapter, we present our research to meet such new needs. We developed a test-bed consisting of 100 networked computers, none of which were specially provisioned for visualization. While all the distributed processors involved are heterogeneous, freely available, and independent of each other, our work shows that they can be formed into a generic, shared infrastructure on which 10 concurrent users can visualize and interact with a 128 time-step simulation dataset totaling 250 GB.

Our contributions include the following. First, we designed middleware that combines loosely coupled, distributed resources into a common execution environment that dynamically discovers the most efficient computing resources available in the system. Using a novel scheme of data replication and distributed caching, it also reduces runtime data movement by leveraging the data access patterns of volume visualization.

Second, for parallel visualization algorithms operating in the master-worker model, we devised a novel scheduling algorithm that runs on a user's local computer, i.e. on the client, and orchestrates a parallel visualization run on distributed heterogeneous processors. The scheduling algorithm implements mechanisms for performance and fault-tolerance. In addition, the scheduler is designed with a robust protocol of distributed flow-control to maintain the scalability and stability of a large-scale shared system. The flow-control mechanism involves a two-level back-off scheme, i.e. system-level back-off as well as application level back-off. The system level back-off (less aggressive task assignment) regulates every client's use of the system to ensure fairness of resource utilization and at the same time avoid overloading the overall distributed system. The application level back-off dynamically trades lowers rendering quality when necessary to reduce the total required workload. The effectiveness of our scheduling scheme is tested with 100 distributed processing nodes, made available through PlanetLab (PlanetLab (n.d)) and the Research and Education Data Depot Network (REDDnet).[1]

The remainder of this chapter is organized as follows. After describing the background of our research, we discuss the overall system. We then present details of the scheduler. Finally, we present testing results and conclude this chapter.

BACKGROUND

Data-Intensive Applications

In order to effectively handle large datasets, parallel visualization algorithms need to optimize the entire overhead incurred during rendering, including costs of out-of-core operations (Yu, Ma, & Welling, 2004). For this purpose, efficient systems level support, for instance parallel I/O by MPI-IO available on parallel clusters, is very beneficial (Gropp, Lusk, & Thakur, 1999).

Since our focus is large-scale parallel visualization using heterogeneous processors distributed across administrative boundaries, no existing system-level tools are readily available for our use to optimize I/O overheads. Instead, we developed a novel architecture that incorporates replication and caching capabilities on distributed processors. All distributed caches collectively are maintained using distributed hash table (DHT). In order to effectively operate in distributed environments, our system also uses a coarser granularity than that used by MPI-IO. While MPI-IO supports accessing an arbitrary block in a file on a parallel virtual file system (Carns, Ligon, Ross, & Thakur, 2000), the smallest unit of data in our system is data blocks, partitioned during pre-computation.

Distributed Infrastructure

Finding a system infrastructure that uses widely distributed resources and is capable of supporting large scale research on parallel visualization for data-intensive applications is a non-trivial challenge. While a variety of distributed system software exists for many specific applications, such as peer-to-peer data sharing and public-resource computing (Anderson, 2004; Sarmenta, 2001), our needs are unique in several ways. First, we want the infrastructure to be lightweight so that a large community of users might find it reasonable to adopt and easy to deploy. If the infrastructural software is too resource hungry, large-scale deployment becomes problematic. Second, redundancy is crucial to fault-tolerance in distributed systems, but managing redundancy can be a tedious process. It would be highly advantageous if the underlying infrastructure provided a simple interface for managing redundancy. Third, and most importantly, in data-intensive visualization it is not advisable to constantly move the entire raw dataset, as this is always a long, error-prone process. Hence, it would be ideal if system infrastructure provided co-located resources for both processing and storage.

Among the possible alternatives, Logistical Networking (LN) fits these conditions especially well (Plank et al., 2001). LN's design philosophy parallels that used for protocols like TCP/IP in order to be lightweight and easy to deploy. It provides an interface that facilitates managing redundancy, and naturally lends itself to minimizing data movement in distributed processing scenarios.

The suite of LN mechanisms includes two generic components, IBP (Beck. Moore, & Plank, 2002) for storage and NFU (Beck, Moore, & Plank, 2003) for processing. The Internet Backplane Protocol (IBP) provides distributed storage service IBP (Beck. Moore, & Plank, 2002). As with IP datagram service, the service that IBP defines is both generic and limited. By running an IBP process, a node provides IBP service and is then referred to as a depot. The depot manages some share of the node's local storage resources (ranging from a small portion to the vast majority of it) and provides storage in pieces or slices, per external requests. A common file can be divided into multiple partitions, with each partition replicated onto several different depots for redundancy. However, all storage slices of the file, on different computers are represented and referenced collectively through a (XML encoded) network file descriptor called an exNode. As standard Unix inodes contain information about all the disk blocks used in a Unix file, exNodes contain information about how a data object is mapped into a set of allocated blocks on a network of IBP depots.

While IBP depots can be set to allow permanent allocations, the usual depot policy is to make allocations time limited in order to facilitate resource sharing. However, before a "lease" on an allocation expires, LN services can renew it on the same depot, or, if the renewal fails, move the partition to another depot with a new allocation. This process is transparent to a user program. Data movement, from a depot to a user client (downloading), from a client to multiple depots (uploading) and between depots (augmenting) can use multiple TCP streams in parallel for optimal network efficiency.

Network Functional Unit (NFU) provides processing power through an orthogonal extension to the IBP protocol (Beck, Moore, & Plank, 2003). It offers an abstract compute service based on computational fragments (e.g. OS time slices) that are managed as "operations" applied to data stored in local IBP memory buffers. In fact, NFU operations can act only on data stored in IBP allocations at the depot where it is invoked. NFU operations run in a sandboxed mode disallowing most calls, such as those that access local file system and network. Executing NFU operations are also bounded in terms of the amount of memory they can allocate and their total running time. These limits are established by local depot

policy. An operation attempting to over-allocate any resource or running for too long may be terminated by the depot.

Both IBP and NFU abstract the details of the local platform. Instead of offering permanent storage, IBP offers fixed storage segments and aggregates them across multiple computers. Instead of offering fixed OS time slices, NFU aggregates them; instead of providing a multiplicity of failure modes, a faulty operation simply terminates with unknown state.

Thus in LN, both storage and computation are essentially "packetized," and the multiplexing of the service must be characterized statistically. To obtain more robustness or high performance processing using the limited NFU protocol, end users need to apply techniques such as replication and scheduling. In this work we show how this can be done for data-intensive parallel visualization.

Scheduling

Our use of the term scheduling strides over two separate domains: master-worker model of parallel visualization and resource scheduling in operating systems.

Parallel Visualization

In parallel visualization, algorithms are often specific to the underlying system architecture, e.g. whether all processors share the same address space (distributed shared memory) or not (distributed memory). Since our intended system is inherently a distributed memory system, we begin by focusing on previous methods on distributed memory systems.

In those methods, the common way to achieve parallel acceleration is to partition a visualization job into sub-tasks, which are then assigned or distributed, together with the data that each requires, to different processors. Either explicitly or implicitly, a scheduling method determines the distribution with load-balance being the primary goal. Scheduling, or task distribution, may take place at runtime or be pre-determined offline.

Several methods to distribute sub-tasks have been developed. Just as a few representative examples, previous researchers have used static distribution (Ma, 1995), run-time job stealing (Whitman, 1993), dynamic job queue based distribution (Challinger, 1993), etc. A job distribution can be further refined by setting a time-stamp for each processor. If a processor cannot complete the assigned list of tasks before the time-stamp expires, the remaining jobs in its list can be re-partitioned and re-distributed (Corrie & Mackerras, 1993). If the scheduling is performed explicitly, this model of operation is referred to as master-worker. Our work herein uses this model.

Much previous work assumes that a parallel visualization run has exclusive access to a parallel system and all processors are homogeneous. Hence the time to complete a sub-task directly correlates with the amount of work required by the sub-task, independent of which processor a sub-task is assigned to. The primary goal of a scheduler is then to achieve maximal parallel acceleration.

This assumption of homogeneity greatly simplifies the scheduler, but unfortunately ceases to hold in the heterogeneous systems of interest in our research, where the amount of time needed to complete a sub-task is dependent on speed as well as current workload of the corresponding processor. In addition, a processor may become sporadically faulty and fail to complete an assigned task. Few previous researchers included this type of scenario in their design goals.

Resource Scheduling

In resource scheduling, for instance to schedule CPU cycles, the goal is multi-fold. Resource utilization, system throughput, as well as fairness in assigning resource to each consumer (e.g. process) are a few typical objectives of optimization (Silberschatz & Galvin, 1994).

While resource utilization (e.g. 85% of CPU cycles) and throughput (e.g. number of processes completed in an hour) can be measured in a straightforward manner, fairness cannot. One would have to use some indirect metrics. As an example, the response time incurred by all interactive processes, when averaged, in a way shows the overall performance of a system. The difference between maximum and minimum of response time incurred by all interactive processes could reflect the underlying fairness of the scheduler (Silberschatz & Galvin, 1994).

However, little previous research exists to measure the overall quality of a scheduler operating on a system composed of distributed heterogeneous processors. Furthermore, most previous scheduling methods in parallel visualization and resource management are entirely centralized.

Our scheduler is different that it is not centralized. Each client serves as the master node (scheduler) of its own parallel visualization run, aiming to achieve fault-tolerance as well as parallel scalability. At the same time, all schedulers abide by the same two-level flow control protocol to ensure the overall system is shared in a fair, efficient and robust manner.

AN ON-DEMAND SYSTEM

Design Goals

To optimize a data-intensive application, it is crucial to carefully consider the underlying pattern of data access. In this work, we target the following scenario:

- A group of users in separate locations need to share a few large datasets.
- Users start and stop their own visualization jobs on-demand, without synchronizing with each other.
- Each user focuses on the part of the data relevant to the user's individual interests.

Figure 1. An illustration of our system design

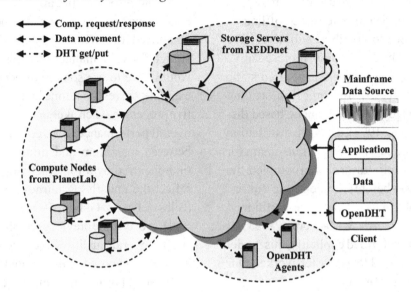

While each user accesses only a subset of the entire dataset at any particular time, there could be considerable overlaps among the subsets accessed by all users.

System Design

Since distributed resources cannot make absolute service guarantees (all stronger services are implemented at higher layers, end-to-end), the quality of service delivered by a given depot resource is a function of its inherent characteristics and its workload. In this respect, our testbed has two basic types of resource: (i) those that are well provisioned and lightly burdened, and therefore tend to be reliable and deliver good performance, and (ii) those that are modestly provisioned and relatively heavily used, and therefore tend to be slower and less reliable.

REDDnet servers are good examples of the first type of resource. They are stable and have a substantial amount of storage, on the order of tens of Terabytes (TB). REDDnet servers also have considerable processing power. PlanetLab (PlanetLab (n.d)) nodes are of the second type. Those nodes provide rather limited storage (5GB

per slice); and since they are shared by a vast community, those nodes tend to stay moderately to heavily burdened. Blanket assumptions about the availability of PlanetLab nodes at any given time are dubious.

The two types of resources are used for different purposes in our system (illustrated in Figure 1). REDDnet servers are mainly used as "working" storage servers to provide medium-term access to the original datasets for distributed communities. By contrast, PlanetLab nodes are used to compute visualization. Parallel visualization jobs will cause the needed data partitions to be streamed from REDDnet servers on the fly for processing. After a computation is done, the result is transmitted back to the client, and the data partition is cached on the PlanetLab nodes. All the caches, collectively a distributed cache, are managed using OpenDHT (Rhea et al., 2005). Subsequent visualization jobs would only need to move the partitions from REDDnet servers that do not exist in the distributed caches on PlanetLab nodes. All other needed partitions are already on PlanetLab nodes. In both REDDnet storage servers and the temporary distributed caches, redundancy is implemented for fault-tolerance.

Of course, due to abrupt increases in workload or loss of network connection, PlanetLab nodes can fail sporadically to complete an assigned task. As with volunteer nodes in public-resource computing systems (Anderson. 2004; Sarmenta, 2001), they can freely join or leave any experiment. REDDnet nodes can also participate in computations on the condition that they do not become overloaded.

The system essentially matches the distributed memory multiprocessor architecture. Every server (either from REDDnet or PlanetLab) is mapped to a parallel node, with NFU acting as the processor, IBP as the processor's main memory, and storage space provided by REDDnet servers as external disks.

However, unlike large-scale I/O modules on conventional parallel systems, each processor in our system (via NFU) caches previously used data for later use on a processor specific basis. Additionally, cache coherence is simplified, since the data cached in memory is read only.

We use DHT to achieve scalability as well as fault-tolerance, while maintaining the whereabouts of data partitions on 100's of distributed nodes. Similar to the Translation Lookaside Buffer (TLB) in classic computer architecture (Patterson & Hennesy, 1994) which converts a virtual memory address to physical memory address, DHT converts a logical name (i.e. which data partition) to a set of memory addresses (i.e. IBP capabilities pointing to cached replicas). Mappings between partition name and capabilities are maintained in the OpenDHT network, avoiding single point failures.

The System in Operation

A dataset generated on a mainframe or a cluster is partitioned and the MD5 hash of each partition is calculated. We use the terms "partition" and "block" interchangeably. As a onetime operation, partitions are uploaded into REDDnet storage servers with a small replication ratio (e.g.

two) for permanent storage. The resulting data capabilities are stored in the OpenDHT network. The client gets data capabilities by querying the underlying OpenDHT agents, uses the queried capabilities to direct data movement and assign visualization tasks.

When a partition is available on an IBP depot, a <key, value> pair is inserted into the OpenDHT network, where key is the MD5 hash of the partition and value is the set of IBP capabilities (a part of exNode) for the partition. The owner of the dataset may choose not to put the write capabilities and manage capabilities into value, making allocations read only. The time-to-live (TTL) value of the <key, value> pair is set to be the duration of the IBP allocation. The entire list of <key, name> pairs of all partitions of a dataset is then published among interested groups, for example, via the web. The field name describes the partition. For example, tsi09.29.bin.ub indicates that the key field is the MD5 of partition 29 in time step 09 of a simulation data called "TSI". It is unsigned byte in binary.

To use the system, a client needs to obtain a <key, name> list of the dataset he is interested in. For the best performance, the client also needs to obtain a list of PlanetLab nodes that can potentially be involved in his visualization. The list is either a static file or is dynamically exported by a resource discovery service. To invoke a computation on a particular partition, the client queries the OpenDHT network using the MD5 hash key and chooses one of the returned read capabilities as a pointer to a copy of the data to work on.

Initially, OpenDHT queries return only capabilities to allocations on REDDnet servers, since all PlanetLab nodes are blank. To balance workload between REDDnet servers and PlanetLab nodes, the client starts to move some of the partitions from REDDnet servers to PlanetLab nodes when doing computations on REDDnet servers. Destination servers are chosen randomly or by some performance metric from the list. Again, when the new replica is made, the resulting <key, value>

pair is inserted into the OpenDHT network with duration of the IBP allocation as TTL. Computation on this partition can now be assigned to the PlanetLab node that the replica is made on. Later on, when other clients come in and do computation on the same data partition, OpenDHT queries will also return capabilities of replicas made during previous executions on PlanetLab nodes as well as capabilities on REDDnet servers.

IBP capabilities of the partition and the corresponding <key, value> pairs in the OpenDHT network are refreshed (if the manage capability is available in value) to keep the frequently used data on PlanetLab nodes.

THE SCHEDULER

Different clients independently initiate parallel visualization processes, with each operating in the master-worker model. Overall, this on-demand mode of operation creates a dynamic set of concurrent computing tasks. Every client runs its own scheduler and serves as the master node in its own parallel visualization session.

The first goal of a scheduler is to ensure fault-tolerance, i.e. completion of a parallel visualization. After a job has been partitioned into sub-tasks to be computed in parallel, the scheduler is provided with a to-do list of sub-tasks. When a sub-task gets assigned to a processor, a time-out stamp is also set. If the result of the sub-task is not returned to the client before the time-out stamp expires, we consider that processor to have failed. The scheduler re-issues the uncompleted sub-task to another processor. To do so, all tasks being computed but unfinished are maintained in a separate job queue (i.e. Un-Finished Queue, UFQ). This queue is of lower priority than the job queue holding all un-assigned sub-tasks (i.e. Un-Assigned Queue, UAQ). After a sub-tasks is assigned, it is demoted from UAQ to UFQ. When a job in the UFQ is determined to have failed, it is

then appended back to the UAQ. Only tasks in the UAQ are assigned to processors of the scheduler.

The dataset is originally distributed on REDDnet servers with K-way (K=2 in our system) replication (Samanta, Funkhouser, & Li, 2001). At runtime, scheduler assigns tasks to workers on the fly. When a processor does not have the necessary data for any remaining tasks in UAQ (e.g. initial startup), the scheduler dynamically directs moving a data partition to the processor. As long as there are tasks in the UAQ that a processor already has data for, possibly cached from a previous run, the scheduler assigns all those tasks to that processor first, no matter the location of those tasks in the UAQ. In a real-world scenario, processors will get an un-even distribution of partitions due to variance in their capability and/ or previous workloads.

Besides fault-tolerance, the scheduler must also provide several system-wide features to be practically useful and deployable. Those include parallel scalability (e.g. parallel acceleration), fairness among all users and stability of the overall system. Given a finite amount of computing resources, the more concurrent users there are, the less a share every user will get. Our scheduler allows a user to provide a deadline for a job to complete. When the scheduler determines that completing a visualization job at full resolution is unrealistic for a given deadline, it switches to use lower resolution (level-of-detail) for less important partitions.

All the extra system-wide features described above require advanced designs in the system. As a special note, our scheduler design considers an unprecedented scenario. That is a large number of schedulers operate in parallel from geographically separated sites to achieve those system-wide features. It is not just one scheduler operating at any time. From this perspective, the design of our scheduler can be regarded as defining a protocol for operating a distributed set of resources, and this protocol is optimized for use in large-scale visualization.

The detailed methods of our scheduler to achieve parallel scalability, fairness and stability as well as enforcement of deadline (e.g. time-critical visualization) are described in the following sections. Borrowing terms from the networking community, the scheduler considers flow control in the overall system, occurring on two levels: (i) system-level back-off and (ii) application-level back-off.

Parallel Acceleration

Parallel visualization jobs issued on-demand by geographically separate users in our system invariably compete for the same pool of shared resources. This causes high variability in resource consumption and performance over time, which, unfortunately, is hard to accurately predict. When shared resources cannot be brought under the control of a single global scheduler, distributed schedulers need to make necessary runtime adaptations.

Since partitions of a dataset for parallel visualization usually have similar sizes, we can define processing throughput as the number of partitions processed in a unit time. The scheduler dynamically computes a running average of measured processing throughput of each processor, with older measurements given an exponentially decreasing weight. In this way, processors that are fast at the current moment are discovered on the fly.

We would like the fastest processors to work on as many data partitions as possible, and avoid stalls caused by slow or faulty processors. Our scheduler achieves this design goal in the following steps.

For each processor, the scheduler maintains a list of pointers for all un-assigned tasks that the processor can compute, i.e. already have the necessary data cached locally. Those pointers point directly to the corresponding tasks in UAQ. This list is sorted in increasing order, with the key being the maximum processing throughput of all the processors that hold the required data partition.

When a processor becomes available, it always picks the first element in its list, to "rob" this sub-task from the other processors that can also process this sub-task; i.e. this processor grabs the first sub-task, whose other potential nodes are all relatively slow, while saving sub-tasks also available on faster processors for later.

The current throughputs of processors vary over time. Every time a new measurement has been taken, the processor-specific list is re-sorted to reflect the change. When a sub-task is completed, it is deleted from the lists of all processors holding its data partition.

Finally, when all sub-tasks available on a processor have been completed, this processor gets fresh tasks from the scheduler. This time, with each new assignment, however, the necessary data has to be moved first across the network.

Pipelining

To enable resource sharing, NFUs impose limits on the time and storage needed by a computation. The size of byte arrays that any computation can transform is bounded and so is the execution time. Large datasets need to be partitioned into smaller pieces, so that each partition can be handled by an NFU operation. It is the job of the client, or the master node, to orchestrate the parallel run and assemble the overall final result.

In the wide-area, network latencies between the client and the compute nodes can be too expensive. If synchronous communication/signaling is used, the performance will suffer. Thus, besides directing more work to more efficient resources, a client also needs to overcome network latency.

To resolve latency issues and increase resource utilization, we use low-level parallelism in the form of pipelining. For instance, instruction pipelining is used to address high instruction issue latency (Patterson & Hennessy, 1994). In that technique, multiple instructions populate different stages, or modules, of the hardware of the processor.

Our scheduler also leverages pipelining to achieve a finer granularity of parallelism. Our scenario is unique because resources available on a processor vary over time. Not all sub-tasks, or partitions, take the same amount of time to complete, nor do they incur the same amount of network communication. Hence, it is hard to statically define how many and what stages to use in the pipeline.

Instead, we devised a pipeline with a variable depth, d. A client initially issues $d+1$ sub-tasks to a processor. When a sub-task is completed, the client assigns one more sub-task to keep the pipeline full until the priority queue is empty. If d is sufficiently large, the client can keep a remote processor busy without incurring bottlenecks related to network latency. But if all clients use too large a value of d, the system could get overloaded. At runtime, our system-level back-off scheme (described in the next section) determines the proper d value to use on the fly.

System-Level Back-off

By combining techniques described previously, a single client can achieve load balance and make full utilization of available resources on distributed and heterogeneous processors if its work is purely CPU-limited. But when multiple users contend for resources, especially with deep pipelines, aggressive clients can cause situations similar to network congestion. Throughput of the overall system, as well as on each individual processor, could significantly decrease due to the overhead of extensive task switching and even worse: thrashing.

By treating each node as if it were a special router that also transforms incoming data, our overall system can be viewed as a data-intensive network. The source consists of data servers on REDDnet nodes. The intermediate PlanetLab nodes are the routers and the client, which is the master, is the sink where all final results are assembled. This analogy provides a bridge for us

to apply the concept of flow control, first studied by the networking communities.

In a familiar case, TCP manages limited network bandwidth with flow control to pace data transfer at acceptable speeds. Similarly, our scheme dynamically increases/decreases the pipeline depth used by each client to make sure that servers do not get overloaded. Most importantly, we make pipeline depth processor-specific. When a client orchestrates a parallel run, it treats processors offering different levels of performance differently, and adjusts the pipeline depth over time as well.

However, our challenge here is to define when a depot should be considered as "being overloaded". In TCP congestion control, congestion is indicated by a timeout or the reception of duplicate ACK messages. But in our system, due to the high temporal and processor-specific variability, it is difficult to find a timeout value that reliably indicates an overloaded system. Instead, for each processor, we start with $d = 0$, i.e., no more requests are sent until the response of the previous request has been received. When a task is finished successfully, the processor's current processing throughput τ is calculated. Supposing the previous processing throughput being τ', d is updated by the following rules:

- if $\tau < (1-\rho) \times \tau'$, $d = d-1$
- if $\tau > (1+\rho) \times \tau'$, $d = min(d+1, MAX\_DEPTH)$
- otherwise, $d = d$

ρ is a tolerance of acceptable variations in the measured performance, e.g. $\rho = 10\%$. Any changes in measured throughput lesser than 10% will not cause d and τ' to be updated. When τ drops by ρ, we decrement d. Note, we allow d to be negative, which means the scheduler cannot make any new request to the corresponding node right now. Instead the scheduler waits for a delay of $1/(\tau' \times 2^{d+1})$. $1/\tau'$ corresponds to the time to compute one partition by that processor. A d

value of -1 sets the delay to $1/\tau'$, while $d = -2$ causes the delay to be $2/\tau'$.

When previous assigned tasks are successfully returned to the scheduler and causes τ to increase by ρ, d is incremented, until d reaches *MAX_DEPTH* (in our system we use *MAX_DEPTH* = 5). If d is positive, the scheduler issues new tasks to fill up the pipeline. But if after incrementing d is still negative, the scheduler still waits a delay of $1/(\tau' \times 2^{d+1})$ before sending new requests to that processor.

In this manner, the scheduler gradually "starts" or "stops" a remote processor, according to how much work that processor has been able to provide. Slow, overloaded processors, or processors with policies limiting usage by the client can be discovered on the fly and treated differently.

The above process iterates over time until the to-do list of subtasks is depleted for a processor. Initially, since there are no outstanding job requests, we set τ' to a negative value, thus the scheduler is guaranteed to update every processor's τ' with the first processing throughput and starts the pipeline with two concurrent requests ($d=1$).

ρ needs to be carefully selected. A large ρ makes the scheduler less adaptive to performance changes due to pipelining depth change. In contrast, a small ρ makes the scheduler sensitive to even performance fluctuation within reasonable range. We use a ρ value of 10% in our experiments.

Application-Level Back-off

In time-critical situations, the visualization has to complete within a user-specified time frame. Image quality may need to be sacrificed in order to guarantee a timely delivery of visualization results. To ensure the highest affordable visual quality, we prioritize sub-tasks, or data partitions, according to an importance metric. This importance metric, measured for each data partition, is based on the visual contribution of the partition to the final image. Guided by the importance metric, we designed an application-level back-off scheme

that schedules more important data partitions to be rendered earlier and in higher resolution. Less important partitions are rendered later, close to the deadline. In many cases to meet the deadline, resolutions of those less important partitions are compromised.

The importance of a data partition depends on a number of factors that can be application-dependent, value-dependent or view-dependent. The importance metric is a relative term, not on absolute scale, solely for sorting purposes. Specifically, the rules are:

- A more transparent block is less important;
- A block with higher variance in voxel values is more important;
- An invisible block has zero importance and is not accessed or processed at all;
- A block closer to the eye is more important;

Our system always chooses the highest affordable resolution for a block as allowed by the specified time limit. Once the system gets a visualization request, it computes importance values for all visible data blocks and then produces a sorted list of tasks ranked in decreasing importance. This list is then provided to the scheduler for constructing the UAQ in the same sorted order.

Periodically, the system compares the user-specified time limit with the estimated time to finish all the required tasks under the current system throughput, calculated as a summation of all processors' throughput. If the deadline cannot be met, the scheduler marks less important tasks are marked to switch to a lower resolution.

The application-level back-off is supported by a hierarchical data structure, essentially an octree. The root of the tree represents the lowest resolution of the data and the leave nodes of the tree correspond to the full resolution of the data.

When a back-off decision needs to be made, the scheduler starts with the tail of UAQ and search backwards for blocks that can be combined into lower resolution (higher in the octree). Those

Figure 2. An example of the application-level back-off

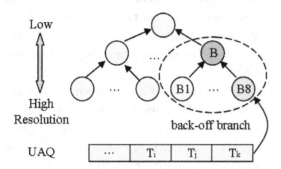

partitions are marked for resolution reduction. If the throughput of the system later improves, those partitions can be de-marked. We illustrate this scheme in Figure 2 with a simple example. When a back-off operation is necessary, the back-off task, T_k, is chosen from the tail of UAQ. Suppose T_k, corresponds to data block B_8. The octree branch $(B, B_1, ..., B_8)$ is selected as a back-off branch. All higher resolution tasks B_i ($i=1 \sim 8$) are then marked. During rendering, B_i's are replaced by the lower resolution block B.

RESULTS

To demonstrate the effectiveness of our system and the dynamic scheduling scheme, we made parallel volume visualization runs on 90 depots (as compute nodes) from PlanetLab and another 10 depots (as both storage and compute servers) from REDDnet. Visualization operations were made into sandboxed NFUs operations. The scalability results we obtained in volume rendering (ray-casting) and isosurface extraction (marching-cube) are similar.

Here we discuss results of parallel software ray-casting in detail. Our approach uses early ray termination when rendering each block. Occlusion culling at the block level is computed using plenoptic opacity function (POF) (Gao, Shen, Huang, & Kohl, 2003). An Enhanced Time-Space

Partitioning (ETSP) tree (Gao, Shen, Huang, & Kohl, 2004) provides a hierarchical data structure that encodes data variation as well as temporal coherence in visibility.

For our experiments we use 128 time-steps (250GB in total) of a simulation data set produced by the Terascale Supernova Initiative (TSI) project (Irion, 2006). Each time-step is of 864×864×864 spatial resolution. We partitioned data and then generated the multi-resolution hierarchy. In total, there are 417 non-empty blocks of 128×128×128 resolution. Each block was roughly 8 MB, totaling 2.9 GB per time-step. The 2.9×128=371 GB data, including the multi-resolution hierarchy, was distributed on 10 REDDnet depots with 2-way replication for high availability and streaming performance.

A third replication will be created dynamically at runtime in the distributed caches managed by DHT. After the third replica is fully created, we have roughly up to 1TB of data to manage during experimental runs with all three replicas together. In all cases, the test runs use image resolutions of 800×800 with a step size of 1.0 along each ray.

Distributed Data Caching

Data caching in the system works as follows. When the first user starts to use the system, visualization operations can be invoked directly on REDDnet depots. At the same time, the system also streams a relevant subset of the entire dataset to PlanetLab depots and starts visualization operations there when data blocks are available. Data blocks used in previous operations are then cached at PlanetLab nodes so that subsequent computations on the same data blocks could be invoked directly on PlanetLab nodes without streaming data blocks from REDDnet depots again.

First let's look at the effects of distributed data caching. Figure 3 shows the computation and data movement throughput of seven consecutive visualization jobs, run back-to-back. At any particular time, there is only one job. Each job runs

Figure 3. Computation and data movement throughput of the first seven sequential visualization jobs

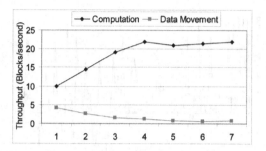

Figure 4. System throughput with different number of users and pipelining depth

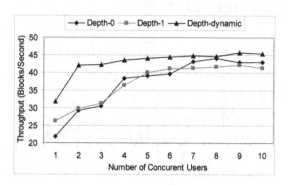

ray-casting from a constant view angle on the same 10 time steps of the TSI dataset. However, the view angles used by the seven parallel jobs are 10 degrees apart. On average each parallel job involves about 918 data blocks. In total, the seven parallel runs processed 1019 unique data blocks.

The system discovers fast processors on the fly and directs more computation to them. This set of processors changes over time, although there are rather significant overlaps from one time to another. Thus, constant re-use of cached data is not guaranteed. However, as more jobs get completed and more data get populated on the processors with an increasing number of replicas, subsequent jobs enjoy increasing flexibility while assigning tasks. Fewer data blocks are streamed from storage servers to compute nodes. As a result of these factors, over time computational throughput steadily increases while the amount of data movement decreases.

Note that data blocks are not evenly distributed among PlanetLab compute nodes. Data blocks are incrementally replicated and cached in compute nodes. Fast nodes with good network connections and large storage space tend to cache more blocks than less well-provisioned servers. During the entire test, 772 blocks were moved to PlanetLab nodes, while the other 247 blocks were completed on the REDDnet nodes. Without caching, up to 918×7 = 6426 blocks would have needed to be moved.

In every subsequent experiment in the following sections, we ran all tests after the distributed caches have stabilized, to isolate the effects of those schemes being evaluated.

System-Level Back-off

Computational throughput can be improved by pipelining requests. However, a universal pipelining depth would be too restrictive because proximities between the client and servers are different and because servers may differ in their capability to handle multiple requests. When multiple users contend for resources on the same node, the resulting system workload is hard to predict. Thus, it is better for a client to dynamically decide proper processor-specific pipelining depth in order to get the best performance out of non-dedicated and possibly heterogeneous compute nodes.

To isolate the effect of pipelining, in all tests we ensured the same scenario of data distribution, without any runtime data movement.

In Figure 4, we show the system throughput with up to 10 concurrent users using different pipelining depth. The 10 users asynchronously start their jobs at random instants within a 10 seconds span of time. The overall system throughput increases as more users enter the system and peaks when serving 10 concurrent users. Right now, we assume each user has only one connection to

Figure 5: A snapshot of pipelining depth of all processors in the system, from the perspective of one user, with 3 other concurrent users in the background (left) vs. no other concurrent users (right). In all cases, MAX_DEPTH = 5

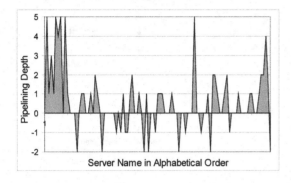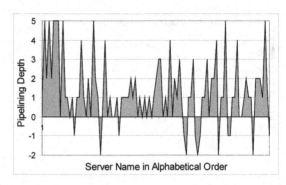

each depot, hence avoiding the possibility of one single user overloading the entire system. Due this design choice, when there is only one user in the system, the peak system-wide throughput is lower than that of multiple concurrent users. Pipelining allows more overlap between CPU and I/O operations, and resulting better system throughput.

Tests with pipelining depth 1 and depth 0 behave similarly except in the single user case. When there is only one user, pipelining does increase system performance since network communication and computation can overlap. The extent of overlapping depends on the nature of the visualization operation. Tests with dynamic pipelining depth performed best among the three. With dynamic pipelining depth, the system reaches its capacity quickly with two concurrent users, delivering more computing power to each user.

Overall, the maximum throughput achieved by the set of 100 shared and heterogeneous processors in our system was 45.8 data partitions (blocks) per second. By comparison, though not a rigorous one, we tested the job list of one of the users in Figure 4 on a standalone 2.2 GHz P4 computer in dedicated mode. That job list had 918 data blocks and took 1080 seconds to complete, so the resulting throughput on that dedicated 2.2

GHz computer was, 0.85 blocks per second. As a rough extrapolation then, our testbed provided throughput equivalent to a 64-node cluster of 2.2 GHz processors, assuming 85% parallel utilization for the same job list.

To further illustrate the dynamics of task assignment, in Figure 5 (left diagram) we plot variations in the pipelining depths of all processors, when there are four concurrent users. This diagram shows the snapshot of a random time from the perspective of one of the four clients, i.e. the other three clients appear as background users. Processors with negative pipelining depth have reached their full capacity and the client is performing back-off on those nodes. For comparison, in the right graph of Figure 5, we provide a similar snapshot of processor-specific pipelining depth when there is only one user. Less system-level back-off means a lot more active processors can be used for computation.

Application-Level Back-off

User-specified deadline decides the eventual number of blocks at each resolution level that are rendered. This experiment involved up to five concurrent users in the background, running large-scale visualization without any deadlines. We monitored one other client's behavior. This client requested a volume rendering of the first 10 time steps of the TSI simulation. In Figure 6, we plot the actual number of blocks rendered for this user at each resolution level with different number of background users.

When there were no background users, this rendering job at the highest quality could almost always finish within 55 seconds (on average around 41~42 seconds in most cases) on 100 shared depots. To observe application-level back-off, we then used 55 seconds as the deadline, and added a different number of background users. Note that none of those depots were reserved for our tests. So, there were already other background jobs consuming computing and I/O resources. Our background users simply add to that amount of dynamic overhead.

As shown in Figure 6, as the number of users increased, it became less likely that an intended job could be finished within the user specified deadline. Fewer concurrent users allowed more data blocks with full resolution (e.g. level 0) to be rendered. Conversely, more users would force the scheduler to back-off and select lower resolution blocks (e.g. level 2) in order to meet the deadline of 55 seconds.

CONCLUSION AND FUTURE WORK

We explored the possibility of developing parallel visualization algorithms that can use distributed, heterogeneous processors to visualize cutting edge simulation datasets. As a novel contribution, we studied how to effectively support multiple concurrent users operating on the same large dataset, with each focusing on a dynamically varying subset of the data. From a system design point of view, we found that a distributed cache offers various advantages, including improved scalability. In addition, from the algorithm design perspective, we developed basic scheduling mechanisms that were able to achieve fault-tolerance and load-balancing, optimal use of resources, and flow-control us-

Figure 6. The number of data blocks at each level rendered with 55 seconds as the deadline vs. different number of concurrent users. The total number of blocks rendered, on all levels, is 918, 818, 634, 580, 510 and 421, respectively

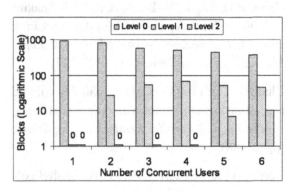

ing system-level back-off, while still enforcing deadline driven (i.e. time-critical) visualization.

In the future, we plan to investigate the possibility of actually deploying a system in the nature of our testbed. We recognize that results obtained from up to 10 concurrent users may not be sufficient to fully understand the underpinnings of a large-scale system, especially considering that data access patterns of other visualization applications, e.g. flow visualization, or even analytical applications beyond visualization, will be different. A systematic study of this area is necessary.

REFERENCES

Anderson, D. P. (2004). BOINC: A system for public-resource computing and storage. *Proceedings of the 5th IEEE/ACM International Workshop on Grid Computing* (GRID'04), (pp. 4-10).

Beck, M., Moore, T., & Plank, J. (2002). An end-to-end approach to globally scalable network storage. *Proceedings of ACM SIGCOMM.*

Beck, M., Moore, T., & Plank, J. (2003). *An end-to-end approach to globally scalable programmable networking*. ACM Workshop on Future Directions in Network Architecture.

Carns, P. H., Ligon, W. B., Ross, R. B., & Thakur, R. (2000). PVFS: A parallel file system for Linux clusters. *Proceedings of the 4th Annual Linux Showcase and Conference*, (pp. 317-327).

Challinger, J. (1993). Scalable parallel volume raycasting for nonrectilinear computational Grids. *Proceedings of Parallel Rendering Symposium*, (pp. 81-88).

Corrie, B., & Mackerras, P. (1993). Parallel volume rendering and data coherence. *Proceedings of Parallel Rendering Symposium*, (pp. 23-26).

Gao, J., Shen, H.-W., Huang, J., & Kohl, J. (2003). Visibility culling using plenoptic opacity functions for large data visualization. *Proceedings of IEEE Visualization Conference*.

Gao, J., Shen, H.-W., Huang, J., & Kohl, J. (2004). Visibility-based acceleration for large-scale time-varying volume rendering using temporal occlusion coherence. *Proceedings of IEEE Visualization Conference*.

Gropp, W., Lusk, E., & Thakur, R. (1999). *Using MPI-2: Advanced features of the message passing interface*. MIT Press.

Irion, R. (2006). The terascale supernova initiative: Modeling the first instance of a stars death. *SciDAC Review*, *1*, 26–37.

Ma, K.-L. (1995). Parallel volume ray-casting for unstructured-grid data on distributed-memory architectures. *Proceedings of Parallel Rendering Symposium*, (pp. 23-30).

Patterson, D., & Hennessy, J. (1994). *Computer organization and design: The hardware/software interface*. Morgan Kaufmann Publishers. *PlanetLab*. (n.d.). Retrieved from http://www.planet-lab.org

Plank, J., Bassi, A., Beck, M., Moore, T., Swany, D., & Wolski, R. (2001). Managing data storage in the network. *IEEE Internet Computing*, *5*, 50–58. doi:10.1109/4236.957895

Rhea, S., Godfrey, B., Karp, B., Kubiatowicz, J., Ratnasamy, S., Shenker, S., et al. (2005). OpenDHT: A public DHT service and its uses. *Proceedings of ACM SIGCOMM*.

Samanta, R., Funkhouser, T., & Li, K. (2001). Parallel rendering with k-way replication. *Proceedings of IEEE Symposium on Parallel and Large-Data Visualization and Graphics*.

Sarmenta, L. F. G. (2001). *Volunteer computing*. MIT Dept. of Electrical Engineering and Computer Science PhD Dissertation.

Silberschatz, A., & Galvin, P. (1994). *Operating system concepts*. Addison-Wesley.

Whitman, S. (1993). A task adaptive parallel graphics renderer. *Proceedings of Parallel Rendering Symposium*, (pp. 27-34).

Yu, H., Ma, K.-L., & Welling, J. (2004). A parallel visualization pipeline for terascale earthquake simulations. *Proceedings of the Supercomputing Conference*.

ENDNOTE

[1]	Infrastructure for this project was funded by two NSF infrastructure grants, an 2002 award (NSF CNS-024441) from the CISE Research Resources program for the National Logistical Networking Testbed (NLNT) and a cross-cutting Major Research Instrumentation award (NSF PHY-0619847) for REDDnet. REDDnet's storage infrastructure built on the same Logistical Networking technology as the NLNT and the resources of the latter were easily folded into the former.

Compilation of References

2MASS. (2008). *Two Micron all sky survey.* Retrieved from http://irsa.ipac.caltech.edu/Missions/2mass.html

Abramovici, A., & Althouse, W. (1992). LIGO: The laser interferometer gravitational-wave observatory. *Science, 256,* 325–333. doi:10.1126/science.256.5055.325

ActiveMQ. (2009). Retrieved December 2009, from http://activemq.apache.org/

Adams, D. L., Harrison, K., & Tan, C. L. (2006). *DIAL: Distributed interactive analysis of large datasets.* Conference for Computing in High Energy and Nuclear Physics (CHEP 06).

Adya, A., Bolosky, W. J., Castro, M., Cermak, G., Chaiken, R., & Douceur, J. R. … Wattenhofer, R.P. (2002). FARSITE: Federated, available, and reliable storage for an incompletely trusted environment. In *Proceedings 5th USENIX OSDI,* (pp. 1–14).

Afsarmanesh, H., Belleman, R. G., Belloum, A. S. Z., Benabdelkader, A., Brand, J. F. J., & van den Eijkel, G. B. (2002). Vlam-g: A grid-based virtual laboratory. *Science Progress, 10*(2), 173–181.

Allcock, B., Bester, J., Bresnahan, J., Chervenak, A., Foster, I., & Kesselman, C. … Tuecke, S. (2001). Secure, efficient data transport and replica management for high-performance data-intensive computing. *Proceedings of IEEE Mass Storage Conference.*

Allcock, B., Foster, I., Nefedova, V., Chervenak, A., Deelman, E., & Kesselman, C. … Williams, D. (2001). High-performance remote access to climate simulation data: a challenge problem for data grid technologies. *Proceedings of the 2001 ACM/IEEE Conference on Supercomputing.*

Allcock, W., Bester, J., et al. (2001). Secure, *efficient data transport and replica management for high-performance data-intensive computing.* Mass Storage Conference.

Allcock, W., Bresnahan, J., Kettimuthu, R., Link, M., Dumitrescu, C., Raicu, I., & Foster, I. (2005). *The Globus striped GridFTP framework and server.* ACM/IEEE SC05.

Allcock, B., Bester, J., Bresnahan, J., Chervenak, A., Foster, I., & Kesselman, C. (2001). Data management and transfer in high performance computational grid environments. *Parallel Computing, 28*(5).

Allcock, W., Bresnahan, J., Kettimuthu, R., Link, M., Dumitrescu, C., Raicu, I., & Foster, I. (2005). *The Globus striped GridFTP framework and server. IEEE Supercomputing (SC05).* Seattle, WA: Conference.

Allen, G., Goodale, T., Masso, J., & Seidel, E. (1999). The Cactus computational toolkit and using distributed computing to collide neutron stars. *Proceedings of Eighth IEEE International Symposium on High Performance Distributed Computing,* HPDC-8. IEEE Computer Society.

Allen, G., MacMahon, C., Seidel, E., & Tierney, T. (2003). *LONI: Louisiana optical network initiative.* Received from http://www.cct.lsu.edu/~gallen/Reports/LONI ConceptPaper.pdf

Alonso, G., Casati, F., Kuno, H., & Machiraju, V. (2003). *Web services - Concepts, architectures and applications.* Springer.

Alspaugh, S., Chervenak, A., et al. (2008). *Policy-driven data management for distributed scientific collaborations using a rule engine* (poster). International Conference for High Performance Computing, Networking, Storage and Analysis (SC08), Austin, TX, USA.

Altman, E., Barman, D., Tuffin, B., & Vojnovic, M. (2006). Parallel tcp sockets: Simple model, throughput and validation. *Proceedings of IEEE Conference on Computer Communications (INFOCOM06)*, (pp. 1-12).

Altschul, S. F. (1990). Basic local alignment search tool. *Journal of Molecular Biology*, 3(215), 403–410.

Altschul, S. F., Gish, W., Miller, W., Myers, E. W., & Lipman, D. J. (1990). Basic local alignment search tool. *Journal of Molecular Biology*, 3(215), 403–410.

Anderson, D. P. (2004). BOINC: A system for public-resource computing and storage. *Proceedings of the 5th IEEE/ACM International Workshop on Grid Computing* (GRID'04), (pp. 4-10).

Anderson, T. E., Dahlin, M. D., Neefe, J. M., Patterson, D. A., Roselli, D. S., & Wang, R. Y. (1996). Serverless network file systems. *ACM Transactions on Computer Systems*, 14(1), 41–79. doi:10.1145/225535.225537

Andrade, H., Kurc, T., Sussman, A., Saltz, J. (2007). Active semantic caching to optimize multidimensional data analysis in parallel and distributed environments. *Parallel Computing Journal*, 33(7-8).

ANL/UC. (2007). *TeraGrid site details*. Retrieved from http://www.uc.teragrid.org/tg-docs/tg-tech-sum.html

Apache Hadoop. (2009). Retrieved December 2009, from http://hadoop.apache.org/

Arpaci-Dusseau, R. (2003). Run-time adaptation in river. *ACM Transactions on Computer Systems*, 21(1), 36–86. doi:10.1145/592637.592639

Arsanjani, A. (2004). *Service-oriented modeling and architecture*. IBM developerWorks.

ASC. (2008). *Alliances Center for Astrophysical Thermonuclear Flashes*. Retrieved from http://www.flash.uchicago.edu/website/home/

ATLAS. (2010). A *Toroidal LHC ApparatuS Project* (ATLAS). Retrieved from http://atlas.web.cern.ch/

Babu, S., Shivam, P., & Chase, J. (2006). Active and accelerated learning of cost models for optimizing scientific applications. *Proceedings of International Conference on Very Large Data Bases (VLDB)*.

Bae, S.-H. (2008). Parallel multidimensional scaling performance on multicore systems. *Proceedings of the Advances in High-Performance E-Science Middleware and Applications Workshop (AHEMA) of Fourth IEEE International Conference on eScience* (pp. 695-702). Indianapolis, IN: IEEE Computer Society.

Bahsi, E. M., Ceyhan, E., & Kosar, T. (2007). Conditional workflow management: A survey and analysis. *Science Progress*, 15(4), 283–297.

Bajaj, C., Ihm, I., Park, S., & Song, D. (2000). Compression-based ray casting of very large volume data in distributed environments. *Proceedings of the Fourth International Conference on High-Performance Computing in the Asia-Pacific Region* (HPC00), 2, (pp. 720–725).

Balakrishman, H., Padmanabhan, V. N., Seshan, S., Katz, R. H., & Stemm, M. (1998). TCP behavior of a busy internet server: Analysis and improvements. *Proceedings of IEEE Conference on Computer Communications (INFOCOM98)*, (pp. 252-262).

Balman, M., & Kosar, M. (2007). From micro- to macro-processing: A generic data management model. *Proceedings of the 8th IEEE/ACM International Conference on Grid Computing, (Grid2007)*, Austin, TX, USA.

Banga, G., Druschel, P., & Mogul, J. C. (1999). *Resource containers: A new facility for resource management in server systems*. Symposium on Operating Systems Design and Implementation.

Barham, P., Dragovic, B., Fraser, K., Hand, S., Harris, T., Ho, A., et al. (2003). Xen and the art of virtualization. *Proceedings of the Nineteenth ACM Symposium on Operating Systems Principles, Bolton Landing* (pp. 164-177). New York, NY: ACM Press.

Barish, B. C., & Weiss, R. (1999). LIGO and the detection of gravitational waves. *Physics Today*, 52(10), 44. doi:10.1063/1.882861

Barker, K. J., Davis, K., Hoisie, A., Kerbyson, D. J., Lang, M., Pakin, S., & Sancho, J. C. (2008). Entering the petaflop era: The architecture and performance of roadrunner. *Proceedings of the 2008 ACM/IEEE conference on Supercomputing (SC'08)*, (pp. 1–11). IEEE Press.

Barnes-Hut Simulation. (2009). Retrieved December 2009, from http://en.wikipedia.org/wiki/Barnes-Hut_simulation

Barrass, T. A. (2004). *Software agents in data and workflow management. Computing in High Energy and Nuclear Physics (CHEP) 2004.* Switzerland: Interlaken.

Baru, C., Moore, R., Rajasekar, A., & Wan, M. (1998). The SDSC storage resource broker. *Proceedings of CASCON'98 Conference,* Toronto, Canada.

Baud, J. P., Casey, J., et al. (2005). *Performance analysis of a file catalog for the LHC computing grid.* 14th IEEE International Symposium on High Performance Distributed Computing (HPDC-14).

Beck, M., Elwasif, W. R., Plank, J., & Moore, T. (1999). The Internet backplane protocol: Storage in the network. *Proceedings of the 1999 Network Storage Symposium NetStore99,* Seattle, WA, USA.

Beck, M., Moore, T., & Plank, J. (2003). *An end-to-end approach to globally scalable programmable networking.* ACM Workshop on Future Directions in Network Architecture.

Bent, J. (2005). *Data-driven batch scheduling.* PhD thesis, University of Wisconsin- Madison.

Bent, J., Thain, D., Arpaci-Dusseau, A. C., Arpaci-Dusseau, R. H., & Livny, M. (2004). Explicit control in a batch-aware distributed file system. In *Proceedings of the 1st USENIX NSDI,* (pp. 365–378).

Berg, I. (2009). *Simulation of N-body problems with the Barnes-Hut algorithm.* Retrieved December 2009, from http://www.beltoforion.de/barnes_hut/barnes_hut_de.html

Berman, F., Casanova, H., Chien, A., Cooper, K., Dail, H., & Dasgupta, A. (2005). New grid scheduling and rescheduling methods in the grads project. *International Journal of Parallel Programming, 33*(2), 209–229. doi:10.1007/s10766-005-3584-4

Bernholdt, D., Bharathi, S., Brown, D., Chancio, K., & Chen, A. Chervenak, L..., Williams, D. (2005). The Earth system Grid: Supporting the next generation of climate modeling research. *Proceedings of the IEEE, 93*(3), 485- 495.

Berriman, G. B., Deelman, E., et al. (2004). Montage: A Grid enabled engine for delivering custom science-grade mosaics on demand. *SPIE Conference, 5487, Astronomical Telescopes.*

Berriman, G. B., et al. (2003). Montage: A Grid-enabled image mosaic service for the NVO. *Astronomical Data Analysis Software & Systems (ADASS), 13.*

Berriman, G. B., et al. (2004). *Montage: A Grid enabled engine for delivering custom science-grade image mosaics on demand.* SPIE Conference on Astronomical Telescopes and Instrumentation.

Bester, J., Foster, I., Kesselman, C., Tedesco, J., & Tuecke, S. (1999). GASS: A data movement and access service for wide area computing systems. In *Proceedings of the Sixth Workshop on I/O in Parallel and Distributed Systems.*

Bethel, W., Tierney, B., Lee, J., Gunter, D., & Lau, S. (2000). Using high-speed WANs and network data caches to enable remote and distributed visualization. *Proceeding of the IEEE Supercomputing 2000 Conference.*

Beynon, M., Chang, C., Catalyurek, U., Kurc, T., Sussman, A., Andrade, H., Ferreira, R., & Saltz, J., (2002). Processing large-scale multidimensional data in parallel and distributed environments. *Parallel Computing, Special issue on Data Intensive Computing, 28*(5),827-859.

Beynon, M., Kurc, T. M., Catalyurek, U. V., Chang, C., Sussman, A., & Saltz, J. H. (2001). Distributed processing of very large datasets with DataCutter. *Parallel Computing, 27*(11), 1457–1478. doi:10.1016/S0167-8191(01)00099-0

Beynon, M., Kurc, T., Catalyurek, U., Chang, C., Sussman, A., & Saltz, J. (2001). Distributed processing of very large datasets with DataCutter. *Parallel Computing, 27*(11), 1457–1478. doi:10.1016/S0167-8191(01)00099-0

Bhat, V., Parashar, M., & Klasky, S. (2007). Experiments with in-transit processing for data intensive grid workflows. In *GRID* (pp. 193-200). IEEE.

Bhat, V., Parashar, M., Liu, H., Kandasamy, N., Khandekar, M., & Klasky, S. (2007). A self-managing wide-area data streaming service. *Cluster Computing, 10*(4), 365–383. doi:10.1007/s10586-007-0023-x

Bialecki, A., Cafarella, M., Cutting, D., & O'Malley, O. (2005). *Hadoop: A framework for running applications on large clusters built of commodity hardware.* Retrieved from http://lucene.apache.org/hadoop/

Bishop, C. M., & Svensén, M. (1997). GTM: A principled alternative to the self-organizing map. *Advances in Neural Information Processing Systems*, 354–360.

Bishop, C. M., Svensén, M., & Williams, C. K. (1998). GTM: The generative topographic mapping. *Neural Computation, 10,* 215–234. doi:10.1162/089976698300017953

Blondin, J. M., Mezzacappa, A., & DeMarino, C. (2003). Stability of standing accretion shocks, with an eye toward core collapse supernovae. *The Astrophysical Journal, 584*(2), 971. doi:10.1086/345812

Blythe, J., Jain, S., Deelman, E., Gil, Y., Vahi, K., Mandal, A., et al. (2005). Task scheduling strategies for workflow-based applications in grids. In *CCGRID '05: Proceedings of the Fifth IEEE International Symposium on Cluster Computing and the Grid (CCGrid'05) - Volume 2* (pp. 759–767). Washington, DC: IEEE.

Borg, I., & Groenen, P. J. (2005). *Modern multidimensional scaling: Theory and applications.* Springer.

Branco, M. (2004). *DonQuijote - Data management for the ATLAS automatic production system.* Computing in High Energy and Nuclear Physics (CHEP04).

Brandic, I., Pllana, S., & Benkner, S. (2006). An approach for the high-level specification of qos-aware grid workflows considering location affinity. *Science Progress, 14*(3/4), 231–250.

Brandic, I., Pllana, S., & Benkner, S. (2008). Specification, planning, and execution of qos-aware grid workflows within the Amadeus environment. *Concurrent Computing: Practice and Experience, 20*(4), 331–345. doi:10.1002/cpe.1215

Braun, T. D., Siegel, H. J., Beck, N., Boloni, L. L., Maheswaran, M., & Reuther, A. I. (2001). A comparison of eleven static heuristics for mapping a class of independent tasks onto heterogeneous distributed computing systems. *Journal of Parallel and Distributed Computing, 61*(6), 810–837. doi:10.1006/jpdc.2000.1714

Broberg, J., Buyya, R., & Tari, Z. (2008, August). *MetaCDN: Harnessing 'storage clouds' for high performance content delivery* (Tech. Rep. No. GRIDS-TR-2008-11). GRIDS Lab: The University of Melbourne.

Brown, D. A., & Brady, P. R. (2006). A case study on the use of workflow technologies for scientific analysis: Gravitational wave data analysis. In Taylor, I., Deelman, E., Gannon, D., & Shields, M. (Eds.), *Workflows for e-Science*. Springer. doi:10.1007/978-1-84628-757-2_4

Buck, J., Ha, S., Lee, E. A., & Messerschmitt, D. G. (2002). *Ptolemy: A framework for simulating and prototyping heterogeneous systems* (pp. 527–543). Norwell, MA: Kluwer Academic Publishers.

Butt, A. R., Johnson, T. A., Zheng, Y., & Hu, Y. C. (2006). Kosha: A peer-to-peer enhancement for the network file system. *Journal of Grid Computing: Special issue on Global and Peer-to-Peer Computing, 4*(3), 323–341.

Butt, A., Johnson, T., Zheng, Y., & Hu, Y. (2004). Kosha: A peer-to-peer enhancement for the network file system. In *Proceedings of Supercomputing Conference.*

Buyya, R., Yeo, C. S., & Venugopal, S. (2008). Market-oriented cloud computing: Vision, hype, and reality for delivering it services as computing utilities. In *HPCC '08: Proceedings of the 2008 10th IEEE International Conference on High Performance Computing and Communications*, (pp. 5-13). Washington, DC: IEEE.

Cabral, B., & Leedom, L. C. (1993). Imaging vector fields using line integral convolution. *Proceedings of the 20th Annual Conference on Computer Graphics and Interactive Techniques (SIGGRAPH'93)* (pp. 263–270).

Cai, M., Chervenak, A., & Frank, M. (2004). *A peer-to-peer replica location service based on a distributed hash table.* SC2004 Conference, Pittsburgh, PA.

Calder, B., Chien, A., Wang, J., & Yang, D. (2005). The Entropia virtual machine for desktop grids. In *Proceedings of the 1st ACM/USENIX International Conference on Virtual Execution Environments.*

Callaghan, B. (2000). *NFS illustrated.* Essex, UK: Addison-Wesley Longman, Inc.

Camahort, E., & Chakravarty, I. (1993). Integrating volume data analysis and rendering on distributed memory architectures. *Proceedings of 1993 Symposium on Parallel Rendering* (PRS '93), (pp. 89–96).

Campbell, N., & Atchley, W. R. (1981). The geometry of canonical variate analysis. *Systematic Zoology*, 268–280. doi:10.2307/2413249

Cao, J., Jarvis, S. A., Saini, S., & Nudd, G. R. (2003). Gridflow: Workflow management for grid computing. In *CCGRID '03: Proceedings of the 3st International Symposium on Cluster Computing and the Grid* (pp. 198–205). Washington, DC, USA.

Cappello, F., & Bal, H. (2007). Toward an international "computer science grid". In *CCGRID '07: Proceedings of the Seventh IEEE International Symposium on Cluster Computing and the Grid* (pp. 3–12). Washington, DC: IEEE.

Carena, F., Carena, W., Chapeland, S., Divia, R., Fuchs, U., & Makhlyueva, I. ... Vyvre, P. V. (2008). The ALICE DAQ online transient data storage system. *Journal of Physics: Conference Series, 119*(2), 022016 (7pp).

Carns, P. H., Ligon, W. B., Ross, R. B., & Thakur, R. (2000). PVFS: A parallel file system for Linux clusters. *Proceedings of the 4th Annual Linux Showcase and Conference*, (pp. 317-327).

CAS. (2007). *SkyServer*. Retrieved from http://cas.sdss.org/dr6/en/tools/search/sql.asp

Castro, M., Druschel, P., Kermarrec, A.-M., & Rowstron, A. (2002). Scribe: A large-scale and decentralised application-level multicast infrastructure. *IEEE Journal on Selected Areas in Communications, 20*(8), 100–110. doi:10.1109/JSAC.2002.803069

Catlett, C. (2006). TeraGrid: Analysis of organization, system architecture, and middleware enabling new types of applications. In Grandinetti, L. (Ed.), *High performance computing and Grids in action*. IOS Press.

CCSP. (2003). *Strategic plan for the US climate change science program*. CCSP Report.

CERN. (2008). *Large hadron collider*. Retrieved from http://lhc.web.cern.ch/lhc

Ceyhan, E., & Kosar, T. (2007). Large scale data management in sensor networking applications. *Proceedings of Secure Cyberspace Workshop*, Shreveport, LA, USA.

Ceyhan, E., Allen, G., White, C., & Kosar, T. (2008). A grid-enabled workflow system for reservoir uncertainty analysis. *Proceedings of Challenges of Large Applications in Distributed Environments (CLADE 2008) Workshop*, Boston, MA, USA.

Challinger, J. (1993). Scalable parallel volume raycasting for nonrectilinear computational Grids. *Proceedings of Parallel Rendering Symposium*, (pp. 81-88).

Chang, F., Dean, J., Ghemawat, S., Hsieh, W. C., Wallach, D. A., & Burrows, M. ... Gruber, R. E. (2006). *Bigtable: A distributed storage system for structured data*. Symposium on Operating System Design and Implementation (OSDI'06).

Chappell, D. (2004). *Enterprise service bus*. O'Reilly Media, Inc. DataONE. (n.d). *Enabling data-intensive biological and environmental research through cyberinfrastructure*. Retrieved from http://mediabeast.ites.utk.edu/mediasite4/Viewer/?peid=38558e47202247bd847456b047cedfbd

Chawathe, Y., Ratnasamy, S., et al. (2003). *Making Gnutella-like P2P systems scalable*. ACM SIGCOMM 2003, Karlsruhe, Germany.

Chen, S. E. (1995). *Quicktime VR: An image-based approach to virtual environment navigation*. Proceedings of the 22nd Annual Conference on Computer Graphics and Interactive Techniques (SIGGRAPH '95), (pp. 29–38).

Chen, Q., Zhao, H., Hu, K., & Douglass, S. L. (2005). Prediction of wind waves in a shallow estuary. *Journal of Waterway, Port, Coastal, and Ocean Engineering, 131*(4), 137–148. doi:10.1061/(ASCE)0733-950X(2005)131:4(137)

Chervenak, A. L., Palavalli, N., Bharathi, S., Kesselman, C., & Schwartzkopf, R. (2004). *Performance and scalability of a replica location service*. Thirteenth IEEE Int'l Symposium High Performance Distributed Computing (HPDC-13), Honolulu, HI.

Chervenak, A. L., Palavalli, N., Bharathi, S., Kesselman, C., & Schwartzkopf, R. (2004). *The replica location service.* International Symposium on High Performance Distributed Computing Conference (HPDC-13).

Chervenak, A., Deelman, E., Foster, I., Guy, L., Hoschek, W., & Iamnitchi, A..... Tierney, B. (2002). *Giggle: A framework for constructing sclable replica location services.* SC2002 Conference, Baltimore, MD.

Chervenak, A., Deelman, E., Livny, M., Su, M., Schuler, R., & Bharathi, S. ... Vahi, K. (2007). *Data placement for scientific applications in distributed environments.* 8th IEEE/ACM Int'l Conference on Grid Computing (Grid 2007), Austin, Texas.

Chervenak, A., Deelman, E., Livny, M., Su, M.-H., Schuler, R., Bharathi, S., et al. (2007, September). Data placement for scientific applications in distributed environments. In *Proceedings of the 8th IEEE/ACM International Conference on Grid Computing (Grid 2007).* Austin, TX: IEEE.

Chervenak, A., Schuler, C., Kesselman, C., Koranda, S., & Moe, B. (2005). Wide area data replication for scientific collaborations. *Proceedings of the 6th IEEE/ACM International Workshop on Grid Computing.*

Chervenak, A., Schuler, R., et al. (2009). The Globus replica location service: Design and experience. *IEEE Transactions on Parallel and Distributed Systems.*

Chervenak, A., Schuler, R., Kesselman, C., Koranda, S., & Moe, B. (2005). *Wide area data replication for scientific collaborations.* 6th IEEE/ACM Int'l Workshop on Grid Computing (Grid2005), Seattle, WA, USA.

Chervenak, A. L., & Schuler, R. (2009). The Globus replica location service: Design and experience. *IEEE Transactions on Parallel and Distributed Systems, 20*(9), 1260–1272. doi:10.1109/TPDS.2008.151

Chervenak, A., & Bharathi, S. (2008). Peer-to-Peer approaches to grid resource discovery. In Danelutto, M., Fragopoulou, P., & Getov, V. (Eds.), *Making Grids work* (pp. 59–76). New York, NY: Springer. doi:10.1007/978-0-387-78448-9_5

Chervenak, A., Deelman, E., Kesselman, C., Allcock, B., Foster, I., & Nefedova, V. (2003). High-performance remote access to climate simulation data: A challenge problem for data Grid technologies. *Parallel Computing. Special Issue: High Performance Computing with Geographical Data, 29*(10), 1335–1356.

Chervenak, A., Foster, I., Kesselman, C., Salisbury, C., & Tuecke, S. (1999). The data grid: Towards an architecture for the distributed management and analysis of large scientific datasets. *Journal of Network and Computer Applications, 23*, 187–200. doi:10.1006/jnca.2000.0110

Chien, A., Calder, B., Elbert, S., & Bhatia, K. (2003). Entropia: Architecture and performance of an enterprise desktop grid system. *Journal of Parallel and Distributed Computing, 63*(5). doi:10.1016/S0743-7315(03)00006-6

Cho, H. (1997). Catalog management in heterogeneous distributed database systems. *Proceedings of IEEE Pacific Rim Conference on Communications, Computers and Signal Processing.*

Choi, K. M., Huh, E., & Choo, H. (2005). Efficient resource management scheme of TCP buffer tuned parallel stream to optimize system performance. *Proceedings of Embedded and Ubiquitous Computing.*

Choy, D. M., Selinger, P. G., et al. (1991). A distributed catalog for heterogeneous distributed database resources. *Proceedings of the First International Conference on Parallel and Distributed Information Systems.*

Chu, C. T. (2006). *Map-reduce for machine learning on multicore. NIPS* (pp. 281–288). MIT Press.

Chun, B. G., Dabek, F., et al. (2006). Efficient replica maintenance for distributed storage systems. *Proceedings of the 3rd Symposium on Networked Systems Design and Implementation.*

Cipar, J., Corner, M. D., & Berger, E. D. (2007). TFS: A transparent file system for contributory storage. In *Proceedings of the 5th USENIX FAST,* (pp. 215–229).

Clarke, I., Sandberg, O., Wiley, B., & Hong, T. W. (1999). *Freenet: A distributed anonymous information storage and retrieval system.* Retrieved from http://freenetproject.org/freenet.pdf

CMS. (2010). *The US Compact Muon Solenoid Project.* Retrieved from http://uscms.fnal.gov/

Cobb, J. W., Geist, A., Kohl, J. A., Miller, S. D., Peterson, P. F., & Pike, G. G. (2007). The neutron science teragrid gateway: A teragrid science gateway to support the spallation neutron source: Research articles. *Concurrency and Computation*, *19*(6), 809–826. doi:10.1002/cpe.1102

Cohen, A., & Cohen, R. (2002). A dynamic approach for efficient TCP buffer allocation. *IEEE Transactions on Computers*, *5*(3), 303–312. doi:10.1109/12.990128

Conseil Europ'een pour la Recherche Nucl'eaire (CERN). (2007). *LHC– The large hadron collider.* Retrieved from http://lhc.web.cern.ch/lhc/

Corrie, B., & Mackerras, P. (1993). Parallel volume rendering and data coherence. *Proceedings of Parallel Rendering Symposium*, (pp. 23-26).

Couvares, P., Kosar, T., Roy, A., Weber, J., & Wenger, K. (2007, January). Workflow management in condor. In Workflows for e-Science (pp. 357–375). London, UK: Springer. doi:10.1007/978-1-84628-757-2_22doi:10.1007/978-1-84628-757-2_22

Couvares, P., & Kosar, T. (2006). Workflow management in Condor. In Taylor, I., Deelman, E., Gannon, D., & Shields, M. (Eds.), *Workflows in e-Science* (pp. 357–375). Springer.

Coyne, R., & Watson, R. (1995). The parallel i/o architecture of the high-performance storage system (hpss). In *Proceedings of the IEEE MSS Symposium.*

Crowcroft, J., & Oechslin, P. (1998). Differentiated End-to-end Internet services using a weighted proportional fair sharing TCP. *ACM SIGCOMM Computer Communication Review*, *28*, 53–69. doi:10.1145/293927.293930

Cruz-Neira, C., Sandin, D. J., DeFanti, T. A., Kenyon, R. V., & Hart, J. C. (1992). The cave - Audio visual experience automatic virtual environment. *Communications of the ACM*, *35*(6), 64–72. doi:10.1145/129888.129892

Culler, D., et al. (1997). *Parallel computing on the Berkeley now.* Symposium on Parallel Processing.

Czajkowski, K., Fitzgerald, S., et al. (2001). *Grid information services for distributed resource sharing.* 10th IEEE International Symposium on High Performance Distributed Computing, IEEE Press.

Dabek, F., Kaashoek, M. F., Karger, D., Morris, R., & Stoica, I. (2001). Wide-area cooperative storage with CFS. In *Proceedings of SOSP*, (pp. 202–215).

DagMan. (2002). *Online.* Retrieved from http://www.cs.wisc.edu/condor/dagman/

Dayal, U. (1994). *Active database systems: Triggers and rules for advanced database processing.* Morgan Kaufmann Publishers Inc.

dCache.org. (2009). Retrieved from http://www.dcache.org/.

de Leeuw, J. (1977). Applications of convex analysis to multidimensional scaling. *Recent Developments in Statistics*, 133-145.

de Leeuw, W. C., & van Wijk, J. J. (1993). A probe for local flow field visualization. *Proceedings of the 4th Conference on Visualization (VIS '93)*, (pp. 39–45).

de Leeuw, J. (1988). Convergence of the majorization method for multidimensional scaling. *Journal of Classification*, *5*, 163–180. doi:10.1007/BF01897162

Dean, J., & Ghemawat, S. (2004). *MapReduce: Simplified data processing on large clusters.* USENIX OSDI'04.

Dean, J., & Ghemawat, S. (2008). MapReduce: Simplified data processing on large clusters. *Communications of the ACM*, *51*(1), 107–113. doi:10.1145/1327452.1327492

Deelman, E., & Chervenak, A. (2008). Data management challenges of data-intensive scientific workflows. In *CCGRID '08: Proceedings of the 2008 Eighth IEEE International Symposium on Cluster Computing and the Grid (CCGRID)* (pp. 687–692). Washington, DC: IEEE Computer Society.

Deelman, E., Blythe, J., Gil, Y., Kesselman, C., Mehta, G., Patil, S., et al. (2004). Pegasus: Mapping scientific workflows onto the grid. In *European Across Grids Conference* (vol. 3165, pp. 11–20). Springer.

Deelman, E., Callaghan, S., et al. (2006). Managing large-scale workflow execution from resource provisioning to provenance tracking: The CyberShake example. *E-SCIENCE '06: Proceedings of the Second IEEE International Conference on e-Science and Grid Computing*, (p. 14).

Deelman, E., et al. (2003). *Grid-based galaxy morphology analysis for the National Virtual Observatory*. SC2003.

Deelman, E., Mehta, G., et al. (2006). Pegasus: Mapping large-scale workflows to distributed resources. I. Taylor, E. Deelman, D. Gannon & M. Shields (Eds.),*Workflows in e-Science*. Springer.

Deelman, E., Singh, G., Atkinson, M. P., Chervenak, A., Chue Hong, N. P., & Kesselman, C. … Su, M.-H. (2004). *Grid-based metadata services*. 16th International Conference on Scientific and Statistical Database Management.

Deelman, E., Singh, G., Livny, M., Berriman, B., & Good, J. (2008). The cost of doing science on the cloud: The montage example. In *SC '08: Proceedings of the 2008 ACM/IEEE Conference on Supercomputing* (pp. 1–12). Piscataway, NJ: IEEE.

Deelman, E., Blythe, J., Gil, Y., Kesselman, C., Mehta, G., & Vahi, K. (2003). Mapping abstract complex workflows onto grid environments. *Journal of Grid Computing*, *1*(1), 25–39. doi:10.1023/A:1024000426962

Deelman, E., & Gil, Y. (2006). *Managing large-scale scientific workflows in distributed environments: Experiences and challenges*. Amsterdam, The Netherlands: Workflows in e-Science.

Deelman, E., & Singh, G. (2005). Pegasus: A framework for mapping complex scientific workflows onto distributed systems. *Scientific Programming Journal*, *13*(3), 219–237.

Deelman, E., Singh, G., Su, M.-H., Blythe, J., Gil, Y., & Kesselman, C. (2005). Pegasus: A framework for mapping complex scientific workflows onto distributed systems. *Science Progress*, *13*(3), 219–237.

DeFanti, T. A., Brown, M. D., Leigh, J., Yu, O., He, E., & Mambretti, J. (2003, August). Optical switching middleware for the OptIPuter. *Institute of Electronics, Information and Communication Engineers (IEICE) Transactions on Communications (Special Issue on Photonic IP Network Technologies for Next Generation Broadband Access)*. *E (Norwalk, Conn.)*, *86-B*(8), 2263–2272.

Dempster, A., Laird, N., & Rubin, D. (1977). Maximum likelihood from incomplete data via the EM algorithm. *Journal of the Royal Statistical Society m Series B*, 1–38.

Ding, J., Huang, J., Beck, M., Liu, S., Moore, T., & Soltesz, S. (2003). Remote visualization by browsing image based databases with logistical networking. *In the Proceedings of SC2003*, Phoenix, AZ, USA.

Disco Project. (2009). Retrieved December 2009, from http://discoproject.org/

DOE. (2004). *The data management challenge. Report from the DOE Office of Science Data-Management Workshops*. US Department of Energy.

DOE. (2008). *Advanced networking for distributed petascale science. Technical report*. US Department of Energy.

Douceur, J., & Bolosky, W. (1999). A large-scale study of file-system contents. In *Proceedings of SIGMETRICS*.

DPOSS. (2010). *The Palomar Digital Sky Survey (DPOSS)*. Retrieved from http://www.astro.caltech.edu/~george/dposs/

Drools Project. (2008). *Drools*. Retrieved from http://www.jboss.org/drools/

Duan, R., Fahringer, T., Prodan, R., Qin, J., Villazon, A., & Wieczorek, M. (2005, February). *Real world workflow applications in the Askalon grid environment*. In European Grid Conference (EGC 2005). Springer Verlag.

Duan, R., Prodan, R., & Fahringer, T. (2006). Run-time optimisation of grid workflow applications. In *GRID* (pp. 33-40). IEEE.

Dunigan, T., Mathis, M., & Tierney, B. (2002). A TCP tuning daemon. *Proceedings of IEEE Super Computing Conference (SC02)*.

Earth System Grid (ESG). (2006). Retrieved from http://www.earthsystemgrid.org

EarthScope. (2001). Retrieved from http://www.earthscope.org/

Eggert, L., Heideman, J., & Touch, J. (2000). Effects of ensemble TCP. *ACM Computer Communication Review*, *30*(1), 15–29. doi:10.1145/505688.505691

Ekanayake, J., Balkir, A., Gunarathne, T., Fox, G., Poulain, C., Araujo, N., et al. (2009). *DryadLINQ for scientific analyses*. Fifth IEEE International Conference on eScience: 2009. Oxford, UK: IEEE.

Ekanayake, J., Gunarathne, T., & Qiu, J. (2010). Cloud technologies for bioinformatics applications. *Invited paper submitted to the Journal of IEEE Transactions on Parallel and Distributed Systems*.

Ekanayake, J., Pallickara, S., & Fox, G. (2008). MapReduce for data intensive scientific analyses. *Fourth IEEE International Conference on eScience* (pp. 277-284). IEEE Press.

Ekanayake, J., Gunarathne, T., Qiu, J., Fox, G., Beason, S., & Choi, J. Y. (2009). *Applicability of DryadLINQ to scientific applications*. Community Grids Laboratory, Indiana University.

Ekanayake, J., Qiu, X., Gunarathne, T., Beason, S., & Fox, G. (2010). High performance parallel computing with clouds and cloud technologies. In Ahson, S. A., & Ilyas, M. (Eds.), *Cloud computing and software services: Theory and techniques. CRC Press*. Taylor and Francis. doi:10.1201/EBK1439803158-c12

Elvins, T. T. (1992). Volume rendering on a distributed memory parallel computer. *Proceedings of the 3rd Conference on Visualization '92*, (pp. 93–98).

Epema, D. H. J., & Livny, M. (1996). A worldwide flock of condors: Load sharing among workstation clusters. *Future Generation Computer Systems*, •••, 12.

Erlang Programming Language. (2009). Retrieved December 2009, from http://www.erlang.org/

European Molecular Biology Laboratory. (2008). Retrieved from http://www.embl.org

F. 180-1. (1995). *Secure hash standard*. Technical Report Publication 180-1, Federal Information Processing Standard (FIPS), NIST. Washington D.C.: US Department of Commerce.

Fagg, G. E., & Dongarra, J. J. (2000). Lecture Notes in Computer Science: *Vol. 1908. FT-MPI: Fault tolerant MPI, supporting dynamic applications in a dynamic world* (pp. 346–353). Springer Verlag.

Fan, L., Cao, P., Almeida, J., & Broder, A. Z. (2000). Summary cache: A Scalable wide-area Web cache sharing protocol. *IEEE/ACM Transactions on Networking, 8*(3), 281–293. doi:10.1109/90.851975

Feller, M., Foster, I., & Martin, S. (2007). *GT4 GRAM: A functionality and performance study*. TeraGrid Conference.

Feng, J., Cui, L., et al. (2006). *Policy-directed data movement in Grids*. 12th International Conference on Parallel and Distributed Systems (ICPADS 2006).

Feng, J., Wasson, G., et al. (2007). *Resource usage policy expression and enforcement in Grid computing*. 8th IEEE/ACM International Conference on Grid Computing (Grid 2007).

Feo, T. A., & Resende, M. G. (1995, March). Greedy randomized adaptive search procedures. *Journal of Global Optimization, 6*(2), 109–133. doi:10.1007/BF01096763

Flynn, M. J. (1999). Basic issues in microprocessor architecture. *Journal of System Architecture, 45*(12-13), 939–948. doi:http://dx.doi.org/10.1016/S1383-7621(98)00045-9.

Foster, I., & Kesselman, C. (Eds.). (1999). Chapter 2: Computational Grids. In I. Foster (Ed.), *The Grid: Blueprint for a future computing infrastructure*. Morgan Kaufmann Publishers.

Foster, I., & Kesselman, C. (2001). The anatomy of the Grid: Enabling scalable virtual organizations. *International Journal of High Performance Computing Applications, 15*(3), 200–222. doi:10.1177/109434200101500302

Foster, I., Kesselman, C., & Tuecke, S. (2001). The anatomy of the Grid. *The International Journal of Supercomputer Applications, 15*(3), 200–222. doi:10.1177/109434200101500302

Fox, G., Bae, S.-H., Ekanayake, J., Qiu, X., & Yuan, H. (2008). *Parallel data mining from multicore to cloudy grids*. High Performance Computing and Grids Workshop.

Fox, G., Qiu, X., Beason, S., Choi, J. Y., Rho, M., Tang, H., et al. (2009). *Biomedical case studies in data intensive computing*. The 1st International Conference on Cloud Computing (CloudCom 2009). Springer Verlag.

Fox, G. C., Williams, R. D., & Messina, P. C. (1994). *Parallel computing works!* Morgan Kaufmann Publishers, Inc.

Frank, S., & Kaufman, A. (2005). Distributed volume rendering on a visualization cluster. *Proceedings of the Ninth International Conference on Computer Aided Design and Computer Graphics*, CAD-CG '05, (pp. 371–376).

Frankel, J., & Pepper, T. (2003). *The Gnutella protocol specification* v0.4. Retrieved from http://www9.limewire.com/developer/gnutella protocol 0.4.pdf

FreeFluo. (2003). *Online*. Retrieved from http://freefluo.sourceforge.net/

Freire, J., & Silva, C. T. (2006). Managing rapidly-evolving scientific workflows. *IPAW, 4145*, 10–18.

Frey, J., Tannenbaum, T., Foster, I., Livny, M., & Tuecke, S. (2002). Condor-G: A computation management agent for multiinstitutional grids. *Cluster Computing, 5*, 237–246. doi:10.1023/A:1015617019423

Fuhrmann, P. (2004). *dCache, the commodity cache*. Twelfth NASA Goddard and Twenty First IEEE Conference on Mass Storage Systems and Technologies.

Funkhouser, T., & Li, K. (2000, July). Large format displays. *IEEE Computer Graphics and Applications, 25*(4), 20–21. doi:10.1109/MCG.2000.851745

FUSE. (n.d.). *Filesystem in userspace*. Retrieved from http://fuse.sourceforge.net

FutureGrid Homepage. (2009). Retrieved December 2009, from http://www.futuregrid.org

Gaither, K. (2007). Visualization's role in analyzing computational fluid dynamics data. *IEEE Computer Graphics and Applications, 24*(3), 13–15. doi:10.1109/MCG.2004.1297005

Gao, J., & Shen, H. W. (2001). Parallel view-dependent isosurface extraction using multi-pass occlusion culling, *Proceedings of the IEEE 2001 symposium on parallel and large-data visualization and graphics (PVG '01)* (pp. 67–74).

Gao, J., Shen, H.-W., Huang, J., & Kohl, J. (2003). Visibility culling using plenoptic opacity functions for large data visualization. *Proceedings of IEEE Visualization Conference.*

Gao, J., Shen, H.-W., Huang, J., & Kohl, J. (2004). Visibility-based acceleration for large-scale time-varying volume rendering using temporal occlusion coherence. *Proceedings of IEEE Visualization Conference.*

Gao, J., & Huang, J. (2005). Distributed data management for large volume visualization. *Visualization, 2005*, 183–189.

Gara, A., Blumrich, M. A., Chen, D., Chiu, G. L.-T., Coteus, P., & Giampapa, M. E. (2005). Overview of the Blue Gene/L system architecture. *IBM Journal of Research and Development, 49*(2/3).

GenBank. (2008). Retrieved from http://www.psc.edu/general/software/packages/genbank

Ghemawat, S., Gobioff, H., & Leung, S. (2003). The Google file system. In *Proceedings of the 19th Symposium on Operating Systems Principles.*

Ghemawat, S., Gobioff, H., & Leung, S.T. (2003). *The Google file system*. 19th ACM SOSP.

Ghemawat, J. D. (2008, January). Mapreduce: Simplified data processing on large clusters. *ACM Communications, 51*, 107–113.

Gil, Y., & Deelman, E. (2007). *Examining the challenges of scientific workflows*. IEEE Computer.

Gil, Y., Deelman, E., Ellisman, M., Fahringer, T., Fox, G., & Gannon, D. (2007). Examining the challenges of scientific workflows. *Computer, 40*(12), 24–32. doi:10.1109/MC.2007.421

Glatard, T., Montagnat, J., Lingrand, D., & Pennec, X. (2008). Flexible and efficient workflow deployment of data-intensive applications on grids with moteur. *International Journal of High Performance Computing Applications, 22*(3), 347–360. doi:10.1177/1094342008096067

Gleicher, M. (n.d). *HSI: Hierarchical storage interface for HPSS*. Retrieved from http://www.hpss-collaboration.org/hpss/HSI/

Globus Project. (1996). *Online*. Retrieved from http://www.globus.org/

Globus Project. (2002). *The GridFTP protocol and software.*

Goble, C. A., & De Roure, D. C. (2007). myExperiment: Social networking for workflow-using e-scientists. *Proceedings of the 2nd workshop on Workflows in support of large-scale science,* (pp. 1-2).

Gotoh, O. (1982). An improved algorithm for matching biological sequences. *Journal of Molecular Biology, 162,* 705–708. doi:10.1016/0022-2836(82)90398-9

Gray, J. (2003). *Distributed computing economics.* Technical Report MSR-TR-2003-24, Microsoft Research, Microsoft Corporation.

Gribble, C., Parker, S., & Hansen, C. (2004). *Interactive volume rendering of large datasets using the silicon graphics Onyx4 visualization system. Tech. Rep.* University of Utah.

GriPhyN. (2000). *The Grid physics network.* Retrieved from http://www.griphyn.org/proj-desc1.0.html.

Gropp, W., & Lusk, E. (2004). Fault tolerance in message passing interface programs. *International Journal of High Performance Computing Applications, 18,* 363–372. doi:10.1177/1094342004046045

Gropp, W., Lusk, E., & Thakur, R. (1999). *Using MPI-2: Advanced features of the message passing interface.* MIT Press.

Grossman, R. L., & Gu, Y. (2008). Data mining using high performance clouds: Experimental studies using Sector and Sphere. *Proceedings of the 14th ACM SIGKDD International Conference on Knowledge Discovery and Data Mining* (KDD 2008).

GSC-II. (2008). *Guide star catalog II.* Retrieved from http://www.gsss.stsci.edu/gsc/GSChome.htm

Gu, Y. G. (2009). Sector and Sphere: The design and implementation of a high performance data cloud. *Crossing boundaries: computational science, e-Science and global e-Infrastructure I. Selected papers from the UK e-Science All Hands Meeting 2008 Philosophical Transactions of the Royal Society of America, 367,* 2429-2445.

Gu, Y., Grossman, R. L., Szalay, A., & Thakar, A. (2006). Distributing the Sloan digital sky survey using udt and sector. In *Proceedings of e-Science 2006.*

Gyulassy, G., Bremer, P.-T., Hamann, B., & Pascucci, V. (2008). A practical approach to Morse-Smale complex computation: Scalability and generality. *IEEE Transactions on Visualization and Computer Graphics, 14*(6), 1619–1626. doi:10.1109/TVCG.2008.110

Hacker, T. J., Noble, B. D., & Atley, B. D. (2002). The end-to-end performance effects of parallel tcp sockets on a lossy wide area network. *Proceedings of IEEE International Symposium on Parallel and Distributed Processing (IPDPS02),* (pp. 434-443).

Hacker, T. J., Noble, B. D., & Atley, B. D. (2005). Adaptive data block scheduling for parallel streams. *Proceedings of IEEE International Symposium on High Performance Distributed Computing (HPDC05),* (pp. 265-275).

Hadoop Distributed File System HDFS. (2009). Retrieved December 2009, from http://hadoop.apache.org/hdfs/

Hadoop. (n.d). Retrieved from http://hadoop.apache.org/core/

Hammond, S. (1999). *Prototyping an Earth system Grid.* Workshop on Advanced Networking Infrastructure Needs in Atmospheric and Related Sciences, National Center for Atmospheric Research, Boulder CO.

Hanisch, R. J. (2001). Definition of the flexible image transport system (FITS). *Astronomy & Astrophysics, 376,* 359–380. doi:10.1051/0004-6361:20010923

Hardoon, D. R., Szedmak, S., & Shawe-Taylor, J. (2004). Canonical correlation analysis: An overview with application to learning methods. *Neural Computation, 16,* 2639–2664. doi:10.1162/0899766042321814

Harvey, N., Jones, M., Saroiu, S., Theimer, M., & Wolman, A. (2003). *SkipNet: A scalable overlay network with practical locality properties.* Fourth USENIX Symposium on Internet Technologies and Systems (USITS '03), Seattle, WA.

Hasan, R., Anwar, Z., Yurcik, W., Brumbaugh, L., & Campbell, R. (2005). A survey of peer-to-peer storage techniques for distributed file systems. *International Conference on Information Technology: Coding and Computing* (ITCC'05), (p. 2).

Hasegawa, G., Terai, T., Okamoto, T., & Murata, M. (2001). Scalable socket buffer tuning for high-performance Web servers. *Proceedings of the International Conference on Network Protocols (ICNP01)*, (p. 281).

He, E., Leigh, J., Yu, O., & DeFanti, T. A. (2002). Reliable blast UDP: Predictable high performance bulk data transfer. *Proceedings of IEEE Cluster Computing 2002.*

Hedges, M., Hasan, A., et al. (2007). Management and preservation of research data with iRODS. *Proceedings of the ACM First Workshop on CyberInfrastructure: Information Management in eScience,* (pp. 17-22).

Henderson, R., & Tweten, D. (1996). *Portable batch system: External reference specification.*

Hennessy, J. L., & Jouppi, N. P. (1991). Computer technology and architecture: An evolving interaction. *IEEE Computer*, *24*(9), 18–29. doi:10.1109/2.84896

Hey, T., & Trefethen, A. (2003). The data deluge: An e-sicence perspective. In Berman, F., Fox, G., & Hey, A. J. G. (Eds.), *Grid computing: Making the global infrastructure a reality*. Wiley.

Hofmann, T., & Buhmann, J. M. (1997). Pairwise data clustering by deterministic annealing. *IEEE Transactions on Pattern Analysis and Machine Intelligence*, *19*, 1–14. doi:10.1109/34.566806

Hollingsworth, D. (1994). *The workflow reference model. (Tech. Rep. No. TCOO- 1003).* Workflow Management Coalition.

Hoschek, W., Jaen-Martinez, J., Samar, A., Stockinger, H., & Stockinger, K. (2000). *Data management in an international data Grid project*. IEEE/ACM International Workshop on Grid Computing. *iRODS: Integrated Rule Oriented Data System*. (n.d). Retrieved from https://www.irods.org/index.php

Hotelling, H. (1936). Relations between two sets of variates. *Biometrika*, *28*, 321–377.

Howard, J. H., Kazar, M. L., Menees, S. G., Nichols, D. A., Satyanarayanan, M., Sidebotham, R. N., & West, M. J. (1988). Scale and performance in a distributed file system. *ACM Transactions on Computer Systems*, *6*(1), 51–81. doi:10.1145/35037.35059

Hsu, W. M. (1993). Segmented ray casting for data parallel volume rendering. *Proceedings of the 1993 Symposium on Parallel Rendering* (PRS93), (pp. 7–14).

Hu, Y. C., Das, S. M., & Pucha, H. (2003). Exploiting the synergy between peer-to-peer and mobile ad hoc networks. In *Proceedings of HotOS IX.*

Huang, X., & Madan, A. (1999). CAP3: A DNA sequence assembly program. *Genome Research*, *9*(9), 868–877. doi:10.1101/gr.9.9.868

Humphreys, G., Eldridge, M., Buck, I., Stoll, G., Everett, M., & Hanrahan, P. (2001). WireGL: A scalable graphics system for clusters. *Proceedings of the 28th International Conference on Computer Graphics and Interactive Techniques,* (pp. 129–140).

Hursey, J., Mattox, T. I., & Lumsdaine, A. (2009). Interconnect agnostic checkpoint/restart in Open MPI. *Proceedings of the 18th ACM International Symposium on High Performance Distributed Computing HPDC,* (pp. 49-58).

Hyde, R. (2003). *The art of assembly language programming - CPU architecture*. No Starch Press. Retrieved from http://web- ster.cs.ucr.edu/AoA/Windows/PDFs/CPUArchitecture.pdf

Iamnitchi, A., Foster, I., & Nurmi, D. (2002). *A peer-to-peer approach to resource discovery in Grid environments*. Eleventh IEEE Int'l Symposium High Performance Distributed Computing (HPDC-11), Edinburgh, Scotland.

Iamnitchi, A., Ripeanu, M., & Foster, I. (2004). Small-world file-sharing communities. In *Proceedings of Infocom.*

IBM. (2008). *BlueGene/P* (BG/P). Retrieved in 2008 from http://www.research.ibm.com/bluegene/

Ino, F., Sasaki, T., Takeuchi, A., & Hagihara, K. (2003). A divided-screenwise hierarchical compositing for sort-last parallel volume rendering. *Proceedings of the 17th International Symposium on Parallel and Distributed Processing* (IPDPS '03), (p. 141).

IPERF. (2010). *Website*. Retrieved from http://iperf.sourceforge.net

Irani, S. (2002). Randomized weighted caching with two page weights. *Algorithmica*, *32*(4), 624–640. doi:10.1007/s00453-001-0095-6

Irion, R. (2006). The terascale supernova initiative: Modeling the first instance of a stars death. *SciDAC Review, 1,* 26–37.

IRODS. (2010). *The Integrated Rule Oriented Data System.* Retrieved from http://www.irods.org/

Isard, M., Budiu, M., Yu, Y., Birrell, A., & Fetterly, D. (2007). *Dryad: Distributed data-parallel programs from sequential building blocks.* European Conference on Computer Systems (EuroSys).

Isard, M., Budiu, M., Yu, Y., Birrell, A., & Fetterly, D. (2007). Dryad: Distributed data-parallel programs from sequential building blocks. *ACM SIGOPS Operating Systems Review, 41,* 59–72. doi:10.1145/1272998.1273005

Ito, T., Ohsaki, H., & Imase, M. (2008). On parameter tuning of data transfer protocol GridFTP for wide-area networks. *International Journal of Computer Science and Engineering, 2*(4), 177–183.

Jaeger, E., Altintas, I., Zhang, J., Ludäscher, B., Pennington, D., & Michener, W. (2005). A scientific workflow approach to distributed geospatial data processing using web services. In *SSDBM'2005: Proceedings of the 17th International Conference on Scientific and Statistical Database Management* (pp. 87–90). Berkeley, CA: Lawrence Berkeley Laboratory.

Jain, M., Prasad, R. S., & Davrolis, C. (2003). *The Tcp bandwidth-delay product revisited: Network buffering, cross traffic, and socket buffer auto-sizing. Technical report.* Georgia Institute of Technology.

Jaligner. (2009). Retrieved December 2009, from Smith Waterman Software: http://jaligner.sourceforge.net

Jeong, B., Renambot, L., Jagodic, R., Singh, R., Aguilera, J., Johnson, A., & Leigh, J. (2006, November). High-performance dynamic graphics streaming for scalable adaptive graphics environment. *Proceedings of Supercomputing, 2006*(SC06).

Johnson, C., & Hansen, C. (2004). *Visualization handbook.* Academic Press, Inc.

Johnston, W. E., Gannon, D., Nitzberg, B., Tanner, L. A., Thigpen, B., & Woo, A. (2000). Computing and data grids for science and engineering. *Proceedings of Supercomputing Conference (SC00),* (p. 52).

Jung, J., & Sit, E. (2002). DNS performance and the effectiveness of caching. *IEEE/ACM Transactions on Networking, 10*(5), 589–603. doi:10.1109/TNET.2002.803905

Kahn, R., & Wilensky, R. (2006). A framework for distributed digital object services. *International Journal on Digital Libraries, 6*(2), 115–123. doi:10.1007/s00799-005-0128-x

Kalyanam, R., Zhao, L., Park, T., & Goasguen, S. (2007). A web service-enabled distributed workflow system for scientific data processing. In *FTDCS '07: Proceedings of the 11th IEEE International Workshop on Future Trends of Distributed Computing Systems* (pp. 7–14). Washington, DC: IEEE.

Kanazawa, M., et al. (2003). *Ultrahigh-definition video system with 4000 scanning lines.* NHK Technical Report.

Karger, D. R., Lehman, E., et al. (1997). *Consistent hashing and random trees: Distributed caching protocols for relieving hot spots on the World Wide Web.* Symposium on Theory of Computing, ACM.

Karger, D., Sherman, A., et al. (1999). *Web caching with consistent hashing.* The Eighth International World Wide Web Conference (WWW8), Toronto, Canada.

Karrer, R. P., Park, J., & Kim, J. (2006). *Adaptive data block scheduling for parallel streams. Technical report.* Deutsche Telekom Laboratories.

Kearsley, A. J., Tapia, R. A., & Trosset, M. W. (1995). *The solution of the metric STRESS and SSTRESS problems in multidimensional scaling using Newton's method.* Houston, TX: Rice University.

Keating, B. (2001). *Challenges involved in multimaster replication.* Retrieved from http://www.dbspecialists.com/files/presentations/mm_replication.html

Keen, M., Moore, B., Carvalho, A., Hamann, M., Imandi, P., Lotter, R., ... Telerman, G. (n.d.) *Getting started with Websphere enterprise service bus V6.* IBM Press

Kiehl, J. T. (1998). The national center for atmospheric research community climate model: CCM3. *Journal of Climate, 11*(6), 1131–1149. doi:10.1175/1520-0442(1998)011<1131:TNCFAR>2.0.CO;2

Klock, H., & Buhmann, J. M. (2000). Data visualization by multidimensional scaling: A deterministic annealing approach. *Pattern Recognition, 33,* 651–669. doi:10.1016/S0031-3203(99)00078-3

KNB. (1999). *The knowledge network for biocomplexity.* Retrieved from http://knb.ecoinformatics.org/

Kohonen, T. (1998). The self-organizing map. *Neurocomputing, 21,* 1–6. doi:10.1016/S0925-2312(98)00030-7

Kola, G., Kosar, T., & Livny, M. (2004). A fully automated fault-tolerant system for distributed video processing and off-site replication. *Proceedings of the 14th ACM International Workshop on Network and Operating Systems Support for Digital Audio and Video (NOSSDAV 2004),* Kinsale, Ireland.

Koranda, S., & Moe, M. (2007). Lightweight data replicator. Retrieved from http://www.ligo.caltech.edu/docs/G/G030623-00/G030623-00.pdf

Korkhov, V., Vasyunin, D., Wibisono, A., Belloum, A. S. Z., Inda, M. A., & Roos, M. (2007). Vlam-g: Interactive data driven workflow engine for grid-enabled resources. *Science Progress, 15*(3), 173–188.

Ko, S. Y., Morales, R., & Gupta, I. (2007). New worker-centric scheduling strategies for data-intensive grid applications. In Cerqueira, R., & Campbell, R. H. (Eds.), *Middleware* (*Vol. 4834,* pp. 121–142). Springer. doi:10.1007/978-3-540-76778-7_7

Kosar, T. (2005). *Data placement in widely distributed systems.* Ph. D. Thesis, University of Wisconsin-Madison.

Kosar, T. (2006). A new paradigm in data intensive computing: Stork and the data-aware schedulers. *Proceedings of Challenges of Large Applications in Distributed Environments (CLADE 2006) Workshop,* Paris, France.

Kosar, T., & Livny, M. (2004). Stork: Making data placement a first class citizen in the grid. *Proceedings of IEEE International Conference on Distributed Computing Systems (ICDCS04),* (pp. 342-349).

Kosar, T., Balman, M., Suslu, I., Yildirim, E., & Yin, D. (2009). Data-aware distributed computing with stork data scheduler. *Proceedings of the SEE-GRID- SCI'09,* Istanbul, Turkey.

Kosar, T. (2006). *A new paradigm in data intensive computing: Stork and the data-aware scheduler.* IEEE CLADE.

Kosar, T., Kola, G., Livny, M., Brunner, R. J., & Remijan, M. (2005). Reliable, automatic transfer and processing of large scale astronomy data sets. In *Proceedings of Astronomical Data Analysis Software and Systems.* ADASS.

Kruskal, J. (1964). Multidimensional scaling by optimizing goodness of fit to a nonmetric hypothesis. *Psychometrika, 29,* 1–27. doi:10.1007/BF02289565

Kruskal, J. B., & Wish, M. (1978). *Multidimensional scaling.* Sage Publications Inc.

Kubiatowicz, J., et al. (2000). Oceanstore: An architecture for global-scale persistent store. In *Proceedings of ASPLOS,* (pp. 190–201).

Kunszt, P., Laure, E., Stockinger, H., & Stockinger, K. (2003). Advanced replica management with Reptor. 5th International Conference on Parallel Processing and Applied Mathematics, Czestochowa, Poland, Springer Verlag.

Kunszt, P. F., & Badino, P. (2005). *Data storage, access and catalogs in gLite.* Local to Global Data Interoperability-Challenges and Technologies.

Kwok, Y. K., & Ahmad, I. (1999). Static scheduling algorithms for allocating directed task graphs to multiprocessors. *ACM Computing Surveys, 31*(4), 406–471. doi:10.1145/344588.344618

Lancellotti, R., Colajanni, M., & Ciciani, B. (2002). *A scalable architecture for cooperative Web caching.* Workshop in Web Engineering, Networking 2002.

Laser Interferometer Gravitational-Wave Observatory (LIGO). (2008). Retrieved from http://www.ligo.caltech.edu/

Lassila, O., & Swick, R. R. (1999). *Resource description framework (RDF) model and syntax specification.*

Laszewski, G. V., Amin, K., Hategan, M., Hampton, N. J. Z. S., & Rossi, A. (2004, January). Gridant: A client-controllable grid workflow system. In *37th Hawaii International Conference on System Science (HICSS'04)* (pp. 5–8). IEEE.

Lawler, J. P., & Howell-Barber, H. (2008). *Service-oriented architecture: SOA strategy, methodology, and technology*. Auerbach Publications.

Lee, J., Gunter, D., Tierney, B., Allcock, B., Bester, J., Bresnahan, J., & Tuecke, S. (2001). Applied techniques for high bandwidth data transfers across wide area networks. *Proceedings International Conference on Computing in High Energy and Nuclear Physics (CHEP01).*

Lee, J., Ma, X., Ross, R., Thakur, R., & Winslett, M. (2004). RFS: Efficient and flexible remote file access for MPI-IO. In *Proceedings of the IEEE International Conference on Cluster Computing*.

Lee, J., Ma, X., Winslett, M., & Yu, S. Active buffering plus compressed migration: An integrated solution to parallel simulations' data transport needs. In *Proceedings of the 16th ACM International Conference on Supercomputing*.

Leibowitz, N., Bergman, A., Ben-Shaul, R., & Shavit, A. (2002). Are file swapping networks cacheable? Characterizing p2p traffic. In *Proc. 7th International Workshop on Web Content Caching and Distribution (WCW7)*.

Leigh, J., & Brown, M. D. (2007, December). Cyber-commons: Merging real and virtual worlds. *Communications of the ACM, 51*(1), 82–85. doi:10.1145/1327452.1327488

Levoy, M. (1988). Display of surfaces from volume data. *IEEE Computer Graphics and Applications, 8*(3), 29–37. doi:10.1109/38.511

Liang, J., R. Kumar, et al. (2005). The KaZaA overlay: A measurement study. *Computer Networks Journal, 49*(6).

LIGO Project. (2004). *Lightweight data replicator*. Retrieved from http://www.lsc-group.phys.uwm.edu/LDR/. from http://www.lsc-group.phys.uwm.edu/LDR/

LIGO Project. (2004). *LIGO - Laser interferometer gravitational wave observatory*, Retrieved from http://www.ligo.caltech.edu/. from http://www.ligo.caltech.edu/

Ligon, W. B., & Ross, R. B. (1996). Implementation and performance of a parallel file system for high performance distributed applications. *HPDC '96: Proceedings of the 5th IEEE International Symposium on High Performance Distributed Computing*, IEEE Computer Society, (p. 471).

Lindsay, B. G. (1987). A retrospective of R: A distributed database management system. *Proceedings of the IEEE, 75*(5), 668–673. doi:10.1109/PROC.1987.13780

LINQ Language-Integrated Query. (2009). Retrieved December 2009, from http://msdn.microsoft.com/en-us/netframework/aa904594.aspx

Litzkow, M., Livny, M., & Mutka, M. (1988). Condor - A hunter of idle workstations. In *Proceedings of the 8th International Conference on Distributed Computing Systems*.

Liu, D. T., & Franklin, M. J. (2004). Griddb: A data-centric overlay for scientific grids. In *VLDB '04: Proceedings of the Thirtieth International Conference on Very Large Data Bases* (pp. 600– 611). VLDB Endowment.

Liu, D. T., & Franklin, M. J. (2004). The design of GridDB: A data-centric overlay for the scientific grid. *VLDB04*, (pp. 600-611).

Livny, M., Basney, J., Raman, R., & Tannenbaum, T. (1997). Mechanisms for high throughput computing. *SPEEDUP Journal, 1*(1).

Lombeyda, S., Moll, L., Shand, M., Breen, D., & Heirich, A. (2001). Scalable interactive volume rendering using off-the-shelf components. *Proceedings of the IEEE 2001 Symposium on Parallel and Large-Data Visualization and Graphics* (PVG '01), (pp. 115–121).

LONI. (2010). *Louisiana Optical Network Initiative*. Retrieved from http://www.loni.org

Lorensen, W. E., & Cline, H. E. (1987). Marching cubes: A high resolution 3D surface construction algorithm. *ACM Computer Graphics, 21*(4), 163–169. doi:10.1145/37402.37422

Lu, D., Qiao, Y., & Dinda, P. A. (2005). Characterizing and predicting TCP throughput on the wide area network. *Proceedings of IEEE International Conference on Distributed Computing Systems (ICDCS05)*, (pp. 414-424).

Lu, D., Qiao, Y., Dinda, P. A., & Bustamante, F. E. (2005). Modeling and taming parallel TCP on the wide area network. *Proceedings of IEEE International Symposium on Parallel and Distributed Processing (IPDPS05)*, (p. 68b).

Ludäscher, B., Altintas, I., Berkley, C., Higgins, D., Jaeger, E., & Jones, M. (2006). Scientific workflow management and the kepler system: Research articles. *Concurrency and Computation, 18*(10), 1039–1065.

Lustre. (2010). *A scalable, high performance file system.* Retrieved from http://wiki.lustre.org/index.php/Main_Page

Lv, Q., Cao, P., et al. (2002). *Search and replication in unstructured peer-to-peer networks.* 16th ACM International Conference on Supercomputing(ICS'02), New York, USA.

Ma, K. L., & Camp, D. M. (2000). High performance visualization of time-varying volume data over a wide-area network. *Proceedings* of *Supercomputing 2000*, (p. 29).

Ma, K.-L. (1995). Parallel volume ray-casting for unstructured-grid data on distributed-memory architectures. *Proceedings of Parallel Rendering Symposium*, (pp. 23-30).

Ma, K.-L. (1999). Parallel rendering of 3D AMR data on the SGI/Cray T3E, *Proceedings of 7th Annual Symposium on the Frontiers of Massively Parallel Computation 1999*, (pp. 138–145).

Ma, X., Vazhkudai, S., Freeh, V., Simon, T., Yang, T., & Scott, S. L. (2006). Coupling prefix caching and collective downloads for remote data access. In *Proceedings of the ACM International Conference on Supercomputing.*

MacQueen, J. B. (1967). Some methods for classification and analysis of multivariate observations. *5-th Berkeley Symposium on Mathematical Statistics and Probability* (pp. 281-297). University of California Press.

Maechling, P., & Chalupsky, H. (2005). Simplifying construction of complex workflows for non-expert users of the Southern California Earthquake Center Community Modeling Environment. *SIGMOD Record, 34*(3), 24–30. doi:10.1145/1084805.1084811

Ma, K.-L., Painter, J. S., Hansen, C. D., & Krogh, M. F. (1994). Parallel volume rendering using binary-swap compositing. *IEEE Computer Graphics and Applications, 14*(4), 59–68. doi:10.1109/38.291532

Ma, K.-L., Wang, C., Yu, H., & Tikhonova, A. (2007). In situ processing and visualization for ultrascale simulations. *Journal of Physics, 78*, 2007. doi:10.1088/1742-6596/78/1/012043

Mathis, M., Semke, J., Mahdavi, J., & Ott, T. (1997). The macroscopic behavior of the TCP congestion avoidance algorithm. *Computer Communication Review, 27*(3), 67–82. doi:10.1145/263932.264023

MCAT. (2000). *Metadata catalog.* Retrieved from http://www.npaci.edu/dice/srb/mcat.html

McCormick, B. H., DeFanti, T. A., & Brown, M. D. (1988). Visualization in scientific computing. *ACM Computer Graphics, 21*(6).

Meyer, L., Annis, J., Wilde, M., Mattoso, M., & Foster, I. (2006). Planning spatial workflows to optimize grid performance. In *SAC '06: Proceedings of the 2006 ACM Symposium on Applied Computing* (pp. 786–790). New York, NY: ACM.

Middleton, D. E., Bernholdt, D. E., Brown, D., Chen, M., Chervenak, A. L., & Cinquini, L..... Williams, D. (2006). Enabling worldwide access to climate simulation data: the earth system grid (ESG). *Scientific Discovery Through Advanced Computing (SciDAC 2006), Journal of Physics: Conference Series, 46*, (pp. 510-514).

Miles, S., Deelman, E., et al. (2007). *Connecting scientific data to scientific experiments with provenance.* e-Science.

Miles, S., & Groth, P. (2006). The requirements of using provenance in e-science experiments. *Journal of Grid Computing, 5*(1).

Moab Cluster Tools Suite. (2009). Retrieved December 2009, from http://www.clusterresources.com/products/moab-cluster-suite.php

Mockapetris, P., & Dunlap, K. J. (1988). *Development of the domain name system.* ACM Symposium on Communications Architectures and Protocols (SIGCOMM '88), Stanford, CA, USA.

Monti, H., Butt, A. R., & Vazhkudai, S. S. (2008a). Just-in-time staging of large input data for supercomputing jobs. In *Proceedings ACM Petascale Data Storage Workshop.*

Monti, H., Butt, A. R., & Vazhkudai, S. S. (2008b). Timely offloading of result-data in HPC centers. In *Proceedings of 22nd ACM International Conference on Supercomputing (ICS '08)*.

Moore, R. (2002). Preservation of data, information, and knowledge. *Proceedings of the World Library Summit*, Singapore.

Moore, R. W., & Rajasekar, A. (2007). *Rule-based distributed data management*. Grid 2007: IEEE/ACM International Conference on Grid Computing.

Moore, R. W., Wan, M., & Rajasekar, A. (2005). Storage resource broker; generic software infrastructure for managing globally distributed data. *International Symposium on Mass Storage Systems and Technology*, IEEE Computer Society, (pp. 65 – 69).

Moore, R., & Rajasekar, A. (2001). *Data and metadata collections for scientific applications*. High Performance Computing and Networking (HPCN 2001). Amsterdam, NL.

Moore, R., Conrad, M., Marciano, R., Rajasekar, A., & Wan, M. (2009). *Transcontinental preservation archive prototype*. Indo-US Workshop on International Trends in Digital Preservation. Pune, India.

Moore, R., Prince, T. A., & Ellisman, M. (1998). Data-intensive computing and digital libraries. *Communications of the ACM, 41*(11), 56–62. doi:10.1145/287831.287840

Morajko, A. (2004). *Dynamic tuning of parallel/distributed applications*. PhD thesis, Universitat Autonoma de Barcelona.

Moreau, L. (2007). The first provenance challenge. *Concurrency and Computation, 20*(5).

Moreau, L., & Freire, J. (2007). *The open provenance model*. University of Southampton.

Moreau, L., & Ludaescher, B. (2007). *Concurrency and Computation: Practice and Experience*. Special Issue on the First Provenance Challenge.

Moretti, C. (2007). *Flexible object based filesystems for scientific computing*. M.S. Thesis, University of Notre Dame.

Moretti, C., Bulosan, J., Thain, D., & Flynn, P. (2008). *All-Pairs: An abstraction for data-intensive cloud computing*. IPDPS'08.

Moretti, C., Bui, H., Hollingsworth, K., Rich, B., Flynn, P., & Thain, D. (2009). All-Pairs: An abstraction for data intensive computing on campus grids. *IEEE Transactions on Parallel and Distributed Systems, 21*, 21–36.

Mount, R. (2004). *The office of science data-management challenge*. Report from the DOE office of science data-management workshops, Tech. Rep.

MPI. (2009). Retrieved December 2009, from Message Passing Interface: http://www-unix.mcs.anl.gov/mpi/

MSCFD. (2010). *Multiscale Computational Fluid Dynamics at LSU*. Retrieved from http://www.cct.lsu.edu/IGERT/

Müller, C., Strengert, M., & Ertl, T. (2006). Optimized volume raycasting for graphics-hardware-based cluster systems. *Eurographics Symposium on Parallel Graphics and Visualization* (EGPGV06), (pp. 59–66).

Munro, C., & Koblitz, B. (2006). Performance comparison of the LCG2 and gLite file catalogues. *Nuclear Instruments and Methods in Physics Research Section A, 559*(1), 48–52. doi:10.1016/j.nima.2005.11.103

Muraki, S., Lum, E. B., Ma, K.-L., Ogata, M., & Liu, X. (2003). A Pc cluster system for simultaneous interactive volumetric modeling and visualization. *Proceedings of the 2003 IEEE Symposium on Parallel and Large-Data Visualization and Graphics* (PVG '03), (pp. 95–102).

Muthitacharoen, A., Morris, R., Gil, T. M., & Chen, B. (2003). *Ivy: A read/write peer-to-peer file system*. In *Proc. 5th USENIX OSDI*, (pp. 31–34).

Nagle, D., Serenyi, D., & Matthews, A. (2004). The Panasas ActiveScale storage cluster: Delivering scalable high bandwidth storage. *SC '04: Proceedings of the 2004 ACM/IEEE conference on Supercomputing*, IEEE Computer Society, (p. 53).

Nakada, H., Matsuoka, S., Seymour, K., Dongarra, J., Lee, C., & Casanova. (2007, June). *A GridRPC model and API for end-user applications*. GridRPC Working Group of Global Grid Forum.

Napster. (n.d). Retrieved from http://www.napster.com/

National Center for Biotechnology Information (NCBI) (n.d). Retrieved from http://www.ncbi.nlm.nih.gov/

NCCS.GOV File Systems. (2007). Retrieved from http://info.nccs.gov/computing-resources/jaguar/file-systems

NEES. (2000). *Network for earthquake engineering simulation.* Retrieved from http://www.eng.nsf.gov/nees/

Newman, H. (2003). Data intensive grids and networks for high energy and nuclear physics. *Nuclear Physics B - Proceedings Supplements, 120,* 109–112. doi:10.1016/S0920-5632(03)01889-9

Nielson, G. M., Hagen, H., & Muller, H. (1997). *Scientific visualization, overviews, methodologies, and techniques.* IEEE Computer Society.

NumRel. (2010). *Numerical relativity at LSU.* Retrieved from http://www.cct.lsu.edu/numerical/

NVO. (2001). *National virtual observatory.* Retrieved from http://www.srl.caltech.edu/nvo/

NWS. (2010). *The Network Weather Service.* Retrieved from http://nws.cs.ucsb.edu/

OASIS. (n.d). *Web services business process execution language* (WSBPEL). Retrieved from http://www.oasis-open.org/committees/tc_home.php?wg_abbrev=wsbpel

Ocean Observatories Initiative. (n.d). Retrieved from http://www.oceanobservatories.org/spaces

Oinn, T., Addis, M., Ferris, J., Marvin, D., Senger, M., & Greenwood, M. (2004, November). Taverna: A tool for the composition and enactment of bioinformatics workflows. *Bioinformatics (Oxford, England), 20*(17), 3045–3054. doi:10.1093/bioinformatics/bth361

Olson, D., & Perl, J. (2002). *Grid service requirements for interactive analysis.* PPDG CS11 Report.

Open Science Grid (OSG). (2008). Retrieved from http://www.opensciencegrid.org/

OpenESB. (n.d). Retrieved from https://open-esb.dev.java.net/

Otoo, E. J., Rotem, D., & Romosan, A. (2004). Optimal file-bundle caching algorithms for data-grids. In *Proceedings of Supercomputing.*

Ousterhout, J. (1998). Scripting: Higher level programming for the 21st century. *IEEE Computer Magazine,* March 1998.

Pallickara, S., & Fox, G. (2003). *NaradaBrokering: A distributed middleware framework and architecture for enabling durable peer-to-peer grids.* ACM/IFIP/USENIX 2003 International Conference on Middleware. Rio de Janeiro, Brazil: Springer-Verlag New York, Inc.

Palmer, M. E., Totty, B., & Taylor, S. (1998). Ray casting on shared-memory architectures: Memory-hierarchy considerations in volume rendering. *IEEE Concurrency, 6*(1), 20–35. doi:10.1109/4434.656777

Papazoglou, M. P. (2007). *Web services: Principles and technology.* Prentice Hall.

Pathchirp. (2010). *Website.* Retrieved from http://www.spin.rice.edu/Software/pathChirp/

Pathload. (2010). *A measurement tool for the available bandwidth of network paths.* Retrieved from http://www.cc.gatech.edu/fac/Constantinos.Dovrolis/pathload.html

Patterson, D., & Hennessy, J. (1994). *Computer organization and design: The hardware/software interface.* Morgan Kaufmann Publishers. *PlanetLab.* (n.d). Retrieved from http://www.planet-lab.org

Pautasso, C. (2005). Jopera: An agile environment for Web service composition with visual unit testing and refactoring. In *VLHCC '05: Proceedings of the 2005 IEEE Symposium on Visual Languages and Human-Centric Computing* (pp. 311–313). Washington, DC: IEEE Computer Society.

Peterka, T., Ross, R., Yu, H., Ma, K.-L., Kenall, W., & Huang, J. (2008). Assessing improvements in the parallel volume rendering pipeline at large scale. *Proceedings of SC 08 Ultrascale Visualization Workshop.*

Peterka, T., Yu, H., Ross, R., & Ma, K.-L. (2008). Parallel volume rendering on the IBM blue gene/p, *Proceedings of Eurographics Parallel Graphics and Visualization Symposium 2008.*

Pike, R., Dorward, S., Griesemer, R., & Quinlan, S. (2005). Interpreting the data: Parallel analysis with sawzall. *Scientific Programming Journal Special Issue on Grids and Worldwide Computing Programming Models and Infrastructure, 13*(4), 227–298.

Pinheiro, E., Weber, W.-D., & Barroso, L. A. (2007). Failure trends in a large disk drive population. In *Proceedings of USENIX FAST*. USENIX Association.

Plank, J., Beck, M., Elwasif, W., Moore, T., Swany, M., & Wolski, R. (1999). The Internet backplane protocol: Storage in the network. In *Proceedings of the Network Storage Symposium*.

Plank, J., Bassi, A., Beck, M., Moore, T., Swany, D., & Wolski, R. (2001). Managing data storage in the network. *IEEE Internet Computing, 5,* 50–58. doi:10.1109/4236.957895

Podlipnig, S., & Böszörmenyi, L. (2003). A survey of Web cache replacement strategies. *ACM Computing Surveys, 35*(4), 374–398. doi:10.1145/954339.954341

Ponomarev, S. Y., Bishop, T. C., & Putkaradze, V. (2009). DNA relaxation dynamics in 1ID3 yeast nucleosome MD simulation. (n.d). Retrieved from http://protege.stanford.edu/. *Biophysical Journal, 96,* doi:10.1016/j.bpj.2008.12.3019

Porter, T., & Duff, T. (1984). Compositing digital images. *Proceedings of the 11th Annual Conference on Computer Graphics and Interactive Techniques* (SIGGRAPH'84), (pp. 253–259).

POSS-II. (2008). *Palomar observatory sky survey.* Retrieved from http://taltos.pha.jhu.edu/~rrg/science/dposs/dposs.html

PPDG. (1999). *The particle physics data Grid.* Retrieved from http://www.cacr.caltech.edu/ppdg/

Prasad, R. S., Jain, M., & Davrolis, C. (2004). Socket buffer auto-sizing for high- performance data transfers. *Journal of Grid Computing, 1*(4), 361–376. doi:10.1023/B:GRID.0000037554.67413.52

Price, A. L., Eskin, E., & Pevzner, P. A. (2004). Whole-genome analysis of Alu repeat elements reveals complex evolutionary history. *Genome Research, 14,* 2245–2252. doi:10.1101/gr.2693004

Prohaska, S., Hutanu, A., Kahler, R., & Hege, H. (2004). Interactive exploration of large remote micro-CT scans. In *VIS '04: Proceedings of the conference on Visualization '04.* Washington, DC: IEEE Computer Society.

Project, C. M. S. (2005). *The compact Muon Solenoid, an experiment for the large hadron collider at CERN.* Retrieved from http://cms.cern.ch/. from http://cmsinfo.cern.ch/Welcome.html/

Project, E. S. G. (2005). *The Earth system Grid.* Retrieved from www.earthsystemgrid.org

Pruhs, K., Sgall, J., & Torng, E. (2004). Online scheduling. In Leung, J. Y.-T., & Anderson, J. H. (Eds.), *Handbook of scheduling: Algorithms, models, and performance analysis.*

PubChem Project. (2009, December). Retrieved from http://pubchem.ncbi.nlm.nih.gov/

Pucha, H., Das, S. M., & Hu, Y. C. (2006). Imposing route reuse in mobile ad hoc network routing protocols using structured peer-to-peer overlay routing. *IEEE Transactions on Parallel and Distributed Systems, 17*(12), 1452–1467. doi:10.1109/TPDS.2006.174

QCDGrid Project. (2005). *QCDGrid: Probing the building blocks of matter with the power of the Grid.* Retrieved from http://www.gridpp.ac.uk/qcdgrid/

Qiu, X., & Fox, G. C. (2008). Data mining on multicore clusters. In *Proceedings of 7th International Conference on Grid and Cooperative Computing GCC2008* (pp. 41-49). Shenzhen, China: IEEE Computer Society.

Qiu, X., Ekanayake, J., Beason, S., Gunarathne, T., Fox, G., Barga, R., et al. (2009). *Cloud technologies for bioinformatics applications.* 2nd ACM Workshop on Many-Task Computing on Grids and Supercomputers (SuperComputing09). ACM Press.

Qiu, X., Fox, G. C., Yuan, H., Bae, S.-H., Chrysanthakopoulos, G., & Nielsen, H. F. (2008). Performance of multicore systems on parallel data clustering with deterministic annealing. *Computational Science – ICCS 2008* (pp. 407-416). Kraków, Poland: Springer Berlin / Heidelberg.

Rabinovich, M., Chase, J., et al. (1998). *Not all hits are created equal: Cooperative proxy caching over a wide-area network.* Third International WWW Caching Workshop.

Raicu, I., Foster, I., & Zhao, Y. (2008a). *Many task computing: Bridging the gap between high throughput computing and high performance computing.* IEEE Workshop on Many-Task Computing on Grids and Supercomputers (MTAGS08).

Raicu, I., Foster, I., Zhao, Y., Little, P., Moretti, C., Chaudhary, A., & Thain, D. (2009). *The quest for scalable support of data intensive applications in distributed systems.* To appear at ACM HPDC09.

Raicu, I., Zhang, Z., Wilde, M., Foster, I., Beckman, P., Iskra, K., & Clifford, B. (2008b). *Towards loosely-coupled programming on Petascale systems.* IEEE/ACM International Conference for High Performance Computing, Networking, Storage and Analysis (SuperComputing/SC08).

Raicu, I., Zhao, Y., Dumitrescu, C., Foster, I., & Wilde, M. (2007). *Falkon: A Fast and Light-weight tasK executiON framework.* IEEE/ACM International Conference for High Performance Computing, Networking, Storage, and Analysis (SC07).

Raicu, I., Zhao, Y., Foster, I. T., & Szalay, A. (2008). Accelerating large-scale data exploration through data diffusion. In *DADC '08: Proceedings of the 2008 International Workshop on Data-Aware Distributed Computing* (pp. 9–18). New York, NY: ACM.

Raicu, I., Zhao, Y., Foster, I., & Szalay, A. (2007). *A data diffusion approach to large-scale scientific exploration.* Microsoft eScience Workshop at RENCI.

Raicu, I., Zhao, Y., Foster, I., & Szalay, A. (2008c). *Accelerating large-scale data exploration through data diffusion.* ACM International Workshop on Data-Aware Distributed Computing.

Raicu, I. (2007). *Harnessing Grid resources with data-centric task farms. Technical Report.* University of Chicago.

Raicu, I., Foster, I., Szalay, A., & Turcu, G. (2006). *AstroPortal: A science gateway for large-scale astronomy data analysis.* TeraGrid Conference.

Rajasekar, A., Moore, R. W., & Wan, M. (2009). *Event processing in policy oriented data Grids.* AAAI Spring Symposium, Stanford, CA, USA.

Rajasekar, A., Moore, R. W., Wan, M., & Schroeder, W. (2009). *Universal view and open policy: Paradigms for collaboration in data grids.* International Symposium on Collaborative Technologies and Systems. Baltimore, MD, USA

Rajasekar, A., Wan, M., & Moore, R. (2002). *MySRB & SRB - Components of a data Grid.* The 11th International Symposium on High Performance Distributed Computing (HPDC-11). Edinburgh, Scotland.

Rajasekar, A., Wan, M., Moore, R., & Schroeder, W. (2006). *A prototype rule-based distributed data management system.* HPDC Workshop on Next Generation Distributed Data Management.

Rajasekar, A. (2003). Storage resource broker - Managing distributed data in a Grid. *Computer Society of India Journal. Special Issue on SAN, 33*(4), 42–54.

Rajasekar, A., & Wan, M. (2003). Storage resource broker-managing distributed data in a Grid. *Computer Society of India Journal. Special Issue on SAN, 33*(4), 42–54.

Ramakrishnan, A., Singh, G., et al. (2007). *Scheduling data-intensive workflows onto storage-constrained distributed resources.* Seventh IEEE International Symposium on Cluster Computing and the Grid — CCGrid 2007.

Ramakrishnan, A., Singh, G., Zhao, H., Deelman, E., Sakellariou, R., Vahi, K., et al. (2007). Scheduling data-intensive workflows onto storage-constrained distributed resources. In *CCGrid '09: Proceedings of the 7th IEEE Symposium on Cluster Computing and The Grid* (pp. 14–17). Brazil: IEEE.

Ramakrishnan, L., & Reed, D. A. (2008). Performability modeling for scheduling and fault tolerance strategies for scientific workflows. In *HPDC '08: Proceedings of the 17th International Symposium on High Performance Distributed Computing* (pp. 23–34). New York, NY: ACM.

Ramanathan, R. M. (2006). *Extending the world's most popular processor architecture - New innovations that improve the performance and energy efficiency of Intel architecture.* Retrieved from http://download.intel.com/technology/architecture

Ranganathan, K., & Foster, I. (2002). Decoupling computation and data scheduling in distributed data-intensive applications. In *Proceedings of the 11th IEEE International Symposium on High Performance Distributed Computing.* USA: IEEE.

Ranganathan, K., & Foster, I. T. (2001). Identifying dynamic replication strategies for a high- performance data grid. In *Proceedings of the Second International Workshop on Grid Computing.* UK: Springer-Verlag.

Ranganathan, R. & Foster, I. (2004). Computation scheduling and data replication algorithms for data Grids. *Journal of Grid Resource Management: State of the Art and Future Trends,* 359-373.

Ranganathan, R., & Foster, I. (2002). Decoupling computation and data scheduling in distributed data-intensive applications. *Proceedings of the 11th IEEE International Symposium on High Performance Distributed Computing HPDC-11,* (p. 352).

Ranganathan, K., & Foster, I. (2003, March). Simulation studies of computation and data scheduling algorithms for data grids. *Journal of Grid Computing, 1*(1), 53–62. doi:10.1023/A:1024035627870

Ratnasamy, S., Francis, P., Handley, M., Karp, R., & Schenker, S. (2001). A scalable content-addressable network. In *Proceedings of SIGCOMM.*

Ratnasamy, S., Shenker, S., & Stoica, I. (2002). *Routing algorithms for DHTs: Some open questions.* IPTPS02, Cambridge, USA.

Ratnasamy, S., Francis, P., Handley, M., Karp, R., & Shenker, S. (2001). *A scalable content-addressable network.* ACM SIGCOMM.

Ravi, M. K., Cynthia, H. S., & William, E. A. (2002). Reliable file transfer in grid environments. *Proceedings of the 27th Annual IEEE Conference on Local Computer Networks,* (pp. 737-738).

Rehn, J., Barrass, T., et al. (2006). *PhEDEx high-throughput data transfer management system.* Computing in High Energy and Nuclear Physics (CHEP) 2006, Mumbai, India.

Renambot, L., Johnson, A., & Leigh, J. (2005). *Techniques for Building Cost-Effective Ultra-high-resolution Visualization Instruments.* NSF CISE/CNS Infrastructure Experience Workshop 2005. Retrieved from www.cs.uiuc.edu/events/expwork-2005/Luc_Renambot_Abstract.pdf

Renambot, L., Jeong, B., Hur, H., Johnson, A., & Leigh, J. (2009). Enabling high resolution collaborative visualization in display rich virtual organizations. *Future Generation Computer Systems,* •••, 25.

Rhea, S., Eaton, P., Geels, D., Weatherspoon, H., Zhao, B., & Kubiatowicz, J. (2003). Pond: The Oceanstore prototype. In *Proceedings of 2nd USENIX FAST,* (pp. 1–14).

Rhea, S., Godfrey, B., Karp, B., Kubiatowicz, J., Ratnasamy, S., Shenker, S., et al. (2005). OpenDHT: A public DHT service and its uses. *Proceedings of ACM SIGCOMM.*

Riedel, E., Gibson, G., & Faloutsos, C. (1998). Active storage for large scale data mining and multimedia. In *Proceedings of Very Large Databases.* VLDB.

Ripeanu, M. (2001). *Peer-to-peer architecture case study: Gnutella network.* IEEE 1st International Conference on Peer-to-peer Computing (P2P2001), Linkoping, Sweden, IEEE.

Ripeanu, M., & Foster, I. (2002). *A decentralized, adaptive, replica location mechanism.* 11th IEEE International Symposium on High Performance Distributed Computing (HPDC-11), Edinburgh, Scotland.

Ripeanu, M., Foster, I., & Iamnitchi, A. (2002). Mapping the Gnutella network: Properties of large-scale peer-to-peer systems and implications for system design. *IEEE Internet Computing Journal, 6*(1), 50–57.

ROOT, Data Analysis Framework. (2009). Retrieved December 2009, from http://root.cern.ch/

ROOT. (2006). *Object oriented data analysis framework.* European Organization for Nuclear Research Journal. Retrieved from http://root.cern.ch.

Rose, K. (1998). Deterministic annealing for clustering, compression, classification, regression, and related optimization problems. *Proceedings of the IEEE, 86,* 2210–2239. doi:10.1109/5.726788

Rose, K., Gurewitz, E., & Fox, G. (1990). A deterministic annealing approach to clustering. *Pattern Recognition Letters, 11*, 589–594. doi:10.1016/0167-8655(90)90010-Y

Rose, K., Gurewitz, E., & Fox, G. C. (1990). Statistical mechanics and phase transitions in clustering. *Physical Review Letters, 65*, 945–948. doi:10.1103/PhysRevLett.65.945

Ross, R., Peterka, T., Shen, H.-W., Hong, Y., Ma, K.-L., Yu, H., & Moreland, K. (2008). Visualization and parallel I/O at extreme scale. *Journal of Physics, 125*(1).

Rowstron, A., & Druschel, P. (2001a). Pastry: Scalable, distributed object location and routing for large-scale peer-to-peer systems. In *Proceedings of IFIP/ACM Middleware*, (pp. 329–350).

Rowstron, A., & Druschel, P. (2001b). Storage management and caching in PAST, a large-scale, persistent peer-to-peer storage utility. In *Proceedings of SOSP*, (pp. 188–201).

Saito, Y., Karamanolis, C., Karlsson, M., & Mahalingam, M. (2002). Taming aggressive replication in the Pangaea wide-area file system. In *Proceedings of 5th USENIX OSDI*, (pp. 15–30).

Sakellariou, R., & Zhao, H. (2007). Scheduling workflows with budget constraints. In Gorlatch, S., & Danelutto, M. (Eds.), *Integrated research in Grid computing. CoreGrid series*. Springer-Verlag. doi:10.1007/978-0-387-47658-2_14

Salmon, J. K. (1991). *Parallel hierarchical N-body methods. PhD*. California Institute of Technology.

Samanta, R., Funkhouser, T., & Li, K. (2001). Parallel rendering with k-way replication. *Proceedings of IEEE Symposium on Parallel and Large-Data Visualization and Graphics*.

Sandberg, R., Goldberg, D., Kleiman, S., Walsh, D., & Lyon, B. (1985). Design and implementation of the Sun network file system. In *Proceedings of Summer USENIX*, (pp. 119–130).

Sarmenta, L. F. G. (2001). *Volunteer computing*. MIT Dept. of Electrical Engineering and Computer Science PhD Dissertation.

Saroiu, S., P. Gummadi, K., & Gribble, S. D. (2002). *A measurement study of peer-to-peer file sharing systems*. Multimedia Computing and Networking.

SCEC Project. (2005). *Southern California earthquake center*. Retrieved from http://www.scec.org/

Schmuck, F., & Haskin, R. (2002). GPFS: A shared-disk file system for large computing clusters. *FAST '02: Proceedings of the 1st USENIX Conference on File and Storage Technologies*. USENIX Association, 19.

Schroeder, B., & Gibson, G. A. (2007). Disk failures in the real world: What does an MTTF of 1,000,000 hours mean to you? In *Proceedings of USENIX FAST*.

Schroeder, W., Martin, K., & Lorensen, W. E. (2006). *The Visualization Toolkit* (4th ed.). Kitware, Inc.

SCOOP. (2010). *SURA Coastal Ocean Observing and Prediction*. Retrieved from http://scoop.sura.org

SDSS Project. (2000). *Online*. Retrieved from https://www.darkenergysurvey.org

SDSS. (2008). *Sloan digital sky survey*. Retrieved from http://www.sdss.org/

Semke, J., Madhavi, J., & Mathis, M. (1998). Automatic TCP buffer tuning. *Proceedings of ACM SIGCOMM '98, 28*(4), 315-323.

Sen, S., & Wong, J. (2002). Analyzing peer-to-peer traffic across large networks. *Proceedings of the Second ACM SIGCOMM Workshop on Internet Measurement*.

Shah, S., & Elerath, J. (2005). Reliability analysis of disk drive failure mechanisms. In *Proceedings of RAMS*.

Shankar, S., & DeWitt, D. J. (2007). Data driven workflow planning in cluster management systems. In *HPDC '07: Proceedings of the 16th International Symposium on High Performance Distributed Computing* (pp. 127–136). New York, NY: ACM.

Shankar, S., Kini, A., DeWitt, D. J., & Naughton, J. (2005). Integrating databases and workflow systems. *SIGMOD Record, 34*(3), 5–11. doi:10.1145/1084805.1084808

Sharman Networks. (2004). *Kazaa media desktop*. Retrieved from http://www.kazaa.com/index.htm

Shepler, S., Callaghan, B., Robinson, D., Thurlow, R., Beame, C., Eisler, M., & Novec, D. (2003). *Network file system version 4 protocol*. Retrieved from http://tools.ietf.org/html/rfc3530

Shoshani, A., Sim, A., & Gu, J. (2003). Storage resource managers: Essential components for the grid. In Nabrzyski, J., Schopf, J., & Weglarz, J. (Eds.), *Grid resource management: State of the art and future trends*.

SiCortex. (2008). Retrieved from http://www.sicortex.com/.

Silberschatz, A., & Galvin, P. (1994). *Operating system concepts*. Addison-Wesley.

Simmhan, Y. L., Plale, B., & Gannon, D. (2005, September). A survey of data provenance in e-science. *SIGMOD Record, 34*(3), 31–36. doi:10.1145/1084805.1084812

Singh, G., Vahi, K., et al. (2007). Optimizing workflow data footprint. *Scientific Programming Journal, Special issue on Dynamic Computational Workflows: Discovery, Optimization, and Scheduling, 15*(4).

Singh, G., Kesselman, C., & Deelman, E. (2005, September). Optimizing grid-based workflow execution. *Journal of Grid Computing, 3*(3-4), 201–219. doi:10.1007/s10723-005-9011-7

Singh, G., Vahi, K., Ramakrishnan, A., Mehta, G., Deelman, E., & Zhao, H. (2007). Optimizing workflow data footprint. *Science Progress, 15*(4), 249–268.

Sit, E., Haeberlen, A., et al. (2006). *Proactive replication for data durability*. 5th International Workshop on Peer-to-Peer Systems (IPTPS 2006).

Sivakumar, H., Bailey, S., & Grossman, R. L. (2000). Psockets: The case for application-level network striping for data intensive applications using high speed wide area networks. In *Proceedings of IEEE Super Computing Conference (SC00)*, (p. 63).

Sloan Digital Sky Survey (SDSS). (2005). Retrieved from http://www.sdss.org

Smarr, L. L., Chien, A. A., DeFanti, T. A., Leigh, J., & Papadopoulos, P. M. (2003, November). The OptIPuter. *Communications of the ACM, 46*(11), 58–67. doi:10.1145/948383.948410

Smith, T. F., & Waterman, M. S. (1981). Identification of common molecular subsequences. *Journal of Molecular Biology, 147*(1), 195–197. doi:10.1016/0022-2836(81)90087-5

Spallation Neutron Source (SNS). (2008). Retrieved from http://www.sns.gov/

Sparql Query Language for RDF. (n.d). Retrived from http://www.w3.org/TR/rdf-sparql-query/

Squid-Cache Project. (2008). *Squid: Optimizing Web delivery*. Retrieved from http://www.squid-cache.org/

SRB. (2010). *The Storage Resource Broker*. Retrieved from http://www.sdsc.edu/srb/

SRM. (2010). *The Storage Resource Managers*. Retrieved from http://sdm.lbl.gov/srm

Stamey, B. H., Wang, V., & Koterba, M. (2007). Predicting the next storm surge flood. *Sea Technology*, 10–15.

Steel, G. L. Jr. (1995). Parallelism in Lisp. *SIGPLAN Lisp Pointers, 8*(2), 1–14. doi:10.1145/224133.224134

Stockinger, K., Schikuta, E., Stockinger, H., & Willers, I. (2001). Towards a cost model for distributed and replicated data stores. *Proceedings of 9th Euromicro Workshop on Parallel and Distributed Processing (PDP 2001)*, IEEE Computer Society Press, Mantova, Italy.

Stockinger, H. (2005). *Data management in data Grids - Habilitation overview*. Research Lab for Computational Technologies and Applications.

Stockinger, H., Laure, E., & Stockinger, K. (2005). Performance engineering in data Grids. *Journal of Concurrency and Computation: Practice and Experience, 17*(2-4), 171–191. doi:10.1002/cpe.923

Stoica, I., Morris, R., Karger, D., Kaashoek, M. F., & Balakrishnan, H. (2001). Chord: A scalable peer-to-peer lookup service for Internet applications. In *Proceedings of SIGCOMM*.

Stoica, I., & Morris, R. (2001). *Chord: A scalable peer-to-peer lookup service for Internet applications*. ACM SIGCOMM.

Stoica, I., Morris, R., Karger, D., Kaashoek, M. F., & Balakrishnan, H. (2001). *Chord: A scalable peer-to-peer lookup service for internet applications*. ACM SIGCOMM.

Stokes, J. M. (2003). *Inside the machine - An illustrated introduction to microprocessors and computer architecture* (p. 320). No Starch Press.

Strickland, J., Freeh, V., Ma, X., & Vazhkudai, S. (2005). Governor: Autonomic throttling for aggressive idle resource scavenging. In *Proceedings of the 2nd IEEE International Conference on Autonomic Computing*.

Sun Constellation Linux Cluster. (2008). Retrieved from http://www.tacc.utexas.edu/resources/hpcsystems/#constellation

Sun, S., Lannom, L., et al. (2003). *Handle system overview*. Internet Engineering Task Force (IETF) Request for Comments (RFC), RFC 3650, November 2003. Retrieved from http://hdl.handle.net/4263537/4069

Sun. (2005). *Sun Microsystems, Ultra Sparc III Cu - User manual*. Retrieved from http://www.sun.com/processors/manuals/USIIIv2.pdf

Sun. (2005). *Sun Microsystems, Ultra Sparc III Cu Processor - Overview*. Retrieved from http://www.sun.com/processors/whitepapers/USIIICuoverview.pdf

Suslu, I., & Kosar, T. (2007). Balancing the use of remote i/o versus staging in distributed environments. *Proceedings of the 9th International Conference on Enterprise Information Systems Doctoral Symposium (DCEIS 2007)*, Madeira, Portugal.

Suslu, I., Turkmen, F., Balman, M., & Kosar, T. (2008). Choosing between remote i/o versus staging in large scale distributed applications. *Proceedings of International Conference on Parallel and Distributed Computing and Communication Systems*, New Orleans, LA, USA.

Swift. (2008). *Swift workflow system*. Retrieved from http://www.ci.uchicago.edu/swift

Szalay, A., Bunn, A., Gray, J., Foster, I., & Raicu, I. (2006). *The importance of data locality in distributed computing applications*. NSF Workflow Workshop.

Szalay, A., & Gray, J. (2001). The world-wide telescope. *Science, 293*(14), 2037–2040. doi:10.1126/science.293.5537.2037

Takane, Y., Young, F. W., & de Leeuw, J. (1977). Nonmetric individual differences multidimensional scaling: an alternating least squares method with optimal scaling features. *Psychometrika, 42*, 7–67. doi:10.1007/BF02293745

Tatebe, O., et al. (2003). *Worldwide fast file replication on Grid Datafarm*. 2003 Computing in High Energy and Nuclear Physics (CHEP03).

Tatebe, O., Morita, Y., Matsuoka, S., Soda, N., & Sekiguchi, S. (2002). Grid datafarm architecture for petascale data intensive computing. *IEEE/ACM International Symposium on Cluster Computing and the Grid* (CCGrid 2002), (pp. 102-110).

Tatebe, O., Soda, N., Morita, Y., Matsuoka, S., & Sekiguchi, S. (2004). *Gfarm v2: A Grid file system that supports high-performance distributed and parallel data computing*. Computing in High Energy and Nuclear Physics (CHEP04).

Taylor, I., Wang, I., Shields, M., & Majithia, S. (2005). Distributed computing with triana on the grid: Research articles. *Concurrency and Computation, 17*(9), 1197–1214. doi:10.1002/cpe.901

Temporal Dynamics of Learning Center. (n.d). Retrieved from http://tdlc.ucsd.edu/portal/

Thain, D. (2005). Identity boxing: A new technical for consistent global identity. *IEEE/ACM Supercomputing*, 51-61.

Thain, D., & Moretti, C. (2007). Efficient access to many small files in a filesystem for Grid computing. In *Proceedings of IEEE Grid Computing*, (pp. 243-250).

Thain, D., Arpaci Dusseau, A., Bent, J., & Livny, M. (2004). Explicit control in a batch aware distributed file system. *Proceedings of the First USENIX/ACM Conference on Networked Systems Design and Implementation*, San Francisco, CA, USA.

Thain, D., Klous, S., Wozniak, J., Brenner, P., Striegel, A., & Izaguirre, J. (2005). Separating abstractions from resources in a tactical storage system. In *Proceedings of Supercomputing*.

Thain, D., & Livny, M. (2005). Parrot: An application environment for data-intensive computing. *Scalable Computing: Practice and Experience, 6*(3), 9–18.

Thain, D., Moretti, C., & Hemmes, J. (2009). Chirp: A practical global filesystem for cluster and Grid computing. *Journal of Grid Computing, 7*(1), 51–72. doi:10.1007/s10723-008-9100-5

The Numerical Relativity Group. (n.d). Retrieved from http://www.cct.lsu.edu/numerical/index.php

The SURA Coastal Ocean Observing and Prediction. (n.d). Retrieved from http://scoop.sura.org/

Thekkath, C. A., Mann, T., & Lee, E. K. (1997). Frangipani: A scalable distributed file system. In *Proceedings of SOSP*, (pp. 224–237).

Thiebaux, M., Cox, D., & Patterson, R. (2000). *Virtual reality 3D interface system for data creation, viewing, and editing.* (Patent No. 6,154,723).

Thomas, M. (2008). *Ultralight planets tutorial.*

Thompson, B. (1984). *Canonical correlation analysis uses and interpretation.* Sage.

Tierney, B. L. (2005). *TCP tuning techniques for high-speed wide-area networks.* nfnn2 talk.

Tierney, B. L., Lee, J., Crowley, B., Holding, M., Hylton, J., & Drake, F. L. (1999). A network-aware distributed storage cache for data-intensive environments. *Proceedings of the Eighth IEEE International Symposium on High Performance Distributed Computing*, (pp. 185-189).

Torng, E. (1998). A unified analysis of paging and caching. *Algorithmica, 20*, 175–200. doi:10.1007/PL00009192

Torvalds, L. (2010). *The Linux kernel.* Retrieved from http://www.kernel.org

Tricoche, X., Kindlmann, G., & Westin, C.-F. (2008). Invariant crease lines for topological and structural analysis of tensor fields. *IEEE Transactions on Visualization and Computer Graphics, 14*(6), 1627–1634. doi:10.1109/TVCG.2008.148

Tu, T., Yu, H., Ramirez-Guzman, L., Bielak, J., Ghattas, O., Ma, K.-L., & O'Hallaron, D. R. (2006). From mesh generation to scientific visualization: An end-to-end approach to parallel supercomputing. *Proceedings of Supercomputing 2006.*

Tummala, S., & Kosar, T. (2007). Data management challenges in coastal applications. *Journal of Coastal Research, 50*(Special Issue), 1188–1193.

Twister. (2011). Retrieved July 2011, from www.iterativemapreduce.org

Tyson, J. A. (2002). Large synoptic survey telescope: Overview, survey and other telescope technologies and discoveries. *Proceedings of the Society for Photo-Instrumentation Engineers, 4836*, 10–20.

Ubiquitous Computing and Monitoring System. (n.d). Retrieved from http://www.ucoms.org/

UC/ANL Teragrid Guide. (2004). Retrieved from http://www.uc.teragrid.org/tg-docs/user-guide.html#disk

UCoMS. (2010). *Ubiquitous computing and monitoring system for discovery and management of energy resources.* Retrieved from http://www.ucoms.org

US National Virtual Observatory. (n.d). Retrieved from http://www.us-vo.org/.

Van Keken, P., & Schwarz, N. (2001). Visualizing seismic wave propagation. *EOS Transactions AGU Fall Meeting Supplement, Abstract ED31E-01, 84*(46).

Vazhkudai, S., Schopf, J., & Foster, I. (2002). Predicting the performance of wide-area data transfers. In *Proceedings of the 16th Int'l Parallel and Distributed Processing Symposium (IPDPS 2002).*

Vazhkudai, S., Ma, X., Freeh, V., Strickland, J., Tammineedi, N., & Scott, S. (2005). Scavenging desktop storage resources for bulk, transient data. In *Proceedings of Supercomputing, 2005.* Freeloader.

Vazhkudai, S., Ma, X., Freeh, V., Strickland, J., Tammineedi, N., Simon, T., & Scott, S. (2006). Constructing collaborative desktop storage caches for large scientific datasets. *ACM Transactions on Storage, 2*(3), 221–254. doi:10.1145/1168910.1168911

Venugopal, S., Buyya, R., & Winton, L. (2004). A grid service broker for scheduling distributed data-oriented applications on global grids. *Proceedings of the 2nd workshop on Middleware for grid computing,* Toronto, Canada, (pp. 75-80).

Venugopal, S., Buyya, R., & Ramamohanarao, K. (2006). A taxonomy of data grids for distributed data sharing, management, and processing. *ACM Computing Surveys, 38*(1). doi:10.1145/1132952,1132955

Venugopal, S., Buyya, R., & Winton, L. (2006). A grid service broker for scheduling e-science applications on global data grids: Research articles. *Concurrency and Computation, 18*(6), 685–699. doi:10.1002/cpe.974

Vishwanath, V., Burns, R., Leigh, J., & Seablom, M. (2008). Accelerating tropical cyclone analysis using LambdaRAM, a distributed data cache over wide-area ultra-fast networks. *Future Generation of Computer Science, The International Journal of Grid Computing: Theory, Methods and Applications, 25*(2).

Vishwanath, V., Leigh, J., Shimizu, T., Nam, S., Renambot, L., & Takahashi, H. … Kamatani, O. (2008b). *The rails toolkit (RTK) - Enabling End-system topology-aware high end computing.* 4th IEEE International Conference on e-Science.

Vishwanath, V., Zuck, L., & Leigh, J. (2008a). Specification and verification of LambdaRAM: A wide-area distributed cache for high performance computing. *In Proceedings of the 6th ACM/IEEE International Conference on Formal Methods and Models for Co-Design, 2008 (MEMOCODE 2008),* 5-7 June 2008, 187 – 198.

Vishwanath, V., Shimizu, T., Takizawa, M., Obana, K., & Leigh, J. (2007, November). Towards terabit/s systems: Performance evaluation of multi-rail systems. *Proceedings of Supercomputing, 2007*(SC07).

von Funck, W., Weinkauf, T., Theisel, H., & Seidel, H.-P. (2008). Smoke surfaces: An interactive flow visualization technique inspired by real-world flow experiments. *IEEE Transactions on Visualization and Computer Graphics, 14*(6), 1396–140. doi:10.1109/TVCG.2008.163

Wan, M., Moore, R. W., & Rajasekar, A. (2009). *Integration of cloud storage with data.* The Third International Conference on the Virtual Computing Initiative. Research Triangle Park, North Carolina, USA. *WebSphere.* (n.d). Retrieved from http://wwww.ibm.com/software/websphere/

Wang, X., & Kosar, T. (2009) Design and implementation of metadata system in petashare. *SSDBM09: Proceeding of the 21ˢᵗ Scientific and Statistical Database Management Conference,* (pp. 191-199).

WCER. (2010). *Wisconsin Center for Education research digital video processing project.* Retrieved from http://www.wcer.wisc.edu/

Weber, G. H., Hagen, H., Hamann, B., Joy, K. I., Ligocki, T. J., Ma, K.-L., & Shalf, J. M. (2001). Visualization of adaptive mesh refinement data. *Proceedings of IS&T/SPIE Visual Data Exploration and Analysis, VIII,* (pp. 121–132).

Weber, G. H., Kreylos, O., Ligocki, T. J., Shalf, J. M., Hagen, H., Hamann, B., … Ma, K.-L. (2001). *High-quality volume rendering of adaptive mesh refinement data.*

Wechsler, O. (2006). *Inside Intel Core microarchitecture – Setting new standards for energy efficient performance.* Retrieved from http://download.intel.com/technology/architecture

Weigle, E., & Feng, W. (2001). Dynamic right-sizing: A simulation study. *Proceedings of IEEE International Conference on Computer Communications and Networks (ICCCN01).*

Weise, A., Wan, M., Schroeder, W., & Hasan, A. (2008). Managing groups of files in a rule oriented data management system (iRODS), *ICCS '08: Proceedings of the 8th international conference on Computational Science,* Part III, (pp. 321–330). Springer-Verlag.

Wei, X., Li, W. W., Tatebe, O., Xu, G., Hu, L., & Ju, J. (2005). *Integrating local job scheduler – LSF with Gfarm. Parallel and Distributed Processing and Applications, LNCS 3758/2005* (pp. 196–204). Berlin, Germany: Springer.

Wheeler, D. L., Barrett, T., Benson, D. A., Bryant, S. H., Canese, K., Chetvernin, V., et al. (2006). Database resources of the national center for biotechnology information. *Nucleic Acids Research, 33*(1). xCAT. (2009). *Extreme cluster administration toolkit.* Retrieved December 2009, from http://xcat.sourceforge.net/

Whitman, S. (1993). A task adaptive parallel graphics renderer. *Proceedings of Parallel Rendering Symposium*, (pp. 27-34).

Wieczorek, M., & Prodan, R. (2005). Scheduling of scientific workflows in the ASKALON Grid environment. *SIGMOD Record, 34*(3), 56–62. doi:10.1145/1084805.1084816

Wolski, R., Spring, N., & Hayes, J. (1999). The network weather service: A distributed resource performance forecasting service for metacomputing. *Future Generation Computer Systems, 15*(5), 757–768. doi:10.1016/S0167-739X(99)00025-4

WSDL. (n.d). *Web service definition language.* Retrieved from http://www.w3.org/TR/wsdl

Xiaohui, W., Li, W. W., Tatebe, O., Gaochao, X., Liang, H., & Jiubin, J. (2005). Implementing data aware scheduling in Gfarm using LSF scheduler plugin mechanism. *International Conference on Grid Computing and Applications* (GCA'05), (pp. 3-10).

Xiong, C., Leigh, J., He, E., Vishwanath, V., Murata, T., Renambot, L., & DeFanti, T. (2005). LambdaStream – A data transport protocol for streaming network-intensive applications over photonic networks. *Proceedings of The Third International Workshop on Protocols for Fast Long-Distance Networks.*

Yang, M. Q., & Yang, J. Y. (2008). High-performance computing for drug design. *IEEE International Conference on Bioinformatics and Biomedicine Workshops*, (p. 120).

Yu, H., Ma, K.-L., & Welling, J. (2004). A parallel visualization pipeline for terascale earthquake simulations. *Proceedings of the Supercomputing Conference.*

Yu, J., & Buyya, R. (2004). A novel architecture for realizing grid workflow using tuple spaces. *Proceedings of the Fifth IEEE/ACM International Workshop on Grid Computing.*

Yu, Y., Isard, M., Fetterly, D., Budiu, M., Erlingsson, U., Gunda, P., et al. (2008). *DryadLINQ: A system for general-purpose distributed data-parallel computing using a high-level language.* Symposium on Operating System Design and Implementation (OSDI).

Yu, A. (1996). The future of microprocessors. *IEEE Micro, 16*(6), 46–53.

Yu, J., & Buyya, R. (2005). A taxonomy of scientific workflow systems for grid computing. *SIGMOD Record, 34*(3), 44–49. doi:10.1145/1084805.1084814

Yu, J., Buyya, R., & Ramamohanarao, K. (2008). Workflow scheduling algorithms for grid computing. In *Metaheuristics for Scheduling in Distributed Computing Environments* (*Vol. 146*, pp. 173–214). Berlin, Germany: Springer. doi:10.1007/978-3-540-69277-5_7

Yu, L., Moretti, C., Thrasher, A., Emrich, S., Judd, K., & Thain, D. (2010). Harnessing parallelism in multicore clusters with the all-pairs, wavefront, and makeflow abstractions. *Journal of Cluster Computing, 13*(3). doi:10.1007/s10586-010-0134-7

Zhang, R., & Hu, Y. C. (2003). Borg: A hybrid protocol for scalable application-level multicast in peer-to-peer networks. In *Proceedings of the 13th NOSSDAV Workshop.*

Zhang, Z., Espinosa, A., Iskra, K., Raicu, I., Foster, I., & Wilde, M. (2008). *Design and evaluation of a collective I/O model for loosely-coupled Petascale programming.* IEEE Workshop on Many-Task Computing on Grids and Supercomputers (MTAGS08).

Zhang, C., Leigh, J., DeFanti, T. A., Mazzucco, M., & Grossman, R. (2003). TeraScope: Distributed visual data mining of terascale data sets over photonic networks. *Journal of Future Generation Computer Systems, 19*(6). doi:10.1016/S0167-739X(03)00072-4

Zhao, B. Y., Kubiatowicz, J. D., & Joseph, A. D. (2001). *Tapestry: An infrastructure for fault-resilient wide-area location and routing.* Technical Report UCB//CSD-01-1141, U. C. Berkeley.

Zhao, Y., Hategan, M., Clifford, B., Foster, I., von Laszewski, G., & Raicu, I. … Wilde, M. (2007). *Swift: Fast, reliable, loosely coupled parallel computation.* IEEE Workshop on Scientific Workflows.

Zhao, Y., Raicu, I., & Foster, I. (2008). Scientific workflow systems for 21st century, new bottle or new wine? In *SERVICES '08: Proceedings of the 2008 IEEE Congress on Services - Part I* (pp. 467–471). Washington, DC: IEEE.

Zhao, B. Y. (2004). Tapestry: A resilient global-scale overlay for service deployment. *IEEE Journal on Selected Areas in Communications*, *22*(1). doi:10.1109/JSAC.2003.818784

Zhao, B. Y., Kubiatowicz, J. D., & Joseph, A. D. (2001). *Tapestry: An infrastructure for fault-resilient wide-area location and routing*. Berkeley: U.C. Berkeley.

Zhao, Y., Raicu, I., Foster, I., Hategan, M., Nefedova, V., & Wilde, M. (2008b). Realizing fast, scalable and reliable scientific computations in grid environments. In Wong, J. (Ed.), *Grid computing research progress*. Nova Publisher.

Zhuang, S. Q., Zhao, B. Y., Joseph, A. D., Katz, R. H., & Kubiatowicz, J. (2001). Bayeux: An architecture for scalable and fault-tolerant wide-area data dissemination. In *Proceedings of 11th NOSSDAV Workshop*.

About the Contributors

Tevfik Kosar is an Associate Professor of Computer Science and Engineering at University at Buffalo (SUNY). He holds a Ph.D. degree in Computer Science from University of Wisconsin-Madison under the guidance of Prof. Miron Livny. Dr. Kosar's main research interests lie in the cross-section of petascale distributed systems, eScience, Grids, Clouds, and collaborative computing with a focus on large-scale data- intensive distributed applications. He is the primary designer and developer of the Stork distributed data scheduling system which has been adopted by many national and international institutions, and the lead investigator of the state-wide PetaShare distributed storage network in Louisiana. He has published more than fifty academic papers in leading journals and conferences. Some of the awards received by Dr. Kosar include NSF CAREER Award (for his work on "data-aware distributed computing"), LSU Rainmaker Award, LSU Flagship Faculty Award, Baton Rouge Business Report's Top 40 Under 40 Award, 1012 Corridor's Young Scientist Award, College of Basic Science's Research Award, and CCT Faculty of the Year Award. Dr. Kosar's work on data intensive computing has been funded by NSF, DOE, ONR, DoEd, SURA, and Louisiana Board of Regents.

* * *

Ismail Akturk is a graduate student in the Department of Computer Engineering at Bilkent University in Ankara, Turkey. Before joining Bilkent University, he was a research assistant in Center for Computation and Technology at Louisiana State University where he worked on distributed data storage and management systems. He got his M.S. degree from Louisiana State University in 2009 and B.S degree from Dogus University in Istanbul, Turkey in 2007.

Michael Albrecht resides in Los Alamos, NM developing filesystems and workload managers for exascale supercomputers. From a young age, Michael knew he wanted a job programming computers, so he earned a BS in Computer Science at the University of Notre Dame. He then decided to stay at Notre Dame in pursuit of a PhD with a specialty in Distributed Systems and Filesystems, and is working on his dissertation proposal.

Seung-Hee Bae is a Ph.D. candidate of the School of Informatics and Computing at Indiana University, Bloomington, and he has been Bloomington for the Ph.D. degree since Fall 2005. His advisor is Professor Geoffrey C. Fox, and he is working at the Community Grids Lab in Pervasive Technology Institute as a graduate research assistant. Before joining IU-Bloomington, he had been in the School of Computer Science and Engineering at Seoul National University for his Master's degree and in the

School of Computer Science and Electronic Engineering at Handong Global University for his Bachelor degree. His research interests cover parallel and distributed computing, data mining and machine learning, dimension reduction and data visualization, data intensive computing, and optimization algorithms. In specific, he is focusing on applying high-performance parallel computing and optimization methods to data mining algorithms when dealing with large high-dimensional data, and searching for efficient parallel runtime models in various parallel and distributed environments.

Mehmet Balman is a researcher in the High Performance Computing Research Department of the Computational Research Division at Lawrence Berkeley National Laboratory (LBNL) in Berkeley, California. He received his Ph.D. degree in Computer Science from Louisiana State University (LSU) in 2010, under the supervision of Dr. Tevfik Kosar. He holds Bachelor of Science and Master of Science degrees in Computer Engineering from Bogazici University, Turkey, and a Master of Science degree in System Sciences from the Department of Computer Science at LSU. During his study at LSU, he worked as a teaching assistant in the Department of Computer Science, and as a research assistant in the Center for Computation & Technology, LSU, where he has contributed to the Stork data scheduler and PetaShare data storage projects. His recent work at LBNL includes high performance data transfers over next-generation high-bandwidth networks, network-aware data management for scientific data-intensive applications, and developing federated system infrastructure for climate sciences. His research interests are data access, scheduling, coordination, and network management in distributed environments.

Scott Beason is with Computer Sciences Corporation. Before joining Computer Sciences Corporation, he was with the School of Informatics at Indiana University. His research interests include cloud technologies for bioinformatics applications, biomedical case studies in data intensive computing, and windows multicore systems with threading and MPI.

Micah Beck began his research career in distributed operating systems at Bell Laboratories and received his Ph.D. in Computer Science from Cornell University (1992) in the area of parallelizing compilers. He then joined the faculty of the Computer Science Department at the University of Tennessee, where he is currently an Associate Professor working in distributed high performance computing, networking, and storage.

Hoang Bui received the B.S. and M.S. in Computer Science in 2004 and 2007 from Midwestern State University. He is currently a PhD student of Computer Science and Engineering at the University of Notre Dame, where his research focuses on building a distributed storage system to archive scientific repositories.

Peter Bui received his B.S. and M.S. in Computer Science in 2006 and 2010 from the University of Notre Dame. He is currently a Computer Science Ph.D. Student at the University of Notre Dame, where he works in the Cooperative Computing Lab investigating methods of combining various distributed system tools and services into a programming framework for constructing scientific workflows.

Ali R. Butt is an Assistant Professor of Computer Science at Virginia Tech. Ali received the BSc (Hons) degree in electrical engineering from the University of Engineering and Technology Lahore, Pakistan, in 2000 and the PhD degree in Electrical and Computer Engineering from Purdue University in 2006. At Purdue, he also served as the President of the Electrical and Computer Engineering Graduate Student Association for 2003 and 2004. His research interests are in experimental computer systems, especially in data-intensive high-performance computing (HPC) and the impact of technologies such as massive multi-cores, Cloud Computing, and asymmetric architectures on HPC. His current work focuses on I/O and storage issues faced in modern HPC systems. Ali is a recipient of the NSF CAREER Award (2008), an IBM Faculty Award (2008), an IBM Shared University Research Award (2009), a Virginia Tech College of Engineering "Outstanding New Assistant Professor" Award (2009), a best paper award (MASCOTS 2009), recognition as Virginia Tech "Scholar of the Week" (2011), and a NetApp Faculty Fellowship (2011). Ali was an invited participant (2009) and an organizer (2010) for the NAE's US Frontiers of Engineering Symposium. He is a member of USENIX, ACM, and ASEE, and a Senior Member of IEEE.

Rajkumar Buyya is Professor of Computer Science and Software Engineering; and Director of the Cloud Computing and Distributed Systems (CLOUDS) Laboratory at the University of Melbourne, Australia. He is also serving as the founding CEO of Manjrasoft, a spin-off company of the University, commercializing its innovations in Cloud Computing. He has authored 400 publications and four text books. He also edited several books including "Cloud Computing: Principles and Paradigms" published by Wiley Press, USA in Feb 2011. He is one of the highly cited authors in computer science and software engineering worldwide (h-index=56, g-index=122, 16000+ citations). Software technologies for Grid and Cloud computing developed under Dr. Buyya's leadership have gained rapid acceptance and are in use at several academic institutions and commercial enterprises in 40 countries around the world. Dr. Buyya has led the establishment and development of key community activities, including serving as foundation Chair of the IEEE Technical Committee on Scalable Computing and five IEEE/ACM conferences. These contributions and international research leadership of Dr. Buyya are recognized through the award of "2009 IEEE Medal for Excellence in Scalable Computing" from the IEEE Computer Society, USA. Manjrasoft's Aneka Cloud technology developed under his leadership has received "2010 Asia Pacific Frost & Sullivan New Product Innovation Award" and "2011 Telstra Innovation Challenge - People's Choice Award".

Rory Carmichael graduated from the University of Notre Dame in 2009 with a B.A. in English and a B.S. in Computer Science. After graduation, he continued on as the Analyst for the Notre Dame Bioinformatics Core Facility, where his work focuses on harnessing distributed systems for problems in computational biology.

Amitabh Chaudhary is an Assistant Professor in the Department of Computer Science and Engineering at the University of Notre Dame since 2005. Before this, he was an Associate Specialist in the Donald Bren School of Information and Computer Sciences at University of California, Irvine. He received a B.Tech in Electrical Engineering from Indian Institute of Technology, Kharagpur, an M.Tech in Computer Science and Engineering from Indian Institute of Technology, Bombay, and a Ph.D. in Computer Science from Johns Hopkins University, Baltimore. Dr. Chaudhary's research is directed at the design, analysis, and application of algorithms, primarily *online algorithms*—algorithms that compute under incomplete information. His algorithms have addressed fundamental problems in resource allocation, distributed databases, scientific computing, network routing, fault-tolerance, spatial data management, inventory control, and graph theory. He has over 35 publications in high-impact journals and conferences. He is a member of the ACM and IEEE. He has received research grants from the NSF and a National Scholarship from NCERT, India. Recently he received the Outstanding Teacher Award from his department at the University of Notre Dame.

Ann L. Chervenak is a Research Associate Professor in the Computer Science Department at the University of Southern California and a Project Leader at the USC Information Sciences Institute. Dr. Chervenak's research interests include data management for large, distributed scientific communities. Her group is part of the Biomedical Informatics Research Network Coordinating Center (BIRNCC), which works with BIRN application scientists to deploy services and infrastructure to support data publication and sharing. Dr. Chervenak is part of the Earth System Grid (ESG) project, where her team provides tools for data cataloguing and replication management of large climate simulation data sets. Her team works with the Laser Interferometer Gravitational Wave Observatory project (LIGO) to provide services for data cataloguing and management of more than 140 million data files stored across ten LIGO locations. Dr. Chervenak's group has a long history of developing robust, open source software and services for data management and replication that are used successfully in production environments for data intensive scientific collaboration. This software includes the Replica Location Service (RLS), a distributed, highly scalable catalog for replicated data items in a distributed system. Currently, her research group is studying policy-driven data management that improves the performance of scientific workflows.

Jong Youl Choi is a graduate student pursuing Ph.D degree in Computer Science department of Indiana University at Bloomington. He earned his MS degree in Computer Science from Courant Institute, New York University in 2004. His areas of research interest span data mining and machine learning algorithms, high-performance data-intensive computing, parallel and distributed systems for Cloud and Grid computing. More specifically, he is focusing on developing high-performance data mining algorithms and researching efficient run-time environments in Cloud and Grid systems.

Ewa Deelman is a Research Associate Professor at the USC Computer Science Department and a Project Leader at the USC Information Sciences Institute. Dr. Deelman's research interests include the design and exploration of collaborative, distributed scientific environments, with particular emphasis on workflow management as well as the management of large amounts of data and metadata. At ISI, Dr. Deelman is leading the Pegasus project, which designs and implements workflow mapping techniques for large-scale applications running in distributed environments. Pegasus is being used today in a number of scientific disciplines, enabling researches to formulate complex computations in a declarative way. Over the years, Dr. Deelman worked with a number of application domains including astronomy, bioinformatics, earthquake science, gravitational-wave physics, and others. As part of these collaborations, new advances in computer science and in the domain sciences were made. For example, the data intensive workflows in LIGO (gravitational-wave physics) motivated new workflow analysis algorithms that minimize workflow data footprint during execution. On the other hand, improvements in the scalability of workflows enabled SCEC scientists (earthquake science) to develop new physics-based seismic hazard maps of Southern California. In 2007, Dr. Deelman edited a book on workflow research: "Workflows in e-Science: Scientific Workflows for Grids," published by Springer. She is also the founder of the annual Workshop on Workflows in Support of Large-Scale Science, which is held in conjunction with the Super Computing conference. In 1997 Dr. Deelman received her PhD in Computer Science from the Rensselaer Polytechnic Institute. Her thesis topic was in the area of parallel discrete event simulation, where she applied parallel programming techniques to the simulation of the spread of Lyme disease in nature.

Jaliya Ekanayake received his Ph.D. from the School of Informatics and Computing at Indiana University, Bloomington. His research advisor was Prof. Geoffrey Fox, and his Ph.D. research focused on architecture and performance of runtime environments for data intensive scalable computing.

Saliya Ekanayake is a Ph.D student in Indiana University, Bloomington and works as a Research Assistant under Prof. Geoffrey Fox in SalsaHPC group. Ekanayake's research tasks have been mainly on solving large scale Bio-Informatics analyses and developing frameworks to seamlessly integrate existing applications. Ekanayake is interested in researching about higher level language support for high performance computing.

Scott Emrich received the B.S. in Biology and Computer Science from Loyola College in Maryland and the Ph.D. in Bioinformatics and Computational Biology from Iowa State University. He is currently an Assistant Professor of Computer Science and Engineering at the University of Notre Dame with research interests including computational biology, bioinformatics, and parallel computing. This work focuses on arthropod genome analysis with applications to global health and ecology.

Patrick J. Flynn is Professor of Computer Science & Engineering and Concurrent Professor of Electrical Engineering at the University of Notre Dame. He received the B.S. in Electrical Engineering (1985), the M.S. in Computer Science (1986), and the Ph.D. in Computer Science (1990) from Michigan State University, East Lansing. He has held faculty positions at Notre Dame (1990 – 1991, 2001 – present), Washington State University (1991 – 1998), and Ohio State University (1998 – 2001). His research interests include computer vision, biometrics, and image processing. Dr. Flynn is a Senior Member of IEEE, a Fellow of IAPR, an Associate Editor of *IEEE Trans. on Information Forensics and Security*, a past Associate Editor and Associate Editor-in-Chief of *IEEE Trans. on PAMI*, and a past Associate Editor of *Pattern Recognition and Pattern Recognition Letters*. He was the Vice-President (Finance) of the IEEE Biometrics Council in 2008 – 2009 and is serving as its Vice-President (Conferences) in 2010 – 2011. He has received outstanding teaching awards from Washington State University and the University of Notre Dame.

Ian Foster is Director of the Computation Institute, a joint institute of the University of Chicago and Argonne National Laboratory. He is also an Argonne Senior Scientist and Distinguished Fellow, and the Arthur Holly Compton Distinguished Service Professor of Computer Science at U.Chicago. His research deals with distributed, parallel, and data-intensive computing technologies, and innovative applications of those technologies to scientific problems. He has led the development of methods and software that underpin many large national and international cyberinfrastructures. Dr. Foster is a fellow of the American Association for the Advancement of Science, the Association for Computing Machinery, and the British Computer Society. His awards include the British Computer Society's Lovelace Medal, honorary doctorates from the University of Canterbury, New Zealand, and CINVESTA V, Mexico, and the IEEE Tsutomu Kanai award.

Geoffrey Fox received a Ph.D. in Theoretical Physics from Cambridge University and is now distinguished Professor of Informatics and Computing, and Physics at Indiana University where he is director of the Digital Science Center and Associate Dean for Research and Graduate Studies at the School of Informatics and Computing. He previously held positions at Caltech, Syracuse University, and Florida State University. He has supervised the PhD of 62 students and published over 600 papers in physics and computer science. He currently works in applying computer science to bioinformatics, defense, earthquake and ice-sheet science, particle physics, and chemical informatics. He is principal investigator of FutureGrid – a facility to enable development of new approaches to computing. He is involved in several projects to enhance the capabilities of minority serving institutions.

Jinzhu Gao is an Assistant Professor of Computer Science at the University of the Pacific. She has received her Ph.D. in Computer and Information Science from Ohio State University in 2004 under the guidance of Dr. Han-Wei Shen. Her research focuses mainly on large data management, analysis, and visualization for collaborative science. Over the past ten years, she has been working closely with application scientists to study the design of a collaborative platform that would help advance scientific discovery and collaboration.

Thilina Gunarathne is a PhD candidate at the School of Informatics and Computing of Indiana University. Thilina has engaged in research in the many fields of distributed and parallel computing including MapReduce & other data intensive computing frameworks, cloud computing, web services, scientific & business workflows, GPGPU, and HPC scientific applications. He has contributed to many open source projects in Apache Software Foundation as a committee and a PMC member starting from 2004. His current research focuses on exploring architectures for efficient execution of data intensive iterative applications on cloud and many core environments. He received his B.Sc. (Computer Science and Engineering) from the University of Moratuwa, Sri Lanka in 2006 and M.Sc. (Computer Science) from the Indiana University in 2009.

Jian Huang is an Associate Professor in the Department of Electrical Engineering and Computer Science at the University of Tennessee. He is also the director of the SEELAB, and associate director of the NSF Teragrid Remote Vis (RDAV) Center. His research expertise includes ultrascale scientific visualization areas such as large data visualization, multivariate data visualization, and time-varying data visualization, as well as systems oriented areas of visualization such as parallel, distributed, remote, and collaborative visualization. His research has been funded by Department of Energy, National Science Foundation, NASA, and UT-Battelle.

Andrew Johnson is an Associate Professor of Computer Science and member of the Electronic Visualization Laboratory at the University of Illinois at Chicago. His research and teaching focus on interaction and collaboration, using advanced visualization devices such as high-resolution walls, tables, and 3D virtual reality displays, the development of those display devices, and the application of those display devices to enhance discovery in areas such as geoscience and biomedicine, as well as to enhance learning from K-12 through college in formal and informal settings. His research has been funded by the National Science Foundation, NASA, the National Institute for Nursing Research, the Department of Energy, the Office of Naval Research, and the State of Illinois. Recent work includes the development of a next generation CAVE virtual reality display; the creation of a real-time core description, correlation, and data visualization system for marine, terrestrial, and Antarctic core data; the creation of mission planning, visualization, and analysis tools for bio and geo-chemical data collected from ice-covered Lake Bonney in Antarctica; and the integration and visualization of data mining and statistical results into a system to improve the hand-off of patients between nurses.

Jason Leigh is a Professor of Computer Science and Director of the Electronic Visualization Laboratory and the Software Technologies Research Center at the University of Illinois at Chicago. Prior projects and research for which he is best known include, the OptIPuter, GeoWall, CoreWall, Lambda-Vision, Tele-Immersion, Reliable Blast UDP, and lifelike avatars. His research since 2000 focused on Cyber- Commons- ultra-resolution display-rich collaboration environments amplified by high performance computing and networking. His work in lifelike avatars has been featured on the Popular Science's *Future Of,* and he has been profiled on Nova *ScienceNow.* His current area of research is human augmentics—the science and technology of expanding the capabilities and characteristics of humans.

Philip Little is a PhD student in Computer Science and Engineering at the University of Notre Dame. He received a BS in Computer Science from the University of Portland and an MSCSE from the University of Notre Dame. His research interests include online and randomized algorithms, natural language processing, and genetic algorithms.

Huadong Liu received his Bachelor's and Master's degree in Engineering in 1999 and 2002 from Nanjing University of Post and Telecommunications. In fall 2002, he started his Doctoral study at the University of Tennessee, Knoxville on data-intensive network computing. In spring 2003, he joined the Logistical Computing and Internetworking Laboratory where he completed his Ph.D. degree in 2008. He interned at Global Software Group Motorola China in 2001. During his Ph.D. study, he worked as a Google Summer of Code programmer in 2005 and a research intern at NEC Labs America in 2006. He has been working at NetApp Inc. on high performance storage server clustering since 2007.

Xiaosong Ma is currently an Associate Professor in the Department of Computer Science at North Carolina State University. She is also a Joint Faculty in the Computer Science and Mathematics Division at Oak Ridge National Laboratory. Her research interests are in the areas of storage systems, parallel I/O, high-performance parallel applications, cloud computing, and self-configurable performance optimization. She received the DOE Early Career Principal Investigator Award in 2005, the NSF CAREER Award in 2006, and an IBM Faculty Award in 2009. Prior to joining NCSU, Xiaosong received her Ph.D. in Computer Science from the University of Illinois at Urbana-Champaign in 2003, and her B.S. in Computer Science from Peking University, China.

Reagan Moore is a Professor in the School of Information and Library Science at the University of North Carolina at Chapel Hill, Chief Scientist for Data Intensive Cyber Environments at the Renaissance Computing Institute, and Director of the Data Intensive Cyber Environments Center at UNC. He coordinates research efforts in development of policy-based data management systems for data grids, digital libraries, and preservation environments. The developed software systems include the Storage Resource Broker (SRB) data grid and the integrated Rule-Oriented Data System (iRODS). An ongoing research interest is use of data grid technology to automate execution of management policies and validate trustworthiness of repositories.

Terry Moore is Associate Director of the Center for Information Technology Research (CITR) at the University of Tennessee. He has received a Ph.D. in Philosophy from the University of North Carolina, Chapel Hill, and has been with CITR since 2001. He is also responsible for the Innovative Computing Lab (ICL) project development, especially focusing on the creative process of proposal development, from the identification of new ideas and opportunities, through the coordination and execution of the collaborative writing process. In this capacity, he serves as ICL and CITR's representative at many conferences and workshops and coordinates their annual participation in the Supercomputing Conference.

Christopher Moretti is a Lecturer in the Department of Computer Science at Princeton University. He has received his Ph.D. in Computer Science and Engineering from University of Notre Dame in 2010. At Notre Dame he worked in the Cooperative Computing Laboratory under the guidance of Professor Douglas Thain. His research interests include distributed and grid computing, cooperative computing systems, and distributed storage.

Suraj Pandey is a research fellow at The Commonwealth Scientific and Industrial Research Organisation (CSIRO), Australia. Before joining CSIRO, he was a post-doctoral fellow at the Cloud Computing and Distributed Systems (CLOUDS) Laboratory at the University of Melbourne, Australia. His PhD thesis focused on scheduling data intensive application workflows on Grids and Cloud computing environments. He completed his PhD from the University of Melbourne, Australia in 2010. He received Master's degree from Inha University, Korea in 2007 and Bachelor's degree from Tribhuvan University, Nepal in 2003. Dr Pandey's research spans many areas of distributed computing, including data intensive applications, workflow scheduling, resource provisioning, and accelerating executions of scientific applications using distributed computing paradigms. He has published his work on these areas at top tier journals and conferences. He has participated in international software competitions and has been awarded at several occasions. For his outstanding performance, he received educational grants from industry leaders such as Amazon and Microsoft.

Tom Peterka earned his Ph.D. in Computer Science from the University of Illinois at Chicago in 2007, where he researched the use of virtual environments for scientific visualization at the Electronic Visualization Laboratory. In his Ph.D. dissertation, Peterka invented a new method of producing autostereoscopic display systems (3D without glasses) by introducing a programmable, active parallax barrier that offers greater flexibility than previous methods. He joined the Mathematics and Computer Science Division at Argonne National Laboratory in 2007, where he researches the efficacy of performing visualization on leadership-class architectures such as the IBM Blue Gene/P and scaling scientific visualization algorithms up to the maximum number of available processors.

Judy Qiu is an Assistant Professor of Computer Science in the School of Informatics and Computing and an Assistant Director of Digital Science Center at Indiana University. Her research interests are parallel and distributed systems, cloud computing, and high performance computing. Dr. Qiu leads the SALSA project (http://salsahpc.indiana.edu) involving both professional staff and PhD students from the IU School of Informatics and Computing. SALSA focuses on data-intensive computing at the intersection of cloud and multicore technologies with an emphasis on life science applications using MapReduce and traditional parallel computing approaches. Dr. Qiu is also active in program service and supporting diversity in computing, which include serving as a Program Co-Chair of the 2nd IEEE International Conference of Cloud Computing Technology and Science 2010 and on editorial board of *International Journal of Cloud Computing*.

Ioan Raicu is an Assistant Professor in the Department of Computer Science (CS) at Illinois Institute of Technology (IIT), as well as a guest research faculty in the Math and Computer Science Division (MCS) at Argonne National Laboratory (ANL). He is also the founder and director of the Data-Intensive Distributed Systems Laboratory (DataSys) at IIT. He has received the prestigious NSF CAREER award (2011 – 2015) for his innovative work on distributed file systems for exascale computing. He was a NSF/CRA Computation Innovation Fellow at Northwestern University in 2009 – 2010, and obtained his Ph.D. in Computer Science from University of Chicago under the guidance of Dr. Ian Foster in 2009. His research work and interests are in the general area of distributed systems, with a focus on defining and exploring the theory and practical aspects of Many-Task Computing across a wide range of large-scale distributed systems. He is particularly interested in resource management in large-scale distributed systems with a focus on data intensive computing, cloud computing, grid computing, and many-core computing. His work has been funded by the NASA Ames Research Center, DOE Office of Advanced Scientific Computing Research, the NSF/CRA CIFellows program, and the NSF CAREER program.

Arcot Rajasekar is a Professor in the School of Information and Library Science at UNC-CH and a Chief Scientist at the Renaissance Computing Institute. He leads the development of the iRODS data grid, and leads the development of policy initiatives for data management projects.

Luc Renambot received a PhD at the University of Rennes-1 (France) in 2000, conducting research on parallel rendering algorithms for illumination simulation. Then holding a Postdoctoral position at the Free University of Amsterdam, till 2002, he worked on bringing education and scientific visualization to virtual reality environments. Since 2003, he joined EVL/UIC first as a PostDoc and now as Research Assistant Professor, where his research topics include high-resolution displays, computer graphics, parallel computing, and high-speed networking.

Yang (Ryan) Ruan is currently enrolled in the Ph.D. program in the Computer Science Department at Indiana University School of Informatics and is a research assistant of SALSA HPC group in Community Grids Lab. Ruan's major research areas are high performance computing, distributed systems, MapReduce frameworks, and distributed algorithms. Ruan has been working on several projects: improving distributed algorithms such as hierarchical multidimensional scaling; latent dirichlet allocation using iterative mapreduce framework (Twister) and message passing interface; evaluating high performance computing framework (Dryad) for Microsoft; integrating mapreduce framework with TORQUE; and performance testing on deploying virtual machine using different infrastructure such as Eucalyptus and OpenNebula. Currently Ruan is working on a project funded by National Institutes of Health to form a clustering pipeline using Needleman-Wunsch, pairwise clustering, multidimensional scaling and interpolation under Linux for clustering millions of sequences and developing a scientific workflow for bioinformatics computing based on TORQUE and Twister.

Mina Rho is a postdoctoral associate in School of Informatics and Computing at Indiana University Bloomington. She completed her Ph.D. in Bioinformatics under the guidance of Prof. Haixu Tang from Indiana University Bloomington (2009), and has been working with Prof. Yuzhen Ye since then. Her research interests lie in developing computational frameworks based on probabilistic models and machine learning methods that incorporate comprehensive information from genomic sequences and experimental data. She is currently working on the prediction and analysis of repetitive elements and genes in metagenomic data sets and microbial genomes.

Wayne Schroeder is the architect and implementer of several key aspects of iRODS including the database interface (metadata catalog), administrative functions, authentication and security functionality, and the testing sub-system, and helped design and maintains the installation sub-system. Schroeder manages the iRODS team at UCSD.

Robert Schuler is a Senior Systems Developer for the USC Information Sciences Institute. He has worked in a variety of academic research and technology industry roles over the past 15 years, including previous positions with Xerox Research, Dynamx Technology, and Candle Corp. Rob has a M.S. and B.S. in Computer Science from USC where he is currently a Ph.D. candidate. His research interests include large-scale scientific data management and cyberinfrastructure for wide area scientific collaborations.

Nicholas Schwarz is a Software Developer at Northwestern University's Department of Physiology. He received his MS in Computer Science from the Electronic Visualization Laboratory (EVL) at the University of Illinois at Chicago (UIC). His research interests include the acquisition, analysis, and visualization of very large multi-dimensional data collected from fluorescence microscopy and electrophysiology devices.

Alexander Szalay is a Professor in the Department of Physics and Astronomy of the Johns Hopkins University. He was born and educated in Hungary, and he spent postdoctoral periods at UC Berkeley and the University of Chicago before accepting a faculty position at Johns Hopkins. Szalay was elected to the Hungarian Academy of Sciences as a corresponding member in 1990. He is the architect for the Science Archive of the Sloan Digital Sky Survey and project director of the NSF-funded National Virtual Observatory. He has written more than 340 papers that have appeared in various scientific journals, covering areas such as theoretical cosmology, observational astronomy, spatial statistics, and computer science. In 2003 he was elected as a Fellow of the American Academy of Arts and Sciences. He received an Alexander von Humboldt Prize in Physical Sciences in 2004 and a Microsoft Award for Technical

Computing in 2008. He is a Corresponding Member of the Hungarian Academy of Sciences, and a Fellow of the American Academy of Arts and Sciences.

Haixu Tang is an Associate Professor of Informatics and Computing. He earned his Ph.D. in Molecular Biology at the Shanghai Institute of Biochemistry; between 1999 and 2001 he was a post-doc with M.S. Waterman in the Department of Mathematics at the University of Southern California. He worked as an assistant project scientist in the Department of Computer Science and Engineering, University of California, San Diego. His current work focuses on computational problems arising in molecular biology, in particular in mass spectrometry. Besides having published many books and articles, Tang is a recipient of the National Science Foundation Faculty Early Career Development Award (2007), as well as a recipient of grants from the National Institutes of Health and the National Cancer Institute.

Douglas Thain is an Associate Professor in the Department of Computer Science and Engineering at the University of Notre Dame. He received the B.S. in Physics from the University of Minnesota and the M.S. and Ph.D. in Computer Sciences from the University of Wisconsin. His research focuses on the design of large scale parallel and distributed systems for data intensive applications in science and engineering.

Sudharshan S. Vazhkudai is a Research Scientist in the Computer Science and Mathematics division at Oak Ridge National Laboratory, a US Department of Energy facility. In addition, he is also a joint faculty at the University of Tennessee. He is broadly interested in storage systems, HPC I/O architectures, multicore systems, and distributed computing. He obtained his Doctorate and Master's from the University of Mississippi, in 2003 and 1998, respectively. His Doctoral research work was conducted at Argonne National Laboratory, where he was a Wallace Givens Fellow. He received a Bachelor of Engineering degree in Computer Science from Karnatak University in India. Sudharshan is a recipient of the "Outstanding Mentor Award" (2008) from the Oak Ridge Institute for Science and Education.

Venkatram Vishwanath is an Argonne Scholar and the Director's Fellow at Argonne National Laboratory. His interests are in the areas of largescale scientific data analysis and visualization, I/O systems, exascale systems, and collaboration technologies. He is currently working on scalable solutions to enable scientists to glean insights from their large scientific simulations and experiments. His work has lead to publications in *ACM/IEEE Supercomputing*, *IEEE Cluster Computing*, and others.

Michael Wan is the chief architect and developer of the SRB and iRODS data grids, which support internationally shared collections that manage petabytes of data and hundreds of millions of files. The iRODS data grid provides generic infrastructure that supports manipulation of structured information, transmission of structured information, and query interfaces to structured information. These capabilities form the basis for federation of independent data management systems.

Xinqi Wang is currently a PhD student at Center for Computation and Technology and Department of Computer Science at Louisiana State University, Baton Rouge, Louisiana, United States. Since January 2007, he has been involved in Petashare project. His research mainly focuses on large-scale data discovery, management, and placement in collaborative cloud and distributed computing environment.

Tak-Lon (Stephen) Wu is in the Computer Science PhD program at School of Informatics and Computing, Indiana University Bloomington. He is also working as a Graduate Research Assistant of SalsaHPC Team, Community Grids Lab at Indiana University Bloomington. Major research interests are Distributed system, MapReduce technologies, Cloud Storage (especially NoSQL type), Cloud system architecture, and high performance computing. He has written a bioinformatics data generator, analyzed the performance of bioinformatics application on different infrastructures such as Cluster, built a small test-bed private Cloud using Eucalyptus and OpenNebula infrastructure, created a dynamic provisioning framework to deploy VM with TORQUE PBS batch queue, written a Classic Cloud framework to run performance analysis test on Amazon EC2, S3 & SQS, implemented a remote scientific workflow on Microsoft Azure Platform, and is currently acting as the programmer and coordinator of Digital Library Research Project using Django open source framework.

Esma Yildirim is a Researcher working with the Data Intensive Distributed Computing group in the Department of Computer Science and Engineering, University at Buffalo, SUNY. She holds a B.S. degree (2004) in Computer Engineering from Fatih University, Istanbul, Turkey and a M.S. degree (2006) in Computer Engineering from Marmara University, Istanbul, Turkey. She received her Ph.D. degree (2010) in Computer Science from Louisiana State University, Baton Rouge, LA, USA where she also worked as a Research Assistant in the Center for Computation and Technology in Stork, Petashare and Cybertools projects. Dr. Yildirim's research interests include high-speed networks and computing, data scheduling, Grid computing, and Clouds.

Yong Zhao is a Professor, and Director of the Extreme Scale Network Computing and Service Laboratory at the School of Computer Science and Engineering, University of Electronic Science and Technology of China. Before joining the university, he worked at Microsoft on Business Intelligence projects that leveraged Cloud storage and computing infrastructure. He obtained his Ph.D. in Computer Science from The University of Chicago under Dr. Ian Foster's supervision, and was the key designer of the Swift parallel scripting system, a programming tool for fast, scalable, and reliable loosely□coupled parallel computation. It comprises a simple scripting language, called SwiftScript, to represent complex scientific workflows, and a scalable runtime system to schedule hundreds of thousands of jobs onto distributed and parallel computing resources. Yong's research areas are in Cloud Computing, many□task computing, and data intensive computing. He is especially interested in providing resource management, workflow management, high level language, and scheduling support for large scale computations in Cloud and Grid environments.

Index